The Adopted Child Grows Up

# $\mathcal{C}$OMING HOME TO $\mathcal{S}$ELF

Nancy Newton Verrier

Author of
*The Primal Wound:*
*Understanding the Adopted Child*

GATEWAY PRESS, INC.
BALTIMORE, MD

The poem "Please Call Me By my True Names" by Thich Nhat Hahn is reprinted with permission of Parallax Press, Berkeley, CA, www.parallax.org

Please direct all correspondence to:
Nancy Verrier
P.O. Box 208
Lafayette, CA 94549
email: nverrier@sterling.net
website: www.nancyverrier.com

Library of Congress Control Number 2003113220
ISBN 978-0-9636480-1-3

Published for the author by
Gateway Press, Inc.
3600 Clipper Mill Rd.
Baltimore, MD 21211-1953

Printed in the United States of America

Eleventh Printing 2019

*Those who do not have power*
*over the story that dominates their lives,*
*power to retell it,*
*deconstruct it,*
*joke about it,*
*and change it as time changes,*
*truly are powerless,*
*because they cannot think new thoughts.*

*Solomon Rushdie*

*We don't see things as they are,*
*we see them as we are.*

*Anais Nin*

# CONTENTS

# PREFACE

This book is meant to be a sequel to my first book *The Primal Wound: Understanding the Adopted Child.* Therefore, in order to understand the observations, thoughts, and ideas presented in this book, it will be important to have read *The Primal Wound.* In it I present how I believe that being separated from the original mother is a trauma, the ultimate loss and rejection, and an experience which has life-long consequences for both mother and child. This trauma has been ignored because we, as a society, have deluded ourselves into believing that adoption has little or no effect on children and, therefore, does not have to be addressed as a way of understanding these children's feelings and behaviors.

As adoptees become adults, the problems, especially those dealing with relationships, do not diminish. Fear of rejection (abandonment) affects intimacy, with adoptees employing various distancing techniques to avoid the vulnerability of intimate relationships. These distancing maneuvers bewilder parents, spouses, and partners. They even bewilder the adoptees themselves. For too long, adoptees have been puzzled by their attitudes, feelings, and behaviors. They have felt shame for those feelings and behaviors because of the altruistic view of adoption perpetuated by our society. Since the advent of my first book in 1993, I have received thousands of phone calls, letters, and e-mails from adoptees thanking me for validating their feelings, for explaining the reasons for their behaviors, and for giving them a context and explanation for their experiences. In *The Primal Wound,* I make it clear that it is not the feelings of adoptees about the loss of their birth mothers, heritage, and history which is abnormal; it is the *experience* of this separation and secrecy which is abnormal. In other words, *they are and have been reacting normally to an abnormal experience.*

This does not mean that adoptees' responses to that early trauma, which get triggered and reenacted over and over in various relationships in the present, are at all helpful to them. In fact, the belief system which keeps these responses going is false and hinders the normal progress and process of relationships. For this reason, it is necessary to change certain behavioral patterns and integrate new, more positive experiences in order to reexamine and challenge the beliefs which have been holding adoptees hostage for so long.

In a broad sense, this work has two main objectives: one is to help adoptees find the authentic Self, a self which has been distorted by living without genetic markers and mirroring (being reflected back) as they grew up in non-biologic families; the other is to help them go beyond the victimhood of their beginning of life and come into their own power and sense of responsibility. One step in that process is recognizing that they have an impact on those around them and therefore must take responsibility for that impact. Both of these objectives, if successful, should help immensely with relationships. It is difficult to have a good relationship with a false self who does not take responsibility for his or her impact on those who love him or her.

A word about how all these ideas are presented. I ask the indulgence of grammarians for the method I use in this book. I know my English professors would be alarmed! However, I am trying to convey ideas, not write a scholarly tome. Therefore, I may use different persons (such as *third person* and *second person*) within one paragraph and certainly within each chapter. I do this because I want to write generally about some things, yet talk directly to whomever I am addressing about others, or to emphasize certain ideas. I will also be trying to find a balance between the genders, so will use *he* sometimes and *she* at others. I didn't do this in *The Primal Wound* and was rightfully chastised for it.

The first two chapters, although sometimes challenging, set the stage for what comes after. The first chapter is about separation trauma but is presented in a different mode—more scientifically—than it was in *The Primal Wound*. The second chapter is what I believe to be the most exciting research going on today: brain research. It is in the beginning of our lives that most of our neurological connections are made, and it is the early experiences of the first years of life which determine how our brains are wired. This chapter gives insight into the reasons for our attitudes, feelings, and behaviors, as well as hope for change. A gentle introduction to the subject of brain research is *A General Theory of Love* by Lewis, Amini, and Lannon. This is a gem of a book, one everyone should read.

Many people from all over the world have contributed to this work. The information and insights, which have come my way from the many conversations, letters, and other means of communication I have had with adoptees, birth parents, adoptive parents, and those who have been closest to them, have added a great deal to my understanding of separation trauma and adoption issues. These brave souls have been my teachers. I am simply communicating their insights and observations to help bring light to this very important subject. I wish to acknowledge and thank all of those who have opened their hearts and souls to me by contributing their experiences to this work.

# PART ONE

## Checking the Foundation

In dreams a house is often a symbol of the psyche. People dream of houses with many rooms, most of them unexplored. Some of the rooms are sunny and bright, and some are dark and mysterious. Exploring the depths of our being for hints of the true Self can seem like opening those closed doors into the unknown. One thing is certain—to build a house that will withstand the elements, it is important to first build a strong foundation. Part I of this book represents the foundations of that house/psyche. For our purposes, the foundation consists of knowledge and awareness of the manifestations of our life's circumstances.

Before changes can be made in the psyche, there must be some understanding of the circumstances and events that created the attitudes, beliefs, and behaviors that keep one from attaining the kinds of relationships, occupations, and lifestyles that promote satisfaction and even happiness. Change cannot take place without the acknowledgment of the issues which prevent satisfaction, and acknowledgment cannot take place without the awareness of these issues, their causes, manifestations, and impact.

The first eight chapters are an effort to make clear the obstacles in the path of finding your authentic Self, assuming the power that comes from discovering this Self, and taking responsibility for the impact you have on those people in your life who matter to you. Those of you who have read *The Primal Wound* (and I hope that includes everyone who attempts to read this book) will wonder if I will be repeating the contents of that book. Some of the ideas in the first chapter will sound familiar, but this time I present them differently and include many of the lessons you have taught me since the writing of that book. I also include the wisdom of other authors who have explored the many aspects of trauma.

One of the reasons that the first two chapters may sound somewhat academic is that the works I have cited pertaining to trauma and brain research are scholarly works meant mainly for the eyes of professionals. Thus the quotations are more academic in nature than I like to use for a book that is meant for the trades. However, it is important that you become aware of these works, as they pertain to your issues. I ask you to bear with me in pursuing these chapters. They are vitally important to the understanding of what transpired to cause the triggers which many of you experience, triggers which interfere with living a full, healthy, and satisfying life. This understanding is also important for the people who are in relationships with adoptees because they may have a tendency to think that it is simply a question of mind over matter. Their edict may be: "Shape up!" While I may say this at times, I know this is not easy to do. It can be easier, however, if there is some understanding of what causes distorted beliefs, unpleasant feelings, and the reactions to these feelings.

From brain research has come the understanding that in order to be emotionally healthy, we have to be able to regulate our emotions. This does not mean either repressing or suppressing them, but reacting appropriately to stimuli, and then responding to our feelings in a mature manner. The third through the seventh chapters give insight into the most troubling emotions and how to deal more effectively with them. The eighth chapter is a synopsis of the importance of regulating our emotions. Having a greater understanding of the workings of the brain and our brain chemistry should make affect regulation a high priority for everyone. "Letting it all hang out" ain't where it's at anymore! But neither is "stuffing it." Although insight isn't the whole answer to affect regulation, it is a start. Awareness is a key to making lifestyle changes that make it possible to allow and keep good relationships, as well as to reinstate relationships that may have gone awry.

Many adoptees have written to tell me how much *The Primal Wound* has helped them understand their feelings and behavior. It has helped normalize their responses to their experience of relinquishment and adoption. It has made them realize that *it was the experience that was abnormal, not their responses to it.* It has allowed them to look deeper into their motives and intentions. It has allowed them to have compassion for the wounded child they were and still may be. This has, no doubt, been helpful, but understanding without a way to change is not enough. Now it is time to help that inner wounded child grow up and respond to the environment in a more appropriate and mature manner.

When your whole life has been one of coping with trauma, it is difficult to know where your coping mechanisms end and the authentic you begins. As you go through life, you adapt more and more, and you identify more and more with this adaptation. This adaptation—these coping skills—seems like a lifeline to a safe existence. Too many of you have been held hostage by your early victimization and the adaptation you have made to that victimization. You believe you *are* that adaptation, no matter how uncomfortable this seems. You have now become a victim, not only of your initial trauma, but also of the adaptation you made to the trauma. Remaining a victim is no longer tenable. It leaves you on the treadmill of self-hatred, failed relationships, inappropriate occupations, and wasted talents. It obscures the true Self and leaves you in the realm of the false self.

In writing this book, I am assuming that the majority of you want to escape the prison of the false self and emerge into your authentic Self. These first few chapters are designed to give you more insight into the stones that hinder the path out of victimhood into an authentic, mature, satisfying adulthood. It will not be as much fun to read as Part II, but it is the foundation for the second part. It is meant to instill the kind of knowledge and awareness which can lead to the changes necessary to obtaining authenticity, responsibility, and personal power.

# CHAPTER I
## Separation Trauma

Although more and more attention is being paid to the effects of trauma on the human psyche, separation between mother and child is rarely recognized as a trauma. Authors have written about rape, incest, battering, the holocaust, natural disasters, and war, but not about perhaps the most devastating trauma of all: being separated from one's mother at the beginning of life. Yet, when else in life is one so helpless and in need of the one person to whom one feels connected—the one who is still part of the Self? The fact that the mothers of these babies were discouraged from seeing, touching, or being available to their infants meant that no one paid attention to the babies' crying and going into shock.

Fortunately, there are now means to measure some of the physical responses to this trauma, such as monitoring blood pressure, heart rate, and neurological changes. A drop in the serotonin level and elevations in adrenaline and cortisol levels have been noted in many trauma victims. According to James Prescott, "One of the brain neurochemical transmitter substances—serotonin—has been shown to be significantly reduced under conditions of failed mother-infant bonding" (Prescott, 1997). This reduced serotonin level influences conditioned avoidance, sleep regulation, and impulse control (van der Kolk, McFarlane, & Weisaeth, 1996), all problems which are often mentioned by adoptees. Brain imagining can also bring insight into the ways in which dendrites and axons connect to form synapses in the developing brain, and how that is affected by the environment and by emotional trauma.

## Manifestations of Trauma

What is trauma and how does it manifest in the lives of its victims? Trauma is reality. Trauma is not an intrapsychic phenomenon which results in neurosis. Trauma is part of the history of the victim and can affect all aspects of the victim's life thereafter. "Trauma can affect victims on every level of functioning: biological, psychological, social, and spiritual" (van der Kolk, et al., 1996). This is what I tried to convey in my first book. It seems so obvious, and yet the unavailability of conscious recall of the event by the victims themselves has certainly contributed to many of the misperceptions about relinquishment and adoption. As we look at the ways in which trauma manifests in the lives of its victims, you can decide for yourselves if separation from mother is indeed a trauma.

Trauma is an event in the life of the victim which overwhelms her ordinary human adaptations to life. Who could be more easily overwhelmed than a helpless newborn infant whose very existence was tied symbiotically to that of her mother? An infant has no way to adapt to the sudden disappearance of its mother/self, especially when it has just entered a world which no longer includes the safety of the mother's womb. Anyone except this original mother, whose rhythms and resonance the infant knows and is in tune with, is foreign and dangerous. Just as a transplant patient needs special medications to keep from rejecting the foreign organ, adoptees need special emotional responses to overcome the impulse to reject the "foreign" family.

In her book *Trauma and Recovery*, Judith Herman tells us, "Traumatic reactions occur when action is of no avail ... the human system of self-defense becomes overwhelmed and disorganized" (1992). The baby who cannot get his mother back, despite his cries (protesting her disappearance and beseeching her return), is helpless, overwhelmed, thrown into chaos, and eventually goes into shock. Joseph Chilton Pearce, author of *Magical Child* and *Evolution's End*, reminds us that it takes about 45 minutes for an infant separated from his mother to go into shock (Pearce, 1992). After rage comes despair and then shock. This helplessness turns to hopelessness and a belief that the world is not safe. One cannot trust. Babies in incubators may experience the same sense of helplessness, where "neither resistance nor escape is possible" (Herman, 1992). While all kinds of physically and emotionally painful procedures are perpetrated upon these infants, there is nothing they can do. Defenses against any future reoccurrence of these traumas are being put into place, many of which are almost impossible to eradicate from the psychological/neurological systems.

*Symptoms of Traumatic Response*

There are definite responses to trauma that help to differentiate traumatic events from ordinary difficult circumstances. One is the persistent intrusion of memories traces related to the trauma that often interfere with attending to other incoming information. In their wonderful little book *A General Theory of Love*, Lewis, Amini, and Lannon say, "If an emotion is sufficiently powerful, it can quash opposing networks so completely that their content becomes inaccessible" (2000). In other words, given a choice, our brains conjure up old responses to new events that bear even a slight resemblance to old painful experiences. The authors go on to say, "Because his mind comes outfitted with Hebbian memory (neurons that fire together wire together) and limbic attractors, a person's emotional experience of the world may not budge, even if the world around him changes dramatically." This is the reason that even the best of adoptive mothers often cannot eliminate anxiety about abandonment in her children.

Another response is the tendency to compulsively expose oneself to situations reminiscent of the original trauma (called repetition compulsion). Juxtaposed to this compulsion is the avoidance of any situation which might evoke the emotions of the original traumatic event. This usually results in the numbing of emotions. Because there are elevated levels of adrenaline and cortisol in the body, one loses the ability to utilize the bodily signals as a means of modulating one's physiological responses to stress; in other words, the fight or flight signal is always on, so that one can't rely on it to tell if danger is actually present. (Herman, van der Kolk, et al.) These symptoms can result in behavior which is often interpreted as personality changes, such as disturbed affect regulation, aggression against self and/or others, dissociative problems, somatization, and an altered relationship with self and others (van der Kolk, et al., 1996). The problem for adoptees, as will be discussed in more detail later, is that there is no "pre-trauma self" to which they can refer. This lends itself even more to the belief that the post-traumatic coping behavior is representative of the personality.

*Hyperarousal*

Furthering the difficulties for victims of trauma is their inability to regulate their arousal levels. There is a restlessness, a perceived need to be constantly on the alert, although in the case of early trauma, the victim seldom knows what the danger is. Herman states, "Traumatic events produce profound and lasting changes in physiological arousal, emotion, cognition, and memory." Hypervigilance and hyperarousal are manifestations of separation trauma. Adoptees can attest to their constant need for vigilance. There is a prevailing feeling of dread, a need to be on the alert for disaster. Because this hypervigilance is continuous, the world is seen as an unsafe place. Van der Kolk, et al. state, "These hyperarousal phenomena represent complex psychological and biological processes, in which the continued anticipation of overwhelming threat seems to cause difficulties with attention and concentration" (1996). This is evident in adoptees' problems with focusing (especially in school). They are easily distracted and have difficulty with stimulus discrimination. The inability to discriminate among the various stimuli constantly occurring in the environment means that adoptees, as well as other trauma victims, have difficulty sorting out relevant from irrelevant stimuli. What most of us would ignore, they must check out as a possible danger. Van der Kolk contends that this makes it difficult for individuals to respond flexibly to the environment and that this loss of flexibility "... may explain current findings of deficits in preservative learning and interference with the acquisition of new information" (1996). This may explain why so many adoptees are diagnosed with attention deficit disorder (ADD).

*The Formation of Beliefs*

To make things more difficult, the emotion of the traumatic event often gets disconnected from the memory (if there is a memory). For most adoptees, the trauma takes place during the period of childhood amnesia or implicit memory. This means that the events of their lives are having a profound effect on their perceptions and on neurological connections in the brain, but there will be no recall of the events. Many adoptees, as well as birth mothers, will react to a reminder of the traumatic event as if it were the event happening in the present. For adoptees, who experienced their trauma before conscious memory, these are feelings and emotions which they can't seem to connect to any event. These are the implicit memories (which will be explained in more detail in the next chapter), which influence one's sense of Self and others, one's emotional responses and behavior, and in some cases physiological responses without there being any hint about the cause of these manifestations. Feelings of anger, hostility, panic, and sadness can come, seemingly, out of nowhere.

Dissociation often occurs, accompanied by distortions in perceptions. These distorted perceptions become disorganized and imprinted as beliefs about oneself. The "defective baby" belief is one of these. Because babies instinctively know that mothers don't give up their babies, most adoptees seem to blame themselves for their own relinquishment. This belief is consistent with the way that children respond to trauma. As van der Kolk, et al. say, "Many traumatized individuals, especially children, tend to blame themselves for having been traumatized" (1996). The "bad baby" belief allows the child to organize in his own distorted way something which had been completely disorganized. The inexplicable begins to make sense, and the victim can believe that he or she was not completely helpless in the situation. (If I had been a better baby I would not have lost my mother.) There is the illusion of control and the preservation of the idea of the birth parent as good. Yet there is an altered perception of self and others. This is manifest in a sense of being unworthy, flawed, undeserving. Equally distorted are the adoptee's perceptions about others who matter in her life. The adoptive mother seems to bear the most distortion, probably because she was the first person with whom the adoptee interacted and because she was not the mother to whom the baby was connected.

*Anxiety*

When traumatic events become disconnected from their source, as is the case in any trauma happening in infancy, they begin to take on a life of their own. For example, a child waiting for his mother to pick him up from school begins to feel anxious when she is late. He doesn't associate that anxiety with the fact that once a long time ago his first mother disappeared, never to be seen again. He just knows that he becomes more and more anxious, until he begins to feel panicky. Most adoptees' symptoms take on a life of their own because they were too young to remember the original precipitating event. However, because trauma itself produces amnesia surrounding the event, even those children who were old enough to remember the separation will seldom connect it to their panic about mother's being late to pick them up from school or baseball practice. For this reason, being late is a grave offense against adoptees.

It is important for adoptees to understand the amnesia aspect of trauma before they get angry at their birth mothers for not remembering exactly what day they were born or the events surrounding the birth and surrender. Many birth mothers, being traumatized themselves by the separation from their babies, have very hazy memories of the birth and the days following that event. Even if the connection is made cognitively, the intellectual understanding for the anxiety doesn't always do away with the fearful feelings. That's because the reptilian brain is in charge of the responses to trauma. The reptilian brain acts nanoseconds before the neocortex, which could add reason to the mix. The reptilian brain is the survival brain, in charge of the four Fs: fight, flight, freeze, and ... er ... reproduction. If one responds to one of those messages before one can think, difficulties often arise.

"Traumatic memories lack verbal narrative and context; rather, they are encoded in the form of vivid sensations and images" (Herman). A lack of verbal narrative makes memories difficult or impossible to talk about. It would be especially true of adoptees, who, at the time of the traumatizing event, were not yet able to speak. But even if the trauma occurred later, when speech had been mastered, the events surrounding a trauma are difficult to put into words. This may be why war veterans seldom talk about the war, or holocaust victims about the camps. When an experience defies the human brain's capacity to integrate it, it floats around without context in the never-never land of dissociated images, vivid sensations, and puzzling behavior. It is like living in one's nightmare. And no one is immune to trauma. Because trauma has the element of surprise, it can happen to anyone. Not only that, but specific events often cause specific responses in trauma victims. The consequences of trauma are predictable.

## The Consequences of Trauma

There are three main consequences of a traumatic event. They are *terror, disconnection, and captivity.* Using Herman's model, which I believe fits the abandonment experience the best, it will become evident how these characteristics apply to the trauma of the separation between mother and child.

## Terror

The immediate response to trauma is terror. Something is not right and no amount of effort makes it right. In the case of the separated child, the inability to reestablish connection to the mother is a terrifying experience. Infants who are placed in hospital nurseries experience this terror to some extent. Babies live in the moment; they do not know that in time they will again be with mother. The same is true for infants in daycare. They have no object constancy, the ability to hold mother in memory when she is absent. Every separation from the mother seems like forever for the infant. This is terrifying.

Some of the physical responses to terror are an elevation in pulse rate and blood pressure, as documented by Kate Burke Cleary in a 1995 unpublished study of 400 infants in a San Francisco hospital titled "Before Attachment: The Effect of Infant/Mother Separation on Adopted Newborns." Sleep disturbance, irritability, and gastro-intestinal problems are also noted in babies separated from their mothers. There may be elevated levels of adrenaline and cortisol circulating throughout the central nervous system, which makes this experience more pronounced and may result in memory traces being more deeply imprinted.

Even in situations where the mother and baby will be going home together, the practice of putting babies in the nursery, instead of keeping them with their mothers, creates tension and fear for the babies, and a sense of sadness and unease for the mothers. In extreme cases, that separation can result in post-partum depression for mothers and a difficulty in bonding between mother and child. At the very time when the mother and baby should be bonding, they are in separate rooms yearning for one another. In the case of premature births, there is an even longer separation, which often results in a wound which resembles that of adoptees: an impaired bond and a lack of trust in the mother's ability of meet the needs of her child and to protect her from danger.

For a birth mother who may not see her child again there may be a response close to terror. She certainly feels the loss as a devastating grief, which is seldom recognized by anyone else. She often has no acknowledgment for her loss and no advocates for her need to grieve. Even today, when there are groups being formed to help women who have experienced miscarriages, abortions, or still births, nothing is mentioned about the birth mother and her need to grieve. Or, if she does have people who are sympathetic to her loss, their sympathy is often accompanied by assurances that she has done the right thing. They don't realize that there is no connection between her intellectual understanding of her need to make this decision and her instinctive sense that it is not normal—that even to her who made the decision, it feels *not right*. As we know, in the past many birth mothers were not allowed to make their own decision about keeping their babies. That decision was made by a judgmental society and the parents who were influenced by that society. Birth mothers have begun to form their own groups, but they often feel that the general population doesn't understand their grief.

## Hypervigilance

All victims of trauma feel terror and will have several responses to that terror. Two, which adoptees will certainly recognize, are hypervigilance and hyperarousal. A traumatic experience is recorded in the reptilian brain, as mentioned before. This is the part of the brain which deals with self-preservation or survival. The level of serotonin is reduced and adrenaline is elevated. There is a sense of being on permanent alert, as if the danger (trauma) might return at any time. This is experienced as anxiety by many adoptees and birth mothers. Adoptees, because they have experienced it all their lives, may not even know that it is not a normal state. Van der Kolk, et al. state, "Trauma interferes with children's capacity to regulate their arousal levels. This seems to be related to a wide spectrum of problems, from learning disabilities to aggression against self and others" (1996). When one senses danger at every turn, one often overreacts to stimuli. Something which would simply annoy anyone else will create a sense of danger in a trauma victim. Trauma victims tend to react rather than reflect. It is not a very good idea to surprise an adoptee.

## Intrusion or Re-experiencing

One of the most problematic manifestations of terror is that it keeps intruding into one's life as if the original trauma were recurring in the present. Van der Kolk, et al. remind us, "Because of this timeless and unintegrated nature of traumatic memories, victims remain embedded in the trauma as a contemporary experience, instead of being able to accept it as something belonging to the past" (1996). Whereas most of us will be only slightly annoyed by repetitive stimuli and just ignore them or tune them out, the traumatized person responds to each repetition as though it were a new and dangerous situation. Unresolved traumatic memories never reach the point of becoming part of the narrative of one's life. Instead, they remain unstable reactions which tend to intrude into one's personal relationships and internal experiences. Daniel Siegel, author of the seminal work *The Developing Mind,* says, "Repeated experiences of terror and fear can be engrained within the circuits of the brain as states of mind. With chronic occurrence, these states can become more readily activated (retrieved) in the future, such that they become characteristic traits of the individual. ... We simply enter these engrained states and experience them as the reality of our present experience" (1999). The triggers don't have to be particularly significant.

Herman says, "... seemingly insignificant reminders can also evoke these memories which often return with all the vividness and emotional force of the original event." It doesn't even need to be events in their own lives which trigger traumatized children. Robert Pynoos points out, "Even fictional portrayals in fairy tales, in novels, or on television may further challenge the child" (Pynoos, 1991). Many adoptees have told me that certain stories, such as *The Ugly Duckling, The Runaway Bunny, Peter Pan, Are You My Mother?,* and *Pinocchio* have had a dramatic effect on them. These intrusions take different forms, such as intense emotions—fear, panic, anger, or rage; somatic sensations, such as stomachaches, headaches, or asthma; nightmares; interpersonal reenactments; and unhealthy behavioral patterns. The reactions to these intrusive flashbacks are often misunderstood by those close to the trauma victims, and many relationships are jeopardized by overwhelming and inappropriate responses to seemingly innocuous stimuli.

Because traumatic memories lack verbal narrative and context, they are most often experienced as sensations and images and expressed as behavior. These acts often incur the frustration or wrath of the recipient and, again, cause difficulties in relationships. It is very difficult for an adoptee, for instance, to say exactly what he is experiencing, so he acts out in response to the stimulus. An adoptee has two strikes against him: not only is he traumatized, but the trauma occurred before he had words. It is important for a traumatized person to learn to halt the behavioral reaction to the imagined danger until the neocortex can get in gear and modify the response. This can be learned, but it is not easy, especially since, as van der Kolk, et al. remind us, "Over time the triggers may become increasingly more subtle and generalized." It becomes difficult to recognize the stimuli as that which is causing the reaction. This, in combination with the adoptee's biased perceptions about events in favor of the more negative aspects, makes interactions more and more confusing and difficult. Van der Kolk, et al. point out that trauma victims "... respond preferentially to trauma-related triggers at the expense of being able to attend to other perceptions." This can be noted in adoptees, who latch onto anything that can be construed as a rejection, rather than seeing some word, action, or attitude in a more positive light. It also plays into their inability to distinguish between suggestion and control. The most innocuous suggestions are often interpreted by an adoptee as an attempt to control. This can result in an adoptee's refusing to participate in an activity she might ordinarily enjoy, just because it was suggested by someone else.

### Repetition Compulsion

Complicating the difficulties of intrusion is something which Freud called the *repetition compulsion*. This is the often unconscious compulsion for one to relive in present life a traumatic experience that happened in the past. Van der Kolk, et al. remind us that unlike ordinary memories that change and become integrated over time, traumatic memories are relived with the intense sensory imagery and emotional intensity that makes a person feel as if the event were taking place in the present. This is true even when the experience is not consciously remembered. Herman claims that this reliving of the experience is an attempt to integrate the traumatic event and master the overwhelming feelings caused by the original experience.

In my correspondence with adoptees, the four most common feelings which they are attempting to master are fear, rage, helplessness, and bottomless sorrow (the abyss or black hole). Unfortunately these attempts are usually unsuccessful. Instead, the present situation is experienced as if it were the original event, the feelings are again overwhelming, and the beliefs which resulted from the original trauma are reinforced. As the adoptee emerges from a failed relationship with an emotionally unavailable partner, he again experiences the beliefs: "I am unworthy, I don't belong, I am unlovable."

### Dissociation, Numbing, or Constriction

At the moment of the traumatic event, when one experiences a state of helplessness or powerlessness, when physical escape is not possible, the person escapes from the terror by an altered state of consciousness called *dissociation*. When fight or flight are not options, then freeze is all that is left. This altered state of consciousness is similar to hypnotic trance and restores a state of calm to the person. Young children will often sit mesmerized in front of the television, oblivious to anything happening around them. They are putting themselves into the drama happening on the screen in order to escape for a little while their own pain. Sometimes this escape is noticed as a kind of daydreaming, something about which many teachers complain. As they get older, more sophisticated forms of avoidance are employed. Trauma victims start organizing their lives to avoid having unwanted emotions by the use of alcohol, drugs, or food, or by promiscuity or pornography.

An example of how this works with adults is the case of prostitutes who learned to dissociate as incest victims and who can subsequently feel untouched by their johns. They simply escape from their bodies and watch the events in the room as if they are happening to someone else. Perceptions are distorted, they are numb, and even physical pain can be anesthetized in the loss of sensation. Men have told me that they are sure that prostitutes really enjoy what they are doing. They might want to remember that they are paid to give that impression.

Some types of dissociation are spontaneous and result in a "... surrender of voluntary action, suspension of initiative and critical judgment, subjective detachment or calm, enhanced perception of imagery, altered sensation, including numbness and analgesia, and distortion of reality, including depersonalization, derealization, and change in the sense of time" (Herman). It is thought that these spontaneous and uncontrolled trance states may trigger the release of chemicals within the central nervous system, such as opiates, which diminish the distress caused by pain without eliminating the sensation of pain.

When she cannot seem to dissociate spontaneously, the trauma victim often turns to alcohol or narcotics in an attempt to avoid the pain of loss. In my research, although I haven't attempted to gather statistics, it seems to me that there is an inordinate number of birth mothers and adoptees who have been addicted to either drugs or alcohol. Whereas many incest victims resort to cutting themselves in an attempt to externalize internal pain, victims of separation trauma may abuse their bodies with narcotics and alcohol. While it may be argued that they are not really helping themselves by behaving in this manner, they will retort that at the time anything is better than experiencing the pain. This behavior is often isolating and causes many adoptees to become withdrawn. Trauma victims may become "... more and more sensitized to environmental stimuli that remind them of the trauma ... and less and less responsive to various stimuli which are necessary for involvement in the present" (van der Kolk, et al., 1996). It is often difficult to integrate present experiences as foils to the beliefs created by the original trauma. Joseph LeDoux, in his book *The Emotional Brain*, suggests that trauma somehow "... biases the brain in such a way that the thalamic pathways to the amygdala (feeling part of the brain) predominates over the cortical (thinking) ones, allowing these low-level processing networks to take the lead in the learning and storage of information." Not only that, but he also says, "It is possible for emotions to be triggered in us without the cortex knowing exactly what is going on" (LeDoux, 1996). This is what many adoptees have complained about. They feel hurt, sad, or angry, but they have no idea where these feelings are coming from. They often overreact to certain stimuli without knowing why. This is puzzling and sometimes frightening to them and to those who are close to them. John Ratey, author of *The User's Guide to the Brain*, says, "We automatically and unconsciously fit our sensations into categories that we have learned, often distorting them in the process" (Ratey, 2001). This is one reason that becoming conscious is so important—distorted assumptions are made about the origin of the sensations which have little to do with the present situation.

Even if, and it is a very big if, the more intrusive symptoms subside, the sense of helplessness continues to plague the adoptee. This is often seen by outsiders as a lack of motivation, laziness, passivity, or apathy. As these symptoms begin to predominate, there is more and more sensation that a long time ago, the baby soul died. Some adoptees call themselves the "walking aborted." This is a dreadful image, but one which, nevertheless, is vivid for some adoptees.

Many of them feel more dead than alive, and some even try to concretize this sensation by attempting suicide. According to communications I have had from thousands of adoptees, suicidal ideation is common among adolescent adoptees.

Terror, in the forms of hypervigilance, intrusion, and dissociation, is tremendously debilitating. When the numbing of feelings occurs, it can even lead to psychosomatic symptoms. It can also lead to a kind of apathy, which precludes getting any therapeutic help "… since the inability to imagine a future for oneself kills the capacity to look for new solutions" (van der Kolk, et al, 1996). Numbing produces a "what's the use" mentality, which must be overcome to even begin the healing process. However, Ratey reassures us when he says, "The brain is amazingly plastic. … Rewiring is possible throughout life." He warns against repeating the same activities that brought us grief in the first place. "To change the wiring in one skill, you must engage in some activity that is unfamiliar, novel to you, but related to that skill, because simply repeating the same activity only maintains already established connections" (Ratey, 2001). Besides consciously responding differently to everyday situations, creative activities, such as learning to paint, sculpt, write poetry, or play a musical instrument, can redirect our neurons and help to form new patterns in the brain.

## Disconnection

The severing of the bond with the birth mother has a lifelong impact on adoptees, as well as the mother. It calls into question basic human relationships. This is especially severe for the adoptee because her earliest postnatal experience is that of disconnection from the mother/self. She learns that the world is unsafe, perhaps even hostile. Trust, the cornerstone of all relationships, is destroyed. Mother, the one with whom she was connected for nine months and whom she should be able to trust to nurture and protect her as long as she needs her, has disappeared. How then can she trust anyone else? Connection or intimacy is experienced as a precursor of abandonment and must be avoided at all costs!

### Basic Human Relationships

It appears that trust in the safety of relationships is learned in stages, like ripples on a pond. First is the relationship with the mother/self, then the mother as other, then the father and the rest of the family, rippling out to relatives and frequently seen friends, the community, and society. When that first stage is interrupted, even with a substitute mother being provided right away, the ripple effect is disturbed. The interruption of the first relationship alters the perception and meaning of the attachment which connects an individual to the community and society. Adoptees often describe themselves as floating, never feeling connected to anyone, alone even when surrounded by friends or in the arms of a lover. There is no sense of belonging, of fitting in. Sometimes there is no sense of existing.

Adoptees are very good at sabotaging relationships by distancing themselves from their partners via various destructive behaviors, then feeling an immediate need to get into another relationship. Sometimes the end of a relationship causes a sense of loss far beyond the norm—as if the mother has disappeared all over again—and they fall again into the abyss. There is an urgency to get into another relationship immediately in order to still the terror of the abyss. But then the anxiety begins all over again: "Will he/she leave me?" Herman says of trauma victims, "Their capacity for intimacy is compromised by intense and contradictory feelings of need and fear." There is a desperate yearning for intimacy, yet an intense fear of allowing that kind of connection.

### The Value of Self

Besides a lack of trust, the separation from the mother calls into question the value of self. "How can I be of value if my mother did not want me?" Infants neither understand nor are interested in reasons which adults may find acceptable for relinquishment. They perceive the disappearance of the mother as a rejection of them. A belief system begins to form: "I am not good enough; I am flawed, unworthy, unlovable." That belief is so deeply imprinted, both because of its accompanying trauma and of its being so early in the person's life, that it makes it very difficult to banish. For some adoptees, years of positive nurturing does not make a dent in it. Mother provides an infant with his first sense of self-esteem. With her disappearance—whether that disappearance is physical or emotional or both—goes the positive value of self. Questions arise about one's competence, initiative, identity, worthiness, and relatedness. Herman points out, "The traumatic event thus destroys the belief that one can *be oneself* in relation to others." Adoptees usually operate from the *false self.* How often have I heard them lament, "But if she knew who I really am, she wouldn't like me anymore"? This devaluation of self, stemming from the "rejection" by the birth mother, makes it almost impossible for one to really get to know an adoptee, who may be afraid that the rejected part of him, the real self, is defective.

### Continuity of Life

A sense of basic continuity of life appears to be compromised by traumatic events. For adoptees in the closed adoption system, not only are they separated from their original, biological mothers, but also from their entire genetic history. It seems that an inordinate number of adoptees never conceive a child, perhaps a refusal or inability to carry on a heritage about which they have no knowledge. Birth mothers, also, have a high incidence of secondary infertility. Although proven to be fertile, according to various studies, from 35–60 percent of them never again conceive. Various reasons have been given for this, including a feeling of guilt about having given up the first baby, accompanied by doubts about her right or ability to be a mother, and a sense of loyalty to that lost baby. Perhaps, with the casting out of a member of the family comes a lost sense of continuity of the birth mother's family also.

## Cause and Effect

One of the complaints adoptive parents have of adolescent adoptees is that they seem to have no sense of cause and effect. Consequences are of no consequence, so to speak. This phenomenon even appears with adoptees who until adolescence had been perfect children. Suddenly, the parents feel betrayed by a child who no longer cares about the consequences of his behavior. It often appears as if there is no sense that there is a consequence. There is a mysterious lack of a sense of cause and effect. It appears that for the adoptee the destruction of the meaningful order of creation has lead to a sense of chaos and confusion about the natural order of things. One can no longer trust the natural order because the event which normally follows birth is that the infant is locked into sublime symbiosis with the mother. They are one, the mother/baby about which Winnicott speaks. The mother's disappearance is like falling through the universe, floating, floating through space with no grounding. There is no order, only chaos and confusion. That confusion is further reinforced by being placed in an alien place with strangers. Nothing is familiar. One looks into the faces of strangers. There is no reflection of self, no assurance that the infant is all right. Not only has the adoptee been betrayed by the mother, but also by God. There can be no more trust in the transcendent order of the divine. The adoptee may feel abandoned, disconnected, alone, and cast out of the human and divine systems. He feels counterfeit or false. Many adoptees feel as if they do not really exist, or, at the very least, as if they have no right to exist. For many the risk of connection is synonymous with the risk of annihilation.

For some adoptees the labels that are attached to them, such as illegitimate, bastard, etc., add to the sense of having no right to exist. Even though the secrecy laws were supposed to prevent this illegitimacy by providing a false birth certificate and doing away with any knowledge of the birth family, the labels often persisted. One young woman told of her attempt to justify her existence and overcome the label of illegitimacy by becoming a nun. She wanted to be a missionary, thus making her feel like a worthwhile member of the human race and worthy of God. However, when she applied to a Franciscan order in

Iowa, her admission was denied solely because of her illegitimate birth. This reason was actually written in a formal letter of rejection. Naturally, this only added to her feelings of being unworthy even of God and brought about her first suicidal thoughts.

Basic trust is destroyed by the severance of the bond with the original mother. This disconnection, as well as other traumas, calls into question basic human relationships. As Herman says, "Basic trust is the foundation of belief in the continuity of life, the order of nature, and the transcendent order of the divine. ... A secure sense of connection with caring people is the foundation of personality development." There are two things which further compromise the development of personality for the adoptee. One is that in the adoptive family the caregivers cannot mirror the adoptee's personality, character traits, or physical features. The other is that there is no "before trauma self" as a reference point for the personality. Thus the adoptee often assumes that his coping behavior, which is designed to ward off another disaster, is his true personality. He is constantly reacting to the early abandonment experience. Siegel states, "These implicit recollections are not usually subject to a process or self-reflection, as in 'Why am I doing this or feeling this way?' Individuals may sense these experiences as just defining who they are" (1999). This is one of the beliefs which needs to be challenged. There is a big difference between personality (who we are) and behavior (what we do), especially as it pertains to coping behavior.

## Captivity

I have talked about the separation from the birth mother as a single traumatic event in the life of an adoptee that results in terror and disconnection. There is another form of repeated, chronic, or prolonged trauma, which occurs only in captivity, where the victim is unable to flee or escape. For most of us, our thoughts go to prisons, concentration camps, cults, brothels, or abusive families. What has this to do with an adoptee in a normal, caring, nurturing family?

### Not Belonging

Because the adoptee is living in a place where he is not mirrored or reflected, he begins to feel as if he doesn't belong, doesn't fit in. He is confused by the conflict between his genetic self, which is authentic but not reflected, and his adaptive self, which feels false, but is more encouraged and accepted. The sense of not fitting in, not belonging, of being reminded over and over again that one is not like those with whom one is living creates a sense of alienation or a form of trauma which is chronic or prolonged. This can be true even in families where there is consistent nurturing and care. And it is true for adoptees who have not been told that they are adopted. The more there is a difference in the basic personality of the adoptee and his parents, the more traumatic his struggle becomes. There is a constant desperate attempt to try to figure out *how* one is supposed *to be* in this family in order to fit in.

In what possible way can an adoptive family resemble a concentration camp or prison? First of all, no matter how alienated the adoptee feels, until he is old enough to run away, there is no escape from the situation. Herman says, "In situations of captivity, the perpetrator becomes the most powerful person in the life of the victim, and the psychology of the victim is shaped by the actions and beliefs of the perpetrator ... (who) relentlessly demands from his victim professions of respect, gratitude, or even love." Not all adoptees feel like captives in their adoptive families, but I have heard from enough of them who do to think that this category is applicable. Whereas many adoptees feel genuinely loved and respected by their adoptive parents for who they are, there are some who feel as if they have been used to fulfill their parents' wishes for a child without regard for who they are or how different they might be from the parents. These adoptees express attitudes very similar to that last statement by Herman, where they feel that their lives were manipulated by people to whom they are not related, but who expect gratitude, respect, and love.

Although some adoptive parents are aware that a person's personality may be genetic and that adoptees are not a blank slate when they came into their lives, others have the idea that they can mould or convert the child, capture his inner mind, and reshape his allegiances. In sometimes subtle and sometimes not-so-subtle ways, the parents may let the child know that any allegiance to his birth family is not all right. He must sacrifice this relationship, however much a fantasy it might be. In trying to be like the members of the adoptive family, the child destroys a sense of self, and innate characteristics begin to atrophy. Some adoptees try to hang onto a sense of self by fighting, while others appear to be malleable, not changing their true character, but just shutting down. Their behavior is different from their personality; often they unconsciously choose a role that they can enact, but when activities alien to the family are seen as insubordination, the child's initiative, planning, and implementation become constricted.

Adhering to the rules of the adoptive family, the adoptee may have been asked, "If it weren't for us, where would you be?" This question reinforces the idea that she might have died as a result of abandonment. The adoptee's sense of abandonment is often experienced as a kind of death. Not only is there a fear of death, but the adoptee is made to feel grateful for being allowed to live. This mirrors the reactions of prisoners of concentration camps, where the prisoner is made to feel grateful for being allowed to live, as he begins to identify with his captors. There are often alterations between intense attachment and terrified withdrawal.

Just as with other captives, time is altered both by the original trauma and by experience in the adoptive family. The past (the genetic past) is obliterated, and the adoptee may be discouraged from trying to find out about it. By obliterating the past, the link to the future becomes tenuous. "Memory, like hope, brings back the yearning for all that has been lost" (Herman). For the future to exist, the past must also exist, but in closed adoption the past has been completely erased by means of a false birth certificate and closed records. In closed adoptions identity is contaminated by secrecy and lies. The child's personal history now includes the sense of the captive self. This leads to preoccupations with shame, self-loathing, and a sense of failure, as if the adoptee could have somehow escaped this captivity. Many adoptees report waiting for rescuers when they were children. They were paradoxically elated and fearful of these fantasies.

Feeling like prisoners in their adoptive homes is not the case for all adoptees or even most adoptees. My guess is that it is more likely to be true when there is a bad fit between the personalities and proclivities of the adoptee and her parents. The less she is mirrored, the more alien she feels, and the more she feels as if she needs to get out of that alien space. This is the fault of neither the adoptee nor the parents. It is something which happens as a result of the hodge-podge way in which adoptions are accomplished. There may be no good way of determining the relative fit between the adoptee's authentic self and her adoptive parents' selves, but there certainly needs to be more care taken as to the parents' understanding of issues like this. If adoptees cannot be mirrored, at least they have a right to be understood.

Let us not forget the effect captivity has on birth mothers, who were often hidden in work-wage homes or spirited away from friends and family to unwed mothers' homes. Isolated and literally held captive by the shaming mechanisms of society, birth mothers were isolated with their unborn children from any other source of information, emotional support, or maternal aid. Many birth mothers lost faith in their ability to make decisions. Their ability to trust their own judgment was often shattered.

*Blaming the Victim*

As with other victims of manipulation, adoptees and birth mothers are often blamed for their responses to trauma. The birth mother is between a rock and a hard place. At the time of surrender, she was told in no uncertain terms that to keep her baby would be a selfish act, and the best interest of her baby would be to give it to a deserving couple who could rear it in a stable home. Later, she has been admonished for giving away her baby. "How could she have done that?"

people ask. The very society which condemned her for getting pregnant and punished her by insisting that she give up her baby is now criticizing her for having done what was required of her at the time. How hypocritical a society we are! According to Ricki Solinger in her seminal book *Wake Up Little Susie*, during the 40s, 50s, and 60s, 90–95% of white unmarried women were giving up their babies, whereas at the present time it is about 3%. What has changed? Two of the most obvious are abortion and "the pill." But not to be ignored is that moral attitudes have changed. Certainly the feelings of the mothers haven't changed. If the birth mothers of the 40s, 50s, 60s, and early 70s had been given a couple years of help from families or agencies, many of them would have gladly kept their babies (and saved themselves years of anguish).

So far as adoptees are concerned, not only are they not understood as having suffered a loss, but they are supposed to be grateful for having been adopted. In the altruistic view still held by much of our society, adoptees' grief is often overlooked, as the joy of the adoptive parents is celebrated. Although, as a society, we are beginning to understand that childhood experiences such as sexual, physical, and emotional abuse are harmful, and that women are not responsible for their own rapes, adoptees are still seen as ungrateful if they don't see adoption as a wonderful experience. Thus, we as a society still view adoption as beneficial without any acknowledgment of the trauma which precedes it or the pain and confusion which accompany it.

A result of this gap in understanding the pain of separation and adoption is that the helping professions often label adoptees as having character disorders. But the concept of personality development does not include "… any understanding of the corrosion of personality that occurs under conditions of prolonged terror" (Herman). It is difficult to develop one's personality when one is constantly fearful, as are many adoptees and birth mothers. Birth mothers have the advantage of having a pre-trauma reference for their personalities: "I know that before this happened to me I was not so fearful, untrusting, and guilt-ridden. My attitudes were different, my behavior was different. I knew who I was." Unfortunately, that knowledge does not always translate into a healthy personality for the birth mother, because her present behavior is influenced by the memory of the trauma. Adoptees, on the other hand, experience the trauma at the very beginning of their lives, before long-term memory develops. There is no "before the trauma" for them, no reference point for who they were/are. They often get confused between their post-trauma coping behavior and their authentic personalities.

Many psychotherapists, including psychiatrists and psychologists, use the DSM (*Diagnostic and Statistical Manual of Mental Disorders*) when diagnosing patients. The problem with this tool is that it is a manual of symptoms only, which means that there is no information as to the etiology or cause of the symptoms. This, I believe, is a very dangerous protocol. As I will demonstrate in Chapter 19—Defining Adult Pathology—the symptoms of adoptees and borderline personalities are almost identical, which is the reason that so many adoptees are falsely diagnosed as borderlines. This is a dangerous and erroneous assumption, because the treatment plans for each is different and for the most part diametrically opposed.

When discussing the various diagnoses of trauma victims, Herman is vehement: "The most notorious is the diagnosis of borderline personality disorder. This term is frequently used within the mental health professions as little more than a sophisticated insult." She believes, as do I, that we desperately need a new paradigm. What has to be understood thus far is that separation trauma is an insidious experience, because, as a society, we fail to see this experience as a trauma. This has kept adoptees and birth mothers locked in the prison of their feelings and fears, without any acknowledgment of the pain they are experiencing.

But what is all this talk of victimhood, when this book is about getting out from under the burden of being a victim? We cannot heal from something unless we acknowledge that it exists. There is no one, in my opinion, who is more traumatized (i.e., victimized) than a newborn infant who is separated from her mother, her heritage, and her genetic history. It is like experiencing a terrific implosion, then growing up with genetic amnesia, no reference points for one's being, no reflection of one's Self. Some adoptees are keenly aware of this, yet feel abnormal for this awareness. Other adoptees, never having known anything else and not being in touch with their feelings, may think that whatever they are experiencing is normal and "no big deal." All trauma is a "big deal," and has an influence on one's basic sense of Self. As we shall see in the next chapter, trauma also influences the way in which our neurons connect in our brains, or, to put it in the vernacular, the way we are wired. No one is immune from trauma. The element of surprise and the danger of annihilation make everyone vulnerable to trauma. "The key is surprise, the unexpected, the interruption in the natural order" (Herman). This is especially true of a helpless infant or child. A child who is separated from her mother in infancy is affected by this separation and sees the world, herself, and others through the lens of that abandonment, whether she understands it or not.

It is this understanding which has to come before one can move out of the role of victim, through the role of survivor, and into the role of participant in life. For as Ken Watson so eloquently put it:

*People cannot recover from the pain of their past until they have faced it, and they can be helped to do this in an empathic relationship or environment. In order to lead more satisfying lives and to achieve their optimum potential, however, people must move beyond the empathy phase and become empowered to change. The energy formerly needed to deny their pain is now available to them to make choices and to take action to reach desired goals. In the empathy phase people see themselves first as victims and then they move on to viewing themselves as survivors. But true healing comes only when one is not just a survivor, but a participant.*

*Watson,* AAC Decree, *summer 1997*

It is only through acknowledging, understanding, and addressing our pain, in the presence of others, that we can participate in a life of empowerment and peace.

Before we can do that, we must first understand how our experiences affect the ways in which our neurons are connected in our brains. This is the key to understanding why we act as we do. At the same time, this understanding can give us hope that we can change the things we want to change.

# CHAPTER 2
Adoption and the Brain

Brain research is in its infancy, but already it is adding scientific validity to aspects of human development that many of us who deal with human emotions for a profession have intuited for a long time. After birth our brains are wired in large part as a result of our experiences and the meaning we place on these experiences. When this meaning is predicated upon a perception introduced during the stage of primary narcissism in infancy, it follows that the person responsible for one's experience and the results thereof must be oneself. Even after infancy, children usually blame themselves for all the things that happen to them during the earliest stages of development.

This, of course, helps explain why so many adoptees blame themselves for their own relinquishment. Even when they *know* this can't be true, they still *feel* as if it is true. They *believe* it to be true. This early belief leaves them with the sense that they are not good enough—unlovable and unworthy. Because this belief was ingrained during a traumatic event and when so many neurons were firing, the imprinted belief is very difficult to change. Let us see why this is so.

## The Development of the Brain

Neurobiology has helped us to understand the tremendous changes that take place in the human infant's brain, beginning before birth and continuing at a terrific rate through age three. J. Madeleine Nash, in a *Time* magazine article titled "Fertile Minds," reminds us that, unlike a computer, the brain begins working before it is finished. The processes that begin before birth help propel the tremendous learning, which occurs immediately after birth (1997). It is to be noted that at birth, the infant's brain is the most undifferentiated organ in the body. Whereas at birth the brain contains all the nerve cells it will ever have, which is roughly 100 billion, the wiring or how those cells are connected has yet to be established. The forming of synapses, an activity that until birth has been more or less spontaneous and genetically driven, is now driven by sensory experiences. These experiences will determine the pattern of wiring, which will be unique to each individual, and after a drastic pruning somewhere between age ten and eighteen, will last a lifetime.

## The Impact of Experience

It is this wiring that is so tremendously important in the first months after birth, when the number of connections explodes. The early experiences of the infant greatly influence the ways in which the neurons connect. Daniel Siegel, in his very important book, *The Developing Mind*, says, "Genes and early experience shape the way neurons connect to one another and thus form the specialized circuits that give rise to mental processes. In this way, experiences in early life have a tremendously important impact on the developing mind" (1999). This has special significance for adoptees who are separated from their mothers, often at birth, so that their earliest postnatal experience is one of separation and loss. We are reminded that studies of animals have demonstrated that even short periods of maternal deprivation "... have powerful neuroendocrine effects on the ability to cope with future stressful events. ... In a direct way, experience shapes the structure of the brain" (Siegel, 1999). Or, as Canadian psychologist Donald Hebb describes it: "Neurons that fire together, wire together" (Siegel, 1999, Restak, 2000, Lewis, et al., 2000).

## Implicit Memory

During the first three years of a child's life, her experiences have a tremendous effect on how she will view herself and others, how she will act or behave, how she will respond emotionally and, perhaps, physically to events and relationships, and the kinds of generalizations she forms from her experiences. Given the importance of this neurological phenomenon, it is a bit disconcerting that much of the memory we have of this time is implicit memory: experiences that greatly influence our responses to the world and those in it, but that we cannot recall. In defining memory, Siegel makes what I consider one of the most profound statements in his book: "Memory is more than what we can consciously recall about events from the past. A broader definition is that *memory is the way past events affect future function*" (italics Siegel's). And remember what he said about repeated experiences of terror and fear: "(they) can be engrained within the circuits of the brain as states of mind." What this means for adoptees is that the separation from mother can be reexperienced as repeated patterns of responding to relationships as if everyone were going to leave them. Siegel offers these encouraging words, however: "Knowing about implicit memory allows us the opportunity to free ourselves from the prison of the past."

## Limbic Regulation

Traumatic experiences that go unnoticed by the mother or unattended by her can make a child more vulnerable to loss. This is because infants cannot regulate their emotions themselves, but need the interdependence of their mothers to help them. In biological mother/child relationships, high levels of oxytocin signal that the pair belong together and help form the ties between them. Adoptive mothers don't have this chemical advantage. For this reason it is very important that the adoptive mother be keenly tuned in to her new baby. The baby cannot regulate himself to the emotions caused by the trauma that has just happened. Because a baby begins life as an open loop, the mother provides the child with the synchronization for these affective or limbic rhythms. Lewis, et al. caution us that "Lengthy parental absence deprives a child of limbic regulation ... attachment interruptions are dangerous. ... Our society overlooks the drain on emotional balance that results from severing attachment" (2000). The interaction between mother and child has vital meaning to the infant. She is helping him regulate his feelings and soothe himself. A young child cannot soothe himself. It takes thousands of interactions between him and his soothing mother for him to learn to self-soothe. If the mother is not attuned to his emotional state, she will not be able to soothe him. As Lewis, et al. put it, "One of a parent's most important jobs is to remain in tune with her child, because she will focus the eyes he turns toward inner and outer worlds." Limbic regulation not only provides a basis for security within the family, but helps prepare a child for life outside the family.

It cannot be overstated that limbic (emotional) attunement and regulation are crucial to emotionally healthy children and adults. Lewis, et al. warn, "As a society, if we do not attend to the limbic needs of our own young, we risk creating an epidemic of loss vulnerability." They further state that a nation which doesn't heed this warning will be a nation depending on serotonin reuptake inhibitors, or as they put it, "Serotonin agents will then become not just a remedy to retrieve those few teetering on the brink of desolation's abyss, but a way of life for a culture that has settled on the lip of the precipice itself." Are we not already there? Not only do we rely on prescription drugs to keep us from falling over the brink, but many people use illegal drugs for the same reason. These authors posit something which I have often wondered myself: "America expends billions to protect our borders against the influx of small packets of limbic anesthesia. Those sums might be better spent ensuring that our children harbor brains minimally responsive to such agents" (Lewis, et al.), to which I say, "Amen!"

*Early Learning*

Although we often think that the development of the brain is directly connected to having a great deal of stimulation, there may be other criteria involved. It certainly is important to have toys and other stimuli in a child's environment, yet it may be equally important to have a sense of safety and security as well. The push now to send young mothers out into the world of commerce, leaving their babies and children in daycare, may in the long run have a detrimental effect on these children's learning. As Nash points out, without excellent programs for these children "... the current drive to curtail welfare costs by pushing mothers with infants and toddlers into the work force may well backfire." It is my belief that even with excellent programs, the separation from the mother, especially during the first three years of life, will adversely affect the formation of synapses. Children need one person with whom they can learn limbic regulation, someone they can count on. Although the best person to regulate an infant is the biological mother with whom he has a shared chemistry, a well-attuned adoptive mother can be of tremendous help in this kind of regulation so long as she is attuned to his emotional states. What isn't helpful is having different people who are not tuned in to the child's emotional states taking care of him.

Because of the child-rearing practices in this country, even biological mothers are probably not as attuned to their infants as African women might be. During a conference on pre- and perinatal psychology I heard an interesting study comparing the learning styles of African and Western babies. It was observed that African babies progressed much faster than their Western counterparts due to the proximity of the baby to its mother over prolonged periods of time and the stimuli which they encounter due to this arrangement. African mothers frequently attach their babies to their bodies right after birth and go about their business. A story related by one visitor to a tribe in Kenya is illustrative of how much more "tuned in" to their babies African mothers are than are Western mothers. The man was walking along talking to the mother, who had a naked baby attached to her, when all of a sudden she held the baby away from her while the baby urinated in the bushes on the side of the path. "How did you know your baby had to pee?" the astonished man asked the mother. The mother looked at the man as if he were demented and asked, "How do I know *I* have to pee?" Who else would be that connected and in tune with that particular infant? This kind of mother/child symbiosis is repeated over and over in less dramatic ways even in our own less attuned relationships with our infants. In a new study, Salvatore Mancuso of Rome finds that mothers retain cellular material from each of their children after the baby is born. This cellular connection is thought to improve communication between the mother and child.

It seems that African babies sleep a great deal less than Western babies, probably because all the stimuli keep them from being bored. They feel safe and secure, being close to their mothers, so they do not go into terror mode or shock. This combination of safely and sensory stimuli seem to make African babies "smarter" than Western babies at an earlier age. This makes a great deal of sense to me as I observe the effects of neglect and sensory deprivation on children. Putting a child in a room by himself and hanging a colorful mobile over his head just doesn't do it! I believe that babies learn best when there is almost constant proximity to the mother, stimulating experiences, and lots of "conversation." As they grow into toddlers, they need father and others in their lives to create more connections and stimulation, as well as a great deal of undirected play, where they can use their imaginations and work out their problems.

*Explicit Memory*

It is during the second year of life that explicit memory begins to form. Unlike implicit memory, explicit memory means there is a sense of being able to recall something. Explicit memory has two parts: semantic and episodic. Semantic memory involves factual information, such as what one is required to memorize in school: the capital of California is Sacramento. Episodic recall is more personal, as it is the retrieval of autobiographical material, a sense of self in time and space. As one delightful three-year-old daughter of a good friend has repeated over and over long after the event, "Your kitty pounced on me, but then said she was sorry." Even if a memory is recalled for some time after the event, that doesn't mean that it will be there forever. Not all long-term memory becomes permanent memory. We'll see if Julia remembers my cat pouncing on her twenty years from now and just *how* she remembers it.

Even as we begin to retain memories, the filtering process which dictates which memories are retained and which are forgotten depends, not only on our interpretation or perception of the event and its meaning, but also on our brain chemistry. Candace Pert asks, "Since our sensing of the outer world is filtered along peptide-receptor-rich sensory way stations, each with a different emotional tone, how can we objectively define what's real and what's not real?" She tells us, "Emotions are constantly regulating what we experience as 'reality.' The decision about what sensory information travels to your brain and what gets filtered out depends on what signals the receptors are receiving from the peptides" (1997).

Those signals from the receptors can be determined by emotion, and emotion is determined by experience. Remember the earlier quotation from Ratey: "We automatically and unconsciously fit our sensations into categories that we have learned, often distorting them in the process. ... Experience colors perception." This last is very important, because victims of trauma often have a very different view of the world than those who are not victims. Sometime they feel rejected if everyone doesn't see the world as they do. It is important to remember that *trauma distorts reality.*

How parents talk with children about experiences in their lives can have a direct effect on the ways in which these events are organized and integrated into their memories. This is one of the ways that interpersonal experiences influence explicit memory. Parents' responses to events can trigger emotional responses in their children. Whether or not an alarming event is perceived as trauma may have something to do with how the parents reacted to it and whether or not there was encouragement to talk about it. The earlier one talks about a traumatic event, the less likely that it will cause post-traumatic stress disorder (PTSD). Even if one doesn't have explicit memories of traumatic events, there are often fantasies about them. Adoptees need to be able to talk about their relinquishment, their difficulty in feeling as if they belong, and their biological families: "Where is my birth mother? Does she think about me? Will I ever see her?" without the adoptive families shutting off their attempts to come to terms with their losses. Parents need to keep the lines of communication open, even if it makes them uncomfortable. Adults also need to have the opportunity to talk about loss. How many birth mothers might have been able to find solace in being able to talk about the horror of having to give up their babies? Being allowed to process the event by talking about it and mourning their loss may have made them better able to integrate their experience.

## The Accuracy of Memory

Memory is not always an accurate recorder of truth. It changes over time. Events which we may recall as facts actually evolve over our lifespan, which may be one reason that no two people in a family remember events in the same way. Even in the present, people see, interpret, and retain as memory different versions of the same event, which is the reason eye-witness accounts of crimes are not always a good indicator of what actually happened. Another memory modifier may be the present mood we're in when we recall an event. And just the passage of time will change the way we remember our experiences. As Richard Restak reminds us, "In short, memory isn't at all like a videotape that you insert into a biological VCR within your brain; memory is a creative reconstruction of the past. ... Preconceptions, prejudices, unexamined assumptions—all influence memory" (2000). Memory, like life itself, is ever changing.

If mood is one of the things which influences memory, what is mood? Lewis, et al. define mood as "a state of enhanced readiness to experience a certain emotion." It stands to reason, then, that our readiness may depend upon old memories which produced certain emotions, so that we have a tendency to experience the same emotions over and over. In addition to our mood, new experiences may also alter our memory. Restak quotes Stuart Zola, a psychologist at U.C. San Diego, who says, "Memories for personally experienced events can be altered by new experiences. Perfectly detailed memory, flawlessly preserved through decades, sitting unchanged as if in a time capsule, appears unlikely to occur" (Restak, 2000). It is important for everyone in the adoption triad to understand this, because the perceptions of an adoptee about his life in his adoptive home as a child may be colored by the lenses of abandonment and loss. Certain events may have a different interpretation as seen from the point of view of the adopted child than from the point of view of the adoptive parents or other siblings. Remember Ratey's statement: "Experience colors perception." When one's first experience outside the womb is the disappearance of the mother, one's perception is going to be very different from someone who remained with mother. In addition, the memory connected to that experience will change over time. Lewis, et al. tell us that "the nature of the brain's storage mechanism dictates that memories *must* change over time." As our experiences and understandings change, so do our memories. Siegel points out, "The degree of conviction about the accuracy of a memory may not correspond to its accuracy … memory is social and suggestible, and … the act of retrieving a memory may alter its form for subsequent storage." No one remembers events exactly as they happened. How many of you have been astounded by rereading entries in your diaries five, ten or twenty years later?

The accuracy of memory has been called into question in some child molestation cases. The suggestibility of memory has been cited as a reason to doubt childhood accounts of abuse. My experience in working with molested patients makes me believe that the *emotional reactions* and *behavior* of a child or adult can more accurately demonstrate repressed memory than an actual narrative account of an incident. Remember from the last chapter that trauma does not lend itself to narrative accounts of the event. So far as suggestibility is concerned, I've been told that if one adoptee in a support group talks about having been abused in his adoptive home, several other adoptees may also interpret what happened to them as abusive, and the whole group will be filled with anger and rage. While there is no doubt that some adoptive parents have been and are abusive, it must be remembered that the implicit memory of having been separated from the birth mother may register as a form of abuse on the infant mind and may color the interpretation of future interactions with adoptive parents.

## Brain Development and Stress

The quality of the relationship to their parents seems to be an important aspect in informing the ways in which synapses are formed in children. This is especially true when it comes to the setting up of a child's regulation of his responses to stress. We know that children who are abused carry an inordinate amount of the stress hormones *cortisol* and/or *catecholamines* in their systems. They also have elevated amounts of adrenaline acting on the central nervous system and remain in a constant state of alert to danger. Siegel reminds us that "… excessive stress hormone or catecholamines release appears, respectively, to impair the hippocampal and amygdala contributions to memory processing. Under some conditions, explicit memory may be blocked from encoding at the actual time of the experience. Trauma may be proposed to be such a situation. ... Unresolved traumatic experiences from this perspective may involve an impairment of the cortical consolidation process, which leaves the memories of these events out of permanent memory" (1999). Of course for infants relinquished at birth, these memories would remain solely in implicit memory because of the early time at which the separation took place. It is important to point out that, although explicit memory changes over time, implicit memory does not. This is one reason it is so difficult to overcome the imprints of implicit memory. The earlier the trauma, the more damaging the effect on the brain. In her *Time* magazine article, Madeleine Nash, quotes Dr. Bruce Perry of Baylor College of Medicine, who says, "Because the brain develops in sequence, with more primitive structures stabilizing their connections first, early abuse is particularly damaging" (Nash, 1997). He goes on to say, "*Experience is the chief architect of the brain*" (italics added). This certainly makes a great deal of sense and can inform us in the ways in which neglected or abused children relate to the world. It also says a great deal about how the wiring of the brain of infants in incubators may be affected by that experience. And what of adoptees?

If, as Dr. Perry claims, "experience is the chief architect of the brain," what does this mean for children whose first postnatal experience is the disappearance of their mother? Trauma which occurs during the period of normal childhood amnesia, which includes immediate postnatal separation from mother, will be processed as implicit memory, affecting behavior and emotional responses, although remaining in an unresolved, unconsolidated form. The danger here is that, as Siegel says, "These implicit recollections are not usually subject to a process of self-reflection, as in 'Why am I doing this or feeling this way?' Individuals may sense these experiences as just defining who they are." This is extremely important for adoptees to hear because, as I will be explaining later, many adoptees define themselves as the way they respond behaviorally and emotionally to the experience of their trauma, rather than who they are intrinsically or genetically. "It is clear that certain early experiences create a fundamental impairment in self-organization" (Siegel). An impairment in self-organization is often experienced by adoptees as chaos and confusion. Something intruded upon the natural order of things to interrupt the natural flow of their lives. After awhile chaos may become the way in which they know they are alive.

If the trauma occurs later in life, then talking about it and allowing the child to integrate it is extremely important. One often hears stories in which a family member dies and no one talks about it. This aura of silence occurs for both birth mothers and children who are adopted at an age when explicit memory has "kicked in." "Let's pretend" seems to be the order of the day. The birth mother is to pretend that nothing has happened and that she can just get on with her life, and the child is to pretend that he never had a life before adoption. In neither case is the event integrated as permanent memory, but lingers in the limbo of unresolved, unconsolidated form, negatively influencing future relationships. Furthermore, according to Daniel Goleman, author of *Emotional Intelligence*, "Victims of a devastating trauma may never be the same biologically." This may be especially true if the traumatized person feels completely helpless. He says, "All *uncontrollable* stress can have the same biological impact. The operative word is *uncontrollable*. ... It's the feeling that your life is in danger *and there's nothing you can do to escape it*—that's the moment the brain change begins" (Goleman, 1995). For the children who were relinquished at birth, a sense of helplessness and anxiety often pervades the completion of even the simplest task. For birth mothers, there is often a lack of faith in their own decision-making ability. We can only surmise and hope that those birth mothers who have some say in the choice of the adoptive parents of their children will have a feeling of more control, and thus less stress and biological change in their neurological systems.

One of the things I have noticed, as I work with many adult adoptees, is that after a couple of visits, I can usually tell if they had some postnatal time with their birth mothers. There seems to be more of a sense of security among these adoptees, and a less anxious attitude. (I am not talking about children who were taken away from abusive parents, but adoptees whose birth mothers held or even breast-fed them in the hospital right after birth.) Having read several articles about the ways in which the brain develops right after birth, I am beginning to understand just how important this postnatal contact is. Although any human contact is better than no contact or abusive contact, as demonstrated by the positive effect of having people touch and massage infants in incubators, could it be that the ultimate experience for infants is the loving touch of their own biological mothers? Is this what will ensure the best neurological development?

As reported in the last chapter on trauma, adoptees appear to react to the experience of the separation from mother the same way that children respond to other traumas, such as physical or sexual abuse. The conclusion drawn from this may be that separating an infant from her mother is a form (although not intentional) of abuse. At the very least it is trauma. This does not mean that this separation is not at times necessary. There are, after all, many forms of abuse, and children who are subjected to constant abusive behavior in their biological homes may not thrive as well as children who have been traumatized by the initial separation, but are then placed with calm, nurturing, and understanding adoptive or foster parents. Separating children for reasons other than neglect or abuse, however, may be abusive to both parents and child. During the middle of the 20th century, the main reason for separating mothers and babies for placement in adoption was the moral climate of society, not abuse or neglect. Is it possible that some day we may acknowledge that by separating babies and their mothers, we have set two people up for a traumatic experience?

Much of what is now being "proven" by technology has been intuited by some of us much earlier. Until now, however, our intuition and anecdotal observations have largely been ignored. However, new brain studies may change this. Lewis, et al. note that recent studies "… have intuition leading comprehension by a country mile." Or as Pascal observed before any of these brain studies were begun, "Reason is the slow and tortuous method by which those who do not know the truth discover it" (Lewis, et al.). Sociologists, psychologists and psychiatrists have long been saying that the first three years of life, much of which are not consciously remembered as actual memories, are the most important years in the development of the "personality." (Rather than personality, I would prefer to say the development of attitudes, behaviors, and beliefs. The personality may be part of the genetic code, although it can be obscured or modified by the attitudes and behaviors formed by the beliefs based on our experiences.) As demonstrated in this chapter, neuro-scientists are now able to provide hard, quantifiable evidence of the effects of negative experiences on the brains of human beings. As Nash warns, "Just last week, in the U.S. alone, some 77,000 newborns began the miraculous process of wiring their brains for a lifetime of learning. If parents and policymakers don't pay attention to the conditions under which this delicate process takes place, we will all suffer the consequences …" (1997).

Along those lines, Lewis, Amini, and Lannon pose a couple of questions: "Does it make a difference with whom a young child passes his time? So long as his attention is occupied and he keeps out of harm's way, does it matter whether his caretaker is a parent, a grandmother, a nanny, a stranger, an electronic device? These questions revolve around an inconvenient center of gravity: the specificity of a child's limbic needs. … Decades of attachment research endorse the conclusion that children form elaborate, individualized relationships with special, irreplaceable others." So the answer is Yes, it matters. And we forget this at our peril.

## A Conscious Attitude

There are some people who are aware of this. More state governments need to follow the lead of North Carolina's former governor James Hunt, who wisely pushed for funding for a program called Smart Start in which parents, teachers, doctors, nurses, and others involved in caring for children work together to ensure the best environment for children under age six. In a *Times* article about

"The Day Care Dilemma," James Collins extols the Smart Start program in North Carolina where many counties are providing subsidies to new parents so the mothers can stay home for the first year of their infant's life. By adding hard science to the arguments of social scientists, Governor Hunt hoped to be able to add to the funding of this program (and now that he is no longer governor, we can only hope that this very important program will continue to be funded). He reminds us of the revolutionary aspect of the new sciences as they inform us about the sensitivity of babies' brains to their early experiences, especially during the first year of life. He says, "Now that we can measure it and prove it, and if it can be made known widely so people understand this, then they'll understand why their schools aren't going to work for them, their technical training isn't going to work, other things we do later on aren't going to work fully unless we do this part right and do this at the appropriate time" (Collins, 1997). Other states are trying to find ways to help educate parents in their parenting skills, rather than taking the children away and paying someone else to rear them. It has never made any sense to me that states spend thousands of dollars paying foster parents to take care of other people's children, yet balk at paying for programs which teach the real parents how to parent their own children. That has always sounded punitive to me. At last science may show that *it is punitive to the children as well as their parents.* Lewis, et al. comment, "Our society overlooks the drain on emotional balance that results from severing attachment." We cannot keep handing children around willy-nilly as if they are not affected by this insensitive process. Their limbic systems won't be able to handle it.

## Attention Deficit Disorder

So far as adoptees are concerned, we have to ask why so many are labeled as having ADD (attention deficit disorder). Besides the experience of trauma interfering with stimuli discrimination, what effect has the separation from mother and the comfort of her presence had on the developing brain of the adopted child? One woman who works a great deal with children said of her experience of adopted children, "These kids have weird wiring." This "weird wiring" seems to be confined to the emotional or limbic parts of the brain, because basic intelligence doesn't appear to be affected. However, what this means is that the limbic wiring may affect a child's ability to put that basic intelligence to its best use. The problems with attention and concentration due to deficits in stimulus discrimination and distractibility result in a loss in flexibility in their capacity to respond to their environment. Always being in a state of fight or flight makes it difficult to focus on problems which take concentration and memory. Van der Kolk, et al. tell us, "This loss of flexibility may explain current findings of deficits in preservative learning and interference with the acquisition of new information, as well as an inability to apply working memory to salient environmental stimuli" (1996). It is noted that these same problems may lead to impulsivity, the purpose of which may be to keep from remembering trauma. Van der Kolk: "They have problems with keeping thoughts in mind without becoming aroused." There needs to be a great deal more study on the effects of separation trauma on the developing brains of children. It has been noted that the brain is quite malleable in many ways, and, although delayed, many early deficits can be overcome. But only if we know what we are doing.

*Nature Versus Nurture*

Most scientists today are not very interested in the old controversy of whether nature or nurture is more influential in the development of a person. Matt Ridley, author of *Nature via Nurture,* says, "For more than 50 years sane voices have called for an end to the debate. Nature versus nurture has been declared everything from dead and finished to futile and wrong—a false dichotomy. Everybody with an ounce of common sense knows that human beings are a product of a transaction between the two. ... The discovery of how genes actually influence human behavior, and how human behavior influences genes, is about to recast the debate entirely. No longer is it nature versus nurture but nature via nurture" (Ridley, 2003). The Human Genome Project has changed our understanding of genes and their role in our development.

It is much more complicated than was once thought. We know that children do not come into the world as a blank slate; nor do they come in as genetically programmed automatons. Dr. Stanley Greenspan, a psychiatrist at George Washington University, says, "It's not a competition; it's a dance" (Nash, 1997). Genes are important, and so is the environment of the womb for the developing fetus. We know that prolonged anxiety, drugs, alcohol, malnutrition, and viral infections can all affect the developmental process of the fetus. What happens right after birth is also important, and separating the mother and the infant, which has been the practice in most hospitals in the U.S. until recently, may be one reason that the United States is considered the country with the highest incidence of neuroses in the industrialized world.

Between the ages of one and three a tremendous burst of activity is recorded in human brains, as the synapses are formed. Trillions of connections are made. Then about age ten, many of these connections begin to atrophy. This process continues until about age 18, when the brain declines in plasticity but increases in power. Nash notes, "Talents and latent tendencies that have been nurtured are ready to blossom." This is very important for adoptive families to know, because "The experiences that drive neural activity," says Yale's Rakic, "are shears, conjuring up form from a lump of stone or a length of cloth. The presence of extra material expands the range of possibilities, but cutting away the extraneous is what makes art" (Nash, 1997). This conjures up a wonderful vision for me, one of shaping the future creativity of the child. "It is the over-production of synaptic connections followed by their loss that leads to patterns in the brain," says neuroscientist William Greenough of the University of Illinois (op. cit.). Nash goes on to comment, "Potential for greatness may be encoded in the genes, but whether that potential is realized as a gift for mathematics, say, or a brilliant criminal mind depends on patterns etched by experience in those critical early years." Both nature and nurture play essential roles in the development of a human being.

We can see from these important discoveries that how an adoptive parent approaches his or her child can be crucial. Despite the terror of the beginning of their lives, repeated experience of understanding and love can help to form new pathways in the neurological system of children. Nothing can be forced, however. And, as adoptees tell me over and over, *love is not enough*. What I have found to be the glue of the adoptive family bond is *understanding and validation*. No matter how much love a couple have to give, if there is no understanding of the loss their child has suffered or validation for his feelings about that loss, if there is no attunement between mother and child, there will be a tenuous bond. These children need parents who are emotionally balanced and available to their children. Lewis, et al. say, "A child of emotionally balanced parents will be resilient to life's minor shocks. Those who miss out on the practice find that in adulthood, their emotional footing pitches beneath them like a deck of a boat in rough waters. ... The end of a relationship is then not merely poignant but incapacitating." In fairness to adoptive parents, because of the distrust separation trauma causes for their children and the behaviors which ensue, even in the most stable of relationships their job of establishing a balanced emotional environment is difficult.

Nevertheless, it is essential to the well-being of a child for the parents to tune in to her emotions and to try to understand her experience. To be constantly misunderstood creates anxiety, which adversely affects the forming of synapses. Siegel points out, "Emotion is a fundamental part of attachment relationships in the early years and throughout the lifespan. The earliest forms of communication are about primary emotional states." Even as parents know they cannot take away their child's pain, they can empathize with it and validate the feelings the pain brings up. Siegel goes on to say, "The experience of being understood develops a mental model or inner expectation that needs are important and goals are achievable. Also, the child's system requires the parent's attunement to help organize the child's own mind" (Siegel, 1999). Parents who are oblivious to what their child is going through will forever be wondering why the child does not seem to be closer to them. There has to be acknowledgment, understanding, and empathy. And this means a *real understanding* of her pain, not just a superficial response to it. A child knows the difference between parents who are truly in tune with her feelings and parents who just want some relief from their own discomfort about their child's behavior—her external response to her pain.

Genes, then, determine what happens in the brain before birth. But after birth, the environment, including the presence or absence of the biological mother, plays a very important part in the billions of connections that are made. How adoptive parents handle the loss may have a great deal to do with how those synapses are formed. The experiences of the next eighteen years will help determine what the child ultimately does with the innate talents and potential he was born with. This means that adoptive parents need to be exquisitely aware of what those talents and aptitudes are so that they can be encouraged, rather than discouraged simply because they do not match the parents' own ideas of what is or is not important. Will the parents' attitudes act as chisels, sculpting the latent talents of their child, or will they, by their neglect or disparaging remarks, place those talents on the chopping block, leaving their child feeling unappreciated—eventually losing track of his native talents or aptitudes?

### Nurturing Natural Talent

In my travels around the world I have met many adoptees who have tales of having their special talents unappreciated by their adoptive parents. One young woman in New Zealand lamented that she was a champion athlete, winning many trophies and medals, yet her parents never attended her meets. They didn't consider sports a worthwhile activity. The same was true for a young man in Australia, who had always wanted to play the piano. His parents were not interested in music, so they never allowed him to take lessons. He had decided just a couple of months before speaking to me that he would begin lessons on his own, for which I commended him. He can certainly enjoy playing the piano, but he will probably never be the concert pianist he might have become had he been encouraged to play from an early age. There are many adoptive parents who are encouraging their children to pursue any talent they may have, even when they know little about it. These parents are to be commended because they are acknowledging they don't expect that just because a child is reared in a particular family, he will have the same interests and talents as other family members. It may actually be much more interesting to have a child with different interests, because this can give the parents opportunities to expand their own horizons!

It is important to understand that for adoptees there may have been some delay in the forming of synapses, due to the experience of separation from the biological mother. It does not appear that this delay affects the innate intelligence of a child, but this delay may have an effect on the scholastic performance of adoptees. There is, however, another phenomenon that may have a great deal to do with the ability of adoptees, as well as other people who have abandonment issues, to perform certain types of functions, to interact with other people, or to form intimate relationships. This has to do with the predominance of the right or left brain in signaling responses to stimuli.

## Hijacking the Neocortex

One of the purposes of this book is to help adoptees and other physically and/or emotionally abandoned people gain more control over the behaviors which are making it difficult for them to function and form relationships. Before getting to that, however, it is necessary for adoptees themselves and those with whom they work or are in relationship to understand the reasons this is so difficult. It is very easy for those who have not been traumatized to sit in judgment of those who have and think that if they just put their minds to it (whatever "it" represents in their minds), they could "do it." That might be true if the neocortex—the rational part of our brains—were always in charge. Unfortunately, this is not true. There is a tiny, almond-shaped part of the limbic brain called the amygdala, which often hijacks our best intentions before they even have a chance to become thoughts (Siegel, 1999). The amygdala may be the reason that the usual techniques of psychotherapy, such as reframing, active listening, and insight, do not always work. It is why "mind over matter" seldom works for victims of trauma. (Are you listening, Dr. Laura?)

The re-experiencing of traumatic events in the forms of flashbacks, nightmares, or the repetition compulsion can unleash intense emotions such as fear or rage, which in turn can lead to paralysis, self-destructive behavior, inappropriate interpersonal behavior, or somatic sensations. The reactions to these stimuli seem almost automatic. Van der Kolk points out that "traumatized people go immediately from stimulus to response without being able to figure out what makes them so upset." Many adoptees will recognize this phenomenon as feeling as if they are in another state of consciousness (or perhaps unconsciousness might be more accurate). They seem to have very little control over their reactions to the trigger, even if that reaction is inappropriate to the situation. As Siegel puts it, "… emotion directly influences the functions of the entire brain and body, from physiological regulation to abstract reasoning." Going from stimulus to response or reaction without thinking or even understanding the cause of the feelings makes overcoming these behaviors very difficult. I am enlisting the help of all who are in relation to trauma victims to help them. They need understanding, encouragement, and help, not criticism. On the other hand, they also need to be reminded of their own responsibility in learning to overcome or modify their reactions.

## Emotion or Reason—Which Comes First?

For a very long time man in his ignorance and arrogance has believed that human beings had the capacity to reason before reacting. It was thought that we were not instinctive like the lower animals, but reflective, rational beings. For the most part this is true. And it is to be expected that we should think before we act. But sometimes, under certain circumstances this doesn't seem to work. Why not and how do we know this?

With the invention of more and more refined imaging techniques which can be used to study the brain and its functions, neurobiologists have discovered that the wiring of our brains may, indeed, be more inclined to favor emotionality, rather than reason. This discovery has shattered previously held theories. It may even be called a revolution in our understanding of the human brain. Although lay people seem fascinated by this new science, the use of these new discoveries is not always reflected in psychotherapy, which of late has been in a hurry to "cure" people through the use of cognitive and behavioral techniques. One of the reasons that this may not work is stated by Lewis et al.: "While having emotions is under limbic control, speaking of them falls under the jurisdiction of the neocortex. That division of labor creates translation troubles." Besides the fact that trauma does not lend itself to narrative, the limbic and cortical parts of the brain do not speak the same language. And, as Lewis et al. point out, the limbic brain is a slow learner. In speaking later about therapies, we will see why it may be that Freud and others espousing analysis or long-term "psychodynamic" psychotherapy were on to something that the HMOs, in their haste for quick fixes, have forgotten or neglected. With depression causing the loss of billions of dollars in corporate profits (at last something to catch everyone's attention!), there may be a reason for HMOs to rethink their policies!

Although this new understanding of the relationship between the neocortex and the amygdala is in its infant stage, it should not be ignored because it could answer some of the questions many therapists and law enforcement personnel have been asking about the relationship between childhood traumatic experiences and violent behavior and crime. Understanding the power of the amygdala to influence behavior should not be used as an excuse for traumatized people to act in an anti-social manner. Instead, any out-of-control behavior pattern should act as a red flag pointing to the need to seek help before the behavior becomes destructive. This warning is driven home as we see children acting out their rage and sorrow in more and more violent ways.

This is only the tip of the iceberg so far as neurobiology is concerned. It is a fairly new science with a long way to go as far as mapping the brain's activities is concerned. As mentioned earlier, the brain has an astounding 100 billion neurons, each of which in turn can interact with thousands of other neurons. This is a staggering thought and needs to temper our conclusions about the limbic system. In an excellent article for *Family Therapy Networker* titled "The Emotional Imperative," Brent Atkinson points out, "... the newly charted links between our neural circuitry and our most primitive passions merit an open-minded and thoughtful response" (1999). The mind and body can no longer be seen as separate, but as parts of a whole. Emotions, too, have to be acknowledged as valid interpreters of our world. Pert says, "We can no longer think of the emotions as having less validity than physical, material substances, but instead must see them as cellular signals that are involved in the process of translating the information into physical reality, literally transforming mind into matter. Emotions are at the nexus between matter and mind, going back and forth between the two and influencing both"(1997). Emotions that are vestiges of old traumas, however, must be tempered with new information about life as it is today.

## A New Paradigm

It may be that we will have to rethink our old beliefs about which came first: the emotion or the thought. For while it may be true that giving a certain belief a great deal of thought will magnify an emotion—anger, for instance—the thought does not necessarily arrive first on the scene. In the past, our understanding of the way the brain worked reinforced our fantasy that we are in control. Sensory information was routed through the thalamus, the brain's central relay station, and sent directly to the neocortex, where the incoming signals were assigned meaning, then sent on to the limbic system for an appropriate emotional/visceral response. As Atkinson points out, "In this tidy, reassuring scenario, emotion is the dutiful servant of the rational brain. Thought proposes, emotion disposes."

While this may be true much of the time, it is not true all of the time. There are times, when a traumatic experience is triggered, for instance, that the information is sent via a back alley directly to the amygdala, the brain's alarm system. Here the information is scanned for potential danger. If danger is perceived, the body goes into fight or flight mode. Although this same information is simultaneously traveling the longer route from thalamus to neocortex, the back alley approach is faster, producing an instantaneous physiological response: elevated heart rate and blood pressure, and the release of adrenaline and cortisol, as well as an accompanying emotional response. Siegel tells us, "The amygdala can rapidly bias the perceptual apparatus toward interpreting the stimuli as dangerous. ... Nonconsciously, the brain is wired, at least with regard to the fear response, to create a 'self-fulfilling prophecy'"(1999). This is well-documented in my studies of adoptees, who frequently seem to operate from a place of fear and to do a great deal of self-sabotaging: "If I allow myself to get too close to this person, she will leave me," thereby making sure that he keeps his distance, which in turn makes the other person feel unloved and perplexed by the relationship. Eventually she gives up trying to have more intimacy with him and leaves, which will then allow him to say, "I knew it!" He can fool himself into believing that it was the closeness that he *did* allow that made the separation so difficult for him, when it was actually the distance he kept that caused her to leave in the first place. If a situation can be perceived as fearful, it becomes fearful. Logic or reason doesn't seem to play much of a part. And the reaction is often instantaneous. Atkinson says, "Within milliseconds, we explode with rage or freeze in fear, well before our conscious mind can even grasp what is happening, much less persuade us to take a few deep breaths and maintain our cool. ... By the time the neocortex gets into the act, the damage has been done—you have already called your late-to-dinner partner an inconsiderate jerk, shrieked at your smart-mouthed child, snapped at your critical colleague or simply shut down, shaking inside, in the face of someone else's rage." He adds that not only are these actions out of our control, but due to the flooding of the neocortex by the amygdala-triggered emotional information, its centers for logic and judgment are overwhelmed, making one think that one's actions were entirely accurate and justifiable. Anyone who has ever listened to a batterer explain why he had to hit his wife will understand this last statement. We have a tendency to try to rationalize almost any action on our part, even when the logical part of our brains are shut down by emotional flooding!

### Emotional Dysregulation

How one reacts to stimuli depends on many things. One of them is one's state of mind when the trigger occurs. This may not be static, but may depend in part on one's present state of mind and one's previous experiences, as well as the social context in which the emotion is generated. For instance: humiliation. If one feels somewhat humiliated by a seemingly innocuous remark by a friend in a one-to-one setting, a person may feel slightly annoyed. However, if the remark is made in the presence of other people, the response may become highly explosive. The rage which is ignited can shut down the higher cognitive, rational functions and descend into the realm of reflexive responding or what Siegel calls "a state of emotion dysregulation." I know a couple of people who ended up in jail because of this very phenomenon. In neither case could the person remember exactly what happened to set him off. They both mentioned feeling as if they were in a different state of consciousness than they had been only seconds before. This apparent inability to regulate one's reaction to emotion is often seen as a psychiatric problem. Alan Schore, in a seminar on "Affect Regulation and Repair of the Self," said that good mental health might be defined as the ability to regulate our affect (emotions). Two such disturbances caused by an inability to do so are mood disorders (dysfunctions in perception, memory, beliefs, and behaviors) and anxiety disorders (excessive sensitivity to the environment, impaired stimuli discrimination, and a sense of impending disaster).

When shame and/or humiliation are enacted over and over again, Siegel points out, "We could almost say that the activation of this state had become a personality trait." This is so obvious in the case of some adoptees, who often identify with their feelings and behaviors as if these define who they are. Of course, there is a great deal of controversy as to what constitutes "who we are," but because I see trauma as causing most of the destructive, outrageous, or secretive behavior, I don't see the behavior as who the person is at all, but only how he is reacting to the trauma (coping). Identifying with behavior can damage self-esteem and keep a person from realizing his potential. In the case of adoptees for whom that feeling of shame (not being kept) begins in the earliest years of life there is no earlier reference point for who they are. Many identify with that shame-filled self and live their lives as undeserving, unworthy, unlovable people. Birth mothers also may experience the belief that they are unworthy because they didn't keep their babies. However, the advantage birth mothers may have is that there was a time when they experienced themselves differently, so that they have a reference to a truer self. It is essential to remember that this is *not* a personality trait; *it is a state of mind predicated upon an emotional response to trauma.*

### States of Mind

Daniel Siegel defines *states of mind* as"… the total pattern of activations in the brain at a particular moment in time. … *States of mind allow the brain to achieve cohesion in functioning*" (1999). He emphasizes the importance of the alignment of the child's and parent's states of mind to help the child organize and regulate his states with that of the parent in order to learn how to respond to various difficult or ambiguous situations. The most common form of communication used is nonverbal behavior: "Facial expression, eye gaze, tone of voice, bodily motion, and the timing of expression are fundamental to emotional messages" (Siegel, 1999). TVs Dr. Phil McGraw says that only 7% of our communication is verbal; the rest is non-verbal. Although certain facial expressions are thought to be universally identical—happiness, sadness, anger, and fear—other non-verbal forms may be cultural. In any case, infants seem to have an easier time discerning their biological mother's expressions than anyone else's. This is borne out by hundreds of accounts from adoptees in reunion, who seem to have an easier time understanding the non-verbal language of their birth family members than their adoptive family members, even after having lived with the adoptive family for many years. Because of the lack of genetic mirroring that adoptees experience in their adoptive families and the adoptive mother's ignorance about her child's loss issues, the regulation of a child's state of mind or limbic functioning may be difficult to achieve. A misreading of signals and the "dance" that the child and mother have to do to try to understand *how to be* with one another often cause confusion for both mother and child. This *lack of knowing* may result in fearful states of mind in both of them. For a child, whose first experience in life was trauma resulting in devastating loss and terror, it may be very easy to fall into that fearful state of mind where hypervigilance, emotional arousal, and self-as-victim become dominant. As the adoptee matures into adulthood, those close to him may be perplexed by his "overreactions" to certain stimuli, because as a child he had no help in learning to regulate his limbic responses.

As mentioned above, one of the most-heard comments told me by adoptees in reunion is how much easier it is to understand the gestures, facial expressions, and body language of their biological family members than it was with their adoptive family members. There is a sense of "coming home," being able to relax just knowing the emotional states of family members. In almost all the cases that I've known, there is usually one parent or sibling to whom the adoptee feels especially close. There is a symmetry of states of mind, of being able to finish one another's sentences, of liking the same things, or of nonverbal understanding which comes as a great relief. A great deal less energy is needed in understanding those whose genetic markers are similar than those who have a different way of expressing themselves nonverbally. *I don't think those of us who have grown up in biological families appreciate that difference.*

How important is this? When one considers that a state of mind demonstrates one's perceptions, memories, thoughts, feelings, attitudes, and beliefs and that those elements determine the ways in which we behave and interact with others, it becomes very clear that our state of mind is very important. What are the beliefs, perceptions and attitudes of a person who has experienced loss at the beginning of life? Is it any wonder that there is a sense of helplessness, rejection, shame, despair and danger? It is noted that children who are neglected or abandoned are especially sensitive to any perceived lack of interest on the part of another individual. Does this feel familiar to adoptees who want to bolt from relationships in which the other person may signal just a wee bit of disappointment or rejection? Because the mind is a dynamic and complex organism, it is important to remember that states of mind can change over time. We are constantly responding to both internal constraints and to external signals from the

environment. In order to overcome the powerful control that early experience
has on one's state of mind, it is important to allow and integrate new experiences,
both internal and external.

### The Importance of Self-Regulation

The fact that adoptees and birth mothers have reasons for the way they act in
the world does not "cut it" with partners, bosses, or law enforcement personnel.
As Siegel says, "An inability to regulate emotions can be a major problem in
both one's personal and professional lives" (1999). Although it may be important
for us to understand the historical value of certain emotional and behavioral
responses, it cannot be an excuse for inappropriate behavior in our public lives.
Friends and colleagues usually don't care about the meaning of bad behavior.
That is why I have said that no matter how much one's pain is not the fault of the
one in pain, it is, nevertheless, the responsibility of that individual to heal the
pain and to gain some control over emotional and behavioral responses to it.
That means learning to self-regulate. Because of the importance that I assign to
this part of brain development, I have given it a chapter of its own. We will get
to the importance of self-regulation after looking at some of the emotions which
have given adoptees problems so far as regulation is concerned. Meanwhile, we
will conclude this chapter with information about the need for each of us to
strive for complexity and integration, the goal of emotional growth.

### Emotional Growth—Toward Complexity and Integration

Emotional growth requires a balance, not only between the neocortex and the
amygdala, but also between continuity and flexibility, so that there is a flow of
experiences reflecting familiarity and innovation, stability and change, certainty
and uncertainty. The idea is to move toward complexity and integration. This
means moving toward a dynamic system of adaptation to environmental changes.
Instead of reacting "the same old way" to situations which remind us of previous
experiences, we are able to form new patterns of responding to these changes.
This is not easy, of course, when one has had the old pattern imprinted during a
traumatic event. "Old habits die hard" is a very mild cliché, when we are referring
to the imprints of traumatic experiences. Our amygdalae, which truly want to be
helpful and protect us from getting hurt again, make certain that we do not again
fall victim to an old situation. This, of course, makes changing our pattern of
response difficult. Let's review what LeDoux says: "It is possible for emotions to
be triggered in us without the cortex knowing exactly what is going on." He has
shown that the amygdala specializes in such preconscious fear recognition.
"The amygdala is programmed to react without benefit of input from the thinking

part of the brain, the cortex" (1996). There is value in this protection by the amygdala in that it can make us react to danger before we really have a chance to understand it. However, if our previous experiences with certain sensory input, such as noise, for instance, is traumatic, we will constantly be reacting to similar noises as if they were dangerous. A Vietnam veteran will react differently to a car backfiring than someone who was never in combat.

Because trauma has a component of helplessness attached to it and interferes with the achievement of self-regulation and the integration of self-states, it can have a negative impact on one's expectations for the future. Remember what Siegel said, "... *memory is the way past events affect future functioning.*" This is partially because the imprint of the trauma forms a bias for anticipating the future. Perhaps this is the reason so many adoptees feel unable to think about the future; it seems so futile—nothing will change. The bias gets reinforced over and over again in a kind of feedback loop, so that imagining a different outcome for the future seems impossible. Because interpersonal relationships are essential to the achievement of complexity and integration, I have tried to make adoptive parents, birth parents, and partners of adoptees aware of the need for validation of their experiences and the feelings connected with those experiences. This validation creates a cross-over of mind states, in which the mind states of the adoptee and that of the significant other are similar, thus creating space for a more subjective experience of Self. The constant reminders that their subjective experience is not acknowledged or validated by anyone else has the effect of making the adoptee feel unreal, false, or invalid. At the very least he feels misunderstood. Not only does this impair the relationships themselves, but makes impossible a movement toward complexity and a more appropriate response to environmental conditions and interpersonal interactions.

Although many adoptees experience some forms of dissociation, I have not known any who were multiple personalities unless they were also sexually or severely physically abused. We all have many aspects to our personalities. So long as we are aware of those various aspects, we are fine. Siegel reminds us that we all have at least two selves: "The self is capable of at least two contextual states: a private, inner, core self and a public, external, adaptive self." We often speak of adoptees' adaptive, adoptive self as a false self, but as Siegel says, "There is nothing 'false' about a mechanism of survival." However, the absence of mirroring for the inner self and the constant need to try to fit in make allowing the core self any latitude seem like a risk even in family life. In order for the brain to develop toward a more complex and integrative whole, there must be an attempt to access that inner self and form a sense of cohesion among the various "selves." The whole process involves not only our sense of internal integrity, but also our interactions with other minds. We usually begin this process as children, when we begin to see ourselves in time and space and to tell stories about our experiences. This may be called the narrative process. The narrative process is an integral part of making meaning of our life experiences. Again, this is one reason it is so important for adoptive parents to pay attention to their children's stories (or pictures, playing, or poetry) about their interpretation of their experiences. They are trying to work them out, to have mastery over them, to make meaning of them. As adults, there is a need to continue the process through art, poetry, journals, stories, myths, metaphors, and music. Telling our stories, whether through an epic poem, an autobiography, or an opera can be a pathway to healing. A child in the narcissistic phase of development cannot make meaning of the trauma of separation except to believe that he was unworthy of being kept. That belief is hardwired into the neurological system. Many adult adoptees try to gain mastery over the belief by reenacting the traumatic event over and over again in their relationships, only to have it reinforced instead. Perhaps taking more control over the situation in the form of one of the artistic endeavors mentioned above would be a better way of integrating it. Then there is the possibility of a more cohesive self composed of the many aspects inherent in all of us. This can then lead to a less fearful approach to relationships and intimacy.

The mind is a miraculous, complex organ, which responds to our experiences from, or perhaps before, birth. It is up to us to help change old, imprinted patterns which resulted from false interpretations of those experiences, so that we can become confident, secure, and loving individuals.

Before learning more about self-regulation, let us look at some of the emotions which cause the most problems for adoptees. They are fear, anger, guilt, sorrow, and joy. Why is joy a problem? Joy itself isn't a problem; the allowing of it is the problem. Let us take these emotions one by one as we learn more about our affective states.

# CHAPTER 3
## Fear: The Great Paralyzer

---

Fear is one of the most influential aspects of our psyches. Fear is the basis for the majority of a trauma victim's feelings. This is unfortunate, because fear leads to paralysis. Fear is the main reason that so many adoptees get stuck in their careers, their relationships, and their own personal growth. They are being controlled by a very scared child inside. Although they may be determined not to let others control them, they are not really in control of themselves, at least not the adult part of themselves. They are instead being controlled by the child who constantly fears abandonment, rejection, and his own inadequacy. These irrational fears can be present even in the face of overwhelming evidence to the contrary: i.e., a very successful career, a good marriage, or other successes which point to a talented, warm, competent person. What the neocortex may be registering is not necessarily what the limbic system is reflecting.

*It All Comes Back to Control*

The "being out of control" which anger produces can lead to acting out in destructive ways, both to self and others. Some of the people in prisons and jails today are good people who allowed their anger to get out of control. (To them, it didn't feel like "allowed" but that they didn't have a choice.) Yet it all comes down to fear. Beneath the anger are pain and fear. People get on what Rhonda Britten, the author of *Fearless Living*, calls the Wheel of Fear: a *trigger* that activates the fear response; this *response* causes them to do something (usually unconsciously) to ward off the dreaded outcome; when that doesn't work, it creates a *negative feeling* about themselves—which is the true fear; which leads to their doing some *self-destructive behavior* such as drinking, over-eating, or isolating. Does this sound familiar?

Fear creates a filter through which its victims view the world and renders them incapable of acting on things they would like to do. Relationships become nightmares, as those caught up in the web of fear sabotage themselves by either getting angry out of proportion to the situation and making their partners wonder what kind of "Alice-in-Wonderland" world they are living in, or distancing themselves in a way which makes relationships inoperable.

But who is in control in these situations? Is it the adult self, who truly wants a good relationship or is it the scared child, who is sure everyone will leave her? If it is not the adult self, then it isn't really being in control ... not unless a person really wants to be controlled by a two or three-year-old.

## The Origin of the Fear of Control

It is easy to understand the reason that the adoptee fears being controlled. He had no control over the original separation from his birth mother, and his life changed forever. He *never* wants to be in that position again. In other words, *he fears helplessness.* In the original scenario, he didn't have any control over being placed in a family where there was nothing familiar. Everything about his life was dictated by others. Although this may be true of all children, most children have the security of knowing that they can see themselves reflected back and know that they belong. For the adoptee every day is a challenge of trying to figure out how to be, although he probably doesn't understand the difficulty this presents for him. It has been true his whole life and, therefore, feels normal. However, it takes a great deal of energy and concentration. And it never feels quite right. He never quite fits. Therefore, he feels as if *he* is never quite right. This may undermine his faith in himself as a person capable of normal things. It may make him doubt himself. So now, not only does he not trust others to do the right thing by him, but he also distrusts himself. This renders him paralyzed in a great many situations. "I don't want you telling me what to do!" but, "I don't know what to do either. What if I make a mistake?" It is a dilemma.

## Fear of Being Disliked

Part of that fear is the fear of rejection—the need the adoptee has to have people like him. Now, we all want to be liked, but we don't all think that we will be annihilated if someone doesn't like us. We aren't all people-pleasers. People-pleasing comes from the constant vigilance the adoptee keeps in his adoptive family as a way of not being abandoned again. The constant alertness to the environment in order to fit in sets up a pattern that the adoptee employs in almost all situations: "I need to find out *how to be* in this situation." That's why adoptees call themselves "chameleons." They are very good at adapting, because they spent their childhoods perfecting the art of adapting to their adoptive families.

It isn't as if all adoptive families require this adaptation. But how does anyone act when in a "foreign" situation? We don't want to stick out too much and we don't want to offend anyone, so we learn the cultural patterns, rules, and mores of whatever culture we find ourselves in. That is what adoptees do. But just as it is easier for someone from California to adapt to Ohio than to Calcutta, it is easier for children to adapt to their biological families than to adoptive families. There is something familiar there. It is easier to become socialized in familiar situations than in foreign ones. It is easier to know we fit. There is less fear of doing something wrong, of making mistakes. Making mistakes is much more fearful for someone who feels like a mistake than for someone who does not. It is much more fearful if one feels as if they either *were* a mistake or *made* a mistake at the beginning of their lives. Because they don't know what that mistake was, there is a constant need to be on the lookout for mistakes. This renders one paralyzed.

### Fear of Inner States of Mind

Sometimes fear is necessary and useful. If we are truly in a dangerous situation, fear may keep us from doing something which will get us in trouble. This is fear of a situation, such as a mugging or holdup. But most of what adoptees fear is in their own minds. This fear is nebulous and undefined. This is because it comes from an experience during the stage of implicit memory—something experienced and very influential but unrecalled. Therefore there has to be a constant vigilance in order not to be surprised again by whatever it was that overwhelmed and devastated them. This causes anxiety and is a drain on their energy and on the freedom to act on their own behalf.

The most difficult fears to overcome are those that happened during childhood amnesia because we can't recall what it is that scared us so badly. If at age six, we were frightened by a dog, we have an idea why we are afraid of dogs. This can be managed in a better way than being left as an infant and forever fearing that anyone close to us may leave us. However, as most adoptees know, just becoming apprised of this reason doesn't eliminate the fear.

### Everyone Fears Something

According to Michael Moore in his provocative movie *Bowling for Columbine*, fear is fed to U.S. citizens in all kinds of ways every day. We are a violent, fear-based society. We seem to be a gullible people, believing everything the media feed us about what we should or shouldn't be doing. Every new study makes us wonder ... should we eat apples? Eggs? Is cholesterol really the culprit or is it inflammation? This keeps us guessing, keeps us off balance, keeps us from thinking deeply about things. It is playing with our heads ... with our minds. It makes us paralyzed in the sense that we don't know what to do. Every day something changes: what we were to fear yesterday is not what we are to fear today.

Even if reports in the media were not making everyone fearful, everyone fears something. Although it may seem to the adoptee as if the rest of the world is going around being in control and not being afraid, that is not true. Except for the people intimately connected to adoptees, most other people are not aware of adoptees' fears either. They don't wear fear on their shoulders. In her book *Feel the Fear and Do It Anyway*, Susan Jeffers begins by talking about her fear of public speaking. She, too, believes that fear is epidemic in our society: "We fear beginnings; we fear endings. We fear changing; we fear 'staying stuck.' We fear success; we fear failure. We fear living; we fear dying" (1987). She talks about the "nonstop, little voice" inside her head that kept telling her things like "Don't take a chance. You might make a mistake. Boy, will you be sorry!" Until one day she looked in the mirror at the reflection full of self-pity and said, "Enough!"

This is similar to the epiphany that Rhonda Britten had two decades after the grizzly death of her parents—her father shot her mother, then himself in front of Rhonda when she was 14 years old—rendering her paralyzed by fear. She began to notice that, although many people had traumatizing events in their lives, not everyone made decisions based on fear. She decided to research what made the difference and wrote a book on the subject titled *Fearless Living*.

### Saying "Enough!"

Perhaps it is time for some of you to say "enough" to some of your fears, at least the fears that were learned. It is more difficult to eliminate the fears that are psychological—that fear of abandonment, for instance. Although that fear was also learned, because you can't remember the "lesson" where you learned it, it makes it much more difficult to overcome. However, there are many fears that are easier to overcome.

A great deal of time is spent by some of you in worrying about things that "might happen." Jeffers states that about 90% of the things we worry about never happen. What a waste of energy! Many adoptees are intuitive, and intuitives can think of endless possibilities. I know, because as an intuitive person, I was often that way myself. I worried about all the possible things that could happen in this or that situation. Although my anxiety wasn't constant the way it is for many adoptees, it would come up in situations where I felt that I had no control over what might be going on, such as my husband's airplane being late without any explanation from him or the airline. Then, like Jeffers, one day I thought "enough!" I realized that most of what I was worrying about never happened and just put me in a state of anxiety. And even if something did happen, in most cases I couldn't have done anything about it anyway. Are you harboring these kinds of fears?

There is something almost superstitious about some of these fears: It feels that if we keep worrying about them, we *will* have some control over them. Of course, that is nonsense! A constant stream of worry will not keep a plane in the air or a burglar from entering our homes. But this belief is coupled with the idea that whatever happens, we won't be able to handle it. For adoptees this fear may come from that helplessness experienced as a baby trying to get mom back. Yet as adults we have a great many resources at our command to help in any situation in which we might find ourselves.

The trouble is that many adoptees are their own worst enemies when it comes to helping themselves. They are the ones who sabotage their own relationships, successes, and talents. They can do something about it, but it will take a change of attitude. It will take a dedication to saying "enough" to the mindset that prevails in them. It is acknowledging that it is easier to keep on doing nothing than to really try to do something about the situation.

*Fearing the Unfamiliar*

Most people are uncomfortable in new situations. They don't know exactly what to expect, so it puts them ill-at-ease. Although there may be various gradients of fear involved, almost everyone has some degree of discomfort or fear in new situations. Adoptees, as well as other trauma victims, may have more fear than others in new situations. But even though this may be true, an honest evaluation of the situation needs to be made. This situation may be new, but is it really something to fear? What might actually come up that can't be handled? *It is very important to make sure that the fear of the unfamiliar situation doesn't become global, that it is realistic and manageable.*

When dealing with the unfamiliar, it is important to take one thing at a time: "What is actually going on here, and what can I do to solve it?" It doesn't help to become the victim and say, "I can't do this. It is too much for me." After all, adoptees, of all people, have had a great deal of practice in dealing with the unfamiliar. Therefore all of you who are adoptees should be really good at dealing with anything new. Use what you have learned. Adapt where you have to; be innovative where you can. Try not to mistake instruction, suggestion, and constructive criticism as complete control over you or rejection of you. *Adoptees have to be very aware of these differences because they may all feel the same.* This is why many adoptees have difficulties in retaining jobs, especially as adolescents (and adolescence for adoptees may be prolonged). The ordinary things that everyone has to put up with, such as getting to work on time and having a good attitude toward clients, customers, and fellow workers often seem like control to adoptees, and they quit in a huff. Or they get fired for not complying. Then they feel very self-righteous and blame the "offending" boss or supervisor. "Well, he was a jerk anyway!" Rarely do they question their own integrity: "I wonder if I got fired because I came to work late every day and took a couple of days off without permission." Self-reflection is often absent in these situations. Remember what Siegel said about self-reflection when feelings are generated by implicit memories: "These implicit recollections are not usually subject to a process of self-reflection, as in 'Why am I doing this or feeling this way?'" Individuals may sense these experiences as just defining who they are. This is why adoptees so often feel personally rejected by ordinary circumstances, such as being fired for non-compliance: They believe "this is just the way I am."

This belief increases their fear of interviewing for another job. There is that little knot of doubt about their own competency. It isn't competency that needs to be questioned, but compliance. My experience with adoptees is that they are very good workers, but that they do have problems with the simple rules listed above. Therefore, they sabotage their positions at work by noncompliance rather than incompetency. This is a direct result of their misunderstanding simple rules of conduct which everyone has to follow, and seeing those same rules as an attempt to control them personally. This is very destructive and totally unnecessary. It calls for a reality check and a vow to take responsibility for their actions.

As long as a person wants to grow and assume more power in his life, there is going to be fear. Unless a person wants to feel helpless all the time, he is going to have to push through the fear and, as Jeffers says, "do it anyway!" As she points out, "Pushing through fear is less frightening than living with the underlying fear that comes from a feeling of helplessness." Feeling helpless means being the victim and feeling powerless. How scary is that?!

*What Having Power Is and Isn't*

Power is not always seen as a positive word in our culture. After all doesn't the Mafia have power over helpless proprietors of business? Don't adults have power over children? Don't the leaders of our country have power over all of us? What is power anyway?

Power, as I am referring to it, has to do with personal power, the power within. It means having control over our own impulses and darker behavior. Sovereign power, to paraphrase Alfred, Lord Tennyson, is having self-reverence, self-knowledge, and self-control. It is being in touch with our own creative spirit and our own authentic identity. This need for authenticity is endemic to having true power. In her book *The Wish for Power and the Fear of Having It*, Althea Horner writes, "People who do not have a clear sense of their own identity often report that they do not know what they want, that they feel as though they have no will of their own. Distortions of identity lead to a loss of intrinsic power. It may be replaced by illusory power that is destructive in its expression, or that becomes essential as a protection against a terrifying awareness of the fragility or helplessness that goes with a poorly defined identity" (1989). Knowing oneself, then, is essential to having true power. The failure to know oneself leads to other forms of control, which have nothing to do with authentic power.

What are the disguises that are used when authentic power is missing? Some of them are manipulation, intimidation, and control. True power actually has very little to do with other people, but with oneself, with identity, competence, and self-restraint. We often mistake intimidation for power. Intimidate is what the Mafia does. Adolescent adoptees seem to have a great deal of power over their parents because they intimidate them by making *huge* fusses over little things. In order to avoid those mind-boggling clashes, many parents allow their children to do things they don't like them to do ... or allow them to not do things they should be doing. Getting their children to comply is just too much trouble and causes too much fuss. It disrupts the whole household and, therefore, needs to be avoided. This may feel good in the moment to the adoptee, but it is also scary. She really doesn't want her parents to be wishy-washy about things. And she is certainly not aware of having any power. What the adoptee is keenly aware of is that she does not want anyone to have any control over her. At the same time, there is an awareness of not being in control herself. It is very confusing and a source of fear. And the control is projected onto the parents. Almost all of these adoptees will tell you that they have very controlling parents.

Many partners of adoptees are absolutely astounded by the ways in which their loved ones manipulate and intimidate them even when it is not necessary. Something that can be simple and straightforward often becomes complicated and confrontive. What happened? What was the landmine he stepped on to cause such a huge confrontation out of what seemed like an innocuous question or suggestion? Again, it is a nebulous fear that usually causes that kind of reaction in an innocuous situation. It is what the partners of adoptees call living on the roller coaster, walking through a minefield, or walking on egg shells. It is not a very pleasant way to live.

## Taking Responsibility

Many partners of adoptees decide that they do not want to live this way. They leave, thus fulfilling the adoptees' greatest fear: abandonment. How can trauma victims learn to stop doing what it is they are doing to cause the very thing they fear the most? The first thing is to become aware of what they are doing, acknowledge it, and then take steps to change what they are doing or not doing. This is difficult because they are very sure that the problem is being caused by the other person. Again, there is a lack of self-reflection.

Another reason this is not easy is because many of those patterns have become second nature. It seems as if it is impossible to stop. But it isn't. Behavior is something that *can be controlled,* even if the feelings which precipitate the behavior cannot. There do seem to be some people who have so much rage that they cannot control their behavior. Many of these people are behind bars. But most people do not shoot others or even hit them. There is a limit to their use of force or intimidation in relation to others. If there is a limit, then it can be controlled, and the behavior, whether it is shouting, throwing things, or pinning someone against the wall, can be changed. But ... it takes effort. It takes giving up the "high" or exhilaration one gets when one "lets go" with one's anger. It takes a commitment to the relationship one is in and a giving up of the childlike acting out. Always think of the two-year-old having a tantrum when you feel like acting out like that. Is that really the age you want to be? Does your partner, wife, husband want to be in a relationship with a two-year-old? Would you?

It is difficult to think that it might be fear that is fueling the rage: the fear of one's lovability, worthiness, and competence. Because of one's own questions about that, any hint that someone else may be questioning it is cause for rage. In Chapter II—Reality Check—it is pointed out that many adoptees exaggerate normal interpretations of things, so that *observations are seen as criticisms, disappointments are interpreted as betrayals, disagreements are seen as rejection, suggestions are felt as control,* etc. These are the landmines that many people who are in relationships with adoptees complain about. Because not all people react this way, others get caught off guard at the reaction adoptees have to seemingly innocuous statements. Any adoptee who is doing this must STOP, really look at the situation, and honestly evaluate it. It means taking responsibility for knowing when you are *not* taking responsibility for what you are doing to others ... how you are affecting others.

## Assigning Blame

One of the most prevalent things which happens in a fear-based life is assigning blame to everyone except oneself. This, of course, negates any power one may have. When everyone else is responsible for what happens to you, then you really don't have any power. "Well,' you will say, "I didn't abandon myself when I was born." No, and you aren't responsible for that abandonment either (although deep down inside, you may feel that you are). In talking about using our traumas as excuses for inappropriate behavior, Britten says, "Whatever the excuse is, it did actually occur. In that sense, it is true. But the problem is that it is only true in regard to the way it shaped your life *in the past" (Britten, 2001).* She reminds us that these excuses, however true in the beginning, only serve to take away any sense of personal responsibility or accountability. In addition they also "... give you permission to ignore your own values, beliefs, and commitments, thereby setting aside any sense of personal integrity."

It is a conundrum that adoptees take responsibility for that over which they had no control (their separation from mother) and do not take responsibility for things over which they do have control (being fired from a job, getting a low grade on a test, getting a speeding ticket). Think about it, really think about it: What could you have done differently in those situations? How could you have had some control (i.e., power) over what happened? Could you have gotten to work on time, studied for the test, driven the speed limit? In many, many cases (not what happened at the beginning of your life, to be sure) but in many cases now as an adult, you have choices in your life. You don't have to blame others for what happens to you—how you are acting, feeling, thinking, or being. In fact you should *never* blame others for those things because most of what is going on is your perceptions of situations and people and those perceptions may be distorted by your original abandonment and the filter of fear.

*Changing Your Perceptions*

How can you change perceptions which have prevailed for so many years? Most people who have early trauma see things in a negative light. On a sunny day, they will see the one cloud in the sky. I remember one professor, who, after looking at all his end-of-semester evaluations, could not stop obsessing about the *one* negative evaluation he got out of over a hundred. Ninety-nine plus good evaluations, and he focused on the one bad one: "What could I have done differently? Why didn't this person like me?" It was amazing! This was a person who always had full classes because he had a great reputation as a teacher, yet he was so insecure that he couldn't get that one bad evaluation out of his mind. When you hear something like that, it seems absolutely silly, doesn't it? But how many of you focus on the negative about yourselves and others (projection). How many of you see the glass as half empty?

Perhaps it is time to challenge this way of looking at the world. I realize that it is a legacy of having such a devastating beginning of life, but with practice (like doing scales on the piano) you can change. Every time you notice yourself being negative (get your friends to help you with this) make yourself see the positive side as well. If you find yourself being critical of one of your friends, ask yourself what it is about yourself that is mirrored in that person? This, again, takes honesty and self-reflection. If you find that trait in yourself, change it if you really don't like it. You have choices. That is part of losing your fear and taking on your power. It means that you have to start liking yourself. You cannot have inner power without having self-love. And every time you criticize someone else, you may be projecting something you don't like about yourself onto them.

I know this to be true because I used to be very judgmental. I would find things I disliked about people and criticize them for it. I was not a happy camper. After several years of therapy and confronting "the shadow" in myself and learning to love and accept that shadow, I no longer feel judgmental toward others. It just ceases to be there. Instead, I feel compassion and empathy. This doesn't mean that I approve of everything others do. We can certainly have discernment, but discernment is there without a "charge." When we disapprove of another's behavior yet don't *feel* strongly about it, then we can believe that we are no longer projecting our shadow onto others. You know what I mean. When you are charged up about another's behavior, there is a great deal of energy behind the disapproval. You are mad about it, incensed. When you notice yourself feeling that way, it is a hint that this is something you don't like about yourself. There is a fear that you are not all right.

### Living with Fear

As much as we may like to, we cannot eliminate fear from our lives, even irrational fear. We have to live with a certain amount of fear, the way one might have to live with some other handicap. When trauma happens at such an early age, fear is part of the residue. Remember, though, the brain can learn new things and new patterns, but it takes practice. This means that you have to push through the fear of unknown things and allow new patterns to form and become habitual. The old patterns have been there for a long time and are difficult to overcome. You can't get rid of fear, but you can form new ways to deal with it. Eventually the brain may get the idea that some of the things you have been fearing are not worth bothering about anymore. New patterns will have formed that are as strong as the original patterns of fear. Remember that you can't learn to play complicated pieces on the piano unless you practice scales over and over again. They form patterns that will be found in every piano piece you will play. Learning those scales will make it possible for you to play the piano well. How does one learn to type? No one was born with the keyboard type pattern in her brain. That pattern seems to have been thrown up on the keyboard somewhat randomly. Yet when we have practiced for awhile, we don't have to think over and over again, "Where do I put my fingers when I want to type *The quick brown fox jumps over the lazy dog?* It becomes automatic. The brain has a pattern that it follows. No one was born knowing how to ride a bicycle, yet one can learn, stop riding for a long time, then pick up a bicycle years later and ride as if one had never stopped.

### Taking Risks

Forming new patterns in the brain means taking risks and doing things we aren't sure we can do. Maybe we don't do them very well at first, but we can learn—our brains can learn. Every new thing requires practice so that we can do it better the next time. Notice a one-year-old toddling across the floor. He is learning how to walk. No one fears that he will be toddling as a 20, 30, or 40-year-old. He will learn how to walk and walk well. Our brains are very pliable. They learn. But they can't learn if we don't try. That may mean overcoming some ancient belief we have that we *can't* or we *shouldn't,* and just *do*! Britten has an acronym for the word R*I*S*K:

*Release* your attachment to the outcome.

*Invest* fully in your intention.

*Stand* for the truth.

*Keep* kindness a priority.

These are all good things to strive for. Keeping these ideas in mind can help us overcome some of the old ways of dealing with life's challenges. They are not easy to achieve, but it is important to begin.

Do little things at first. Deal with your fear of being different by telling a friend who your favorite author is without knowing what kind of literature he likes. You will find out that the world doesn't end when you take a bold step out of the chameleon role. Your friend may disagree with you, but that doesn't mean that he doesn't like you. It doesn't mean that he is rejecting you. It just means that he has a different taste in literature. How do Britten's ideas apply? What were you expecting as an outcome of your declaration? Did you expect the other person to agree with you or simply to learn something about you? What was your intention? Are you being honest about it? Can you stand up for your choice, even if the friend doesn't agree? Is it your truth? If he doesn't agree, can you accept his difference with kindness, allowing for the differences between you? By taking this step, you are allowing someone to know you better. It may be a risk, but it is one worth taking.

Now, if the person becomes abusive and tells you that you are crazy or stupid or a jerk for liking your favorite author, you can be assertive (not abusive) and say that you are sorry he feels that way, but everyone has his own tastes in literature as well as ice cream, and that it is not a federal offense. Whatever you do, don't take it personally, but realize that people who get offensive when they are not agreed with are insecure, not right. (That includes you!)

### The Fear of Change

Many people are afraid to enjoy themselves because they fear that the happy situation they are in will not last. Therefore, they miss the joy of the moment by worrying about when it will end. Well, everything ends. Everything changes. So why waste a perfectly good moment by worrying about when it will pass? For people who have had a trauma so early in their lives that they cannot remember it, it is the element of surprise that worries them. After all, all trauma is a surprise, by its very definition. (Remember, trauma is something that happens unexpectedly, affects one adversely, and over which one has no control.) Again, there is an almost magical thinking in not allowing oneself to enjoy the moment, as if by anticipating something bad happening, one can have some control over it. "Well," you might say, "at least I won't be surprised by whatever it is." Perhaps, but you won't have much fun either.

Think about it: How much control do you have over the things you worry about? What happens when they occur? Did it help to worry? There is a paradox in all of this, because adoptees, although inveterate worriers, are often not very good planners. There is a *big* difference between planning for the future and worrying about things that might happen. Planning for the future involves thought, purpose, and strategy. Doing one's homework might fall into that category: "My purpose is to pass my test, therefore I must think how to do that, and studying seems to be the best thing to do in this situation." Becoming a musician might also fall into that category: "My purpose is to entertain others by playing the saxophone. The best way to do that is to practice until I become very good at playing, find a venue to begin in, and always do my best."

Worrying about nebulous things doesn't do any good because you can't worry about everything and you might be worrying about the wrong thing. How many times has worrying about something done you any good? Were you able to have a better outcome as a result of your worrying? Were you hurt any less when your partner left you because you worried during the entirety of your relationship that it would happen? Did all that worrying do you any good? Do you feel better because of it? I guess you could say "I told you so" to yourself. I guess you could believe that you were right. But what if your constant worrying got in the way of your relationship … got in the way of intimacy and love? What if your worrying *caused* the relationship to end? I believe that in the case of many adoptees and birth mothers this is what happens. It is a self-fulfilling prophecy because it is caused by the very thing that is feared. Siegel says, "Nonconsciously, the brain is wired, at least with regard to the fear response, to create a 'self-fulfilling prophecy.'" We keep recreating the very situations that we fear the most in order to gain mastery over them, yet instead we most often reinforce them. We can only gain mastery over them if we react differently, if we push through the fear. President Franklin Roosevelt said, "There is nothing to fear but fear itself." It is true that fear is sometimes the greatest disabler of careers and relationships.

*The Fear of Intimacy*

The fear of connection or intimacy is the most destructive fear in relationships. There is nothing more intimate than the relationship between a mother and her baby. That trace memory or implicit memory of the subsequent separation from her, when it was much too early to separate, is a real barrier to intimacy with others in one's life. This begins with the relationship with the adoptive mother. There is always a little wedge of separation between the child and her adoptive mother. This drives the mother to distraction, as she become obsessed with filling that gap. What she doesn't understand is that she can't fill this gap, because the gap is what is keeping her child safe. (Of course, this is not true because if anything happens to the mother, the child will be devastated, despite the faithful maintenance of that gap.) Nevertheless, there is a magical belief that if the adoptee makes sure that she doesn't get too close to her mother, she will never again feel the devastation of loss that she did the first time. She is surprised and perplexed, then, when if the mother dies, she is nonetheless devastated. Even adoptees who profess to dislike their adoptive mothers are surprised at their reactions to her death. Once in awhile there is someone who really feels relief at the death of an adoptive parent, but that is a rare case. Most of the time, even with that heavily guarded heart intact, adoptees are inconsolable when their mothers die.

This scenario continues in every relationship the adoptee has. "If I don't love too much, I won't lose too much," is the way the saying goes. Unfortunately, what actually happens is that the adoptee keeps herself from loving too much (i.e., becoming truly emotionally intimate with her partner), yet still becomes devastated when something happens to the relationship. *It was all for nothing!* It didn't work. And although this lesson is felt over and over again, it seems not to be learned. She still believes in the magic of disconnection or distancing.

There is another saying, which might be much more beneficial to listen to: *"It is better to have loved and lost, than never to have loved at all."* Now, you can get to age 95 and be proud of the fact that you never gave in to intimacy and connection. "At least I never felt loss that way again." But is that true? Was it easy to just walk away? Was it easy when she left you because you didn't let her get close? Did you think she would put up with your distancing behaviors forever? Did those distancing techniques really keep you safe, or were they the cause of the demise of the relationship? I guess if one is in a relationship with someone else who fears intimacy, it might all work out. But what kind of a relationship is that going to be? Safe and sterile? Safe and anonymous? Safe and unexciting? Safe and dead?

*The Secret Self*

Of course becoming intimate means knowing yourself so the other can also know you. I have heard many adoptees say, "I will never let someone really know me." They believe that keeping themselves secret is keeping themselves safe. There is a fear that the real self is some kind of monster that if known to others would make them run away. Come on, adoptees. Stop being so grandiose! You have no more claim on "the shadow" than any of the rest of us. We all have a shadow—those unacknowledged aspects of ourselves that we believe others will not like. Yours is no more monstrous than anyone else's. It isn't really what got you kicked out of paradise. Remember, you were a helpless infant. It was the grownups who did it!

Intimacy is all about sharing yourself with those close to you. It means first learning who you are, so that you can share your authentic self and not that false self you fashioned out of trauma-based behavior that at one time helped you to cope. You are afraid of leaving that behind, because you are afraid there is nothing else. Believe me, there is. I have met thousands of adoptees, and I've never met one who didn't have an authentic self worth knowing. Sometimes it is difficult to see beneath the false self that is so firmly placed over the real self, but what is there is definitely not a monster. I have met thousands of loving, warm, talented, intelligent people, most of whom did not feel that way about themselves. They could let me know them, because I was a stranger. Yet many would admit that there seems to be an almost instinctive need to keep themselves secret from those who care most about them.

What we are talking about is a boundary problem. An adoptee will tell the mailman, who doesn't give a hoot about her, all the problems she is having with her boyfriend, yet she won't tell her parents, who truly care. Part of this may be that the adoptee won't feel judged by the uncaring mailman. He won't offer advice or intrude in any way into her life. Parents, on the other hand, caring about the way their child is being treated, may have opinions or suggestions (read: control) about the situation. This is abhorrent to the adoptee. She habitually misreads their concern for control.

This is not to say that some parents aren't controlling. There are controlling adoptive parents as well as controlling biological parents. Adoptive parents may *seem* more controlling because their kids seem more out of control. These parents are scared, and the helplessness that their children feel about their lives is often projected onto them, so that they, too, feel helpless. But part of the feeling of helplessness comes from the fact that their children are so secretive. They are responsible for children who seem to be leading a secret life. This is not an enviable position to be in.

Part of the secrecy which the adoptee seems prone to maintain may be a reaction to the secrecy surrounding her own birth family. "If I can't know about them, then you can't know about me." Every adoptee should understand something: When your mother left you, you may have felt that either your soul died or you had to become someone else. You may be truly afraid that the authentic self that I am talking about doesn't really exist. You built your own existence out of your adaptation to your environment. Without that, it feels as if there is no self. Daniel Siegel says that certain states of mind, such as shame/humiliation, when activated almost become personality traits. Traumatized people begin to identify with their reactions to their trauma and believe that this is who they are. What I am saying is this is not true. Feelings and behavior are results of experiences; personality is more intrinsic, genetic. It has been there all along. What happened to it? Because there didn't seem to be any reflection for that self in your adoptive family, it stayed hidden. Yet the real self was there all along. *It stayed hidden inside you like a treasure buried beneath a mountain.* It was more hidden for some adoptees than for others, depending on the match between their true characteristics and those of their adoptive parents. It also depended on how safe the adoptee felt in expressing her true self in her family, despite the differences there. Were those differences seen as interesting and good, or something to be feared and bad? Did the parents understand the difference between trauma-based behavior and true personality or were they convinced that their child's behavior reflected her personality? And what of the adoptee? Did she assume that because her mother didn't keep her the true self was flawed? Perhaps it wasn't the adoptive parents who were disapproving; perhaps it was the adoptee herself. Whatever it was, there are plenty of reasons that the authentic self of the adoptee has remained hidden like a treasure beneath a mountain. *It is time to dig up that treasure.* Or, as Robert Bly says, now that we are adults, to retrieve all those aspects of our personality that we threw into that big sack we were carrying behind us as we journeyed through childhood and adolescence. That sack full of shadow ... that sack full of treasure.

When I get a peek at that treasure—when I see that real self beneath that false self—*I like it a lot better than the false self.* I cannot relate to the false self, all that posing and inappropriate (either outrageous or perfectionistic) behavior, because it is like relating to a ghost. There is no substance. But I can see substance beneath all that posing. I can see substance in the real self. *And I like it.* Adoptees need to stop thinking they have a corner on the "shadow" market. Adoptees are neither any better nor any worse than the rest of us. Sorry, adoptees. I can't let you think you can do "bad" better than the rest of us. You may be able to act that way, but you can't *be* that way.

*What to Do*

How do you get from secrecy to advocacy for your own true Self? The first step is to acknowledge the pain which creates the fear and secrecy. Pain is always the source of fear, just as fear is the source of most of our feelings. This is true even if it is pain unremembered, fear unacknowledged. Because it has been there all their lives, many adoptees do not believe that there is any pain. Many adoptees with whom I have spoken believe that everyone feels anxiety most of the time. They have a hard time pinpointing a time when they did not feel anxious, so they see anxiety as normal. Yet it is not normal on a regular basis. Anxiety should be circumstantial, not habitual. In order to overcome the pain and fear that accompany separation trauma, there has to be an acknowledgment of that pain and fear. There is no room for denial. To deny either personal or societal pain creates inactivity and stops positive action. It gives an excuse for doing nothing. It fosters the "why bother" mentality. It is an excuse for laziness and uninvolvement. It negates power.

*Chronic Negativism*

Stop believing that negative is realistic and positive is pie in the sky. Be honest about your general mood. Daniel Siegel defines mood as "the general tone of emotions across time," whereas, Lewis, et al. define mood as "a state of enhanced readiness to experience a certain emotion." Although somewhat different, each definition explains the rut many people are in when it comes to the way they see the world. For example, many people insist on interpreting everything bad that happens to them as proof that they are a failure. They begin to recount the many times they have failed in the past and look upon the future with dismay. Siegel says, "The influence of mood upon all of these cognitive functions reveals how general emotional tone reinforces itself in a feedback loop that keeps one's mood spiraling in the same direction. This may explain the tenacious nature of emotional disturbances such as depression or chronic anxiety, in which a given mood becomes a relative fixed and disabling state." If you find yourself always focusing on the negative about yourself or your circumstances, force yourself to find something positive to think about. *Train your mind.* Positive thoughts create a more positive chemical reaction in your body. Positive thoughts are good for you. Don't be afraid of them.

You can't count on your feelings to be a true state of things. As Britten says, "Our feelings lie. I'm talking about the feelings that are derived from fear-based thinking, and sad to say, that's most of our feelings. Yet the majority of people believe their fear-based feelings define who they are. They do not. Feelings move through you in the same way that a head cold or a thought does. Feelings do not sum up who you are." How do you begin to get beyond the control your feelings have in running your life? Britten says to remember the four A's: *Acknowledge* you are having feelings. *Allow* yourself time to process the feelings. *Ask* yourself, "What am I committed to?" *Act* on your commitments. These are important points to remember, because overwhelming feelings often make it difficult for adoptees to make choices and decisions.

*Decision-Making*

Decision-making is another area which becomes paralyzed by fear. Many of you report being petrified when faced with even the most innocuous decisions. Yet decision-making is an integral part of adult life. Not making a decision can be dangerous. Remember the proverbial donkey who starved to death while trying to decide which bale of hay to eat? Opportunities can slip by while you are trying to "make the right decision." It is important to remember that *not* choosing is a choice. It is a choice to be a victim of fate. It is better to make a choice to do something than a choice not to. This entails your allowing that there is more than one right way to do things. The one you choose doesn't have to be wrong, it doesn't have to be what someone else would choose, but it could be one of the right ways. Once you have chosen, stop wondering "what if" I had chosen the other way or one of the other ways. This is a waste of time and energy. You don't have time for it. Go with your decision and keep going. If you made the wrong one, then learn from it. If you made one of the right ones, then be happy with it. You won't be able to control every aspect of your choice. Whenever you run into something you didn't expect, then it is time again to make a choice about what to do. You don't have to worry about it ahead of time. Just have faith in yourself to be able to handle whatever comes up.

Many birth mothers have difficulties with decision-making because of their "decision" to give up their babies. The pain of that decision makes many of them wary of their ability to make decisions. For many birth mothers, however, the choice was not theirs, but society's or their parents' (and thus society's). In the present state of values in our society, many of them would have made a different decision. It is important for birth mothers to realize that they need to live in the present and that they can make good decisions for themselves today. If this is not happening, then some counseling to help them with this would be advised.

For both adoptees and birth mothers, it is essential to incorporate experiences that happened since the one "fatal" decision which seemed to stop everything in its tracks. How have you handled difficult situations or crises in your life since then? Were you able to stop and analyze the true situation and make an intervention that worked? Were you able to take one step at a time, rather than seeing the whole thing as overwhelming? Were you able to ask for help? (This is a big no-no for many adoptees. There is a creed: I shall never ask for help! This, as they go about rescuing everyone else!) Well, take a chance. Ask for help. You get no points for "doing it yourself." Remember that human beings were meant to be *interdependent*: to help one another. Are you human? Of course you are. Then act like it. Take a chance and give and take.

It may be difficult to make decisions about your life if you don't know who you are. One of the barriers to adoptees' making decisions may be their vagueness about who they really are. Spending your whole life trying to figure out how others have wanted you to be or to act makes listening to intuition and instinct about how you really feel a novelty. And, again, it may be stifled by fear, fear of disappointing or hurting or angering someone else. This book is for adults, and adults have to begin doing what is best for them, not what everyone else wants them to do. But we go again to the place where we have to know who we are before we can make good decisions about what we should do. *Self-knowledge is essential to the decision-making process.*

Remember that trying and failing is better than not trying at all. Not trying is a zero. Trying and failing is a lesson and earns points. Remember than no matter how things turn out, you will be better off no matter what your decision because you will have learned something. You will have grown in your outlook. At least have as much courage as you did when you were a year old and got up on your feet and took that first step. What if you had never taken that risk?

There are steps you can take to ensure a better result when you have to make a decision. For adoptees being impulsive isn't one of them. Acting on an impulse is not always a bad thing, but too many of the impulses that adoptees act on are self-destructive or inappropriate. So for adoptees, decisions should be well thought out. This doesn't mean that adoptees should not pay attention to intuition. Many times intuition is better than rationality. Knowing the difference between intuition, impulse, and projection is essential when using intuition for decision-making. People who act on impulse usually act in spite of their intuitive or rational knowledge.

Making a decision involves either a strong intuitive certainty that some action will be the right one, or it involves taking several steps to ensure that a rational decision is made. Investigating a situation is the smart thing to do. Decide on a procedure that you can live with by establishing priorities. What do you need to do first? Find different resources for your idea: books, journals, professionals, the Internet, etc. Don't be afraid to ask for help. Someone may have ideas that you never thought of. If an idea doesn't work, don't be afraid to try something else. Don't be like so many scientists over the ages and stubbornly protect your sacred "truth" by denying the fallibility of it. When new information is introduced, it may change the way you want to proceed. This is a good thing. It is not a good thing to get all hot and bothered because your first idea didn't work and you are going to make it work no matter what. Remember that *you are succeeding if you are learning.*

Don't try to predict every outcome of every aspect of your decision. That takes all the fun and excitement out of trying new things. Expect the unexpected, then deal with it. If your expectations didn't happen, don't have a fit. Maybe something better is about to happen. Many really helpful things have been discovered while something else was being worked on. Most inventors will vouch for that. So will pharmaceutical companies. You really don't have to control every aspect of whatever is going on. All you have to do is *have faith that you can deal with whatever does happen.* And you can. You have before.

### From Expectation to Intention: Dealing with Change

Britten recommends turning expectations into intentions. She defines expectations as, "... what you think ought to happen as a result of what you do, say, or plan." Fear is built into every expectation because we can't always predict the outcome of what we expect, especially when other people are involved. When we change that expectation into an intention, which Britten defines as "... living purposefully. On purpose, with purpose. Proactively, responsibly, and intuitively. ... When intention is our mode of operation, we give up the idea that our past dictates our future. Intention is living in the present, actively choosing the future while being aware that in each moment your state of mind is up to you. ... Intention is the pathway to shift your focus from fear to freedom" (Britten, 2001). What this means is that real freedom is realizing that your future is in your own hands and doesn't have to depend upon "wishing, waiting, and hoping" for a different outcome, but being proactive in your own life. If this sounds scary, it can't be more scary than leaving your life up to fate. This would be like bobbing around on the ocean without a rudder. You have to provide your own rudder.

In an interview with Georgia Rowe in the *Contra Costa Times* about his new book *What Should I Do with My Life?*, author Po Bronson, who interviewed 900 people from various walks of life, talks about the things that stop people from changing even when they know they are going down the wrong track. He says, "I began to make lists of fears that people have—fear of choosing, fear of irreversibility, fear of what your parents are going to say, fear of being broke, fear of failing and destroying your fantasy." He doesn't imply that overcoming these fears is easy. He did say, "But it did seem that for most of their lives, these people had made certain assumptions about who they were, about the notion that their talent should have manifested itself early in life. Then they heard an urge, and that urge slowly erupted in their lives. And they discovered talents they didn't even know they had. So I think the notion that our talents should be clear keeps us from finding things we can devote ourselves to. Finding things that can make us happy" (Rowe, 2003). How true this last statement can be for adult adoptees, who have spent much of their lives trying to fit into a family that may have had different criteria for professions, lifestyles, and values than that which might have been native to the adoptee. I know myriad adoptees who have studied for and acquired a profession because it was what they assumed their parents wanted them to do. In some cases this was true, but in others it was only a perception. It is time for everyone to reach deep inside and discover those talents which may have lain dormant for the past twenty plus years. It is hoped that by the end of this book some methods for doing so will be evident.

*Summary*

Fear and its little brother, anxiety, keep many adoptees and birth mothers from doing what they need to do in their lives, from learning to love themselves and thus being prepared to love others and allow intimacy into their lives, to discovering and actualizing their potential in a meaningful profession or lifestyle. Most of that fear, which is most often felt as anxiety, is coming from an ancient place in their history: the separation of one from the other. This trauma created imprints in the brain, which get triggered whenever any event with the slightest similarity to the original trauma is encountered. The feelings that this engenders are very difficult to ignore. No one is saying to ignore these feelings, but we are saying to feel them and push through them to form a new pathway. Then practice until that pathway is more deeply imprinted and can supersede the original pathway.

Taking steps to form new patterns in the brain seems like a big risk, but in order for adoptees and birth mothers to have a fuller and richer life, risk is necessary. Remember that the brain is pliable until death and able to form new pathways. As John Ratey says, "The brain is amazingly plastic. ... Rewiring is possible throughout life." He also emphasizes that we must do something unfamiliar in a situation which is similar to an experience that no longer serves us well. See it as an adventure, not without risks, but exciting and beneficial to your well-being.

# CHAPTER 4
Anger and Rage

Anger is the second universal emotion. It is also the most difficult emotion to deal with, especially in its extreme form, rage. It is difficult to deal with because we either repress it or we explode. We seldom know the cause of our rage, but often act upon it anyway. It is the source of much unhappiness and violence; yet it is also the initiator of change both personal and societal. What is anger and how can we use it in constructive, rather than destructive, ways?

*The Four Components of Anger*

As with many other feelings, anger appears as a part of a series of experiences. Because it suits my paradigm best, I see these experiences as having four different components. Those four components are *an event,* which precipitates *a belief,* which causes *a feeling or sensation* (including *a physical sensation),* which results in *action—a behavioral reaction or response.* An event occurs, which one interprets through the lens or filter of one's culture and previous experiences. Depending upon what that experience has been, anger may occur if the event gets translated into a belief, such as "I am being threatened" or "I am being trespassed against." That belief causes an emotion (anger or fear), which may be a cause for action.

Events are occurring in our lives all the time. The way we interpret those events has a great deal to do with how we respond to them. Someone sent me an example on the Internet: Four people have pooled their money and have won the lottery. Each is going to get $1,000,000. Anna, who has had a fairly uneventful life and has a positive attitude toward other people, is delighted and begins to plan how she will spend some of it and invest the rest. She is generally excited and positive about her win. John, who feels as if people take advantage of him and who is suspicious of others' motives, begins to worry that people will want him to share his winnings or that he will be cheated out of them by having to pay so much tax on them. Instead of excitement, John begins to feel anger. Donna has never had much money and has lived from paycheck to paycheck, both in her family of origin and in her present life. She begins to feel overwhelmed by the prospect of how she is going to handle this money and becomes anxious. Bob, although glad that he is going to have so much money, thinks about how it would have been if he had won the whole pot for himself and experiences his $1,000,000 as a loss. He begins to feel sad, discontented, and resentful. All four of these people experienced the same event, but all four interpreted it differently and thus had different emotions about it.

Epictetus of the first century said, *"Men are disturbed not by events, but by the view they take of them."* That view, belief, or meaning causes an emotion. If the event is seen as a need or desire having been satisfied, the emotion may be one of joy, satisfaction, contentment, happiness, excitement, or other positive feelings. If the event is interpreted as a threat, the emotions which ensue may be anger or fear. If, on the other hand, the event is seen as a loss, the feeling may be sorrow, sadness, grief or despair.

Our bodies, too, respond to our interpretation of events. If anger is evoked, the body responds with tense muscles, elevated heart rate and blood pressure, cessation of digestion, a surge in adrenal and cortisol activity, and the brain goes into attack mode. If a person experiences anger very often, *these physical responses can be damaging to our health.* Our bodies respond chemically to our emotions, which is the reason it is important to be able to control the negative emotions. Having elevated levels of adrenaline or cortisol in the body is not a good thing over time.

Sometimes controlling our responses isn't very easy. If the belief, which starts this chain of events, is related in even the smallest way to trauma, the information is hijacked by the amygdala in the limbic system before the neocortex can provide caution, and violence may occur. In the event of trauma, the emotions connected with the trauma seem to be hard-wired into the central nervous system. In this case, one's ability to interpret the event becomes compromised, and the event is responded to as if it were a case of life or death. (Review Chapter 2.) In that case, we may want to end the trespass by wounding or even killing the trespasser. If the event is wired into the brain and central nervous system, one may respond with an immature, unsocialized reaction, in which there may be a physical attack where things or people may be destroyed. If, however, one has learned to exercise a certain level of self-restraint, one may employ a more socialized, mature response such as a controlled verbal response or silence.

### Beliefs about Anger

Three things which enter into the feeling of anger are attitude, perception, and belief. The advent of the theories of Darwin and Freud changed our beliefs about anger from the belief that we *can and must* control anger to the belief that we *cannot*, and in fact *should not.* In the 70s, Americans took to the latter theory like ducks to water. Rather than a society of community, cooperation, and self-restraint for the good of the whole, in America we have had a society of individualism and self-indulgence (the "me generation" or the "looking out for

#1" crowd). This paradigm not only creates anger by limiting the wish to act on our desires without considering others, but also encourages the release of that anger in violent and destructive ways. This can be witnessed over and over in movie and television programs, in video games, and in the news. Daniel Goleman says,

> *Unlike sadness, anger is energizing, even exhilarating. Anger's seductive, persuasive power may in itself explain why some views about it are so common: that anger is uncontrollable, or that, at any rate, it should not be controlled, and that venting anger in "catharsis" is all to the good. The contrasting view, perhaps a reaction against the bleak picture of these other two, holds that anger can be prevented entirely. But careful reading of research findings suggests that all these common attitudes toward anger are misguided, if not outright myths.*
> Goleman, 1995

We have a tendency in America to polarize our points of view. We look to extremes, to black or white thinking, to guide us. This can be very dangerous. We need to find balance.

Unlike fear, the rules governing anger serve one's culture. People get angry because of what they believe about the offender or the intent of the offender. Things which are insulting in one culture may not be in another and will not engender anger. Our culture is an angry culture, and as a result there are some facilitators of support or therapy groups who insist that all the members must feel anger in order to heal. I believed this at one time myself. It was what I was taught. However, I now believe that anger is an emotion which requires a certain amount of self-restraint. *Allowing* for the appearance of anger in therapy-type setting where there is containment and control can be very helpful. However, *goading* someone into feeling anger is never recommended.

I did research for a woman who investigated cults in a case against one of the more well-known encounter groups which sprang up during the 80s. One member died as the result of a heart attack apparently brought on by the rage he was prodded to feel toward his birth mother. (Remember what anger does to us physiologically: heart rate, blood pressure, hormones, neuropeptides, and so forth!) Now, I don't know if that adoptee died of a heart attack as a result of his anger or not, but I do know that it is unconscionable to manipulate someone into a feeling. That particular adoptee may have been feeling more rage toward the facilitators who were goading him than at his birth mother. There is a big difference between allowing and supporting someone in his feelings and forcing him to feel something that the therapist or group facilitator thinks he should feel.

There is also a difference, as I have said before, between having feelings and acting upon them. Children should never be told that they shouldn't feel something, but they must be given appropriate ways of expressing those feelings. Self-restraint is often missing in our society, yet it is something for which all adults should strive. Seneca was a believer in self-restraint. He believed that because we are in love with our vices, we uphold them and prefer to make excuses for them rather than shake them off. Why do we make excuses for them? In her book *Anger: The Misunderstood Emotion*, Carol Tavris answers, "Because they excuse us." Alcohol is a good example of this idea. Alcohol does not so much incite anger and outrageous behavior as it simply gives one an excuse for such behavior. Tarvis goes on to say, "While anger serves our private uses, it also makes our social excuses." We have all heard someone say, "Well, I couldn't help it; I had been drinking." By now everyone should know that drugs and alcohol distort reality and impair judgment, so if you choose to drink, you choose to have your reality distorted and your judgment impaired. You have to suffer the consequences for that choice.

Anger is easily displaced—projected upon the wrong person. In his essay *"Nicomachean Ethics,"* Aristotle said, "Anyone can become angry—that is easy. But to be angry with the right person, to the right degree, at the right time, for the right purpose, and in the right way—that is not easy." This is the key to righteous anger. And Aristotle is right—it is not easy. Most of the time our anger has 20% to do with the current situation and 80% to do with past injustices or trespasses.

## Anger Myths

There are many myths about anger, which have been circulated for several decades and certainly for the past thirty years. The emphasis on the individual in America has produced a variety of myths, which serve to excuse the individual at the expense of the community. I will discuss four of those myths.

### Venting Anger Is Healthy and Cathartic

Because many people have been denied their feelings of anger during childhood, as adults they believe that they must express those feelings whenever they occur in order to be emotionally healthy. While it may be appropriate to express anger in certain situations, the perimeters surrounding the expression of that emotion are clear. To paraphrase Aristotle, *the anger must be directed toward the person who made one angry, it must be about the current situation with that person, it must be appropriate to the situation, and it must be acknowledged and not retaliated.* There is no satisfaction in venting anger if there is no acknowledgment and apology for the offense.

Research has shown that talking about anger doesn't get rid of it or reduce it, it rehearses it and often inflames it. Venting anger may feed the anger. It may cause severe depression and even suicide. By talking, I don't mean just expressing an angry feeling to someone. I am talking about endless repetitions of recounting the anger. Lewis, et al. say, "The most common precipitant of this reiterant emotionality is cognition: people tend to think about emotionally arousing occasions afterward, recirculating the experience and stimulating the consequent emotion just as if the inciting event had actually reoccurred. The human penchant for this post hoc cogitation can magnify the physiologic impact of an emotion many times." This is the problem with some adoption support groups; they do nothing but vent—at birth parents, at adoptive parents, at social workers, etc. This seldom exorcises the anger or makes the participants feel better. Lewis, et al. also say, "Because limbic states can leap between minds, feelings are contagious, while notions are not." Many adoptees I know won't go to these groups anymore, because they feel so bad by the time they leave that they can't sleep all night. Even if they weren't angry when they arrived, they often are by the time they leave. Goleman notes, "Anger builds on anger; the emotional brain heats up." If anger is contagious, as Lewis states, then everyone present at those meetings may end up with emotional and physiological reactions to anger, theirs or someone else's. Adoptees at those meetings have noted that some people have been venting anger for years, which doesn't say much for the cathartic value of venting.

In *The Primal Wound*, I mention that adoptees may have baby rage at their birth mothers. After reunion, the mother may ask, "How long do I have to listen to this?" Good question. Two or three months ought to be enough. Then it is time for both the adoptee and the birth mother to go on to a new phase of the relationship. One thing which has to happen first, however, is that the birth mother must validate the adoptee's anger *without giving any reason or excuse for her actions.* Giving the reasons at that point will make the adoptee feel as if she is not understanding the *infant self,* which cares nothing for reasons. Later, when the mother senses that the adoptee has matured in their relationship, they can discuss the moral climate at the time of the relinquishment and talk in more adult terms. If the adoptee is still angry after a few months of raging or the silence of "abandoning the birth mother" (i.e., not answering phone calls, letters, or e-mail), the birth mother should ask "What would you like me to do about it now?" And I don't mean for this to be a rhetorical question. Wait for an answer. Although the anger may still be there, it is important for both adoptee and birth mother to realize that history cannot be changed and, in order for them to continue their relationship, there must be some kind of pardon or forgiveness.

This is true also for birth mothers who are still angry at their parents for encouraging or even forcing them to give up their babies. At an adoption conference, Rickie Solinger, who wrote *Wake Up Little Suzie,* the classic book about the social and historic reasons so many white unwed women gave up their babies during the 40s, 50s, and 60s, reminded birth mothers that if they want forgiveness from their children, they also have to be forgiving toward their own parents. Forgiveness isn't only for the targets of our anger; it is also for us. Carrying anger around is a burden.

Venting anger is often an excuse for poor anger management. Managing anger means taking responsibility for one's emotions and behavior. It means refusing to play the blame game, or to be stuck in the fury or the silent treatment mode. If anger is used to belittle the nearest (and probably most vulnerable) target instead of to change a difficult situation, it is no longer credible or powerful. It feeds only on itself. When one already has an underlying stratum of anger (that baby rage), then each time anger is provoked in the present, the explosion may be greater than if there were no underlying anger. Anger builds upon itself so that a seemingly innocuous event may provoke an angry response completely out of proportion to the precipitating event. In fairness to the people in one's life, *it is important to respond to the event rather than to the feeling.* It is also important to have all the information necessary to make a fair response, since many responses are premature and based on partial data. One of the most prevalent reasons for anger in relationships is assumptions. People act on assumptions without checking them out. This is an immature and self-serving way to relate because it simply gives one an excuse for childish reactions to feelings.

In experiments with both children and college students, it has been noted that being encouraged to vent anger, rather than control it, does not assuage the anger, but instead inflames it. Most kids on the playground get angry regularly, yet five minutes later all the feelings have dissipated and everyone is playing harmoniously again. Yet if anyone points out the transgression of the offending party and makes a "big deal" out of it, the anger can linger into the next day.

In a study of college students, contrary to the prevailing and popular idea that repressed students would be mentally unhealthy and the expressers more healthy, it was found that those students who didn't take everything personally and were slow to anger, were more dependable and socially mature than those who were quick to anger and showed little self-restraint.

Because a surge of adrenaline accompanies anger, it is important to allow the adrenal surge to subside before proceeding with any discussion. When one is in the throes of intense anger and the accompanying adrenal rush, perceptions get distorted and one may act or say things for which one is sorry later. This is not to say that one should suppress anger. But allowing oneself to feel anger and allowing oneself to act on it are two different things. If you feel that your anger is legitimate (i.e., that it follows Aristotle's model), then it might be important when calmed down to talk to the person about whatever caused it. Remember that the only thing that really dispels anger is an appropriate response to it. Just venting at anyone in any way only serves to make it worse.

Life is not fair. To think otherwise sets one up for being angry most of the time. We want to think so, and at times we screen out any information which is contrary to our beliefs. Isn't this what happens in adoption? If we want others to stop believing in the altruistic value of adoption, what are we doing to become realistic about a number of things ourselves? We want order and consistency in life—for it to have meaning. On the other hand, many people who have suffered adversity early in life tend to filter out the good things in life and see only the negative aspects. "Life is always unfair, and I am always its victim." That is enough to make anyone angry!

### Aggression Is Instinctive and Unavoidable

Believing that aggression is the instinctive catharsis for anger is a fallacy equating anger with aggression, or the hiss with the bite, as Tavris puts it. It is a good thing to be able to know when one is angry, to feel anger, but it is not a good thing to act it out aggressively. To believe that aggression is inevitable when one is angry: "I couldn't help myself ..." is to believe that anger is instinctive like fear. Anger, however, involves a judgment that an injustice, insult, or trespass has been committed. It also involves cultural understanding of just what is insulting. A certain gesture, which will provoke anger in one culture, will be ignored by another. It also involves a voluntary choice of reactions. Tavris says, "Judgment and choice distinguish human beings from other species; judgment and choice are the hallmarks of human anger."

When it comes to the "baby rage" that the adoptee feels, there is a belief, no matter how primitive and perhaps correct, that the baby has been wronged. This feeling of being wronged exists, paradoxically, with the belief that she was left because she wasn't good enough to keep. Thus the anger is directed both at the birth mother (or her representative, the adoptive mother or significant other) and at the adoptee herself. The presence of these two simultaneous ideas creates a climate of anger in many adoptees, which seems to be permanent and pervasive. In my experience, feeling trespassed against, discounted, or criticized will send some adoptees into a rage. The "discounting" of the abandonment is such a tremendous wound that anything resembling a discounting of their person is given much more importance than it is with most people. And it isn't hard to trip that trigger because adoptees often take everything personally. Thus, a great deal of perplexity exists among those in relation to adoptees who feel the wrath of this anger (the angry child). However, adoptees are every bit as apt to turn the anger on themselves—they have a very short fuse when it comes to their own shortcomings. It must be noted that self-blame restores control. If I can blame the "bad baby" for getting kicked out, then I won't have to feel so helpless. I just have to be a better baby (or the adult version, a people-pleaser). However it is experienced, anger is one of the most difficult emotions for some adoptees to gain some control over.

A great deal of anger is displaced or misdirected. It has been noted that retaliation works only for those at the same or lower position in life as our own. There is no release of tension if the person retaliated against is in a superior position to ours. For instance, let's say that someone is very angry with his boss, but is afraid of expressing it to him because he may be fired or at least reprimanded. So he waits until he gets home and vents his anger at his wife, his children, or his dog. There is nothing healthy about this kind of displaced anger because it just causes more anger and misunderstanding to be generated within the family and does nothing about the situation with the boss. It is simply indulgence and a lack of self-restraint. There is absolutely no acceptable reason to vent anger at someone other than the perpetrator of the injustice. Nor is there any sense of restitution or resolution. Ratey reminds us, "Learning to control anger is a natural and important step for toddlers, and yet one out of five people experience attacks of rage that they report they cannot control." In other words, the adult is being controlled by a toddler within.

### Venting Anger Prevents Neurosis

Some people, even therapists, encourage some kind of physical expression of anger, such as hitting pillows or a punching bag. While this might be appropriate for children, who have less self-control than adults, it usually doesn't work for adults in the long run. The one physical activity I might suggest for adults is a long walk, which will often restore perspective and lower the adrenaline and cortisol levels. Intense emotion distorts reality and judgment. A cooling-off period is called for. Not only will a walk or run de-escalate the chemicals of anger, but it can be a distraction from the anger-causing trigger. Distraction is important. If you just use the time walking to carry on a running monologue about the cause of the anger, it only serves to escalate the feelings. It is important to notice one's surroundings or other people or think about something else. You can actually begin to have a pleasant time. It is hard to stay angry when you're having a good time.

Some people will say, "But I don't want to be distracted. I am angry, damn it!" Well, while you are angry, you are not thinking straight. So it is better to cool down if you are trying to deal with your anger toward another person. Having a tantrum is not the answer. Tantrums are for two-year-olds. And they are awesome to behold. Anyone who thinks, however, that this form of expressing anger is instinctive and unavoidable has not closely observed a child having a tantrum. For one thing, there is no tantrum without an audience. For another, they can begin, become violent, then be interrupted by some curiosity on the part of the child, and then be resumed. For instance, a child may be screaming, beating his fists on the floor, kicking, and so forth, then in the middle of it all, calmly ask his mother, "When is daddy coming home?" then go right back to the "fit." If anyone doesn't think this is calculated, take another guess! Some cultures tolerate tantrums from children under the age of four because they cannot reason. But as soon as children are at an age when they can reason, they are expected to control their reactions to anger. Carol Tavris recounts that in the Eskimo culture "... the only adults who are exempt from this expectation are idiots, the insane, the very sick ... and *kaplunas*—white people." This is quite an indictment of our ability to control our behavior. It must also be noted that there is more neurosis among white people than among other cultures.

When adults have tantrums, throwing things, hitting, kicking or screaming, they are acting like two-year-olds. They are not taking responsibility for their actions or the way their actions affect others. Again, it is usually in the presence of another that these tirades take place. If alone, it might be more usual for the person to cry or become depressed. For the most part, these behaviors can be controlled. I remember the story I heard once of a couples' therapist who was questioning a man about hitting his wife. "I just can't help it," the man kept saying. "She provokes me." "Then why don't you shoot her and get it over with?" the therapist asked. "Because I would go to jail," the man replied. "Exactly!" exclaimed the therapist. If the consequence is great enough, then one can often control the behavior. Railing against the boss, for instance, may result in being fired, so one doesn't throw a fit in the boss's office. One may go home and hit the wife instead. It is easy to retaliate against someone physically unable to defend herself. If anyone believes that he doesn't have that kind of control, it is grossly irresponsible to go one more day without enrolling in an anger management class.

Adults need to express their anger verbally, but not inappropriately or abusively. Remember that if the idea is justice and catharsis, it does not serve to simply make the other person defensive or angry. Some kind of satisfaction needs to be a result of the expression of anger. Anger is a sign of attachment and connection. People rarely feel angry with people who are of no consequence to them. The people we get the most mad at are our family members. Many times for adoptees this is a way to connect to parents without risking the vulnerability of love. It is intense and safe—at least safer than love. The same may be true of any significant other in your life. If you are expressing anger instead of love, it isn't fair and your partner really doesn't have to put up with it. This is the sabotaging behavior that adoptees often employ. The fear of being rejected causes the kind of behavior which often precipitates that very rejection. It is time to realize that a change in behavior is needed.

### "I'm Just Being Honest"

The "let it all hang out" crowd during the 70s said that they were just being honest in "telling it like it is." But telling it like it is when one is angry may neither be honest nor about truth. Being angry results in distorted thinking. An easy example of this is being cut off on the freeway. Some people become enraged by this and take it as a personal insult. Yet who is this person who is insulting you? You can say that you're being honest by being angry, but it may not be truthful because that person may not, *probably was not*, trying to do anything to you. *Sometimes an innocent action is viewed as a trespass and triggers a reaction.* That reaction is not about truth, even though the anger may seem honest. A great many of our reactions to anger, the finger on the freeway, throwing things, or hitting people are simply indulging in childish responses. It exhilarates us, makes us feel good in the moment. It makes us feel less helpless. *But it is not powerful; it is not taking responsibility for our behavior.* Ratey warns us, "Research has shown that there is little health benefit from this kind of behavior. Anger can get out of control and create both mental and physical health risks. Unreasonable anger is a symptom of many disorders ... psychologically, we know that anger can create an unhealthy environment for anyone in contact with an angry person." So go ahead and be angry, but don't react in an immature manner and say that you are being honest. If getting cut off on the freeway enrages you, then you probably have a great deal of undifferentiated anger which needs to be addressed rather than acted upon.

Although we often believe that all we want is justice, justice predicated upon anger, instead of being righteous, is self-righteous. It is self-interested and self-indulgent. *Anger is a disorganizing emotion.* This is very important for everyone to understand. What it means is that however we attempt to settle an argument while in the thralls of this emotion, it will probably not turn out very well. People will say, "I was so angry that I couldn't see straight." And yet they will justify their reaction while not seeing straight. Pert warns us that reality is distorted by our chemistry which includes emotional tones from our past history. This makes it difficult to know what is real and what is not. That being the case, there is no justification in the adult world for reacting to these perceptions while caught up in an emotion without allowing thought to kick in. *Justice seen through distorted eyes is not justice.*

# The Dangers of Anger

*Anger Fuels Violence*

There are two things which lead to or fuel violence: anger and fear. If one lashes out in anger, one is often out of control. A synonym for anger is *mad*. "I was mad at my wife for wrecking the car." Another synonym for mad is *insane*. When we are mad, we often feel insane or out of control. That's why a lot of men want to cool off before talking about whatever made the couple mad. If a wife insists on talking things out in the moment, when both are still angry, not very much is going to be accomplished except an escalation of anger. In studies of both men's and women's reactions to anger, it was observed that men tend toward retaliation and women tend toward reparation, which is probably a hormonal response. Because of this difference in attitude, it is important for women to understand that men may not be reacting the same way they are. Therefore, they need to allow men time to gain some perspective on the situation. Now, before I get a basket of mail from gentle men, I want to say that not all people react according to gender-specific paradigms. But hormones do play a part in our emotional reactions to events, so we can't just ignore that aspect of a situation.

Our culture, which sanctions anger, is a violent society. We see it everywhere. Children grow up watching violent cartoons. They graduate to violent movies and video games. If the violence is performed by the "good guys," it is condoned. Societies in which the venting of anger is encouraged have five times the crime rate of those where it is not. In the U.S. today, murder, assault, rape, spousal and child abuse are rampant. Yet we continue to "let it all hang out." According to Martin Seligman, out of control anger ruins more lives than most other things, including AIDS and alcohol. Manners and courtesy have become as rare as hens' teeth. Given what is going on in our schools, as well as in the workplace and sporting events, it might be time for manners to make a comeback. As silly as some rules of etiquette may seem, they are there to slow us down, to show respect, to make others feel comfortable. Please note that *these rules take someone other than the individual into account*. We are, after all, social beings meant to interact with one another, not simply to look out for ourselves.

It was noted that after the terrorists' acts of September II, 2001, people began to appreciate one another and to cooperate with one another. Yes, there were some who wanted to retaliate against anyone who remotely resembled the terrorists, but most people were feeling truly connected, empathic, and loving toward their families and their fellow human beings. Although I am skeptical that this attitude will have any staying power, wouldn't it be wonderful if it did? Then, perhaps when one got cut off on the freeway, instead of having thoughts of outrage and revenge, one could reflect and wonder, "Does he have an exit right away that he was unaware of? Is he on the way to the hospital? Perhaps he didn't see me. Have I ever done that to anyone?" These kinds of reflections are much more gentle to our bodies and psyches than the rage that some people allow themselves to feel.

## The Anger of Others Causes Depression in Children

Recent studies have shown that parental anger causes pessimism and depression in children. It may have about the same effect as divorce. The upheaval when parents fight causes a loss of security in children, which leads to dysphoria (dejection and unhappiness). Pretending that the children are unaware of what is going on is either naïve or dishonest. Even if the fights are contained within the parental bedroom, children know that something is going on. They are intuitive and sense the atmosphere of the home. They are exquisitely tuned in to their parents' and especially their mother's feelings. Rather than having endless, pointless, angry discussions, parents should find another way of airing their grievances. Children don't have to believe that their parents do not have arguments. That would be dishonest and would model deception. However, the manner in which these disagreements are conducted is very important. Honest discussions and attempts at solving marital problems have a calming effect on children and give them role models for solving their own problems. But anger scares them and leaves them feeling that there are no adults in the family. It may also make *them* angry, and they are liable to lash out at their fellow students at school or at younger brothers and sisters. Remember what Lewis, et al. said about feelings being contagious! Also remember that behavior is learned and that parents can't expect from their children more emotional control than they are able to demonstrate themselves.

## Anger Damages Relationships

There are two things which I see as being especially destructive to relationships. One is unchecked assumptions (about behavior, thoughts, feelings, etc.), and the other is anger. Anger is hot, quick, and destructive, whereas judgment is cool, patient, and constructive. When a person is old enough to be in a chosen relationship, a partnership or marriage, he is old enough to use judgment, rather than anger, when trying to find justice or solutions to differences in the relationship. This does not mean that he should not be angry. There are certain situations where anger is appropriate. Yet, remembering that anger distorts his ability to think rationally, it isn't a good idea to act on the immediate feeling. In order to effect change in a mature relationship, it is important to be civil, to let the trivial things go by, and to wait for calmness to return in order to discuss important issues. There must be emotional respect and integrity. Expressing anger, although exhilarating, shows disingenuousness toward the resolution of disagreements.

## Distorted Thinking

Pert reminds us that our emotions regulate what we perceive as reality. She says, "The decision about what sensory information travels to your brain and what gets filtered out depends on what signals the receptors are receiving from the peptides. There is a plethora of elegant neurophysiological data suggesting that the nervous system is not capable of taking in everything, but can only scan the outer world for material that it is prepared to find by virtue of its wiring hookups, its own internal patterns, and its past experience." We have discovered that these brain wirings have a bias toward a certain way of viewing events based upon past experience. This often leads to distorted thinking.

Reneau Peurifoy, in his book *Anger: Taming the Beast,* lists six types of distorted thinking that he says "can awaken the beast of anger and cause it to run wild" (Peurifoy, 1999). Because most of our emotions are triggered by our interpretations of events, and because by the time we are adults many of our behavior patterns have become automatic, there is a great deal of distorted thinking going on which results in inappropriate behavior. It is important to become aware of this distorted thinking in order to gain some control over our reactions to it. What are some of these distortions? I have listed them with some modification.

### Overgeneralizing

Although generalizing or forming concepts is an important part of our being able to deal with situations which we don't always have time to analyze, sometimes we use absolutes to carry these generalizations to the extreme. If one was traumatized early in life and grew up with a sense of helplessness, this tendency to generalize becomes even more problematic. There may be a bias towards negative interpretations of what may be innocuous situations.

Some of the clues to an overgeneralization are the words *always* and *never.* People who overgeneralize cannot seem to see the situation, but see their whole existence as being challenged. "I didn't get a raise this year," becomes, "I never get raises. No one ever appreciates me." Or even more extreme, "Nothing good ever happens to me." If you have a tendency to feel undeserving or unworthy, the thought might be, "I am no good." If you find yourself thinking these things, it would be important to test the validity of the thought. What actually happened?

Is this really about your whole life or only an aspect of it? What parts of your life *are* working? What steps can you take to remedy the part that is not? This last question is very important because it reins in that feeling of helplessness and allows you to feel as if you have some control.

Overgeneralizing can be detected in the therapeutic setting when the therapist makes a comment about something specific, but the patient takes it as a blanket statement about his choices or behavior. For example, one may say, "I wonder if you could have reacted differently to what happened." The patient may then reply, "Why do you always think I over-react?" With certain patients, this form of statement can degenerate into a whirlwind of chaos and distorted thinking. It is very important to have the patient mirror what the therapist says and return to the specific idea being discussed.

This form of self-degradation can get very old. It can be very manipulative in discussions between two people. If a wife or husband complains about a very specific behavior of the other spouse, the offending spouse may answer, "Oh, I never do anything right. I may as well leave." This is a ploy, which often gets the complaining spouse to correct and rectify the offending spouses' perception, and the whole discussion gets lost in the chaos of false starts and wrong turns. What the complaining spouse should do, rather than trying to correct the perception of the offending spouse is to ask, "What exactly did I say?" Asking questions is a much better method of getting things back on track than any kind of reiteration or justification.

### The "Shoulds"

As a therapist, I am amazed by the number of times a day I hear the word "*should*." I am not a person who thinks that one can never have obligations or that guilt is a dirty word. However, we do have choices in life, and there are probably very few things which must always be done. Circumstances will often dictate what our choices will be. Where is the word *should* coming from when used in connection with something that must be done? Who is thinking that it should be done?

When the shoulds are coming from an old tape being played in a person's head, it is time to question the validity of that *should*. Is it something that someone else thinks is necessary? Do you have the same values as the person who instilled that *should* in your head? To be honest, I believe there are times when *shoulds* need to be *inserted* in some people's heads. For instance when one member of a family is always the one to help an infirm relative and everyone else just allows that and does nothing—contributes neither time nor money— guilt is the correct response. The uninvolved members should be made to pitch in and help or feel guilty about it. Guilt is appropriate here!

Most of the time, however, when I hear *should* mentioned in my consulting room, it has nothing to do with the values of the person sitting there or helping a family member. It is some vestigial *should* left over from childhood, when mom and dad were in charge of one's life. What is being felt is a form of manipulation perpetrated upon the individual by someone wanting some form of control. Often that manipulation is not even going on in the present but is a tape running in the person's head. I know adults who live alone, earn their own living, and are generally independent, yet who still won't allow themselves to do something, buy something, or change something because there is an old tape from childhood playing in their heads that says, "You shouldn't do that!" If you were advising that person, what would you say? Are you willing to say it to yourself?

As long as an individual realizes that his choices may run up against another's choices, it is better to use phrases such as *I want, I like, I choose,* or *I prefer,* rather than *I must* or *I should.* However, if we take a job where we are obligated to be there on time and stay until a certain time and we choose not to do so, the boss may also make a choice—to fire us. In other words, we have to choose wisely.

*Personalization*

A person who has experienced helplessness such as having been removed from her biological home, family, and ancestry, has a tendency to personalize things. She may ask endless questions, all having to do with her. "Why didn't Jan call me back. I left a message two days ago. What did I do? She must be mad at me." It doesn't occur to the caller that Jan may be sick, away, or busy. She formulates endless scenarios in her head without taking the time to check out her assumptions. She becomes hurt and angry that Jan has not called back. She is afraid to call again to find out what happened. Everything is based on a personalized assumption. It all has to do with me, me, me. The idea that Jan may have a life that includes others equally important to her may be a scarier thought than "I must have done something to make her mad." To put things in perspective and gain a modicum of control, she must call Jan and ascertain just why she didn't call back. That takes her out of the victim role (waiting for Jan to do something) and into a place of power (doing something herself). She may find out that Jan's delay in returning her call was due to something other than herself, or she may find out the reason that Jan is upset with her and talk about it. Either way, taking the risk is better than the feeling of helplessness.

*Catastrophic Thinking or Discounting*

People often aggrandize their response to a trivial event by using such phrases as "That's terrible!" or "I hate that!" or "I can't stand it when that happens." Although it is important not to minimize painful events in people's lives, when those phrases are used in situations that are clearly not catastrophic, it is important to get them back in perspective. If this event is terrible, what is *not* terrible? What is there to hate about it? When people see life in negative terms, they often use such phrases in response to many events or situations in their lives. This is the "boy who cried wolf" response. After a while no one pays any attention to them because their utterings have lost meaning. When something really does seem catastrophic to them, they will have a difficult time convincing anyone.

Conversely, discounting events or circumstances can be as annoying to others as aggrandizing may be. For people with low self-esteem, the discounting is usually about themselves. They cannot take compliments to heart, but discount the importance of what they did or said. They have a difficult time being enthusiastic about things that others find wonderful or important. In other words, they can be a wet blanket at times. People who minimize their own contributions in the workplace, for instance, will usually maximize others' contributions.

*Circular "Why" Questioning*

There are two parts to something called circular thinking or questioning. The question usually begins with "why" or "how could." The questions are often rhetorical in nature, such as "Why did this happen to me?" or "How could she do that to me?" They are victimizing questions about fate or other people's intentions and are often based on assumptions. They are based on a belief that life isn't fair, which is true. The question is, at this time in history, why would one think that life is supposed to be fair?

Sometimes these questions are a foil to looking closely at oneself and how one puts oneself in certain positions. It is a way to avoid responsibility for one's circumstance. It can be a way of blaming others for something that is inconveniencing oneself—a form of disappointment. "Why isn't Janet here yet? She promised to pick me up at seven." Then five minutes later, "Why is she doing this to me?" One can allow oneself to be come angry over the fact that Janet is late or to label her as inconsiderate. Before doing that, however, it is important to closely examine the situation and the person involved. One way to do that is to answer the question you are asking. Don't just ask the question over and over like a mantra.

There are many reasons that Janet may be late other than trying to annoy or inconvenience you. Is it crucial that Janet be on time? Is Janet usually inconsiderate? If so, it might be important to talk to her about how that irritates you. If Janet is habitually late, she may be exhibiting passive aggressive behavior, and it would be important to call her on it. But if she is usually punctual and considerate, then it might be time to think about something else that might be going on—she had to get gas, or the phone rang as she was leaving, or the babysitter was late. It might not be about you. It is important to return to some kind of perspective on the circumstance based on facts and not on a perceived sense of victimization.

The other form of circular questioning is the kind of questions that four-year-olds ask: "Daddy, why is Grandpa old?" When daddy answers, "Because he has lived a long time," the question comes up, "But why has he lived a long time?" ... and so on. This kind of questioning in adult form can be tremendously annoying because one gets the impression after awhile that the questioner doesn't really want an answer to the question, but only wants to argue about something or to make the person attempting to answer the question wrong. The questions go round and round until someone gets angry, perhaps the answerer. Then the question is "Why are you mad at me? I just wanted to know why you didn't answer your phone last night." Of course, we already know that the original answer did not satisfy her. And no matter what the answer would have been, it would not have satisfied her, because she was angry and wanted to make the "perpetrator" wrong.

I usually advise people to avoid asking a question beginning with the word "why." For some reason that word puts people on the defensive. Of course in the above scenario, that is exactly what the questioner wants. But if one really wants an answer to a "why" question, a better way of asking it would be to start out by saying, "I'm curious about what happened last night. You didn't answer your phone and I was a little worried about you." Or "I'm wondering what happened last night. I thought we had an agreement to talk on the phone, but you didn't answer." These kinds of open-ended inquiries take away the blame tone and present a sincere concern for the missed appointment and the person involved. In other words, it isn't just about me, me, me!

Whenever someone over the age of seven starts in with the "whys," after the second or third question it is time to stop answering. Perhaps asking, "What is it you really want to know?" or "What is it you really want to say?" would be a good way to respond about then. The circular questioning gets nowhere and is only a game usually ending in anger on one or both people's parts.

*Name-calling*

One of the lowest forms of communication is name-calling or labeling. It is used when a more effective argument isn't forthcoming. Instead of formulating a rational argument to counter what someone has said, the name-caller is more likely to say, "What a dummy Bert is; he doesn't know what he is talking about." But name-calling can also be a habit learned in childhood. It is a form of verbal abuse and one often used by parents on their children. It is terribly debilitating and discounting and leaves scars on children which can persist into adulthood. Calling a child "stupid" or "dumb" can result in his calling himself that years later. Whenever he makes a mistake or is disappointed in himself, he may say something like "I am such an idiot!" or "How can I be so dumb?" This kind of rhetoric is self-defeating and makes others very uncomfortable.

This negative type of communication can also extend to others. It often becomes distorted, magnifying a problem which may be only annoying. For instance, when confronted by a confused salesclerk, calling him an incompetent idiot would be a form of labeling that may be out of proportion to the magnitude of the mistake he may have made. Whatever the reason for the name-calling, it is usually a response to a feeling of anger that probably has very little to do with the present situation. Whenever a person finds herself getting angry out of proportion to whatever situation she is in, it is time to look for the real source of the anger and learn to control her responses to that anger.

In order to counter the inappropriate responses to anger caused by the different ways of interpreting the events listed above, it is important to be honest with yourself about just what is going on. If you are using the words "always" or "never" a lot, then stop and think about what you are doing. Stick to the specific situation at hand. If you frequently find yourself assuming that everything others are doing or not doing is about you, reconsider. Most people are more interested in themselves than in others. If you catch yourself telling yourself that you *should* be doing this or that, ask yourself who is saying so. How old are you, and should you really be allowing mom and dad to dictate to you through those tapes you are playing in your head? They probably don't even want to anymore. Their days of socializing you are over. You need to realize that you do have choices, and interpreting your response as a "should" or an obligation *may be your way of avoiding the responsibility that comes with making choices.*

If you have difficulty accepting compliments and are frequently discounting your good qualities or your achievements, ask yourself what you are getting out of doing so. Do you feel undeserving of accolades, and if so, why? Get to the bottom of it. On the other hand, if you find yourself using terms such as "That's terrible" or using other overemphatic ways of expressing yourself, think about the context of your remarks. Does it really call for such a strong statement or comment? Save those comments for things that really warrant them, so that they will retain their meaning. And if you hear yourself calling people names or labeling them, try to be more specific. Use constructive criticism or helpful comments instead of labeling the other guy.

## Swearing

In addition to using overemphatic ways of expressing oneself, there is the tendency in our angry society to use swear words on a daily basis as common language. The f-word is so common that many people don't even notice it anymore. Yet what is the point? Despite that it is becoming more commonplace, if one pays close attention, one can detect the anger behind the utterance. People are angry, and they are expressing it with more and more impolite language. I, for one, am tired of it. If one is so angry that every other word is "fuck" then it is time to find out what is making one so angry. Becoming more commonplace does not make that word acceptable. It is still offensive and unnecessary.

This is not to say that there may not be certain circumstances where a well-placed swear word is appropriate. However, if you find yourself using this kind of language on a daily basis, find a better way of expressing yourself. Find out what is making you so mad. But don't condemn the rest of us to having to listen to that kind of language. More people should speak up and tell the foul-mouthed people that we really don't want to hear it. Certainly teachers and others in charge of children should not allow it in their sphere of influence. It is truly sad to hear little children making these utterances. By the time most kids today are twelve years old, they use these words as fluently as they breathe. Do we really want that? What does this say about our society?

## Anger and the Brain

Part of the problem with anger, and indeed with any emotion, is that it comes from a different part of the brain than that used to reason or speak. Remember, our ability to reason and to speak (as well as a host of other things) came with the evolution of the neocortex. Yet, our feelings and sensations come from the limbic system, which is a completely different part of the brain. I often have people in my office saying that they *know* that something is true, but they *feel* as if it is not. "I know John won't leave me. He has shown that so many times, but every time he goes on one of his business trips it *feels* as if he is never coming back." That feeling, imprinted before the neocortex was developed, is activated over and over again, often in completely inappropriate circumstances. Because the amygdala, which is part of the limbic system, gets messages before the neocortex, the feeling part often acts on the belief before the neocortex has a chance to be "heard." Even after it is heard, the feeling is often so strong, especially if it was imprinted during trauma, that it is difficult to pay any attention to the rational part of the equation.

The early imprinting of the "baby rage," when the most intense sobbing did not result in mommy coming back, can be reactivated in the blink of an eye. In combination with an increased input of adrenaline and cortisol, this reactivation can become a self-fulfilling prophecy. The most innocuous trespasses on the part of a partner can activate that 'baby rage" and make an adopted person lash out in an inappropriate manner, stunning the partner and, over time, leading to his leaving. Many actions on the part of others get exaggerated in the minds of those who have suffered trauma. (Please see the chapters A Reality Check and A Definition of Terms.) Trauma victims, if they don't want to remain victims, must begin to compare their own interpretations of things with that of others, and then make more appropriate responses. It is not normal to feel angry, sad, ashamed, or anxious most of the time. People whose trauma occurred early in life may not realize this, because "it has always been this way." My fear is that because more and more children feel disenfranchised and alienated from the people who are supposed to be taking care of them, in the future more and more adults are going to feel and act in inappropriate ways.

Peurifoy lists six things which can result from using anger to feel strong or to avoid painful emotions or realities. He says it can "(a) prevent you from dealing with the source of the problem, (b) stop you from correcting distortions in your thinking, (c) keep you helpless by stopping problem-solving, (d) prevent you from processing and releasing painful emotions, (e) poison your relationships, and (f) increase the overall pain you experience." None of these results sound as if they would be beneficial to anyone, yet anger is employed every day with similar results. It may be time to try something new. You know what Dr. Phil says, "If it isn't working, change it!" Many adoptees use anger to avoid having to feel their helplessness or sorrow.

## What to Do

During the course of this discussion of anger, I have listed some ideas for acting differently ... for changing. What other ideas or methods of controlling this destructive emotion can you use? First of all it would be important to know the level of your anger. If it seems out of control, then enrolling in an anger management class seems essential. If you find yourself losing your temper and saying and doing things which you later wish you hadn't, then perhaps being more observant and responsible for your effect on others can be managed without a class or therapy. You have to be honest about your degree of anger and the control you really have over it. Ask someone else, if you're not sure.

## Marrying the Two Sides of the Brain

Find ways of making a connection between the part of the brain that controls feelings and that which can describe them. This may mean painting or poetry. It may mean doing EMDR (described in a later chapter). There must be a connection so that describing your feelings and understanding their source become possible. Remember that the part of the brain which engenders feelings and the part which uses words to describe them don't always communicate very well. Activities which engage the right side of the brain may be more effective in creating vocabulary for understanding your anger. Lewis, et al. make this suggestion: "... people just strain to force a strong feeling into the straitjacket of verbal expression. ... Poetry, a bridge between the neocortical and limbic brains, is simultaneously improbable and powerful. Frost wrote that a poem 'begins as a lump in the throat, a sense of wrong, a homesickness, a love sickness. It is never a thought to begin with.'" Poetry, while using words, uses them in a very different way from prose. Poetry is often intuitive and is a good bridge between the two sides of the brain.

## Identifying Physical Symptoms and Anger-Producing Situations

What are the physical sensations that precede or accompany anger? Learn to identify those sensations and be forewarned. Before the feelings become full-blown do something to defuse the situation. Take a walk. Go to the gym. Usually some physical activity can help defuse anger. Remember that if you choose to ignore the warning signs, you are *choosing* to suffer the consequences of your anger. The immediate exhilaration or "high" you may feel as a result of letting off steam will be short-lived, and the more long-term consequence may not be something you will want to live with.

Learn to identify recurring situations or circumstances where you find yourself getting unduly angry and behaving inappropriately. I have had adoptees tell me that they become incensed at certain family celebrations, and they do or say outrageous things, which stun everyone within hearing distance. What is it about family celebrations that makes you so angry? Please go back and review the paragraphs about attractor states in the chapter on the brain. Remember that we have a tendency to react to holidays as if we were younger. This is a normal thing that happens in the brain. It is, therefore, important to try not to blame parents or other siblings for the feelings you are having. You, too, are reacting as a younger version of yourself. Use humor to get things back on track. "Oh, my gosh! We are all feeling and acting as if we were children. And Mom and Dad, you are falling right into the whole thing and treating us that way! Let's start over." Holidays can be pleasant if everyone lowers their expectations and rolls with the punches. It can also be fun to act like kids again, if everyone is joking and playing. The important thing to remember is that our brains are falling back into an old groove. *It is no one's fault.*

For many adoptees there may be a feeling of not really fitting in or belonging to the family. Everyone is acting as if they are members of the family, when the adoptee may not feel that way! "What is the matter with everyone? Can't they see that I feel different? Can't they tell that I don't really belong?" Making outrageous remarks may be a way to delineate that difference. "See, I'm not really like you." Or perhaps it is a way of drawing attention to yourself—to make you feel as if you exist. With all the family around, it is easy to get lost, to feel unimportant and invisible. For some adoptees, being invisible is the preferred mode, but for others there is a constant need for a sonar test, making sure that one registers on the existence scale. A well-placed absurdity or inappropriate swear word ought to do the trick! If you are still doing this type of thing after age 16, it is time to find a new way to prove your existence—perhaps something worthwhile. The important thing to remember is that no matter what the reason for these kinds of outrageous remarks, they have nothing to do with *you.* So don't you dare ever tell me, "I can't help it. That's just the way I am."!! That just won't fly with me.

*"It's Just the Way I Am ..."*

Which brings me to two erroneous beliefs: (I) "I can't help it; that's just the way I am;" and (2) "It doesn't matter; I don't have any impact anyway." These two statements, although coming from a sense of unworthiness, are absolutely false. Take my word for it. Not only do they discount who you are and how you affect others, but they let you off the hook so far as your taking responsibility for yourself. If you can make inappropriate behavior an intrinsic part of your personality, then perhaps you just "can't help it." But remember that from the time we are born, everything that has anything to do with behavior is learned. Thus, it can be unlearned. You have to take responsibility for how you act. Even if it isn't your fault that you became this way, as an adult it is your responsibility to respond to your feelings, including anger, differently. It's called *accountability.*

If, on the other hand, you are convinced, perhaps because you couldn't get mommy back, that you don't count, are unimportant, don't have an impact, again, you don't have to be responsible for how you affect others. After all, you *won't* affect others! Well, wake up. You do! Just check around you. Did you ever find out why your last partner left you? Could it have been because throwing the telephone into the china cabinet was the last straw? If you didn't affect others, they wouldn't leave you for your bad behavior. Don't cry and say "I'm unlovable."

You are making yourself unlovable by your actions. *And you can stop.* Go to Chapter 10 to see if any of the criteria fit. Those criteria have nothing to do with one's personality; they have to do with behavior—something that can be changed. In that chapter, you will find out that the person who is controlling you is about three years old and resides inside you. How long is this going to go on?

I don't mean to discount the tremendous forces which come into play when you are experiencing these feelings. But I do want to emphasize that no matter how strongly you feel a certain thing, you must learn to control your response to it. That is your adult responsibility. We all exist on this planet with one another. We can't act as if we are here alone, even if it feels that way to some of you. We are all connected, and we all have to take responsibility for that connection. Can you imagine the world if we all did that?!

# CHAPTER 5
## Guilt and Shame

*The Differences Between Guilt and Shame*

Different authors define guilt and shame differently. I want to define what I mean so it is clear what I am talking about in this chapter. When I refer to guilt, I am referring to a sensation that has to do with transgressing a societal, cultural, or penal boundary. In other words, doing something that offends or insults someone in some way. The worst offenses are considered crimes. When we feel guilty, we know that we have intentionally wronged someone. Our perception of having wronged comes from our understanding of the moral code of our society or culture. Guilt is about *what we do.*

Shame, on the other hand, is a sense that we personally are flawed in some way. There is a sense of inferiority, inadequacy, or incompetency which we believe comes directly from being who we are. Accompanying these senses is the feeling that we are undeserving, unworthy, and unlovable. There is nothing that we have done that makes us feel this way; it is *who we are.*

Shame and guilt get confused in our minds, because we sometimes don't know if what is wrong is something we did or who we are. This is especially true if it is something about which we need feel neither shame nor guilt (i.e., something over which we had no control). For instance, some adoptees believe that they are guilty of something or their mothers would not have left them. Yet what can a tiny baby do? Well, it must be shame then. It must be who we are. We must be intrinsically flawed. There are some events which seem so unfathomable that we take on some kind of responsibility for them, because otherwise they defy explanation.

Three of the most confusing and chaotic events that happen for children are being separated from their mothers too early, being abused by a parent, and having parents get a divorce, thus splitting up the family. For each of these events, children often take on the responsibility and thus feel either guilty or shameful. It is a huge burden, and one children need not assume. Yet the pattern established in the brain by either trauma is so entrenched that it is very difficult to change. Even as adults, if someone was separated from a mother or a father by adoption or divorce, the belief remains the same: "I must have caused this." Even the reasoning of the neocortex: "I couldn't have caused this; my mother just couldn't take care of me" or "I was so little," or "My parents just didn't get along," does not eliminate the belief that it was "my fault." These beliefs are useless and debilitating. Yet they often persist for years. Many adoptees and other people were deeply affected by the scene in the movie *Good Will Hunting* when the psychiatrist kept telling Will, "It is not your fault. It is not your fault. It is not your fault." He would not allow Will to just say, "Yeah, I know," because he knew that the belief was still there. It wasn't until Will broke down that the psychiatrist (brilliantly played by Robin Williams) felt that he had actually "gotten it." This is the belief carried by many adoptees, children of divorce, and others who have been the victims of adult decisions, neglect, or abuse.

Another reason that guilt and shame are confusing is that one can be ashamed for a guilty act. Many birth mothers feel guilty for having given up their babies. Yet the feeling they get is often shame. I believe their shame is in their not having been able to override all the "advice" they were getting from parents, social workers, and others. In other words, they feel that there must be something intrinsically wrong with them if they could not defy everyone and keep their babies. The guilt they carry is debilitating enough, but the shame that resides within them is even more burdensome.

*The Uses of Guilt*

Guilt is a very useful sensation when it is warranted. The problem is that much of the time, the guilt adoptees feel has nothing to do with behavior that needs to be changed. Rather, it has to do with events over which they had no control. Adoptees' guilt or shame for having been relinquished by their birth mothers is not useful. Their belief that had they been better babies their mothers would not have left them is not true. There was nothing wrong with them as babies. Yet, even when they know their belief makes no sense, it remains.

On the other hand, adoptees are very good at blaming others for actions over which they *do* have control. "Why did you fail your test," a mother may ask. "The teacher asked about things we didn't go over in class," her child will reply. There is no mention of the fact that he did not study for the test. "Don't tell me you got another speeding ticket!" a father may exclaim. "That rotten cop was just needing to fill his quota," replies the unrepentant young driver. No mention that he was going twenty miles above the posted speed limit.

These are examples of how guilt is misguided. Some things over which a person has no control are taken on as the adoptee's fault, while things over which he does have control are not. The question to ask is "What could I have *done* differently? As an infant you could not have "been a better baby." Babies are perfect. At least they start out that way. I believe in original sin only in the sense that we all have the capacity for good or evil. However, I believe that whichever road we take has a great deal to do with how we were treated—that includes being (feeling) rejected by the birth mother. If a newborn is not perfect it is because she was wounded in utero or postnatally. Everything that happens to infants after they are born affects them in profound ways. Some things that happen to them in utero affect them as well.

However, no matter what wounds a baby suffers either in utero or postnatally, the wounding is not the baby's fault. She did nothing to deserve it. She was born guilt-free. She gets to be guilt-free for a while. Young children do not know the rules of society by osmosis. They must be taught. Each culture has its own values and rules. While they are learning, children make mistakes. Parents often forget this and treat children as if they were little adults with all the understanding and training of someone who has inhabited this world for a long time. This is grossly unfair. What if we, as adults, were to go to another country with different values, rules, and traditions than ours. Do we think we would not make mistakes in that culture? If we do make mistakes, should we be punished or gently reminded? Which would we prefer? (Of course, some Americans are so arrogant they think our culture is the only one, that everyone should be like us, and they can act the way they want. But that's another story.) My point is that children are being socialized into the culture of their parents. As they are learning the values and rules, they are not going to be perfect. Parents must be patient in teaching the rules of society and *they must do most of their teaching by example.* Respect, courtesy, honesty, and integrity are best learned by example. Parents cannot expect anything of a young child that they are not capable of themselves. (I am often reminded of this when I see a young mother or father trying to discipline a child in a supermarket by screaming at him.)

When they reach the age of reason—about age seven or eight—children can begin to take responsibility for how they affect others. At that point it would be appropriate to feel guilty for deliberately hurting a friend, cheating on a test, or stealing a toy from the five-and-dime. These are acts over which a child of this age can have some control. It is only when we actually have age-appropriate control over our actions that we need to feel guilty. This doesn't mean that we wait until seven or eight to begin teaching the differences between right and wrong. It just means that we have to have patience for the lessons to take effect. Some rules and values can be learned by rote, but others are best learned in the context of rationale. Four-year-olds are trying to learn the rationale for things. That's why they are always asking "why?" They ask the same questions over and over because they are not yet capable of truly understanding and integrating the answers. Repetition is important for the teaching of values and rules. So is patience.

Children have very little control over the important things that happen to them for the first 10–12 years of their lives. They can voice their opinions, but ultimately parents make the decisions. No control—no fault! This does not mean that everyone up to age twelve can feel guilt-free. Around age six, children should be made aware of how they affect others and be held responsible *in a gentle and appropriate manner* for the impact they have on friends, family, and others in whom they come into contact. As they get older, the methods of correction can be more direct. It should always be immediate and appropriate to their age. Remember, they are still learning the mores and rules of their culture. They may have no responsibility for the big decisions in their families, but they do have a responsibility to conduct themselves in a manner acceptable to others and the rules of our society. Why doesn't this always happen?

*Behavior as Communication*

Behavior isn't always just a matter knowing or not knowing the rules. Behavior is often a form of communication. Sometimes, especially when trauma is involved, a person's behavior is an indication of early wounding. It is a cry for understanding—an acted out message. Some of you remember playing charades. Well, children play charades all the time, yet they don't know that is what they are doing. Unfortunately, most of the time, neither do their parents. However, if they were to treat their child's behavior as a game of charades and try to discern what it is the child is trying to convey to them, they would be on the road to understanding and connection.

Even people who have suffered trauma as adults behave in ways that they don't understand. How much more confusing it is when there is no memory of the trauma! Adoptees' inability to get mom to come back right after separation left them with the sense that they have no impact, no importance. Therefore, there is the perception that what they do doesn't really affect others. It didn't then; it doesn't now. This belief, in concert with the fact that trauma victims seldom reflect on what they are doing or why they are doing it, results in their being oblivious of the impact they are having on others. This is where the ability to figure out whether or not to assume guilt is important. Remember: guilt is not a bad thing *if it is warranted.* It takes self-reflection to make that judgment: "Why is she reacting that way? Could my behavior have anything to do with how she is reacting?" Remember that adoptees are experts at projective identification; they are able to get others to assume their feelings by the way they act, by creating little scenarios that provoke others into feelings they didn't have five minutes earlier.

*Guilty or Not Guilty?*

One way to discern whether or not you should assume responsibility for the way someone is reacting to you is to ask yourself: "Does my friend, parent, colleague feel hurt by my actions?" (Be sure to ask!) "Is this something I can apologize for? Is this something over which I had some control? Could I have acted differently?" If you answer "Yes" to these questions, then you are guilty of something, intentional or not. Remember that as an adult you should have control over your actions. If you find yourself having little self-restraint, enroll in an anger management class or a yoga class. The good thing is that you can rectify the situation by sincerely feeling remorse and apologizing. If you don't want to do that, then guilt is what you may be left with. Or perhaps not.

If you don't feel guilty for hurting others, then you are worse off. Anyone who really doesn't care about anyone but himself has a much bigger problem than someone who cares, but has little control. Not caring, having no empathy, is sociopathic. Most adoptees whom I've met do not fall into that category. However, some of our most notorious serial killers are sociopathic adoptees: David Berkowitz (Son of Sam), Joel Rifkin (the ripper), and Jeffrey Dalmer (the cannibal) come to mind. In addition to serial murder, more adoptees are likely to kill their parents than nonadopted people. B.J. Lifton, in her book *Journey of the Adopted Self*, informs us that according to criminal attorney Paul Mones, adoptees are 15 or 20 to 1 more apt to kill their parents (adoptive) than nonadoptees. Many adoptees have told me that they can understand the rage which propels people to commit murder. However, most of them have enough empathy and self-restraint not to commit these crimes. If they had an empathic adoptive mother, even if she didn't really understand her child's wounds, there will be empathy. Empathy is very important in the ability to have self-restraint because it means that we care about others. Empathy is taught only by example. If a child has been hurt over and over again, if there has been no understanding or empathy in his young life, it becomes more and more difficult to instill empathy after a certain age. This may be especially true of children who have been sensory deprived, such as children who have spent two or three years in foreign orphanages. Some adoptive parents go overseas to adopt children in order to avoid having to deal with the birth mother, as many U.S. birth mothers are asking for open adoptions. However, dealing with a birth mother is nothing compared to dealing with a sensory-deprived child. Many unsuspecting adoptive parents are beginning to discover this. There are many failed adoptions which can be attributed to sensory deprivation in early childhood.

*Victimless Guilt*

In the case of doing something for which only you have suffered the consequences, such as getting a speeding ticket for which you have to pay or failing a test for which you didn't study, the consequence may lead you to be more careful next time. In any case, you need to begin taking responsibility for the consequences of your actions. Often it is the inability or unwillingness to get beyond the victim role—the "why did this happen to me?" mentality—that keeps adoptees from reaching their potential or accomplishing what they want to in life. If you find yourself repeatedly blaming others for what happens to you, you are not taking responsibility for your part in this "unfairness." It is true that as a child you had no control over what happened to you. However, as adults you have a great deal more control than you may be taking responsibility for. Every time you find yourself saying, "It's not my fault," take a minute to challenge this statement to find out if perhaps part of what is happening *is* your fault. It is a great deal more satisfying to be able to see what we may be doing wrong and rectifying it than it is to feel helpless.

### The Problem of Cause and Effect

Being aware of one's responsibility in certain circumstances may be difficult for trauma victims because they have had the natural order of their lives interrupted. At one time (or many times) in their lives, they have had something so devastating happen that life made no sense. When this happens at the beginning of life, when mother leaves, for instance, it is very difficult to deal with because there is no explicit memory to help understand what went wrong. Normal life was yanked off course, and it became difficult to understand what is supposed to happen in sequence. *Cause and effect is a casualty of this phenomenon.* This is the reason that it is so important for parents to very carefully and consistently teach consequences to their adopted children. These children do not have the advantage of a naturally occurring life pattern to help them "get" cause and effect. They have had a big interruption in this pathway and need careful tutoring to form a new pathway. This takes patience, firmness, fairness, and consistency. Because this is such an important lesson for future relationships and because adoptees' pain is sometimes a barrier to the parents' resolve, there must be a genuine commitment on the part of parents to patiently and persistently teach of the lessons of cause and effect.

These lessons cannot begin in adolescence but must continue into adolescence. This can often be daunting because teenagers can be very intimidating. Parents of teenaged adoptees often just let things go by because they don't want to "rock the boat" and have to face the screaming, swearing, blaming, and disrespect of their children. Calling them on the carpet for their bad behavior may unleash an additional barrage of blaming, unacceptable language, which is what the mother is trying to avoid. Yet avoiding the escalation of anger in the moment will only keep the child from learning about cause and effect and that they *do* have an impact: "You said unpleasant things to me; I am hurt." Because adoptees have a very short attention span when it comes to what they have just said or done, it is important to bring attention to the impact of their behavior right away. There must be consequences to unacceptable behavior, including verbal abuse by adolescent children. They desperately need to learn that they do affect others. Some mothers who have finally burst into tears at the horrible names their children have called them, find their children surprised and repentant, because they had no idea that what they said hurt their mothers! Pretending that the teenager is having no effect ("I'm not going to give her the satisfaction of knowing that she got to me!") is counterproductive and short-sighted. She will just continue her cycle of guilt-free abuse.

If there has been good limit-setting and boundary-keeping around acceptable behavior all along, adolescence should not be as difficult for parents as it will be for parents who let things go by until the stakes get high (drugs, alcohol, sex, and stealing). In addition to letting the child know the effect he is having on them, the parents themselves have to use emotional integrity when dealing with out-of-control children. They cannot scream, yell, or call names back, but must speak softly yet firmly. I would suggest that they wait until their teenager runs out of steam, then quietly inform him that they understand that he is angry, but he cannot go out/miss his appointment/drive the car. It doesn't always work, but out-of-control parents are even scarier than out-of-control adolescents.

What I want to say to adult adoptees is that you may not always be aware of actions or words that you need to feel guilty about. You may be surprised that there are circumstances during which *I want you to feel guilty.* Remember, guilt is not a bad thing. It is sometimes appropriate and sometimes not. The trick is to discern the appropriate guilt from the inappropriate guilt. The question to ask is "*Could* I have done anything differently?" Ask this question even if you *don't want* to have done anything differently. If you could have had no effect on the situation, then you need not feel guilty. However, it is important to be honest in your assessment of your part in whatever took place. Just saying, "I can't help it" or "I couldn't help it," may not be true. And please, don't ever say, when excusing behavior, "That's just the way I am."!! *The way you are* gets us into *shame.* That is something altogether different.

### The Sources of Shame

Shame is very harmful in an adoptive family because *it inhibits attachment.* What does one do when one is shameful? One hides, slinks away, lowers the head, tries to become invisible. Adoptive parents have to be very careful not to contribute to this attitude if they want to encourage attachment. Shame is even more debilitating than guilt because there is no recourse. Shame is based on a belief about who we are, not what we do. Shame often begins with a perception of having disappointed someone important to us. It has little to do with societal norms. It is more personal. Often the reason for the disappointment is not understood. Therefore, we believe that it must just be something wrong with us that is causing the disappointment. We thus have the feeling: "I am a disappointment to my parents." There is a feeling of inadequacy or inferiority involved in shame. "Something is wrong with me or they wouldn't be disappointed." For adoptees, this belief often begins with the perception that he was a disappointment to his birth mother. "Something must be wrong with me or she wouldn't have let me go."

The feelings of shame *can* involve things that we do. For instance, an adoptee may feel shame for having disappointed his parents about his performance in school even though he studied hard and did his best. Because he is having a difficult time, he assumes that the reason that he isn't doing better is that something is the matter with him. He tries, and still he fails. He must be incompetent at learning. What is going on here is that neither is it who the child is or something the child is doing that is at fault. *It is something that happened to him.* He may be having trouble in school because the dynamics that were set in motion at relinquishment create a sense of hyperalertness in him that precludes his being able to concentrate or focus.

### Creating a Good Learning Environment

Learning is very difficult if one always has to be alert to the environment, if one cannot "tune out" distractions. When one has to be hypervigilant, it is difficult to concentrate on a math problem or the correct spelling of a word. Because this understanding is not available to the child (or to his parents or teachers), he often feels shameful about how he is doing in school: "I must be dumb." This is not the case. I know adoptees with IQs of 130 and above who have felt dumb because they haven't been able to get better than Cs and Ds in school. They simply can't concentrate on the task at hand. There is so much anxiety about *what might happen next*—that Sword of Damocles hanging over their heads—that they simply can't focus.

It is very important for parents of adoptees to make sure that the environment in which they study is calming and not distracting: no TV, loud music, or other children playing in the vicinity, no quarreling parents or other distractions. Victims of trauma are exquisitely sensitive to distractions and have little stimulus discrimination. In other words, they cannot discern the dangerous stimuli from the innocuous stimuli. What may be merely annoying to us may feel potentially dangerous to them. Even if parents don't understand this, it would be helpful if they just believed it and acted appropriately. Their child's attention is constantly being drawn to noises and movement. Studying in a room without other children, with a white-noise machine, or soft classical music to help block out other noises might be helpful. Having the child help figure out what calms him can be a good idea. Some children, for instance, will not feel calm if they are isolated.

Being in the same room with mom, with another child who is studying, or with a pet, but without other distractions may be more ideal. This may be difficult to achieve if there are younger children in the household. Each family will have to discover the best atmosphere for its children.

As I was writing this chapter, a friend of mine called to talk to me about a colleague of hers who has six children living in a relatively small house. She reported that it is difficult for the older children to study because of all the commotion that is inherent when there are so many children in a limited space. Her solution was to offer her home as a place for a couple of the children to study. I thought, "What a wonderful idea. Why can't some people who live alone or who have an extra room offer their homes as a place for students to study?" Elderly people in the neighborhood might be good people to ask. Everyone would have to understand that the child is there to study and not to talk or entertain the homeowner (although spending 10 or 15 minutes after studying to talk to the person would be courteous). It is an idea that could really work. In small towns with limited budgets, libraries are often closed early or are not open every day. Finding people who would be willing to allow a friend's child or children to study at their homes would be a good solution. In any case, finding a quiet place is important for children with distractibility or stimulus discrimination problems (perhaps more prevalent than actual attention deficit disorder—ADD) is a must. It only adds to a child's shame to be unable to concentrate and do better in school.

*Shame for What Others Do to Us*

It is well known that victims of sexual abuse, no matter how young when abused, feel shame and guilt about what happened to them. They feel that they are bad. They often hate themselves. This is reinforced by the abuser telling them they are special, but their relationship must be kept secret: They must not tell anyone of their special relationship. There is something intrinsic about the feeling that secrets are bad and that what is going on is wrong. The child might be too young to understand the cultural or societal rules that dictate this. It is more an internal sense of right and wrong. "What daddy is doing to me is wrong." Yet because it is daddy and the body is responding to what daddy is doing, it feels as if what is happening must be the child's fault. "It feels good, so I am bad." Of course not everything that fathers do to their children feels good, but often the stimulation of sexual organs does feel pleasant to the child. This paradox of the act seeming bad but at the same time feeling good makes a child confused about who is wrong. The child is led to believe that in order to gain her father's love, she must allow him to "love" her the way he wants. As adults, victims of sexual abuse are often confused about the difference between love and sex and tend to sexualize all subsequent relationships. It is believed that most prostitutes have been sexually abused as children. Some of them even ran away from home to avoid the abuse, only to find that this is the only way they have of supporting themselves. Many of them dissociate in order to avoid the pain of what they are doing. Other abused people find it difficult to have normal sexual relationships in their marriages or partnerships. The effects of sexual abuse are long-lasting, although the punishment for such crimes often is not.

A similar sense of being bad may be going on for adoptees who assume the burden of responsibility for the separation from their mothers. There is no place in the infant's psyche for an understanding of a mother's leaving her baby. Out of the chaos and confusion that follow separation, the baby mind conjures up a "reason." That reason is often herself: "I am somehow at fault. I am flawed. Mothers do not leave their babies." It is often the adoptive parents who are seen as the heroes in this scenario. They rescued the baby. That the baby had to be rescued is additional proof that she is flawed. There is a real need for the adoptee to keep the parents from discovering the "bad baby" and to try to be someone else. This feeling is reinforced by the child's not being mirrored in her adoptive family. In his book *Shame: the Underside of Narcissism*, Andrew Morrison says that one cause for shame in children is a failure in mirroring. Mirroring, as we have said before, is a big problem in adoptive families. Parents can certainly mirror the expressions and actions of their young children. However, because the adoptive parents are genetically different from their child, they can't mirror him as well as he might be mirrored in his biological family. Instead of seeing this as a failure of the parents or, more accurately, a result of being placed with non-genetic parents, the child assumes responsibility for this failure: "I can't see anything of me in this family, therefore there must be something wrong with me." When information about the birth family is kept secret, this again reinforces the sense of something being "wrong with me." People don't keep secrets about things that are not shameful. "My birth family is shameful, therefore, I must be shameful, too." All of these beliefs, no matter how flawed, are deeply imprinted in the human brain. Remember what was said about how experience influences how our neurons are connected. Our *perceptions* about those experiences also influence those connections. And those early connections are very difficult, *but not impossible*, to change.

## Eliminating Shame and Inappropriate Guilt

Changing what has been profoundly imprinted upon our neurological system is not easy. However, I would like to remind everyone about what was said in the chapter on the brain. *It is possible to form new pathways.* We just have to remember that the limbic system is a slow learner, therefore we have to have patience and tenacity. I believe that the process can be speeded up with different types of therapy. However, there are other ways of overcoming the effects of shame and inappropriate guilt that can be employed immediately.

### Acknowledging the Narcissistic Wound

The roots of shame occur during the narcissistic phase of development, the first few years of life. Morrison reminds us, "Whereas guilt reflects a hurtful thought or action, shame is an affective response to a perception of the self as flawed, and thus inevitably involves narcissism, vulnerability, and their various manifestations." There are all kinds of scenarios that create a sense of shame in a vulnerable child. Having one's mother leave is definitely up there at the top of the list. Being neglected by one's mother is near the top. Abandonment and neglect are reported to be the two most devastating experiences that children endure—even more devastating than sexual or physical abuse. That's why some neglected children do naughty things to get attention. Even though the attention is hurtful—being yelled at, hit, or otherwise harmed—it is better than neglect. *Anything* is better than abandonment. Abandonment is a child's greatest fear. For adoptees it is also reality, embedded in their implicit and unintegrated memory.

Almost anyone will tell you that they didn't get all their needs met as children. No parents are superhuman enough to meet all their children's every need. But abandoned and neglected children have an especially difficult time because very basic needs were not met. In the case of neglected children, this was because the mother or primary caretaker did not or could not meet those needs. In the case of some adoptees, there can be several causes. Most of the time with adopted children, the physical needs of clothing, food, and shelter were met, but the emotional needs were deficient. Some mothers were unwilling to try to understand their children and thus missed the boat emotionally. Others tried but were unable to affect their children. Oftentimes, having suffered the devastation of losing one mother, adoptees were unable to trust the second mother to meet those needs and disallowed her attempts to do so. Or they couldn't respond because the mother felt "wrong"; they were not attuned to one another. Adoptees who believe their mothers were unaffectionate need to check out the accuracy of that belief: Was she truly unaffectionate (which may be true) or did she give up because of a lack of response or even active resistance by you? No one is to blame here. It just needs checking out because "perception isn't always reality," as the saying goes. And memory, as we found out in the chapter on the brain, is often inaccurate.

## The IOUs from Childhood

One problem that occurs later in people who have narcissistic wounds is that there is an almost constant yearning to get some of those narcissistic needs met. This often drives people who are in relation to adoptees to distraction. Because these needs are the needs of a child, partners of adoptees often feel as if they are expected to parent the adoptee in some way. This precludes their having a reciprocal, mature relationship. People with narcissistic injuries are concerned for the most part only about themselves. This may be very deceptive because there is often a perception that they are interested only in others. They are great rescuers. This is often a projection: "I need rescuing, therefore I will rescue." Many of you have observed the person who is always doing things for other people. The question is: *Is he doing it for others or is he doing it because he needs others to like him?* If it is the latter reason, then it is being done for narcissistic, rather than altruistic, reasons. The term people-pleaser is often a misnomer.

This doesn't mean that a person doesn't have empathy or is not interested in other people. It just means that the overriding concern is to have one's needs met. It is built into the timing of the wounding. It is no one's fault!! If you were traumatized when you were an infant, then you automatically have a narcissistic wound. You have no choice any more than a child has a choice about having spina bifida, a malformation which usually occurs before the fetus is three months old. For the narcissistically wounded child, certain emotional needs cannot be met by the adoptive mother because the child no longer trusts mothers. There may be a resistance to allowing the nurturing that the mother tries to provide. Some mothers can sense this disallowing—by the child's avoiding eye contact or stiffening up when she tries to hold or hug him—yet others seem oblivious to it. For the children who allow a certain amount of hugging and cuddling there are other ways that distancing is achieved: being secretive about his inner life, spending lots of time alone reading or listening to music and, during adolescence, spending most of his waking moments away from home. Sometimes the distancing takes the form of dissociation, such as daydreaming and, later, drugs, alcohol, sex, or pornography. These addictions serve two purposes for the adoptee: to dull the pain of separation and to distance himself from others. In case someone wants to argue that sex is an intimate act, recreational sex or "needy" sex is not at all intimate; it is very impersonal. It doesn't really matter who the other person is. This is true even though the adoptee may feel as if she is close to someone for a little while. The same adoptee who will allow sexual contact will withhold intimate information from a partner whom she is supposed to love. Intimacy is about emotional vulnerability and connectedness. Sex can be a part of that but only if it is in tandem with emotional closeness.

Whatever the needs left by early wounds and whatever the behaviors that emanated from those wounds during the early years, it is impossible to rectify the failure in having those emotional needs met. You can't expect the partners in your life today to make up for those losses. In their book *Mapping the Terrain of the Heart*, Stephen Goldbart and David Wallin put it very succinctly by reminding us that the people in our adult lives are not responsible for picking up the emotional IOUs left from childhood. This doesn't mean that a partner can't help heal early wounds. It just means that it can't be done unless the wounded person is participating in the healing and not just expecting to be healed.

### Overcoming Narcissism/Eradicating Shame

If shame is based in narcissism, how can we deal with something which has been a part of our lives for so long? How can we deal with the absence of something—the absence of attention, nurturing, and love? How can we deal with the shadow—that dark part of ourselves that we believe to be the cause of our shame? *Where there is darkness, what is needed is light.* The aspects of ourselves that we are keeping hidden may contain some of the gold of our beings, yet we may be afraid to let these aspects see the light of day.

Adoptees are especially good at keeping large parts of themselves hidden. I remember one of the first patients I saw as an intern. Her shame came in the door with her, and she decided to get it over with and have me reject her outright. The first thing she said to me after she sat down is "I am an adoptee, a lesbian, and an alcoholic." Then she looked at me as if expecting me to toss her out of the office. What I said (typical shrink talk!) was "Uh huh ..." and waited for her to go on and tell me what was bothering her. She just looked at me as if I hadn't heard her. When I refused to boot her out of the office, but instead wanted to help her, not to overcome the shame-based parts of her, but help her accept herself and understand the origins of her shame, she began her healing journey. Most people would have taken months to tell me the things this woman did in the first session. What she did was to shed light on her *shadow* (a term coined by Carl Jung to denote the aspects of ourselves which we disown or consider intolerable) so that it no longer haunted her. My immediate and continuous toleration of her shadow eventually led her to be able to tolerate it herself. In fact, she ended up being quite fond of herself!

### Me and My Shadow

Shedding light on the shadow is one of the ways to overcome the power it has over us. When I was dealing with my shadow in my own therapy, I would write about it and hand it to my therapist. I was too afraid to just tell him about sexy Suzy, vindictive Vicky, or spiritual Anya (who, although very spiritual, didn't adhere to all the tenets of the church, so was thrown out when I was about twelve or thirteen). I named all my shadow selves and had dialogues with them. The first time I ever used profanity was when Suzy was talking. Her vernacular and syntax were quite different from my normal way of speaking. She really surprised me. She definitely had a different voice! Anya, on the other hand, wrote some wonderful philosophical essays. Just knowing that Vicky existed helped me understand some of my behaviors, which I could then modify. The various parts of my shadow came up one by one, some of them scaring me to death. I was sure that they would scare my therapist. But he just read my "confessions," looked up at me, and said the equivalent of "Uh huh. ..." He was never thrown by my shadow selves, even when I acted them out. I eventually got so that I could just tell him about them. When I began to allow them into the light of day, they stopped being so scary and I stopped projecting them onto others.

Remember what Robert Bly said about our shadows: When we are born, we have a 360 degree personality. But as we go through life, we perceive that others disapprove of aspects of that personality. Therefore, little by little, we discard parts of ourselves, and toss them into a sack we drag along behind us, until, according to Bly, by age 20 we have only a small, pie-shaped piece left. Then we spend the rest of our lives trying to get back all those discarded aspects of ourselves—the gold of our personalities.

What I learned about the shadow was that it is those discarded parts of ourselves that give us character—a more interesting personality. And when they are conscious and no longer denied we have a great deal more control over them than when they are unconscious. The unconscious shadow can really wreak havoc on our relationships. Once brought up to consciousness—brought into the light—the shadow can make us much more interesting people. How can we become aware of that which is unconscious? We pay attention to how the behavior of others affects us. Do we have a "charged" reaction to their behavior or do we just yawn and say, "that's ridiculous"? Those behaviors that have a charge might be in our own sack. We need to examine ourselves honestly and determine if this is true. We can then allow those aspects of ourselves to be a part of our conscious personality, and in doing so we modify them so that they are not only tolerable, but wonderful. There's gold in that there sack!

So, adoptees, stop being so secretive with those you love and those who love you. When is the last time you told your parents something really important about what you are doing? I'll bet you told the mailman! The mailman doesn't care, so he can't really judge you, right? Well, just maybe if you were to tell someone who does care, they wouldn't judge you either. Maybe they would delight in you. Most of the things we discard into the sack of the shadow are things that only *we* think are terrible. But whether aspects of the shadow are bad or good, bringing them into consciousness is necessary to have more control in our lives.

*Transmuting Shame*

Narcissism needs to be transformed from a shame-based model into a more acceptable view of ourselves. Remembering that the main sources of shame are having intrinsic flaws and a failure in mirroring, we need to look realistically at those sources. We have no control over either what happens to us as infants or how our mothers mirrored us. How can an adoptive mother truly mirror her children? She can surely mirror behavior and expressions, yet those expressions will be a bit "off." Not being mirrored properly may add more shame to the already self-blaming belief in the cause of the first mother's abandonment. Perhaps using Morty Lefkoe's method of questioning our belief systems (see Chapter 19) will help. The beauty of his method is that he doesn't say, "You are wrong to believe you are a bad baby." Instead, he says, "Well, perhaps you were a bad baby, but what else might have been true?" Having other possibilities in addition to the long-held belief can be liberating.

Instead of relying on external signals for determining what is best for us, we need to turn inward and examine our own expectations and the ways in which we evaluate them. The whole world is not going to agree with us. There are as many realities as there are people. How another person perceives or interprets who we are or what we do is dependent upon his experiences in life, the meaning he gave to them, and how his brain is wired as a result. What we can do to help ourselves overcome guilt and shame is to examine our own self – determine who that self is, and evaluate our own behavior. Although we need to take note of how we affect others, if we continue to rely on others' ideas of us, or our perception of others' ideas of us, we will always be found wanting. Very few people in the world are seen as wonderful by everyone else. Perhaps Osama bin Laden would find something wrong with Mother Teresa.

How can you transform the "bad baby" of adoptee fame into a wiser and more empathic view of yourselves? You could start with humor. Try to picture a baby trying to be better than a baby is. What could the baby do? How could the baby be? Was the baby bad because she cried her eyes out trying to get mom back? Was she bad for going into shock when that didn't work? What exactly constitutes a bad baby? Perhaps picturing a baby trying to be a better baby can conjure up a sense of humor. What can the baby do: wink at mom? make faces hoping she will see how much fun she is and not be able to part with her? grin and make cute noises? You can see where a sense of humor can be used here. Just observe a baby sometime. What do you see? Perhaps realizing the absurdity of trying to be a better baby will make you laugh. It should, because it *is* absurd.

Instead of trying to figure out how you as that baby were bad or defective, how about beginning to have empathy for the plight of that baby, newly out of the womb and trying to cope with a new world without the help of mom? You can see your baby-self as intrinsically flawed or you can see him as absolutely devastated and inconsolable by the loss of his mother. He is the victim here. He didn't discourage his mother from keeping him. It is society that did that. And, although your baby self may not be able to distinguish between these two ideas on the feeling level, it is important to get in touch with that terrified baby and take him in your arms to comfort him. Having empathy for that wounded baby is the beginning of acceptance and love for self.

Self-acceptance and self-love are crucial to the capacity to love others. Anything else is the need to have others love you. Why is it that many of you adoptees are devastated when a partner leaves you? Is it because you loved your partner so much or is it because *you needed him so much to love you*? A continued belief in the "bad baby" is self-indulgent. It hinders your ability to love and be loved. It gives you an excuse for not truly connecting with others. It renders you an eternal victim. Perhaps if you see it as part of your narcissism rather than something to be either hated or pitied, it can help shake you out of your insistence on hanging on to that belief.

I am the last person to think that mind over matter is always useful in the kinds of irrational beliefs that result from early trauma, beliefs that were imprinted in infancy. I know how difficult they are to shake. But there is something to be said for acting *as if*. At least if you still can't shake your belief in your defective baby self, try to act *as if* it were not true. Remember that acting as if can help to form new pathways in the brain. At some time in the future, the new pathways can become the preferred pathways. I know that even getting close to that inconsolable baby may be more difficult than retaining the belief in the bad baby. But give it a try. Consider it as an alternative belief. To the rest of us, the inconsolable baby is the truth, whereas the defective baby is a myth thought up by your baby mind, just as shameful child is the myth perceived and believed by the sexually abused child/adult.

Sometime in our lives, it is necessary to accept our mortality. An acceptance of our mortality is useful because it is important to realize that we don't have forever to make connections, to let others in. Adoptees are experts at keeping others at bay. The thinking sometimes goes: "If I don't truly connect, I won't get hurt if she leaves." Of course, this doesn't work. You will be devastated anyway. The only thing you have accomplished is that you managed to get this far in life without a meaningful connection. You can keep on doing that until the end of your life and say, "Whew, I did it! I managed not to become intimate with anyone." Wow, what an accomplishment! It saved you from nothing, but it kept you from enjoying the relationships you had. All your relationships may not have lasted forever, but they may have been meaningful relationships nonetheless. Remember that even relationships that end don't *really* end. You still retain some of the memories and influences of whomever you allowed into your life. They changed you and added to aspects of your personality that otherwise may not have been allowed to see the light of day. *Whether or not a person stays in your life, he or she has an effect on your life.* It is up to you to make those influences the best they can be by choosing well and being the best you can be in those relationships. If someone is abusive, they must not be allowed to stay. Just be sure that it is not you who is being abusive. We don't live forever. Whether or not you believe in reincarnation, this is the life you have now. Live it to the fullest. Allow yourself to love and be loved. Don't wait for the end of life to notice that this never happened to you. Look at the people in your life and let them in. This means people whom you may have keep at bay for a long time, including partners, siblings, and birth and adoptive parents, who may not deserve your distancing. No one lives forever, including you. Live now! Love now!

## Gaining Wisdom

As we mature, we are supposed to become wiser. This includes realizing that our youthful ideas and beliefs were not always correct. We see more of the world, have many relationships, and broaden our perspectives about life. Yet, many adoptees retain a belief that originated just out of the womb: "My mother didn't keep me, therefore I am unworthy, undeserving, unlovable." They take on guilt and shame for events that were out of their control. Engel and Ferguson call these self-imposed ideas *imaginary crimes,* from their book of the same name. They note that "… hidden guilt is the price we pay for our imaginary crimes. … Those who suffer from massive unconscious guilt may wreck their marriages, alienate their families, sabotage their careers, become chemically dependent, or may be afflicted with overwhelming feelings of anxiety or depression" (Engel and Ferguson, 1990). Does any of this seem familiar to any of you? They further add, "Taking the blame may be less frightening than facing the truth." For adoptees, the truth may be that they had no control over their separation from mother. They were helpless and at the mercy of others. This is why control is such an issue for them. They are often thinking that others are trying to control them because a lack of control was so devastating in infancy. Yet many adoptees are observed (often in passive aggressive ways) as trying to control others, needing to be in control of every situation. It may feel like a matter of life or death. Yet these beliefs and behaviors are no longer useful and inhibit meaningful relationships.

If we have been able to give up some of our more naïve, youthful beliefs about the world, why is it that so many of us hang on to our archaic beliefs about ourselves? Many of these beliefs were formed by the immature baby-mind or child-mind and are no longer useful. You know the old story about why cousin Hazel cuts off the ends of the ham before putting it in the oven: because her mother and her grandmother did it. Why did grandma do it? Because her pan was too short for the ham. Why did mom do it? Why does cousin Hazel do it? Because Grandma did it. Hazel (and probably mom) had pans big enough to accommodate the ham but simply copied the behavior of their mom and grandmother. It makes no sense and serves no purpose. That is the way with many of the beliefs and habits that we allow to continue in our lives. They are vestiges of times past. They serve no useful purpose. No, they don't keep you safe; *they just keep you separate.*

We need to tune in to our wisdom, not our habitual repetition of old behaviors and beliefs. What does your wisdom tell you about what is going on in your life? What does experience, real clear-eyed experience with others, not your jaded view of that experience as seen through distorted lenses, tell you? Do others see you as a good person, accomplished and capable? Do you still believe in the bogey man or monster who is ready to jump out at any minute and prove that the wonderful you that others see is a fraud? Okay, let's say that the bogey man exists. Let's say that at crucial times in your life you lash out in rage, have tantrums, resort to promiscuity or revenge, collapse in self-pity or otherwise set out to destroy all that you were trying to achieve in your relationships. Then acknowledge that shadow side of yourself and take control of it. As long as it remains the bogey man—jumping out at any time because you have not taken the time to allow it into the light of day and control it—this can happen. You can lose control. But remember what I said about the value of becoming conscious of our shadow! It is only then that you can gain control over it. The "bad baby" bogey man doesn't exist. However, the rageful baby may. The needy baby may. The inconsolable baby may. There may be some behaviors over which you need to gain control. Really think about this and be honest about it. Let your more adult wisdom enter into your perception. Don't allow the child to take control, with his rages, tantrums, and acting out.

What does your adult self have to say about your present circumstances? How has the influence of others aided in your attaining the wisdom you have? What experiences have contributed to your accumulated wisdom? Being wise means being mature. It means acknowledging and utilizing the accumulated knowledge that you have gained over the course of your life and no longer allowing the child to run your life. It means acknowledging your power and taking responsibility for your life. A big task, yes! But it means getting out of the abyss of victimhood into the light of self-hood and mature, loving relationships. It's up to you to choose: the darkness or the light ...

*Guilt and Reunions*

Conscious guilt is knowing that we have done wrong or hurt another. It is acknowledging that wrong-doing, making it right it in some way with an act, an apology, or some other overt behavior, and then having a sense of resolution about our transgression. Hidden guilt, unconscious guilt, or neurotic guilt are useless burdens that keep us from having fulfilling relationships. It has been my observation in working with people in reunion that the guilt birth mothers carry has a great deal to do with the success or failure of reunion relationships. Some birth mothers do have a real choice today, but the choice for birth mothers in the 40s, 50s, 60s, and 70s was limited or absent. It is a good idea to allow their children to express their anger at her "choosing" as she did, but it isn't a good idea for her to continue to carry the burden of that guilt around for the rest of her life. Very few women who became pregnant during that era were able to keep their babies. I believe it was around 3%. That means that 97% of unwed (white) women were being forced by society's moral code to give up their babies. Today it is more like 3% that are relinquishing. What has changed is society, not mothers. Yet, many mid-century birth mothers are still carrying the guilt of relinquishment. It is notable that birth mothers almost universally refer to relinquishment as "surrender." It was at the gunpoint of the mores of the times which caused their separation from their babies. So, why can't these mothers *just get over it?* Why can't they drop the burden of their guilt? It is probably for the same reason that adoptees have a difficult time forgiving them for that separation: It seems inconceivable that there is any reason a mother could allow her baby to be taken away. This disbelief is built into our psyches.

However, this guilt is causing a chasm in many reunions. It is hindering the acceptance between mother and child. It is causing many adoptees to feel that they have to "take care" of that guilt in their mothers. They cannot tell their birth mothers about the sadness and difficulties they faced growing up in a genetically unfamiliar or, sometimes, abusive family because this only reinforces their mother's guilt. She thought she did the right thing. She was told that she was doing the only loving thing. Yet her child has suffered. How can this be? This can only increase her guilt! Instinctively she knew that she needed to keep her baby, yet the times were such that she was at the mercy of parents, priests, nuns, and social workers. Young women were not as independent then as they are today. There was so much shame connected to just having sex, let alone getting pregnant. Some psychologists and social workers actually believed that young women who got pregnant were mentally ill. (I doubt that diagnosis was pinned on any of the birth fathers.) When one is deep in the throes of shame, one just does what one is told. So, after the initial rage that the adoptee may hurl at her mother, and the mother's acceptance of that rage, both must forgive. The adoptee must forgive her mother, and the mother must forgive herself and her parents. It is only through that forgiveness that the relationship can flourish.

This guilt for relinquishing is sometimes exacerbated by the birth mother's being a "wounded child" herself. Sometimes the birth mother was an adoptee herself, and sometimes she was a victim of abuse, neglect, a mother who died when she was a child, or some other form of abandonment. This often means that there is no mother in the reunion relationship, only two children yearning for something they never had. This can be disastrous, because it means that an adoptee, who may have had to take care of her adoptive mother in some way, if only in her perception of having to be the perfect child, will now have to take care of her new-found birth mother. Many adoptees have the fantasy that when they at last reunite with their original mothers, she will be the nurturing, caring mother they didn't have or they couldn't allow themselves to accept. They yearn to be taken care of, if only for a little while. They have had fantasies of burrowing themselves in the bosom of her love and care. Finding a needy birth mother is devastating because it means this fantasy will never come to fruition. It may mean, instead, that the adoptee will again have to become a caretaker. This often leads to a very stilted and resentful relationship. It is fraught with unfulfilled dreams and unrequited longings.

If the birth mother is unable or unwilling to seek help in healing her own wounded child, then it is probably best if both mother and child grieve the loss of what they didn't have and treat one another as adults. This is not easy because it means giving up the hope of ever attaining that lost nurturing. It means giving up something that has been like a talisman for years and years. Many people are not willing to assume the kind of maturity this requires. It takes a kind of maturity that neither may be ready to attain. If not, then the relationship may be limited to a surface or superficial one. Although not desirable, it may be better than either one of them having expectations of being parented by the other. It is imperative that both mother and child honestly evaluate their own as well as the other's capacity for relationship. It is neither fair nor helpful to expect more from the other than she is capable of.

Guilt and unmet childhood needs can ruin a reunion between mother and child. It is important to find the best path to follow for each. This will mean compromises on both sides. Although this may seem unfair to the adoptee, who had no choice in the beginning, it is better than the kind of relationships I sometimes see in reunions where there is an impasse, a refusal to budge on both sides and a paralysis in the relationship. This is a no-win situation. Because I truly believe that a relationship between an adoptee and the birth family is better than none at all, I think that compromise must be achieved. Admittedly, there are some birth families that are unhealthy for the adoptee to become involved in, just as there are certain circumstances where the adoptee no longer wants to have anything to do with the adoptive parents, but those are rare exceptions and should be honestly evaluated. Just not getting one's way is not a good reason for "throwing out the baby with the bath water." Adoptees, too, have to grow up. That is what this book is all about. This means acting maturely in reunions, which all of you have to do at some point. Some of you will get to be "baby" for a little while, and some of you won't. Sacrificing the reunion for any except the most egregious behaviors is not worth it. There is something to be gained in reuniting with one's child or with one's birth family. Take the beneficial nuggets, and leave the rest. And everyone remember to be respectful!

### Summary

Genuine guilt, the kind that needs to be acknowledged and resolved, comes from transgressions over which we actually have some control. It is a means by which we know if we have transgressed against another. It also means that we can do something about it. Even if the person about whom we feel guilty is dead and we are unable to apologize, we can do something related—do penance—for our behavior. Find out what the person's favorite charity was and do some work for it (not just send money). Then allow yourself to feel the burden of that guilt being lifted. Too many people hang onto guilt as if it were their last friend.

If you find yourself feeling guilty for things over which you had no control—for imaginary crimes—then let go of it. Even if as a child you were sometimes mean-spirited, you can forgive yourself. Engel and Ferguson say, "Being selfish, malicious, angry, or unmindful of the feelings of others is well within the repertoire of all normal children. Although we are each responsible for our own actions from the time we can tell right from wrong, it is ultimately up to parents to set meaningful limits." Children are children and do not have the wisdom of having lived very long or having been completely socialized to take total responsibility for their actions. As adults, you can forgive your own childish transgressions as a means of letting go of neurotic guilt. However, you must assume responsibility for rejecting, violent, cruel, or other unacceptable forms of behavior in the present. My motto is *treat everyone with respect*. To treat others with respect doesn't mean that you have to agree with them; it just means that you have to be respectful in your disagreement. It means practicing emotional integrity, which will be discussed in another chapter.

Shame can be debilitating, because it doesn't originate from what we do but in how we perceive ourselves to be. It is based in narcissism and makes truly relating to others impossible. It keeps parts of ourselves hidden, which means that others are forced to try to relate to a false self or a partial self. This prevents attachment, bonding, and true relationship. It creates a never-ending sense of yearning that we want others to assuage. This impedes a mature, reciprocal relationship, and instead fosters a parent-child relationship. This is not what the adult adoptee wants, but may be what the inner child adoptee still yearns for. It does not make for a lasting relationship because eventually even the most nurturing of partners gets tired of always having to be parent to her partner-child. Remember about those IOUs from childhood.

One antidote to narcissism is community service. Get out of the clutches of your own needs and administer to others. Go to a nursing home and read to elderly people who can no longer read for themselves. Or help them to write letters to loved ones or just talk to them. It is amazing what one can learn from older people! Work as a Pink Lady in a hospital. Tutor kids in school. (You really know more than you think, and teaching others is a good way to prove that to yourself. When you are teaching, you won't feel the anxiety that you may have felt as a student.) There are a myriad things you can do to help others. Just make sure that it involves people. Picking up refuse along the highway or riverbank, while worthwhile projects, won't have the same result. The narcissistic wound was the result of a severance of an early relationship. It is only through relationship that it can be healed. I have heard too many adoptees say, "I have to do this myself. When I get my act together, then I can be in a relationship." You can't "get your act together" by yourself no matter how many self-help books you read. It won't happen!

Remember that we are all born blameless. It is the circumstances of our early life that wire our brains for certain types of emotional and behavioral responses. We have to let go of narcissistic shame, and take responsibility for our lives today. If you have the chance, look at a newborn baby. Should that baby feel shame? That baby should be cherished, because everything that happens to him or her will influence future behavior. Nothing is intrinsically wrong with the baby. Even if a baby has some kind of disability, it is not the baby's fault. Can you blame a disability on a baby? If not, then stop blaming imaginary defects on yourself. Perhaps if you reinterpret blame as an excuse you are using for not doing all that you are capable of doing, it will help move you out of that paralysis. "I'm not worthy, therefore I can just sit in the puddle of my worthlessness and do nothing." Do you still believe you have an excuse for hanging on to it? I've met many of you and heard your stories, and I have yet to meet anyone who has a true, ironclad reason to feel shame. Guilt? Sometimes, but not irrevocable guilt and certainly not shame.

Leave shame behind and take control of your guilt. A heartfelt apology is such a wonderful thing! Write to your old girlfriend. Talk to your parents—birth and/

or adoptive. And above all, talk to yourself. You don't have to apologize for the way you acted as a child. You couldn't have acted any differently. But you are no longer a child and are now responsible for your actions. If you feel guilty for any of those actions, apologize to the appropriate people. And apologize to yourself for the ways you have judged yourself, both as a child and as an adult. Then allow forgiveness to enter in. Forgive, and allow yourself to be forgiven.

# CHAPTER 6
## Sorrow: The Ubiquitous Emotion

It is natural for an adoptee to feel sorrow. He has lost his mother and has never been able to complete the grieving process. It's as if he is carrying around a well of sorrow somewhere in the background of his life. His was a private loss and an isolated grief, neither witnessed nor acknowledged by anyone else. Somehow, everyone missed it; missed the reality that a newborn would know his own mother, would be aware of her disappearance, and would need to grieve his loss. The expectation was that he would be unaware of his first mother and adapt quickly to his adoptive mother. Yet, his first mother's disappearance sent him headlong into a world of terror, confusion, and chaos. And sorrow—deep, deep sorrow. It is impossible for anyone who has not lost a mother early in life to understand the depth of the sorrow of that loss.

### The Grieving Birth Mother

And what about his mother? No one acknowledged that the mother was going to be devastated by having to surrender her baby and not know what was going to happen to him. It was assumed that she could get on with her life as if nothing had happened. And this assumption was coming from the very same mother who had given birth to *her*. How, one might ask, could a mother have made such an assumption about her own daughter? Did she not feel bonded to her own child before birth? Didn't she even entertain the idea that her daughter might have bonded with her child, too? What kind of denial did it take for her to be able to miss the sadness and devastation in her daughter's eyes? How could she not be a witness and solace to her grief? Was her concern about what the neighbors would think more important to her than being able to see, truly see, her own daughter? Many a birth grandmother has lived with the guilt of giving in to society's mores at a time when her child most needed her. Her daughter, too, like her daughter's child, was left to grieve alone or to deny her own grief because everyone expected her to.

These two beings then—mother and child yearning for one another—were left to grieve without any validation for their loss or compassion for their sorrow. Because this grief was unacknowledged and incomplete, it remains in an unresolved state. This may leave both the adoptee and the birth mother with a chronic, low-level depression, technically called dysthymia. This symptom, as well as anxiety, is common for anyone who has suffered loss without being able to mourn the loss. The anxiety is a constant reminder that another devastating loss might happen any time.

*The Birth Father's Grief and Helplessness*

No one talks about the birth father's grief. It is assumed that he "hit the trail" and hasn't had a thought about his child or the mother of his child since. Yet it has come to my attention that many birth fathers have been in pain about the loss of their children as well. Some of them didn't support the mother in her wish to keep the baby and some of them, wanting to keep the baby, felt helpless in the decision to relinquish. Often the father wasn't consulted. Sometimes his parents, like the birth mother's parents, were adamant about their giving up the baby for adoption. Whatever the scenario, very few of the relationships between birth fathers and birth mothers survived. And the adversarial aspect of the relationship that resulted from the surrendering of the baby often persists into adulthood. Twenty years later, many birth mothers are still very angry at the birth fathers for their lack of support at the time of the birth of their child.

What has transpired for him lo these many years? Many fathers did what many mothers have done: become numb. They pushed all thoughts of their children out of their minds and "got on with life." Others have never stopped thinking about the babies they never got to see. They have lived with a veiled wish that someday they would meet their children and begin a relationship. Many have been left with a guilt they find difficult to verbalize. I will talk more about this in the chapter on Reunions. What I want to emphasize here is that we should not assume that birth fathers don't have feelings and a sense of sorrow about what happened to them, to the mother, and to the baby. Some of them realize that they forced the girls to have sex against their will and know this was wrong. Some of them genuinely loved their girlfriends and wanted to marry someday. As they matured, the enormity of the act of relinquishment, the loss of their children, became more clear. Although some of them can forgive the youths they were who could allow that to happen, there is a certain sense of responsibility as men that they still feel, or that they now feel and about which they may always have a sense of guilt.

But what about the sorrow? Sometimes birth fathers don't realize the enormity of the sorrow until the child comes back into their lives. It may be easier for the fathers to get on with life than the mothers. But the bursting into their lives of the child (who is now an adult) can bring up a host of feelings, not the least of which is sorrow. Although aware that those lost years can never be retrieved, the loss of the experience of watching his child grow up can plunge a birth father as well as a birth mother into an abyss of sorrow. The father, too, needs to allow himself to grieve and to have a ritual for healing some of that grief.

*Unacknowledged Adoptive Mother Sorrow*

Sorrow can also be a part of what the adoptive mother is feeling. She may have been trying for years to get pregnant or to remain pregnant, if she had multiple miscarriages. Unfortunately, many pre-adoptive parents do not mourn their losses before they decide to adopt. This leaves them, too, with unresolved grief about lost children or lost generativity. The advent of their new little adopted baby assuages some of the grief, but there may still be a vestige of sorrow for them as well. As time goes on, they may begin to feel that their children are not allowing the depth of connection they had hoped for. Therapists will tell them they are not feeling entitled to their children, as if it is their fault. The implication is that if they would only do so, the bond would deepen. No one realizes that the children need distancing, especially from the mother, as a way to feel safe. It has nothing to do with this particular mother, and the best way for her to deepen the connection with her child is to acknowledge and validate the child's loss and his need for distancing. The distancing that many adoptees experience between themselves and their mothers may be brought on by their own fear. So here, again, we have a mother and child experiencing sorrow in isolation with no one to offer solace.

*A Dearth of Information*

The adoptive mother was not alerted to her child's grief. No one told her that she was taking home a child who was suffering a devastating loss. After all, what does a grieving baby look like? Human beings don't seem to be able to recognize grief in infants. The baby may have desperately cried out for his first mother, then retreated into shock and despair, but he was never allowed the solace of having a witness to and comforter for his grief. Many adoptive parents go through their child's entire childhood oblivious to his unresolved grief. Others see it, but don't know what to do. Sometimes they feel guilty because they think they have caused the pain they see in their child's eyes. And in their ignorance, they add to that grief by failing to acknowledge it.

It is sometimes difficult to spot grief in children. After all, it isn't as if the child sits in a puddle of tears his entire childhood. As one adoptee said, "Of course I played, laughed, and sang. Do people think that if you're not sitting in a corner with your head on your knees, you are not sad? I had happy times, but the sadness was always there, even when I was having fun." In another chapter I will outline ways in which adoptive mothers can help their infants and children deal with this loss. It is very important to do so because it sets the tone for the relationship with the mom and with all significant others in the future.

Adoptive parents need to acknowledge the loss involved in not conceiving and giving birth to their biological children. Although it may not seem like a very big problem to some, the loss is still there in some form or another. It is only in grieving the child-that-will-never-be that some adoptive parents can truly allow their adopted child to be different from them. The loss of generativity is no small thing. It should not be dismissed as insignificant. Adoptive parents, as well as birth parents, can benefit from grieving rituals. Their children will benefit as well.

## Rituals for Grieving

Even when the adoptee and birth parents are reunited, sorrow often remains as a theme in their relationship. For the adoptive parents, reunions may bring reminders of the distancing that has taken place in their relationship with their child. There needs to be a means of resolving everyone's sorrow—a ritual of grieving and healing. It is helpful if there can be a finalizing of the loss: the birth parents' physical loss of the child, the adoptive parents' emotional loss of biological generativity and/or a secure connection to their child, or the loss of any part of the relationships that collapsed under the burden of that long-ago decision. A constant state of yearning for *what was not to be* isn't healthy.

Often the reunited pair continue to despair for the years they missed. This may interfere with the time they have in the present. Over and over again, they have to be reminded that history cannot be changed. But neither does it have to be lived and relived. Also, it has to be acknowledged that our history is not accurately remembered. Many adoptees went through their childhoods in a trancelike state. It wasn't that they didn't play and laugh and learn and so forth; it is just that all of this took place under a haze of sadness and anxiety. I can look at pictures of an adoptee laughing and having a lot of fun, yet that same person will tell me, like the adoptee quoted above, that she can't remember a time when she wasn't sad.

I agree with Judith Herman, who believes that we need witnesses and allies to our pain. It is up to each individual to ascertain if they feel safe doing this exercise together. The exercise is based loosely on Herman's strategy for recovery from trauma. She emphasizes the need for safety. There will be a great deal of vulnerability for all concerned, so each has to be empathic and receptive to the others. It is not for those who are still regressed—either the mother or the child. If one is ready and the other is not, perhaps the exercise can be processed with someone else—someone in one's support group, a good friend, or a therapist.

We don't "do" grief very well in this country. The advice we hear over and over is "You just have to get on with your life." Perhaps that is why so many millions of people are on antidepressants. We may be getting on with our lives, but we are doing so with underlying sadness and/or chemicals. Alan Jones, in his book *Soul Making*, reminds us of the gift of tears: "Tears flow when the real source of our life is uncovered, when the mask of pretense is dropped, when our strategies of self-deception are abandoned. ... Weeping, then, has a triple function. It softens the hardened and dried-out soul, making it receptive and alive. It clears the mind. It opens the heart" (1985). Awakening the soul, clearing the mind, and opening the heart are what I have in mind in the exercises which follow. I will write with the adoptee and birth mother in mind, but want to recommend it for birth fathers and adoptive parents as well. If possible, having everyone in the triad present and taking part in the ceremony might be the most healing.

*A Narrative of Loss and Hope*

What I would ask adoptees and birth mothers to do is write a history of their time apart. Birth mothers will want to begin with the events leading up to the separation. Narrative is an important part of the healing process. This may seem difficult, because, whereas normal memory may be like telling a story, traumatic memory is, in Herman's words, "wordless and static." It is revealed in images and sensations. It is difficult to find words for these memories, if there *are* memories. Many adoptees can recall very little about their childhoods. Many birth mothers have amnesia around the birth and cannot remember either the exact date of the birth or very much that happened immediately before or after. Adoptees not only have traumatic amnesia to contend with but the natural childhood amnesia that occurs for much of the first three years. That is why it is sometimes best to create the story in a form other than a straightforward autobiography. It is also all right to call on others to help fill in the parts of one's life that seem hazy.

The story might be written in the form of a poem, myth, or fable. This would make use of the right brain, which would tap into emotional memories. Some people find the kinetic act of writing by hand jogs or enhances the memory. Pictures, such as a collage of photographs or a series of paintings, might accompany the text. The story should include good times as well as sad times. It should include feelings as well as events. It should be as honest as possible. In other words, an adoptee should not write a story that leaves out the positive aspects of her history with her adoptive parents just to make her birth mother feel better. Believe me, she won't feel better. She doesn't want her daughter or son to have had a life devoid of fun or happy times. On the other hand, neither should the adoptee leave out the sadness and loneliness she may have felt in order to assuage her mother's guilt. Everything should be included. The same for the birth mother. She may have gone on to college and a successful career. She may have had other children who brought her joy. She cannot exclude the happiness those children brought her just to please the child she surrendered.

Some adoptees have trouble thinking of anything positive to say about their childhoods. The underlying sadness keeps them from labeling even good times as happy times. Martin Seligman tells us, "There are three ways you can lastingly feel more happiness about your past. The first is intellectual—letting go of an ideology that your past determines your future. ... The second and third are emotional, and both involve voluntarily changing your memories. Increasing your gratitude about the good things in your past intensifies positive memories, and learning how to forgive past wrongs defuses the bitterness that makes satisfaction impossible" (*Authentic Happiness, 2002*).

You may say, "But wait! Didn't you tell us in your first book that we have a right to our feelings of anger, sadness, and fear? Didn't you say that we don't have to be grateful? Why are you changing your tune?" Yes, you certainly do have a right to those feelings which were unacknowledged and not validated. And you need to know that these feelings were normal and shared by others with your experience. However, I didn't mean for you to be a prisoner of these feelings and chew on them forever like a sacred cud. You certainly don't have to feel grateful for being adopted, but there are probably things that happened in your adoptive life for which you *may* feel grateful. Just don't forget these, is what I am saying. So, I am not changing my tune, but rather saying that as adults you now have a chance to participate in your own healing process, and part of this means really looking honestly at the past, but not dwelling there. Seligman says, "Frequent and intense negative thoughts about the past are the raw material that blocks the emotions of contentment and satisfaction, and these thoughts make serenity and peace impossible." The idea of this exercise is to bring you to serenity and peace, not to block them.

This exercise will certainly provide an opportunity to experience again or at least remember a panoply of feelings, but it is meant to be used as a healing process not as a hair shirt. That's why I encourage you to remember positive as well as negative experiences and feelings. Too often the positive gets trumped by the negative, which is the brain's way of helping you avoid another devastation. But sometimes the brain is overly cautious, harkening back to its primitive beginnings, and thus causing you to get stuck in negative thinking.

After the stories are complete you should read them out loud to one another. It is important to respect each other's perceptions of "how it was." There should be no interruptions (in the form of criticism or questioning) during the reading of the stories. You can laugh and cry together. You can realize that for whatever reason, you were not able to spend the first years of the adoptee's life together.

You can grieve for those lost years. Then it is important to find meaning in this part of your lives. Tell how the event of relinquishment/surrender changed your lives—for better and for worse. Look realistically at the issues of guilt and blame. Look realistically at past and present relationships. Forgive others for having hurt you and yourself for having hurt others. It is very important, for instance, for the birth mother to forgive her parents if she wants her child to forgive her. It is very important as well for the adoptee to take a mature look at his mother's options at the time of relinquishment and to walk in her shoes. (Remember, this exercise is not for adoptees who are still regressed, but if you have been regressed for more than a year, it is time to move on.) Look realistically at your own and the other's pain. Have compassion for one another. How has the experience of separation and adoption helped form your values? Are there any values you want to change as a result of this exercise? Review your values and principles and vow to live up to them as you understand them today.

### A Ritual Rite of Passage

Create a ritual for formalizing the loss of each other. This should be planned in advance. It can include items that are meaningful to each of you. It can include prayers, songs, poems, or other artistic works that you love. It can include what you love about one another and what you feel you have missed by not spending those lost years together. Be creative and personal with your own ritual. It would be a good idea to have some symbolic gesture included which would put the past to rest—burning or burying something which represents the old sorrow and grief. Then have something which symbolizes the new sense of hope, trust, optimism, and joy for your future life together—a lighted candle, a flower, an exchange of lockets.

When you have finished reading and discussing your stories, partake of the ritual you have devised as a symbol of your loss and of your new beginning. For instance, the adoptee might grieve for the loss of her first mother, the loss of Self, the loss of a safe childhood, and the loss of the foundation of basic trust. The birth mother might grieve for the loss of her child, the loss of motherhood, the loss of trust in those closest to her, a loss of faith in herself—her intuition and ability to make good decisions. Both must try to shed the burden of "if only" and realize that, for whatever reason, your lives happened the way they did. Neither of you had control over what happened, and you both need to stop trying to find the "key" to how you could have made it different. *You can't. It is over.* You have a future ahead of you. You need to be fully *present* in order to enjoy your new life together.

*The Adoptive Family Ritual*

Many adoptees feel a great deal of sorrow because they realize they weren't able to allow their adoptive parents to get close to them. Some defining moment in their lives brought this to their attention and they don't know what to do with this realization. Sometimes it is too late, the death of the adoptive mother, for instance. Sometimes it is seeing the mother with the grandkids ... she is so loving and nurturing with them and the wish is that you had allowed her to be that way with you. Whatever the circumstances, writing or talking about this discrepancy in the way you wish it had been and the way it was can be healing. Adoptees and their adoptive parents can devise their own rituals for healing whatever wounds were between them. They can write their stories, read them, and have a ritual of healing. Then they can begin a new way of relating.

This can also be the case in sibling relationships. I know of many adoptees who are sorry that they weren't closer to their siblings. Perhaps the sibs were so different that they never got along. Perhaps there was a mixture of bio and adoptive sibs and they were jealous of one another. Now that they are older and more mature, many of the things that split them as children no longer seem important (or shouldn't). As adults it is time to give up childish things, such as the kinds of quarrels that drive children apart. I can't believe the number of adults who actually still hang on to hurtful things that happened in childhood. Everyone needs to get over it. Children are not adults, and the hurts that children inflict on one another must be forgiven when they become adults.

My advice as far as connecting with parents or siblings is to write a note saying what is in your heart. Don't go into details about all the problems you had, but just say that you are interested in reconnecting. Life is too short to hold grudges. The most important things we have in this world are relationships. It is a good idea not to squander them. Don't wait for the other person to make the move toward reconciliation; do it yourself.

*A Warning*

There are some people who don't want to give up their old feelings and ways of being. They may be afraid, or they may feel that those feelings are too much a part of them. Perhaps it would be like giving up an old friend. And, indeed, the dysfunctional way of life can feel like an old friend because it is so familiar. But it is *not* a friend. It is a burden holding each of you back. Often it is one or the other of the reunited pair who hangs on to the old "stuff." This makes it difficult for the other person to make any progress in the relationship. While no one can deny the past, everyone has to let go of the burden of the past. Seligman says,

"To the extent that you believe that the past determines the future, you will tend to allow yourself to be a passive vessel that does not actively change its course" (2002). This is the point where you want your life to change its course—from a life of sadness, fear, and paralysis to a life of joy, hope, and participation. This process can be started through writing and reading your histories and the rituals of mourning and renewal; in other words, in actively participating in your own recovery.

*Reconnecting and Reconciling*

After the reading of the stories and the ritual of grief and renewal, it is time to reconnect and live in the present. It is time now to begin a new phase of your lives. Reconnection means not only reconnecting with each other and the rippling pond of important relationships, but reconnecting with the authentic Self. After years of trying to be what others wanted or what the trauma elicited, it is difficult to answer the question, "who am I?" The adoptee has been the adoptive, adaptive self; the birth mother may have been the unmother, emotionally paralyzed at whatever age she was when she surrendered her child; the adoptive mother may have become a raging maniac, a role totally foreign to her normal way of being. All have been playing roles dictated by their traumas. All need to find out who they really are and trust in the goodness of that person.

Reconnecting and reconciling has two parts: reconnecting and reconciling with those closest to you and reconnecting and reconciling with yourself. The healing ritual of remembrance and mourning will have a connecting effect on the adoptee and birth mother. But there are others with whom each also has to reconnect. Both the adoptee and birth mother may have unfinished business with the birth father. Don't leave him out. There are a lot of grieving birth fathers out there. They have grown up, too. They are no longer the impetuous youths who caused problems for the mother and child. Many birth fathers feel that their most important healing needs to be done with the birth mothers.

As I pointed out, for the adoptee there is probably some healing and reconnecting which has to be done with his adoptive parents. It is important to get the input of others about what was going on in the adoptive home. Although there are some adoptive homes which are truly abusive, in many cases the very fact of living without genetic markers and mirroring; living with a mother whose resonance, voice, heartbeat, skin, and so forth were genetically unfamiliar; always having to figure out *how to be* each day, often feeling misunderstood—all this may have felt abusive. All of these things take a great deal of energy and vigilance. They make life harder than it should have to be. Add to this the constant fear of abandonment and rejection and it can feel very much like abuse. And it is. But it isn't the fault of either parent that this has been so. They, too, have suffered from the disparity in genetic makeup. Most of the adoptive parents I have met have really done their best. And no parent is perfect. We all make mistakes—sometimes big mistakes. Often, these mistakes are inadvertent. However, it is important for parents to ask their children about their most egregious mistakes and ask for forgiveness. They should not argue about them or try to explain them. They should just say they are sorry. However innocuous the event might have seemed to the parents, obviously it had another meaning to their child. It is this meaning which has affected the child and needs to be acknowledged and addressed.

## A Personal Story

Perhaps I can demonstrate this best by recounting a personal story of a difference in meaning between a mother and child. When my adopted daughter was in first grade, I made her several matching pants and tops. They were pretty and colorful with rickrack and other trim. I was very proud of them and thought I was demonstrating my love for my daughter by taking the time to make these outfits. I honestly don't remember her objecting to them at the time. But she suffered a great deal from having to wear these clothes. She wanted to wear jeans like the other kids. Now, not all the other kids were wearing jeans. Some of the parents even made their little girls wear dresses. But the point is that most of the kids were wearing jeans and my daughter was not. For years I heard about how terrible this was. Every time my daughter brought it up, she again expressed her anger at me. I couldn't understand it. The effect it had on her seemed so out of proportion to what it was. She was not at the age that clothes mattered all that much. So what was the big deal? It had happened so long ago. Was I going to be hearing about this for the rest of my life? She made me feel as if I had ruined her life.

Well, one day, I think my daughter was 30, she added a sentence to her angry accusations which made a light bulb go off in my head. She said, "But I needed to fit in!" At last I understood and could honestly ask her forgiveness. I had said I was sorry before, but didn't really know what I was sorry for. Now I did. Adoptees are always looking for ways to fit in wherever they are. My making those outfits for my daughter and her feeling different from the other kids was much more of a "big deal" for her than it might have been for other first graders. Ever since I truly said I was sorry, I haven't heard about it. My daughter *needed* me to know what this meant to her, how it affected her at the time. And I finally got it. But look how long it took me! I am the one who writes about adoption and it took me years to "get" this message.

I know that if an adoptee in my practice had told me this story, I would have seen it right away. But because my intentions were so good, I let those intentions get in the way of my seeing the impact they were having on my daughter. This is very important for everyone: *Although it is all right to tell the other person of your intention, it is essential that you then allow yourself to acknowledge the impact the event had on the other person, which may have been very different from your intention. Then ask for forgiveness for the impact and your lack of understanding, no matter the intention.* I know how difficult this is. I know how we want to say, "But. ..." and again recount our pure intentions. Remember, it is the impact for which we are asking forgiveness, not our intentions. My daughter knows it was not my intention to hurt her by sewing those clothes for her to wear to school, but it was *very important* to her to have me understand how it actually affected her.

*Forgiveness*

I believe I have been forgiven by my daughter for not having understood what it was she needed in first grade. However, for some people forgiveness is very difficult. "People, in general, would rather die than forgive. It's *that* hard. If God said in plain language, 'I'm giving you a choice, forgive or die,' a lot of people would go ahead and order their coffin." (Fourteen-year-old Lily in *The Secret Life of Bees* by Sue Monk Kidd, 2002). Lily is right: Sometimes it is *that* hard. Yet carrying around the burden of an unforgiving heart may be harder. Harboring anger, resentment, or hostility can poison one's spirit.

If the offending person has honestly said she is sorry, if she is beginning to understand, then the offended person is urged to forgive anyone who may have inadvertently hurt her. Many adoptees find it difficult to forgive anything. They hang onto ancient wrongs with a death grip. Sometimes there is even a wish for revenge. Jones describes a vindictive attitude as dangerous: "But the most hidden, and therefore the most dangerous form of neurosis is that of revenge, the desire for vindictive triumph over others." Hanging on to old anger will result in a smoldering resentment and eventual bitterness which will color relationships and life. It is not worth it. If you've ever met a bitter old man or woman, you will know that you don't want to become one. Now is the time to make sure this doesn't happen. As hard as it may be to understand, forgiving others is healthy for you. Seligman says, "You can't hurt the perpetrator by not forgiving, but you can set yourself free by forgiving." Forgiveness is good for the forgiver, as well as for the one forgiven.

The birth mother may have to reconnect in a new way to her parents. She may have never forgiven them for the part they played in the decision to surrender her child. As years have passed, many of these grandparents of the lost child have come to see the error of their ways. Times have changed, and with it attitudes toward unwed pregnancies. They, too, have felt sorrow. Whatever the reason for the surrender, a reconciliation needs to take place between the birth mother and her parents. Again, no explanations have to be given. Most birth mothers know about the climate of the times. They just need to have their parents say that they are sorry for playing a part in their daughter's sorrow.

There are other people with whom both the adoptee and the birth mother may want to reconnect and reconcile. Perhaps you will want to get everyone together who is important to you and with whom there is healing to do. The main thing is to look honestly at these relationships and acknowledge what part each of you may have played in what makes them difficult. An adoptee often slams the door on a friend who made a mistake which was construed as a betrayal. Perhaps in reviewing the incident, it will become clear that, although the friend did indeed disappoint her, betrayal was perhaps too strong a label to place on what happened. It is time to reevaluate and reconnect. Some good relationships may have been lost because of an overreaction to an innocuous incident.

*Summary*

There is a great deal of sorrow connected with the adoption experience. Holding on to it can have a deadening effect on all aspects of your life. You don't have to wait for a reunion to begin the process of remembering, recounting, and mourning your losses. Healing can begin as soon as you become tired of carrying around the burden of sorrow. Some of you will be afraid that letting go of the sorrow will separate you from the one who is being mourned. That doesn't have to be true. Perhaps all sorrow will not be banished, but renewal cannot take place until grieving has taken place. And the grieving needs to have some kind of form or ritual to it. That is why we have funerals for memorials for people who have died. Otherwise, there is just an endless, isolated grief which permeates your life. It is something that should be done with someone else in order to have a witness to it and to help contain the grief. So begin, and don't skip any steps. *It is difficult and many of you will not want to do it.* However, it will help prepare you for the next step, which is to find and allow joy into your lives.

# CHAPTER 7
Joy: The Elusive Emotion

Joy, it seems, is an elusive commodity for adoptees, as well as many birth mothers. It has a superstitious quality, as if feeling joy will cause some great tragedy. Sometimes setting up barriers to joy is a way of quelling disappointment, the way that distancing oneself is a way of avoiding loss of love. Of course, all that really happens is that one lives one's life without intimacy and without joy. Neither betrayal nor disappointment is kept at bay. It is magical thinking to believe that this would work. But it is like knocking wood. This old superstitious gesture against bad luck is still used by many people. Knocking wood is quite harmless, but the avoidance of love and joy is not harmless. It deprives a person of living life to the fullest.

Although it may seem like something that happens to only a few people, I have dealt with many adoptees and birth mothers, as well as others who have suffered one kind of tragedy or another, who truly believe that they have to be very careful not to feel too joyful, or not to feel joyful for too long. They begin to feel very uneasy, as if sorrow, anxiety, or numbness is all they are allowed to experience. Joy seems unfamiliar, therefore wrong. Having too good a time? Then it must be time to shut down. Can't let that happen. Joy may be unfamiliar, but it is not wrong. Like all things which need to be imprinted over the old familiar pathways in the brain, it is a good idea just to notice that having a good time did not harm you. Then do it again.

## Avoidance as Talisman

The important thing to learn here is that shutting down joy has never saved anyone from a tragedy or from "impending doom." It simply saves us from truly having a good time. We may bring some of our bad times on ourselves, but we don't do it by having fun. We do it by sabotaging ourselves. We do it by not believing in ourselves. We do it by thinking negative thoughts all the time. We do it by undermining our own best efforts and stopping short of success. Having a good time is free. And it is good for us. It gets the right neurotransmitters going in our bodies. It changes our brain chemistry. It enhances us.

By having a good time, I am referring to fun without chemical substances. Any ingested or inhaled chemical substances will interfere with the good natural chemicals which can enhance a person's well-being. I am also referring to fun without risking our lives. There is a difference between joy and a thrill. When we mix adrenaline with norepinephrine, the result may be a diluted sensation of joy or at the very least a confusing mess of joy and anxiety. Anyway, contrary to the popular opinion of adoptees and other trauma victims, having fun is good for your health. Try it, you'll like it.

### Nature as a Pathway to Joy

How can you start allowing unfettered joy into your life? First of all, you have to know what makes you happy. Sometimes it is a good idea to begin with something in nature. Does it make you happy to walk along the seashore? To meditate among the redwoods? To work in your garden? Start there. Do it as long as you want. Remember, you are doing soul work, having experiences that feed your soul. How can you feel guilty about this, or think that it will trigger doom? I recall a sentence in a book by Alice Walker titled *In Search of our Mothers' Gardens* in which she described her mother working in her garden: "She is involved in work her soul must have." What a wonderful description of what we are doing when we are finding joy in creative endeavors! Our souls *must* be fed, just as our bodies must be fed. Often feeding our souls brings us joy. What Walker was talking about was the tremendous spiritual strength African American mothers showed in the types of activities in which they engaged in their sparse spare time during a certain era in history. It was what kept them alive. It fed their souls, when so much of what was going on was bent on destroying them. Finding what feeds your soul is not only a good idea, *it is necessary.*

Go out on a clear night and experience the joy of looking up at the stars and allowing yourselves to feel a part of the universe. Some of you may say, "But it makes me feel so small, so insignificant." Well, the atom is small, too, but look how powerful it is! You are a part of the universe, the cosmos. It is time to take your rightful place in it. No more excuses! Look up and participate in the life force that is there.

Go into a forest and see how harmonious nature is. Experience the joy of seeing how everything depends on everything else. Look, really look at a flower and see how perfectly each petal fits into the next and how beautiful the colors are. Listen to the birds. Look under a log. Feel the velvety smoothness of the moss beneath a fallen tree. Watch a beetle busily scurrying around a rock. Smell the pungent odor of the ferns and pines. Be present, experience things fully, allow all your senses to participate in this joyful activity.

### Creative Joy

One of the ways we can find joy in our lives is to tap into our creativity.

Everyone has creative talents, and needs to discover what they are. Remember what I said earlier about studying people with multiple personalities—it has led us to the realization that we have multiple talents. Usually the "alters" of the multiples have each developed a different talent: one will be a pianist, another a painter, another a computer whiz. This is all one person, remember! Usually we don't have or take the time to develop more than two or three of our creative talents, but we should at least do that. The propensities for these talents usually show up in childhood, but sometimes not. And they are not always developed then. There are various reasons for this. For adoptees, sometimes it is because the parents don't value their child's particular talents. (This can be true for non-adoptees as well.) Or maybe it is because the adoptee is trying to be more like the parents and doesn't seek to develop what he would really like to do, or even allow himself to know what that might be. Whatever the reason, you are now an adult, and it is time to find joy in whatever you like to do: play the piano, sing, paint, watercolor, sculpt, dance, write poetry, short stories, or essays, take photographs of nature or people, play tennis. Whatever it is, it is time to begin. Do it with joy. Do not try to find perfection in it because perfection is not an absolute. It is a relative thing, everyone having his own definition. Find the joy, instead. What brings joy into your life is personal to you and only you can know what it is.

## Joy in Physical Activity

For some people, there is freedom and joy in physical activities. Some may be solo activities: running, bicycle riding, or skating. Some may be group or team activities: playing tennis, basketball, soccer, or baseball. When the game is only for fun and not competitive, then one can find joy. Competition usually brings forth all the stress hormones which get in the way of joy. Just the sheer joy of the physical activity itself is what one is after. But it may also be the camaraderie of playing with others. Bocce ball and horse shoes may be two of these types of games—competitive, but mostly fun. For some of you it may be the more meditative forms of physical activity such as yoga, tai chi, or tae kwan do. Whatever the activity, take note if it is bringing you joy or stress. Find and take part in those that give you joy.

## The Joy of Giving

Sometimes what we need to do is get out of ourselves a bit and turn toward others. I don't mean that we need to be rescuers of people. I just mean that we can help on a limited basis, but one that can really make a difference. Some of those activities are volunteering at a hospital or nursing home, mentoring or tutoring kids, reading to the blind, or writing letters for stroke victims. These kinds of activities are usually purer than those which involve people with whom we are in relation. We do these things strictly for the other. Our benefit is the joy we experience in helping others who are not connected to our lives—where there will be no other "pay off" except satisfaction and joy.

Sometimes it is good to know the difference between passing pleasures and a lasting sense of satisfaction, keeping in mind that it is important to include both in our lives. In *Authentic Happiness*, Marty Seligman delineates a difference between pleasure and what he calls gratification. Pleasures are fleeting things which make us momentarily happy, but are not lasting. He says, "The afterglow of the 'pleasurable' activity paled in comparison with the effect of the kind action. ... The pleasures are about the senses and the emotions. The gratifications, in contrast, are about enacting personal strengths and virtues" (2002). He lists six core virtues which are valued in almost every culture, are valued in their own right, and are malleable. These core strengths are *wisdom and knowledge, courage, love and humanity, justice, temperance, and spirituality and transcendence.* Seligman notes the difference between virtues and talents. Talents, such as an ability to play the trumpet or sing, paint or play baseball, are innate— we are born with them. Whether we enhance and use them or waste them is up to us. Strengths or virtues, on the other hand, can be acquired and "built on even frail foundations." He identifies the good life as "... the identification and the use of your signature strengths. ... You cannot squander a strength." The important thing to remember here is that these strengths are within us and only need be accessed and practiced.

One of the deterrents to joy or peace is self-absorption. Seligman says, "One of the major symptoms of depression is self-absorption. The depressed person thinks about how she feels a great deal, excessively so. ... 'Get in touch with your feelings,' shout the self-esteem peddlers in our society. Our youth have absorbed this message, and believing it has produced a generation of narcissists whose major concern, not surprisingly, is with how they feel. ... Gratification dispels self-absorption" (2002).

Although I encourage people to get in touch with their feelings, I don't mean for them to get stuck in the negative emotions of anger, frustration, or fear. Seligman says, "Expressed and dwelt upon. ... emotions multiply and imprison you in a vicious cycle of dealing fruitlessly with past wrongs. Insufficient appreciation and savoring of the good events in your past and overemphasis of the bad ones are the two culprits that undermine serenity, contentment, and satisfaction." If you are dwelling on past wrongs, it can hold you a prisoner to the past and paralyze you because the past cannot be relived or redone. Remaining paralyzed in past negative emotions can inhibit forgiveness and keep relationships in limbo. Instead of wanting to find someone to blame for a multitude of past wrongs, look within to see what good times you can remember and try to get back the feelings they elicited.

Usually it is not the outbursts of anger and rage that adoptees and birth mothers talk about, but the vague feelings of sadness and anxiety that hang like a veil over everything they do. These don't seem like feelings at all, but rather a state of being—a mood—the origin of which many are just beginning to understand. Most people I know do not want to hang onto these feelings, but don't know how to dispel them. I agree with Seligman that focusing on others and acknowledging positive experiences and feelings are good ways to allow the brain to begin imprinting new patterns. Using our virtues and strengths to refocus our attention from our own situations and feelings and allowing ourselves to become more genuinely involved in the lives of others can begin the process of imprinting different patterns in our brains, patterns that will infuse our lives with calmness instead of anxiety.

If this sounds like the opposite of what I have been saying in *The Primal Wound*, it is only the grown up version of that message. Remember, the subtitle of that book is *Understanding the Adopted Child*. This book is for adults only. It is presuming that you are ready to gently say goodbye to the child and allow the adult to come forth. It means taking a genuine interest in the lives of others that may not reflect back on you. Remember that extolling virtues in the manner described by Seligman involves not being concerned with approval, acceptance, or love. Acts of virtue are freely given and freely received. No strings attached! They are acts of kindness, valor, and/or restraint.

*Just for Fun!*

Well, enough about virtue! Sometimes it is important to just be silly, to laugh and squeal with joy, the way we did when we were kids. One of the most hilarious times I had was at a San Francisco Symphony Chorus retreat. I can't even remember where it was. I know that we were there to practice for an upcoming concert and to get to know one another better. What I remember most about that retreat was playing a game called Spoons at two o'clock in the morning and laughing so hard I could hardly get my breath. It was a card game which, in addition to a deck of cards, required spoons. I don't even remember how to play it. I do remember that we didn't have any spoons, so we used rolled up socks, which seemed to add to our hilarity. The game required absolutely no skills, but was entirely a game of chance. That was one of the beauties of it. It didn't matter who won. We all won, because we all had such a rip-roaring good time. (No, we weren't drinking. We were "drunk" on good clean fun.) It is important to have this kind of fun every once in awhile. Just silly, child-like fun. This, too, feeds the spirit.

Although pleasure will not be as lasting as the kind of gratification Seligman is talking about, there is nothing wrong with having a good time. Laughing is good for your health! Everyone must find his own tickle-trigger, the things that make him laugh. Not everyone will laugh at the same things. One of my daughters would laugh herself silly whenever Burt and Ernie would appear on Sesame Street. The other daughter couldn't have cared less and rarely watched the show. Not everyone will feel joy at the same events. Some people love slapstick and others can't stand it. Each person is different and that is good. Just think how boring and tragic it would be if we were all alike! The key is to know what brings joy into *your* life. And then *let it in.*

If you find yourself feeling uneasy at feeling too much joy or happiness, take the risk of staying with it anyway. The superstitious feeling that makes you believe you can ward off tragedy by avoiding joy is just that—superstition. Joy is one of life's greatest experiences. Why would you want to miss out on it? If joy were not meant to be experienced, why would we have such a good chemical reaction to it? Why would it be such "good medicine" for body and soul?

Seligman describes the good life as "... deriving happiness by using our signature strengths every day in the main realms of living. The meaningful life adds one more component: using these same strengths to forward knowledge, power, or goodness. A life that does this is pregnant with meaning, and if God comes at the end, such a life is sacred" (2002). Both gratification and pleasure are parts of joy. Both are necessary in attaining a satisfying life.

*Risking Joy*

Like everything else, starting new pathways in the brain by allowing joy into our lives means taking risks. There will be bad things that happen in the world— to us personally, to our nation, and to our planet. Avoiding happiness, fun, and joy will not magically stave off these events. We don't have that kind of power. Neither will it make the bad times, when they come, any easier. On the contrary, when we are having difficult experiences, it is sometimes helpful to remember the good times, the joyful, happy times, so we can get through the more difficult times. It seems that it was the more optimistic, happy people who were able to get through the 9/11 tragedy the best. It isn't that it didn't affect them. It did. But they did not dwell on it too long, and didn't generalize it into a "Chicken Little" event. They were able to allow themselves to feel joy in other parts of their lives. They were able to find a sense of balance, instead of seeing life as a continuous pall of gloom.

Life is made up of joy and sadness, of good times and bad. The key is to bask in joy when and where we find it. If a starving man suddenly comes upon a loaf of bread, should he avoid eating it because then it will be gone? If he doesn't eat it, it will become moldy and inedible. He will miss his chance. He will miss the nourishment it could give him. You don't want to miss the chance of having joy in your life, to miss the chance of nourishing your soul. You need to take it where you find it and enjoy it to the fullest. The opportunity will pass, and you will not have accomplished a thing. Instead you will have missed a wonderful experience for your soul.

So take joy whenever and wherever it presents itself. Create it for yourself. Create it for others. Know that joy is part of life, one of the best parts. It is meant to be. So, go forth and be joyful!

# CHAPTER 8
Emotion and the Regulation of Self

*All psychopathology constitutes primary or secondary disorders of bonding or attachment and manifests itself as disorders of self and/or interactional regulation.*
*James Grotstein (1986) as found in Schore (1994)*

Now that some of the most troubling stones in the path to Self have been discussed, it is time to talk about how these stones can be made into smoother pathways. There are many neuroscientists who suggest that it is the ability to regulate affect or emotion which constitutes good mental health. Conversely, difficulty in the regulation of affect inhibits the development of the true Self and the ability to attain and sustain meaningful relationships.

The regulation of affect is a major problem for many adoptees. What is affect and why is it so important? Affect is defined by Robert Campbell as "... the 'feeling tone,' the fluctuating, subjective aspect of emotion" (Campbell, *Psychiatric Dictionary*, 1989). It is closely connected to mood. It is important because it has a great deal to do with the way in which a person interacts in the world. For many adoptees, the presence of overwhelming feelings has resulted in either acting out behaviors or distancing behaviors, causing difficulties in personal relationships and in a belief in the goodness of Self. This doesn't mean we have to resort to suppression to eliminate inappropriate responses to feelings. Some of the important work we do in therapy is to unearth repressed feelings which may have been expressed in unconscious ways. Allowing these feelings to come up to consciousness doesn't mean, however, that we want them unleashed in an unmanageable way. It means that we want to know what these feelings are, where they originated, and to work them through (revise the limbic pathways) so that they don't interfere with the normal pursuit of goals and relationships. Many of the out-of-control feelings that come up for adoptees have very little to do with the situation that triggers them. This often makes the way these feelings are expressed inappropriate in the present situation. Thus, self-regulation has to be a goal of any adult.

*Neural Integration and the Sense of Self*

In order to formulate a true sense of Self, self-organization is essential. This means that neural integration has to be achieved. This will allow a person to select which rules are maladaptive and which are useful in his present life. This, in turn, will allow for new behavioral responses to old stimuli. Although the neurological system is biased toward old patterns of responding, it is hopeful to know that the neural circuitry which facilitates integration is believed to continue to develop throughout our lifetimes. This is the reason that avoidance is such a hindrance to the forming and maintaining of good relationships for adoptees and other trauma victims; *new experiences of connection and intimacy can be integrated as new patterns of behavior and response.* However, this is dependent upon one's allowing connection and intimacy to be experienced in the first place, no matter how unfamiliar and "wrong" it seems. Remember: practice makes perfect!

Even if an adoptee experienced an insecure attachment and lack of attunement in childhood, the deficits which this causes in adult relationships can be overcome if close interpersonal experiences are allowed and fostered. The goal is to form collaborative and linked functions within his own mind and between himself and others. This means that he has to allow others to know his true emotional states, which can be achieved through non-verbal cues, verbal testimony, or behavioral interactions. As he matures, the process should become more and more verbal and less and less behavioral. The idea is to have witness to and empathy for his true states of mind. Any false state will only alienate him from others because there is no true connection. It is in a true connection or understanding of his emotions by others that he can more easily achieve the kind of self-regulation necessary for the blossoming of the authentic self.

### Self-Regulation

Regulating our emotions is part of the natural maturation process. However, it doesn't begin with the self, but with the calming, soothing adults in our lives. It takes thousands of calming touches and words of a mother to help an infant begin to self-regulate when upsetting things happen. She intuits what her infant is feeling and calms him down. Her understanding and calmness are what eventually help the young child begin to become more emotionally organized. Lewis, et al. say, "A baby's physiology is maximally open-loop. ... When the mother is absent, an infant loses all his organizing channels at once ... (and) his physiology collapses into the huddled heap of despair. ... Given the open-loop physiology of mammals and their dependence on limbic regulation, attachment interruptions are dangerous" (2000). By "open loop," the authors mean that certain aspects of our physiology are not self-sufficient, but rely on others to help become regulated. Although becoming more self-regulated as we mature is a goal, human beings will always do better if there is another person to help with limbic regulation. Because human beings are basically social animals, we will be more emotionally stable if we are close to someone who can help regulate us. Sometimes this need has been misunderstood. Misunderstood humans sometimes turn to pets as a substitute for soothing as a pathway to self-regulation.

We have gone through eras when self-regulation was considered unhealthy. During the "let-it-all-hang-out" era of the 70s, adults were allowing themselves to act like very young children in the name of "honesty." There was little self-restraint. In actuality, this was nothing more than a license to act discourteously and then to blame any discomfort and negative response to selfishly indulgent behavior on the recipient: "If you don't like the way I'm acting, that's *your* problem," was the *me generation's* answer to negative responses to their words and actions. Or "That's just how I am," which really meant: "This is the way I am choosing to behave." It was a time of self-absorption and childishness. It had nothing to do with true states of mind. And it was dishonest.

Perhaps there was a reason for this huge pendulum swing, however. Perhaps it was a response to the "uptight" fifties, when feelings were seldom expressed and social decorum was the order of the day. Instead of finding a nice, happy medium and adding a bit of emotion to our civility, Americans, in typical fashion, went to the other extreme and decided that all feelings had to be expressed and damn the consequences. This allowed for a trend toward narcissism and discourtesy that continues even today. Although at the present time there isn't a movement to this effect such as the encounter groups of the 60s and 70s, we still experience the vestiges of that lack of self-restraint in road rage, adolescent violence, domestic violence, and so forth.

Does anyone have any idea where our present era of disrespect, polarization, negativism, and fascination with "reality TV" is going to end up? We are headed toward incivility, disrespect, cynicism, alienation, and even anarchy. We have to pay more attention to the early years of our children's lives. We have to help them regulate their emotions by really paying attention, by being there for them, by sacrificing for the stability of their early years. One of the most disconcerting commercials on TV is the one for orange juice, where we first see a black and white version of life in the fifties: the mother serving breakfast to her family, politely calling the children to the table, everyone saying "Good morning" and being civil. It is quiet, calm, and polite. Then the narrator says, "Get real!" And (in living color) we see a modern family in the morning ... with everyone going in all directions, no one really sitting down to breakfast, no one really paying attention to one another, but rushing around in a tizzy. Perhaps both scenes are exaggerated, but there is enough truth to them to make one rethink "What are we doing today? What kind of effect is all this chaos and confusion doing to our children? Is it necessary?" As much as we make fun of life in the 50s, I don't recall raunchy language on the playground or children shooting one another then.

Although we don't want to go back to the more rigid time of the fifties, there is a need for us to think more about what we might be doing to avoid the chaos and "disconnect" of our present way of life. This calls for a greater understanding of the importance of interdependence and community. Working together to help with the more appropriate expression of feelings and a better interaction in all areas of our lives is necessary if we are going to survive as individuals, as families, and as a nation. It is up to each of us to take control of our emotions and to learn to self-regulate. We can ask for help, but as adults the responsibility for beginning the process is ours.

### The Amygdala: Our Savior and Our Nemesis

Self-regulation is an important element in gaining control in one's life and one's relationships. When trauma is involved, this task becomes even more daunting. It is necessary to overcome the effect of that "back alley" process: the hijacking of the amygdala. Let us review how this little almond-shaped hijacker works. Besides giving us insight into our emotions and behavior, it can be used to help people "… arm themselves against future cranial abductions" (Atkinson). Arming ourselves means having a bit more understanding about the amygdala. The current wisdom is that the amygdala, not being a patient, thoughtful part of the brain, makes snap judgments based on past experiences that resemble current situations. An "if it walks like a duck, it must be a duck" kind of mentality. It is a response based on emotional memory. This emotional memory may be completely disconnected from any conscious memory of the original experience, as in the case of separation trauma.

Until the most recent brain research, it was believed the hippocampus was the repository for our emotional memories. However, Atkinson reports that Joseph LeDoux of the Center for Neural Science at New York University and other neuroscientists now believe that "… the hippocampus is actually more concerned with registering factual and contextual data, while the amygdala is the repository of primitive feelings linked with those facts and situations. So while the hippocampus will remember what your ex-partner looks like—the jerk who dumped you for a new lover—the amygdala is responsible for the surge of fury that floods your body when you see someone who looks even vaguely like your former mate" (Atkinson, 1999).

"Vaguely" seems to be the operative word. In its attempt to judge whether a current situation is dangerous, "… it compares that situation with its motley collection of past emotionally charged events. If any key elements are even crudely similar—the sound of a voice, the expression on a face—it instantaneously unleashes its warning sirens and accompanying emotional explosion" (Atkinson).

While this kind of automatic response may have saved the lives of cavemen, it no longer serves us very well. It is one of the chief reasons that victims of trauma have a difficult time establishing and maintaining lasting relationships.

## The Window of Tolerance

Siegel says, "*One's thinking or behavior can become disrupted if arousal moves beyond the boundaries of the window of tolerance.*" How much emotional disturbance can one tolerate and remain able to function normally? It is up to each one of us to discover our own window of tolerance and then gradually decrease the disorganizing effects of the emotional response. This will eventually lead to our developing some control over these out-of-control states. Because exceeding our window of tolerance results in a breakdown or shutdown of the neocortical circuits, the natural inhibition of our higher perceptions, thoughts, and attitudes no longer come into play. Instead, the sensory perceptions and beliefs overpower the higher thought processes, and we may act impulsively and emotionally to a situation, rather than acting thoughtfully and rationally. LeDoux calls these two different pathways the high road and the low road, the problem being that the high (neocortical) road is a longer road than the low (limbic) road, so that we sometimes act before we think. Or as Atkinson so colorfully puts it, "By the time the neocortex gets into the act, the damage has been done— you have already called your late-to-dinner partner an inconsiderate jerk, shrieked at your smart-mouthed child, snapped at your critical colleague, or simply shut down, shaking inside, in the face of someone else's rage." To add insult to injury, the neocortex itself has been overwhelmed with the emotion-laden information from the amygdala, further compromising our reasoning ability. So if anyone points out that this seems like a bit of an overreaction to whatever is going on, the perpetrator denies this, *feeling perfectly justified in his behavior.* His neocortex is still out of commission. Does this sound familiar to anyone??

If this is such a natural reaction to our brain's workings, how then can we gain some control over these cranial machinations? The key is being able to *respond to a situation, rather than to an emotion.* This is a tall order. When one can't remember the original source of the emotion, the current situation will *seem* like the source. Why is there a discrepancy? While the amygdala is mature at birth, the hippocampus, the memory bank for factual data, doesn't develop until we are two years old. This is why we don't remember much of what happened during the first years. It is always frustrating to think that although the first three years of life are probably the most influential in the development of our attitudes and beliefs, we have very little memory of that time. Atkinson says, "This means that during that early childhood, when relationships with caregivers have such profoundly life-shaping impact, the amygdala is busy making emotion-charged associations about events that the embryonic hippocampus never even records. ... Once, in our helpless infancy our need to stave off abandonment truly was a matter of survival. So when our partner says or does something that telegraphs *This person doesn't love me! This person is leaving me!* our amygdala scrambles blindly, frantically to the rescue." This scenario will sound familiar to many adoptees as a re-enactment of their most profoundly wounding experience. Yet it is an experience often ignored by the rest of society, including clinicians. For this reason, many adoptees who have gone to clinicians in an attempt to gain some control over overwhelming feelings have had little success.

The inability of the hippocampus to record early experiences is the reason that it is futile to try to get people to remember abusive or traumatic events that occurred before age two. (It should be remembered that trauma itself can cause amnesia around an emotionally charged experience for people of any age.) People who have been sexually or physically abused as infants or toddlers may never remember the events which caused their trauma. Our bodies remember the pain, and our limbic brains remember the emotions, but there is no picture to go with those somatic/emotional memories. This is very important information for therapists, physicians, and law-enforcement officials.

Learning what our window of tolerance is for certain emotions in particular situations can be the first step in gaining some control over our reactions to old wounds. We must become aware of the subtle signals of an impending "take over" of the mind by the amygdala. What are the intense emotions that get triggered, and at what point are we in danger of crossing that boundary between reason and emotion? Self-awareness is essential. But significant others can be of immense help in making another person aware. Too often we allow the "offending person" to get by with hurtful words or behavior just to avoid an unpleasant scene. This only reinforces the person's belief that what he does has no impact and he can continue the hurtful or outlandish behavior. Anyone who colludes with adoptees or others who display this kind of attitude must take some responsibility for the deepening of the belief pattern of "no impact" which pervades the adoptee's state of mind. Remember that anyone who has had the natural order of things interrupted by a traumatic event has more trouble discerning cause and effect or consequences than someone who has not suffered trauma. What that means is that parents and siblings, then friends, colleagues and partners of trauma victims must help to reeducate the brain of those whose patterns are so deeply imprinted with "I don't matter, so what I do doesn't matter."

A group of people I hear from more often than one may imagine are the partners of adoptees, be they men or women. (I hear more often from female partners of male adoptees than the other way around, probably because women are more apt to see how they are placed in the position of the "abandoning mother.") Over and over again, they say such things as the excerpt from an e-mail I received from the partner of an adoptee overseas:

> I have tried to understand and to love him. I have tried to make him feel secure and I have tried to accept him. But ... he has made it impossible to love him and impossible to receive love in his life. I have felt that I have been living with a child, and I hate to say it, but a monstrous child at times. The violent, uncontrollable outbursts, and the 'tests' he has set for me have been a normal part of our life for two years. I am exhausted with the battle and now understand how he can comfortably continue participating in it: From three months after we first met, he has been working towards the day when I will leave. And it has come.

This is the self-fulfilling prophecy of many adoptee relationships. This woman recognized many wonderful qualities of her partner: "gifted, intelligent, and passionate." Yet he could not trust in those qualities, but instead needed to act out the testing behavior which eventually drove her away. When her boyfriend finally realized that she was actually going to do what he had been both fearing and working toward, he had put my book out for her to read. And she did read it, all in one sitting. But it was too late. Too much damage had been done. Adults can't expect the same kind of tolerance for acting-out behavior that children can expect. People are usually drawn intuitively to the *essence* of the other and are stunned and bewildered by the testing behavior which eventually contaminates the relationship. The trauma-driven behavior must be modified in order for the person to again be seen and appreciated. Sometimes, as in the above case, it is too late. As much as a partner may love and appreciate the true essence of her partner, she doesn't have to accept inappropriate behavior. The adoptee needs to realize that this behavior is not coming from the mature adult who wants a relationship, but from the inner rejected, fearful, angry, hurt child.

What can be done? How are adoptees to overcome the power of the neurological connections which leave them prone to emotional reactions, rather than more measured responses? How can new neurological pathways be established? How can trauma be integrated as memory and not experienced as an ever-present danger?

## Consciousness and Attractor States

In a later chapter there will be a discussion about specific therapies which may help in overcoming the effects of trauma, but in the meantime, it is important to again stress the role of consciousness in affecting change. Some consciousness can come from our own recognition of a change in our feelings under certain circumstances, during certain situations, at certain times, or with certain people. Neurologists talk about *attractor states* in which we tend to return to old patterns of feelings and behavior. One that everyone will probably recognize and relate to is going home for the holidays. People (not just trauma victims) will say, "I feel so competent and intelligent at work, then I go home for Christmas, and I feel as if I'm ten years old again." What is happening? Why does this always seem to ruin holidays? What is happening is whatever emotions and responses predominated during childhood will be reactivated upon returning to the childhood or parental home. For the people who had a happy childhood with lots of interaction among siblings, joking and support from parents, and friendly debates with relatives this will be a time of fun and even giddiness, a time to let down their hair and be young again.

However, if childhood felt like a time when nothing you did was right, when every meal was filled with discounting, belittling, and arguing, then going home for Christmas will be felt as a burden, something to be avoided if possible. Even if the relationships between the parents and children have improved over the years, with mom offering support and encouragement and dad now listening to and respecting his children's opinions, when the setting is the same as in childhood, old states of mind are likely to reoccur. This may happen automatically, without there being any intention or awareness. As Siegel puts it, "The family now functions as a whole system, reinstating its old attractor states" (1999). *This in no one's fault.*

Why is this information important for adoptees? I have noticed that going home, especially for the holidays, is quite stressful for many of them. This doesn't mean that there was anything particularly wrong going on at home during childhood. But it may mean that the old sad, lonely, unacknowledged feelings of unresolved grief will reappear. In addition to many adoptees' not having a sense of fitting in or belonging at a time when family is emphasized, there may be a sense of "nothing's changed," when going back home. Despite an improvement in the relationship which may have taken place since the adoptee moved out, returning home may bring back old sensations and attitudes. It may seem as if there is just as much tension between mother and son, just as much discounting of ideas from dad. The parents may see their adult child in much the way they viewed him in childhood—outrageous, impulsive, disrespectful, and oppositional or sullen, uncommunicative, and withholding. He, on the other hand, may again experience his parents as insensitive, controlling, unsupportive, and invalidating.

If these states are allowed to continue with no one becoming conscious of what is going on, if no new possibilities are presented, then no change is possible. There is, instead, a returning to the old attractor states, where everyone goes back to the old roles. This doesn't have to happen, but it takes a conscious effort on everyone's part, and note here, adoptees, that I'm saying *everyone* and not that it is up to the parents to make everything right or different. I say this because it is so often the case that adoptees wait for everyone else to act, as if they are again helpless. If you adoptees want things to be different, then *you* have to be different and not return to the old withholding, distancing, and avoiding methods of relating. This goes for birth mothers as well, who may feel helpless and distrustful of their own ideas and opinions, an emotional return to that fateful decision to give up the baby, which didn't seem like their idea at all.

The parents also have to be willing to look at their behavior and change. I personally know how easy it is to get into the old mode and say things which are totally inappropriate given that my children are now adults. Sometimes I say them in spite of myself. It is so easy to get back into the trap of *being the parent.* So, although I can have empathy with parents who do this, I also believe that it is up to us to gain awareness and control over these tendencies. Apologize when you catch yourself doing the "old thing." This goes for parents and children alike. And it is up to the offended person to remind the other that the old behavior is not all right. This can all take place in a civilized fashion. "Hey, Mom. I'm not fifteen anymore." Or "Linda, I'll bet you don't say those things to your co-workers." Just gentle reminders that *everyone present is an adult and needs to act like one and be treated like one* can go a long way toward a more enjoyable holiday. It takes giving up old beliefs, such as "I'm right and they are wrong" or "nothing's changed." At such times, humor comes in very handy! (And alcohol doesn't.)

The activation of attractor states is a natural phenomenon of the brain; no one is to blame. However, since it can make family get-togethers difficult and unpleasant, it is important to become aware of it and overcome its effects. This is everyone's job, but it is up to the most aware person to bring it to everyone else's attention. Again, humor can play a big part in a family's overcoming old states of being.

### Some Precursors to Self-Control Issues

Self-regulation is one of the most difficult tasks of adoptees. Although many may seem rigidly controlled, this may be a way of keeping them from flying out of control, not true self-regulation. I have heard adoptees say over and over again, "I'm afraid if I really get angry, I could kill someone." Or, "If I allow myself to cry, I'm afraid I'll never stop." The quiet adoptee, especially, may be a volcano of suppressed feelings which he is terrified to experience. The "in charge" person co-workers see in the workplace may only be the outer trappings of a simmering caldron of volatile feelings. How many adoptees have said the equivalent to "Everyone thinks I am so 'together,' but they just don't know how I feel inside"?

Because adoptees have difficulty with stimulus discrimination and are often in hypervigilant mode, they are sometimes overwhelmed by stress hormones. This can interfere with the development of self-regulation. Siegel says, "Psychological trauma can overwhelm affect regulation mechanisms, and various forms of adaptation may be required to maintain equilibrium. The flood of stress hormones can produce toxic effects on the development of brain systems responsible for self-regulation." This puts the adoptee in a position of needing to be hypersensitive to what is appropriate and what is inappropriate behavior. The limbic brain may be preparing him for one thing and the neocortical brain may be telling him something else.

Two conditions set the stage for separation trauma's having a tremendously disorganizing effect on the child: *the loss being kept out of conscious awareness and there being little or no acknowledgment or sharing of the grief connected to that loss.* I have seen in adopted children a kind of unreal sense of themselves in time and space, an almost ethereal quality. Adoptees themselves sometimes describe this as a feeling of floating. Others have described feeling as if they went through their childhoods in a trance.

The loss experience also has an adverse effect on a person's *expectations for the future.* Maintaining a structured environment is important to the development of expectations for the future. This is the reason routine and consistency are so necessary for children. Writing in *Focus*, an educational journal, Ruby Payne quotes Feuerstein, an Israeli educator: "If an individual cannot plan, he or she cannot predict. If an individual cannot predict, he or she cannot identify cause and effect. If an individual cannot identify cause and effect, he or she cannot identify consequence. If an individual cannot identify consequence, he or she cannot control impulsivity. If an individual cannot control impulsivity, he or she has an inclination to criminal behavior" (Payne, 1999). We already know that adoptees are over-represented in juvenile halls and prisons. Even those who are not committing crimes are often impulsive and as children get into trouble at home and in school. One of the arguments against trying children as adults (besides the absurdity of it—what exactly is an "as adult"?) is that even in normal development, the ability to curb impulses doesn't mature until about age 20.

A deficit in expectations for the future creates impairments in the ability to regulate internal states. One reason for this impairment is that the child may be in survival mode. Having to be sure that one is not abandoned again is a form of survival. Because so many parents are working and have little time or patience for mediating their children's emotions and behavior, more and more children are having difficulty with self-regulation. Feuerstein gives some interventions which parents or teachers can use:

- Point out the stimulus
- Give it meaning
- Provide a strategy to deal with the stimulus.

He gives these examples:
"Don't cross the street without looking." (Stimulus)
"You could be killed." (Meaning)
"Look twice both ways before you cross the street." (Strategy).

This type of intervention can get the child thinking in more strategic patterns and help him to plan his daily life more effectively. Although very young children can't really understand the meaning behind directions from their parents, as the child reaches the age of reason (around age seven), it is important to begin teaching him to think in this way. Planning for future actions is one form of self-regulation. It must be pointed out that these types of directions have to be made over and over again. This requires patience and consistency on the part of parents.

### The Cost of Dysregulation in Adult Life

As many adoptees have discovered the hard way, an inability to regulate their emotions can interfere with both personal and professional relationships. In running into difficulties in both realms of interpersonal relationships, adoptees often misunderstand cues from the people with whom they are interacting and overreact to whatever is going on. Disorders of self-regulation can take the form of dysfunctions in perception, beliefs, memory, and actions. This may result in the end of a relationship or being fired from or quitting a job. By doing a reality check, such as talking the situation over with a therapist or close friend, perhaps the loss of job or relationship would not have had to happen. I can't count the number of times I have interjected a reality check to an adoptee who was just about to sabotage a relationship for some innocuous action on the part of a partner. The degree to which he overvalued the event was remarkable. Yet it is truly felt by the adoptee as a major transgression—not innocuous at all. However, to anyone else it would be something to talk about, something to check out for validity (remember that assumptions play a major role in miscommunication between partners), not something over which to end the relationship.

Although understanding the trauma which created the problem gives the adoptee an explanation for his behaviors, those in relationship to him couldn't care less about the *meaning* of his actions. Or even if they care, they become weary of the repetitive behaviors and outbursts, and decide to leave anyway. Partners, although caring and often helpful, are not responsible for changing the behavior. It is up to the individual who has the problem to do that. These dysfunctions, in addition to having a lack of stimulus discrimination in the environment and a generalized sense of impending disaster, contribute to the adoptee's difficulty in social and work situations. Most of these dysfunctions have to do with an event which has happened, not one which is about to happen.

Both constitutional and environmental factors can influence the intensity and sensitivity in which a person experiences something. A person with a genetically calm personality, if living with raging parents, can experience difficulty in regulating the intensity of his emotions. On the other hand, an extroverted, excitable child living with calm, introverted parents who have little patience or understanding for her exuberance, may find herself feeling ashamed of her exhilaration and emotionally isolated within her family. This mismatch creates a difficult living situation in an adoptive family and increases the difficulties the child has in self-regulation. Siegel says, "At a moment of intensity, a failure to be understood, to be connected with emotionally, can result in a profound feeling of shame ... not being understood may lead to a sense of isolation." Remember that shame inhibits connection or attachment. Many adoptees can relate to this sense of isolation. Although matching personality traits may be more important than matching hair or eye color, this is rarely considered when finding parents for children (or children for parents!).

The terror of having mom disappear may permanently alter the sensitivity of the adoptee to even slightly similar stimulus related to abandonment. Part of the reason is, as Siegel puts it, "Once we are hurt, our amygdalas will to do everything they can to keep us from allowing it to happen again." What happens, then, is that adoptees will respond to a stimulus even slightly similar to the one which perpetrated the separation trauma. This may be the amygdala's way of protecting the adoptee from further trauma, but it is what others call overreacting, and often ends up causing the very thing which was feared—abandonment. The fear of connecting often results in an adoptee's distancing herself from her partner, and a fear of abandonment causes her to cling. Adoptees often go back and forth between these two states, the push-pull syndrome, causing their spouses and partners to feel as if they were riding on a roller coaster.

## How to Begin to Self-Regulate

Although some early traumas that sensitize the arousal system to respond may never be fully desensitized, there are ways of diverting the arousal system so that a more flexible life can be achieved. When we experience reflexive responding ("I couldn't help it"), as opposed to integrative processing ("It didn't seem like a good idea"), we are experiencing emotional dysregulation. We have to begin to notice the cues which lead to this state in order to regulate the emotional response or behavioral reaction to stimuli. In learning to do so, it becomes necessary to know our *window of tolerance* or the boundaries at which we become unable to function appropriately when faced with certain emotional situations. Going beyond the window of tolerance means an alteration in thinking and behavior. It means being out of control. In order to gain control over the situation, it is necessary to divert the energy that goes into an inappropriate response to a more useful image or thought which creates distance from the original trauma. This can be practiced in therapy or with close friends and should eventually decrease the disorganizing effects of various episodes of emotional arousal. It means paying close attention to how and why we respond the way we do. It means challenging or questioning the validity of our responses and making deliberate and overt changes in those responses. This is the beginning of a long process of creating new pathways in the brain. It is not easy, but *it is possible!*

Unconscious processes often influence our sense of Self, our behavior, and our emotional responses. Therefore, becoming more conscious is requisite to allowing us a more flexible and meaningful life and giving us a sense of choice in our responses. Consciousness has to come before emotional and behavioral responses can be regulated. Because human beings have the capacity to self-reflect, we can reflect upon the sources of our emotional and behavioral problems. There is a need to have some input from others to help regulate the impressions and perceptions which come from a traumatic experience. Because trauma victims have difficulty with self-reflection, without others' offerings it is difficult to modify faulty belief systems. It is important to remember that perceptions and ideas can change with the help of new experiences and others' perceptions. There has to be an allowance for the possibility that our own perceptions are not a hundred percent valid. One does not have to be a slave to the past or a puppet to the perceptions of that fearful child within.

Contrary to the seventies dictum of "let it all hang out," which meant allowing the emotions to run wild, it is now understood that regulating our emotions is an integral aspect of our mental health and our sense of Self. It is difficult to allow ourselves to *be* ourselves if we are constantly afraid that we will spin out of control. It is equally difficult to become ourselves if we are tied up emotionally, not being able to connect with others. There must be a balance between excessive, nonregulated arousal and excessive inhibition of emotions for a healthy process of brain development. As Siegel says, "Emotions are the contents and processes of interpersonal communication early in life, and they create the tone and texture of such communications throughout the lifespan. ... In their essence, primary emotions are the beginning of how the mind creates meaning. ... The regulation of emotion, or the regulation of the flow of information and energy within the brain, creates the self" (1999). Or, as I would prefer, *allows* the Self to emerge. Self regulation is an essential part of feeling authentic and in control.

Regulating our emotional responses allows for a wide range of feelings while maintaining appropriate, flexible, adaptive, and organized behavior. Although early childhood trauma makes achieving emotional self-regulation more difficult, it must be remembered that the perceptions which caused the emotional turmoil may have been inaccurate. Challenging the beliefs which emanated from these perceptions can be a helpful step. "Perhaps my mom wasn't unaffectionate. Perhaps she just gave up trying to cuddle a fearful child." It would be easy to check this out by noticing if mom is affectionate with other people. If so, then she probably tried to be affectionate with her child as well. If not, then she probably did not have affectionate behavior modeled for her in her family. Although they must exist because I've heard about them, I've never met an adoptive mother who was innately hostile to her child. There are many who are frustrated by their inability to reach their children emotionally, and some react irresponsibly, but there has usually been an initial feeling of warmth and caring on her part.

*The Importance of the Narrative Process*

Narration is an important part of achieving self-regulation and self-organization. We have to try to make sense of events in our lives. Even if they don't seem to make sense, we have to be able to tell others how these events affect us. This is the reason that talking about important milestones, such as birth and death, are so important to our being able to self-regulate. This is *essential* for children, but also important for adults. When speaking of adoption, of course, we only have to look as far as the separation of mother and child to know there is a lot to talk about. The birth mother's inability to talk about her loss has been tremendously influential in her being unable to regulate certain emotions which lead to mature relationships. There was no narrative for her experience, only a void, an absence, a nothingness. If she had been able to process her grief, she could eventually have felt some kind of integration of the experience, although she would always feel the loss.

For the adoptee, talking about the experience of separation is more difficult, for there is no memory of it in the sense of conscious recall. He feels a void, but he doesn't know what is causing it. Nevertheless, when other events happen in his life that scare or puzzle him, it is important to provide a forum for his being able to process them as long as he wants. When a grandparent dies, for instance, what happens in the family? Do they sit around reminiscing about grandpa's life, or does everyone act as if he never existed? Do they talk about why grandpa died and what it means, or do they act mysterious and withholding about his illness and demise? Does everyone think he has to mourn in private? Acknowledging and communicating our grief in conjunction with others is a faster pathway to healing than suffering alone. We could learn a great deal from other cultures when it comes to grieving.

Adoptees are especially good at acting as if loss means nothing to them. How many times have I heard that an adoptee has not mourned the loss of his parents or grandparents? Well, has he witnessed the grief of other family members, or have they too been secretive about their loss? Over and over I have heard people say, "After Aunt Lucy died, no one ever spoke of her again." Why do parents think they have to be "strong" or stoical in front of their kids? Are they afraid the kids will be upset? Isn't it more upsetting to think that if something happened to us, no one would acknowledge that we had mattered? *That we would be forgotten?* Isn't this one of adoptees' greatest fears—that they are forgotten? If grief is shared, it is going to benefit the regulation process. We can help one another. We can cry together, laugh together, and share our feelings about the person who is no longer with us. This enhances feelings of connection for all who are experiencing the loss.

Sometimes written narrative is helpful. Writing about our losses, our fears, our hopes, and our joys can help us integrate these experiences. If prose doesn't seem to work, perhaps poetry will. As difficult as it may seem, sharing our words with others is necessary to the integration process. We need others to bear witness to our experiences in order to integrate them and feel connected. One reason therapy is so powerful is that it is a sharing of our innermost thoughts and feelings with another who can have an empathic response to these experiences. For some people, it is the first time they have ever experienced this kind of attention.

There are many ways to attain self-regulation and self-integration. With certain techniques and practices, a better integration is attainable. The first step is consciousness—becoming aware that a problem exists and having the courage and motivation to begin the processes which will lead to healing. Healing has to do with consciousness, self-reflection, and connection to others. Forming connections with others is infinitely important and possible. It is possible because our brains are wired not only for defense, but also for connection. (The amygdala has more than one trick up its sleeve.) This is very hopeful information. And it may seem paradoxical, but being connected is essential to the discovery and integration of the authentic Self.

# PART TWO

Exploring the Many Rooms

Now that you have an the knowledge you need to understand the foundation for your coping style—the experiences which dictated your neurological connections, attitudes, behaviors, and emotional responses—it is time to explore the many rooms that may better represent *you*. Too often we allow the baby mind to dictate the rooms we are allowed to enter. That baby mind has decided that some rooms are too dangerous to explore. These rooms are shut tight and locked against a possible accidental entrance. But now you are adults and need to be more adventuresome. You have to question the baby mind and its narrow view of those rooms and the fear that they engender. It is time to take the risk of opening a few doors … many doors!

The first chapter of Part Two is just such an exploration. It is time to get out of the cramped closets of adaptation and coping you have been occupying and into the sunny, bright rooms of your more authentic self. This is a call to challenge your habit of surveying the environment to know what it is you should be doing, saying, or believing, and, instead, I encourage you to look within for that more true representation of your needs, desires, and beliefs. You no longer have to be concerned with adaptation, but more with authenticity. In order to have true and lasting relationships, you need to be more true to your authentic self. This chapter is a pathway into those many locked doors … doors that lead to exciting rooms lying within the wonderful house that is you.

Along with authenticity comes the responsibility for how you affect others. It is no longer all right to continue ignoring your effect on others as you go through life. You can never be powerful if you do not take responsibility for your actions. True inner power requires accountability as well as vulnerability. If this sounds like a paradox, be aware that life is full of paradoxes and it is a good idea to accept and even welcome them. They make life interesting and exciting.

The next three chapters will help to correct some misconceptions about feelings we all have and words we all use. It is hoped that exploring these rooms will provide some balance in your emotional life and better ways to respond to your feelings and experiences. Some of the rooms will help you know how to set up permeable, yet firm boundaries, rather than concrete walls or none at all.

The two chapters on Reunions and Relationships, are perhaps the most important of this section. However, in order to fully be able to take advantage of entering these rooms, you must first do your work on the previous five chapters. You cannot truly be in a relationship if you are not being authentic. And a successful reunion requires that you are at least on the road to adulthood. Chronic childlike behavior in either reunions or other relationships will only lead to your worst nightmare—rejection. Being able to distinguish between the nursery and the master bedroom is important. It is time to tiptoe out of the former and walk proudly into the latter.

The last room in this section is the chapel. This is a chapter about your spiritual life. This room is not designated as a church, synagogue, mosque, or temple, but as your very own private place for spiritual contemplation. Everyone has a spiritual life, even if he doesn't label it as such. If you have values, worldviews, beliefs, or are in awe of nature, you have a spiritual life. Spirituality is about all these things as well as about your relationship with the whole of humankind and the universe.

Begin! Explore these many exciting and challenging rooms. There is treasure here.

# CHAPTER 9
## The Search for the Authentic Self

We have talked about the trauma of separation and the effects this trauma has on the adoptee's neurological system, as well as on her psychological, emotional, and spiritual life. It also has a tremendous effect on just who she believes herself to be. Why is this and how can she discover the core of her being? First of all, she has to rediscover her lost soul.

*Reviving (or Retrieving?) the Lost Soul*

I like to think of the discovery of the authentic Self like the metamorphosis of a butterfly. The word *psyche* in Greek means both butterfly and soul. The growth of the soul may be like the emergence of the butterfly, developing in stages. We all become part of the world's soul, yet many adoptees feel cut off from this larger picture. As we look at the state of the world, many may even wonder if they *want* to be part of the world's soul. Yet it may be through our souls' connections that we can finally bring peace—both inner and outer peace—into our lives. Why is it that so many adoptees feel separate and isolated in their lives? How can they revive their lost souls and find a sense of Self?

The problem may have begun before they were born or shortly thereafter. Birth mothers who were subjected to various unwed mothers' facilities rightly claim that there was a lack of soul in what they experienced there. Even though many of them were in facilities run by religious groups, rather than experiencing understanding and compassion, many experienced judgment and condemnation. This may have affected their emotional lives and that of their unborn children. Then, babies who were in the hospital nurseries awaiting release either to adoption agencies or adopting parents, instead of being placed in the caring, soothing arms of a nurse or other warm human being, were often subjected to doses of Phenobarbital when they cried for their mothers. Adoptive parents, instead of receiving understanding and support concerning the difficulties of rearing a child who feels as if he doesn't belong, were instead told, "If you had just loved him enough or disciplined him more, he would have been fine." There seems to be no way any of these people can make others, even other members of the triad, understand what they are or have been experiencing.

But what others have done to adoptees, birth parents, and adoptive parents is no worse than what they subsequently do to themselves. There is a tendency to label oneself, rather than label the experience, so that one's entire way of seeing oneself is in terms of "abandoning birth mother," "uncaring birth father," "rejected child," or "infertile woman."

How else can you look at yourself? You can look at yourself as Joan or Jim or Ann or David, who had experiences which impacted you, but which are not the total of who you are. These experiences may greatly affect the ways in which you view the world and other people, as well as yourself, but these experiences do not change the basic characteristics of Joan, Jim, Ann, or David. What these experiences do is to delay the emergence of your true personality, stunting its growth, in favor of the "more acceptable" false self.

In other words, each of us is born with the potential personality we are going to have for our entire lives. Any mother is able to discern, right from the beginning of her child's life, individual characteristics of her child. No two children are alike, even at birth. Some people believe that it has to do with the star under which one is born. This many have some validity. I don't rule it out. Yet because of the ways in which adoptees notice similarities in their personalities, gestures, body language, and facial expressions when they find their birth families, I am inclined to believe that the true personality is mostly genetic.

Before I go on, I want to hastily remind you of what I've said before. Behavior is not genetic, but is the result of experience and environment. We act in certain ways in order to cope with or communicate various experiences in our lives. Hence the difficulty for adoptive parents to know the true personalities of their children. What they see instead is coping behavior, their child's way of dealing with loss and the potential for future loss. The acting-out child is dealing with loss and his fear of a further abandonment by distancing himself in an externalized, overt, provocative manner; while the compliant adoptee is dealing with his fear of abandonment by distancing in an internalized, withdrawn, acquiescent manner. Neither is exhibiting his true personality. This doesn't mean that the personality is totally obscured by the behavior, but that the personality is *skewed* by the behavior.

One adoptee, in imaging herself as an infant confused by the sudden disappearance of her mother, put it this way:

> When I was born, I was a whole person, a wonderful little human being. But after having been given up by my birth mother I began to see myself as flawed. Something was wrong with me or she wouldn't have left me. So I had to change who I was to someone else. I had to hide that flawed baby self and be someone whom my new parents wouldn't give away. I began to act differently. I began to be very, very good to try to please everyone. I had to constantly be on the alert to what was expected of me. It was exhausting. I had little energy for anything else. I did

poorly in school, even though I knew I was smart. All my energy went into being that good adopted child. Now I want to be me. Good or bad, I just want to be me.

Being you is what this is all about. Not identifying with your coping behavior or your experience, but identifying with the true Self, hidden from everyone, especially yourself. And this suggestion is not just for triad members, but for anyone who has felt as if she has had to compromise her true Self in order to survive in her family. Trauma comes in many forms, and trauma transforms one from who one truly is to someone else.

### Early vs. Late Trauma

The effects of trauma are tremendous. It doesn't matter at what time in our lives a trauma happens, it changes our lives in profound ways. If a woman is raped at age 30, she finds herself profoundly affected by that event. She, in fact, demonstrates all the manifestations of trauma listed in the first chapter of this book. She no longer trusts anyone, she is hypervigilant, she finds the world unsafe, she feels ashamed, alone, and disconnected from others. Her attitudes and behavior reflect this new way of being in the world.

So how is this different from how an adoptee sees himself and the world? The manifestations are the same, but there are three important differences: 1. The 30-year-old rape victim can remember the traumatic event, whereas the adoptee can't. For him, as well as for incubator babies and other victims of early childhood trauma, the event happened before their capacity for recall was developed. 2. He doesn't have the advantage of a reference point for authenticity. The rape victim can think back to herself at 25 or 29, before the rape occurred and know herself as she was then. She cannot go back to being that person without a lot of hard work, but she has that person as a reference point. She knows who she was before she was raped. The adoptee didn't have time to develop a self before his trauma occurred. 3. In addition, she probably has her biological family in her life so she is surrounded by familiar people, people who are like her or the person she knew herself to be before the trauma. This again is not true for the adoptee. Not only has he suffered a trauma at the most vulnerable time of his life, but he is then placed with strangers who cannot reflect him at all. He has no reference point either from memory or genetic markers. A rape victim may or may not have the support of her family. Much depends upon whether or not she has told them and whether or not they are sensitive and empathic. An adoptee rarely has parents who understand his loss and help him grieve.

The adoptee, then, has not only been devastated by an unnatural, life-threatening event, but he has then been left with strangers. He has neither a reference point for his authentic Self nor is he surrounded by familiar people to help him sort it out. In fact, the people who are now in charge of him are not only strangers, but are probably oblivious to the significance of what has happened to him. There is no acknowledgment of the effects of that devastation. To these new parents, he is a blessed event, a miracle. They are happy that their dream of having a child has finally come true. He feels completely alone and terrified. He has begun his life with a trauma, and the way he relates in the world will be forever affected by this event, the significance of which isn't even acknowledged by anyone else. He is alone in his loss, sorrow, and fear.

Where does the birth mother fit into this scenario of trauma? She is a combination of both. She certainly can remember the event of pregnancy and birth, although her memory may have gaps in it because of trauma-induced amnesia. She has a reference point for who she was, but in most cases this reference was a very young person. Some birth mothers have told me that they feel as if they haven't grown emotionally since that event. They are emotionally paralyzed at age 14, 17, or 21. So far as her biological family helping her with regaining her true Self or assisting in her grieving process, this has rarely happened. Usually she is treated as if she has gotten rid of a bad situation and can now get on with her life. The parts of her family she may see as part of her are not the parts she wishes to imitate: insensitive, oblivious, callous, and indifferent. Although she may have the advantage of partial explicit memory around the event of conception, pregnancy, birth, and surrender, she is not much better off than the adoptee.

### The Coping Mechanisms

The adoptee has thus lived with the trauma all his life. He began to identify with the traumatized child because that is all he knew. If he reacts to his trauma by acting out, he believes himself to be bad or difficult. He doesn't like himself very much. He gave his parents a hard time and made his own life difficult as well. He may have gotten into legal troubles. He may have tried to kill the pain with drugs, alcohol, sex, or porn. And in all probability, he identifies with all these actions and maneuvers and thinks "this is who I am."

The quiet, compliant adoptee believes she always has to please others, to be very, very careful not to offend others or put herself in a position to be criticized or shunned. She becomes the people pleaser, never having a diverse opinion, always trying to fit into every situation in which she finds herself. Yet she feels as if she fits into none of them. She may believe herself to be introverted and shy. She may try not to be too visible.

Neither of these characterizations has anything to do with who the adoptee really is. In fact, being an adoptee isn't who she is either. It is a word which designates what happened to her. Many adoptees have objected to being "categorized" by this label. I can't blame them. It isn't who they truly are. However, it may be how they have been acting. When something so catastrophic happens to a person, there are certain manifestations of that event which affect those to whom it happened. There are certain ways in which they are similar in their responses to that event. These are called coping mechanisms. They emanate from the trauma. But coping mechanisms have nothing to do with who one truly is.

*A Caveat*

At this point I want to say three things:

1.  I apologize for referring to those of you who were relinquished as *adoptees*. It is only a label I use to clarify a group of people who have a *similar experience*. It is a matter of clarity, *not identity*.
2.  You are not your *coping mechanisms* any more than you are your *experiences*. If you acted out, it is because this was the only way you felt able to cope with the pain of separation and your determination not to let that happen again. If you were compliant, you felt that you had to avoid annihilation by never making waves. Neither of you was being true to your original encoded personality. That got lost in the shuffle. Some of you were able to hang on to more of your true personality than others. It probably had a great deal to do with how similar you were to your adoptive family.
3.  I also realize that some mothers who relinquished object to the term *birth mother*. Again, it is used in my book as a way to distinguish between the birth and adoptive mothers. It is only for clarity. I have separated the word birth mother into two words in order to designate that *birth* is an adjective modifying *mother*. As I say to birth mothers on my Web site, you *are* mothers. Adoptees and adoptive parents, as well as the rest of society, need to recognize and acknowledge this.

*Labels Have to Do with Experience, Not Personality*

The problem for adoptees is that most have not known anything before they entered their adoptive families. They were traumatized at the beginning of their lives, so they cannot look to a non-traumatized self and know that they are simply reacting to the devastation of having been separated from their first mothers. To make matters even more confusing, they have lived all their lives with genetic strangers. Even the modicum of authenticity that has come through to them over the years may never have been validated or encouraged. And even if their adoptive parents delighted in the ways in which they were different from everyone else, it may have seemed dangerous to them. "After all, what was it anyway that caused my original abandonment?" As children, they most likely decided that it was something that was wrong with them. That is what children do. They blame themselves for anything that happens to them early in their lives. This includes separation from mother, divorce, abuse, etc. If it happened in the narcissistic phase of their development, they will blame themselves. That is all they know how to do.

What this means is that they will try to fit into the family by being as much like everyone else as possible, even if it isn't required. The compliant kids are best at this, of course. They don't like to make waves. The acting-out kids aren't being any more authentic, but they are coping by, paradoxically, distancing themselves and connecting via anger and hostility. This means that if you are still acting from those coping mechanisms, you are still not acting from your true Self. No one is born always needing to please others. This is a coping mechanism. No one is born making outrageous statements meant to shock people. That, too, is a coping mechanism. Those of you who think you are being authentic because you have come to terms with your coping mechanisms and "like myself as I am" are in for a shock. *It isn't who you are.* I'm glad you like the you that shocks, upsets, or appeases others, but that still doesn't make it *you.* Many adoptees have gone through years of therapy with unsuspecting therapists learning to come to terms with and like their false selves!

Some of you have additional labels, such as alcoholic, incest survivor, drug addict, or porn junkie. None of these labels is who you are either. Some labels, like *incest survivor,* are additional traumatic experiences; others, like alcoholic or drug addict, are ways in which you attempted to dissociate from your pain of separation. Of course they don't work. They may give a bit of respite from the pain, but they don't take it away. Something that is very important for you to know: *You can't "get rid of" your pain. You have to integrate it.* You have to make it work for you. You have to give it meaning. I know that this sounds ridiculous. I have never liked the saying, "Everything that happens has a meaning." This saying has always upset me because I can't see how a tragic event such as having a child kidnapped, abused, and killed has any meaning. Perhaps there are realms that we don't understand and these things will make sense when we enter that realm. Despite how meaningless some experiences seem, in order to heal I do think that we have to *try* to make meaning—not out of the traumatic event—but of our present circumstances. I will talk more about this in the chapter on Spirituality. However, before we do that, we have to know more about ourselves—our true Selves.

*You Are Only Fooling Yourself*

Each of you has a unique personality. It may be very different from those of your adoptive family members. There are people in your lives who know more about your true personalities than you do yourselves. They are the people who love you and know that you aren't your coping mechanisms. Sometimes you try to prove them wrong by testing them. You use all your old coping behavior to see if they will still stick around. You want to prove that you are not worthy of their love. And, although you can't really do that, some of them will leave anyway. You *can* make a relationship untenable. You can prove to *yourself* that you are unlovable. What you are proving to *other people* is that you are not taking responsibility for your behavior, and they are no longer willing to put up with it. You are not proving that you are unlovable; you are proving that your behavior is at odds with your personality and not coming from your authentic Self. But why do that? Is it because you are afraid that if they really find out who you are (*the grown-up version of the rotten baby*) they will leave you? Whatever it is, there is a compulsion to repeat over and over again the abandonment scene.

Sometimes the end of a relationship may not be your fault. There may in fact be something going on with the person with whom you are in relation that causes him to leave you despite how true to yourself you try to be. It may have to do with you only in that you are the one who chose/decided to be with someone who may not have been able to sustain a relationship. And *that* you need to look at. However, the demise of every relationship isn't always your fault. It may be, but not necessarily. How often have I listened to adoptees who list all the things they did to prove to their partners that they were unworthy, then lamented when they left? And how often have I listened to those who have really tried to hold together a relationship that was doomed from the start because the other person was incapable of intimacy? In both cases the adopted person is likely to blame himself for the demise of the relationship. Yet while he was doing all the testing behavior he was not taking any responsibility for those actions. He was busy blaming the other person for what was going on. That was part of the game. In the second case, he will usually spend a great deal of time trying to figure out how he failed to keep things together, never considering that the other person may have been incapable of sustaining a relationship. The constant taking responsibility after the fact is part of the ways in which adoptees try to be in control. It's why the baby believes himself to have been a defective baby. "If I could just figure this out ..." puts him back in the driver's seat. It makes him believe he could have control over the uncontrollable situations in his life if he could just figure out what is wrong.

*Hiding Out*

The paradox is that often an adoptee acts absolutely helpless in many situations. She can't make decisions, she can't offer opinions, she can't make plans. *She feels responsible but doesn't take responsibility.* What if she makes a mistake? The root of this is the almost nebulous belief that she *is* a mistake. The mistake is the *belief* that she is a mistake. Let's clear that up right now: *Not a single one of you is a mistake. Every one of you belongs in this world interacting and connecting with the rest of us.* To believe otherwise just gives you an excuse to sit on the sidelines and try to be invisible. Those of you acting outrageously are hiding just as much as the quiet ones on the periphery. You are hiding who you truly are just as much. So don't think that just because you are "out there" you are really out there. You are hiding behind your behavior as if it were armour. You may be even more hidden than the "wall flowers." At least they are being honest about trying to be invisible. You, on the other hand, are trying to convince the rest of us that what we see is what we get. You are all a bunch of Pagliaccis— acting the clown, while crying inside. Give it up. It isn't working. You are only fooling yourselves.

But who can blame you? As I said, you don't know anything else. There may have always been the nagging feeling that you've felt like two people. That's the dual reality I have mentioned elsewhere. Depending on how terrified you were about being abandoned, you buried various aspects of your true genetic personality in favor of a false self that fit in more with what you assumed was expected of you in your non-biologic family. When you think of it, it is such a crap shoot—the arbitrariness of how babies are placed in strangers' homes. It terrifies me to think about it. And yet it also terrifies me to think of our family without our beloved adopted daughter. What if we had taken the first child offered to us? (It was a boy; we wanted a girl.) She would have gone home with someone else. The very thought makes me break out in a cold sweat. I can't imagine life without her. She is so loved. She is so my daughter. And she is also her birth mom's daughter.

*What Is the False Self?*

Growing up with biological strangers is not easy. People outside the adoption triad don't realize this. Even people in the triad don't realize it, including many of you adoptees yourselves. Because it *was always this way* you may not have understood the difficulties of being true to yourselves. Yet some of you always knew. You knew you were always having to figure out *how to be.* Just being yourselves seemed so dangerous! Let me assure you that when I can see the true Self beneath the coping mechanisms, I am delighted. I have never met an adoptee whom I didn't like. No, it was not the well-honed, "together," false self that I was attracted to, but the vulnerable, authentic self buried beneath that false self. It doesn't take me long to discover that more true self. Yes, I know that many of you convinced many therapists that the false self was the real you, and their goal was to get you to like that false self. And many of you have learned to at least make a stab at it. I have mentioned that Daniel Siegel says there is nothing false about a self that is coping with trauma. And that's true. I guess a better description would be the "coping self." Yet because so many of you can swing back and forth between the defiant coping self and the compliant coping self, it really doesn't seem to have much to do with who you are—not really. You neither coped using defiance nor using compliance because of your personality—who you truly are—for all the reasons mentioned in *The Primal Wound.*

### Stalking the Tame Chameleon

Something else that I've noticed as I've been counseling people for so many years is that some adoptees who were the introverted, compliant ones in their adoptive homes are really extraverted *in real life.* By that I mean that when they have delved deeply inside and mined the true Self from the depths of their being, where it has been buried for so many years, they have been astonished to discover an out-going, extraverted, social self—not the shy, fearful person that they had acted all their growing up years. On the other hand, some adoptees who acted out and seemed quite extraverted to others, are really more quiet, introspective, and introverted than their behavior led others to believe. In therapy, little by little they allowed themselves to take risks with me, then try them out with the people they most trusted in their lives. Therapy isn't just about concentrating on the pain of separation and adoption, but also discovering and delighting in the excitement of *being*—of being who we're truly meant to be. It is a tremendously liberating experience. It is like finally being able to breathe.

Do any of you have any idea just how much energy you used each day trying to figure out *how to be* in your adoptive homes? (How much energy you may still be using in trying to be the chameleon?) It is a tremendously energy-draining activity. It wasn't your parents' fault. They were oblivious to how hard you were working at this. Your mother, too, was having to do the same thing in trying to be a good mother. And many times, no matter how much she wanted to, she never did figure out just how to meet your emotional needs, because she didn't understand that you were suffering loss. Neither of you could recognize in the other any genetic markers which may have helped. Instead, it was a dance you each did in the presence of the other—the dance of desperately trying to figure it out. It is what many people do when they are not in familiar territory. When they are not mirrored. When the faces, voices, energy, skin tones, facial expressions, gestures, and body language are unfamiliar. They try to figure it out. No one in the adoptive family is at fault. It is built into the system of adoption, yet it is a significant problem that needs to be recognized.

One of the problems for adoptees is that this particular form of vigilance doesn't seem to stop when they are out of the family. Once in awhile I talk to an adoptee who really thinks he became more real when he moved out of his adoptive home. But did he really? Or did he just become another coping self—trying to fit into yet another venue? Many adoptees refer to themselves as chameleons. They can adjust to any situation. They can change color to meet the present environment. The fact that they have been doing this for so long in their adoptive families, where it seemed a matter of life or death, makes it practically impossible to stop doing so. It is a pattern of acting in the world. Add to that the fact that many do not even know they are doing so and one can begin to see what a universal problem it is.

The problem is that all of us who are trying to relate to the chameleon are being cheated. After all, the whole idea of the chameleon's changing colors is to remain unseen. It wants to appear to be something else. A leaf, perhaps. Sound familiar? Although an adoptee may not want to appear to be a leaf, he may want to be a ghost of those around him. But this isn't real. We can't relate to someone who isn't real, who keeps changing all the time. It's kind of like relating to Casper the Ghost—you can't quite make out who he is and you can walk right through him. There is no one home. There is only the ever-changing cipher. We feel cheated. I have heard adoptees say, "I would never let anyone know who I *really* am?" What they believe is that they are all *shadow*.

## The Shadow

Everyone who has ever heard of Carl Jung knows what the *shadow* is. It is what we think of as the dark side of our natures. Or maybe the dark side of our coping styles. We are all born with the capacity for good and evil. Yet I believe that all little infants are born with *intention* for good. Any bad action that comes from them comes as a result of difficult experiences. The capacity for bad behavior and even evil may be there, but only the capacity is there at birth. All babies are innocent and full of potential. Sometimes, terrible things happen to little children. Perhaps more often than we realize. Things that aren't always recognized as terrible, such as being put in an incubator to save a life or placed with foster parents to avoid abuse, feel terrible to little children. We know that leaving children with abusive parents is a bad thing, but we don't often recognize that children also suffer when placed with other people, even if those people are good. I am quite sure that many CPS (Child Protective Services) case workers don't recognize the harm in taking children away from their real parents. Yet in the life of the child it is a huge transgression. These actions, although perhaps necessary, create attitudes in children which are sometimes harmful to them. The shadow begins to emerge and makes them act out (cope) in certain ways contrary to their nature. Sometimes social workers have to make these decisions, but they need to understand the pain for the children when they do. Then the children's feelings can be validated by the foster parents. Life is not black and white. Children may be harmed by keeping them in their abusive homes *and* by placing them with foster parents. (I'm not referring to the harm that comes when the foster parents also abuse them. That is unconscionable and happens all too often.) I am referring to the harm that comes from being separated from everything familiar—from family, even a bad family. Whatever the decisions adults make for children, understanding and validating their feelings go a long way toward thwarting difficult behavior. Children do not appreciate martyrs.

The shadow can emerge in other ways. Sometimes it is only a suspicion that the important people in our lives don't approve of aspects of ourselves that seem authentic to us. Some of those things are just the expressions of feelings such as anger. So we begin to believe that feeling anger is bad—that *we* are bad for being angry. What happens is that we begin to repress our anger. We don't express it, but keep it hidden even from ourselves. And we begin to get really charged up about anger in other people. As adults we may point our fingers and say with distain, "Look at how angry he is!" The fact that we are all charged up about it may mean that it is a feeling we are not owning in ourselves. We are projecting it onto others. Often we see anger in the other when it really isn't there. A man may come home from work, look at his wife and say, "Why are you angry at me? What did I do?" To which she may reply, "I'm not angry. What do you mean?" "Yes, you are. I can tell. Don't try to deny it. I always know when you're angry with me." The wife may still be puzzled at this accusation. But the badgering from her husband will continue until she breaks down and exclaims in a loud voice, "I am *not* angry." At which point he will say, "See, I knew you were angry. Why can't you just admit it in the first place?" Of course the wife was not angry in the first place. The husband was, perhaps at something that happened at work, but instead of owning his own feelings, he projected it onto his wife and badgered her until she was indeed angry. This is called *projective identification* and is thoroughly discussed in Chapter 17.

This is part of the shadow—those rejected aspects of ourselves that we feel are too dangerous to own, but which we project onto others. Robert Bly talks about how we are all whole at the beginning of our lives, but little by little become diminished. He explains it as it relates to him and his brother:

*When we were one or two years old, we had what we might visualize as a 360 degree personality. Energy radiated out from all parts of our body and all parts of our psyche. A child running is a living globe of energy. We had a ball of energy, all right; but one day we noticed that our parents didn't like certain parts of that ball. They said things like: "Can't you be still?" Or "It isn't nice to try and kill your brother." Behind us we have an invisible bag, and the part of us our parents don't like we, to keep our parents' love, put in the bag. By the time we go to school our bag is quite large. Then our teachers have their say: "Good children don't get angry over such little things." So we take our anger and put it in the bag. But the time my brother and I were twelve in Madison, Minnesota, we were known as "the nice Bly boys." Our bags were a mile long.*

*Then we do a lot of bag-stuffing in high school. This time it's no longer the evil grownups that pressure us, but people our own age. So the student's paranoia about grownups can be misplaced. I lied all through high school automatically to try to be more like the basketball players. Any part of myself that was a little slow went into the bag. ... So I maintain that out of a round globe of energy, the 20-year-old ends up with a slice. ... We spend our life until we're 20 deciding what parts of ourself (sic) to put into the bag, and we spend the rest of our lives trying to get them out again.*

Robert Bly, A Little Book
on the Human Shadow, *1988*

How much earlier and completely the bag is filled when an infant winds up in a strange environment with no familiar signs! Most of him goes into the bag right away. He then relies on the false or coping self to keep him safe. Later, when he dares to look in the bag, he often can't recognize the value of what is in there. Bly says that instead of courageously opening the bag and examining the contents for treasure, a person may look around him and decry those whom he deems to be doing him in or he may become judgmental about those around him.

Robert Louis Stevenson wrote about what happens when the bag is sealed and the shadow is projected instead of owned and retrieved. His story is called *Dr. Jekyll and Mr. Hyde.* How often I have heard that description from a partner of an adoptee! "I can't understand it; he's like Dr. Jekyll and Mr. Hyde." He may be vacillating between the defiant and compliant child, or he may be fluctuating between the defiant child and the true adult self.

Some aspects of the shadow are very valuable and need to be retrieved. Have you ever envied something about another person? Not just liked, but truly envied— had strong feelings about? Well, those characteristics of the other person are probably also your own characteristics, but ones that you have not developed for one reason or another. Most of what is in the bag is worth retrieving because if integrated it can make a person more whole and interesting. I can vouch for that from my own experience. I am a much more interesting person since finally retrieving those previously unclaimed aspects of myself I told you about in

Chapter 5. It was scary, but necessary and ultimately very satisfying. If left unknown and unowned, the shadow can burst out in unexpected ways and cause a great deal of harm. One needs to ask over and over again: "What feels congruent inside and outside myself? Why am I so adamant about the things I dislike about that person? Why am I so envious of those particular traits in her?" As impossible as it may sound, it is safer to own what's in the bag than to ignore it. *If left unconscious, the Shadow is in control. If made conscious, it can be controlled.*

## The Duality of Human Nature

We all have the capacity for good or evil. We all have our compassionate, loving side, and we all have the shadow side. We have to acknowledge these diverse sides of our natures in order to avoid being controlled by some aspects that we don't want in control.

In his book *Being Peace* Thich Nhat Hanh wrote a poem called "Please Call Me by My True Names" in which he describes the paradoxes which play upon our natures by way of darkness and light. The following are a few stanzas from that poem:

> *I am the frog swimming happily in the*
> *clear water of a pond,*
> *and I am also the grass snake who,*
> *approaching in silence,*
> *feeds itself on the frog.*
>
> *I am the 12-year old girl, refugee*
> *on a small boat,*
> *who throws herself into the ocean after*
> *being raped by a sea pirate,*
> *and I am the pirate, my heart not yet capable*
> *of seeing and loving.*
>
> *My joy is like spring, so warm it makes*
> *flowers bloom in all walks of life.*
> *My pain is like a river of tears, so full it*
> *fills up the four oceans.*
>
> *Please call me by my true names,*
> *so I can hear all my cries and my laughs*
> *at once,*
> *so I can see that my joy and pain are one.*

*Please call me by my true names,*
*so I can wake up,*
*and so the door of my heart can be left open,*
*the door of my compassion.*
                                    *Thich Nhat Hanh, 1987*

We cannot have compassion for others or for ourselves until we understand that we are both the victim and the perpetrator; that we experience joy and sorrow; and that we have to own our projections in order to be able to metamorphose—to mature into the butterfly. We need to stop blaming—blaming the birth mother, her parents, the adoptive parents, social workers, society. Although it may be true that each is partially responsible for what happened, there is nothing we can do about the past. The only influence we have is on the future. What are we willing to do about what is to come?

## The Emerging Butterfly

When describing the journey to the true Self, I use the metaphor of the butterfly because the butterfly goes through three stages of development: the caterpillar, the pupa, and the butterfly itself. Each stage has its tasks. During the caterpillar stage, the insect crawls along at a slow pace, confined to leaves on plants, where it finds its sustenance. It eats, survives, and grows until it is ready for the next stage.

This can be compared to our childhoods, when we have very little freedom away from the immediate environment, and where everything is provided for us so we can survive and grow. Yet childhood is often fraught with dangers, as is the precarious life as a caterpillar that may be eaten by a bird or spider. The caterpillar is protected by camouflage, its protective coloring makes it blend in with its surroundings. Children are supposed to be protected by their parents, but are sometimes the victims of the very people who are supposed to protect them.

If the caterpillar survives, it goes on to the next stage. It finds a nice branch or underside of a leaf, and it spins a cocoon in which it is going to trap itself. Adolescents often do that: They spin webs in which they trap themselves, as they struggle to become the adults they are meant to be. After the softness and suppleness of the caterpillar, the pupa is hardened, paralyzed, looking as if nothing is happening to it. Adolescents often seem hardened, and the confusion about what is happening to them often seems paralyzing. They are not children; they are not yet adults. No one takes them seriously. Adults are prone to believe that they will never grow up.

But meanwhile in the pupa, though everything looks deceptively inert, a great transformation is taking place. The caterpillar is turning to liquid! A caterpillar doesn't' simply grow wings the way a tadpole grows legs. It dissolves into liquid, and then becomes something entirely different from what it was before. That state of being a liquid may be similar to what adolescents feel: a state of confusion of being neither child nor adult—neither caterpillar nor butterfly—but an external presence which belies the magnificent transformation that is taking place within.

What happens when trauma occurs at one or the other of these first two stages? What happens is that one gets emotionally stuck in that stage. One is paralyzed as either a caterpillar crawling (floating?) along endlessly without direction. Or, in the case of the birth mother, a pupa, unable to complete the transformation process needed to facilitate the emergence of the butterfly. The adoptee feels at the mercy of that wounded child-self; and the birth mother may be stuck in adolescence, the stage at which her trauma took place. How do we free the adult self from the confines of that child or adolescent, whose wound paralyzed her?

First of all, we have to observe *what is* and stop trying to undo the past. Rather than trying to get rid of things, whether it is some aspect of our personalities or some portion of our experience, we might do well to take a different view of them. In *Care of the Soul*, Thomas Moore suggests, "… the first point to make about care of the soul is that it is not primarily a method of problem solving. Its goal is not to make life problem-free, but to give ordinary life the depth and value that come with soulfulness. … In care of the soul, we ourselves have both the task and the pleasures of organizing and shaping our lives for the good of the soul." As adults, we have to take on the responsibility for shaping our soul—and our future.

Rather than trying to get rid of a problem, Moore suggests that we look at it in a different way, a way that shows its necessity and value. In other words, instead of being the exterminator of our own life's experiences, we should instead "go with the symptom," to try to figure out what the soul is saying. When I work with adoptees and birth mothers, I sometimes get the feeling that the only thing that will make them feel better is to eradicate their experience of separation. Since that can't happen, since they are stuck with their histories, this leaves them feeling hopeless to change their lives. Even a reunion cannot retrieve those lost years, so they remain stuck at the caterpillar or pupa stage of development, helpless to move forward or backward.

There is, of course, a secondary gain (or advantage) in being stuck there. If we cannot become the butterfly, if we can never grow up, then we never have to take responsibility for ourselves. We can go on blaming others for what our lives are like. Someone once said, "A person doesn't become an adult until he moves from the passive voice to the active voice." In other words, instead of saying, "It got lost," we can say, "I lost it." We can take responsibility.

We all know that there are certain things that happen to us as children or adolescents over which we have no control. But that's the point. As children we often have no idea why we do what we do and have little control over what we do. But as adults we have to stop acting as if we still have no control. Certainly there are events over which we have no control, but we do have control over *how we respond to those events*. We have to stop being victims, and fill our vocabularies with phrases such as "I am choosing ..." and "I have decided ..."

### The Journey: Victim ... Survivor ... Participant

No one wants to remain a victim. It leaves us with no control over what happens in our lives. We are like flotsam on the sea—floating with the tide, having no rudder to allow for direction or purpose. The first step on the road out of victimhood is to survive. Most of you have done that. Yet being a survivor isn't the end of the journey. Although no longer in danger of annihilation, you might only be running on two cylinders. You may still react to triggers of the old wound. You may still not be empowered. Your choices seem limited. People speak with such pride about being a survivor, as indeed they should. But they shouldn't stop there. Being a survivor isn't the end of the journey back from trauma. It is the intermediate step.

What is the goal then? The goal is to be a true participant in life. If one is a survivor of a trauma later in life, he may already have participated in life fully at some time. However, for adoptees there was never a time when they fully participated in life. Some have remained victims and some have become survivors. But anyone who still has strong fears about intimacy, trust, or control is not fully participating. Participating means having control over responses to triggers. It means not having to be loved or approved of by everyone. It means feeling empowered and able to make choices. It requires a change in the belief system.

### The Ugly Duckling

The current belief system may have an adoptee believing that he is the ugly duckling. How many of you adoptees have read all the way to the end of that story? Was the little "duckling" right? Was he in fact an ugly duckling? No, of course not! He was a cygnet, a baby swan. He was judging himself by the family in which he was living. It was a perfectly good family of ducks. But because he didn't look like a duck, he considered himself ugly. Notice that he didn't think that all of them were ugly and that he was beautiful. How typical! When the ugly duckling finally saw his grownup reflection in the water and noticed a flock of swans nearby, he knew that he was all right. He was beautiful and fit in somewhere. Some of you have felt that kind of tremendous relief when you have met your birth family.

The lesson here is clear. Living without any genetic markers can make you feel like an outcast, like the ugly duckling. Whether you have been acting like the ugly duckling or the chameleon or anyone but yourself, no one can really get to know and love you unless you become more real. This is one good reason to find that lost family of swans to whom you belong. Not only may it answer some questions about how you got put into the duck family, but it may make you realize how beautiful you are. Ducks are beautiful, too. But they don't look like swans. You may have to find someone who looks and acts like you to feel all right about yourself.

The important thing to remember so far is that *you are neither your experience nor your coping mechanisms.* There is a basic, genuine person down there somewhere who is aching to get out. Where should you begin?

### Debunking the "Keeping Myself Secret Is Keeping Me Safe" Myth

After a lifetime of adapting, it may seem very scary to stop doing so. In fact, it may seem rather impossible because you don't really know anything else. Just because you were not like your parents doesn't mean that you were being you. Remember that the acting-out adoptee is no more real than the withdrawn adoptee. Both were disguises used for survival. Well, survival time is over. It is time to participate in your life. Participation means being real. You can't really participate if you are full of fear. For as long as you can remember you have believed that keeping yourself, the real you, secret was keeping you safe. After all, wasn't it the real you that got kicked out of paradise in the first place? No, it was not. And frankly, most of us who really care about you are very tired of having to deal with the wounded baby who believes that. We would rather take our chances with the real adult self. We can't relate to the false or child-like self because it isn't real and it is fearful. Fear inhibits the life process. It paralyzes. It keeps you from being who you were meant to be. It keeps us from knowing you and truly relating to you. We really need you to be real. (All in favor, say "aye!")

### Taking Baby Steps

You can begin with the little things which define you. But how do you know who you are? In the five-hundred-year-old *Book of Life*, Marsilio Ficino advised people to begin with very concrete decisions, carefully choosing, for example, "colors, spices, oils, places to walk, countries to visit, etc ..." By the particular choices we make, we either support or disturb the soul. And each of us needs to observe our own souls for that which makes us know that we are being true to ourselves. It has nothing to do with what someone else may like or what supports his or her soul. Although we all pour into the collective soul of our culture and world as streams pour into the river and then the ocean, we need to nurture our own tiny stream with what it needs to flow, so that it doesn't dry up, so that the river keeps flowing into the ocean of soulfulness.

So let's start small. When I do my "Who Am I?" workshops, one of the first questions I ask adoptees is "Who can go into a restaurant and order first?" Now this may seem like a ridiculous question. I'm sure that many of you can easily do this. You know what you like to eat and you are not going to be swayed if everyone else orders something different. But some people cannot do this. Even something as innocuous as what to have for dinner seems like a daunting decision. "What if I order the wrong thing?" There is usually a lot of nervous giggling when I ask this question because even those people who can make this particular decision know what I am talking about. They know that there are myriad other decisions that seem impossible to make, decisions that others may have no problem making. Suffering from trauma creates the paradox of not being able to make decisions and not wanting anyone else to make them for you. It is a dilemma that I want to help you with.

Since we were talking about ordering food in a restaurant, why not start there? What is your favorite food? This is a big category, so let's get more specific. What about, what is your favorite flavor of ice cream? Believe it or not, sometimes when I ask this question, an adoptee will tell me that she doesn't know. Now, how can anyone not know her favorite flavor of ice cream? Well, if a person has always been checking in with other people to make her decisions, she won't know. She will be looking around for clues from the outside instead of peering inside of her own self-awareness to find the answer. She may have to conduct some experiments to discover what she really likes. I recommend those experiments. Do them when there is no one else around, no one who might criticize you for ordering chocolate when their favorite is strawberry. (I am kidding about the criticism because, to be honest, no one else cares what kind of ice cream you order. I'm sorry, but it's true.) Favorites are favorites, and everyone has his own favorite that no one else cares about. Now, someone may try to get you to try his favorite, but he isn't really trying to get you to make it your favorite. He just wants you to experience something that gives him pleasure. It is not criticism, coercion, or control. It is just sharing.

*From Ice Cream to Politics—Getting Real*

You have to be true to yourself and discover what you like or what your opinions are. So here are some open-ended phrases for you to complete. They start out easy and get more difficult. Remember to answer from the depths of your being, not from the self you've been playing at. Remember the question Ficino asked, "Does it support or disturb your soul?" Take your time. Experiment. Don't try to answer too quickly, but think that if no one else were to judge you about it, what would your choice be? What would support your soul? To get you started, here are some phrases to complete:

- My favorite flavor of ice cream is
- My favorite foods are
- My favorite type of ethnic food is
- My favorite color is
- My favorite color to wear is
- My favorite style of clothes is
- I like to read books about
- My favorite type of music is
  (No fair saying that you like all kinds of music; choose a favorite.)
- My favorite singer is
- My favorite composer is
- I like movies about
- My favorite male actor is female actor is
- My favorite TV show is
- I like it because
- My favorite type of art is
- Of that type, I like _____ the best.
- I prefer baths/showers
- My favorite flower is
- My favorite tree is
- My favorite type of furniture is
- My favorite type of house is
- My favorite sport is
- If I had a choice, I would pick _____ as a career.
- I would like volunteering as a
- I find that I am most at peace (in the forest/in the desert/at the seashore/on the prairie/ _____.
- My religious/spiritual beliefs are
- Spirituality means _____ to me.

- I belong to the _____ political party
  because _____.
- I would like to join the _____ party, but haven't
  because _____.
- I would like to vote for _____ _____ _____ for president/
  governor/senator.
- My real opinion about our present president is _____.
- This is my opinion about the present conflict
    guns in our society
    the trade deficit
    the national debt
    corporate greed
    organized religion
    the environment
    global warming
    race issues
    homosexuality
    "free love"
    foreign relations
    the United Nations
    adoption
    working mothers
    other social issues
- Seven qualities in a person (of the same sex) I admire are
- The qualities I would like in a partner or spouse are
- The qualities I admire in a friend are
- Some ideas for improving the world are
- Things I would like to change about how I act in the world are
- Things that get in my way of doing this are
- Steps I will take to change are
- (take one step at a time ... change slowly)

This will get you started. Use as much paper as you need. Take your time. Gather information about the political questions in order to make an informed choice. Think about how your answers make you feel. Some of these questions are difficult and complex. Maybe there are things on this list that you have never considered before. Yet they are choices and issues to which every adult really should seek answers. To be an adult means knowing what you value and believe in as well as what you like or desire. If you really thought deeply about the answers to these questions and didn't just answer the way you've always answered because it seemed easier or safer, you have already begun to make changes in yourself. These changes will lead to your being more authentic. Congratulations!

Sometimes it is a good idea to work on some of these ideas with someone else so that you can discuss them and make sure you are not answering from your false self. You can make the choices in private, then share them with someone you trust. You can be honest about how difficult it may have been to know just what your choices, ideas, or opinions are; how you may now realize how much you have depended on cues from the environment (i.e., other people) to give you the courage to speak up; how scary it is to allow even one other person to know what you really like, think, or believe.

The next step is for you and a friend or support group to do these exercises together, and then discuss the *differences* in your opinions *without having any judgment about others' opinions or choices.* If there were only one right answer to questions of importance, by now we would have all the answers, and politicians as well as philosophers would be out of business. Remember that many of your opinions today are not the same as they were ten years ago and are not the same as they will be ten years from now. You can certainly debate the relative merits of this over that, but only in a genial, respectful way. No put downs, name calling, or other forms of verbal abuse. You will probably discover that all of you survived this exercise—it isn't life-threatening to have a different choice or opinion from others. At least not in this country. At least not yet.

*Being Authentic*

As you discover your *Self,* it is important to allow others to discover *You.* Start with people you may not know well, because it is not such a risk. Perhaps you have been acting more real at work except when opinions that aren't work-related are called for. Allow even more of your Self to come out there. Voice those opinions. Then little by little allow those who really do care about you see beneath the armour to that magical self. This includes your adoptive parents. After years and years of adapting to the adoptive family, adoptees are surprised when they discover that their adoptive parents like being introduced to the real person. To tell you the truth, it may be a relief because they will then have the opportunity to have a real relationship with you. Don't forget to include your best friend and your partner or spouse. Take baby steps in order not to scare yourself too much. Note how you feel. What are the responses from others? Have you been abandoned? Are you still alive? If you happen to have a verbally abusive partner who degrades you when you voice an opinion different from his, this may a good time to "abandon" him. Not allowing for differences is his problem. Your problem would be to decide if you really want to stay with such a person. If it is your parents who are giving you a bad time about your different ideas or opinions, you can draw their attention to it, and if they don't change (remember to use humor) you have a choice about how much time to spend with them. The thing for *you* to remember about others having different ideas from yours is that *they are not rejecting you; they are differing from you.* Not the same thing!

Just for fun and in order to give you an idea of what the characteristics of a mature, well-integrated person might be, I have invented a person I will call Yolanda and have outlined some of her choices, ideas, values, opinions, and beliefs. (Note: Some of these have no value other than she *knows* the answer to the question, such as what kind of ice cream she likes; others may change over time, such as what political party she belongs to; while others definitely show a mature attitude toward life. Please also note that Yolanda's choices, beliefs, and opinions and not necessarily mine—and they don't have to become yours!! Some of her *common sense* ideas might be something to strive for, however.)

Yolanda
- Likes to eat strawberry ice cream, prawns, and broccoli.
- Prefers Thai food to all other ethnic foods.
- Likes to read romance novels, murder mysteries, and biographies.
- Likes to listen to light rock and classical music of the Baroque period.
- Likes movies that develop the characters, rather than those with intricate plots.
- Likes "funky" clothes, but usually dresses conservatively.
- Recognizes when feelings seem out of proportion to the situation she is in and responds to the situation, rather than the feelings.
- Can accept or reject suggestions from others based on the merits of the ideas, rather than a need to avoid control or a need to please others.
- Realizes that she doesn't need everyone's love or approval.
- Knows that everyone has a different reality and that hers isn't the only one.
- Is assertive, but not aggressive.
- Is able to recognize life's crises as specific problems, rather than global catastrophes.

- Has an adult-to-adult relationship with her parents, which she insists upon.
- Seeks out reciprocal relationships with friends who are stable, responsible, and supportive.
- Can ascertain and express her needs: Doesn't expect her partner or friends to be mind-readers.
- Wants to be a "stay-at-home mom" and isn't afraid to express this to her workaholic friends.
- Has changed her political party to better represent her political beliefs (she knows what these are).
- Believes that everyone has a right to his/her own religion, although she was raised to believe that everyone who wasn't of her faith would be doomed.
- Loves to go to the desert to commune with the stars.
- Prefers a walk in the woods to gathering shells on the beach, but enjoys both.
- Is not afraid to state her opinions, but doesn't think others have to agree with her.
- Is interested in learning the Western swing.
- Dislikes square dancing.
- Likes ballet, but not opera.
- Loves the color yellow, but prefers to dress in blue.
- Likes antiques and would like to furnish her home with them.
- Prefers watercolors to oil paintings.
- Has always wanted to learn to carve wood.
- Would like to learn to scuba dive.
- Believes people should be treated with respect, and should be judged according to their character, rather than by their color, sexual orientation, or other superficial means.
- Believes that the sexes are equal, but different.
- Knows that she could be successful at several careers, such as teaching, law, journalism, or engineering.
- Sometimes fantasizes about being a ballerina; may take ballet when the kids are in school.
- Loves volunteering as a tutor.
- Will continue to take time to herself whenever possible (at least once a week)

- Hates to exercise, but will walk with husband.
- Tries to communicate dissatisfactions to her husband, but also tries not to nit-pick.
- Tries to do a random act of kindness everyday.
- Doesn't sweat the small stuff.
- Recognizes that she needs to return phone calls more pomptly ... also needs to find out why her friend hasn't called her back.
- Feels comfortable around strangers as well as friends (because she's herself!)
- Has a wide variety of friends of different ethnic backgrounds and cultures, as well as different political and religious beliefs, but confides in only three best friends (has good boundaries).
- Loves her parents, although she disagrees with many of their beliefs.
- Wants to go to Tibet someday.

You get the picture. This, as I said, is a well-integrated person who truly knows herself. She is a fantasy person and almost too perfect, but her list can give you an idea of some opinions, preferences, behaviors, and attitudes to think about. For instance, how often have you thought about what medium of art you like, or if you like ballet, or whether you *really* like to exercise? It might help you to have some knowledge of your birth parents and your heritage, but only to reflect you, not to influence you—not to turn you into yet another chameleon! And remember, even if this isn't possible for you to reunite with your birth family or it hasn't happened yet, those genes are within you. You just have to allow what they represent to surface. Besides, you won't be just like your birth relatives either. Some of the answers to the above questions will be intrinsic and some will be experiential, but they all deserve deep consideration and honesty. You have to get off the "people pleasing" train and learn to be yourself. (Note: The people who really count will be even *more* pleased!)

You know, I hate to tell you this, but most people really don't care that much about what you like or what you believe. It's the baby, stuck in the narcissistic phase of development, who thinks they do. Most people are more interested in themselves than in anyone else. If they tell you you're an idiot for voting for the party or person of your choice, then they are being verbally abusive and probably feel insecure in their own beliefs and opinions. Just as you don't have to blame others for your problems, neither do you have to believe everything they say about or to you.

We can't love you if we don't know who you are. Loving a false self is like loving a robot. "Oh yeah," you may say, "but my partner loves the person she thinks I am. What do you think she will do if she finds out that person is a fraud?" Well, contrary to your belief that you have successfully hidden your real self (which isn't as flawed as you believe it to be), the person who loves you has probably gotten a glimpse of that real self and has adored it. She is just waiting for you to stop trying to sabotage everything by doing the push/pull thing—acting out, then withdrawing—the roller coaster ride that partners of adoptees complain about. She is waiting for you to *settle into yourself.* The trouble with you is that you believe you are those coping mechanisms we've talked about. But you're not. So, stop already! Act yourself. Act your age. Allow yourself to be loved.

*This Is Only the Beginning ...*

There are other facets of becoming yourselves which will be outlined in other chapters. They have to do with responsibilities, reunions, relationships, and spirituality. This chapter is meant to get you started by making you more aware that you do truly have your own favorites, wants, needs, ideas, opinions, beliefs, and values. Treat it like a treasure hunt, because that it what it is. And you are the treasure. Good luck!

And remember: You are the only *you* in the history of the world, so make the most of you!

# CHAPTER 10
Responsibility and Power: The Road to Possibilities

---

*Men are disturbed not by things, but by the view they take of them.*
*Epictetus*

*The longer I live, the more I realize the impact of attitude on life. Attitude, to me,*
*is more important than facts. ... The only thing we can do is play on the one string*
*we have, and that is our attitude ... I am convinced that life is 10% what*
*happens to me and 90% how I react to it. And so it is with you. ... We are in*
*charge of our attitudes!*
*Charles Swindoll*

Now comes the hard part. We have discussed taking some of the steps necessary for you to become more authentic. Now it is necessary to take another step in order to give up the victim role and be yourselves. The interesting thing about becoming more authentic and empowered is that it necessitates your being willing to be vulnerable. I will explain more about this later. Let me just say that it shouldn't be that big a leap for most of you because you have been vulnerable most of your lives, even if you have tried not to be. Many actions on the parts of others have affected you deeply, whether or not you have been willing to admit it.

In fact, your reactions to the behavior of others may be out of proportion to whatever may be going on at the moment. That's because your feelings have become magnified through the lens of abandonment and loss, which causes an over-reaction to what others would consider innocuous statements or actions. For instance, *disappointment* becomes *betrayal, disagreement* becomes *rejection,* etc. Yet, when it comes to how you affect others, many of you seem oblivious. I have received myriad letters from partners or spouses who really love their adoptee partners, yet they feel as if they are constantly being hurt by them. One woman said it was like a distorted Golden Rule that went something like this: *I can do unto you that which I could never tolerate your doing unto me.* Are you going by that Golden Rule? What is it that makes you apply this double standard to your relationships?

## Recognizing the Wounded Child

Whenever there is unawareness, there is no adult present. Adults take responsibility for their actions and words. Those who refuse to take responsibility are acting like children. Many adoptees are acting from the wounded child-self rather than from the mature adult-self. Adoptees aren't the only ones who do this, and not all adoptees do it. For those of you who do, how many of you want to continue letting a three-year-old run your life?

I can defend the hurt that you adoptees, as children, have done to others because you had no awareness that you were having any effect at all. I know this seems impossible for adoptive parents to grasp. They are sure that much of the behavior they have had to endure was deliberate. But it wasn't. It was more of a desperate attempt to keep yourselves safe. Anyone really looking closely at it could see the desperation behind it. However, as adults you can no longer get by with hurtful behavior because of ignorance. Some of you have walked out of relationships without a backward glance—without ever suspecting that those you left behind were devastated. I know because I have received phone calls and letters from those who have been left behind. Most of them were quite aware that they were being placed in the role of the abandoner regardless of who left whom, yet their biggest astonishment was in how oblivious their partners were to the effect of their actions. There was a level of insensitivity that bordered on callousness. Others of you have been insensitive to your adoptive or birth parents' pain when you have ignored them or treated them badly. If you want to continue to be ignorant of your effect on others, then don't read this chapter because I am going to enlighten you. You will never again be able to hurt someone and be unaware of the impact your behavior has on another person. You will have to take responsibility for what you do. That's the price you pay for becoming more real and leaving victimhood (and childhood) behind.

## Trying to Get Mom Back

What is it that makes adoptees so unaware of their impact on others? I believe it began in those first moments after birth when you cried and cried and cried, trying to get mom to come back. No matter how much you cried, you couldn't get her back. What was imprinted in the neurological system? "*I don't matter. I'm not important. I'm impotent. I have no impact!*" Like all early imprints, this one is very difficult to dislodge. It becomes a belief that takes on even more aspects: *I am unworthy, undeserving, unlovable.* All this is a result of circumstances which neither the mother nor the child could affect. But for the adoptee, for you, it became a deeply held belief: *I do not matter, I have no impact.*

This has made life miserable for anyone who has loved you because it has resulted in a double standard. Because you have been so vulnerable (in spite of the hoopla many of you have put out there), you have been keenly aware that others have affected you. In fact, because the original wound is so sensitive, those who love you have to tiptoe delicately through a minefield in order to avoid triggering you. However, you have not even considered the idea that others may have feelings about the things that *you* do. I really don't believe that most of you want to hurt others. In personal interviews or correspondence with you, I have been cognizant of your unawareness of just how your behavior, whether overt or covert, has affected the people who love you. Perhaps there are times when you deliberately mean to hurt another, but most of the time you have been oblivious of your impact on others. That hasn't made the impact any less potent. In fact, it becomes very frustrating to the people in your lives to keep seeing the same behavior over and over without any acknowledgment of how much it has hurt.

*Avoiding Intimidation*

There are several reasons that the ignorance of your impact has been allowed to continue. One is that we, your parents, friends, and partners, have allowed it. We have been afraid to confront you with how you are affecting us. Why is this? For some it is to avoid intimidation, the fury of your wrath that anyone would dare question you. For others it is ego, not letting you know how much you are affecting us. In both cases what is happening is the belief—"I have no impact"— is being reinforced by a lack of response on the part of the injured person.

For many adoptees who are still living in the childlike self, there is often a volatile reaction to any suggestion that you should take responsibility for your behavior. This reaction often begins in adolescence if it hasn't begun before. Any reminders that you have responsibilities is met with charges that your parents are being intrusive, controlling, rejecting, etc. The problem becomes that of the parents, rather than yours. I tell about one such scene in another chapter, but I will paraphrase it here: A mother suspects her son of doing drugs and searches his room. She finds a cache of marijuana and confronts her son. He immediately turns things around and lashes out at her for "daring to invade his privacy and search his room." The tables have been turned. Now, rather than a drug problem, we have a privacy problem. It is very easy to make present-day parents feel guilty. Rather than reminding the adolescent that they are talking about his drug problem and nothing else, the parents may slink away with their tails between their legs. Parents must be strong to avoid letting this happen. There is too much "killing the messenger" when dealing with adolescents. If parents suspect their child of doing drugs, they have a right and responsibility to search his room. They are concerned about his well-being. End of discussion. As parents who have had a child die of a drug overdose say (you've seen this on TV), there are worse things than "invading your child's privacy" and experiencing the wrath that follows.

However, there are parents who, no matter how suspicious they are about certain behaviors of their children, have been afraid to even go into their child's room because they have been "forbidden" to do so! As I mention in Chapter 18 of this book, therapists are beginning to change the way they've been dealing with adolescents and have been ceasing to advocate for teenagers' privacy vs. anything else. They have been seeing more and more dangerous behavior among this age group and are more concerned about safety than about privacy. They see a real disconnect between parents and their children and are alarmed by this trend. They are more apt to try to reconnect them and support the parents' efforts to keep their kids safe than to "individuate" them. This may be especially true of adoptees, who really need to work toward being able to connect, rather than being so "independent." One thing needs to be made clear: Privacy for minors is a privilege, not a right. It is not granted *carte blanche*, but has to be earned with responsible behavior. (See Chapter 18—*Working with Families*—for more on this subject.)

Another behavior that many adoptive parents have had to endure, or at least thought they had to endure is name calling. How many mothers have been called a f—— b—— been paralyzed by this, and thus have done nothing? After yelling such an epithet, the adoptee may have gone out the door, then a few minutes later stuck her head back in and asked, "Hey, Mom. Can you take me over to Angela's?" without any hint that she realized she had just hurt her mother deeply. And what does Mom do? Well, some moms might get mad and yell and scream and call names back. However, most of the moms I have worked with have just quietly answered, "In a minute, Allison." She is afraid to confront her daughter about how hurt she was just a minute ago and wants to avoid further confrontation and intimidation.

Neither of these responses is a good one. The yelling, screaming, out-of-control mom is only reinforcing the idea that being insulting and out of control is okay. She is not modeling good behavior, but is herself being childlike. On the other hand, the intimidated, silent mom, by ignoring the effect her child has had on her, is reinforcing the belief that the child's behavior *has no impact*. A better response would be to say, "You know what, Allison? You really hurt me a minute ago and I don't feel like doing you any favors right now." Even if the daughter starts in on her about how she never wants to do anything for her and everyone else's mother is nicer than she is, yada, yada, yada, the mother needs to stick to her guns. She should follow up with a question: "Do you have any idea how much it hurts me when you call me names?" Then wait for her answer. Make her respond, because unless she is taught, she won't know that her actions and words have an impact. It takes a thousand such reminders to overcome the original imprint of *I don't matter so what I do doesn't matter*. I can't tell you how many mothers have told me that when they had finally broken down and cried at the thoughtless behavior of their children, the children were absolutely astonished. They had no idea their behavior had bothered their mothers at all. Many kids then become very repentant and affectionate. More mothers (as well as others in relation to adoptees) need to do more crying and less screaming or withdrawing. What am I saying here, adoptees? I am saying that *you have an impact on those around you and it is time to take responsibility for it.*

## The Impact on You

What about how your own behavior has affected you? Many of you have not been happy campers. You have discovered that you have been doing the same things over and over and have not been seeing very good results. Your relationships aren't working, your job seems unsatisfactory, you don't seem to be having much fun. This is especially true when it comes to relationships. What this means is that you have to begin taking responsibility for the impact you have on yourselves (stop sabotaging). What are some of the ideas to consider when trying to take responsibility for yourselves? One thing is to change. This often seems impossible. Because the old way of acting in the world is so ingrained and familiar, anything else often seems wrong. Even when the old ways are not working, it is difficult to give them up. It is very easy to confuse feeling *different* from being *wrong*. Just because something feels different, doesn't mean that it is wrong. Although some of the ideas in this chapter may seem obvious, many are more difficult to do than to say. They are all useful, however, and worth striving for. Rollo May, author and psychotherapist, defined insanity as *doing the same thing over and over, expecting different results.* Or, as Dr. Phil (McGraw) says, "If it isn't working, change it." Some of the ideas in this chapter are easier to change than others, but change is possible.

## Healing Is Your Responsibility

Healing begins with acknowledging what happened to you and knowing that you can't change that. No matter how much some of you adoptees may wish that your birth mothers hadn't given you up, or you birth mothers wish that you hadn't given up your child, this has already happened. It is part of your personal history, and you can't make it "unhappen." Sinking into regret isn't going to change things. In fact, along with fear and shame, regret paralyzes and inhibits change. Regret sometimes enters into the picture when you've been reunited and you have found siblings who weren't relinquished. You may ask, "Why couldn't I have grown up with my brothers and sisters? Why did I have to be the one given up?" Whatever the reason, it doesn't matter at this point because you have to deal with what is, not what might have been. Regret is one of those emotions which hold us back because there is no solution. It is wishing for the impossible—a rewriting of history. It is time to look ahead toward healing and hope.

It doesn't seem fair that most of the things which make relationships difficult for people are caused by events that may have happened before we were old enough to remember anything. Despite what many of you are harboring as a belief, it certainly wasn't your fault that your mother was too young or too intimidated by parents, social workers, or society to keep you and take care of you. No matter. Healing the wounds from relinquishment and other painful experiences is your responsibility. You can see what happens when your parents (birth or adoptive) didn't heal their wounds, nor their parents, etc., etc. Perhaps there are generations of alcoholics in the family, for example. The wounds of the past generations get passed down through the psychological atmosphere, attitudes, and behavior in the home. So, in addition to your own wounds, you have been exposed to those of your parents as well. To be fair to past generations, until the last third of the 20th century, many people did not think about getting psychological help for family problems. It was understood by many that psychological help was only for those with mental illness—psychosis. Family therapy did not even exist until the 1960s. However, now a wide variety of methods and formats is available. In order to safeguard your own children as well as to make your own lives more meaningful and peaceful, it is up to you to heal your wounds.

The first thing you have to do is become aware of how your wounds have impacted your lives. In his book *Men and the Water of Life*, Michael Meade says, "The way to guarantee that someone will continue to wound others is to keep him ignorant of his own wounds. The wounded wounder knows vaguely that there is a wound somewhere, but he can only see it when it appears in someone else. Wounding another makes the wound clear for a moment and seems to move the pain of it from inside the wounder to out in the world" (1993). Is it any wonder that adoptees are so good at wounding others, not to mention spotting and rescuing other wounded people? Although oblivious to their own wounds, they can easily see the wounds of someone else. Meade's description also sounds like projective identification, where the wounded sets up a scenario that makes the other person feel the pain he doesn't want to feel. These methods may work for awhile, but they are not very satisfactory and certainly not for adults. What are the questions you need to be asking yourself about how you are really feeling and how you may be projecting these feelings onto others? What are the ways in which your wounds are interfering with the way you want to live? Are your relationships loving, intimate, supportive, and reciprocal? What are your criteria for good relationships? Are you living up to those criteria?

*Acknowledgment—the Antidote to Denial*

In order to change what isn't working, it is necessary to stop denying that it isn't working. You can't change what you are not acknowledging. If you believe the relationship you are in with all its problems and turmoil is working, why aren't you happier? Do you know how many forms of verbal abuse there are, including belittling, teasing, countering, and discounting? Everyone should read Patricia Evan's book *The Verbally Abusive Relationship* to find out if you are being abused or abusing someone else. Some forms of verbal abuse are very subtle yet take their toll over time. If you are finding yourself making excuses for yourself or your partner, someone is probably being abusive. Stop denying the abuse.

After so many years of the feminist movement, I am discouraged when I hear about the number of high school girls being physically abused by their boyfriends. While we have been worrying about which pronoun to use, have we failed to teach our daughters not to accept abuse? Girls are also being sexually abused, even if they seem to be consenting to some of the more questionable sexual practices. For instance, most boys and men don't like to wear condoms while having oral sex, yet diseases can be transmitted just as readily through the mouth as through the vagina. Women are always more vulnerable sexually than men by virtue of our anatomy and biology. Many girls are being talked into questionable and dangerous sexual practices that have more consequences for them than for the boys. Both boys and girls can be harmed by anal sex, but no one seems to be talking about this. Why are children not being warned against this? Part of the answer is that the parents are also in denial about what their children are doing sexually.

What about your relationships now? Are you finding them satisfactory and beneficial, or are they unsatisfactory and burdensome? Taking a good, long look at your relationships is important to do now that you are becoming more authentic. This is scary, because if you find yourself being too dissatisfied, perhaps you will have to leave. As you grow in becoming more yourself, however, you will want to have a relationship that fits the new you, the real you. Perhaps the false self was willing to put up with some of the things you are now finding intolerable. This doesn't always mean the end of a relationship. Perhaps your partner is waiting for you to become less of a doormat. Regardless of the fear that you may have, it is important to take a realistic inventory of your relationships, try to make changes, and then decide whether to continue the relationships or not.

*Get Out of the Blame Game*

Checking with others as to your perceptions of your relationships and how you are acting in these relationships is important. You have a certain lens through which you are looking at everything. This lens may be distorting the picture so that you could use a different perspective on the subject. Are you used to blaming others for whatever happens to you? How many times a day do you say, "It wasn't my fault"? You may be right, but perhaps not.

There is a difference between blame and accountability. You can be blamed for something if you have shown reckless disregard for the consequences of your behavior. Accountability means that you are in control of the situation and take responsibility for the outcome. You should expect others to be accountable for their behavior, but you must also be accountable for yours. You can excuse yourself for all the things you did as a kid because you were reacting to pain and too young to be able to have the judgment to know how to act differently. However, as an adult who is interested in mature relationships, you can no longer afford to be unaware and irresponsible. What are some of the attitudes and behaviors that get adoptees into trouble? I will make a list of some of those that have been told to me, either by adoptees themselves or by those who have lived with or related to them. Not all these criteria will fit every adoptee, but sometimes they will fit and the adoptee won't be aware of it. That's why this list should be checked out with someone who knows you well—someone who has experienced your attitudes and behaviors and how they have affected him or her. It is important for adoptees and their loved ones to remember that *these are examples of trauma-driven attitudes and behaviors—coping mechanisms—and not personality traits.* They are coming from the wounded child, not from the mature, authentic Self. I say this because it is important not only to elicit awareness on the part of adoptees, but patience on the parts of their loved ones. These things must be acknowledged and the attitudes and behaviors changed, but change will not happen overnight. Feelings are not easy to modify, but the responses to them can be.

*Trauma-Driven Feelings, Attitudes, and Behaviors*

Someone reacting to separation trauma:
- Feels as if each parting with a significant other is an abandonment.
- Often changes his/her whole set of friends when changing partners— leaving old friends bewildered. (May be surprised that it matters to them.)
- Is afraid of intimacy and will not allow others to get very close.
- Has a double set of standards—can do certain things to others (such as borrow things without permission or make hurtful comments) that cannot tolerate others doing to him.

- Feels unimportant—having no impact. (This needs to be checked out with parents, partners, and friends!)
- Often interprets not agreeing as not listening (especially during adolescence). "You never listen to me," really means, "You are not agreeing with me."
- Keeps self secret from others, even those closest to him (perhaps especially those closest) which makes others feel as if *they* are not important to *him*. (Hint to "others": This is a projection—adoptee feels unimportant.)
- Either refuses to recognizes loss or becomes paralyzed by loss.
- Interprets disappointment as betrayal and slams the door on relationships.
- Feels guilty about things over which she has/had no control (such as separation from birth mother), yet refuses to take responsibility for things over which she could and should have some control (such as getting a speeding ticket: "It was the policeman's fault!")
- Has trouble asking for help.
- Has trouble saying "please" or "thank you."
- Always saying "I'm sorry," but inappropriately (not for real offenses—for existing?).
- Interprets not being hired after an interview as a rejection of self, rather than not being qualified for the job, or not as qualified as someone else.
- Takes everything personally—interpreting everything in terms of self. For instance, if someone fails to return a phone call, thinks it must be something she said or did, rather than realizing that the person probably has other things happening in his life, such as illness, travel, etc.
- Feels helpless in the above situation, rather than just calling again and finding out what happened.
- Tends to think in generalities, rather than in specifics: "I lost my job" becomes "the world is falling apart."
- Believes that things which are happening right now are always going to be happening or things that are not happening now will never happen. (Hopelessness: nothing is going to change.)
- Has difficulty with cause and effect—consequences not foreseen. (The future does not exist?)
- Or, conversely, believes that any misstep will be grounds for rejection.

- Will have an outburst of outrageous behavior at inappropriate times (shock value). May be a projection of the shock of losing mom, but that behavior needs to stop after age 16.
- Does not want to be controlled, but has trouble making even simple decisions.
- Feels manipulated (which may be true), but is also manipulative.
- Sabotages relationships in order to prove that he is unlovable.
- Leaves others before being left.
- Has relationships with emotionally unavailable people in order to maintain distance and feel safe, but without having to take responsibility for the distancing.
- Remains in an impossible relationship or a relationship which has run its course because he cannot bear to "abandon" anyone.
- Distrusts women.
- Won't let anyone really get to know her (for fear they'll discover the "monster" inside).
- Doesn't seem to fit in anywhere, doesn't belong.
- Paradoxically, tries to fit in by being the chameleon, agreeing with others, choosing what others choose, etc. (all strange behavior for someone who dislikes being controlled!).
- Often doesn't know what he likes, wants, or needs.
- Tends to be a rescuer.
- Is waiting to be rescued.
- Either has a strong spiritual life or none.
- Interprets mere suggestions as attempts to control.
- Behavior often oppositional as a result of the above.
- Interprets observations as criticism.
- Interprets disapproval of actions as withdrawal of love.
- Has distorted images of adoptive parents, and often birth parents as well.
- Has an intense need to blame others for own indiscretions, especially blames adoptive and birth parents, but teachers and others in authority will do.
- On the other hand, secretly blames self for own abandonment.
- Has low frustration tolerance.
- Has little impulse control.
- Anger and rage are usually out of proportion to the immediate situation.

- Fear rules life (with accompanying dangerous levels of adrenaline and cortisol wreaking havoc on the body).
- Feels and acts like a victim, having no power over events in his life (vestige of helplessness as a child, but unnecessary in adult life).
- Fears failure.
- Fears success.
- If successful, feels like a fraud.
- Has to justify existence (maybe 5 PhDs will do!).
- Feels as if doing something *differently* from what has always been done is doing something *wrong*.
- Is afraid to feel joy.
- Has to be alert for something which is about to happen.
- Interprets a request for respect and responsibility as manipulative, as if having to pay a price for acceptance, rather than as confidence in maturity.
- Longs to be intimate, but cannot risk rejection; thus lives a life without intimacy in order to avoid losing it!!??
- Uses short, curt answers in order to keep distance, but would be deeply hurt if anyone did that to him (again, the double standard).
- Fails to note the difference between intent and impact when relating to others.
- Interprets inquiries about what's happening in life (especially from parents) as intrusions, rather than interest.
- On the other hand, sometimes shows a lack of boundaries when talking to strangers, telling them more than they want to know.

I will be discussing some of these ideas in Chapters 11 and 12—*Reality Check* and *Definition of Terms*. Some of these behaviors and attitudes will be true for other trauma victims, not just those suffering separation trauma. However, none of them is an acceptable attitude or behavior for mature adults. No one who loves you has to accept difficult or tentative behavior, abusive or couched language, or vague or destructive attitudes. Besides, these are not your authentic personal attitudes and behaviors, but vestiges of archaic coping mechanisms (trauma-driven attitudes and behaviors left over from childhood). How many of you are willing to allow the wounded child to be in charge of your life forever? Another year? Another day? Another minute? She isn't real, you know. She took possession of you when you were separated from your birth mother, but she isn't real. I can find hundreds—no thousands of her in any direction I look. These attitudes and behaviors are generic to anyone having suffered early childhood trauma and are quite predictable. It is the true personality which is unique. It is the predictable and persistent trauma-driven behaviors to which many people in relationships with adoptees object and get weary of enduring. It is the true personality to which they are attracted. Yet many adoptees will allow others to see these distancing, destructive attitudes and behaviors, but be afraid to let anyone see the authentic Self. Note: *If you think that keeping yourself secret is keeping you safe, you are wrong.* Just the opposite is true. The people in your life who care about you will take the risk of learning who you really are. Quite frankly, we're all tired of having to deal with the wounded baby. We can't relate to the false self. We all want to get to know that unique person—*you.*

### The Truth About Power

Victims feel powerless. They constantly feel as if others are trying to control them. They feel as if they need to control others. They don't always have control over themselves. They mistake control for power. They mistake intimidation for power. In other words, there is a great deal of confusion about what constitutes power and who has it.

*The only person you need to have power over is yourself.* If you have true inner power, you won't feel the need to control or intimidate others. The bullies of the world are not powerful, they are pitiful. They have considerable insecurities and have to intimidate in order to feel less helpless. The boss who roars at his employees is not powerful; he is intimidating. He has to prove that he is in charge. No one who is truly in charge has to prove it. Some of you have had employers who are truly powerful. They are polite and respectful. They lead, but don't always have to be right. They welcome ideas from others. They trust you to do your work well.

One of the necessities of true power is that of true identity. Althea Horner says, "Distortions of identity lead to a loss of intrinsic power" (1989). We already know that you can't have power over yourself if you don't know who that self is. Self-knowledge is a prerequisite to power. The false self, contrary to what you may believe, is not reliable. It twists and turns as it changes in each new environment. The true self is reliable. It can be true in every situation in which it finds itself because it comes from within, rather than from external cues. It knows how to respond to each new situation because it has authenticity. It relies on intuition and insight, rather than projection. True power also depends on believing that you matter. That's one reason it is so important to check out your impact on others. You can't really be powerful without mattering, without knowing your place in the world and in other peoples' lives. And, believe me, you *do* matter. But you have to matter as adults in an adult world. It is not that the wounded inner child doesn't matter, but it can't be powerful. It will always feel helpless and fearful. The adult can matter and feel powerful, ready to give and receive. It has reverence for itself. It has self-love, so it can see others clearly. It does not always view others with suspicion. The adult can accept suggestions without feeling controlled. "Would you like to go to the movies?" is not an attempt to control you. It is an invitation to share something. I have heard many funny/sad stories about adoptees rejecting an invitation that they would really like to accept because they were afraid of being controlled. The question to ask is *"What does my adult self really want to do?* Do I want to go to the movies?" Or "Do I want to please this person because he means so much to me, even though I don't feel like going to the movies tonight?" The person making these decisions is the mature, adult, real self. The one who is afraid to say yes to others' suggestions is the scared child who needs an adult (you) in her life.

You can't ignore that scared child. You have to acknowledge how scared she is without allowing her to be in charge. You have to soothe her and say, "I know how scared you are, but I will take care of you. I am in charge now." Ignoring or becoming angry at her will only make her more and more anxious. She will become more and more insistent to be heard. Hearing her and soothing her is the way to allow your adult self to flourish. Eventually she will begin to trust that you will make good decisions. Eventually she will become less fearful. Being an adult will begin to feel comfortable; the child will grow up. You will begin to fit into your own skin.

*Authoritative Power*

There are certain positions in business, schools, and organizations which give certain people power over others. Sometimes these people are deserving of that power and sometimes they are not. Your boss has power over you. This is true whether he is a good boss or not or whether you like it or not. I know so many adoptees who have quit their jobs because they didn't want to be "controlled" by a boss they didn't respect. Or even by a boss they *did* respect. They didn't want to be controlled period. Yet that is the nature of being employed by someone else. Most of the people I know who have quit a job because of their boss have quit *many* jobs because of their bosses. In other words, it isn't about how good or bad the boss is, it is about being controlled. This is not helpful if you want to be employed. You have to find a level of freedom within the confines of an atmosphere of control. If you have any creativity, and you all do, you can manage this.

Whenever you are in a situation where you are not the boss, you will have to accept a certain amount of guidance, whether it is in the workplace, in a military service, or in an organization. If you have a real "beef" with an authority figure, it is all right to go to that person in a respectful manner and put forth your grievance. It is not all right to stomp around and complain but never say anything directly to the person in charge, nor it is all right to quit a job before exploring avenues of change that may make it more enjoyable, profitable, or well-run. If you find yourself in an intolerable situation, then you might have to look for new employment, but make sure it is the situation that is intolerable, not your fear of being controlled. Be sure it isn't a pattern. Ask yourself, "Have I done this before? Is it becoming a pattern?"

In family life, parents have power over their children. Although there have been times when families have tried to distribute the power more evenly among the parents and children, it hasn't worked very well. (I remember clearly in the early 70s when the schools tried this. It was a disaster! The kids who were in school at that time later blamed the schools for their poor education.) Children don't have the maturity and experience that their parents (or teachers) have. They can't always make informed decisions about their well-being. That's why human children live with their parents for so long. They need to be taken care of. They need guidance. Some parents, just as some bosses, are better at it than others. Some parents are neglectful or abusive. Some are just incompetent. It is very difficult for children to grow up in such a home. Parents who are neglectful, abusive, or incompetent either have not grown up or they place more value on their careers than on their families. Some are narcissistic and selfish, indecisive and chaotic, or full of self-pity or anger. In such cases, it is important for a child to find another adult whom he can trust to guide him, who can serve as a role model for adult behavior. It isn't all right to think that he is ready to guide himself. He isn't, and he shouldn't have to rely on himself to do so. It is preferable to have good parents, but in their absence there are other adults to turn to as role models and mentors. It is important to remember that there is a difference between an incompetent parent and an imperfect parent. Winnicott talks about the "good enough parent." That's all most of us hope to be. We know we can't be perfect because no one has defined that yet. Good enough parents are those who truly care about the well-being of their children and will sacrifice for them. At the same time, they will take care of their own well-being, individually and as a couple. In other words, they will find balance in their lives.

## Attributed Power

When parents don't assume their parental responsibilities, children sometimes appear to have the power. Here is where the acting-out adoptee comes in. Contrary to what many of them believe, they may have held most of the control in the dynamics of the family. Everything may have revolved around their need for proof of their existence and their subsequent acting-out behavior. Children wield a great deal of control over families, although they feel as if they are being controlled. Children who act out rule by intimidation. Although this is not true power, it seems like it to the parents who themselves feel powerless. Parents who cannot set limits for their children or who fail to teach, earn, and demand respect from them are handing over power to little beings who aren't ready for it. This is a recipe for chaos, confusion, and failure in the family. It makes children very, very afraid. It makes them feel unsafe. By virtue of their authority, parents are supposed to have formal power over their children. By this I mean mature guidance and integrity, not intimidation and negative control or abusive coercion. When the tables are turned, everyone loses.

Adult relationships is another arena where power may be given away or attributed to another. In theory, relationships should reflect interdependence and reciprocal power, neither partner having more power than the other. Sometimes, however, one partner feels subservient to the other, or the other decides he has to have more power in the relationship than his partner. In every relationship there will be a power struggle. It is part of the relationship dance, but it need not go on forever and it needs to end in a balance of power between the couple. More will be said about this in the chapter on relationships.

One of the most destructive forms of attributed power in present family life is the power people give to the company or organization for whom they work. I am not talking about giving power to the boss per se. I am talking about allowing one's occupation to take precedence over everything else including the family itself. Europeans say that they *work to live*, but Americans *live to work*. That is a crushing indictment and doesn't speak well of our values. People will say, "Well, if I don't work a 60- (or 70- or 80-) hour week, then someone else will and I will lose my job." That is true only if we as a society agree to it. In Europe, no one I know would think of giving up his 5-week vacation so that he could stay at work either to make overtime or to curry favor with the boss. No one. Europeans work their 7½-hour days and take their 5-week vacations. They spend time with their families. They enjoy their friends. They work to live, and then they really live. (Europeans have the annoying habit of copying the worst habits of Americans, so who knows how long this will last!)

*What It Means to Be Empowered*

There are several truths about being empowered. Some of them have already been discussed. No one is going to endow you with power. You have to claim it. You begin by ensuring that you *know who you are*. Go back to the previous chapter and add to the list of things which help you know who you are. The answer is deep within you. You are a product of your genetics and your environment. You can now choose the values you've learned as a child that you wish to retain, and reject those which don't fit who you really are or what you really believe. The answers you need are right there—within you.

As you learn more and more about yourself, you have to *begin acting from the authentic Self*. It doesn't do any good to know yourself if you keep that self hidden from others. This doesn't mean that you have to convince everyone that you are right about everything. You might not even agree with yourself a few years from now! Not everyone will be on the same page as you. This does not mean people don't like you. This is a difficult lesson for adoptees because so many of you fear being rejected and you may be mistaking disagreement for rejection. It is important to keep in mind that everyone has his own reality. Not everyone sees the world in the same way. It isn't important for others to see your version of the world. What is important is that *you know what your version is.* By that, I mean your adult version, not the scared-child version. We know the scared-child version is distorted. It hasn't served you very well in your relationships so far. It is time to find and act from the adult version of your world view.

Speaking of world view, remember that *reality is really perception.* What may be reality for you may not be for someone else. Everyone grows up in a certain culture and has her own experiences in life. Your perceptions of those experiences, *the meaning that you gave them,* not only had a great deal to do with how your neurological connections were made (how you are wired), but how you see the world. Some people believe the world is safe, others believe it's dangerous. It depends upon your perceptions of your early experiences. Even children reared in the same households do not perceive their lives the same way. You have a specific filter through which you view the world, and each and every person has his own filter. These filters are like fingerprints or snowflakes—no two are alike. Therefore, it should not be a big surprise if everyone does not agree with you. The meanings others gave to their life experiences were different from yours, even if they grew up in the same household. This should make those who disagree with you or disappoint you a little less threatening. It should also make it easier to take things less personally. Acknowledging different realities can make life much, much easier. It makes room for individual power, because your inner power doesn't have to depend upon others agreeing with you.

Another aspect of your life which needs *acknowledging* is your *vulnerabilities*. You cannot become powerful if you get sabotaged by the vulnerabilities that you are failing to acknowledge. Once you acknowledge your vulnerabilities, you can begin to challenge whether or not they are currently genuine or vestiges of your childhood. Do they exist in your adult life, or are many of them memories of the helplessness of childhood? We all have vulnerabilities. We cannot be powerful without knowing and acknowledging them. Without vulnerabilities, we cannot have empathy. Without empathy we cannot have power. Remember that power comes from within. Not knowing our vulnerabilities makes us subject to being blindsided. Being blindsided doesn't feel very powerful. But what may have been a threat of annihilation in infancy, may not be so now. Those of you waiting for some dreadful thing to happen need to realize that it already did and it never can again. You can be left by someone, but you will never be as helpless as you were as a baby. As an adult you have resources, support, and inner strength.

*You must stop allowing the fearful, inner child to rule your life.* Please repeat after me: "I will no longer allow my fearful, inner child to rule my life." Without having to shut her out or ignore her, you can leave her out of the decision-making process. You can listen, validate, and then assure her that, although you hear her fear, your adult self will take care of her. Acknowledging her is not the same as allowing her to tell you how to conduct your life. She has ruled for too long. It is time for the adult to take over her care. The key is to become more aware of when she is taking over and when you are being more adult. If you are becoming whiny, angry, and oppositional, or fearful, sullen and withdrawn, then the child is probably in charge.

*The antithesis of power is helplessness.* Remember the three warning signs of helplessness: *permanence,* where it seems as if things will never change; *pervasiveness,* where individual problems become global catastrophes; and *personalization,* where everything is about you. If you find yourself caught in the web of any of these signs, challenge your perception, demand evidence that it is true or not true, find alternatives that may be just as true, and then use an intervention to take care of the real problem. You have it within you to meet the challenges of your life, but it is important to ascertain what those challenges really are as seen from your adult perspective.

*Become realistic about control.* What are the things over which you really do have control? Paying your bills on time, driving carefully, getting to work on time and doing your best when you get there, taking time for your family—these are all things over which you have control. Sometimes you may have to make an extra effort to do some of the things that others find easy. For instance, an adoptee I know tells me that she used to be "chronologically impaired." In other words, she had a hard time getting anywhere on time because time didn't seem to have the same meaning for her as it does for others. It is true that trauma can cause a distortion in time. However, the trauma happened a long time ago. If necessary, you may have to make a special effort to make sure you arrive places on time such as buying a watch with an alarm.

You didn't have any control over anything that happened to you in the first three years of your life, and not much in the next few years after that. It is time to stop beating yourself up about this. If you feel you want to apologize to someone about your childhood behavior, go ahead. But much of it was beyond your control. How do I know? Because it was so predictable. It was trauma-driven coping behavior and unconscious. However, now you can and must gain control over behaviors that are detrimental to your well-being and that of your loved ones. Practice the wisdom in the Prayer of St. Francis: *Give me the strength to take responsibility for the things I can control, the ability to give up control over those that I can't, and the wisdom to know the difference.* You can't control whether or not there will be an earthquake, but you can control your response to it. Will you become sullen and paralyzed or energized and helpful? It is up to you. We can't change certain circumstances of our lives, but we can change our attitudes and our responses to them.

Part of having control over yourself is to *take responsibility for your words and behavior.* Have you ever counted the number of times in a day that you say or do something you regret? Do so. Count them. Does anyone hold you in higher esteem because of them? Do you? When you lash out at your husband or scream at the children or kick the dog, do you feel powerful? I didn't think so. What about the times you didn't speak up for yourself when someone falsely accused you of something? Are you angry at him or at yourself for being so unassertive? If you allow yourself to continue behaviors that you later regret, you will be postponing your ability to empower yourself. Please notice your effect on those around you. Remember, you do have an impact and must take responsibility for it. Don't forget to count those passive-aggressive things you might be doing: being chronically late for appointments, dates, or meetings; ignoring people who speak to you; procrastinating about things you don't like to do; or other inactions that cause inconvenience or hardships for others. People who exhibit passive-aggressive behavior are people who feel powerless. It is an insidious way of controlling others. It is true, if I have to wait around for you I won't be able to make good use of that time. But do I think of you as powerful? No, I think of you as inconsiderate. Being passive-aggressive means controlling others by what you *don't* do. You don't need to control others; you only need to control yourself. That will be a big enough challenge.

Powerful people are people with integrity *who give and expect courtesy, dignity, and respect.* You are neither powerful if you treat others poorly nor if you allow others to treat you poorly. Power demands respect, but it also gives respect. Remember that neither intimidation nor control over others is powerful. You can see a serene quality about people who are truly powerful. They radiate inner peace as well as inner power. And no one questions it. It is too obvious. It is inclusive. It harbors no prejudices. It makes no enemies. It is considerate of others without caring what they think because the consideration comes from respect, not from the need to be liked. It is unselfish, demonstrating true humility. With genuine inner power, you can be at home having a meal with the homeless under a bridge or in a castle with the queen of England. It is a truly liberating experience.

*Being true to yourself* and taking care of yourself are necessary if you want to have power. You must *do what is in your own best interest,* at the same time being sure that you are *not harming others.* It is never in your best interest to act to the detriment of others. This introduces guilt, and guilt interferes with power. Know what you want and take the steps to get it. Don't wait around for it to drop into your lap. This probably won't happen. If you take care of yourself, you will be able to give to others. This necessitates your knowing what you want specifically, not some generalized mumbo jumbo. If you constantly feel frustrated by your life, you won't be able to give to others. But make sure that what you want is really what *you* want and not what you believe others think you *should* want. If what you want seems unrealistic as a way of life or a profession, then introduce it into your life in some other way such as an avocation or hobby. Perhaps you think you don't have time for the many things you want to do in life. If they are really important to you, you can find a way to make them fit. For instance, you can realize these things sequentially or consecutively rather than simultaneously—take a painting class one year and sing in a chorus the next. Make use of your talents and skills. When it comes to your emotional health, you must be specific about what you need and how others can help you get it.

In Don Miguel Ruiz' book *The Four Agreements,* he lists the first agreement as *being impeccable with your word.* This is so powerful. How can you have power if you are dishonest, equivocal, or evasive? Here is what he says: "Speak with integrity. Say only what you mean. Avoid using the word to speak against yourself or to gossip about others. Use the power of your word in the direction of truth and love" (1997). Being impeccable with your word also means honoring your agreements. Don't promise things you can't deliver. It is better to say, "Let me think about that," than to say, "Yes," then break your world. Saying what you mean does not mean being brutal or needlessly "honest" and wounding the psyches of others. Having tact is a good quality because it shows sensitivity toward others. Ask yourself what your motivation is before giving yourself permission to speak your word. Integrity is the key. Finding a tactful way of saying something is as important as what it is you say. "Have you ever thought of doing it this way?" is a better way of criticizing a person's work than, " You idiot! That's ridiculous! What ever made you think that would work?" And did you notice what Ruiz says about not speaking against yourself? How many of you run negative tapes in your head about yourselves? This is a real anti-power agent.

*Avoid making assumptions,* or, to be more realistic, *check out your assumptions.* People make assumptions all the time. Assumptions can be the ruination of relationships. They take on a life of their own. Because we all have different perceptions (realities), we don't all interpret things the same way. On top of this we may be projecting onto others. There are many, many reasons we may misinterpret one another. Then, why is it that we believe we understand without asking questions, without checking things out? The majority of couples' relationships could be salvaged if each partner would stop making assumptions, begin to check out what they believe, and ask questions to clarify the other's position. Too many people make an assumption then ride off into the sunset with it, reacting without ever checking on their interpretation of another's feelings, words, or actions. Now, everyone makes assumptions, and no one is going to discontinue doing so altogether. But the idea is to check out whatever you assume the other person said, or their motivation for what they did, or what their feelings really are. Do not react before you know. You cannot be powerful when you are riding off into the sunset upon the back of a wrong assumption.

A trigger from the old wound can leave you feeling powerless and reactive. If you feel *overwhelmed by a trigger*, try to stop yourself from reacting and ask, "What am I *doing?*" Then stop to consider, "What am I *feeling?*" And last ask, "What do I *believe?*" You will be asking the questions in the reverse order of how you got to the point of reacting the way you did: A *belief* triggers a *feeling* which triggers a *behavior or action*. You may *believe* that someone insulted you. You *feel* angry or hurt. You *lash out* with an x-rated comment or *sink into* a depressed mood. If you have true inner power, even if someone does try to insult you, you don't have to allow yourself to be insulted. Others' actions and words can hurt you only if you believe them. What people do and say have more to do with them than with you. You can avoid taking those kinds of comments personally and remain serene.

What if you trigger a strong reaction in others? If people get excited about something you said or did and want to lash out at you, it usually means they are feeling a lot of pain about it. People don't get all charged up about things that don't touch them personally. You can respond to their outburst by saying something like, "You seem to be having strong feelings about this. Do you want to say more about how it is affecting you?" If you don't get defensive or tell them they are wrong, they usually calm down and you can have a discussion about what it was that was so painful to them. It helps not to take things personally and not to expect everyone to agree with you. *You* get triggered by things people do and say. *You have to realize that other people do too.*

When dealing with triggered feelings, it is important to remember to *respond to situations, rather than feelings.* Remember from reading chapters 1 and 2 about Trauma and the Brain, the slightest suggestion of an old situation can trigger a feeling. Sometimes a person will say or do something that reminds our amygdala of an old wound. Instead of reacting to the triggered feeling, ask yourself, "Is this feeling appropriate to the situation I'm in right now, or is it out of proportion to what's going on?" Often, the intensity of the feeling will be inappropriate to the present situation. Therefore, it would be unfair to whoever is in that situation with you for you to react as if it were the old situation. This takes practice because that little amygdala can get overzealous in its need to protect you from a repeat of the pain of the original situation. It is up to you to use your power and control to ascertain the true nature of each situation and then respond appropriately.

*Summary*

You can see how power and responsibility are connected. It all hinges on your being more true to yourself. It means living the paradox of vulnerability and strength. It means taking the risk to change. It means changing your attitudes toward yourself, others, and life events. Remember what Charles Swindoll said in the introduction to this chapter: "We are in charge of our attitudes!" How long are you going to allow your present attitudes toward life keep you in a prison of negativity?

Making changes can be daunting, but if your life is not going the way you want it to, why not risk it? Change is demanding and takes courage and commitment. You can choose to remain where you are in the various aspects of your life or you can choose to change. If you choose to do nothing, remember *this is a choice* you are making. All choices have consequences. Retaining your old habits and thinking patterns will have consequences. You already know what some of these are. They are being dictated by old, false beliefs that are obsolete and crippling your adult life. Stop giving yourself excuses, rationalizations, and justifications for what is going wrong in your life. Take responsibility. It is time to stop blaming your birth mother, your adoptive parents, your partner or spouse, or anyone else. Whatever they did has affected you, but that is history. The healing is up to you. It takes effort, it takes commitment, it takes persistence, it takes patience. In the long run, you will be happier and so will those who love you.

# CHAPTER II
Reality Check

---

It is difficult to take responsibility for your behavior when you are oblivious to how others are perceiving your actions. In order to change, you have to begin to understand the wounded child and how he or she is taking over and affecting others. That child may feel invisible and totally incapable of affecting others. A reality check is definitely in order, because, contrary to those baby beliefs, you have a tremendous impact on those who love you.

In order to get started, I would like to expand upon some of the attitudes and behaviors which were created by a belief system formed right after birth. Unfortunately, it is my observation that many of you have not changed the beliefs which were imprinted or encoded during that early period. This is understandable when one understands the consequences of trauma. Nevertheless, those beliefs are not helping you in your relationships. The attitudes and behaviors mentioned previously were predicated upon those early, untrue, and archaic beliefs which are still dictating the way you live your lives. It is time for a reality check. Each of you will need someone with whom to do this. You cannot do it alone. (Sometimes others see us more clearly than we see ourselves.)

Not all beliefs can be changed simply by awareness. Some are perceived more as sensations and feelings than as attitudes and beliefs and are so entrenched that they are difficult to change. However, the attitudes and behaviors I will be talking about are those which can and should be changed, even if the sense is that it won't matter. It does matter to the people who mean the most to you, and it is essential that you take responsibility for the impact your behavior has on those people. Remember that in order to have power, you have to take responsibility for your actions.

## The Double Set of Standards

The first is the *double set of standards*. Many of your parents and partners have told me that interacting and talking with you is like walking through a mine field. They never know when they are going to step on one of those long-buried mines and set off an explosion of anger or an implosion of withdrawal. Even after years of living with you, there are still sensitive areas which get triggered with an explosion of rage, hostility, or indignation or a veil of silence, rejection, and disapproval. There is a sense in each case that you are feeling rejected, even though the person acting or speaking neither intended to hurt nor reject you, nor understands how you perceived it that way. Often there is no way to talk about this, because you are closed to opening it up to discussion, sure that you are right. Communication is closed!

On the other hand, you can, with impunity, say or do exactly the same thing to your loved ones and not have any qualms about it at all. You give the impression that nothing you do matters, so the other person will not be affected by it. This is where the reality check needs to come in. Really observe the other person's response to your action or comment. This is not to make you feel guilty. As one who has observed this phenomenon, I believe in most cases there is no intent to harm. Yet you really need to check out just what your *impact* truly is, because others are deeply hurt by some of the things you do and say.

Where does this come from, this strange idea of your impotence in matters dealing with people important in your life? As I mentioned in the previous chapter, I believe it comes from that very first imprint of helplessness you experienced as an infant when no amount of protesting (crying) could bring mommy back. This is called learned helplessness. The imprint upon your neurological system was: "I am ineffective, helpless, impotent, invisible, don't matter. I cannot affect the person I need the most." You gave up hope of changing the situation. Not only does this make you feel helpless in any number of situations (read Martin Seligman's *Learned Helplessness* or *Learned Optimism*), but it makes you feel as if you have no impact upon the people most important in your life. Whereas you know that you are deeply affected by any slight or perceived slight perpetrated upon you, you have no idea that others are also deeply affected by you. Please believe me when I say *you have a great deal of influence upon those with whom you are most intimately connected.*

To check this out, you will have to go all the way back to your childhood in your adoptive family. As impotent as you may have felt in your family, you had a tremendous impact on the family dynamics. And you have a tremendous impact on the feelings of those with whom you are in relationship today. You cannot trust your own feelings about this because they are based on a false belief. It is vitally important that you keep checking this out, because you may sometimes be quite insensitive and sometimes even cruel in your attitudes and behavior towards those you love. Many times I have heard adoptees tell me that if someone did to them what they just did to their partner, they'd be "out of there." *It is time to take responsibility for that and put a stop to it!* Remember, part of getting rid of the victim mentality is to take responsibility for your actions and their effect on others.

The other thing that you must do is listen when others apologize for stepping on one of your many landmines. The feeling which is triggered for you may have nothing to do (or very little to do) with the situation at hand. If you find yourself getting very hurt or overly angry at something someone did to you, check it out. You cannot simply cut off everyone who inadvertently offends you, because we all do this sometimes. It is time to question your own perceptions of the intentions of others. *It is time to apply the same set of standards to yourself that you apply to others.*

### Being Controlled by the Fear of Being Controlled

Being controlled by others is a fear many of you adoptees experience. This results in what appears to be oppositional behavior as children and stubbornness as adults. The fact that the feeling for you is much more intense than anyone can imagine—that it feels like a matter of life or death that you not comply with whatever the other person is proposing—is never understood by the person making the suggestion. He or she just feels perplexed by the vehemence of the response to the suggestion. This response, too, is probably a result of having not been in control when unseen forces separated you from your mother. Never again do you want anyone to have that kind of control over your life. It was devastating, and you have been hypervigilant ever since to ensure that it doesn't happen again. Of course, nothing so devastating can ever happen again, but it *feels* as if it could. The trauma has generalized and become separated from the event which gave rise to the belief: If I let someone else control me, I can be annihilated.

The tragedy is that even as you ensure that you are not being controlled by that other person, *you are not in control*, at least not the adult person you see in the mirror. You are being controlled instead by your fear of being controlled—by the little scared child inside, who is still in the grips of the fear of that first loss. How many of you have refused to do something you really would like to do because someone else suggested it? Ah, ha! Thought so!

I remember a woman named Alice who told me about the day her husband suggested that the family go on a picnic to the park. It was a beautiful day, and the kids really wanted to go. She said, "No, I need to clean the house. I really don't think I can go." "Oh, come on," said her husband. "The kids and I will help clean the house when we get home." "No," she repeated, "I really don't think it is possible for me to go today." All the while she was telling me this, she was laughing at herself. She realized how ridiculous it sounded, because she really had wanted to go. She just felt she couldn't. And it wasn't just a feeling of being stubborn and difficult. It wasn't just that she wouldn't. She really did feel as if she couldn't. *It felt important not to.*

The problem with this is that she wasn't really being controlled by her husband, who only wanted the family to have a nice outing. She was being controlled by her fear of being controlled. She was being controlled by that *enfant terrible* known as the generic traumatized child. Alice had nothing to do with it. Alice wanted to go, but she was held hostage by that infant self.

The key to this kind of dilemma is to ask yourself (as you hear yourself rejecting a suggestion, plan, or idea), "What do I want to do?" Not what is the baby afraid of, but what does the mature, adult person I am want to do? You can, at the same time, acknowledge the baby's fear. (It is best not to ignore it; the protests will only get louder.) But ultimately, you need to do the mature, responsible thing. After all, giving in to the fearful child is not freedom. It is a trap and keeps you from doing many of the things you might otherwise enjoy doing.

### The Appearance of the Chameleon

The paradoxical thing about the fear of being controlled is that it is in direct opposition to two things: the difficulty in making decisions and the need for approval. This is a real dilemma. The very person who cannot go on a picnic with her husband might have a difficult time ordering from a menu in a restaurant before anyone else. After all, what if she makes a mistake! What if she orders prawns and everyone else orders chicken? What will they think of her? As ridiculous as this may sound, this problem exists in tandem with the fear of being controlled.

As children, many adoptees aren't able to get ready for school if their mothers tell them what to do. Of course, they don't do it without being told either, so they are setting up a situation which is lose/lose all around. "I can't decide what to wear, but I won't be able to wear anything you suggest." As a daily routine in the mornings, this can get old pretty fast! But it goes on in many families day after day, year after year. It continues into high school where a student is not doing his homework, but will not be able to do it when the parents, finally frustrated by their child's lack of initiative, suggest that it is getting late and it might be a good idea to get started. This, in addition to a deficit in understanding consequences, makes the school years a nightmare for some parents and their children.

As adults, this phenomenon translates into a lack of initiative and difficulty in making decisions about a host of things. Coupled with the need for approval, we get the chameleon—someone who tries to fit into every situation by taking note of the prevailing atmosphere and by agreeing with others, having no distinct opinions or ideas. He goes to the movies others choose, eats what everyone else is eating, acts as if he has the same political opinions as others, etc., etc. He may seem "nice," but there is nobody home. Again, it is the scared child who is making an appearance. The adult, with ideas, opinions, and suggestions of his own is nowhere to be found. Sometimes the adult doesn't even know what his opinions are; sometimes he is afraid to voice them. In neither case is he allowing anyone the chance to get to know him ... even himself!

What needs to be checked out here is the reality of your perceptions. How many people do you think really care whether you order prawns or chicken? Just ask, "How many of you would be upset if I order prawns?" Put that way, I'm sure you see the absurdity of the situation. But it felt real, didn't it? Many of you will say you don't know what you like. You have spent so many years trying to figure out what others expect of you, beginning with your adoptive family, that you haven't figured out what the real person inside likes, thinks, or believes. Try asking—asking yourself, that is. Say, "Joe" (meaning you), "what do you feel like eating tonight?" Trust me, no one else will care!

### "You're Not Listening to Me!"

Many feelings of rejection which adoptees experience are a result of their misinterpreting what is said or done. For instance, something which adoptive parents of adolescents hear all the time is "You're not listening to me!" This mantra sometimes continues into adulthood within conversations between husbands and wives. What the adoptee is actually experiencing is that someone is not *agreeing* with him. Because he is so closely identified with his ideas and opinions and needs so much to be validated, he tends to interpret not agreeing with not listening. *Attention adoptees: If someone is answering you, they are listening.* They may not be agreeing, but this doesn't mean they have forsaken you. It just means they are interpreting what you are saying through a different filter or lens, which we all do. Just because you believe that you have to agree with the prevailing wisdom doesn't mean everyone does. *Stop saying that people aren't listening when they are simply disagreeing.*

We all see things differently, depending on our experiences. Our experiences determine our frame of reference. They give each of us a different perception of the world and the people and events in it. There are no absolute realities about life events. There are only perceptions, individual realities. This is true both intellectually and psychologically. Our belief systems help form our realities. These may be skewed because of early trauma. Whereas you may experience the world (and especially relationships) as dangerous because of your early experiences, I may experience it as safe and enjoyable because of mine. It is important to allow for these differences as we interact with others because otherwise we will always be disappointed in others and feel personally rejected. It would be arrogant to expect that everyone experiences the world as we do. We can all find valid "proof" of our points of view in myriad examples from life. It is important to check out other people's viewpoints, because it can expand our frame of reference and make us less afraid.

In speaking of these separate realities as it involves couples' work, it can be freeing to understand this dynamic. This understanding can create an atmosphere for expanding one's world view. Couples come into their relationship having had different experiences. This will create in each person a specific perspective on the world. Being in a relationship allows us to explore another's world view with someone whom we trust more than others. This gives us an opportunity to expand our perspectives. Yet in order to do so we need to see how our individual thought systems have created our perspective on the world. We then know that this is true for others as well. This can make us feel less threatened or rejected when someone disagrees or is disappointed with us because, recognizing beliefs as a result of past experiences and conditioning, we understand the inevitability of this dynamic. Understanding the nature of biases, beliefs, opinions, and philosophies of life allows us to take things less personally. This understanding is absolutely necessary if one is to be successful in relationships. When separate realities are not understood, differences in opinions can be interpreted as rejection.

## Support Does Not Require Agreement

Because we all have our own filters through which we create our realities, it is safe to say that we will not all agree with one another on everything. This does not mean that we cannot be supportive of another's point of view. Any therapist knows this. We need to validate our patients' perceptions because that is the basis for their feelings. Those feelings are real, even if the beliefs which precipitated them are not. Slowly but surely, we want to eventually change the false beliefs which cause unwanted feelings, feelings which are no longer helpful to the people we are seeing. But first it is necessary to validate that the feelings make a great deal of sense in light of their experiences and the attitudes formed from those experiences.

This can be true in personal relationships as well. Some people believe that if you haven't experienced the same thing or have the same attitudes towards it, you can't be supportive. This idea would spell the end of relationships, because even when two people experience the same thing, they often interpret it differently. Just ask siblings about what it was like growing up in their family. You will get a different response from each one. It isn't as if there aren't certain things they will be able to agree upon, but their attitudes and beliefs about the events—*the meaning they gave to them*—can be worlds apart. Even their memories may differ. Because each interpreted what happened differently, what seemed important to remember will vary. It is like the story of several blind people describing an elephant—it depends on what part of the elephant they are able to feel.

What is required for support? It is important to listen intently to the other person, recognize the effect the event is having on her, and empathize with her feelings. If your best friend's husband has just left her, even though you know that she gave him a hard time sometimes, it is important to listen and empathize with how this loss is affecting her. The events leading up to the separation were not happening to you, so there is no way that you will be feeling the same way your friend is feeling. If you have had a similar experience, of course it will be easier to empathize, because you will be able to access those feelings of loss yourself. However, it is not necessary to experience the same thing to be supportive.

If you are the one who has just experienced a loss, don't discount your friend's support just because she has not had the same experience. Or if it is a matter of talking about an argument you've had with your partner and you know that your friend has some doubts that it is entirely your partner's fault, don't discount whatever support she may be offering. It is unnecessary to assign fault to what is going on in any situation. If your friend refuses to agree with your blaming your partner for everything, that's okay. She can still be supportive of your feelings. It may be disappointing to you that she doesn't agree wholeheartedly with you, but this is not a betrayal. Accept her support; you need it!

*The Closed Door Syndrome*

Exaggerating a simple disappointment into a sense of betrayal is another way in which adoptees sometimes sabotage themselves. I've mentioned the landmines which people dealing with adoptees are forever stumbling upon. Sometimes, stepping on those mines can mean the end of a relationship. Inadvertently someone may do or say something which makes the adoptee feel betrayed, even though there was no intention to betray on the part of the perpetrator. He may have disappointed his friend in some way, but the "sin" is rarely bad enough to warrant a total rejection. Yet this happens more often than one might think. Adoptees often have a hair trigger for rejection and interpret many innocuous acts as a betrayal. This is quite unfair to the other person, as well as to the adoptee himself, because it can mean the end of a friendship that doesn't really need to end.

What to do? Well, you adoptees have to ask yourselves why the person would have wanted to betray you. Then check it out with her. You can say, "What you did really hurt me. Did you mean to do that?" Talk it over *in a mature manner*. Again, it is important not to let the child be in charge. Most of the time you will discover that the problem was simply a misunderstanding which can easily be rectified. If something really is irreconcilable, then at least you tried to straighten it out. You can feel proud of yourself.

I experienced a situation like this. A friend of mine had lost both of her parents in an automobile accident when she was fifteen. This, too, is interpreted by the psyche as an abandonment. Several years ago, she and I had a misunderstanding of a professional nature. For some reason, she interpreted something I said as a betrayal of some kind, and slammed the door on our friendship. All my efforts to talk it over with her were to no avail. She wouldn't take my phone calls, sent back my letters unopened, and refused to discuss it at all. This was a therapist who was in the business of helping couples learn to communicate. And she was a very good therapist. Let me make that clear. Yet she could not apply to her own life that which she could teach others, because the "betrayal" of her parents' dying in that crash kept getting repeated over and over in her life. I am sorry the friendship ended. It was completely unnecessary, and I still care about her.

The point for anyone who has experienced such a loss to understand is that people do things which they don't know will be magnified from a small misunderstanding or indiscretion into a huge betrayal. If you've shut someone out of your life, think about it. Was it worth it? You have to understand that you have a much lower tolerance for differences than most people. This is a problem for you, one that you need to address. Is there someone out there you really liked to whom you no longer speak? Why not give them a call? (Don't think they've forgotten you! That's a different issue.) Tell them that you over-reacted, that you'd like to talk things over. If they are too hurt by your rejection of them to reconcile, take this as a lesson that dismissing people from your life too quickly and without "due process" is hurtful and mystifying to others, and may needlessly end basically good friendships.

### Keeping Myself Secret Is Keeping Myself Safe

Many adoptees believe that if they can continue to ascertain from their environment how they should be and not allow anyone to know the dark secret of who they truly are, they will be safe. Because as children they had no external reference (no mirroring or reflection of genetic traits and markers) for who they are, many of them still assume that they are some kind of monster who was rejected by their mothers. It is therefore imperative that no one discover the existence of this monster. Thus we have the false self, the chameleon, or the wounded child instead of a mature, reasonable, adult human being to relate to.

As I mentioned earlier, most of us would rather take our chances with the "monster" than have to continue to experience the emptiness of the false self, the unreliability of the chameleon, or the emotional roller coaster of the wounded child. There is nothing safe (for you or for us) about any of them. (Remember the landmines!) We cannot honestly relate to any of those adaptations. They are not real. They have no place in mature relationships.

We know that because your trauma happened before you had a Self (at least for most of you), you honestly don't know that Self either. You are hiding it from yourself as well as from us. However, by doing so *you are abandoning yourself.* You are repeating the trauma which so wounded you in the first place! Stop, already!! I will leave it to you to use the exercises in Chapter 9 to step by tiny step explore your genetic, mature, authentic self. If you aren't annihilated when you order a different kind of ice cream than everyone else, take another risk tomorrow.

Allowing those who love you, and eventually other people, to know your genetic, authentic Self does not mean that you cannot have privacy in your life. There is a difference between secrecy and privacy. It is a matter of understanding and establishing boundaries with people. (Learning how to establish and maintain healthy boundaries will be discussed in Chapter 13.) Despite the fact that you are secretive, you often have a poor understanding of appropriate boundaries. You may either be withholding and stingy with your emotions and attitudes, or you may exhibit inappropriate behavior as a result of crossing boundaries. Some of that behavior can be terribly inappropriate to the point of being shocking. There may be a compulsion to say or do something outrageous (to make everyone around as uncomfortable as you may be feeling?).

Although the person who is constantly crossing other people's boundaries may seem more genuine, neither she nor the withholding person is real. Both are being secretive because both are defending against the authentic Self, which they believe to be flawed, unworthy, and unlovable. Attention adoptees: Please believe me when I say that we would all rather relate to your authentic Self than to the wounded child. As adults, we really can't relate to that child and maintain a mature relationship (such as marriage, partnership, or genuine friendship). Take the time to observe who it is that is getting you into trouble in your relationships. Is it really your true Self, or is it the child? (And also remember that the child was never authentic either, even when you *were* a child. It has always been responding to your trauma and to having to adapt to a non-genetic family.) You have never had an authentic childhood and you never will, but why not at least give yourselves a chance to have an authentic adulthood? Why continue the falseness and deception into your adult relationships? Do you want to end your lives *never* having been real? Please don't deprive us and don't deprive yourselves. (I know you have been unaware, at least some of you, that you have not been genuine, so you are not to blame. But now that you know, it is time to so something about it.)

*"I'm Sorry!"*

Although it may be difficult to get an adoptee to take responsibility for some of her actions, there is a mantra that one often hears when interacting with her: "I'm sorry!" Now, this is not said at appropriate times when she has actually offended someone, but is like a filler such as "you know" thrown seemingly indiscriminately into conversations. It is perplexing to the person having a conversation with her, because we are never sure what she is apologizing for. There doesn't seem to be anything specific to apologize for at the time, yet there is that ubiquitous "I'm sorry." I finally forbade a woman I used to converse with in New York from uttering those words.

There are times when we might want to hear "I'm sorry," such as after a hurtful remark or deed. But that is seldom when we hear it. Hurtful remarks seldom register on the conscience of adoptees, because, as I said earlier, they feel they have so little impact on us that they don't need to apologize. No, it is at unexpected times that the "I'm sorry" comes, and it is my guess that the adoptee is unconsciously apologizing for her existence—as if she is a mistake and has no right to be here.

Adoptees, pay attention! Most of you had the experience of separation from your birth mothers because of societal norms at the time of your birth. You are not a mistake. You don't have to apologize for your existence. You have as much right to be here as anyone else. There are many famous people in history who could be considered "illegitimate." Remember that this is a legal term and means nothing spiritually. It just means that some men, usually men in power, could weasel out of taking responsibility for their actions, actions which resulted in the miracle of a new life. These men were so cowardly that they not only refused to take responsibility for this beautiful new life, but then attached labels to the innocent newborn and his mother, names which are now used derogatorily as insults.

If you continue to feel like a mistake, perhaps this just gives you an excuse to remain a victim and not take your place in history. Taking your place in history doesn't mean that you have to do something heroic. It just means that you need to take responsibility for finding out who you truly are and for having conscious control in the areas of your life over which you can have control. It means being respectful of others and expecting respect *from* others. It means having integrity and dignity. It means learning how to love and be loved. We all have a place in history, and we all have an effect on other people. John Donne said: "No man is an island entire of itself; every man's death diminishes me." We are all connected; we all affect one another.

*Fear of Change*

Often when adoptees try to change a habit or pattern in their behavior, they stop after a time or two because it feels wrong to them. The reason we keep doing the things we do, even if they are not working, is that they are familiar to us. When we try something new, it just doesn't feel right. It's unfamiliar. This can happen even when our rational minds tell us the feeling is crazy. For instance, if you have been the one to end your relationships in an insensitive way but a way in which you feel as if you are in control, then changing and having a mature discussion with your partner and coming to a mutually agreeable arrangement may seem wrong. This may be true, even though your adult self and your friends all know that this is the mature way to handle the situation. It will begin to feel as if your partner took advantage of you, as if you were not ultimately in control. Of course the truth is that the mature, adult self was much more in control than if you had just walked out without any explanation after an argument. The person in control during one of those altercations in which you self-righteously walk out of the room and out of your partner's life is the scared child. In therapy this is called acting out and is not a mature way to handle anything, although it certainly can give you an adrenaline rush at the time. For a short time, it feels just wonderful.

After awhile, however, old doubts begin to come up. "Did I do the right thing? I feel so lonely now." That grand gesture has been brought back to a reasonable size and seen to have been rather impulsive. Many of the actions adoptees take are impulsive because impulse control is not high on their list of achievements. Although being impulsive may be an outcome of trauma, it needs to be reined in. I know just how frightening it can be to make big changes, so remember what I told you about taking baby steps in making changes in your life. Of course, deciding whether or not to remain in a relationship is a big decision and should not be decided on an impulse. But in order to do it differently, it is necessary to have practiced with other, less crucial decisions.

The idea of something's feeling wrong because it is different needs to be checked out over and over. "What is wrong with this?" you need to ask yourself. Take a step back and review the scene as if someone else were starring in it. What would you think then? Can you picture this scene? *Your best friend has just had an argument with his partner and walks indignantly out of the room, telling her that he's had it; he's leaving. Later she calls him and begs him to reconsider, to talk it over. He is adamant, still riding high on adrenaline, feeling as if he is really in control and showing her!* How would you advise this guy? Since the scene is no longer about you, can you see that while the thing she did which set your friend off was disappointing, it need not be fatal to the relationship? Doesn't he come off as sort of a jerk? Do you feel the helplessness of his partner as she tries to reason with such a jerk? Don't you wonder why she would even want to be with him? Ah, ha! Now we are coming to the crux of the thing. Now you can see that this guy, this jerk isn't worth being with. And this jerk is you. You always suspected as much. You are not worth loving and you have just proven it. I'm a jerk, unlovable, not worth staying in a relationship.

Well, let me burst your bubble. Your friend's behavior is certainly less than ideal, and looking objectively at the scene, it certainly does seem as if the woman in question would be better off without him, but you are looking at it as if your friend and his partner are playing roles. Don't you think you should find out if you haven't been doing the same? Is that really *you* who wants to break up with your partner, or is it the scared child inside who is running the show? If in reviewing your behavior as if it were a scene starring someone else, you don't like what you see, perhaps it isn't really you. Perhaps those changes in the relationship, which feel so wrong, are more your style. Maybe if you make one little change at a time, you will not feel as if they are so wrong. Remember to ask yourself, *"Is what I am doing wrong or just different?"*

Old habits or patterns of behavior, which we hold onto for dear life, seem as if they are keeping us together. We are afraid that if we change something it will change everything, or at the very least that it will put cracks in the foundation of who we believe ourselves to be. But habits and patterns *are not who we are, but what we are doing.* They are patterns of behavior that made us feel safe at one time. Most of these patterns are not very useful to us today. Just the opposite is true. Rather, they are getting in the way of our living a full, rich life. It's a case of "the devil you know being better than the devil you don't know." Some of us are so afraid of the unknown that we would rather do self-destructive or self-deprecating things than to change. Are you in this category? Do you want to stay there? I know that some of you have already discovered this truth and are acting in a manner very different from the one you acted in as you were growing up or when you were in your twenties. You have told me how liberating this is.

Another paradox is that we fear change, yet things are always changing. This has been true since the world began. The one thing we can depend upon is that things will change. This can be exciting and challenging or it can be frightening and paralyzing. If we approach change with a positive outlook, the results will be much better than if we approach change with fear and trepidation. At the same time, every change we make in our lives may not be beneficial. In that case, make another change. If things aren't working, do something different. If the change you made still isn't right, do something different again. It's really that simple! To continue doing things in your life that lead to a negative outcome isn't very smart. It isn't in your best interest, and it isn't being decided by your adult self. Learn the difference between something's being wrong and something's being different, then CHANGE!

*Summary*

There are many behaviors which are not indigenous to you, but which have been coping mechanisms for many years. It is time to examine some of those coping styles and decide which are no longer useful in your present-day life. Some of them you may not be aware of, because you have been doing them so long that you feel as if they are part of you—an old friend. That's where your partner or someone close to you comes in. Check out these ideas with them. Before you say, "Well, that's just the way I am," check whether this is really who you are or just *what you are doing.* Remember that things you do can be changed. Doing is behavior. Behavior is a form of communication. What is it that you are communicating? Is it what you *want* to be communicating? Is it in your best interest or the best interest of your relationship or career? Or is it just an adrenaline rush, a thrill for the moment? Does it reflect who you really are or just the way you have believed you needed to be as you adjusted to your adoptive family and subsequent relationships? Be honest. Trauma creates a change in behavioral patterns. If the trauma happens at an early age, you have no way of contrasting your present behavior with pre-trauma behavior. Remember that ill-fitting shoes can begin to feel all right after awhile, after they're worn in. But are they really good for your feet?

Looking closely at these reality checks is part of determining what is you and what has been adaptation. Adaptation is not all bad, but it can be archaic. A great deal of it may have been in the service of avoiding another abandonment. As an adult, you really can't be abandoned. You can be left, but you will survive. And you won't be left nearly as quickly if you change some of your self-defeating, insensitive behavior as you would be if you continue to do what you've been doing just because you've always done it.

Most of all it is important to remember that you have an impact on those around you. To believe otherwise is self-indulgent and signifies an uncaring attitude toward those who care about you, as well as a lack of responsibility toward them. Everything is not about you. It is the narcissistic wound which often makes it seem that way. Other people's feelings count. And you have a great deal to do with what those feelings are. Think about it! Act on it!

# CHAPTER 12
## A Definition of Terms

Having just discussed some things that need a reality check, it has occurred to me that there are some terms that get confused in the minds of many people. This confusion often leads to assumptions, causing feelings of rejection that may be unwarranted. Understanding everything through the lens of abandonment or loss makes many adoptees and birth mothers extremely sensitive to any hint of rejection. This chapter is meant to clarify the differences between or among common terms used in everyday life. It is hoped that this clarification will ease tension and promote better understanding in relationships.

### Love vs. Approval

*Love is an attitude toward another person for who they are, no matter what they do.* Love endures even while other feelings are taking place within the individual. For instance, a mother loves her child, even when she is angry for something the child did. She may disapprove of a behavior or action of the child, but she still maintains her love for her. Part of a parent's job is to teach children socially acceptable behavior. Children don't just know this automatically. Social behavior is different in every culture, so it must be learned. While a parent is correcting a child's behavior, the parent still loves the child. Being socialized sometimes clashes with an adoptee's fear of being controlled. The need to withstand being controlled sometimes makes teaching adoptees very difficult (except for the compliant adoptees).

Many people will interpret a disapproving attitude toward certain behaviors or opinions as a withdrawal of love. Even if the subject being scrutinized is not personal (i.e., a political view), disagreement is often interpreted as a personal blow. This may be why so many adoptees do not voice their opinions about things, or why they become people-pleasers or "chameleons." Loving someone does not mean giving tacit approval to everything he says or does. A person may be loved, even though he may be demonstrating disappointing behavior or voicing dissenting opinions.

One often hears, "Well, that's just the way I am. You just have to accept me the way I am." The problem is that what the person may be referring to most of the time is behavior, *which no one has to accept.* If someone is acting irresponsibly and claiming that no one loves her, it isn't about love; it's about approval. *Approval is acceptance for one's actions.* Approval may vary, depending on who is doing the judging. The important thing for adults to ask is "Do I approve of my *own* behavior?" If the answer is "No," then it is time to change the behavior. If the answer is "Yes," then it doesn't matter what others think, so long as it isn't harming anyone else.

If one's basic belief is "I am unlovable," then distinguishing the difference between love and approval will be more difficult. If one feels unlovable, then everything may be interpreted as proof of a lack of the capacity to be loved. There will be a super-sensitive response to anything interpreted as disapproval: "You see! I knew I was unlovable." This is unfair to those who do love the person because it places them in a position of having to walk on eggshells whenever they are around that person. One can't have a genuine relationship with someone who so often misinterprets and overreacts to what other people say.

Love and approval are two different things. Beginning in childhood, the two are often confused. Perhaps we need to find more loving ways of informing others that their behavior is hurting us or otherwise unacceptable, so that it will be easy to tell the difference between love and approval. That goes for adoptees as well as for those in relationship with them. It is always important to notice the impact one has on others, then to try to discern whether the impact has to do with the delivery or the receipt. But above all, it is important to remember that others can disapprove of some of the things we do *and still love us.*

*Observation vs. Criticism*

An observation is noticing something about a person, thing, or situation. A criticism is passing judgment upon the person, thing, or situation. The latter often involves blame. When one makes an observation, it doesn't mean that there is any blame involved. If I were to look at someone and say, "George, you have a sunburn," it means just that: I've noticed that George has a sunburn. It does *not* mean, "You shouldn't have gone out in the sun" or "You should have used sunscreen." It is simply an observation. Any judgment or criticism found in this statement would be an assumption made by the recipient of the observation. It usually reflects a critical or disapproving attitude towards oneself, which gets projected onto the speaker.

The reason it is so important to distinguish between the observation and criticism is that making assumptions about another person's observation is a *huge* problem in relationships. This can be observed in marriages, friendships, sibling relationships, parent/child relationships, etc. There is a tendency for people to interpret simple observations as criticisms. This will be especially true of people who don't approve of themselves. If a person doesn't like himself very much, then most of the observations made by others will be interpreted as criticisms. This, like the problem with love and approval, makes communicating with this type of person difficult.

Of course, we all know people who use vague, non-direct observations as criticisms. A woman may say that men just don't understand women. This sounds like an innocuous observation, but what it really means is, "Alan, you don't understand me." It is much more efficient to say what one really means in a non-threatening manner. "Alan, do you realize how much it hurts me when you misinterpret what I am saying? Please check out your assumptions before galloping off into the sunset with them."

Then, too, we all know people who *are* very critical and everything they say evokes guilt. When we have to deal with these people, we must realize that they are people who have no self-love and who project disapproval out into the world and onto everyone else. We can have compassion for them, but try not to engage with them very much, and above all, we don't have to take to heart what they are saying to us.

### Empathy vs. Collusion

This is a tricky one! Many people don't understand the meaning of the term empathy. Like other words, there may be a variety of meanings for it. What I mean is putting oneself in a frame of reference to the person's actual feelings about something and validating those feelings. Collusion, on the other hand, is to conspire in a belief that is fraudulent or untrue. *Empathy is about feelings; collusion is about beliefs.*

There are people who always feel as if no one understands them; no one empathizes with their feelings. When a "feeling" keeps a person in a victim role, it becomes a problem. If one agrees with the ideas which are being presented (that the speaker is somehow a victim), then it reinforces the feeling of helplessness in the speaker. It is being an enabler. If the person disagrees with the victim stance, then she is accused of not understanding.

This is a problem in therapeutic relationships as well as friendships and partnerships. A person pulls for the other to collude with him in his belief that he is a victim, helpless to do anything about his situation. The problem is that the person may originally (as an infant or child) *have been a victim* of some trauma, and because of the repetition compulsion (see Chapter I), keeps getting into situations which repeat the sense of being a victim. In this type of situation, it is best to empathize with the child/victim, but go on to note choices the adult may have.

People who have a fragile authentic Self will have difficulty letting go of the victim role. It defines them. Giving up that role would be like giving up the only self they know. But it is not helpful to collude with a person who believes that the world is always operating against him. On the other hand, it is sometimes difficult to effect any change in these people because they are what Dr. Phil calls the "Yeah, but ..." type of person. He says that these people "*give* frustration and they *get* frustration." Every suggestion which counters their belief that they can't get out of the victim role is met with "Yeah, but ..." This is indeed frustrating to all concerned and often makes people avoid them, which then reinforces their belief that the world is against them.

It is important to differentiate between feelings and beliefs when dealing with the differences between empathy and collusion. Beliefs are often expressed as feelings. Then, when the person listening does not agree with the belief, he is accused of not understanding or caring about the person's feelings. If he goes along with the speaker on some of those excursions, he will simply be colluding with the speaker's attitude toward his life. This eliminates hope and choice.

Another misunderstanding vis-à-vis empathy for another's feelings has to do with the difference between having empathy and actually experiencing the same feeling as the other. Some people are convinced that in order to truly understand them, one has to be experiencing the same feelings at the same time. While empathy requires having had a similar feeling or experience, it is not the same as simultaneously experiencing the feeling that the other is experiencing. In fact, we say that people who do experience others' feelings have difficulty with boundaries—knowing where they leave off and the other begins. It is not necessary to be experiencing the same feeling as the person one is with in order to empathize, validate, and understand those feelings.

*One can empathize with genuine feelings, but one colludes with beliefs.* Although it may help a person to have her ideas, beliefs, and opinions understood, it is not always a good idea to collude with them if the agreement reinforces a negative attitude. It is very important to know the difference between empathy and collusion and to avoid getting caught up in another's angst.

### Feelings vs. Beliefs, Perceptions, Ideas, Thoughts, and Opinions

As stated above, it is crucial to differentiate between true feelings and beliefs, perceptions, thoughts, opinions, or assumptions. People often call something a feeling, when it is actually something else. One way to differentiate between feelings, beliefs, and so forth, is to know that feelings are never preceded by the word "*that.*" When one says, "I feel *that* ... no one likes me," for instance, he is actually expressing a thought or belief. A feeling is an emotion such as joy, sadness, anger, or hostility. "I feel sad." "I feel angry." "I feel happy." It would be more accurate to say, "I *believe* that no one loves me, therefore I *feel* very sad."

It is often our interpretation or beliefs about things which *cause* our feelings. We use the term feeling indiscriminately to mean other things, which is why it gets confusing.

For instance, we may intuit something and call it a "gut feeling." It is a sense about something, but it is not a true feeling. It is not necessary for one to go along with others' thoughts, ideas, intuitions, assumptions, or beliefs. One can agree or disagree with those things, but one cannot empathize with them. On the other hand, one can empathize with another's feelings of sadness, joy, or anger. When pulling for empathy, it is important for the person who wants understanding to know what is really going on, otherwise one can get caught up in another's faulty belief system. One can have a great deal of compassion for another's pain and suffering without going along with the belief system which reinforces the person's sense of helplessness and lack of power.

## Caring vs. Agreement

Have you ever disagreed with another person's perception (which they may be calling a "feeling") and been accused of not caring about that person? It is important to understand the difference between caring about a person and agreeing with that person's ideas. I can and do care about people with whom I have disagreements. In fact, I enjoy debating and expanding my understanding of things when people have different ideas and opinions from mine. I certainly don't expect everyone to agree with me, and I don't believe that I have to agree with others. One *can* change one's mind as a result of debating an issue or receiving more information, but it is not necessary to a healthy relationship.

In marriages, partnerships, friendships, or any relationship, it is essential to know the difference between *caring* and *agreement*. If one has to agree with another in order to convey love and caring, then someone is not being truthful. To argue a point until there is agreement, simply means that someone is finally worn down to the point of *saying* that they agree. This seems like a very specious victory, since it is more a victory of tenacity than meaning. No two people will agree all the time, no matter how much alike they are. Remember about everyone having separate and unique realities (perceptions). It is unrealistic to think that one has to be in agreement with another to retain their love. This harks back to taking everything personally, which is discussed in another chapter.

## Boundaries vs. Rejection

Establishing boundaries is tremendously important, but it may be difficult for people who have suffered certain types of trauma such as early separation from mother and sexual abuse. For people who had boundaries crossed by an abusive or narcissistic parent, establishing boundaries is often interpreted as a rejection. The same thing may be true for anyone who yearns for the merger (the symbiotic relationship) that was cut short by the premature separation between mother and child. For all of these people, the mere act of saying goodbye and hanging up the phone can be felt as a rejection.

An adoptee's yearning for merger and his simultaneous fear of abandonment can cause complications in relationships. A clinginess that comes from wanting to reestablish the closeness severed by the premature severing of the bond with mother may feel intrusive and engulfing to a partner. On the other hand, the fear of abandonment often keeps an adoptee from getting close to those with whom he is in relationship. When he begins to feel connected to another person, he will do something to distance himself from his partner and find a sense of safety again. This is often disconcerting to the other person, who often can't understand what is happening or why. This push-pull relationship often takes on the quality of a roller coaster ride or, as one partner of an adoptee called it, "a bungee cord romance."

When you are feeling rejected by another, it would be a good idea to examine the actions of the other to determine if she is actually being rejecting or if she is only setting boundaries. Setting boundaries is a compliment because it means the person is respecting you as a person, as well as asking for that respect from you. And if someone is often crossing appropriate boundaries, it is a good idea to talk to her about the source of her inappropriate behavior. People who were prematurely separated from mother or who grow up in homes where boundaries were frequently crossed will not have learned what good boundaries are. They have to be (gently) taught.

Having good boundaries allows for intimacy while keeping one safe as a separate person. One can't be intimate *with* the other if the other has become *me*. In *The Prophet* Kahlil Gibran suggests that couples in a marriage should make spaces between them and warns against making a bond of love, but rather allowing love to be "a moving sea between the shores of your souls" (Gibran, 1923). I love that image, because it is as if love is a sea caressing the varied aspects of the shore. This image makes love to be caring, affectionate, and playful, without needing to change or remake the other into oneself.

## Different vs. Wrong

The difference between something's being different and its being wrong is another misunderstanding. This one seems to originate in patterns set early in life which are still operating. It is essential to understand the difference between the two in order to make appropriate changes in one's life. Otherwise every change that is made will seem wrong. This can be true, even if the person *knows* that the change makes sense and is a good one. If it isn't something he has done before, it may *feel* wrong.

What one has to do is try to discriminate between the change being truly wrong, in that it makes life harder or relationships more difficult, and its being simply different from the way the person has operated all along. For instance, if an adoptee is used to being the one to leave a relationship, often without any kind of explanation, warning, or reason (except fear), it may seem wrong to calmly discuss the pros and cons of the relationship with his partner and then make a decision between them that is good for both of them. This scenario actually happened. The adoptee *knew* that the way he and his girlfriend broke up was the mature way to do things, but it absolutely *felt* wrong. It was all he could do not to go over to her house and yell, "Okay, I'm leaving you!" in order to *be in control* of the breakup (i.e., be the one to do all the "breaking up").

It is sometimes difficult to allow the adult to be in charge instead of the little kid. It may feel very, very wrong. It is necessary when this happens to honestly ask the question, "What is wrong with this *really?* Is this the way two mature adults would behave?" If the answer is "yes," then let the behavior stand. It is just a *different* way of acting, not a wrong way. After awhile one can actually get used to and like things that are different and adult!

### Betrayal vs. Disappointment

One of the most astonishing things that happens to some people in relationships with adoptees is the ease with which the adoptee bounces out of the relationship. One day everything is going along fine, then something happens—a misunderstanding or argument—and the door is slammed. The adoptee feels betrayed and doesn't want to continue the relationship.

Now, there are times when we may be betrayed by someone we care about. Infidelity comes to mind. But many times that which is understood by an adoptee to be a betrayal would be only a disappointment to the rest of us. We get disappointed a lot. Others don't live up to our expectations. But, again, in the exaggerated way in which adoptees respond to the things the rest of us would only find annoying, they often want to end a relationship prematurely simply because someone disappointed them.

What is the difference between betrayal and disappointment? How can you be sure someone is only disappointing you and not betraying you? I guess it is a difference in magnitude. If someone fails to arrive at a destination when he said he would, that is a *disappointment*. It isn't enough to get the person kicked out of your life. Even if someone failed to show up for a date, there may be some misunderstanding which prevented the completion of this event. Now, if someone continually fails to show up for a date, then it would be time to end the relationship, perhaps not because of betrayal, but because the person is unreliable.

I've known adoptees who feel betrayed when someone they love disagrees with them—or if someone doesn't have the same feelings about something that they do. There is an inability to distinguish between the lesser transgression of disappointment and the greater transgression of betrayal. Betrayal is a much greater trespass than disappointment. You may rightly feel betrayed when someone divulges some confidence you told them, or sleeps with your girlfriend, or continuously talks about you behind your back. But ordinary mistakes, assumptions, or misunderstandings don't qualify as betrayal. If you have a difficult time figuring out the difference, check with a parent, teacher, minister, or friend. Remember that having suffered a trauma magnifies ordinary transgressions and makes them seem like betrayals. A "minimizing glass" needs to be used to review everything that seems to be a betrayal. Losing friends, good friends, because of a difficulty in discernment is disheartening and puzzling to those who care about you. It keeps you from making close friends, and makes the friends you do have feel as if they are walking on eggshells when around you. Take it easy! Check it out! Cool it! Remember how you feel when someone misunderstands you or accuses you of something you didn't do. Do you want people to judge you so severely? You can't have it both ways. If you want a second chance, if you want to be able to explain yourself, then you have to afford the same privilege to the people in your life.

### Independence vs. Fear of Connection

It is always amazing to me when I hear the parents of a three-year-old say, "My Janice is so independent. She can get her own breakfast and do so many things on her own." What I would like to ask these parents is "How well does Janice connect to other people?"

Little children are not supposed to be independent. They have a right to depend on adults and have the assurance that they will be taken care of. That's what childhood is all about. It is about being able to count on the adults in their lives to do what is necessary to feed, clothe, and shelter them, as well as take care of their emotional, psychological, and spiritual needs. Part of taking care of emotional needs involves forming bonds which ensures connection.

Many adoptees claim that they are very independent. They don't have to ask for help or count on anyone else. This is what they say. What I actually hear is "I am afraid to connect or trust anyone else." It is not that they don't have to ask for help, they are *afraid* to ask for help. They don't trust anyone to be there for them. Not trusting and not connecting is not the same as being truly independent. In fact, one cannot become truly independent without being connected. Being independent means being able to form comfortable interconnections with people, reciprocal relationships where there is trust and safety. It means going back and forth between individualism and connection, between self and others.

Children gradually become independent through the careful guidance of their parents and other adults in their lives. They are totally dependent for the first few years. Ironically, the more they can trust adults to meet their needs, the more independent they will be able to become. As they mature, they gradually begin to do things on their own, with the help and encouragement of their parents. As they approach adolescence, there is more need for independence and self-reliance. Adolescents are preparing for adulthood. However, no one is entirely independent. Not if they are human. We all need one another. Human beings are at their best when they are interdependent. They can rely on and trust others to do the things they cannot do themselves. There is a bartering system of give and take. There is cooperation. To be truly independent is a myth. It is not a human trait. It is not normal or desirable.

America is a country which has put individualism on a pedestal. This is not the way it is everywhere in the world. The cult of individualism and false independence has helped to form a country full of lonely, isolated people. Why should an ill person living in Los Angeles starve because no one was there to help her? This should not happen in a caring society. There should be communities of people helping one another. People can die in this country and no one may find out about it for weeks! This is a disgrace and no tribute to individualism or so-called independence. We need one another and we need to be able to give and accept help from one another. That is true freedom, true independence.

*Intrusion vs. Concern, Caring, or Interest*

Many people who are in relation to adoptees—perhaps most especially adoptive parents and sometimes birth parents—report that adoptees seem unusually secretive or withholding when it comes to telling anything about themselves or what they are doing. Adoptees seem to have difficulty reporting even the most innocuous activities or events to parents. If you ask a biological child what they did on the weekend (with the exception of teenagers!), they will give you a detailed report on going to the lake, with whom they went, the fun they had water skiing, what they ate, funny stories about what went on, etc., etc. If you ask an adoptee what he did, the conversation might go like this:

| | |
|---|---|
| Mom: "Did you have fun last weekend?" | Adoptee: "Yeah." |
| Mom: "What did you do?" | Adoptee: "Not much." |
| Mom: "Weren't you going to go to the lake." | Adoptee: "Yeah." |
| Mom: "Well, did you go?" | Adoptee: "Yeah." |

| | |
|---|---|
| Mom: "Did you have fun." | Adoptee: "Yeah." |
| Mom: "Well, what did you do?" | Adoptee: "Not much." |

By this time the mother is exhausted with her attempt to carry on what she perceives to be a normal, interested conversation with her child and gives up. The adoptee, meanwhile, is thinking how intrusive his mother is.

When talking to adoptees about this, they confess that this is true. For some reason they can't explain, they withhold information from those closest to them and especially their adoptive parents. (Birth mothers have complained of this as well.) They admit that they consider their parents intrusive when they ask these kinds of questions. When I point out that they are being "intrusive" because they (adoptees) are being withholding, they admit that this might be true. In the normal give and take of parent/child relationships (and I am referring to child as a relationship, not as an age), information about activities is reciprocal. They can tell one another about events and activities in their lives. But for adoptees, this seems intrusive and invasive. Here, again, adoptees have exaggerated what is going on and interpret *interest* or *concern* to mean *intrusion*. I have even heard of adoptees that won't let their parents know the destination of a two-week vacation because they think this is an intrusion into their lives.

Adoptees, get a grip! Your parents—or other interested people—want to know where you are going on a vacation because they may need to get in touch with you in an emergency. Besides that, they are interested in you and what you are doing. You are so afraid of being controlled or allowing someone to know something about you, that you go overboard with your responses. What are the differences between intrusion and concern or interest?

Intrusion is wanting to know things about you that are understood to be private in our culture. That doesn't mean everything about you!! That means things that are meant to be private between two people or something very personal, such as your sex life or your spiritual life. (This doesn't mean that you can't talk about your spiritual life with your parents or anyone else, but it means that it wouldn't seem strange if you didn't.) However, not wanting to divulge even a tiny iota of information about a trip to the lake is being withholding and stingy with yourselves. It is totally unnecessary. And it isn't fair, because you then label any inquiries from parents or friends as invasive questions, when they are only questions of interest or concern. Learn the difference. (As in all these examples, not all adoptees are like this, but I have heard from enough people involved with adoptees to believe it to be a phenomenon worth mentioning in this chapter.)

*Summary*

There are many hurt feelings that come from the misinterpretation of terms we use every day. All too often a misunderstanding can end a perfectly good friendship. Before doing something that is irrevocable, ask yourself some questions:

- Am I being fair to think that my dad doesn't love me just because he doesn't approve of my tattoo?
- When Al told me he thought I looked tired, was he criticizing me or just making an observation?
- Is it fair to Ann to accuse her of not caring about my feelings when she wouldn't go along with my "feeling" that I'm unlucky?
- Do I really know the difference between a feeling and a belief, thought, opinion, or perception?
- Do I expect those who care about me to always agree with me?
- Can I expect John to stay in this relationship if I don't give him some space?
- What will happen if I take the risk to do something differently from the way I have always done it?
- I wonder what would happen if I were to approach Jennifer and tell her that I was wrong to end our friendship over her not going to the beach with me last summer.
- Was I wrong to believe that Ben isn't being supportive just because he doesn't agree with the way I handled that situation? After all, he's still here.
- I wonder what will happen if I ask for help with the planning of this party.
- Have I been fooling myself all these years, thinking I'm so independent just because I seem not to need anybody?
- What will happen if I don't do anything to sabotage this relationship, even though it's getting more and more intimate?
- Have I been withholding perfectly innocuous information from my parents when their questions are only showing caring and interest? Am I unfairly labeling them as intrusive for their concern?

Remember to err on the side of a positive outlook, rather than a negative one. Most people, and especially the people who care about you, aren't out to hurt you. Give others the chance you would like them to give you.

# CHAPTER 13
## The Importance of Boundaries

Maintaining healthy boundaries is of great importance in any relationship. It is important in daily life. Knowing what healthy boundaries are seems to be difficult for many people. It is certainly difficult for anyone who was sexually abused as a child. Parents don't always teach healthy boundaries to their children. In the case of adoptees, boundary-keeping presents ambiguous feelings and paradoxical dilemmas.

There is a difference between having healthy boundaries and being walled off. When one has been cut off from the symbiotic relationship with the mother too soon (the mother/child psychological merger present during the first few months of life), knowing the difference between healthy and unhealthy boundaries is difficult. There is the eternal yearning for the merger with another, yet a fear of getting too close. It poses a dilemma for adoptees and others with early childhood trauma due to abandonment, neglect, or abuse.

If yearning for intimacy is coupled with the need for approval, the difficulty is compounded. Many adoptees have gotten into relationships that never should have happened because they wanted to be loved. Someone seemed to like them, so they accepted the overtures of affection and "love" that were offered before knowing anything about the person offering. This leads to one of the greatest paradoxes of separation trauma: the will to merge and the fear of connecting. The converging of these two strong, diametrically opposed inclinations leaves many adoptees feeling continually unsatisfied in their relationships, yet afraid to do anything about it. Boundaries are often blurred. The problem begins during the first few weeks of life when the adoptive mother notices that she has either the "Velcro baby" or the "stiff-armed baby." The infant, right from the beginning of life, has adopted one of these two methods of coping with the yearning for merger and the fear of another abandonment. Neither is healthy and both are accompanied by feelings of anxiety.

Let's look at some of the boundary issues adoptees may experience:

### Trust

The issue of trust is one of the most difficult issues to resolve. As we know, adoptee mistrust comes from the original disappearance of the mother. Her disappearance is so unimaginable to a newborn that it makes it almost impossible to believe that everyone else in their lives won't disappear as well. The original mindset of mistrust is hardwired into the neurological system and very difficult to change. Because it usually begins in the implicit memory stage of neurological development, there is no conscious understanding of why there is so little trust for everyone. There just is.

This phenomenon is first noticed by the adoptive mother who finds her child full of anxiety whenever she is out of his sight. The fear doesn't fade with maturity, but is noticeable in adult relationships as well. There is a lack of trust that important people in the adoptee's life will stay or will return. The need for assurance and reassurance sometimes drives those in relationship with adoptees a bit mad. It also keeps many adoptees from forming close relationships. It is just too dangerous.

The paradox is that sometimes adoptees are too trusting with people they don't even know. They will tell their life story to someone they have just met. The story often includes intimate details of their lives. This has been related to me by many adoptees. They have not really thought about why, but it seems safer to relay intimate details of their lives to strangers than to those whom they love or who love them. This is inappropriate and perhaps even dangerous. It also keeps them from having more intimate relationships with those who really care about them.

Many birth mothers, too, have lost their trust in family and professionals. From the time that their family members urged them to give up their babies for adoption, they began to distrust those relationships. Their own intuitive feelings about who would best love and care for their babies were replaced by intellectual theories that seemed rational at the time, but made them sad and angry (if they allowed themselves any feelings at all). They lost trust, not only in their family members and professionals, but in their own judgment.

Trust of even a very good friend can easily be broken by adoptees. This is because of their inability to discern the difference between disappointment and betrayal (see the last chapter—A Definition of Terms). Although they themselves may disappoint others, their tolerance for being disappointed by those they care for is about zero. Some very important and good relationships have been destroyed by this inability to tolerate some types of disappointment. The door is slammed shut and another notch of distrust is carved into the belt of friendship.

What are healthy boundaries of trust? In the case of good friends and family, it is a good idea to check things out. Instead of galloping off into the sunset of betrayal and rejection, it is best to find out what was really meant by what was said or done. Not everyone has to go along with your ideas. Not doing so is not a rejection of you, but just someone having a different idea. This does not have to be fatal to the relationship. If everyone did this to you every time you were disappointing or expressed a different idea, you would be deeply hurt. Think about it and stop with the double standard!

Intuition can be a great asset in knowing whom to trust and whom to distrust. However, intuition can be confused with projection. Is the person in front of you really who you think he is? Or are you merely projecting someone you want him to be? Although you may be sure that you "know" the person because your intuition is so good, it is always a good idea to entertain the idea that you may be projecting.

It is smart to err on the side of caution. It is never a good idea to spill out your life story to a stranger, even if you believe him to be trustworthy. It isn't appropriate. Why would that person be interested in so much information about someone he just met? Or if he were, what does that say about him? And how much is he telling you? Trust can be earned by sharing innocuous things at first; then, as the person becomes more and more known to you, telling more about yourself. Even then, it is not a good idea to blurt out everything about yourself after a few weeks or months of knowing a person. Be sure to check out the other person's responses to all that information. And don't say things just to shock or test the other person. This is adoptee baby talk. It is not the real you. Enough already!

## Telling All

This brings us to the confessional at the beauty salon or at the cocktail lounge. Some people seem to talk about intimate aspects of their lives in situations where their confessions can be overheard by others. In the case of telling all in a bar, the use of alcohol probably adds to the loosening of the tongue. But, again, telling all, whether to the hairdresser or the bartender, is inappropriate and can be dangerous. I heard recently about some young women at a large hotel who were telling someone they had just met at poolside all about what they were planning to do and what room was theirs at the hotel. This information, if overheard by the wrong people, could lead to trouble for these young women. This is boundary crossing. It is inappropriate behavior.

Contrary to adoptees' perception of reality, it is the people who really care about them who will stand by them regardless of their "confessions," not strangers or near-strangers. I know many adoptees who want to tell everything they perceive to be bad about themselves on their first date with someone. This is the "take me as I am or leave me now" approach. Of course, many people will leave now, because they haven't formed a real caring relationship with the adoptee in order to put those confessions in perspective. And many adoptees' opinions of themselves are so bad that they put the worst light on themselves in order to test the other person.

Now we come to the perception of being "flawed" or "unworthy." I have met many adoptees who tell me that they never let anyone know who they really are because it would be too dangerous. This may include someone to whom they have been married for 15 years! While "telling all" to anyone may not be necessary, letting the person with whom you are in relationship know important things about yourself is appropriate; it fosters intimacy. The problem for adoptees isn't that they have so much to hide, but that they *think* they do. "After all, mom didn't keep me, did she? Therefore I must be intrinsically defective. There are all kinds of things I could tell you about myself that would prove to you that this is true." We can always rationalize our faulty beliefs. Rationalization is a huge problem.

Perhaps, as a way of coping with your loss, you acted out as a teenager. Do you believe this will send your husband out the door forever if he learns about it? As I have mentioned before, the acting-out adoptee isn't you. It was simply a way of coping with loss and an attempt to avoid another loss. It is a coping style. Although it happened, you don't have to pay for it the rest of your life by being afraid that others will reject you because of it. If someone really loves you, they will try to understand and judge you by how you are acting today. This means that it is important to become more and more *yourself* and less and less *the adoptee*. You are not intrinsically bad; you had something intrinsically bad *happen to you*.

Take the *testing aspect* out of your conversations with people. Don't use the first date to confess all, but to get to know the other person and let him know you—how you are now as an adult—what you have discovered about your true self, not the adoptee/child who is always testing people, always daring people to like you. Learn about the other person. Life isn't just about you. Give and take in the exchange of information and ideas. Allow for differences between you as well as looking for things you have in common. Take it easy. Pay attention to the other person's responses to you and be responsive to him. If you can't have a genuine interest in the other person, a relationship will not be reciprocal. Really get to know the other person before becoming sexual. *Sex changes everything.*

### Falling in Love with Love

Inappropriate boundaries can be seen in some of the relationships that adoptees form. This may be especially true during adolescence, but sometimes it carries over into early adulthood; that is falling "in love" with anyone "who will have me." The need for approval is sometimes so great and the self-esteem so low that some adoptees will agree to a relationship with the first person who shows an interest in them. "Why did you start to 'go' with him?" "Because he asked me." This is the scenario in more adoptees' lives than one would wish to believe. I have heard from several people who have even agreed to marry someone "because he asked me." They were afraid no one else would ask, so even though they weren't in love with the person, they agreed to the marriage. This scenario is not limited to adoptees, but includes others who have low self-esteem as well.

Because it may not have felt safe to trust the love of the people entrusted with their upbringing, many teenagers find themselves desperately seeking love and settling for less-than-good and sometimes quite abusive relationships. They often mistake a sexual interest with love. Girls may be especially vulnerable to this type of deception. Many adolescent adopted girls mistake sex for love. They don't seem to understand about horny teenage boys who will do or say just about anything for sex. (Okay, not all boys are like that, but enough are, and many female adoptees seem to be drawn to them.)

Sex is sometimes used by adoptees as a foil to pain. Just for a little while they can be relieved of the pain connected to their loss. Like drugs or alcohol, sex can be an analgesic. This is why so many adoptees are promiscuous. It isn't that many of them even like sex *per se*, but it is just that they feel loved for a little while.

For many adoptees, their low self-esteem and their need for approval leads to early sex with many partners. This isn't appropriate or healthy. Entrusting one's body to another before getting to know that person is another boundary issue. It isn't healthy and, in the case of STDs, HIV, and hepatitis B and C, can be dangerous.

Girls wanting to please guys can lead to unhealthy boundaries so far as oral sex is concerned. How many parents know if their daughters are "giving head" without the use of condoms? I am sorry if being so explicit is offensive to anyone, but this practice is reaching epidemic proportions. It is finally being brought out into the open on talk shows such as "Oprah" and "Dr. Phil." Guys have found that even if a girl "doesn't want to have sex," meaning intercourse, she may be willing to have oral sex. (Note to the disbelieving: *oral SEX is sex*.) And, of course the guy doesn't want to use a condom. Little can happen to him; she is the one more at risk for STDs. The amazing thing is that girls go along with this idiotic idea. Girls, sexual pleasure is supposed to be reciprocal. If you are giving head just to please the guy, what is your motive? If the guy is someone you really care about and you want to "pleasure him" in this way, then use a condom. If he really cares about you, he will use one. If not, start running. If it is someone you just met at a picnic and he tries to talk you into giving head, don't do it. You have no idea where he has been or what diseases he may be harboring. You can't always tell by looking. Besides, if you don't know him, why on earth would you compromise yourself in this way? Get a grip. This is not the way to prove that you are lovable! It only proves that you are *gullible*.

What are the consequences of acting on sexual impulses? Besides pregnancy,

STDs, HIV, and hepatitis B and C, the results are often feelings of shame, guilt, and being used. Because adoptees habitually have difficulty anticipating the consequences of their behavior, they have to be especially diligent and aware. It is important to think about consequences before doing anything that means giving up control over yourself. Having a pleasurable sexual experience means giving up a certain amount of control. Having a responsible sexual experience means thinking about pregnancy, STDs, AIDS, cancer, and emotional repercussions. It is always appropriate to ask yourself, "Is this experience going to be beneficial or detrimental to me? It is really in my best interest in the long run? Or is it just a temporary band-aid for my pain that will lead to even more pain in the future?" Your body is the temple of your soul. Use it wisely. This goes for boys as well as girls, men as well as women.

The so-called sexual revolution has not helped with this problem. It seems that many teenage girls just want to "get rid of" their virginity. It is like a virus or something to be ashamed of. Many of them are beginning their sexual life much before they are ready for the emotional fallout. "Free love" may not be so free for women. The idea that women can become as casual about sex as men doesn't seem to be panning out. Patricia Dalton, a clinical psychologist, notes: "Women today are being led willingly and blindly down the garden path—and some are doing the leading." She says what many other therapists are saying, which is that many women have "... an almost breathtaking lack of awareness" of the price they pay for casual sex.

The price can be very high. We may finally be getting away from the belief (wishful thinking?) that men and women's sexual natures are the same. They aren't. Besides the differences in the brain and hormones, the ticking clock comes much earlier for women than for men. Many women find themselves going from relationship to relationship without any firm commitment from their partners, then all of a sudden discovering that menopause is just around the corner. Too late they discover the price they pay for having chosen "free love" over commitment, marriage, and children. Being married or at least having a committed relationship is a rite of passage into adulthood. It is also a hedge against loneliness, which is reaching epidemic proportions in this country.

The emotional cost of the sexual revolution, as well as the biological cost, can be high. Recreational sex or sex-as-sport is an expensive way to avoid adulthood. It seems that childhood ends at age nine, yet adolescence seems to last well into the thirties. (Does anyone consider those wacky women on *Sex and the City* to be adults?) Women are much more likely to feel "used" than men when engaging in casual sex. The feminist revolution hasn't been much help either. It may have helped women become firefighters, but it hasn't seemed to help girls (or women) understand about the sovereignty of their bodies. Women today seem to be even less understanding of this idea than women were in the past. Although we don't want to go back to the shame connected with sexuality in past generations, it wouldn't hurt for young people today to understand the responsibilities, as well as the pleasures, connected with becoming sexual. These responsibilities include responsibilities to themselves as well as to their partners.

Having a sexual relationship can be a wonderful form of intimacy, but it needs to be a part of the relationship and not the first part. First comes getting to know things about the person. What does she like to do for fun? What does he hope to become in life? What are her hobbies? What kind of relationship does he have with his parents? How is she doing in school? What does he think about what is going on in the world today? What are her values? his principles? Find out if you are compatible. Find out if you even *like* one another. Keep the hormones in check until you really know that you won't feel ashamed about having sex after the relationship is over. Meaningful relationships don't come from having sex with strangers. They come from going from acquaintanceship to friendship to lovers. That is the order for appropriate boundaries and for self-respect. Although this may sound like a judgment, it is rather an observation of what women have been saying about how casual sex has affected their lives today.

### Obsession and Abuse

Sometimes adoptees become obsessed about someone. It goes beyond the normal headiness of those first weeks of being in love. It means never being able to think of anything or anyone else. It means always having to know where the other person is or what she is doing. It often means becoming engulfing. It certainly means boundary-crossing. The engulfing nature of obsession may *cause* the very thing that it is meant to deter—rejection. Although at first all the attention given by the obsessed person may seem like love, after awhile it becomes more like a prison. The object of the obsession feels more and more trapped in the distrust demonstrated by the other's behavior.

Obsession can lead to abuse. The abuse may not be physical, but verbal and emotional. A man who is afraid of losing his partner may interpret every glance at another man as a betrayal. He may become verbally abusive and controlling. He may demand a constant reporting of his partner's whereabouts and activities. He may gradually separate his partner from relationships with family and other friends, so that she is isolated and dependent solely on him. This leaves her with few options: She finds herself with no one to turn to but her controlling partner.

In the beginning, a woman might interpret her partner's "interest" in her activities as caring. After awhile, however, it becomes evident that it is not interest in her that is paramount, but interest in himself which makes her partner intrude into every aspect of her life. An obsessive person does not really care about anyone but himself. Every aspect of the relationship is interpreted as to how it affects him. There is no "how are you doing?" sentiment coming from an obsessive person. He is running on fear and instills fear into the life of his partner.

Adoptees have to be careful about interpreting "intrusive." To some adoptees, any questioning seems intrusive. This may be especially true in the case of adoptive parents. Some adoptees have never felt as if their adoptive parents were really their parents. Many have admitted that they withhold even innocuous information about themselves or their activities as a way of negating that relationship. Even adoptees who do feel connected to their adoptive parents may do this. It just seems as if their parents' questions are intrusive. They aren't quite sure why. Perhaps it is time to stop doing it!

Whether it is a parent, friend, or a spouse asking innocuous questions about some activity, be reasonable. Their saying, "Hi, Hon. What did you do today?" is not being intrusive. However, asking you questions about every aspect of what you did and whom you saw is being intrusive. If you answer, "I had lunch with Bill, a colleague at work," and your partner asks about everything you talked about, how long you were together, what you did next, and then goes out to check the mileage on your car, it is time to be concerned.

How will you know if your partner is only interested in your activities or is obsessed about them? First of all, you have to be alert to the signs of this kind of abuse. The manifestations of these signs may become evident little by little so that, like the frog that is placed in cold water and doesn't notice the water is getting hotter and hotter until it is too late, you may become isolated before you realize what has been going on. Be alert to the first signs of this kind of abuse.

The following is a list of some of the warning signs of abuse, which comes from different sources:

- *Pushes for quick involvement:* Right away makes you believe that you are special and need to be in an exclusive relationship with him.
- *Jealous and possessive:* Checks on all your activities, friends, and colleagues. Is especially jealous about any contact with male friends, but may even object to socializing with female friends. May check the mileage on your car.
- *Controlling:* Makes you ask permission to go places and questions you about it afterwards. Usually keeps all money and makes you ask for it, then questions you as to how you spent it. Is stingy.
- *Unrealistic expectations:* Expects work to be done the way he wants it done and on his time table. Orders you around. Treats you like a

personal servant. Expects you to meet all his needs and to be perfect.

- *Isolation:* Little by little cuts you off from family and friends so you have to be totally dependent on him. In extreme cases, this may include taking away your transportation and keeping you at home.
- *Blame:* Never takes responsibility for things that go wrong but always blames someone or something else. May admit to hitting partners in the past but always blames the other person.
- *Makes others responsible for his feelings:* Is quick to anger and blame partner for how he is feeling. Uses as an excuse to be abusive. "You made me do it."
- *Hypersensitivity/Paranoia:* Always thinks people are "after" him. Interprets others' motives as wanting to hurt him. Sees the world as an unsafe place. Gets very angry when you disagree with him.
- *Cruelty to animals and children:* May have started being cruel to animals as a child and continues today. May have unrealistic expectations of children, beating them for things that all children do: shaking a baby for crying or hitting a toddler for wetting the bed. Sixty-five percent of abusers who beat their partner will also abuse children. May "play" inappropriately with children such as tickling them until they cry. If you have children and stay with an abuser, you may be in danger of having your children taken away from you because you are putting them at risk. It is called Child Endangerment and is a punishable offense.
- *Sex on demand:* May demand sex even when you don't want it. May like to hold you down or do S&M-type uses of force and claim he is just playing around. Always wants to be dominant. Wants to be served and obeyed. Is excited by the idea of rape.
- *Verbal abuse:* Name-calling, constant criticizing, discounting, belittling, degrading, cursing, shouting, etc. Verbal abuse comes in many guises.
- *Diminishes self-esteem:* Says you are ugly, stupid, unable to care for yourself; humiliates, shames, acts rude to you in front of others, and says that no one else would want you.
- *Sudden mood swings:* Switches from agreeable to violent without warning or provocation. Alcohol may contribute to this but should never be an excuse.
- *Threats of violence:* Says threatening things such as "I'll kill you," or "I'll break your neck." Then denies he means it by saying things like "Everybody talks that way; I didn't really mean it."

- *Frightens you:* You feel frightened of him most of the time and especially when he has been drinking. Don't let alcohol be an excuse: "He is such a sweet guy when he isn't drinking." How is he most of the time with you? Is he doing anything about his anger?

In all of these cases boundaries are being crossed. Neither the abuser nor the abused has good boundaries. There is no such thing as being the peacemaker with an abuser. You will not be communicating on the same wavelength. Abusers can find fault with all your arguments and make the most blatant abusive behavior seem reasonable. And do not wait around for them to change. We are not talking here just about adoptees, although the anger that many adoptees carry makes them good candidates for abusive behavior. Domestic abuse is more universal than previously understood. Women can also be abusive. Usually women are verbal abusers, whereas men may tend more toward physical abuse. This probably reflects the strengths of each—women are more verbal and men are physically stronger. Women may emasculate men with words, which may cause the men to strike out physically. Neither is all right. Passive-aggressive men are often verbal abusers.

It is important to be honest with yourself about these signs. You do not need all the signs to know that you are in trouble. Children should not have to grow up in the presence of an abuser. This might perpetuate abuse into the next generation. Call the domestic abuse hotline at 800-799-7233. Read Patricia Evans' book *The Verbally Abusive Relationship.* You may not know when someone is being abusive with you or you with them, especially if you grew up in an abusive home and everything seems familiar and "normal." Abuse is *not* normal; it does not happen to everyone. It should not happen to you or your children.

### Values and the Chameleon

Usually by the time you have entered adulthood you have some idea of your values, even if they were merely inherited from your parents. Sometimes the chameleon in an adoptee causes him to change his values every time he is in the presence of someone who has different values from those he had yesterday. Part of knowing yourself is knowing your values and sticking to them. Having principles to live by is essential to having a meaningful life. If you change your principles or values every time you are challenged by someone else, you are not keeping good boundaries. If you find yourself changing your ideas to please someone else, you are allowing that person to invade your personal space. Maintaining personal values despite what others want or what they do is part of having good boundaries.

Sometimes confusion about values has to do with drinking, drugs, or sex. This is especially true during adolescence. Many teenagers allow themselves to be talked into smoking, drinking, or having sex when they really don't want to because they want to please someone or they don't want to appear "square." This is never a good idea because you have to live with yourself. Learn to say no to unwanted food, drinks, drugs, sex, or touch that you really don't want. Your real friends will not shun you if you don't go along with the crowd when the crowd is doing something you find offensive. Stick to your values; maintain your boundaries and your self-respect.

### Being Oblivious

Sometimes, when a person has low self-esteem, he is not even aware when others are displaying inappropriate boundaries. There are some people who believe that they deserve whatever is happening to them. There may or may not be a level of discomfort. If this has been true for you, then begin right now to change it.

It is important to pay attention to your level of comfort when interacting with other people. People-pleasers may be especially susceptible to boundary crossing. They may believe that they have to accept inappropriate touch or sex, or offers of food, drink, gifts, or drugs. This is different from just wanting to be one of the gang. It goes into the realm of not understanding the *right of refusal*. It is amazing that so many of you *who don't like being controlled* have so much trouble when it comes to choosing what to allow and what not to allow. It's as if you don't have a choice. Believe me, you do!

Too many women have told me about feeling obligated to have sex with someone who took them out to dinner or showed them a good time. There are certainly men who will try to make you feel as if you owe them your body in exchange for a steak dinner, but get real! What kind of a deal is that? If you really feel as if you owe them something, then offer to fix them a picnic lunch the next weekend. Any man who will try to make a woman feel obligated to have sex because of taking her to dinner or a concert is engaging in prostitution—paying for sex. Only in this case he paid in advance. Do you want to be a prostitute? Even with advance payment??? And, yes, oral sex is sex.

On the other hand, I have heard from men who say that women expect them to be sexual, even on the first date. They report that the woman expects it and provokes it. It is as if she doesn't feel accepted unless the man wants to have sex with her. Something must be wrong. She isn't desirable. The questions both men and women have to ask themselves are: "Do I know this person well enough to begin a sexual relationship? Do I like him/her well enough to have sex with him/her? Will I regret this in the morning?" Men can show their interest and appreciation for a woman without having to take her to bed. Women, listen up? Maybe neither of you wants to have sex and it doesn't mean that you aren't desirable or appreciated. Maybe it means you *are* liked and appreciated and that the man wants to wait to have sex until you both know it is the right thing to do. Not all men like a one-night stand, casual sex, or women who do.

What about gifts? Does a gift make you feel obligated to the other person? Is the gift appropriate to the length of time you have known the person and the level of your involvement? By its very name a gift is given freely, no obligation attached. (That's the reason the term "free gift" is redundant.) A gift is not a gift if the person giving it expects a payback. You have to decide if a gift is appropriate or not. Check on your level of comfort or discomfort. Some people will say, "Well, I didn't want to hurt his feelings by not accepting the gift." Because gifts often do come with strings attached, it is better to hurt the giver's feelings at the time than to feel some kind of obligation and lingering resentment toward him. Trust your intuition. It knows more than all the rationalizations you talk yourself into.

Have you ever been inappropriately touched by someone? What did you do? Did you ignore it and thus allow the other person to violate your sovereignty? Or were you able to tell the other person that you expect more respect from them? It is especially important not to let anyone touch you sexually, even in passing, even as a joke. No one should touch you inappropriately or without your permission. Nor should you touch another without permission. Even if it is just a hug, rather than just throwing your arms around the person, it is best to say, "May I give you a hug?" before hugging someone for the first time. Touch, any kind of touch, can feel dangerous for people who have been sexually abused. You can't tell by looking who this might be.

Touch can be an issue in reunions, especially between mothers and sons. If both regress and she feels like the 17-year-old mother of a newborn, and he feels like that newborn, inappropriate touching may trigger trouble. They just want to touch and hold one another, but they are no longer as young as they feel. Powerful sensual feelings become sexualized and they may find themselves in a compromising situation. As much as both may want skin-to-skin contact, they need to confine that kind of contact to face, hands, and arms. It should be up to the mother to keep the boundaries, since her son is feeling like a baby, but if she is not doing so, then the adoptee needs to take over that responsibility. It is very injurious to the relationship to act on these sexualized feelings. This is true for fathers and daughters as well.

### People-Pleasing and Other Vices

There is nothing intrinsically wrong with wanting to help people. However, *people-pleasing* may be a misnomer. Helping others can be altruistic or it might be selfishly motivated. The question to ask yourself is "Am I doing this because I really want to help this person with no accolades to myself, or am I doing it because I want him to like me?" Perhaps there is no real line of purity in that question, but there can be a pattern which needs to be studied. Some people may believe that they have to accept responsibilities that they really don't want or have the time to carry out. It is amazing the number of people who believe that they have to give an immediate answer to someone making a request of them—from the PTA president asking them to chaperon a dance to the magazine salesman peddling his wares. Not only do you not have to say yes right away, *you don't have to give any answer right away.*

If asked to do something, a well-boundaried person would answer, "I'll have to check my schedule and get back to you later." This gives her time to evaluate whether she indeed has time or whether she even wants to do it. Or, in the case of the salesman, she may answer, "I never buy anything on impulse, but if you will leave information or an order form, I will think about it." If door-to-door sales people insist on an immediate answer (or you won't get the huge discount!) then it might be best to tell them that if you have to make a decision now, your answer is "No." You are never obligated to answer immediately no matter what the other person would *like* and even urges you to do. The pressure is for his benefit, not yours. Take time to think about what you really want to do. This will eliminate anger at both the person making the request and yourself for answering so impulsively. It will eliminate any lingering resentment that ensues when you have said yes to something you later regret.

Have you ever been at someone's home for dinner and the host insisted that you have a cocktail before dinner or a second helping of lasagna, even if you wanted neither? Can you steadfastly say "No"? There are ways of holding your own under these kinds of social pressures without having to offend the other person. Remember your *right of refusal*. Refusals can be firm but light-hearted and humorous. "I appreciate your offer, but I want to stay wide awake through the entire dinner," may get an overzealous host off your back about the cocktail. Remember that you have choices and you do not have to allow others to take away those choices. Insistence from someone is boundary-crossing, and you do not have to allow it. This also means that you have to mean what you say. If you want to be talked into things, then this chapter is not for you. One of the objectives of this book is to make you more aware of what you want and the ways to ask for it. This also means saying what you don't want and not allowing it. Keep practicing.

Part of awareness has to include knowing when others are taking advantage of your generosity. If you have a car and someone asks you to drive them around for errands more than once or twice, then you need to take stock of the situation and decide what you want to do. If you have an agreement with the person to do this because of some disability, then that is up to you. Whenever you make agreements like this, it is always a good idea at first to limit the time you will do it, and then every so often review how it is working out. There are organizations which give aid to people who are not able to do things for themselves. Perhaps after doing a favor for someone who needs help for awhile, you can then help them get in touch with such an organization. Don't let their hesitation to do so obligate you. It is fine to be generous, but not if you begin to feel resentful about it.

### It's Your Life, So Who's in Charge?

For many adoptees, making decisions, even the most mundane decisions, can be difficult. The big questions: "Who am I?" and "What am I supposed to do with my life?" are hampered by a lack of knowledge about biological history and by living so long with genetic strangers. But what about the less important decisions like what color to paint the bedroom or what to wear to the movies? Why is it so difficult for some adoptees to make these kinds of decisions without consulting with three other people?

We have discussed the whys of indecisiveness in another chapter, but for the purposes of being in charge of your own life and establishing good boundaries, it is important to be able to make decisions such as these. There are people, who when noting some hesitation on your part in making these seemingly easy decisions, will take advantage of you. Believe it or not, some people like nothing better than to run someone else's life (despite the fact that their own might not be going too well!).

Do you know people who think they know you and define you in a way that seems incongruent with what you feel is true about yourself? I'm not talking about how you may have been acting, but how you actually *feel* inside. You have had to adapt so often to acting in a way that may have seemed dystonic (not like yourself) that you may not notice that you are constantly acting like the chameleon and others are taking advantage of your adaptability.

Do you allow others to define your reality? Direct your life? Define you? If so, it is time to begin taking responsibility for these things yourself. Even if you have not had the advantage of meeting with your birth family, you can reach within yourself to find what seems best for you. Your reality has been challenged by living in a non-biological family. The more differences there are between the essential you and your adoptive family, the more challenging your hold on your own reality may be. This is when others might take advantage of you and tell you what your reality is. It might begin with your adoptive parents who have decided that you should be an attorney. Have you ever thought about whether or not you want to be an attorney? Are you doing it because you feel obligated to? Or is it because you just don't know what else to do? Do you feel triumphant when you leave practicing law and become a social worker, only to discover you did this to please your partner? Where are *you* in all of this? Perhaps you don't know yourself well enough to decide what your path in life should be. I once met an adoptee who changed her college major six times.

We are all born with talents and aptitudes which could provide us with an idea for an occupation. There are several directions each of us could take. We have to choose because we can't do it all. But if you have been constantly playing down your true talents and interests because they were never encouraged, or were in fact discouraged, then it is time to bring them back to life. If you can't afford to do whatever it is for a living, then do it for an avocation. But start making decisions about your own life. Start defining yourself and choosing your own path. Otherwise, others in your life will cross another boundary and take up the slack and do it for you.

Describing their reality is difficult for adoptees because no one they talk to wants to believe that being adopted, especially if one has good adoptive parents, is painful. They have seen you laughing and having fun. They have met your parents who seem like good people. What do you mean your life has been painful? Thousands of adoptees have told me that reading *The Primal Wound* was the first time they had ever felt their reality had been understood (even by themselves!).

This does not mean you have to go around with a long face and look for sympathy. This is not what you want and the whole purpose of this book is to remove the victim from your view of yourself. But it is hard work always being "up" for people, especially around certain times of the year such as birthdays or the end-of-the-year holidays. It would be nice if at least family members and good friends could understand that you may not feel wonderful at these times. Whatever the case, it is important not to let others decide how you feel on those occasions. Don't feel obligated to put a smile on your face if you are feeling sad. Just explain the situation and let the chips fall where they may. Those who care about you will respect your need for understanding. (I know that many of you will be scared to take that risk, but do it anyway.) Those who insist on telling you that you really feel great are not good friends. If they are family members, it is sad because if they would try to understand it could bring you closer together. There is a tendency in our materialistic society to think that if an adoptee grew up in an affluent family, there is no cause for sad feelings. (This is true of biological families, as well.) As much of a cliché as it sounds, it is still true— money can't buy happiness, folks. And, as advantageous as it is to have wonderful adoptive parents, they cannot eliminate all the pain of the adoptee's separation from her birth parents and roots.

Some of you may have lived your life not wanting anyone to control you, but at the same time wanting others to make decisions for you, or at least help you make decisions. As I said, there are adoptees who will not make any decisions without the approval of someone else. They have become so befuddled about who they are that they can't even chose their own clothes without input from others. This gives others an advantage over them which can backfire later. If you find yourself always having to ask others' opinions about the simplest decision, take the risk of making that decision without anyone's help. The world really won't come to an end, even if no one likes your decision except you. If it is about you, you are the only one who has to like it.

*No One Is a Mind-Reader*

Wanting others to anticipate your needs is another sign of immaturity and unhealthy boundaries. I think I mentioned elsewhere that if you are over a year old, you have to let others know what you want. Expecting that others will automatically fulfill your needs is part of the infant wish. You are only going to be disappointed in others and they are going to become resentful of you. One adoptee told me, "But it isn't fair if I have to tell him what I want. That means that he doesn't really know me." To which I replied, "And how well have you *allowed* him to know you?" She got a sly grin on her face and very softly said, "Not very." Well, even if he had known her, he might not know exactly what she needs at every juncture. For one thing, men and women are notoriously bad at anticipating one another's needs. Even among friends of the same sex, it is not fair to expect others to read your mind. *Adults communicate their needs and wishes verbally.*

What if you ask and your wish is not fulfilled? Well, asking only puts the request out there. A request may either be affirmed or denied. If denied, it doesn't mean the other person doesn't like you. It only means that he can't or won't fulfill your needs or wish at this time. No one has to be a slave to your wishes. All adults know that sometimes their wishes are fulfilled and sometimes they are not. Because adoptees as infants and young children may not have fully been able to participate (as in trusting) in the need-fulfilling duties of their adoptive mothers, they sometimes feel as if they haven't had that experience. They couldn't trust it, so as far as they are concerned, it didn't happen. This makes them want it to happen in adult relationships. However, this scenario is not appropriate in adult relationships.

Some people even fall apart so they can get someone to take care of them. They allow the slightest disappointment to plunge them into the abyss. Some people do this in therapy by refusing to learn and change. They are afraid that if they get better, the relationship with the therapist will end, so they fail to improve. If a person in therapy continues to act like a child or falls apart at the slightest provocation, it is time for the therapist to insist on their growing up. It is not a good idea to collude with this ploy. Regression in therapy is normal in some cases, but continued regression is not helpful. Some therapists will collude with this tactic in order to ensure their continued importance to the patient. This is a problem which the therapist needs to resolve in consultation or his own therapy.

It is not only in therapy that people regress. Some adoptees (and birth mothers) regress in reunions, which is addressed in the next chapter. Some people want someone else to take care of them. They get into relationships with this in mind. If you find yourself in this category, begin to change your behavior. You can do it slowly so that you and your partner can handle the new way of acting in the relationship. Remember that some people are in relationship with a person who needs a caregiver because they are rescuers. You need not be either a victim or a rescuer. What you really need is a reciprocal, mature relationship with another adult, where boundaries are respected and interdependence rules the day.

## Summary

Healthy boundaries are essential to a happy, well-balanced, adult life. You first have to know what these are before you can ascertain whether or not they exist in your relationships. If they do, good. If not, it is time to make some changes. Check your relationships against the information given in this chapter. Make a priority list of changes you need to make. Decide which unhealthy boundary is causing you the most problems and work on that first. Some of the changes may mean letting people in more, not less.

If it feels intrusive to you when a friend or parent asks you harmless questions about your weekend, it is time to change your definition of intrusiveness. Be honest about your response to those who care about you and make the necessary changes to allow for healthy relationships. Good boundaries act neither as a wall to keep others out, nor as a carte blanche invitation to allow all others in, but act like a permeable filter to allow for appropriate interactions with appropriate others. Getting the right balance can take time. There is no time like the present to begin!

# CHAPTER 14
Reunions: The Agony and the Ecstasy

One way of getting to know yourself better is to reunite with your birth family. It isn't just that you may find people who are more like you than your adoptive family, but it will concretize the fact that you were born. According to my mail, many of you regard your birth as only a theory. In order to get rid of that floating sensation and feel as if your feet are firmly planted on terra firma you may have to find your birth mother. Only then may the fantasies of having dropped in from outer space, been found in a file drawer, or just appeared in the hospital as if by magic disappear.

When I published *The Primal Wound* in 1993, reunions were still relatively new and unknown. Although some brave souls had been reuniting since the mid-20th century, it wasn't common. For one thing, in all but a couple of states it was illegal to get original birth certificates or other adoption information. This made searching difficult. On top of this, the guilt that birth mothers carried and the unworthiness that adoptees felt inhibited them from searching for one another. They felt undeserving. They were used to bowing to authority. It wasn't until more and more triad members began to band together in organizations that searching became more common. Now a few more states allow adoptees to have their records, but it is still a sorry situation for a country that prides itself on being more enlightened than most. Our draconian adoption laws are one reason that our claim to human rights is overstated.

Reunions are like other relationships—complex and unpredictable. They evoke both fear and hope, threat and fulfillment, agony and ecstasy. No two are ever alike, just as no two marriages are alike. However, there are some similarities which can help in making adjustments so that they can better serve all parts of the triad. In this chapter I will put forth some ideas from all of you and from my own experience and expertise. None of this is written in stone. It is what seems the best for now from what we know now. With more experience and personal stories, we can increase our knowledge and improve our advice.

## Whose Rights?

I believe that all adoptees have the right to their heritage and to meet their birth families. They had no say in being separated from them or any way of objecting to this crisis in their lives. It was a brutal, devastating separation and needs to be rectified in some way if possible. It doesn't matter if the birth mother hasn't yet told her parents, husband, or other children that she surrendered her baby. That doesn't change the right of the adoptee. *I believe that every person in the world has a right to his or her heritage.* Judging from the thousands of adoptees who have communicated with me, this is basic. It is instinctive. It is healthy. It is much more important than those who facilitate adoptions seem to understand. An adoption decree does not change the DNA nor the biological heritage of an individual. The amended birth certificate is a legal, social document, not a biological, psychological one. As one adoptee told her adoptive parents, "Yes, you are my parents, but your ancestors are not my ancestors." She has a right to know who her ancestors are.

I also believe that birth mothers have a right to search for their children. As has been pointed out before, those who relinquished in the mid-to-late 20th century had very little choice in the matter. Many have agonized for years over the fate of their children. They have suffered great emotional distress resulting in many issues as a consequence of that "decision." They have a right to know whether or not their children are alive or dead; they have a right to know if they had good or difficult lives; they have a right to meet these children to whom they gave birth.

What about the rights of adoptive parents who don't want their children to either search or be found? They have a right to their opinion and can keep their minor children from searching. But when their children become adults, these adoptees have the right to make up their own minds about what they want to do. I can't think of a single instance where the adoptee loved his adoptive parents more because they didn't want him to search. I do know of many adoptees who have resisted searching because they thought they would hurt their adoptive parents. Some waited so long that their birth mothers had died before being found. Some of them went ahead and searched anyway, but the adoptive parents knew nothing about it. Neither of these scenarios foster closeness to adoptive parents. The first often creates resentment towards them. The second perpetuates secrets, which are toxic to all relationships. Adoptive parents should know that in many cases the relationship with them may improve after a reunion has taken place. I have never heard of a relationship improving if a reunion is forbidden.

*Reluctance*

Adoptive parents are entitled to their feelings, just as adoptees and birth parents are. Most are bound to have some feelings of trepidation when a reunion is mentioned. This shouldn't cause them to try to stop their child from searching. Everyone has fears about searching. Both the adoptee and birth mother may fear rejection by the other. One of them felt rejected once before and the other may feel guilty. They, too, are scared. Adoptive mothers do not have to be stoical when it comes to reunions. After all, many have felt a gap in the relationship with their child and know way down deep that that gap has something to do with the birth mother's place in the adoptee's heart. She is entitled to her feelings about that.

However, there are some adoptive parents who are so threatened by the idea of the birth mother's coming back into the life of their child that they issue ultimatums or other threats. In my experience, it is the unstable relationships between adoptive parents and children which most often elicit this kind of reaction to the idea of reunion. But as I said, it begs the question of how the already tenuous relationship can be improved by the parents' going against what the adoptee really wants and needs. Logically it can't. But feelings aren't logical and many adoptive parents give in to their fearful feelings about losing their children. Some become hypochondriacs and others threaten cutting the adoptee out of the will. These are extreme cases, however. Most adoptive parents, although feeling a bit threatened, understand their child's need to search and help if they can. If the parent/child relationship is a solid one, adoptive parents are often happy to help in the search and are eager to know their child's birth family.

Adoptive parents aren't the only ones who may be reluctant to embrace reunions. Sometimes it is the birth mother or father who is reluctant. Opening up the Pandora's box of painful feelings seems overwhelming. I believe that most birth mothers who refuse to meet with their children are trying to avoid pain, not their children. Nevertheless, it is their children who are hurt by this refusal. It is another rejection and is often met with the same kind of physical/emotional pain that was experienced in the beginning. Some adoptees become physically ill at being told their mothers don't want to meet them. Others curl up in a fetal position and sob uncontrollably. They regress back to infancy and are inconsolable.

What I would like to say to birth mothers is that I know your pain is enormous, and I understand your not wanting to face it again. However, it is time to think first of your child. No matter what the circumstances under which the relinquishment took place, your child has suffered tremendous loss, as have you. As the mother, you now have a chance to help your child heal. At the same time, you also can heal. It is not easy, but to continue in hiding is no solution. The lid is already off Pandora's box and it can't be put back on. You may as well face those painful feelings overtly, rather than letting them take over covertly.

Sometimes, and I believe for many birth fathers this is more the case, it is the idea of telling their present family that they have a child "out there" which seems so difficult. Some may have been married and had an affair that resulted in a pregnancy. They may be married to the same woman and don't want her to know about the affair. Other birth fathers have wives who don't want to have to compete for their husband's affection with his daughter who is now a young woman. This may be especially true after a reunion has actually taken place, and even more true if there is any hint of genetic sexual attraction involved (discussed later in this chapter). The wife sees the intensity of the relationship between her husband and his child (especially daughter) and interferes with the relationship. Many men don't seem to be strong enough to stand up to their wives' insecurities. Others form secret relationships with their children, as do some birth mothers. This is not very satisfactory to the adoptee who is tired of being a secret.

When a birth mother finds it hard to tell her family, it may be that she has regressed back to her age of the pregnancy and birth. She can't seem to stand up for herself. She feels shameful and wants to avoid telling her family of origin or her nuclear family. She may be 40 or 50 years old, but she feels 16 and confused. Even though she is living in a different era now, she feels as if she is back in the days when having sex before marriage was frowned upon and getting pregnant considered a sin. She will need help in the form of therapy or support groups to allow herself to grow up emotionally and become to her child the mature adult that she is under other circumstances.

Adoptees are also reluctant at times to be reunited with their birth mothers. I hear things like "I never really thought about her and don't need her in my life." This is usually said with a great deal of feeling, which is a dead giveaway that she *is* important, and this needs to be made more conscious. Many times the adoptee is downright angry, in fact, enraged at his birth mother and doesn't want to have anything to do with her. If this rage is overt, it can be easy for the mother (if she is no longer feeling 16!) to deal with. She can answer the screaming child who says "How could you have given me away?" by saying that she is sorry. If it is true, she can add that she wishes she had made a different choice. (In some cases, the birth mother's circumstances were so bad that she still believes that the choice she made was the right one.) The apology must be made at least once without any "if, ands, or buts" following her apology. It should also be said in the active voice, not the passive voice. ("I made a mistake;" not "a mistake was made." Or "I'm sorry what I did hurt you so much," not "I'm sorry you were hurt by the relinquishment.") The adoptee's baby-self needs for her to take full responsibility and to hear that she's sorry without any qualifications. Later, when the adoptee is not acting from that baby place, the birth mother can explain what little choice she had and what things were like in 1968. I highly recommend that both birth mother and adoptee watch the movie version of Carol Schafer's book *The Other Mother*. The movie conveys better than the book the youth and vulnerability of these young mothers, the tenor of the times vis-à-vis family relationships, and the tenuousness of their situations. This TV movie is played often on Lifetime. Watch for it.

Often the adoptee's anger is covert and unconscious and comes across as passive-aggressive behavior. This is more difficult to deal with than overt anger, because it is what the adoptee *isn't* doing that is causing the birth mother so much pain—in essence not wanting to meet her or never having time for her. As an academic point, I would like to point out to all concerned that what happened 25, 40, or 50 years ago cannot be compared to what is happening so far as women being able to keep their babies today. All adoptees, as well as birth mothers, should read Rickie Solinger's book *Wake Up Little Suzie.* It will give the historical/social background for the tremendous number of white women who were giving up their babies during the second half of the 20th century, at least through the early 70s. Reading this account won't do away with the baby rage, but it can temper it with reason. This explanation will satisfy only the adult adoptee, not the child within.

Even today there may be pressures put on confused young women who find themselves pregnant. Although it is not considered by most people to be morally wrong to give birth out of wedlock, the confusion that a young woman may feel at becoming pregnant can put her at the mercy of unscrupulous adoption facilitators and attorneys. At the height of her confusion and pain, while she is still in the hospital, she may be coerced into signing away her rights to her child. In one or two states, she is given only 12 hours to change her mind! This is unconscionable. Unfortunately, there are fewer safeguards for human babies than for dogs and cats when it comes to separating them from their mothers right after birth. Joseph Chilton Pearce says that because of their vulnerability during childbirth, women have been at the mercy of "... the arrogance of the male intellect in undermining Nature's wisdom" (Pearce, 1992). Pearce was not addressing the problems of unwed mothers, but the whole way birth has been practiced by doctors who whisk babies away from their mothers too soon after birth. And although it is not only men who are making these decisions for vulnerable young women, our society is still dominated by patriarchal norms where motherhood is neither valued nor understood.

Many birth mothers today are promised that they will have access to their children after the adoption has taken place. They sign on the dotted line because they believe what they have been told. However, the reality is that there is no legal obligation on the part of the adoptive parents to keep such an agreement. A booklet all young, unwed, pregnant women should read before making a decision is *What You Should KNOW if You're Considering Adoption for Your Baby.* It can be obtained by accessing the CUB (Concerned United Birthparents) Web site: www.cubirthparents.org. A life-changing decision such as whether or not to keep one's child should never be made while under some kind of sedation or while still emotionally drained from the birth and separation. And, although it may seem as if the mother had several months to make her decision and her plan, it isn't until the baby is born that the reality of that decision can become known to her. It is only then, after the birth and when she has become emotionally stabilized, that a truly informed decision can be made.

What I am trying to say to adoptees is that, although you are allowed your child-felt responses to your birth mother's decision, at some point, as an adult, you will have to understand the true circumstances under which that decision was made.

To all members of the triad I would like to say that reunions are an important part of an adoptee's being able to understand who he/she is. Being cut off from your heritage is a terrible legacy. It can keep a person paralyzed in a state of no-oneness. Without a past—a biological history—it is difficult to plan for the future. We may not understand why this is true, but it is. The adoption decree neither allowed the birth mother to just get on with her life nor afforded the adoptee a free ride in his new family. Both have been suffering the loss of the other and need to be reconnected. But that is only the beginning.

*The Honeymoon*

When we see reunions on television, we see weeping adoptees and birth mothers fall into one another's arms in ecstasy. There is such a sense of relief that they have at last found one another, such a feeling of having come home, that everyone is entranced. Sometimes the two talk for hours and hours. Sometimes they just hold one another. They go on to call on the phone every day and talk for hours. They plan when they can again see one another. And every parting feels like the first separation. They are devastated by the tremendous sense of loss. Some fear that they will never see one another again. Many regress back to that stage when they left one another the first time. The adoptee feels that she needs her mother to be available to her at all times, just as an infant would. The mother feels the need to be available just as she felt when her baby was taken from her. This time can be wonderful for both of them, even though it may be a bit scary. And if they both go through this together, they can do a great deal of healing just by having a lot of contact. (The effect this has on everyone else will be addressed later.)

This stage should not be prolonged, however. In my first book, I mentioned that it is important for the adoptee to be in charge of the reunion at first, because he had no choice in the decision to be relinquished. However, I didn't mean for this arrangement to go on forever. Both the adoptee and the birth mother have to grow in their relationship with one another. The mother has to become more mature, and the adoptee has to give up being the baby. Everyone has to become conscious and aware of what is happening so a successful relationship can be negotiated. This is essential to a satisfactory reunion. Too often, either one or the other, or both the adoptee and birth mother stay in the regressed phase and act out in the relationship. This brings to a close the ecstasy of the honeymoon period of a reunion.

## Different Expectations

Not all reunions begin with a honeymoon period. Sometimes one or the other of the pair is so much in denial, or unconscious, or numb that she doesn't see any reason to cooperate in the reunion relationship. "I don't need this," is the way she may convey her disinterest. But even if both parties are interested, the expectations of what the reunion will be like are often very different between the two. This often has to do with how much time to spend together or how often to write, e-mail, or phone. In many cases, there is a big discrepancy between what each expects from the other. This is when the honeymoon begins to wane.

Sometimes the differences in expectations have to do with how much to talk about "important things" (i.e., feelings). Either one or the other wants to keep everything on the superficial level—talking about what they are doing, the weather, what other members of the family are doing, etc. The other wants to get right down to basics and talk about the relationship and all the feelings that are evoked in their being together. What I recommend when there is a discrepancy between what each wants to do is to set aside a time every once in awhile to check out the emotional content of the relationship, but keep things light most of the time. After all, we don't talk about feelings all the time with other people with whom we are in relationship. Granted, the reunited pair have not had the advantage of years of familiarity to allow for the easy exchange of ideas and emotions. But talking about heavy things all the time, or even most of the time, is draining. If you can agree on a "rationing" of emotional topics, it might satisfy both.

One of the things I've noticed, and in my experience this happens more often with the adoptee than with the birth mother, is that even when feelings are *not* being discussed, there is the accusation that they *are* being talked about. This is why some adoptees don't want to be alone with their birth mothers. What I would like to say to adoptees is that it is *not talking about feelings* that is bothering you. Rather, it is *the actual experiencing of feelings in the presence of your birth mother* that is bothering you. She isn't talking about these feelings, but because they are so present in the one-on-one encounter, it *seems* as if they are being talked about. They are just there—all around you. This is especially true of adoptees who say they can take or leave a relationship with their birth mothers. I have seen this happen over and over again. So what you adoptees need to do is to admit that it is the feelings that are evoked while being alone with your birth mother which are making you so uneasy. What you also need to acknowledge is that these feelings *mean something!* Then, you can give in to them and let them guide you in your relationship with her. Resisting the feelings by avoiding alone time with your birth mother is not the answer. This will only make them more intense the next time and make the relationship more difficult.

Adoptive parents, too, have different expectations of the reunion experience. I talked to an adoptive mother at a conference who told me that she thought once her daughter had all the answers she wanted from her birth mother things would get back to normal. In other words, the birth mother would again fade from their lives. She was perplexed by her daughter's need to keep her birth mother in her life. She was a thoughtful mother who truly loved her daughter, so she was getting used to the idea of the birth mother's being permanently in their lives. She just had a different expectation from that of her daughter.

Or perhaps not. Perhaps it was also the daughter's expectation that she just needed information. Many adoptees have no idea how intense the feelings will be when they reunite. They may have spent most of their lives thinking very little about their birth mothers and believe that they only want information. After all, they have one mother and that is enough. However, when the reunion takes place a truly mystical thing happens between her and her birth mother. She feels unable to leave and devastated when she has been separated again. She can't wait to hear from her birth mother and waits by the phone like a besotted teenager waiting for her boyfriend to call. It is perplexing for her, too, and totally unexpected. She doesn't know what to do. She just knows that she needs her birth mother in a way she never could have expected. She is then faced with the necessity of finding a way to make her relationships with both her mothers work.

### When the Birth Mother Has also Suffered Early Loss

One of the most difficult hurdles to cross in reunions is that of having two babies and no mother. What I mean by that is sometimes the birth mother has either been abandoned (physically or emotionally) as a baby or young child or has had some other early trauma which has left her still needing to have *her* baby needs met. In other words, when there are two people in the reunion with narcissistic wounds the reunion is more difficult. It means that when the adoptee acts out by testing and rejecting the birth mother in some way, she is not able to tolerate the behavior or sustain her maternal feelings for her child. She just wants out.

If a birth mother has matured at least to adolescence, she is able to remain the mother for her reunited child. She can withstand the posturing and testing behavior and not again jump ship. She has an understanding of what her child is doing and like mothers everywhere tolerates it while trying to teach a different way of behaving.

However, if the mother has been in an incubator as an infant, is herself an adoptee who hasn't worked though some of her own issues, or has had some kind of early neglect or abuse, she may very well be unable to sustain the role of mother. She will herself want to be mothered. Or, at the very least, she will want her child to want her and treat her well. She will be very disappointed that her child seems to be selfish and controlling. She will wonder if it wouldn't have been better if they had not met at all. It will all seem very black and white. "Either she loves me and treats me well, or I am out of here."

Whereas many birth mothers may have this same thought, those who are not narcissistically needy will be able to ride out the rejecting behavior, just be glad that their child is safe and well, and wait for things to change. They will keep sending short, innocuous messages once in awhile. They will be patient and understanding. This doesn't mean that they need to accept disrespectful behavior from their children. Quite the contrary. Emotionally mature birth mothers can convey to their children that they expect to be respected. They can discourage bad behavior without becoming too emotional themselves or cutting their children off. It is when the birth mother is herself in that baby place that she feels she cannot tolerate the baby behavior of her child and wants to abandon him again.

### Parenting the Birth Mother

This puts the adoptee in the position of having to be the parentified child, having to take care of the emotional needs of a parent. This makes most adoptees very upset. They thought that when they found their birth mothers they would be able to allow themselves to sink into the embrace of a mother's loving care. Many were too scared to allow this to happen with the adoptive mother. Others had adoptive mothers who were incapable of doing so. So, the reunion was supposed to be the opportunity to have some of those unmet needs met. And lo and behold, instead of a mother, they found a child. Not fair!

Some adoptees are so used to this role, having had that position in the adoptive family, that they fall into it despite themselves. Others are so disgusted that they decide the relationship isn't worth it. Whatever the case, this scenario is the most difficult to handle. Either there is no adult or the roles are reversed. Emotional needs are in jeopardy and everyone loses. This is the reason that any birth mother who has had early childhood trauma or loss needs some counseling before contemplating a reunion. Someone needs to know what is going on and how to proceed with the adoptee/child. In the beginning, it needs to be the mother. Of course, if she is the one found, she doesn't have time to get ready. In this case, she needs to at least realize what is happening and do her best to temper the situation. Getting into a support group as the birth mother, and getting into therapy where the inner child can be satisfied may be necessary. Getting help with the relationship between adoptee and birth mother may also be needed. This is a chance to heal and it should not be wasted.

*Hit and Run Reunions*

On my Web site, I warn anyone wanting to search to be sure that they are willing to be there for the duration. Too many times I have heard about adoptees or birth mothers who open the door to reunion only to close it when things don't meet their expectations. Even if adoptees search with only the expectation of getting information, they have to understand that they will be opening a plethora of feelings for the person for whom they are searching. The adoptees who stops communicating with her birth mother after getting all the data she wants is being unfair to her. She may have spent a great deal of energy trying to bury her feelings of remorse and sorrow about having surrendered her child. Now she has had that door opened and it isn't going to get closed. It is not easy to shut down a second time. Adoptees, too, have to be willing to stay the course and remain in the relationship. They can get help from a therapist in negotiating a satisfactory relationship. The mother/child bond is the strongest bond in the world. It is much stronger than a marriage. You can't divorce your mother or your child. Perhaps you can separate physically, but you can't separate emotionally. Haven't you already tried that? Did it work? How are your other relationships?

Some birth mothers, especially those I described in the above paragraphs, decide after finding their children that they have had enough. The adoptee is a disappointment and she wants to have nothing more to do with him. She thus abandons him a second time. When I try to explain that as adoptive parents many of us have hung in there with an acting out child, they will reply, "Yes, but he is an adult now." This may be true chronologically, but not emotionally and definitely not when he is with you. *Most adoptees regress when with their birth mothers.* They are not acting like adults. They do not have control over their emotions. You need to deal with him as if he were a two-year-old. At the same time, you have to be aware that he is indeed an adult and at times will act like one and resent being treated like a child. It is a tricky situation, one that those living with adoptees call *riding the roller coaster or walking through a mine field.* No one knows when the switch will take place. Some people say it's like living with Dr. Jekyll and Mr. Hyde. It definitely is like living with an adult/child. Adoptees vacillate back and forth between the two. Most of the time they don't realize that they are doing so.

Now, I am not letting adoptees off the hook here. This whole book is an attempt to help adoptees take more responsibility for their effect on others. I am trying to get rid of many of the landmines so that living with an adoptee isn't so hazardous. However, since adoptees have been using coping mechanisms all of their lives, they are blissfully unaware that what they are doing is harmful to others. They definitely need to be taught this, but there has to be some understanding and patience while they are learning. Birth mothers have to understand that the roots of their child's giving them a hard time were formed during the separation from her. This is not a reason to feel guilty, but those of you who feel guilty for having surrendered your child need to take this as an opportunity to set things straight. Abandoning your child a second time will be devastating, even if he is acting like a jerk. You may feel justified, but you are not. *Nothing justifies a second rejection by a mother.*

To adoptees I say, "Knock it off." If you've been giving your birth mother a hard time for awhile, then enough already! Try to get to your adult self. If that isn't always possible, at least become aware that you are acting like a scared child and say so. Then do something different. This is essential in all your relationships, not only that with your birth mother. *All of us are tired of dealing with the baby.*

To anyone contemplating a search, make sure that you are stable enough to deal with the consequences of a reunion. Be sure that you can withstand finding the acting out or reluctant adoptee or finding a childlike mother or a petrified, ashamed mother who can't tell her family about you. Get in a support group or therapy with an informed therapist. Whatever you do, don't search unless you are prepared to hang in there. It isn't fair to either wounded person if you bail out after reunion. No one has a corner on pain here. Everyone needs understanding, compassion, and love.

*Notes from Me to You*

Here is where I would like to address triad members individually. Because I have communicated with so many members of the triad—in the thousands by now—I feel that I have some insight into how many of you feel and fear. It is nevertheless difficult to get through to some of you because denial is such a key component of adoption. Denial isn't something that you can just turn on and off. True denial is an unconscious defense mechanism, meaning that you *don't know* when you are in denial. You just believe certain things as if they were true. We have a tendency to say, "She's in denial," or "He's in denial," with such derision, as if that person could just snap out of it. He/She can't! By it's very definition denial is unknown to the person in its clutches. Denial is a defense mechanism meant to protect the one employing it from psychological harm. Our defense mechanisms are there for a reason—to protect us from deterioration, from meltdown. So those adoptees or birth mothers who say that they don't have any need for the other are probably in more need and are more devastated than those who have been able to allow their feelings to surface.

Having said that, and I am aware that many of you will be angry at me for this statement, I would like to nevertheless encourage each of you who is over the age of 25 and still believes that you do not need to search to allow just a tiny hint of skepticism into your belief. When I wrote *The Primal Wound*, I was convinced that all babies suffer from the separation from their biological mothers. Today, ten years later, I am even more convinced. There is nothing in the latest pre-and perinatal literature or neurological research to convince me otherwise. Quite the contrary. All the latest research is even more convincing of the profound, primal connection which exists between mother and child. Any severing of that connection has tremendous psychological, emotional, and neurological ramifications. And for infants and young children even day-long absences, as in the case of day care, is harmful. We fail to recognize this at our peril. We have to stop denying (in the conscious sense) the consequences of our choices which we can't or do not want to change.

The connection with one's biological mother, father, and heritage is part of our instinctive nature. We *need* that connection. Some people begin to realize this earlier than others. Some young children begin asking about their birth mothers almost as soon as they can talk. Others never mention a word about her until they are 35 or 50. Our society has not fostered the idea of that quintessential connection as being important, especially regarding adoption. It was and may still be believed that the placement of an infant in an adoptive family made him a member of that family and all the ancestors thereof. And it is true that in some adoptive families the adoptee feels loved and included by everyone in the family, including the aunts, uncles, grandparents, and cousins. But there is some small voice down deep within that says, "Yes, but I am not related to them." Now, of course one may be related by deep and abiding attachments. But there is something everlasting, mysterious, and true about blood relationships. *They mean something.* They mean something even if we wish they didn't. I have worked with some people (not adoptees) who would dearly love to divorce their entire biological family. Some have managed the physical separation, but none I have ever worked with has managed the emotional separation. There are always strong feelings connected to their family.

What am I saying, then? I am saying that I truly believe that reunions are an essential part of a person's discovering who he is. They answer so many questions that remain unanswered when reunions are impossible (as in some black market or international adoptions). Some adoptees are so different from their adoptive parents, even when those adoptive parents are wonderful people (which has nothing to do with it), they simply lose all sense of themselves. Or they believe the sense they have of themselves is terribly flawed because it is so different. (Remember the Ugly Duckling!) It is such a relief to meet people who have some of the same qualities as they have. It may not be the birth mother or the birth father. It may be one of the siblings. I have met adoptees who don't relate very well to either biological parent, but have a close relationship with one of their aunts or sibs. Somewhere in the family, in an aunt or an uncle, a sib or a cousin, there will be a person with whom the adoptee can breathe freely. Someone with whom she can feel as if she is okay ... *that all along she has been okay.* It was just that she was different from those around her.

What is it about being different that is so bad? We see it in all the various kinds of prejudice and bigotry that go on in this country—race, sexual orientation, and different traditions and cultures. Can it be any wonder that living in a country where differences, instead of being celebrated and useful, are derided and treated with contempt that an adoptee tries to avoid being different from his adoptive parents? The secrecy of closed adoptions only serves to reinforce that sense of shame. The excuse legislators use to deny adoptees their original birth certificates is a sham—birth mothers were promised confidentiality. I have met thousands of birth mothers and not one has been promised confidentiality. What is more true is that she was told she had better leave her child alone. She was not to bother the new family in some selfish pursuit of her own. Many birth mothers were afraid to search, even in the light of recent reunions, because they were still operating under the fear instilled by social workers and attorneys in the past. Most legislators are attorneys, so they wish to operate under the illusion that they or their colleagues promised confidentiality to these women who were for the most part coerced into giving up their babies.

Granted, there are some birth mothers who do not wish to be found. Some of them claim to have been promised confidentiality. Perhaps some of them were. As I said, I haven't met any among the thousands who have communicated with me over the past ten years. One legislator told someone that even if only one birth mother objected to being found, confidentiality should be maintained. *Only one?* Is that the way we operate in a democracy? What about the thousands who weren't promised and don't want confidentiality? And what about the adoptee? Is it because adoptees had no one to speak for them at the time of their relinquishment that their wishes are secondary to the six birth mothers who do not wish to be found? Those birth mothers know their heritage. They are not languishing in the never-never land of ancestral anonymity. *No one should be forced to be anonymous.*

At this point I would like to speak separately to the three parts of the triad. However, all parts should be read by everyone; you will all learn something! I will begin with the birth mother, because she is where it started. Part of the time I will be speaking to both birth parents. I will try to be clear about this.

## To Birth Parents

*Birth Mothers: From Conception to Birth*

> *The presence of her absence is everywhere.*
> *Edna St. Vincent Millay*

At a time in your lives when you were young and vulnerable you had sex and conceived a baby. If you gave birth in the mid-20th century through the early part of the seventies, you may have been among the 95–97 percent of white, middle-class women who were coerced into giving up their babies for adoption. You really had very little choice. Times were different then. You did as you were told. The fact that you were having sex was shameful enough and that you got pregnant was a crisis. It brought shame on the family. There was not an atmosphere where you could take a stand. The humiliation of having been caught at having sex put you in a position to do as you were told. Keeping the pregnancy from others, even other members of the family in some cases, was paramount. So you, the young mother-to-be, went off to a relative or an unwed mothers' home to give birth. Often there was little support for you and more shame heaped upon that already garnered by your family.

When your baby was born, you were asked to sign papers when you were fatigued by the birthing process, under the influence of meds, in shock, and unable to make an informed decision. Many of you were denied your right to hold or even see your baby. You were lied to, coerced, and shamed. You were made to feel selfish for wanting to keep your baby. On the rational level, it seemed that the only thing to do was to give up your rights to your child and turn them over to a "more deserving couple." You were promised that these were people who would be able to give your child things that you would not, the first of which was a two-parent family. So you tried to still the raging instincts and intuition that told you that you should not be separated from your child, that he would need you and you would be the best person to take care of him. You were made to believe that this permanent solution to a temporary problem (your immediate inability to take care of this infant alone) was the better solution. Most of you overrode your intuition and instincts and signed the papers.

At that point, some of you went to pieces and sobbed for days and finally stopped only when you convinced yourselves that one day you might have a chance to meet your child again. Others of you went numb and didn't have any feelings about anything for 20 years or more. From 40–60 percent of you were unable to conceive again, due to secondary infertility, which was largely due to psychological issues having to do with guilt. Those of you who did have children may have parented your subsequent children differently than you might otherwise have done because of having lost the first one.

Whether you went numb or remained painfully aware of your sacrifice, you have been undeniably scarred by the surrendering of your first child. The rekindling of those painful memories can be devastating. Some of you have fantasies about your lost children. Most of you have clung to the promise by social workers of your child's having a wonderful childhood and upbringing in his life with the adoptive parents.

### The Shock of the Lie

What no one was factoring into the mix was the trauma that the child was experiencing upon being separated from you. Although many of you instinctively believed that your child would be better off with you, being a good American, you allowed yourselves to be convinced that logic was to take precedence over intuition. (Recent brain research contradicts the wisdom of this attitude.) You were convinced of the need for material well-being to create a good atmosphere for a child to grow up in. Again, this is the good, old American way! Never mind that there are happier families in the jungles of Costa Rica than in New York City and that money has never managed to buy happiness.

Some of you, being brave souls who defied the threats of the social workers, decided that you had to know what happened to your children and searched. When you found them, some of you were very upset to learn that your child was not as happy and well off as you had been led to believe. Although many had the educational and social opportunities that you were promised, there was something wrong. There was a hole in the emotional well-being of your child. And in other cases, the educational opportunities were never realized because anxiety and hypervigilance kept your child from focusing well enough to do well in school. Some acted out and got into trouble, in some cases with the law. There was trouble in paradise.

Even for those of you whose children did well in school and later in their professions, there seemed to be a sadness underlying everything. What was this and whose fault was it? Many of you blamed the adoptive parents. What did they do to make your child so sad? So angry? So unable to sustain relationships? Granted, there are some adoptive parents who were totally unsuited to be parents, let alone adoptive parents (which requires even more than mere parenting).

Some were alcoholics, some abusers, some just incompetent, childlike people. Whether they were good parents or incompetent parents, none was given even a hint that the child they were taking home was suffering a loss and would need a witness and comforter to his suffering. None was told that there is a psychological and emotional price to pay for separation trauma and that their child was going to be paying that price. As were they. No one told them that bonding is physiological as well as psychological, or that their child, at the most vulnerable time of her life having suffered a devastating loss, would be unable to trust that kind of connection ever again. So they made mistakes.

Yet most adoptive parents, at least most of the hundreds with whom I have communicated, were deeply caring and loving people. They wanted to do their best for their children. They were puzzled by the difficulties in communication between them. A marvelous quotation from an adoptive mother best explains what many have experienced: "I have grieved anew the confirmation that I cannot be to these children the mother I want to be. *They have both limited my expressions of affection and their own.* I ache for them at times, and feel that I am watching them from a distance. It is the most painful aspect for me, yet I have no regrets. I love them dearly." The sentence which I placed in italics is very telling. Many adoptees find their adoptive parents unaffectionate, but have little or no idea how their own need for distancing may have contributed to this phenomenon. It is not their fault. It is not their adoptive parents' fault. It is not anyone's fault. It is just one of the coping mechanisms which limited the adoptive relationship.

Most adoptive parents had no idea what was happening. They believed, as I did, that all you had to do was to provide a loving home for a child and everything would be fine. We were all very naïve. We were convinced, just as many of you birth mothers were, that adoption would work. And to a certain extent it did. Many adoptees are productive, relatively happy people who are living ordinary lives. Yet the differences cannot all be laid at the feet of the competence of the adoptive parents to nurture their children. Separation trauma, regardless of the abilities of the parents, causes deep, devastating wounds. Children perceive the events in their lives in different ways. A whole system of beliefs is predicated upon these perceptions. These beliefs govern the ways in which adoptees will act in the world. No matter what that is, none has escaped the sorrow of that loss. It has been there all along and plays a part in every aspect of their lives. It is a shadow that is cast on even the most brilliant of days. It shows in their eyes.

Many adoptees don't even know it. After all, they have known nothing else. They believe that everyone lives with anxiety. They have never been a minute without it, so it seems normal to them. And sadness? It is such an integral part of their neurological makeup that they are unaware that it *is* sadness. It just is. It is just the way they have always been. They have been feeling the grief of your absence ever since you left. They just don't label it as such. Or some of them don't. There are some who have been painfully aware for a very long time that they have a hole where you belong. Some of them have figured it out. But not all. Some are in denial in the real sense of the word and actually think that nothing is wrong. They have never known anything else. It just is.

What am I saying then? Am I saying that since the root of the adoptees' pain is the separation from you it is your fault that they have had a difficult time in their lives? No. What I am doing is trying to eliminate blame altogether. We are all victims of our cultures and the moral values that permeate that culture. Sometimes those values help us and other times they are so narrow and judgmental that they harm us. Many of you lived in a time when what the neighbors thought of you was considered by your parents as more important than knowing what happened to their grandchildren. Should we blame them, then?

### Blame: A Foil to Healing

Placing blame just keeps someone a victim. It hampers progress. It creates impasses. It is useless. It allows us to look at someone else rather than at ourselves. How are we now acting? Are we helping with the healing or contributing to the pain? A great deal of an adoptee's problems can be attributed to the separation trauma. It might be a good time to review the manifestations of trauma in the first chapter of this book. Many of you will be familiar with them because you, too, have experienced them. But at least your trauma was conscious. Many of you understood that you were experiencing the loss of your child. Adoptees were infants and totally confused by your absence. They have had no help in knowing the source of their sorrow or anger. The ignorance of social workers and adoptive parents as to the fact and fallout from that trauma has only added to their confusion. With no acknowledgment as to the source of the feelings, there could be no help in alleviating them. So social workers, therapists, and adoptive parents have also contributed to the adoptees' inability to heal. And as adults, many adoptees still do not attribute their difficulties in relationships and their being paralyzed in their lives a result of having been separated from you. Or if they do, many of them do not feel responsible for doing anything about it. They refuse to do anything about their behavior and their effect on others. So, in some ways we are all to blame, but *out of ignorance, not malice.* There is definitely enough blame to go around. We could continue slinging blame at one another, but what would that prove? We all did our part, or are still doing our part. The question is *what are we going to do now?* My suggestion is that rather than blaming one another we instead try to help one another. This way we can all become healers instead of blamers, healers instead of victims.

*What You Can Do*

As birth parents you can help by being available to your children. Yes, you will have to re-experience (or perhaps experience for the first time if you are one of the numb ones) the original pain of the loss of your child. Don't think, however, that you have escaped the influence of that pain, even if you managed not to feel it. What about the secondary infertility? What about the failed relationships with others? What about the unspoken chasm between you and your parents? What about the way you either failed to bond or became smothering with your other children? What about *your* sad eyes?

No one escapes the consequences of trauma. Not your child. Not you. Not the adoptive parents. But now you can help do something about it. You have another chance. You can help your child heal from the consequences of that trauma. You can heal at the same time. Will it be complete? Will it be easy? In many cases, no. Separation is such an unnatural act. It is unnatural for all mammals, all animals including humans who have a gestation period. Birds can imprint with other species because they develop inside a shell but outside the mother. Mammals imprint with the mother in utero, before birth. Anyone besides her seems wrong. There may be a strong attachment to others, but bonding already took place. Any subsequent "bonding" lacks the trust of the original bonding because it happens after the disruption of the natural order of life.

As a result of the unnatural separation, reunions may feel unnatural. At any rate, they will probably be difficult. There have been so many years of separation, so many feelings that need to be felt and expressed, so many words that need to be spoken. Many of you, both mother and child, will regress. There will be a teenaged mom and a baby trying to figure out what to do. Neither will be acting in an adult manner, even if they think they are. Throw genetic sexual attraction, the intense erotic and sometimes sexualized feelings that exist between birth parents and their children, into the equation and reunions can be an emotional minefield. But as the mother or father you owe it to your child to do your best. And you must remember that *you are the parents.* As young and unsure as you may be feeling, you are not feeling as young as your child. Both of you suffered trauma at the time of the separation, but you were older then and you have to act older now. Your child needs you. Don't fail him.

Never mind that you turned over the rights to another set of parents. Those parents, although they may have been wonderful or they may have been terrible, were never going to be able to mirror your child the way you could have. Your child grew up without ever seeing him or herself reflected back. Do you have any idea what a deficit this is? They need that mirroring, even today. The adoptive parents may have done their best, but they could not reflect their children back to them. And they cannot give them a genetic history. Their ancestors are not the ancestors of your child, regardless of that legal document that says they are the parents.

This doesn't mean that you are now to take over as the parents. You child has two sets of parents. You fulfill different aspects of your child's life, and he needs you both. No matter how much he likes or dislikes his adoptive parents, they are the custodians of his childhood history. They were witnesses to his early life. They helped shape that life. We all need witnesses to our lives, especially children because children are wont to perceive things differently from adults. They see things with their baby or child minds. Ask any person about events that happened when she was a child, then ask the parent; you will get different versions of those events. You will even get different versions from various children. In talking to my children, I am sometimes astonished by the ways they interpreted things I said or did. Their interpretations may have had little or nothing to do with my intent. We all have different realities. A child whose first postnatal experience was of separation from mother will have a very different version of her life than a child who didn't have that experience.

## A Right to Know

To get back on point—*everyone has a right to know who they are.* We are none of us a tabula rasa. We have genes and those genes determine a great deal about who we are meant to be. We are not meant to live by coping mechanisms alone. We have a personality embedded in our genetic code. The legal documents known as the amended birth certificate and adoption papers do not change that code. However, growing up without mirroring tends to cover up some of the truth of that code. It tends to foster a false self or an adaptive self. In time, some adoptees begin to identify with that adaptive self because it is all they know. They have done a first class job of covering up the authentic self. They continue to adapt to every new situation. They have become chameleons. It leaves them feeling uneasy, as if something is amiss, but they don't know what to do about it. It feels like life or death to them. The rest of us are left feeling as if we can never get to know the person wrapped so tightly inside that adaptation. Or, if we have managed to see beneath that protective shell, we keep wondering when the adoptee will at last discard it and become real. As a birth parent, you will wonder, too, because your child may be afraid to reveal the "defective" self that you once failed to keep. You, too, will get to deal with the false self, even if you reflect some of your child back to him. He may not be able to uncover his more authentic Self right away and he may not trust it completely. It will take time. But being with both of you—mother and father—can help. You each contributed to the genetic structure of your child. He is part of both of you. His need for you is monumental whether he knows it or not.

There is an inherent need to know who we are and whence we came. It should be a basic human right in this country. In a ruling to allow an adoptee the right to gain access to adoption records, Judge Wade S. Weatherford, Jr. of South Carolina, one of the more enlightened judges in this country, said: "Even now the sands and ashes of continents are being sifted to find where we made our first step as man. Religions of mankind often include ancestor worship in one way or another. For many the future is blind without a sight of the past. Those emotions and anxieties that generate our thirst to know the past are not superficial or whimsical. They are real and they are good cause under the law of man and God." This is a very wise man. You also must be wise, not afraid. You are the only ones who can supply your child with the information he needs.

For birth mothers, this information includes the name of the birth father. Just as you are no longer the naïve teenager who succumbed to those in authority, perhaps he is no longer the jerk who left you in the lurch. You changed; hopefully so has he. Often you are the only one who knows his identity. You must not keep it from your child, even if she was conceived in rape (unless you did not know the rapist, but this is rare). *No one should be anonymous.* Keeping their genetic history from adoptees makes many of them feel like non-persons. They continue to float through life, never feeling rooted. There is a reason we call our biological history a family *tree.* That tree provides roots to all who are members. Adoptees are grafted onto non-genetic root stock. Their roots are different. That difference is felt by them.

Some adoptees will say that they prefer the grafted part of themselves. That is fine so long as they have the chance to find out what the original root stock is. But not knowing is not okay. It is your responsibility as the biological parents of that child to be available to answer questions or to have a relationship. Even though you both may have been young when you decided to have sex, you were not babies. There was a consequence to that decision. The baby is not the one who should be paying the price for it. He has already paid enough in having to suffer the loss of you. It has affected his every relationship. Yes, you were also a victim. But why compound the pain for all of you by again being unavailable to your child? You must not. His yearning is so deep and so instinctive that you must answer his call. To ignore it is unconscionable. And it won't bring you any peace.

The severing of the connection and bond between mother and child is the most devastating loss in the world. Please be a participant in healing that wound.

### Birth Fathers and Healing

Although my first book was primarily about the effects of severing the bond between mother and child, the birth father also has a great deal that he can do in order to help his child heal. In addition, he needs to heal himself. As a boy grows into a man, he begins to realize the tremendous responsibility he has in the lives of those he loves. Many boys/men were not very supportive when they heard they had helped conceive a child. They, too, may have been at the mercy of their parents and their parents' wish for secrecy. Also, they were not feeling the same connection to that growing child in the womb that the mother was feeling. It was easier for them to entertain the idea of just walking away. And many of them did. They walked away from both the mother and the baby. Years later, they are beginning to understand the consequences of that decision.

Just as birth mothers have to be able to say they are sorry to their children without the qualifying phrase that follows, so too do birth fathers have to say they are sorry, both to their children and to the mothers of those children. Randy Wood, a birth father from Oregon who is writing a book on the subject, is trying to do just that. He has given me permission to quote some e-mails he sent to me after we met at a CUB Retreat. What he has to say is very important. He is very articulate, but most of all he is totally honest with himself. Here is some of what he has to say:

> The reason your book had such an enormous impact on me is because, in so precisely identifying the pain caused by the primal wound of separation between my daughter and her mother, I am forced, as a birthfather, to squarely face the tremendous, almost unbearable amount of pain my decision not to support the mother in her desire to keep our baby, caused for them BOTH. A primal wound that forever altered my daughter's life ... forever changed the natural course of her life, which should have blossomed within her original family. That is the legacy I left my child. The unbearable pain of that separation, that is the legacy I left her birthmom. To truly heal, I must face and own the consequences of my actions and the devastating affect those actions had on both their lives.
>
> For a birthfather to come out of the shadows, enter fully into the reunion process and actively seek true healing, he MUST stare the primal wound squarely in the face and come to grips with the life-changing consequences that this wound caused in those two human beings.
>
> You see, intuitively males absolutely understand that wonderful, mysterious connection between a mother and her unborn child. When a father shares in a healthy, wanted pregnancy with his spouse or significant other later in life, he witnesses and experiences this almost holy connection between mother and child. In a healthy relationship,

sharing the life cycle as a vital part of the evolving growth of our child's life in the mother's womb is an honor and a blessing that deeply affects us as the future father of that child.

The Primal Wound is really a lighthouse for birthfathers, highlighting those consequences. It grabs that elusive intuition within our souls, bringing it to life by dramatically describing the trauma of the separation caused by our decision to abandon our baby. ... The birthfather understands that HE is the one responsible for the devastation in those two lives because of the adoption decision he supported ... either actively or by virtue of abandoning the birthmom. In many cases, including mine, if the birthfather had just said "Keep her," that would have changed everything!

With regards to the child, it's not guilt really; it's a profound sense of grief over the loss of that child and that child's involvement in our life. Sure there's an incremental amount of guilt, especially if the child had a difficult time adjusting in his adoptive family or faced abuse or neglect. But the vast majority of guilt that a birthfather feels is almost exclusively reserved for the birthmother and the impact his actions had on damaging her sense of self. A birthmother doesn't feel guilt associated with the birthfather in this same manner, nor that sense of responsibility that a man feels.

As such, a birthfather needs to face the birthmother and ALL her pent up anger along with her anguish and deep, searing pain. He needs to become a man of character this time around, step up to the plate and face and own the devastation his actions caused ... the entirety of the primal wound of the birthmother as she stands there, alone in front of him. Only then can he begin to truly heal the deep wounds in his own Soul.

Although Randy was only 16 when his child was born, he is not using this as an excuse for his actions. He has forgiven the 16-year-old self, yet says:

But the core of what I am learning has nothing to do with age. Birthfathers who were 20, 23, or 28 years old feel in the core of their being the same way I do. I believe it's something unique to a male ... a truth about our creation as men that leaves us with this sense of responsibility. I feel an obligation to try to articulate what on the inside feels like an illusive intuition of sorts. I understand my youth and my situation and have forgiven myself, realizing that I was ignorant and as such couldn't make the best decision at that time. However, that doesn't absolve me, at my core, of needing to accept responsibly ... as a man ... for the trauma that took place. I believe you are going to hear this theme resonate from all birthfathers who gather the strength to come out of the shadows, so it must be addressed head on and not coddled the way society has done these many years. There is something liberating in the center of his being for a man to be able to fully own his part in giving his child away and facing the damage to his child's birthmom. What I need is someone to help me bring this intuition out of the hazy realm of feeling into the clear light of understanding.

This is a birthfather who is willing to do the work needed to heal both his daughter and her birth mother in addition to himself. He also has to be heedful of the effect this reunion and the subsequent need for healing has had on his spouse. She, too, is suffering. More about that later. I just want to add that birth fathers are not immune to the pain which adoption can cause, nor the pain that their lack of responsibility toward their girlfriends had on all concerned. Not everyone has articulated it so well, but I have heard from other birth fathers who have similar feelings. I am glad that Randy is planning to publish a book about this aspect of adoption.

The pain of the relinquishment of their child may not "hit" either the birth mother or the birth father until years after the fact. Many of them just went numb. The advent of the reunion can trigger the hitherto unfelt emotions for both mother and father. Reunions can be a forum for healing for all of them. It takes a great deal of work, however, and everyone has to be willing to take responsibility for how each has affected and is affecting one another.

## To Adoptees

*To Search or Not to Search*

Many of you have known for a long time that you needed to find your biological family in order to know yourselves better and to heal some unfathomable hole in your soul. You have felt an instinctive need to be reconnected with the mother who gave birth to you and whose genes you carry. There has been an emotional hole within you that has been there since you were separated from her.

After you have found her, you begin to feel the need to know about the other half of you. You need to find your birth father. Although the need to find him is often secondary to the need for your mother, he is nevertheless an important part of who you are. Some sperm-donor babies are beginning to feel this need as they enter adolescence. They, too, don't want to be half anonymous. Adults sometimes make decisions the consequences of which they have never thought about. They need to think about them now. We all need to think about them now. You have been made to pay a huge price for their ignorance.

Others of you have adapted so completely that you don't even know that you have this need. You have become a very acceptable adaptive self. No one, including you, has a clue that you are not being real. It feels real to you because you have never known anything else. You have never been reflected. Adaptation and coping are what you know. It is all you know. Or, at least, all you let others see.

"There she goes again," you may say, "telling those of us who are feeling fine and not acting out and being ridiculous that it is just because we are in denial. You can't win with that woman." Well, that's true! I do believe that *all* babies are affected by separation from their mothers. That includes preemies and babies whose parents decided to take a two-week vacation without them when they were 16 months old. It includes babies who spend most of their waking hours in day care. Yes, I believe this affects them. I believe it affected you. You have nothing to compare it to because it has always been this way for you. But it has deeply affected the way you think about yourself and others and the way you respond emotionally and perhaps physically to experiences in your life. It has affected your attitudes and behavior and your relationships. It has affected the way your brain is wired.

As I told the birth parents, no one escapes the consequences of trauma. Trauma is sudden and takes one by surprise. Do you know anyone who likes to say inappropriate things to shock people? This is the projection of that surprise. It was a shock that your mother left you. You need to reconnect with her.

Some of you have searched and found. Others of you have been found. You have had a good beginning of the reunion—the honeymoon period—but then have found things you didn't like about your birth family or have begun feeling the anger that lurks inside the baby-self. Others of you have found a reluctant birth mother whom I have addressed in the above paragraphs. Whatever you have found, it is necessary to keep hold of your adult self, even when the baby tries to take over. Otherwise, things happen in the reunion that are difficult to reconcile. Some of you are too scared of hurting your adoptive parents to search at all. Let me address you first.

### Protecting the Adoptive Parents

I can understand your concern. It is good to be concerned about other people's feelings, especially people you care about. However, *finding your birth parents has nothing to do with your adoptive parents.* It is about finding you. It is about becoming more stable … planting your feet firmly on the ground. It is about knowing your genetic history. And it is about reconnecting with the person who gave birth to you. As much as some of you may want to deny it, that bond is a deep and abiding bond. Even if later you discover that you don't even know if you like your birth mother (which is rare, but happens), there will be primal feelings about her that are normal. None of this has to do with the people who reared you. They are your parents; they are Mom and Dad. But they can't give you everything. They can't give you your heritage and they can't reflect your features and traits. You need both. What they have given you is tremendous. But there is more, and we, as adoptive parents, don't have the right genetic code to fill in those gaps. It is impossible. Therefore, you have to go to the source. You may not even know how important this is because you have never experienced it. But its absence has influenced your life. It has had an effect on your self-image. Something your adoptive parents should know is that many adoptee/adoptive parents relationships are improved upon the reunion. The fantasies are gone and the birth family becomes a real, ordinary (for the most part) family. You need both in your life. And it can be done.

### Some Pitfalls in Reunion

Next I would like to address those of you who have searched and found. These relationships run the gamut from ecstasy to agony. Reunions are not easy. They are like all relationships, full of pitfalls and landmines, miscommunications and false assumptions, accusations and retaliations, and perhaps most difficult, different expectations. I have had all kinds of complaints about birth mothers from adoptees over the years. As I mentioned, expectation is a big stumbling block in reunions. With a few exceptions, it doesn't seem as if the expectations of the birth mother and the expectations of the adoptee coincide. But perhaps that is part of the "push-pull" aspect of the relationship. If you want more time with her, the birth mother pulls away to get some space. If you seem reluctant, she moves in and wants more time. Although these time/space problems may seem monumental, they can be negotiated, *but only when both of you are being adults.*

What I would like you to put limits on is the *abandoning the birth mother* phase of the reunion. I am not saying not to do it, just to set a time limit on it. I realize that most of you are unaware of what you are doing, so I am enlightening you. This is a phenomenon that I've observed in hundreds of reunions. There is the honeymoon period, then after a few months, or maybe a couple of years, there is silence. The birth mother doesn't hear from her child for long periods of time. (One mother in Canada waited ten years for her daughter to decide she wanted a relationship after all!) Well, ten years is too long. Yes, I know you waited 20, 28, 35, or 40 years to hear from your birth mother. I know that unconsciously you want her to know just how difficult that was. You waited, and waited, and waited, and waited. ... Even if you didn't consciously know you were waiting, you were. Now you are trying to get her to understand how difficult that was. So you don't call, you don't write, you don't e-mail, and you ignore or finesse her attempts to get together. If anyone asks you why, you say that you just haven't gotten around to it, you have been too busy, or you were just thinking of doing so. And this is the truth. There is nothing conscious about your abandoning your birth mother. It is one of those *projective identification* phenomena that I talk about in Chapter 17. It is an unconscious, behavioral attempt to communicate the pain of your separation.

Now, I could say to birth mothers, "Well, Carol waited 30 years to hear from you, what is a mere two years for you? If she could tolerate it, why can't you?" I could say that, but I won't because you are both adults now (even though the part of you who is abandoning her is a child), and it is time to act like it. Also, time is going by and enough time has already been wasted. So, if you have been neglecting your birth mother for over a year, it is time to stop. This is acting out; it is not living your true life. It is letting the baby be in control of your life. And maybe you need some of that. That's why I say, do it for awhile, but no more than a year. That's all! Six months would be better. Let your birth mom know that you now know what it is you were trying to do (however unconsciously) and you hope she has some idea of just how difficult it was for you to be without her. Even then, she won't understand completely. You were a helpless infant, totally bewildered, devastated, and terrified by her absence. She is an adult who may have support from family, support groups, and friends. In any case, she is an adult. You can never truly make her feel what you felt. So stop already! Enough is enough!

### Keep a Balance Between Feelings and Fun

It is time to begin the next phase of your relationship with her. You may need help with this. Both of you have been hurt by the long silence. You may be reluctant to begin communicating with her again. You may not know how to start. You will have to take it slowly. Build upon that basic bond you have with one another. Tell her what you've learned reading the last couple of paragraphs. Let her know that you had no idea that you were trying to replicate for her your own experience of separation and endless waiting. Tell her that you are probably still angry, but that you will try to express this more overtly with words instead of passive-aggressively in behavior, as you may have been doing. Tell her you need her help. If you get bogged down, you may need the help of a therapist or counselor who understands these issues. Whatever you do, *get on with it. Time's awastin'!*

As you begin the next phase of your relationship, don't talk about feelings all the time. This will only drain you both. But, adoptees, I will repeat what I said to birth mothers. Sometimes your being together makes you believe that feelings are being discussed simply because you are *experiencing* feelings so intensely. Being with her is bound to elicit intense feelings. Don't fight them or pretend they don't exist. I've met some of you who are so intent on believing that you have no feelings for "this person," sometimes out of anger, sometimes out of loyalty to the adoptive mother, that you project all your own feelings on her and then blame her for them. Be aware of your own feelings and take responsibility for them. Don't project them onto her and don't try to avoid them by avoiding alone time with her. Allow the feelings to surface. No matter how scary and difficult it may seem, you need to have time alone with her to talk about how everything is affecting you and to tell her what you need from her. If you don't take alone time with your birth mother, there will always be something between you that is going to interfere with your relationship—that big, pink elephant known as the mother/child bond. It's there, whether you want to acknowledge it or not. (Note to birth mothers: You need to be the mother here. Don't let *your* inner child surface! This is crucial.) Both of you should suspend judgment of yourselves, of each other, and of the adoptive parents. Each of you has your own "truth" about what happened. You can never completely know the others' truths. Just be there for one another. Just know that each of you has suffered from your separation, and that you have both learned some valuable lessons from the experience.

Limit the topics of phone conversations to mundane things. My experience with reunions has led me to believe that the phone is the worst method of communication for expressing feelings. I'm not sure why this is, but over and over again it has proven to be true. As tempting as it may be to blat out something over the phone, try hard to control that impulse. It will only bring about misunderstandings and alienation. Write, talk in person, or e-mail, but don't phone if you are experiencing intense, negative feelings. Positive feelings are all right to express in any way you want.

Most of the time, just have fun! Send e-mails about ordinary, daily life. Write poems for one another. Send funny stories about your life. Get to know one another. There is a lot of catching up to do. And this means both of you need to talk and to listen. Birth mothers have sometimes told me that their child doesn't seem to be interested in what interests them or in their present life. That's the narcissistic child surfacing—the adoptee is concerned only about himself. Adoptees, you need to learn more about your birth mothers. Everything you don't know, you project. Do you remember talking to her on the phone before you met her? What did you see? A phone suspended in air? I doubt it. I'll bet you pictured a person at the other end of the line. I know you made her up because you hadn't met her yet. We do this all the time when talking on the phone. Well, if you refuse to learn anything about your birth mother, you are making up the deficit with your imagination. You are assuming, probably not very accurately, all kinds of things about her. If you are having a positive relationship with her, those projections will be wonderful. If you are experiencing negative feelings about her, the projections will be unflattering. Neither may have very much to do with reality. Do you want her to do that to you? Take the time to listen to her, not only about the family history or the story of your conception, birth, and relinquishment (which you need to hear only once), but about her life today. What is her job like? What are her hobbies? What are her relationships like? What does she like to do on vacations? What are her values, politics, religion, opinions? What did she dream about when she was your age? This is important. You shouldn't judge any of this. You don't need to agree about things. Just use this information as a way to fill in the blanks about her. (Note to birth mothers: Stop obsessing about the similarities between you. For some reason it makes many adoptees annoyed having these things pointed out all the time.)

### The Futility of Regret

Some of you spend most of your time regretting what didn't happen. Try not to spend too much time here. Regret, guilt, shame, and anger will color your relationship with a gray pall. If you can't get beyond your anger at her, write her angry letters that you don't send. Get all that rage outside yourself. And don't let her pour out her guilt to you every time you meet. After she's said a couple of times that she is so sorry that she relinquished you, tell her that's enough. Her constant retelling of her regret will put you in a position of having to comfort her. That's not your job. You can have empathy for her situation and the climate of the times that caused her to relinquish you, but you are not required to listen to her lament about this every time you meet.

What you do need from her is at least one time when you can tell her how terrible it has been for you to be separated from her (this doesn't necessarily mean that it was terrible living with your adoptive parents, just that the separation left a hole in your soul) without her adding anything to her "I'm sorry." No reasons, no excuses, no history of the times, no nothing. Just "I am so sorry that I hurt you so!" Period. I've told her that she needs to do this, too. It will be difficult for her, but it will be a boon to the relationship if she can. One adoptee described it as magical!

Then your part will be to forgive her. Even if your life with your adoptive parents was abusive and terrible, you need to forgive your birth mother for having made that decision. This is for your benefit, as well as hers. It will allow the relationship to progress without all the guilt and shame. It will help eliminate regret. It will put you in the present where the relationship belongs. If both of you continue to wish that things had been different, you will get nowhere in your reunion. *You cannot change history. You can only live in the present. You can only influence the future.* So do what you can, and let go of what you can't. You both had the experience of living many years without one another. It was terrifying; it was painful; it was unnatural. But it happened. You can't undo it. What you can do is to go forward. Now it is time to make the most of the time you can have together. That means no guilt, no blame, no regrets.

Now, I am not so naïve that I think saying this is like a magic wand wiping out all those feelings of guilt, shame, or regret. What I am saying is that you must not allow yourselves to *dwell* in those feelings. Stop giving them so much energy. Each of you can have empathy for your younger selves, you for that scared, little child that you were, and she for the confused, young mother that she was. However, remind yourselves that you are adults now and each can help take care of that child or that young mother within. You each can listen to that inner younger self, empathize with her fears, and soothe her. Whatever you do, don't ignore her. That will only make her scream louder. But you must not let her take over. That is being indulgent and will get you nowhere. It's where you've been and where you no longer want to be.

### She Is a Mother, Not a Friend

Some of you are secretly (from yourselves as well as others) angry with your birth mother and don't want to acknowledge her as your mother. Others of you have some kind of misplaced loyalty to your adoptive mother. Whatever the reason, you may say, "Well, you can be a friend, but I already have a mother." Now, that sounds reasonable, *but it is not true.* Or rather, it is only partially true. Yes, you have a mother, but in fact *you have two mothers.* That's the way it is. You can define motherhood anyway you want, but your birth mother is one of your mothers. She can never be just a friend. It isn't in her psyche or yours. And it definitely is not in your biology or hers. A mother is a mother. Your feelings about her and hers about you will never be just those of a friend, no matter how hard you try. So forget it!

For one thing, you can never be unrelated to her. It doesn't matter what that piece of paper says. It is a legal document. It did not change your DNA or your ancestry. You can, if you want to make what I consider a bad decision, decide not to have a relationship with her, but you can't change your biology. You can try to make yourself believe that biology doesn't matter, but it does. Why do you think some adoptive mothers are so threatened by a reunion with a woman you may never have seen? They know that biology matters! They know that the birth bond matters. This is what scares them so much. So, stop denying your relationship to your birth mother. Don't try to pretend that she is only a friend. Hey, you're not fooling me. So stop trying to fool yourself.

Why do I insist? Because you are asking something of your birth mother that is impossible for her to do. There is no way a woman who has given birth can pretend that her child, no matter how old, is only a friend. So, you are being unfair in expecting her to do this. You will be angry at her because she won't be able to do it. You will blame her, accuse her, and vilify her. I am telling you that what you are asking is impossible. It can't be done...

### What About Your Adoptive Parents?

I will be writing a personal note to your adoptive parents, as well. But I want to talk to you about them. Some of you have feelings of guilt about wanting to search or having found. Some of you have not told your adoptive parents that you have had a reunion and have an ongoing relationship with your birth family. You have bought into the myth that you need to be grateful that they adopted you. So, you don't want to hurt them. I have discussed this in another part of the book, but it bears repeating—you did not, nor would you have, chosen to be relinquished and adopted by strangers. That decision was out of your hands. Your adoptive parents wanted a child and most of them deserved to have one. But they are the ones who should be grateful. They got what they wanted.

Now, some of you believe that you have disappointed your adoptive parents— you are not who they wanted you to be. Well, I am sorry if they expected that they would get a replica of themselves. That isn't biologically possible. I am sorry that they didn't know that you would be traumatized by the jolting separation from your birth mother and would be mourning her loss and trying to avoid another such loss for the rest of your life. (I am sorry *I* didn't know that.) But, as adoptive parents, we basically got what we wanted—a child. We are the ones who can feel grateful. You can be grateful for all the material things they gave you. The other things are things that all parents owe their children: clothing, food, shelter, nurturing, values, guidance, and acculturation. And love. All parents owe their children love. You can feel grateful that they were good parents if you want. All of you have friends who have less-than-good parents. Perhaps your parents were exceptional. That's definitely a plus for which to be grateful. What all parents owe their children is to do what is in their best interest. For you that includes finding out who you are.

You don't owe your parents a covenant never to look for your original parents. Searching for your roots is part of your legacy as an adoptee. As I said before, it is not about them: not about their not being good enough parents, not about your not loving them, not about their being a disappointment to you. It is about knowing about your ancestral past, so that you can see more clearly into the future. It is about being more accurately mirrored. It is about you and what is in your best interest.

Having said that, it is good to be sensitive about their feelings. Your mother will probably have more feelings about this than your dad. This is because she intrinsically knows that the mother/child bond with the birth mother is profound. It scares her. It will especially scare those mothers whose children acted out. But all mothers, if they are intuitive and sensitive, know that there has always been a bit of a gap in the relationship. It has been heartbreaking for her, even though you couldn't help it. Trust was broken for you upon the original separation, and it has never been completely healed. Sort of like Humpty Dumpty.

I don't recommend more secrets. I don't recommend keeping your wish to search or your having found from your adoptive parents. If this is a temptation for you, you need to question your motives. Sometimes they are pure, and sometimes they are not so pure. It doesn't matter in the long run because no matter, pure or impure, searching is something you have a right to do, and they have a right to know about it. The exceptions to this are rare and may include very ill, elderly adoptive parents.

Those of you who have a good relationship with your adoptive parents will probably find it easier to talk to them about this than those of you who have had a difficult relationship. It is kind of paradoxical ... like how we feel when someone has died. If we had a good relationship with the deceased, it is easier to let them go than if the relationship was troublesome. That's because of the unfinished business of troubled relationships—there is no time to repair them. With troubled adoptive relationships, it is the same. Healing has not yet taken place in that relationship, yet it is time to search. Providing it is possible, it would be a good idea to try to repair some of the damage before searching. If there was extreme alcoholism, abuse, or neglect, this might not be possible. But be certain. Be truthful with yourself. Don't ignore an opportunity for healing if it is possible just because it might be difficult. (Avoid avoidance—.)

In any event, talk to your parents about your reasons for wanting to search. Assure them that you are not looking for someone to take their place. Show them the section of this chapter that I have written for them. After all, I'm an adoptive mother and I survived! The important thing is for all of you to act like the adults that you are. Neither the parents nor the adoptee should allow their whiny inner children to take over. (One thing that made all this easier for me was that my inner child had completely grown up before my daughter's reunion.)

After you have been in reunion for awhile, the next thing is to make your parents a part of the reunion. Not at first. The beginning has to be for you and your birth mother. The first meeting should be just for the two of you. Then you should meet more of her family, preferably little by little. Then, if you want to, your father and his family. He is important to you, too. After all, half your genes came from him. Take it slowly. Meeting all those relatives can be overwhelming. Take time between meetings to assimilate the experience. Write down your feelings about it. Paint, draw, play music, dance. Allow your feelings to be expressed in many different ways.

Let your adoptive parents know that you have met with your birth relatives. Remember, no secrets! This doesn't mean that you have to give them a play by play account of your visits with your birth family. It just means that it is all right to mention that you visited them. And you can tell them as much about your visits as you want. Just don't accuse them of being intrusive if they are curious. Wouldn't you be? They are just showing interest. Interest is not the same as intrusiveness. *Learn the difference.* Ask yourself: "If my best friend asked these questions, would I consider it intrusive?" Ah, ha! See what I mean? (This doesn't mean that some parents—adoptive or birth—are not intrusive. It just means that asking questions doesn't necessarily mean that they are.) After all, they are your parents. They care about you. Here is a little secret I've learned from both birth and adoptive parents: *Many feel as if they are walking a tightrope between appearing intrusive and appearing uncaring.* Are you aware of this? Let them off the hook (to mix metaphors.) Volunteer information ... not all, but some—more than you have been.

When you have been in reunion for awhile, plan for your adoptive parents to meet your birth parents. My notion of an ideal reunion is to have an extended family. This is what we have done in our families. That way, you don't have to always be filled with anxiety about where to go for holidays. If it is geographically possible, you can all be together. Of course this will not always work, but when it does, it is really wonderful. It was such a relief to me that my daughter's birth mom likes making mashed potatoes. Mine always come out the consistency of glue. Thanksgiving dinner is better for having the two of us working on it! (I wish she had been around when it was time to make Halloween costumes!)

It is all right for your two sets of parents to have their own relationship. Don't be afraid of this. It can help. (Well, sometimes it is a pain in the—er—neck to have two sets of parents, but overall it can be very beneficial.) I know that not all parents can be mature enough to do this. There is a certain mentality about not being able to share, as if love were like money in the bank—expendable. Even if your two mothers are quite different, they will have a bond in their love for you. If both are putting your best interests ahead of their own, they will learn to get along and may even learn to love one another. Rejoice in this!

Now, you have to do your part. You can't try to carve out two different relationships and live two different lives. If you ever want to be *you*, you have to allow the assimilation of your two sets of families. Remember that, in his book *Nature via Nurture*, Matt Ridley explains how our genes are influenced by our environment and experiences in life: "No longer is it nature versus nurture but nature via nurture. Genes are designed to take their cues from nurture. ... My argument in a nutshell is this: the more we lift the lid on the genome, the more vulnerable to experience genes appear to be" (Ridley, 2003). Both nature and nurture have been and are important in knowing who you are.

You are the product of both sets of parents and you can best help each of them to understand *you* better by allowing them to know *one another*. It will save you a lot of time, explanations, and grief. There it will all be in living color: the source of your red hair, the way you gesture when telling a story, your opinions about the war on terrorism, and the reason that you took ballet instead of tap. Neither set of parents need criticize any of this. They can just observe it and learn from it. (I will repeat: You're all adults. Don't stoop to pettiness!)

A reunion can be a plus for all parts of the adoption triad. It opens the way for truth and trust. Keeping secrets is not the way to go. You have already found this out. If everyone tries to be mature, it can be a blessing for everyone.

## To Adoptive Parents

*The Fear*

The idea of a reunion in the abstract may seem like a good idea to most of you. However, when the actual search is underway and the whole thing becomes more real, it can produce anxiety. What if she likes her birth mother more than me? What if her birth mother blames me for her drug use? What if her birth mother sees the lack of affection between us as my fault when I wanted so much to just cuddle her as an infant—would give anything for a real hug today? What if she finds a whole lot of sibs that will take her time away from her adoptive sibs? All these questions are valid, but have little to do with what the reunion is really about.

Your child needs to find his birth family because they will reflect a great deal of who he is. You cannot do this. They can give him his ancestral history. You cannot do this. As much as he loves Grandma and Grandpa, they are not really related to him. Their history is not his history. Adoptees need their own history. You cannot provide it, but their birth families can.

Is this the extent of the necessity for a reunion? No, your child needs to be reconnected with his birth mother. When they were separated, each was traumatized by the experience. You have been a witness, whether you knew it or not, to your child's part of that trauma. They need that reconnection to help both of them heal. But they can't do it alone. They need your help. They need your encouragement and love to help make healing possible. If you are reluctant or afraid, if you threaten to disown your child or break off communication with him, he will not be able to heal as well. And neither will you.

Tell me, how can your forbidding your child to search for birth parents make the relationship between you better? Would you have good feelings toward someone who told you you couldn't do something you felt essential to your well-being? This is essential to his well-being. It doesn't have anything to do with you. He isn't looking for new parents; he is looking for himself. You couldn't reflect that genetic part of him which is so much a part of who he is. He needs that. You have done wonderful things for him. But none of us who are adoptive parents can do that kind of mirroring. You probably have no idea what a deficit this has been in your child's life. It has made him unsure of himself. It has made him have to assume a false self. It has covered up essential parts of who he truly is. This wasn't your fault, but you need to be part of the solution, not a continuation of the problem.

At the same time, you have a right to your feelings about searching. You may be scared. That's all right. You may feel threatened. You may be angry. You may be sad. Whatever your feelings, they are all right. How you act on them is up to you. You can take the high road or the low road. If you truly love your child, if you put his well-being above your fears, you will rally behind his wanting to search even if it scares you, angers you, or saddens you. I can assure you, even if your relationship was somewhat tentative before, if you can come through now, your relationship will improve. Both your child and his birth family will be inspired by your generosity. They will have good feelings towards you. They will know that your best intentions are truly for your child. All birth mothers should know that this is scary for you. If they were to put themselves in your shoes, they would know that. I am asking them to put their child first, even when they may be scared of the feelings this may bring up in them ... many of which have remained dormant for 20 or 30 years. I am also asking you to put your child first and tolerate your feelings of fear, anger, or sorrow.

### The Most Vulnerable

Both sets of parents need to understand that at the time of the relinquishment and adoption your child had absolutely no say in what happened. He was a traumatized infant who was separated prematurely from his mother. As I said before, he would never had chosen to leave her, even if she had been a 13-year-old drug addict. That is the strength of the mother/child bond. Also, conscious or explicit memory (see Chapter 2) had not clicked in yet. Therefore, the child has all kinds of reactions to the event of separation but absolutely no conscious memory of it. The rest of you do have some memory of what happened, even if those memories have been distorted over time. You were all adults or almost adults. In other words you were not helpless infants. You had some idea of what was going on.

Your child did not. He has conjured up a whole belief system based on his baby's mind's idea of what happened, without the benefit of explicit memory. That belief system often includes the belief that he was at fault for having been relinquished by his birth mother. A baby's mind cannot imagine any reason that the mother would do this except that something must have been wrong with him. This has permeated his sense of self-worth and undermined his self-esteem. Because no one explained to you that your child was the victim of a trauma, you had no way of helping him recover from that trauma. Although you and the birth families basically knew what was going on, you did not know the consequences of that experience for your child. What you don't know, you can't help. However, now you know (because I and perhaps others have told you). Now you can no longer claim ignorance. And now you can be part of the healing process for your child. This can strengthen you, as well as your child and your relationship with one another.

### Dump the Blame Game

I think I've mentioned this in each section of this chapter—no one is to blame for the ignorance of the past. What you all must build upon is what you have learned. What you must strive for is the truth about the effect relinquishment and adoption has had on all of you. Try not to say, "Well, her birth mother gave her up and now she has to live with the consequences of that decision." As you know, if you've been paying attention at all, most of these so-called decisions were made by parents of the birth mother and by social workers and clergy, not by the young mothers themselves. Remember when you were that age? Most of us didn't defy our parents then. We tried to be good kids. If we wandered off the beaten path, we were mortified if we got caught. Remember? What would you have done if you had gotten pregnant then? Maybe you are one who did. Maybe you are one of the many birth mothers who could never get pregnant again. Whatever the case, it is better to have compassion than to spread blame. This goes for the birth mothers, too. Rather than saying, "Well, if the adoptive parents didn't get pregnant maybe they shouldn't have become parents," birth parents should have some compassion for a couple who tried over and over again to get pregnant, but never could. Good parents are not determined by their ability to procreate, believe me. In my profession I have dealt with many people who were badly abused by parents to whom they were biologically related.

## Getting Started

So what can you do? First of all, it would be good to join a support group for adoptive parents. If there is none in your area, form one. Non-adoptive parents don't understand the issues that adoptive parents face. They have no idea what it is like to rear a child who has been traumatized and who is not genetically connected to you. Only other adoptive parents will be able to understand. They will also be able to understand your ambivalence about a reunion. They know the fear this idea may generate. And they also know the importance reunions may have for their children. They will understand. So get together. Don't isolate yourselves in your experiences.

If she wants you to, help your child search. At the same time that we are striving to make searching easier through the legislative process, there are some people who think that at the present time the adoptee should do the whole thing herself. "It is her journey," they may say. Well, perhaps so, but if we do get legislation to make it easier, her journey will not be so difficult. So why make it more difficult for those searching now? It is a scary ride, so the more people who are in on it, the easier it may be. There can be support there and compassion. These are good things.

Let your child know that no matter how scary it is for him and for you, this is something you know he needs to do. Let him set the pace; don't push him, but keep encouraging him. These searches progress by fits and starts. He may need time to process his feelings after each step. Let him talk openly about his fears without any judgment on your part. Let him know that his fears are understandable, but that most birth mothers are happy to be found. Let him know that you will be there for him no matter what happens. It is tricky to do this without sounding as if it would be all right with you whether he found or not. You have to convey your understanding of his need to search for his birthright and that it has nothing to do with his relationship to you.

## The Reunion

Once the birth mother has been found, it is time for you to back off for awhile. As difficult as it may be for you, you have to allow the two of them to have time alone together. *This is sacred time.* It is the reconnecting of two souls who should never have been separated. You have an idea of how important and significant this is. It is why you are so scared! Just keep remembering that it has nothing to do with your child's relationship to you. You are the witnesses of his childhood. You are the foundation of his values and morals. You have been and continue to be the source of great love for the child that he was. This is very important. The birth mother can never take this away from you. If she is a mature birth mother, she will not want to. She will rejoice in the relationship between you and the child you now share. In any case, in the beginning the adoptee and birth mother need time alone to reconnect. After reconnecting with his birth mother, he will want to meet other members of his birth family. This may take some time, so be patient. You don't have to wait to get involved until everyone in both the birth mother's and birth father's families have been met. It may be quite a while after the reunion with the birth mother's family that your child will want to contact the birth father's family.

While she is meeting members of her birth family, it is all right to ask about how she is doing with it. Ask general questions and be non-judgmental about the answers. Let your child know that you are not trying to pry, but are interested in things that affect her. You know that she will resemble some members of her birth family, so you are sure you will like them, too. It is difficult to find the right balance between interest and intrusiveness when it comes to adoptees, who sometimes misinterpret interest for intrusiveness. I have warned them about this, so hopefully they will be forthcoming with information about their reunion process. How you receive this information will help determine how much more they will tell you.

*Where You Come In*

Once this early period has passed, it is important for you to begin to have a part in the relationship. (Note to adoptees: Don't keep this from happening unless there is a *very* good reason for doing so.) The meeting between a birth and adoptive mother can be very warm or very tentative. Again, I want to encourage both mothers to be supportive and non-judgmental. Neither of you can really imagine the experience of the other. Try to get to know one another as two adult women who love the same child. Your child does not need to get into a situation of having to mediate between you or defend one of you against the other. Your getting to know one another can help alleviate that kind of situation. You may be very different. That's all right. It is good to know people who are different from us. It gives us a broader perspective of life ... gets us out of a rut. In some cases, the adoptive mother may be more educated and come from a more affluent family and in other cases the birth mother may be the educated, affluent one. During the 40s, 50s, and 60s, it was the affluent, middle class families who were mortified that their daughters became pregnant and were worried about what the neighbors would think. Many of these young women went on to a university. Others did not, but in any case getting rid of stereotypes about who the birth mother is would be greatly aided by actually getting to know her. There are basic aspects of women which are similar no matter what the background.

It is also important for the birth family to get to know you. Your child will have a distorted idea of who you are, especially mom. He has always seen you through the lens of his separation trauma. He has always seen you as "not her," meaning not the mother he was expecting. His view of you may be skewed. The birth family needs to get to know you both as a woman and as a man in your own rights. Of course, they will see you through their own lenses of experiences as well. We all do this. But it is important for them to form an opinion of who you are independent of who your child thinks you are. Your child may have denigrated you or he may have idealized you. None of us likes to be known second-hand. Getting to know the birth family is very important to all concerned.

What can you do if the birth family has no interest in knowing you? I would advise e-mailing or writing them and inquiring about this. Let them know that it is in everyone's best interest to keep the important relationships in your child's life as open and connected as possible. There have been enough secrets to last everyone a lifetime. Whatever it is that is making them reluctant needs to be explored. Perhaps it is a misperception. Perhaps it has something to do with their families. Whatever it is, be persistent in trying to achieve a meeting. Ask your child to help with this. All of you should remember that many adoptions today are open adoptions. That sometimes means that the birth and adoptive families have an on-going relationship. This keeps things more honest and true. It gives all the adults a chance to know one another while the child is growing up. You did not have this opportunity. It is not too late to open up the connections now.

What if you are the reluctant one? Well, get over it. One of the first things I told my daughter's birth mother (when my daughter handed the phone to me) was that I felt as if I knew her because I had been living with her daughter for 25 years. This is true. Many of the traits you may have admired in your child can probably be found in some members of the birth family. We fear most what we don't know. Get to know as many members of the birth family as possible. It will eliminate the fantasy of their being bigger than life, and it will help you to get to know and understand the true personality of your child.

### Difficult Behavior

Just as I asked the birth family to suspend judgment about any acting-out behavior demonstrated by the adoptee, I would ask you to do the same. They might cry, "Those parents did not rear my child the way I was promised he would be reared!" And you may have a tendency to say, "I wonder what kind of genes created a child who would put us through so much pain?" Neither of you is correct. What created the acting-out adoptee was the experience of his separation trauma. That was the way he coped. You, as adoptive parents, could not have had a child without your child's having gone through that trauma. (So don't blame the birth mom for that.) On the other hand, neither is it your fault. Perhaps you could have responded differently to your child's loss if you had been aware of it. You could not have eliminated it. It is built into the original separation and the way your child's neurological system is connected. But just as the birth mother was unaware of the pain her child would suffer as a result of her surrendering him, you were unaware of that pain as well. So, she let him go, and you were unable to help him. Neither of you is to blame for the ignorance of the medical, social services, or psychological professions at the time of the adoption. Neither of you was warned.

What both sets of parents can do instead is try to help this child who acted out in order to avoid more pain. You can work together if he is still sabotaging himself. It will never help him for you to point fingers at one another. Just get together, perhaps with a professional, and try to find out how to help him. This does not mean enabling him to keep being irresponsible. It does not mean giving him more and more money. It means sitting down with him to form a plan for him to get on his feet. If both families can work on this together, it is much more effective than if one or the other set of parents does it alone. For one thing, it eliminates the tendency that all children have to pit one parent or one set of parents against the other. You all may have to allow him to hit bottom, and this will be very difficult, but he may not allow himself to avail himself of your help until this happens. You can find comfort in one another at a time like this. Remember—no blame. Work together.

### Holidays and the Extended Family

Adoptees in reunion have one of the same dilemmas that we all find ourselves in when we marry—where to go for holidays. If the adoptee is married *and* in reunion this problem is compounded. A great deal depends on geography. If everyone is within driving distance or is willing to travel, then having everyone together can be lots of fun. Holidays are for families and the more the merrier. Everyone can pitch in and help with the food. It can be a good experience.

However, if the families don't get along or are geographically far apart, then taking turns on holidays may be the answer. As the adoptive parents, it is up to you to be generous about this. I know you are used to having your child home for every holiday. It won't be the same without him. But you may have to share. The easier this is worked out, the better. No one wins when there is a great deal of strife over the holiday season. Holidays are difficult enough for adoptees without added stress. Because of the nature of reunions, having both sides of the adoptee's family (meaning birth and adoptive) can be helpful. Some adoptees have never felt a part of the adoptive family at those "high octane" family events.

Some feel left out of the birth family events because of all those lost years that everyone refers to. Having both families present may help fill the gaps in both genetic material and historical data. There may be comfort in having both sides represented.

Whatever the case, just as in the union of families in marriage, the best scenario is when everyone tries to get along and just celebrates the occasion. Holidays are not the time to talk about problems in the family or problems of any kind. Holidays are celebrations. They should be fun. (This may mean limiting the amount of alcohol that flows.) Everyone has something about him or her which is lovable and holidays are the time to concentrate on those aspects of everyone present.

Reunions can be a great experience for everyone in the adoption triad. They should be centered on the adoptee, but include both families. After the first few months of regression on the part of the adoptee and birth mother, they should strive to act maturely and share in the decisions about when, how often, and how to meet. Everyone should avoid secrets, be tolerant, and rejoice in the fact that everyone is together at last.

## To Siblings and Other Relatives

*Birth Family Sibs*

All the hoopla that is driving you crazy will subside, I promise. If you are a sibling member of the birth family, you may wonder why your mother finds this lost child so fascinating. Why is she obsessed by someone she may have never seen before? Why does she have to call him every night and talk for hours? What can they possibly have to say to one another? Why is she always crying? Does this mean that she loves him more than you? No. She is feeling toward him the same way she felt about you when you were her new little infant. They are experiencing postnatal bonding. Because she has never had any postnatal time with her lost child before, she is feeling it as if the birth just took place. You will have to put up with their being in their own little world right now. You had that time with her, and your new sib needs this time, too. This level of intensity won't last forever. Just as you and your mom got used to one another and your relationship mellowed out, so will this relationship. You will just have to be patient. Things will get back to normal, except that you will have a new sister or brother. This can be very exciting.

For those of you who have just been replaced as the oldest child, this may be a bit of a challenge. There is a certain mentality that goes with birth order. You may have always experienced yourself as the oldest, and you may not want to give up that position. The intensity of the feelings between your new-found sib and your mother may be exacerbating your feelings of jealousy and anger about your demotion. Other kids in the family will not feel this as intensely as the child who always believed he was the oldest. He may be angry at the "new kid" and at his mother. The feelings about this are usually more intense if the adoptee and the former oldest child are of the same sex. If the oldest child is a girl and the adoptee a boy, she may be happy to have discovered an older brother. It might not be quite so joyous the other way around, but mixed gender adoptee/oldest child combinations seem to be easier to handle than a same gender scenario. It is important to remember that you have had your mother all your life. The adoptee, no matter his birth order, can never have that. He would gladly trade his birth order for that opportunity. Whatever the case, you are entitled to your feelings about being displaced as the oldest child. Just don't take it out on your new sibling. And remember, many adoptees have to get used to the idea of not being an only child. That, too, is a big adjustment.

Something you need to know is that an adoptee who has just found her birth family is going to be *very* interested in everything about your family. Things that you have taken for granted will have immense importance for her. You can't possibly imagine what it has been like for her to grow up without any of the genetic markers you are used to—seeing yourself reflected in those around you, whether it is the shape of the face, the color of hair or eyes, the way you walk, the way you gesture when you are excited, or the way you raise your eyebrow when you are being inquisitive. Although the effect of environment on our values is important, sometimes adoptees feel more in tune with the values and politics of their birth families than those of their adoptive parents. And sometimes not. In any case, your new sister or brother will be watching everyone closely. She will be absolutely fascinated by the similarities among you. It will be a relief to her because living without those genetically coded messages means always having to figure out how to be in your family. This can be exhausting.

You have probably never thought about how secure it makes you feel to see yourself reflected back. It means you are okay. You fit. You belong. Your sib has never had that. She has not felt as if she fit, even though she may have known that she was loved. This lack of mirroring has been a huge deficit for her, and her need for that kind of validation is great. It might be fun for all of you to start noticing all the similarities among you ... the things you have taken for granted for so long.

Another thing you need to know—she needs you to phone or e-mail her more than she communicates with you. Or she needs you to initiate communication. She will be feeling unsure of her place in your family. She needs to know that you accept her. This will not be a one-time thing. Your keeping in touch will mean much more to her than to you. You know your family. You know your place in it. You are secure in your place in the family. (I realize that there are families in which no one feels secure or knows their place, but I am talking about ordinary messy, chaotic families, not dysfunctional ones ... and I use the term dysfunctional sparingly.) So, although it may not seem a big deal to you to have frequent communication with your newly found sib, it means the world to her. Please take the initiative here. Be kind. Be understanding. Be compassionate. Be available.

Please, don't ever say, "Sometimes I wish I had grown up in an adoptive family." You have no idea what that means and you would be discounting the pain of living without one's biological parents and one's roots. This doesn't mean that your sibling didn't have a good life. It just means that loss has always been a part of her life—living in a pall of ever-present anxiety and sadness.

You and the brothers and sisters you've grown up with are very important to your "new" sib. She will need you to let her know that she is also important to you. The disappearance of her (your) mother at the beginning of her life left her feeling as if she is forgotten the minute she leaves the room or gets off the phone. She will need you to remind her this is not true. She will need a great deal of reassurance. Take the time to make her feel welcome and a part of the family.

Having said that, I do want to make a note here to adoptees by saying that you need to take some responsibility in the relationship with your new-found family. I know you feel insecure, but they need to know that they are important to you as you want to be to them. If you always wait for them to contact you, they will think you don't care about them. Remember that much of this book is about becoming aware of your impact on others and taking responsibility for that impact. This means you have to be more active in the reunion. It means realizing that the people who have always been a part of this family will have a hard time understanding your obsession with them. Help them out. Talk to them. Don't be withholding, but instead tell them how you are feeling. They can't read your mind. They have not had your experience. They need educating. Only you can do that. So, get started. It might not be a bad idea to invite them to the next adoption conference. This has proven tremendously enlightening to siblings of adoptees. Whatever you do or however you do it, it is your responsibility to help educate your siblings about your experience of living in a non-biological family.

## Siblings in the Adoptive Family

What if he likes his birth brother more than he likes me? What if I am no longer important to him? These are some of the fears that adoptive siblings experience when they hear about a sib wanting to search or having found. "Will the 'real' sibs be more important in his life than I am?" If you are worried about this, probably not. Being worried about it means that you have a relationship with your sibling and you want to keep that relationship strong. A reunion will not ruin good relationships.

It is not always the case that adoptive sibs have good relationships, that they feel like brothers or sisters. If adoptive siblings have never had a close relationship, a reunion will probably have no effect on that relationship. It won't get closer; it might become more estranged. There are some adoptive sibs who never have any contact with one another after they both leave the adoptive home. They are too different and have nothing in common. This can happen when children are brought willy-nilly into a family. There are no genetics to hold them together. There are sibs in biological families for whom this feels true as well. But when there is no relationship through friendship or blood, there can be a real cut-off.

If you are the sib of an adoptee in reunion, you, too, will have to be patient while the newness and intensity of the relationship with the birth family recedes and some kind of normalcy returns. Your brother will be fascinated by the mirroring and reflection of himself in his new-found family. This will seem all-important for awhile. The more he is around them, the more used to this phenomenon he will become and your importance in his life will again emerge.

If you are the biological child of your parents, yet the adoptive brother of your parent's other child, then you have some idea of the advantage of having genetic markers, although you have probably never thought about it. It might be a good idea to try to think how difficult it may have been for your sib to try to be a member of the family without those coded markers, never seeing himself anywhere. This puts you in the position of knowing how important it might be for him to meet people with whom he *will* have that mirroring. Mirroring makes life easier to understand. It makes relationships easier. It fosters self-love and self-esteem.

To ensure this return to your strong relationship, it is important that you support his reunion. As scared as you may be about your importance in his life, you will retain that importance more if you encourage him in his new family than if you complain or act as if you don't understand the importance of it for him. Let him know that you want to meet his new sibs after he has been in the relationship for awhile. If you love your brother, you will probably love his other sibs as well.

*Spouses and Partners of Adoptees and Birth Parents in Reunion*

Many spouses of birth parents will be astonished by the intensity of the relationship between their partner and his or her new-found son or daughter. Many spouses have complained that the long phone calls and need to be connected gets irritating. It may even be scaring them … threatening the marriage. You, too, will do better if you can be patient. Your spouse doesn't want to replace you, but she needs time to do postnatal bonding with her son or daughter. If you have other children and remember what it was like when the new baby came home, that can give you an idea what this is all about. The birth father, too, will need to have time to assimilate the reality of this child into his life.

The overwhelming intensity of feelings connected with reunions may happen more often to birth mothers than to birth fathers. However, birth fathers are not immune to the charms of their "baby girl or boy." Birth, as common as it may be, is a miracle. In the same way, having a son or daughter come into your life after many years (sometimes of not even knowing about him or her, in the case of birth fathers), can seem like a miracle. There is wonder. There is love. There is enchantment. There is difficulty. There is intensity. A birth mother's hormones may begin to play tricks on her. Her moods may be extreme. This, too, will pass.

If you are the spouse of a birth mother or birth father and are suffering from the intensity of the feelings that are going on in the reunion, you have a right to your feelings as well. Many spouses are very jealous of the love that is expressed between the adoptee and parent. There can be extreme insecurity, even in good marriages, and marriages may be threatened by the intense feelings generated by the reunited pair. On top of that may be jealousy and insecurity about the need for some birth parents to have some resolution to what happened so many years ago. Just as the birth father whom I quoted earlier indicated, no one can prepare himself or his spouse for the enormity of the feelings and sense of responsibility he experiences toward his child and her mother. Although this couple had been married for over twenty years and had two grown children, the holocaust of the reunion almost did them in as a couple. While he needed his wife to be supportive as he was going through "this explosive emotional eruption in my life," she was feeling paralyzed by the fear of losing her husband to a former love or to his daughter. I believe it is important to state the normalcy of the spouse's feelings of jealousy and insecurity, because it happens a great deal. No one should feel guilty for having such feelings. However, it is important to realize that the phase that is so difficult will not last. It is not worth ending a marriage over. Spouses, too, must work through their feelings of insecurity and jealousy with someone.

The spouse mentioned above did a great deal of work on her own to get through her jealousy and insecurity, including going to another state and spending a weekend with the birth mom. The birth mother was no longer a fantasy to her, but a real human being who was going through her own difficult feelings. These two women were able to work out a good relationship with one another. Needless to say, they were acting in a mature manner with one another, even if they didn't always feel very adult. I have nothing but respect for all three people involved in this effort.

### Genetic Sensual Attraction

Sometimes there is genetic sensual attraction (better known as genetic sexual attraction—GSA) which can seem like a huge threat to a comfortable, staid relationship. After all, some of these birth parents were very young when they had their baby. They are not very much older than their children. This poses a problem if the birth parents are not very well boundaried. Although the parent may feel sixteen again, the adoptee is feeling like an infant. Whose responsibility is it to set the boundaries?

The feelings of sensual attraction are normal and happen between moms and both sons and daughters. That sensual closeness or symbiotic relationship which was severed can be reactivated upon reunion. Sometimes, with parents of the opposite sex, these feelings are sexualized and acted upon. This can mean disaster for the relationship. Although the feelings are normal, sexualizing and acting upon these feelings is not recommended. For one thing, it is incest. For another, seldom do both people want to end the sexual part of the relationship at the same time. This means that someone is upset and feeling rejected. In some cases, blackmail may even be threatened in the form of telling co-workers of the mom or dad or other members of the family that they had sex with their son or daughter. In any case, it usually ends with hard feelings and a severing of the relationship. It is difficult to get the parent/child relationship back on track when there have been sexual relations between them.

Sexual relations between fathers and daughters is more rare than that between mothers and sons. For one thing, it comes from a different source. This is not the bonding of mother and child, but falling in love with the birth mother again or with a representation of the self. There is the person who reminds the birth father of his first love. Or there is the person who is so much like him. That reflection of himself or of a past love is what he falls in love with. Again, the father, being the parent, needs to be in control. He needs to set the boundaries. A daughter will so want the love of her father that she will often do whatever he wants. This happens in biological homes all the time. The child needs to obey the father, even though it feels wrong. A regressed adoptee is in the same position as the real three-year-old. She needs to please dad. I have never known a case where this has been acted upon and the relationship has been maintained. It is somehow easier for a son to remain connected to a mother with whom this has happened (although it may take years for the relationship to normalize) than for the father/daughter relationship to survive.

It is always the duty of the parent, mother or father, to keep the boundaries clear. Even though you may feel like a teenager, your child feels like an infant. He may look like a wonderfully handsome grown man or a beautiful young woman, but inside s/he is feeling like your little baby once again. He just wants to get as close to you as he can. These feelings are very intense, much more intense than normal sexual feelings. It is up to you, the parent, to keep anything damaging from happening. This often means keeping your clothes on at all times. It may mean never staying in a hotel room together. This can be very hard, because many times all you really want to do is to hold your "baby" in your arms ... to touch him skin to skin. But if those sensual feelings are rampant, it is best not to give in to the temptation and risk going too far. Birth mothers need to understand that adoptees can be very manipulating. Don't fall for any kind of manipulation which puts either of you in harm's way. Be strong. Be the adult. Set limits.

*If It Happened to Your Spouse*

Some of you have married an adoptee who has had incestuous relations with his birth mother. What are you to think? Whatever you do, don't use it against the adoptee. He was the "baby" in the scenario and had little control over the situation. He needed his mommy and that seemed like the price to pay for her love. When one is regressed, it is very difficult to resist what the parent wants. This is true when one really is a small child or just feels like a small child. What you must never do is use this information in a court of law. Believe me, if you don't understand it, attorneys and judges will definitely not understand it. Even though they are the ones who uphold the law saying that the adoptive parents are the parents and the birth parents are not, when it comes to incest they are not going to quibble. Most people have no idea what genetic sexual attraction is or how it manifests in reunions. Using this for gaining the custody of children or other such legal matters is playing dirty pool.

For this reason, I advise all adoptees who have fallen victim to genetic sexual attraction not to tell their spouses. What is the point? They won't understand and it will only make them uneasy. They will think both you and your mother/father are weird. They won't have a clue as to the biological yearning which prompts this phenomenon. They won't understand it as the same feelings they have had for your children while bonding with them, but because of the ages of both you and your parent it has become sexualized. Since they won't receive the information in the manner in which it is presented, why play the fool and tell him or her? Before making any confessions to a spouse or partner, mother or father, ask yourself what your motives are. Be honest. Sometimes silence is golden.

### Sexual Relations Between Siblings

Here, again, the sources of the attraction are a bit different from that with the mother. It is the narcissistic element again—the falling in love with self. Although the acting out of these feelings is not recommended, the reparation of the relationship is probably easier between sibs than between parent and child. And no matter what the amended birth certificate says, you are still brother and sister. It is still incest. It can be damaging to the long-term relationship.

There are two cases I know of where siblings either got married or were planning to get married. This is like snubbing your nose at the legal system which dictates that you are not siblings because of a legal document. That paper makes no difference. You are still related. You are still subject to the same cautions that apply to all brothers and sisters—negative traits in the family can be passed on more readily between close relatives than between genetic strangers. I know those feelings are intense. I know you want to act on them. But my advice is not to. In my experience with sibs who acted upon these feelings, they became disenchanted with one another at some time as their personalities became more real to them. It is like the normal run of the infatuation part of a relationship. After all the intensity wears off, you have to decide if you really like the person. Those sexualized feelings are so strong that the personality doesn't even play a part in the whole scenario. It is all about emotion. In time, the feelings will subside. Let that happen and just have a normal brother/sister relationship. In the long run, this will be much more satisfactory than trying to go back to a non-sexual relationship. If you've ever tried going back to being just friends with someone with whom you've had sexual relations, you may get the idea of the difficulty. It is easier to remain non-sexual in the first place. Sex changes things, folks.

What I am saying to everyone who is caught up in sensual or sexual genetic attraction is that it is imperative not to act on these feelings. It is like a drug. The high can be very high. But eventually you have to come down. And the fall can be fatal to the relationship. Know that *the feelings are normal, but to act on them is dangerous and irresponsible.*

## Etcetera

### Taking the Time to Process

Reunions can be wonderful experiences or added trauma. Much depends upon the people involved taking a deep breath and not reacting to things as they come along. There is so much emotion connected to reunions that it is sometimes difficult to determine just what *is* going on. Certainly at first the key players in the drama are enveloped in a cloud of emotion and have little capacity for rational thinking. There is a great deal of projection going on all around. Nothing is as it seems. There are extreme highs and extreme lows. There is regression. There are multiple misunderstandings. There are fear, frustration, and anxiety. There are sorrow and anger. Because of all the intense feelings, it is imperative for all involved to withhold judgment about one another. No one is acting as he or she does in "real life, real time." No one will be able to truly get to know one another until most of the emotion subsides and everyone can begin to act normally again. Please keep this in mind, because otherwise your reunion may get off track. You may judge your child or your mother or your child's adoptive parents or birth parents in an unfair manner. This will be detrimental to the long-term relationship.

There are some people who seem incapable of being adults. They are narcissistic and selfish. Sometimes they come around and sometimes they don't. Most people who act this way have had some kind of early trauma. We know that adoptees have experienced early trauma, but many birth parents and adoptive parents have, too. Try to suspend judgment. Be sure that *you* are being mature. Make sure you are not contributing to the problem. If after a certain length of time, nothing seems to be changing, then it might be time to sever a relationship with the "offending party." But this decision should be a last resort. And it might be a good idea to try again in a year.

A lot of people would like for me and other professionals to have a magic solution for members of the triad who refuse to cooperate. I have no magic wand. Because feelings sometimes get the upper hand and logic and rationale are put by the wayside, some people cannot be reasoned with. Sending the reluctant party a copy of this chapter may or may not help. Sometimes it just takes being patient and waiting to try again in a couple of years. Not everyone is ready for reunions at the same time. It depends on their level of awareness. Or their level of fear.

Remember that adoptees have never lived without having been influenced by their early trauma. A trauma-driven life is all they know. Therefore it seems normal to them. Many birth mothers, who seem to be able to function at work or in their normal lives, fall apart and become fearful teenagers at the idea of telling their families about a baby whom they have kept a secret from them. They will fear being perceived differently from the way they have always been perceived. They may be swept back to the time when they gave up the baby and cannot take in that things have changed. In both cases, however, having been made aware that the other is looking for them or wanting to meet them can never be put back in the bottle. It will be processed in one way or another. This often takes time, time that the searcher often doesn't want to allow. If a year or two has gone by since the original contact, it might be time to make yourself known again. He or she may be more ready to come around. But what if that doesn't happen?

## Searching for Sibs or Other Relatives

For adoptees: If after several years of waiting for a birth mother to "get her act together" and tell her relatives that you exist, it might be time to bypass her and get in touch with other members of the family. If there are sibs or half-sibs, that might be the best place to start, because they live in the present—an era of more openness and freedom. They are not shocked by the idea of an adoptee finding his family. They see it on TV all the time. It is commonplace for them. They did not live through the trauma of the original pregnancy and relinquishment. They are not influenced by those original feelings of shame, guilt, and fear. They can be more objective. They can even be excited.

Many of you may be afraid to do this because you may be afraid of making your birth mother angry at you. But if nothing has happened for several years, what do you have to lose? She is not coming around herself. Your sibs may be able to help with that. When she finds out that they do not share her feelings of shame or even understand them, she may have the courage to come forward and take part in the reunion.

Even if she doesn't, you will have found a connection with your biological ties. You and your sibs are adults and you have a right to do this. You have a right to contact them, and they have a right to know that they have another sibling. In most cases, this works out very well. The exception is when the siblings are unduly influenced by their mother and are afraid to go against her wishes. Or they may feel that doing so will hurt her too much. But reluctance on the part of siblings is rare. They may be surprised (remember that many children are sure that their parents know nothing about sex, let alone that they knew about it before they got married!), but they are rarely upset about being contacted. And, as I said, they can often be a help in getting their mother to become a participant of this time and place in history, instead of reliving the time and place of the pregnancy and surrender. In my experience, based on communications from many of you, these contacts often work out very well.

Sometimes there are no other siblings on the mother's side. Remember that secondary infertility is a by-product of surrendering. However, there may be aunts, uncles, cousins, or grandparents to contact. Often a sister of the birth mother may be the only one, other than the parents, who knew about the pregnancy. She may have wondered ever since what has happened to her niece or nephew. Contacting her may be another positive way to connect with your biological family. Perhaps she can have a relationship with you herself or she could try to get her sister to see the light. Of course, what you really want is to be with your mother, but it is better to have a relationship with some member of your biological family than no relationship at all.

In cases where the birth mother is taking her time growing up and getting over her fear, the adoptee can use this time to search for the birth father and his family. I know many cases where the relationship with the birth father's family was well-established before the birth mother finally came around. This gives the adoptee a sense of a biological connection and can be very rewarding. Sometimes, too, having this relationship can give the adoptee more courage to contact siblings from her birth mother's family. After all, she now has family that accepts her, so she can afford to be more courageous.

*In any case, you are an adult* and you can contact whomever you want without permission from anyone. Be brave. Be an adult. Go for it!

## Finding the Birth Mother Deceased

Sometimes an adoptee will wait too long to search or has had difficulty finding his birth family and when he does, he finds that his mother has died. This can be devastating, but it doesn't have to be the end of the search. Again, there are other members of the family to get to know. They can help him form a picture of his birth mother. He can have relationships with other members of the family, as I said in the case of the reluctant birth mother. A wonderful book on this subject is *Searching for Charmian* by Suzanne Chick. Suzanne is an Australian adoptee who discovered that her mother, the famous, beautiful, and complex novelist and essayist, Charmian Clift, had committed suicide. She set about discovering who her mother was by getting to know other members of her mother's family and her many friends and colleagues. It is evident that Suzanne inherited her mother's literary talent—the book reads like a novel.

## Summary

Although it is possible for an adoptee to connect with his true Self without a reunion, it is more difficult. Genetic mirroring can be a shortcut to knowing who he is. It can give him a sense that he belongs somewhere. Although this does not always happen because of those lost years and lost personal histories, in many cases it does.

In cases where the adoptee suffered abuse at the hands of her adoptive parents, finding the birth family may allow her to have a family that will love and accept her. It can bring some sense of resolution to a difficult life. It can give her a new start in life, if she will take advantage of it. It can, for the first time, give her a sense of family.

Sometimes a reunion makes the adoptee realize he is glad that he was not reared in his birth family. This knowledge does not eliminate the pain and trauma of his childhood, but it can help him reconcile with his experience and make some sense of it. It can also help the relationship with his adoptive parents. In most cases, whatever the adoptive parents' "sins" may have been, they loved their children and gave them a good start in life. Sometimes this can be appreciated for the first time after a reunion.

No one may ever know how much the birth mother's reaction to her surrendering her first child may have influenced the way her subsequent children turned out. In many cases she, too, had a difficult life. Many adoptees have told me that no matter how painful the separation was, they are thankful that they did not grow up that way. Often they fail to realize that it might not have been "that way" if the surrender had never taken place. The trauma of the surrender has entered into the lives of everyone with whom the birth mother has been in relationship.

Whatever the case, what happened happened! Nothing can change that. Reunions can help explain, connect, and reconcile, but they can't change anyone's history. It is useless to hang on to regret about this. It is time to go on from here—the present—with awareness, maturity, compassion, and forgiveness. These are what will forge a connection and the bonds of love.

# CHAPTER 15
The Power and Pathos of Relationships

Relationships are the basis of our humanity. They are what distinguish us as human beings. Human beings have been social entities from the beginning of time. We have lived in tribes, clans, communities, and families. As a whole, humans have not lived alone. We need one another; we need our relationships with one another. People who were ostracized from the tribe or clan were left to live alone, which was the ultimate punishment. Those who chose to live alone were considered hermits and eccentrics.

Today there is a trend in this country for people to live alone. There is a romantic idea that individualism and independence are the ideal. People think that if they can't live alone, there is something wrong with them. I have heard so many people say, "I have to be able to live by myself just to know that I can do it." Yet what does this prove? In some ways it is easier to live alone than to have to compromise and relate with another person or persons. Sometimes, if a person has a lot of friends and doesn't spend very much time alone, she can do fine. But there are a lot of lonely people in this country who can't seem to find one another. Or they are afraid to find one another. What are we all afraid of? What have we forgotten about relationships?

Difficulties in relationships force many people into therapy. Adoptees seem especially prone to relationship difficulties, often beginning with their relationship with their adoptive mothers. Understanding the role that separation trauma plays in these issues is helpful. Because most adoptees are separated from their mothers at birth or soon after, it is difficult for them to know that what they are experiencing isn't what most people experience. It is difficult to know how their world view has been distorted by that early traumatic experience. When your whole life has been skewed by an event, it seems normal. It is only when they recognize a pattern of relationship failures that many adoptees begin to understand that something is wrong, that perhaps these difficulties are not the norm.

The high divorce rate in this country points to a great many people having difficulties in relationships. There is an inability to find a good balance between independence and interdependence. Many relationships are more adversarial than congenial. There appears to be a war going on with no clear winners. In fact, there seem to be a lot of losers. How can we begin to reverse this trend?

Let's begin with the first permanent relationship and try to understand what happens for adoptees and those who inhabit their world.

## The Relationship with the Adoptive Parents

The relationship with the adoptive mother is one of the most troubling. Most adoptive mothers want nothing more than to be a mother. Most mothers are fully ready to love a baby whether she gave birth to her or not. Yet thousands of adoptive mothers have experienced the feeling that her child has not fully accepted her. Why not? It is forgotten at her peril that the baby she is taking home has already suffered the trauma of separation from a mother. She has not been told that she is taking home a baby who may be afraid to fully connect with her.

### The "Wrong" Mother

In addition, the baby is aware that the person taking her home is not the right mother. Now, before I get hundreds of letters from irate adoptive mothers, what I mean is that she is not the mother the baby had been connected to. She is not the mother that the baby is genetically related to, not the one she is bonded to, not the one who has the right resonance, smell, heartbeat, voice, or skin. No matter what a potentially wonderful mother this new mother may be, to the baby she seems like the wrong mother. Right now she *is* the wrong mother.

So, after being separated from her biological mother, the baby also has to contend with feeling as if she were in an alien place with alien people. Nothing seems familiar. There is no mirroring in the sense of being reflected. The child begins to experience the *ugly duckling syndrome*: "Something must be wrong with me because I don't see myself anywhere. I am different." Since she was not kept by her first mother, she begins to try to adapt so this painful separation will not be repeated. Everyday she tries to figure out how to be in this family. She is anxious, hypervigilant, and fearful.

The mother, too, has to figure everything out. She has neither genetic markers nor the experience of gestation to help her know how to be with this particular baby. Although she may lack the fear of abandonment that her child is experiencing, she may become aware that her child is keeping her at a distance. She may become obsessed by the need to connect with her child more effectively. Even clingy children are holding something back. They don't feel safe. They cling to keep the mother from disappearing. Yet they, too, have to maintain some emotional distance. The real self becomes invisible and they spend every moment figuring out how the mother wants them to be, without allowing her to know them. Intuitive mothers know this. They desperately want to know how to bridge this gap.

*The Bond of Understanding*

The most important thing an adoptive mother needs to know about her baby is that the baby is suffering *loss*. If she misses this monumental truth, she will miss many opportunities to connect with her child. The child, too, will suffer from this deficit. Mothers are the chief teachers of emotional regulation. "When the mother is absent," warn Lewis, et al., "the infant loses all his organizing channels at once." The adopted infant has already experienced the loss of his organizing source. If the adoptive mother doesn't understand the emotional reality of her child, she cannot help him organize and regulate his emotions or his reactions to them. She cannot help him deal with the enormity of these feelings. If she is oblivious, the child feels entirely alone in his suffering. He is unable to learn to regulate his emotions, so he either acts them out or buries them.

If he acts out his feelings, the parents have a chance to experience them and understand them. They can label them and talk about them to the child so he will learn what they are and a better way to deal with them. If the parents don't know that the child's behavior is a form of communication, they may react negatively to these projected feelings and leave the child believing that all his emotions are intolerable. This becomes more of a problem if the parents themselves have some form of abandonment issues. The child's behavior may tap into their own unresolved feelings. The parents may overreact to the feelings and destroy any opportunity they may have had to teach the child that the feelings are tolerable and manageable. These kids can be very provocative, so this is not easy. Birth mothers, as well as adoptive mothers have discovered this.

*Validating Feelings*

After understanding that her child has suffered a tremendous loss, the next thing the mother needs to do is validate her child's feelings. The separation itself has left the infant feeling all alone. Despite whoever else may be in his life, his separation from his first mother is all he can experience at first. He is thrown into chaos, confusion, and terror. He needs empathy and understanding during this experience. The mother must be attuned to his loss and his fear and say soothing things to him. Babies are very sensitive to empathy and tone of voice. They respond to a sincere empathic reaction to their feelings. This empathic response is called *attunement* and is very important in the child's ability to learn to regulate his emotions.

This is one reason that the availability of the adoptive mother is crucial. If she is not around to be attuned and empathic to her child's loss and fear, who will be? Who else will be able to soothe him and connect to him? If the adoptive mother wants to form a bond with her child, she needs to be the one who understands and soothes his emotions. She will not experience the kind of bond that is possible for biological and gestating mothers because that bond is partially biological and physical. But she can form a very important bond with her child if she can be present and attuned to his emotions.

In case some adoptive mothers want to doubt what I am saying, I know of several cases where adult adoptees who are friends of new adoptive mothers have tuned in to the baby's loss and were able to soothe the child when no one else was doing so. They report positive responses from the babies in the form of calming and eye contact. Adoptive mothers need to be the ones to do this. They must take it on faith that their children have suffered from the loss of their first mothers, and proceed with empathy and soothing acts toward their infants.

Validation needs to continue throughout the adoptee's life. This does not mean that parents (or anyone else) have to put up with rude or difficult behavior. Feelings are unconscious, but if early empathy has been demonstrated and a certain amount of emotional regulation has been taught, *behavior is a choice*.

### Adoptive Fathers Have a Unique Role

An infant has the experience of having been profoundly connected to mother. In the case of a normal delivery and uninterrupted bonding with the mother, she is the whole world to her child. In the case of relinquishment and adoption, this world has been shattered by the disappearance of the mother. Father had nothing to do with it. He wasn't even there. Even if he were, he would be inconsequential. The infant is genetically related to the birth father, but has no sense of him. The infant resides in the world of mother/child. Therefore, the adoptive father is off the hook as far as the child's projection is concerned. He is not immediately seen as dangerous, a person capable of abandoning her. Although he may not seem familiar, he is not to be feared the way the mother may be. Because he doesn't seem so dangerous, the child may gravitate toward him and feel safer with him than with the mother. This gives adoptive fathers an opportunity to have an earlier importance to the child than a biological father may have.

Many adoptees have told me that they have felt more comfortable with their fathers than with their mothers. The adoptive father was not unconsciously being compared with the birth father the way the adoptive mother was being compared with the birth mother. (This will not be true with children who have spent time with their biological fathers and were adopted when older.) This puts the adoptive father in the position of being able to have a close relationship with his child. He should not waste this opportunity. Fathers are very important in the lives of their children. They have a different role from that of the mother. This doesn't mean that they cannot be nurturing. Fathers can be nurturing. Adoptive fathers *need* to be nurturing. But they also need to lead the child into a broader world. Both sons and daughters benefit greatly from the kinds of contributions fathers make to their socialization process. And, unless it is abusive, mothers should not interfere with the way fathers do this. Some mothers object when fathers treat the children differently from the way she does. Children need the experience of both mother-love and father-love, of mother-nurturing and father-nurturing, of female and male perceptions of the world. Fathers can give their children a different perception than mothers can. Both are important.

However, an adoptive father has to be careful that he doesn't inadvertently alienate the child from the mother. Children can easily be triangulated, which means in effect, two against one. Because of the difficulty the child is having with the mother, this would be easy to do. Yet the child's relationship to the mother is very important. It will be the father's task to create a safe place for the child without alienating her further from her mother. The best way he can do this is by showing his wife respect and affection in front of the child. He can lead by example. He can demonstrate that loving mom is not dangerous. By having a good, solid, loving relationship with one another, the parents can best create a safe environment for their child.

*Teaching Appropriate Responses to Feelings*

Any traumatized child will have difficulty regulating his feelings. Emotions will come out of the blue to zap him at random times. The vaguest resemblance of a present experience to a past traumatic event will bring on overwhelming feelings. He will be unable to control or understand them, especially if the traumatizing event happened before his explicit memory kicked in. It will be up to the parents to help him with this. An example would be mom's being late picking up her child from school. In this case, a parent might say, "I'll bet it scared you a bit having me come late, didn't it, Joey? I'm sorry, but just remember that I always come." The mother's acknowledging her child's fear makes him feel safer, even if she did scare him to death by arriving late. He needs her to understand the enormity of these events on him. She, on the other hand, needs to try very hard not to be late. Although her understanding and apology will help solidify their connection, her reassurance that she always comes will not eliminate his fear the next time.

Children learn best by example. The best way for adults to help children respond appropriately to their feelings is to respond appropriately themselves. It does no good for a parent to scream at a child to behave when the parent's behavior is also out of control. Even when the child is extremely provocative, the parents must stay in control of their emotions. This is not always easy, but it is essential. Any child knows that parents should not be requiring something of him that they have not mastered themselves.

Although the appropriate expression of adult feelings is speech—talking about what is upsetting rather than acting out—a child, and especially a traumatized child, will be unable to put words to his feelings. Drawing or coloring can be one form of expression for a child. Using puppets to act out the feelings and the source of the feelings is another effective method. Trauma victims of any age have very few verbal skills in dealing with trauma. (Why do you think an adoptive mother, rather than an adoptee, wrote *The Primal Wound?*) The trauma is re-experienced as sensations and images and need non-verbal forms of expression until such time as words are possible. Drama, art, dance, and poetry (which comes from a different part of the brain than prose) are effective in getting to the source of these sensations and emotions. Parents need to encourage these forms of expression, rather than allowing the child to use destructive behavior as his form of expression. For younger children who are doing destructive things, saying something like, "Boy, Bobby, you seem really angry; you must be hurting a lot," can stop the behavior and bring on the tears and a need for comforting. This can reinforce the parent/child connection. Getting angry at the child is a reaction to the behavior and demonstrates no understanding of the underlying emotions. As was mentioned earlier, a parent's staying in control and exhibiting appropriate ways to respond to emotions is the best way to teach this skill. The "do as I say, not as I do" method is seldom effective.

*Rejoice in Your Child's Uniqueness*

Rearing an adopted child is more difficult than many adoptive parents would like to admit. Many would like to believe that there is no difference between rearing a biological child and rearing an adopted child. This belief, although it may be well-intended, is counterproductive. The child needs her parents to recognize and accept the differences between her and them. Genetics plays a key role in her personality. It plays a key role in her talents, inclinations, aptitudes, and intellectual interests. Good adoptive parents stay alert to their child's special characteristics and encourage them. They don't try to mold her in their own image or images.

I have mentioned this in other parts of the book, so I won't belabor it here, but I will say this: Adoptive parents have to remember that there is no reason their child should be anything like them. Unless the social workers really tried to match personalities, talents, and intellectual interests, there may be little in common. This can be a good thing because it can cause the parents to expand their own interests. People should not attempt to adopt children unless they are prepared to develop and encourage interests in aspects of a child's character that may have little to do with them. If parents really love their child and have his best interest at heart, they will be interested in those things indigenous to the child.

*Teaching Empathy, Lessening Narcissism*

One of the tenets of this book is to convince adoptees that they actually have an impact on others. The parents can set the stage for this to be understood by the adoptee by making sure that he understands the impact he is having on his parents. By this I mean allowing the child to know the true feelings his behavior elicits in them. For parents of an acting-out child, the usual response is anger. This is probably not the right emotion. Feeling hurt might be closer. Yet most people who are hurt act out in anger. Adopted children certainly do this because it is safer. When parents do this as well, the real effect of the other's behavior is lost in the adrenaline rush which anger promotes. Adoptees have to be taught to allow themselves to experience pain and sadness. Parents must teach by example. Acting angry when one is hurt shows a lack of emotional integrity. Emotional integrity is crucial to relationships.

Because the infant was unable to affect the birth mother's response to him, he may feel impotent in his ability to affect others. His feeling that he has no impact may be wired into his neurological system. This is discussed more fully for adoptees themselves in a previous chapter, but I want to point out to parents that they can greatly assist their child in being able to have future good relationships if they can convey to the child, beginning at age 10 or 11, the effect he has on them—the real effect, the real emotion. (Younger children will feel at a loss to know what to do about their parents' feelings. Preadolescent children can begin to have some control over this.) Parents will have to keep responding honestly ten thousand times in order to make a dent in the deeply imprinted neurological belief: *I do not matter.* (Remember adoptive parents: The *I do not matter* belief is conveyed to you through the process of projective identification, so you may feel as if *you do not matter to your child.* This is his feeling about himself; let him know in the most sensitive way that you understand this.) A warning here: Adoptive parents should not exploit nor manipulate their children by expressing their feelings. Children are highly attuned to false motives in adult behavior. The only reasons for conveying the true emotion in response to a child's behavior is to teach him that he has an impact and that expressing hurt and sadness will not annihilate him or others. It should not be used to manipulate the child into doing some task or favor: "Johnny, you've made Mommy sad. Would you get me a drink of water?" This teaches children that expressing feelings can be used to manipulate others.

Over and over again I have had adoptive parents report that their child (usually a teenager) was amazed when the abusive behavior she was demonstrating got so bad that the parent finally broke down and cried. The child stopped in her tracks and began to comfort the parent. She was truly sorry for causing the parent so much grief. It scared her. She didn't believe it was possible. The usual scenario was that her parent just got angry, which fueled the child's anger, and round and round it went. However, causing grief, pain, and hurt was something else. It required a different way of reacting. The child was able to experience and express empathy.

This is very important to the child's emerging from the trap of the narcissistic wound. Experiencing a narcissistic wound usually means that the child will be emotionally stuck in the narcissistic stage of development. Learning to have empathy has to be taught. It does not just happen. Parents can teach empathy by *being empathic* and by *eliciting empathy* from their children. Both are necessary to the socialization of the child. Both are necessary for the child to be able to emerge from his narcissism. This is a parent's job, and it is a more difficult job for adoptive parents or other parents of a child who suffered early trauma. It requires persistence and patience.

Feelings that should *not* be conveyed to the child are the mother's frustration and disappointment about the gap in the relationship. The child can do nothing about this. This is not a behavior that can be corrected; it is an attitude formed at the time of relinquishment and is partially biological. The mother needs to talk about and work through her feelings about this with a therapist, a friend, or a support group. I can't emphasize this enough because I know many adoptive mothers who (sometimes unknowingly) blame their kids for their need to distance. It isn't anyone's fault. It just is. Mothers must learn to build a different bridge—one of understanding, validation, empathy, and respect.

## Consistency, Patience, and Integrity

As the child matures, a consistent set of values and rules makes it safer for the child and easier for the parents to deal with behavioral problems. It is sometimes difficult to always follow through with consequences for inappropriate behavior, yet because adoptees have problems with cause and effect or consequences, being consistent is even more essential. At the same time, it is important to be patient. The child is not deliberately baiting his parents. He is reacting to his early experience. He does not experience cause and effect the way children who have not had the natural order of their lives interrupted do. He needs to be painstakingly taught cause and effect, just as he has to be taught that he has an impact. Consistence, persistence, and patience are in order here.

A strategy that was tried during the seventies and still continues in many households today is that families are a democracy. In my opinion this didn't/ doesn't work. Children by their very nature as children are not mature and wise enough to know what is good for them. That they have some kind of intuitive knowing is wishful thinking. Human beings have a prolonged childhood for the very reason that they need guidance longer than most mammals. When we don't provide guidance, they languish or become out of control. Parenting is a hard job and takes a great deal of time and sacrifice. If people don't want to take the time or make the sacrifices necessary to parent, *to really parent*, they should not have kids. And if they didn't want kids, but find themselves with them anyway, then they have to do what is right for the kids—become parents.

I remember watching Phil McGraw on *Oprah* one time when a wife was complaining that her husband wasn't taking his role as father seriously. He was still going out with the boys and spending lots of time away from home. When it was the man's turn to speak he began whining that he hadn't *wanted* to become a parent. He wasn't ready to become a parent. Dr. Phil gave him one of his looks and said something to the effect, "Well, you may not have wanted to become a father, but the child is here, so deal with it. You *are* a father and you need to take responsibility for the child you helped create." In other words, deal with the reality of the situation, not some wishful thinking. (Guys who may have been "out to lunch" most of their lives need to remember that having unprotected sex can result in a child, and bingo—you're a father.)

Parents have certain responsibilities. This means they need to be in control of what is going on at home. Free-floating homes produce free-floating children— children with no direction, sense of responsibility, or control over their impulses. In some cases, when the parents are out of control, the kids become the responsible ones, but in an inappropriate way. They become what we call parentified children, children who sense that their parents can't find their way out of a paper bag so they take over. This is very sad, because it robs them of their childhoods. A great deal of resentment builds up over time and the parent/ child relationship is severely damaged.

For parents who do want to be in control but have a great deal of difficulty with an out-of-control kid, there is help. One book which deals effectively with out-of-control kids is *Parent in Control* by Gregory Bodenhamer. Although I disagree with one of his premises (he believes that some children are just born with a bad temperament and therefore bad behavior, while I believe that early experience has more to do with bad behavior), I think that his methods for correcting difficult behavior can be effective. One of the things he emphasizes is structure. This is very important for adopted kids. In the matter of discipline, Bodenhamer says, "Discipline consists of three elements: clearly defined and stated rules; follow-through and monitoring to make the rules mandatory; and consistency" (Bodenhamer, 1995). I want to add that all rules and expectations for chores need to be written down. This eliminates the arguments about who said what or when things have to be done.

This is where integrity comes in. The chores listed for Saturday morning need to be finite. It is not fair to decide when a child has finished his chores early that there are a couple more things he can now do. That is not fair and kids know it. They become resentful and angry. Wouldn't you? When it comes to inappropriate behavior, the consequences must be fair and immediate. Children in general and adoptees in particular are not very good at remembering their crimes for any length of time. For consequences to be effective, they must be administered at the time of the transgression. Waiting until daddy gets home will not do. Overreacting with impossible-to-follow-through threats also will not do. Grounding a teenager for a month leaves fewer options for the next transgression. Having a young child go without a meal only teaches that food is connected with emotion. This is not a good lesson. Fairness means that the parents take into consideration that much of the behavior to which they object may have to do with reaction to trauma and not with deliberate disobedience or opposition. This does not mean the behavior doesn't have to be corrected. The child has to live in harmony with his family and society; therefore he has to live by his culture's values, rules, and mores. He cannot have a different set of rules from everyone else.

Understanding your child's loss, being attuned to and empathizing with that loss, and validating his feelings is the beginning of the special bond that can occur between adoptive parent and child. Having control over your own emotions and helping your child regulate his are essential in the successful socialization of the child. Teaching empathy by example and showing your own feelings, thus eliciting empathy from your child, will aid in his managing to emerge from his narcissism. Being consistent and having patience and integrity in the socialization process will make the process easier and more meaningful to the child.

Up to this point I have made the relationship the responsibility of the parents. Parents must parent, which means making the sacrifices and taking the time to socialize the child or children. It means teaching through example, guidance, and supervision. It means there is a difference between the expectations of adults and children but those differences become less and less as the child matures. Sometime during adolescence it is time to make the relationship more reciprocal.

### Adolescence: The Dreaded Phase

Somewhere in this book I voiced my opinion that adolescence does not have to be what many Americans seem to believe—total rebellion and alienation from parents. Not all cultures have this experience and perhaps it is time that we no longer expect or foster this idea. This doesn't mean that adolescence is not a difficult stage of development. It is a kind of purgatory for kids. They are not children; they are not adults. They are in limbo. In our society we have few if any rites of passage for our children to help them bridge the gap between childhood and adulthood. We just leave them to fend for themselves. They don't do this very well.

Adolescents are confused by the many changes taking place in their bodies and in their emotions. Hormones are raging, voices are changing, bodies are developing, and emotions are high. After infancy, this is the very time when children need their parents the most, yet it is the time when American children are sometimes abandoned by their parents. (I know many parents will say that it is the other way around, but the parents are still the adults and should have a better handle on things than their moody, confused children.)

Adopted adolescents have an even more difficult time than their unadopted counterparts. After the terror of infancy when the child first experienced the adoptive mother as different, adolescence is the next time when this is brought so poignantly to the forefront. Adolescence is *identity time*. There is a need to become more of an individual, separate somewhat from mom and dad. When a child has never been able to identify with the parent, it is more difficult to separate. Teenage adoptees, in my experience especially the girls, have a difficult time accepting that their mothers are so different from them. They are angry about it. They blame her for it. It feels wrong and they communicate this by making mother wrong about almost everything. Because she feels inadequate, the adoptee makes her mother feel inadequate. The onset of womanhood brings their differences home to adopted girls more than any other time after the perinatal trauma.

All parents could aid their children in their journeys to adulthood if they would listen uncritically to their children's ideas. This is the time for experimentation in opinions and ideas (not drugs and alcohol). Some parents are so insecure themselves that they cannot tolerate their children's having ideas and opinions different from theirs. Yet shouldn't home be the safe environment for expressing a different point of view? Sometimes it is the least safe place. It doesn't mean parents have to agree with their children's opinions. But they should allow them to have different opinions without ridicule or judgment. If they want to be sure that their own opinion is also heard, instead of telling their children that they are crazy for having such an opinion, they could say something like, "Well, that's an interesting idea, Bobby, but did you ever think of it this way?" By shooting their kids down, parents are putting bullet holes in their relationship. Adolescents need their parents. It is not the time for parents to be sabotaging the relationship. Kids want to be respected. They are more likely to give their parents respect if they feel respected themselves. Respect will help hold the relationship together while it is going through all the changes that this phase of development brings.

It is important to remember that a parent's job is very difficult, especially during their children's adolescence. The misunderstandings and the blame which take place make the relationship very difficult. Although not always, mothers are often the most targeted for their children's rage. In an article titled "The Mother Journey," Molly Layton hit the nail on the head when she said:

> *The mother is the object, the bull's eye, of her children's feelings, some of which could stun an ox. She is intensely loved, hated, seized, ignored. I was thunderstruck by the blunt distortions my children made of my motives, and then at other times struck by their keen accuracy. In writing this, it occurs to me that they might say the same of me.*
> *Molly Layton, 1989*

I think every mother can relate to the sentiment in this paragraph. We certainly feel like the bull's eye of our children's feelings—good and bad. During adolescence those feelings sometimes hit a fever pitch. We have to be ready to help our children regulate and appropriately express their feelings without getting out of control ourselves. We also have to be sure that we understand what they are trying to do and say, as misunderstandings permeate the teen/parent relationship.

## The Teenager's Responsibility

As I mentioned a few paragraphs ago, until the age of adolescence I hold the parents responsible for the parent/child relationship. Children have neither the psychological understanding nor the maturity to understand their own feelings or behavior. This is especially true of victims of trauma and even more especially victims of early trauma. However, when children begin to mature and head into adulthood, it is necessary for them to begin learning to understand and assume responsibility for their behavior. Even before they totally understand the source of it or the reasons for it, it is necessary for adolescents to notice, acknowledge, and modify inappropriate behavior. This is not only for the benefit of their parents, but for their own benefit as they begin to form other important relationships.

If the parents did a good job of imparting the impact of their child's behavior on them as he was growing up, this will immensely help when the more difficult age of adolescence occurs. If the child was never taught the true effect of his actions on those around him, it will be very difficult to convey this during the more volatile teen years. However, if the parents were unaware of how important this was and neglected to do so, it is never too late to start. It will just be much more difficult.

To teenagers I say this: You are embarking on the road to adulthood with all its *responsibilities* and *privileges*. You cannot have one without the other. One of your tasks is to prove to your parents and others in authority that you are worthy of the additional privileges they are conferring upon you. Do you want to drive a car? Then you must be willing to drive responsibly. You must be willing to keep your grades up so insurance is affordable. You must abide by the rules of the road and the rules about curfews. *Driving is a privilege, not a right.* You have to qualify with the state in order to drive, and you must qualify with your parents to keep driving. Should something terrible happen while you are driving and someone is hurt or killed, you would live with the guilt for the rest of your life. You and your friends are not immortal. Your parents know this and want to protect you from the consequences of magical thinking. It will be up to you to make good choices and not be unduly influenced by the goading of friends. Your friends would not have to live with your guilt or the consequences of your choices (which could include jail time) . You would. Your present friends might not even be in your life in five years, but the guilt from a tragic accident would still be there for you.

This is only one example. Learning to avoid being talked into drinking or doing drugs or having unprotected sex are other such examples of choices you will have to make. Will you be making these choices as a mature emerging adult or as a follower of some of your more immature and irresponsible friends? There is a big difference between experimenting with ideas and opinions and experimenting with drugs or sex. People can get hurt from the latter two.

*Life With Mom and Dad*

Living with adoptive parents can be pleasant or it can be difficult. A lot depends upon the fit and their understanding of your initial loss. Are they quite a bit like you (the real, authentic you, not the adaptive, false you)? Or are they very different from you? You've been adapting all our life, so do you really know? Have they demonstrated an understanding of your loss issues? They may not have a clue as to the kinds of feelings you have been experiencing while living with them all these years. They may not know how sad you've felt at times or that you haven't felt as if you fit into the family very well, even if you really like everyone in it. You may have been doing such a good job adapting that they have never noticed this. Sometimes it is only as you approach adulthood that the shit hits the fan, as they say, and you begin to really notice the differences between you and your family. Don't blame your parents for this. They are having a difficult time with it, too. They are trying very hard to understand you and are probably missing the mark by quite a large margin. Are you adding to their misunderstanding by being secretive and distant? If so, don't blame them. You probably don't understand *them* either. Your perception of them is distorted by your separation trauma, just as their perception of you is distorted by their idea of their fantasy child. All of you owe it to one another to begin to really get to know one another. It is time to put aside childish ways and childish perceptions and begin to see the world through a more mature lens.

This entails some hard work. It means being more honest with them and with yourself. Are you keeping yourself secret from them? Are you keeping yourself secret from you? Have you tried to get them to understand the difficulties of growing up without seeing yourself reflected back—how hard it is to feel okay about yourself when this is true? Do you let them know some of the things that really interest you? Are you afraid to? Do you know? Before you can invite your parents into your world, you have to discover that world for yourself. Now is the time to begin, to explore, to experiment with being you.

And that *you* is not some loser hanging out on the periphery of life. If that is your opinion of yourself, you have not yet discovered *you*. Believing such a thing is just giving you an excuse for bad behavior. Keep remembering that behavior is a choice. Make good choices for yourself. Look inside yourself. *There is gold there.* Oh yeah, you have a *shadow* like everyone else. But yours is no better or worse. No matter how much your little baby mind has convinced you that your birth mother's leaving you was your fault, it just isn't true. That is just a baby belief which it is time to let go. It isn't helping you. Besides, there are a lot of things you can and should take responsibility for that you can actually have some influence upon. It does no one any good for you to assume responsibility for something that happened when you had just emerged from the womb. Now really! Does that make sense?

Living with mom and dad may have been more difficult for you than living with your birth parents may have been, especially as an infant. You have had to deal with a great many feelings that have left you puzzled and perplexed. Your experience of relinquishment has been the most difficult thing a baby can endure. But you are approaching adulthood now. Whatever the origins of your feelings and behavior, it is now time for you to take responsibility for your impact on the world. And *you do have an impact.* If you don't feel it, take it on faith. And act *as if* ... To do anything else is irresponsible. If you haven't felt as if you have an impact, at least begin to *notice* how you are affecting others. If you had no impact, you wouldn't be affecting others. Ask them, if you don't know. Begin by having a mature and honest talk with your parents. Ask them how aspects of your behavior have affected them. Listen to how puzzled and inadequate they have felt in interacting with you. Ask them if they have ever felt as if you have left them out of your life. Begin to let them in. Unless you have been in a very abusive relationship with your parents (and by that I mean physical, sexual, or extreme verbal or emotional abuse because just living with genetic strangers can *feel like abuse* if the differences are too great), it is time to do your part to repair the relationship. It is time to reintroduce yourselves to one another.

## Finding Other Role Models

There are some people who never should have become parents. They are the people who are emotionally unstable, immature, may never have had good role models for parenting themselves, or who are mentally ill. I don't mean the people who explode once in awhile—most people have parents like that. I mean consistently mean or abusive people. If you have been reared by people like this and can corroborate it, you need to do something about it. Either contact a teacher, principal, or minister/priest/rabbi about getting counseling or ask them to help you with the courts. You should not remain in an abusive home unless your parents are in counseling and making a definite effort to control their behavior. Remember that just being very different from you is not abuse, although it may feel like it.

If you haven't done so already, it is important to find other adults to use as role models—a teacher, scout leader, other parent, or older friend. Look for a person to be a mentor. You need role models other than your abusive parents. Otherwise you will experience adults as either abandoning or abusive. There are other kinds. You deserve to have them in your life. Never, and I mean *never*, think because your birth mom couldn't keep you, you deserve whatever you get. No child deserves abuse. Every child deserves a safe environment in which to grow up. You will have a harder time than non-adopted kids feeling safe, even in a safe environment. But you really know if your parents are safe or not. If they are not, try to get help either through counseling or the courts.

## Adulthood

In our society it seems as if childhood is very short and adolescence very long. Kids want to wear makeup and start dating at ten, but they don't want to take on adult commitments until thirty or thirty-five. What does this mean for the adult relationship with the adoptive parents?

For a lot of people it means that they want to continue blaming their parents for all their difficulties *ad nauseam*. (When they meet the birth parents, they sometimes redirect the blame, but nevertheless don't take it on themselves.) One of my tenets is that there doesn't have to be any blame, just accountability and responsibility. And as adults, we all have to assume responsibility for our behavior in our relationships. We can't continue blaming others for our behavior. It also means, then, that it isn't all right for adoptees to expect their parents to support them or bail them out forever. If they want to be treated and respected as adults, they have to act like adults and take responsibility for their livelihood. I say this advisedly because a number of adoptive parents have contacted me saying that their 20–30 year old "children" are still living at home, waking up at 3 p.m., going out with friends until 3 a.m., and saying they can't find a job! I'd say that they aren't waking up at all! And neither are the parents.

That being said, as twenty-somethings or thirty-somethings, it is important that adoptees, like any other adults, begin having a more mature relationship with their adoptive parents. This will require the cooperation of the parents, so I am speaking to them as well as their adult children. Just as in any other relationship, there has to be more communication. This communication needs to be honest, yet sensitive, informative, non-blaming, and above all respectful. The games need to stop. Integrity needs to be paramount. Parents have to recognize their adult children as equals and stop treating them as uninformed children. Their opinions and values may differ, but that doesn't mean that they can't get along. Men and women have fought long and hard for the idea of *different but equal.* We need to confer the same mantle upon the parent/adult-child relationship.

As already mentioned, for adoptive families this may be more difficult than with biological families (although there are some biological families who defy the rule) because the children may be very different from the parents. However, differences don't mean ostracism. After all, don't we have friends who are quite different from us? I hope so. It makes life much more interesting. If there are great differences, let those differences broaden *both* your horizons. Rather than *either/or,* see your relationship as *and* ... The French say, "Vive la difference!" It is time for adoptive families to say this as well. In any case, it is during adulthood that adoptees and their parents can re-evaluate their perceptions of one another, acknowledge the difficulties that they have lived through, ask and give forgiveness, dust off the love that got damaged during adolescence, and begin their relationship anew based on adult attitudes and behaviors.

## Relationships with Friends ...

Relationships seem to be troubling for many adoptees. Failed or difficult relationships are often what bring them into therapy. Most of these difficulties are based on an event that most of them don't even remember—the severance of the very first relationship with mother. We have already discussed how this first failed relationship affects the relationship with the second mother. How does it impact the relationships with friends and partners?

### The Double Standard

One of the most reported difficulties friends and lovers seem to have with adoptees is their tendency to have one set of rules for themselves and another for everyone else. "They have a double standard," is what I keep hearing. Over and over I hear, "If I did to her what she does to me, she would be so hurt and resentful. Yet she doesn't seem to understand that I have feelings too." This subject is discussed in more detail in Chapter II. But I want to mention it here because it does seem to be a real stumbling block in relationships involving adoptees. It revolves around a paradoxical belief system: *I can't stand anyone doing anything to me that hurts me*, and *I have no impact on others, so I can't hurt them.* These beliefs are not thoughts that come from the neocortex. If they were they would be easy to correct. They are feelings, emotions, or senses, products of the limbic system. Correcting these beliefs, therefore, will take diligence. There needs to be a real effort to correct the resulting behavior even before the beliefs are modified.

Acting solely from emotion is a dangerous thing for people who have experienced trauma. The emotion may have very little to do with the present event which triggered it. This means that the person who triggered it is going to get an over-reaction to the trigger. This isn't fair and is the death of many relationships. It is not just that the reaction is too severe, but the perpetrator of the reaction has no idea of the impact the reaction is making on the other person. This gets very old after awhile. As I've said before, adoptees, it doesn't matter whether or not you believe, feel, or understand that you have an impact; *it is there and must be accounted for.* Adoptees are always talking about fair and unfair. Well, do you think treating someone poorly in your life today because of what happened to you twenty, thirty, or forty years ago is fair? You are smart enough to know that you can't hold everyone you care about hostage to what happened to you as an infant. Apply the real Golden Rule: Treat others as you want to be treated. You might be surprised at the result!

### The Slammed Door

The second thing that I hear a lot about is the *if you disappoint (betray) me, you're out of my life* syndrome. Again, adoptees are so sensitive to others' impact on them, and so insensitive to their impact on others that they dismiss people for minor offenses. Their sense of betrayal is overwhelming. It is so out of proportion that almost anything can set it off. Adoptive parents are always saying that their children don't keep friends very long. They don't understand it. Someone is a bosom buddy one day and *persona non grata* the next. This may be a normal phenomenon during junior high school, but for adoptees it often starts earlier and just keeps on going beyond adolescence and into adulthood. This is not to say that there are not some adoptees who have lifelong friends. There are. But as a whole, small transgressions can destroy a perfectly good relationship for many adoptees. It is time to take another look at this and see if the adult or the "child" is in control. If the reasons for the cutoff cannot be substantiated by logic, you can bet the child is running the show. Do you really want her to be in charge? Was the offense worth destroying a friendship? Would you want someone to get rid of you for such an offense? (Is that what you think happened in the beginning of your life?) Think about it. Think honestly about it! You may want to call up a few ex-friends!

### Keeping in Touch

Because many adoptees don't think they matter much, they often leave it to others to keep in touch. They have a difficult time believing that anyone remembers them after they've left the room. Sometimes this takes the form of their never initiating e-mails or phone calls. Sometimes it means they don't even return messages. It doesn't seem to matter. (Translation: *I don't matter.*) On the other hand, if they are in a serious relationship, it may mean they have to phone or e-mail all the time just to remind their lover that they still exist. The feeling is: *If I don't keep in touch, he may forget me.*

In order to lessen the impact of the overwhelming feelings of fear about the permanency of relationships, you have to take risks and note carefully the results. By that I don't mean doing inappropriate things and daring your lover or friend to stick around. What I do mean is don't call every five minutes when he is spending a night away from you. Does he come around the next day? Okay, let that sink in. Think about it. Integrate it as a new feeling: *I can trust him to come back. He isn't leaving me.* Or call up a friend you haven't heard from for a long time and see what she says. Then try to integrate: *My friends do remember me. They care about me. Sometimes they just get busy, as I do, and forget to call.* It will take many such efforts to make it seem more normal not to worry every time your partner is out of your sight or you haven't heard from a friend. Keep at it. Practice makes perfect or at least tolerable.

### Rules for Friendships

*Friendships should be reciprocal.* This means there is balance in communication and activities. People get tired of friendships that are one-sided: " I listen to her problems over and over again, but she never wants to hear mine." Or "I went bowling with him last time and I just wanted him to go to the ball game with me this time." Whether it is in the area of recreational activities or the need for a shoulder to cry on, there should be reciprocity and balance. For adoptees, this means that you can't be so stingy in allowing people in. Adoptees are great at rescuing other people from the foibles they get themselves into. They are less than good at allowing others to help them or to even allowing others to know what is bothering them (except for the mailman or the bank teller).

*Friendships take time.* In our busy, busy lives, friendships seem be to less important than anything else. So many times I have heard someone say, "I wish I had more time for my friends." I have said that myself. After all, aren't we all busy? Don't we all feel as if there isn't enough time in the day for work and family, let alone friends? Although it seems as if we don't have the time, perhaps we are not making good use of our leisure time. How many times have you watched a TV program rather than calling a friend? Sometimes you just want to "vege out" and not talk to anyone. That is fine. But if we are honest, we could find time to keep in touch, even if it is only with one friend a day. Or three friends a week. There are plenty of times when we could make a phone call, send an e-mail, or stop by to say "Hello." If we value our friendships, we need to take the time for them. When all is said and done, it is the people in our lives who feed us, feed our souls. We need to take the time to nourish ourselves with our friendships as well as to nurture them.

*Friendships take effort.* Closely tied to the need to take time for our friends is the necessity of putting in the effort to maintain friendships. There are some friends, perhaps from an earlier time in your life, with whom you can have an occasional correspondence and know that if you need them they will be there. There is no need to keep up a running dialogue. But for most friendships, the ones that are immediate, it is necessary to make the effort to keep them viable. The people who seem to do the best job at this are the people who have a network of friends who all know one another. There is a feeling of camaraderie and connection that makes keeping up with these friends easier than having disconnected friends here and there. This doesn't mean that having a variety of friends who don't know one another is a bad thing. It is just harder to keep up with all of them. It takes more effort.

### Making Friends

"Well," you say, "that's all fine and good *if you have friends*, but I don't have any and don't know how to get any." I can tell you this: They aren't going to fall out of the sky into your lap, that's for sure. Here, again, it takes effort to find and cultivate new friends. First of all it takes *becoming visible*. In other words, you can't hide out in a classroom, gym, party, church, political rally, or wherever there are people you can meet. In most social gatherings, it is all right to join a group already in a discussion. Unless it seems to be something very, very personal, listen at first, then add a comment or two. At first, if you just want to listen, that's okay. Gradually, however, begin to join in the discussion. Be appropriate. Don't try to sabotage yourself by saying something inappropriate, outrageous, or extremely controversial. That would only give you ammunition to add to your arsenal of self-deprecating comments like "I always knew nobody liked me." Or you could put it into the "I knew I shouldn't have gone to that party; those people are assholes" category. Taking a risk is one thing; testing people is something else. Do you know the difference?

Some people say they have an easier time if they just talk to one person at a time. Look for someone else who seems lost or ill-at-ease. Go over and talk to that person. Ask him questions about himself. Not intrusive questions, but general questions about where he lives or what he enjoys doing. Draw him out and you won't be so concerned about yourself. I read the other day that shy people aren't necessarily intrinsically shy; they are just overly concerned about what others think of *them*. Does this sound familiar? All your life, whether you realize it or not, you have been trying to adapt, and very concerned about how your parents saw you. You can't seem to stop doing that. *Stop making everything about you.* Really focus on the other person.

Don't wait until you have decided that you are finally your authentic self to begin making friends. Others can intuit your real qualities perhaps better than you can yourself. Allow them to get to know you by being honest about your opinions, ideas, and interests. Don't push your ideas on others or become upset if they have different opinions. Just present them as part of who you are right now and find out who the other person is. Perhaps there will be enough similarities to begin a friendship and perhaps not, but whatever the outcome, you will have made a definite step toward authenticity. The next time you are at a party, a break in a class, or lunch break at work approaching someone will be easier. The more you do it, the easier it becomes. I've seen miracles happen!

## Avoiding the Pitfalls

There are definitely things you can do to sabotage fledgling relationships. One is to lose control by using drugs or alcohol. Anything which causes a distortion in reality is not conducive to making or maintaining friendships. It may seem like a good idea to have a drink or two "just to get me over my inhibitions," but you really don't want to get over your inhibitions. You just want to be friendly. You can do that without alcohol. This does not mean that I am against social drinking. I certainly engage in social drinking myself. But allowing yourself to get out of control is never a good idea. And you may not be the best judge of that: Note how many people think they are sober enough to drive when they are not. If someone has told you that you were acting like a jerk at a party, don't get mad at him, take it as a warning to drink less next time. Alcohol can cause people to do and say things they later regret. That is not the way to make friends.

The same is true of drugs. Although the effects of marijuana may be less obnoxious and dangerous (to others) than alcohol as far as substances go, it distorts reality nevertheless. It is not much fun to try carrying on a conversation with a person who is high on pot if you are not. As brilliant as they may think they are being, it all sounds a bit repetitive and simplistic to the listener. Other drugs are definitely out. I am not condoning the use of marijuana by discussing it in this way, but I am not nearly so cautious in the presence of a pot smoker as I am with someone who has had too much alcohol. There was a time (and for people who adhere to some religious beliefs it still exists) when people knew how to have a good time without drugs *or* alcohol. Maybe it takes more effort, but maybe it is also more real.

Expecting others to take on more responsibility for the relationship than you do can make others feel as if *they don't matter to you*. This may seem ironic to adoptees who often don't believe themselves important to others, but it is nevertheless true. We take our cues from one another. If a person doesn't hear from you after a particularly nice evening, whether on a date or just having connected during a social gathering, she won't think she made any difference to you. Adoptees aren't the only ones who feel unimportant to others. "Hey," you might say, "they didn't call me either." And, naturally, it was more their responsibility than yours, wasn't it? Far be it from you to make the first move! Of course, it isn't always appropriate or possible to contact someone whom you've just met at a social gathering, but perhaps it is and you just don't want to bother. (Or *be* a bother ...) Remember: Following up is important if you want to make friends.

Keep it simple. By that I mean don't try to make a huge impression on someone by doing something extravagant if you decide to see him again. For one thing, you don't want to set a precedent that you can't continue. For another, it may make the other person feel uncomfortable. Perhaps he wouldn't be able to reciprocate in the same manner, or perhaps he just doesn't feel at ease in certain situations. Talk it over with the other person if you aren't sure what he would like to do. On the other hand, don't just wait around for the other person to make all the decisions about where to go and what to do.

Don't begin to get clingy if you have decided that you really like this new person. This may sound the opposite of what I was saying about taking the initiative and calling first and so on, but it isn't. If your anxiety begins to get the better of you, talk to another friend or a therapist, but don't give in to your insecurities. None of us really knows how a new person in our lives feels about us. Most of us can tolerate the uncertainty. Adoptees find this more difficult, for obvious reasons. The problem is that if you give in and act on your need to call frequently, you will bring about the very thing you are fearing. Think about the result, rather than the immediate discomfort. No one likes being engulfed. Find the balance you need to stay connected without engulfing and scaring away the other person.

Once you've made a friend, be loyal. Unless there is a very good reason for ending the friendship, why do it? Reread what I have said in several places in this book about the *double standard* and *slamming the door*. Try putting yourself in the other person's shoes. How would you like someone to treat you the way you are treating your friend? Take note of how long your friendships last. If you find that you are always having to make new friends because the old ones are no longer part of your life, really think hard about why this is. Unless you are always making bad choices in your friends, perhaps there is something you are doing that causes this phenomenon. (If you are always making bad choices, that *is* something you are doing!) Did you slam the door after a disappointment? Are you sure you understand all there is to know about the situation? Did she do something you have never and would never do to someone yourself? Be very vigilant about using a double standard on your friends and family. Don't slam the door on a friendship without "due cause."

## ... And Lovers

Everyone or almost everyone wants someone special with whom to share his or her life. It is the reason the species still exists. Yet as long as relationships have existed, we have yet to discover the magical solution to their being satisfactory to all concerned. We all want companionship, safety, a sense of belonging, and love. These are not unreasonable wishes. Why has it been so difficult to fulfill these criteria? What is it especially about adoptees that has made relationships the main reason they seek therapy?

After the relationship with the adoptive mother, perhaps the next most difficult relationship is that with a partner or spouse. Here again, I get lots of complaints about the double standard. Angry adoptees don't make very good partners. They take their partners on an emotional roller coaster ride. Even those partners who have some understanding about the abandonment issues that give rise to these outbursts get tired of the whole thing. And most people don't have a clue. Adoptees often don't have a clue. As far as they are concerned, "That's just the way I am."

Remember that you can no longer get by with this excuse. *That isn't just the way you are; it is just the way you are allowing yourself to behave.* It has to do with attitudes and beliefs, but nothing to do with who you really are. Attitudes and beliefs are formed by experience. That's why it is so important to integrate new experiences. Although old beliefs and attitudes are difficult to overcome, it isn't impossible. Our brains continue to admit and process new information all our lives. This should give everyone hope.

There are many books written about marriage and relationships. Some are good and some are useless. One of the best that I've read recently is *The New Couple* by Taylor and McGee. In it the authors replace the ideas about traditional marriages with "The ten new laws of love." These are not crazy ideas about New Age Relationships. They are pertinent and practical concepts and include *chemistry,* making the relationship a *priority, emotional integrity, deep listening, equality, peacemaking, self-love,* having a *mission in life, walking* (having the willingness and ability to leave if the relationship becomes intolerable), and *transformational education* (a kind of experiential education that both instructs the head and moves the heart). Taylor and McGee's ideas are so refreshing and yet so practical that one will wonder why we haven't known about them all along. Perhaps we have and just haven't known how to implement them.

Another book which is helpful in gaining insight into relationships is *Getting the Love You Want* by Harville Hendrix. His books have led to a method of marriage counseling based on empathy that I often recommend called *Imago Therapy.* This is one of the most effective methods I know of getting both people in the relationship to face their own pain and to empathize with one another. With a good Imago therapist, it is impossible for one person to sit around waiting for the other person to "get his/her stuff together so we can be happy again." Both partners become immediately engaged in their own "stuff." Often this stuff has its origins in childhood pain, and understanding that pain becomes the basis for an empathic connection between the two people. When two people are in a relationship they both contribute to its stability or instability. Therefore, they *both* need to acknowledge and change those things that are making it unstable. Gaining insight into a partners childhood can create the crucible for empathy and a deeper love.

John Gottman has written a book called *The Seven Principles for Making Marriage Work.* In it he recommends such ideas as *enhancing your love maps, nurturing your fondness and admiration, turning toward each other instead of away, letting your partner influence you, solving solvable problems, overcoming gridlock,* and *creating shared meaning.* He claims to be able to predict which marriages will end in divorce by noticing certain signals that the couple emit during an interview. One such sign he calls the Four Horsemen. The first horseman is *criticism,* which he differentiates from complaints in that criticisms are general attacks upon a person, whereas complaints have to do with specific behaviors. The second horseman is *contempt,* which is telegraphed by sarcasm, cynicism, eye-rolling, sneering, etc. The third horseman is *defensiveness.* Although Gottman recognizes that certain criticisms or complaints warrant a defensive posture, he says that being defensive seldom gets the desired results of backing down or an apology. Instead it usually escalates the conflict by shifting the blame onto the other partner. The fourth horseman is *stonewalling.* Stonewalling or ignoring the complaints of the other spouse is more commonly used by men than women. Hiding behind a newspaper or going out to the garage when a wife is trying to discuss something is a typically male thing to do, although women can be guilty of it as well. Gottman's book is a good one and has excellent exercises to help couples learn how to feel closer and be on the same team.

A new book by Rhonda Britten, author of *Fearless Living,* is called *Fearless Loving: 8 Simple Truths that Will Change the Way You Date, Mate, and Relate.* The eight truths that she writes about are Truth 1: Love is up to you; Truth 2: Everyone is innocent; Truth 3: Feelings lie; Truth 4: Chemistry is between your ears; Truth 5: Dating is where you practice being yourself; Truth 6: "Yes" means nothing if you can't say "No"; Truth 7: Loss is a fact of life; Truth 8: Love is a risk you must take. The last two truths will be the most difficult for adoptees, but also essential if they are to live a full life.

There are many other books about relationships. Judith Wallerstein conducted a study into what makes a good marriage. Her book is called *The Good Marriage* and is written in conjunction with Sandra Blakeslee. All of these books offer good ideas concerning what constitutes a lasting relationship and how to help achieve one. I would like to offer some ideas which include my own observations as well as things I've learned from other therapists and authors.

## Chemistry

Chemistry is very important in any committed relationship. It is the basis for intimate friendships as well as great sex in a relationship. There is a kind of connection that makes the two people feel protective of one another. Perhaps it is similar to the bonding that takes place between mother and child. It is said that bonding between mother and child is what makes mothers "fight like tigers" to protect their young. Although it may be possible for a person to have different kinds of chemistry with different people (for instance perhaps one's partner is not one's soul mate), it is certainly a plus if one's lover is also one's best friend. (This doesn't mean that one person is expected to fulfill *all* of another's emotional needs.)

## Falling in Love

One of the things most couples therapists agree upon is that attraction or chemistry or falling in love is either there or not there. *It is not something that can be worked on.* Although there are several theories about why we fall in love with one person and not another who may have many of the same characteristics, falling in love is still pretty much of a mystery. Usually it is the part of a relationship which hits us first. Having chemistry isn't the same as infatuation. Whereas infatuation is fleeting, having chemistry with someone can last a lifetime. Sometimes it is difficult to differentiate between the two in the beginning of a relationship because a kind of intoxication can be present in both types of attraction. However, infatuation will dissipate. Even if difficulties in a relationship make it seem as if it is dissipating, real chemistry between people can be retrieved. However, it can't be manufactured, created, cultivated, or faked.

In the beginning, the chemistry is a kind of intoxication. Our endorphins are having a field day and we feel euphoric. This is the first stage of love. It can last from a couple of months to a couple of years. It is more than great sex, but great sex is part of it. Also important are a trusting friendship and compatibility. These are part of the chemistry and can't be faked.

## Compatibility

Compatibility is an essential ingredient of a strong relationship and is part of the chemistry. It is easy to feel the energy when there is a strong connection. It is not necessary for a couple to like all the same things, but having similar interests can certainly make two people more compatible. Often it is a strong interest which brings them together in the first place. This does not mean there will be chemistry between them. Chemistry can be present in friendships other than that with one's partner and is not always sexual.

## Trust and Intimacy

Chemistry between a couple can strengthen trust. A couple have to be able to trust one another in order for the relationship to survive. They have to be able to be one another's best friends, keeping confidences and allowing for true intimacy to take place. If one cannot trust one's partner, there is no way emotional intimacy will be able to evolve. Without intimacy, there will be a void in the relationship. Intimacy is one of the big problems for adoptees. Writing in *Sacred Romance,*

Brent Curtis admits, "Intimacy requires a heart that is released and mine was pinned down with unknown fears and grief" (1997). Does that sound familiar to you? Opening up the heart to another person may seem terrifying, but the alternative—a life without intimacy—may be more terrifying. If the chemistry is there, it is easier for trust and intimacy to evolve. Although both trust and intimacy can be worked on in a relationship, chemistry cannot. A relationship is missing something essential if chemistry is missing.

## Emotional Integrity

Almost all couples therapists mention emotional integrity as one of the essentials of a good relationship. What does this mean? Emotional integrity means that as adults we take full responsibility for the full range of our emotions. There are several aspects of emotional integrity. According to Taylor and McGee these aspects are *being emotionally honest, acquiring emotional literacy, and becoming skilled at emotional management.*

### Achieving Adulthood

First of all, being able to achieve any of the above means that one has to become an adult. Part of that is what Judith Wallerstein, in her book *The Good Marriage*, calls the first task of marriage: "... to detach emotionally from the families of childhood, commit to the relationship, and build new connections with the extended family" (1995). When Wallerstein says "detach emotionally from the families of childhood," she doesn't mean we no longer love our parents. She means we no longer depend on them in the same way we did before. Some parents make this difficult because they don't feel valuable anymore if their children no longer need them in the same way. It isn't that we no longer need our parents, but we need them in a different way as adults than we did as children and adolescents. When we marry, we are forming a new family. Making the marriage the primary relationship is not being disloyal to the family of childhood. In fact, parents should rejoice in their children's reaching this stage in their lives. It means they have done their job well. It is part of becoming an adult and committing emotionally to the new partner, and it involves establishing different boundaries with other family members.

Emotional integrity is impossible if someone is allowing the inner child to rule. Children cannot be expected to take full responsibility for their emotions, but adults can and should. Do you know when you are acting from the child or from the adult? In Transactional Analysis, Eric Berne divides people's psyches into three categories: child, adult, and parent. Acting from the child or the parent in a mature relationship is not helpful. Even though a parent may be expected to be an adult, acting parental with one's partner puts the partner in the child's role. This often manifests in discounting or belittling verbal abuse and relegates him or her to inequality in the relationship. Although all couples will fall into one of these three roles from time to time, it is important to know when it is happening and to change anything that is compromising the emotional integrity of the relationship.

*Becoming Aware*

Early childhood trauma can interfere with the implementation of emotional integrity. Almost everyone has suffered some emotional trauma during childhood. Children are more easily traumatized than most people realize. We too easily think that kids are not affected by things that actually *do* affect them. That's because children perceive things differently from adults. It is these *perceptions— the meanings children give them*—which cause the trauma. Therefore, it is important for couples to delve into their psyches and discover together (or with a therapist) what those traumas may have been. This is difficult if the trauma happened before age three. You might need help from your parents or others who knew you when you were an infant and young child. Something as innocuous as mom and dad going on a two-week vacation without you when you were two years old may have been traumatic for you, even if you were left with loving grandparents.

We already know adoptees' greatest trauma, but there may be other traumas as well. It can't be overlooked that their partners may also have suffered some kind of trauma. This doesn't mean it will be necessary to go back to mom and dad and read them the riot act about something that happened long ago. As Taylor and McGee say, "First of all, it's the rare father or mother who intentionally traumatizes his or her children. Second, what parent wasn't little once? We can't pass on what wasn't done to us." They quote Bob Hoffman, a pioneer of emotional healing, as saying, "Everyone is guilty, and no one is to blame" (Taylor & McGee, 2000). If you are interested in healing, this is an important concept to remember. After all, you may someday want *your* children to become aware of this idea!

There is a great deal of miscommunication between children and their parents. The lack of genetic clues can make this even more probable in adoptive families. Rearing children is a learn-as-you-go occupation. Even if there are manuals, there is no one-size-fits-all when it comes to relationships with children. Some of these miscommunications may have caused traumas that slid under the radar of the parents. In adult relationships, becoming aware of the ways in which early trauma can evoke feelings from present-day events is the first step in gaining emotional integrity.

*Emotional Literacy*

Why is it important for these traumas to be brought up to the light of day? Because you will still be reacting to them, and your partners may be broad-sided by this fact. Instead of reacting to the traumatic reminder, what is the mature way to handle the feelings which are evoked? After awareness comes acknowledgment. This will necessitate becoming emotionally literate. Emotional literacy gives you a way to express the emotion without acting on it. Again, this is more difficult where trauma is concerned because of an inability for many people to express their trauma-induced emotions in words. It can be learned, however. A couple owe it to one another to practice fluency in talking about feelings. Otherwise they will be constantly bombarding one another with reactions to emotions that have very little to do with the partner or the present situation. This is hard on relationships.

One of the elements of a relationship which creates problems is something that is seldom talked about outside the therapeutic relationship. That is *transference.* Transference is part of every relationship and is responsible for a great deal of the blame that gets placed on contemporary people in our lives. Taylor and McGee say, "In fact, very unscientifically, as much as eighty percent of the emotional juice of each couple conflict is leakage from the mysterious reservoirs of stored feelings from childhood. Only the remaining twenty percent actually pertains to the contemporary situation. This is called the eighty/twenty principle of transference." Transference is a kind of projection that emanates from either parental idealization or parental demonization. At first, during the "in love" part of the relationship, the *transference is positive.* But at some point, the *negative transference* is bound to appear. It is at this time that so many couples begin to have difficulty. The power struggle begins and the idealized person begins to grow warts. When the feeling being triggered is related to a trauma, it is called *traumatic transference.* Adoptees are subject to this kind of transference and their parents or partners are the targets. When a feeling seems out of proportion to the situation, transference is probably playing a part. In none of the kinds of transference mentioned is the feeling or sensation all about the person who triggered it. This is the reason it is so important to identify the issues in our childhoods that may be triggering us today. How might this be helpful?

*Recognizing Transference*

Let's use an example that was first introduced in the chapter on the Brain. Brent Atkinson talks about how our neocortex gets sidetracked by the amygdala whenever a traumatic event is triggered. He uses the example: "By the time the neocortex gets into the act, the damage has been done—you have already called your late-to-dinner partner an inconsiderate jerk ..." It would be easy to understand the child within the adoptee getting very upset by someone's being late for a date or an appointment. But instead of doing what Atkinson asserts might be the reaction, calling the person an inconsiderate jerk, the aware adoptee would understand that the disappearance of her birth mother is what is being triggered here. So she might say instead, "I'm so relieved that you are here. It makes me really nervous for people to be late." She doesn't have to remind him of the origin of that fear because they've already talked about it, but she lets him know in a respectful way that he should try to be on time. The meal can proceed without animosity or further stress.

Emotion is always present when people are communicating. Knowing exactly what emotion is being evoked and how much of it is due to the triggering event is important to our communicating it to another person. Are you acting or speaking angrily *when you are really hurt?* Can you tell the difference? Do you know who it was who really hurt you? Are you afraid that allowing your partner, friend, parent, or child to know you are hurt will make you seem weak? The opposite is true. Only courageous people allow themselves to be vulnerable. If you want the other person to take responsibility for the effect he is having on you, you have to let him know the *true emotion* that is being experienced. And you have to explore how much of it is actually attributable to him. This is known as emotional honesty.

### Emotional Honesty

Some people are not even aware that they are being emotionally dishonest. For so long they have been used to hiding their feelings, because of parental influence or fear of falling into an abyss, that they no longer even know what they are feeling let alone how to communicate it. Emotional honesty is not the same as honesty about ideas, beliefs, opinions, or thoughts. Do you remember what I said in Chapter 12 about the difference? If you follow the word *feel* by the word *that* you are not describing a feeling, but an idea, thought, opinion, etc. Most feelings consist of one word each. In their book *The New Couple*, Taylor and McGee list the six families of emotions:

1. Shock, surprise, and confusion.
2. Anger, rage, resentment, frustration, annoyance, irritation, impatience, and the contempt cluster (hatred, scorn, disdain, contempt).
3. Sadness, grief, disappointment, hurt, and despair.
4. Fear, anxiety, worry, insecurity, panic, jealousy, and toxic guilt, and toxic shame.

5. Healthy guilt and shame, and embarrassment.
6. Love, joy, admiration, appreciation, gratitude, relief, empathy, and compassion.


This list may give you a better idea of what words to use to have emotional honesty. Having emotional honesty means telling your partner the positive feelings, not just the negative ones. How many of you can say, "I feel really happy today"? I have found joy to be almost as frightening for adoptees to allow themselves to feel as love is. It is important to be aware of feelings of happiness and joy, to speak of them, and to savor them.

Knowing the difference between feelings and opinions is very important because so many people claim to be expressing their feelings, yet they begin by saying, "I feel that ..." Or they go on and on about beliefs and thoughts and claim to be stating their feelings. I remember a young man who wanted very much to be part of his birth mother's family. The only problem was that each time he communicated with her, he told her what a rotten person he thought she was. Of course, he was angry at her for having given him away, but he wasn't getting even close to having her want him back when she had to listen to the deluge of negative opinions and beliefs he had about her. All the time, he claimed he had a right to his feelings (which he did) and he wanted her to know what they were (which he wasn't communicating). If he had said, "I feel terribly hurt that you didn't keep me," that would have been an honest feeling. It was easier for him to feel angry than to plumb the depths of his sadness. But even his anger wasn't being communicated honestly.

Adoptees have a difficult time when expressing their feelings to their birth mothers or fathers. Because they are often regressed, there may be no barrier to the blatting out of emotions. Birth mothers of newly reunited children have to keep this in mind and make allowances for it. However, when the relationship has been going on for over a year, it is time for the adoptee to gain some control over the manner in which he expresses his emotions to his birth mother or father. If support groups want to be helpful, the facilitators will supply appropriate language and encourage its use when aiding adoptees and their parents in reunion. It is important to remember that *everyone* in the triad has been wounded by the processes of relinquishment and adoption.


*Emotional Safety*

One of the things I hear all the time is that the expression of feelings was not allowed in families of origin. Although since the 70s there has been more openness for feelings to be expressed, there is still a sense for most people that it would not be a good idea to express negative feelings. This makes emotional honesty difficult.

Whether or not you were allowed to express emotions in your family of origin—adoptive or not—it is essential to feel safe about expressing them in adult relationships. How often I have heard wives say, "He (husband) never lets me know how he is feeling," yet when the husband expresses a feeling in a therapy session, she may retort, "Well, you have no reason to feel that way!" Feelings are what they are. There is no *ought* or *ought not* about them. Many men get discouraged about expressing their feelings when they are immediately shot down. Women can't have it both ways. Sometimes wives have a tendency to elevate their own feelings above their husband's, while giving lip service to wanting to know what their husbands are feeling. We all have to learn to have more compassion for one another's feelings.

Whatever the case, having emotional safety means that you feel safe about expressing your feelings in the partnership. Remember, it is in a committed relationship that emotional honesty and integrity can best be learned. Our mates have insight into our blind spots that we may not have ourselves. They can scope out blind spots by reading facial expressions and body language. If a man has a contemptuous look on his face as he hands his wife a bouquet of flowers, her reaction is going to be quite different from what he might have anticipated. Although on the surface he is conducting an act of love, he may not be feeling love while he is doing it. He may not even be aware of this. His wife needs to help him find the source of his contemptuous feeling, otherwise he will go on conveying a different feeling from the one he intended with most of his communication mechanisms.

The wife, on the other hand, has to be careful that she is not projecting her own feelings onto her husband. Perhaps her father used to bring flowers to her mother after a particularly ugly fight. He seemed to be apologizing, but even as a little girl she could tell that her father was not sincere. He was only trying to get his wife to be nice to him. Therefore, the offering of flowers may have negative connotations for her, thus making her "read" her husband wrong. This is the reason that both partners have to stir up the sediment at the bottom of the pond of their early experiences in order to help one another with emotional integrity.

*Managing Our Emotions*

In Chapter 8, I reminded you that the "let it all hang out" motto of the 70s was not healthy. Rather than promoting an honest expression of emotions, it was an era of self-indulgence and license to avoid taking responsibility for one's effect on others. Because most adoptive mothers (me included) did not know how the disappearance of the birth mother affected their babies, we did not do a very good job of being attuned to our children's emotional states or in helping them to regulate those states. That's why a truly committed partner is so essential for adoptees. And it is reciprocal. Remember what was said about almost everyone having some kind of early trauma. You can help each other. However, you can't do it alone. These are relationship issues and can only be healed in relationship, either with a therapist or in a current relationship with willing parents, partners, or friends.

One of the most difficult emotions for adoptees to manage is anger. Even adoptees who appear to be placid are harboring a great deal of anger. Some of this anger is a true feeling, but some of it is hiding sorrow, sadness, hurt. It is much easier to "cop" to anger than to fall into the abyss of sorrow. Adoptive parents of teenagers are acutely aware of this. Many of their children are set off by every little thing. Living with them is like living in a mine field—explosions all over the place! Seldom do they see the tremendous pain that is being hidden by the barrage of angry outbursts.

But it isn't only adolescents who express anger. Many adult adoptees do as well. Anger is one of the main reasons that so many relationships break up. Couples end up traumatizing one another and their children. Make no mistake—children are traumatized by out-of-control parents. Parents are supposed to keep children safe, but how can they do so if they seem so unsafe themselves? Anger must be kept under control. Just because someone is expressing anger doesn't mean they are either feeling it or acknowledging it. Often, at the same time they are acting out angrily, they are projecting it onto the other person.

There are two ways of acting out anger: active aggression and passive aggression. When anger is acted out overtly, physical, emotional, and verbal abuse are often exhibited. Objects are thrown, threats are made and sometimes carried out, physical violence, such as hitting or shoving, is perpetrated. These acts are easily identified. Passive-aggressive behavior, on the other hand, is more difficult to pinpoint. This is because it is often what a person *doesn't do* that is the aggression. Not being on time, never saying you're sorry, acting like a victim, being sarcastic, teasing, discounting, withdrawing, sabotaging, etc. are examples of passive-aggressive behaviors.

Anger is sometimes justified. If one's rights have been violated, anger is appropriate. The question is, how much anger? And how is it to be expressed? It is always a good idea to ask oneself: *"Is my feeling appropriate to the situation or is it out of proportion?"* Remember the 80/20 rule. It is important to respond to the situation, not just the feeling. If a partner's passive-aggressive anger is demonstrated by his always being late for a date, instead of flying off the handle, the appropriate response might be, "You know, John, it makes me angry when you are always late. It also hurts that you think so little of me that you always keep me waiting." If his being late is habitual, it is also a good idea to follow up with a consequence for his behavior: "The next time I have to wait more than 10 minutes for you, I will leave." *Then do it.* People have a difficult time learning lessons if there are no consequences for their bad habits and behaviors. Remember what I have said about how adoptees have less than average understanding of both their effect on others and cause and effect. They need to be taught. If they weren't taught by their parents, then they have to be taught by their partners.

Anger is one of the easiest emotions to be displaced. Notice how people act on the freeways. Road rage is an excellent example of this phenomenon. Does anyone believe that the person so "het up" over some unfortunate maneuver on the freeway is really that angry at the other driver? Does the angry driver really believe that the other person did that *to him?* Of course not! Everyone knows that this kind of anger is both distorted and displaced. Sometimes (perhaps most of the time) the angry person doesn't even know at whom he really *is* angry. If this happens to you, it is time for an anger management class. Sooner or later allowing this kind of anger to take over will get you into trouble.

When this kind of displaced anger gets out of hand in a family, it can have grave consequences. It often leads to abusive behavior. Most of the time, abusive behavior is assigned to men. But verbal abuse is often perpetrated by women as well. It is my belief that too many therapists ignore this. I have witnessed women berating their husbands in verbally abusive language such as shaming, emasculating, sarcasm, psychoanalyzing, bossing, belittling, nagging, blaming, and so forth. Women are usually more verbally articulate than men, and men often retaliate by being physically abusive. Then the verbally abusive provocation is sometimes overlooked. This is not to say that a physically abusive response is all right if verbal abuse provoked it. *It definitely is not.* I do believe, however, that we cannot overlook the harm that verbal abuse causes for both men and women. All forms of abuse need to be addressed. *If emotional integrity is to be maintained, no abuse is ever justified.*

### Reining in the "Child"

Most acting out is immature behavior. Children aren't able to express their feelings in words, so they communicate them by acting out. However, anyone over twenty (the age when most people's brains have reached their full capacity to curb impulses) who acts out instead of speaking about his feelings is allowing the child to be in charge. Upon meeting someone, the potential partner's childlike behavior can be endearing. However, it soon becomes enslaving. It hinders a mature, loving, caring relationship. It can in fact sound the death knell for a relationship. Remember the letter from the woman overseas about her adoptee partner whom she was leaving after two years? Let me repeat it, because it is the epitome of so many letters I have received on the subject:

> I have tried so hard in this relationship—I have tried to understand and to love him. I have tried to make him feel secure and I have tried to accept him. But … he has made it impossible to love him and impossible to receive love in his life. I have felt that I have been living with a child, and I hate to say it, but a monstrous child at times. The violent, uncontrollable outbursts, and the 'tests' he has set for me have been a normal part of our life for two years. I am exhausted with the battle, and now understand how he can comfortably continue to participate in it. From three months after we first met, he has been working towards the day when I will leave. And it has come.

This is the *repetition compulsion* at its best! Yet how sad that a person who loved her partner so much and tried so hard finally had to give up. But even the most dedicated people finally reach their limits of endurance. I am sure her partner could then feel justified in his assertion that he is unlovable. And even if he were to acknowledge that his behavior had a great deal to do with the outcome, would he bother to change it? Or would he just go on proving over and over again that his baby beliefs about himself are correct? He was allowing the child to be in charge of their relationship. Her attempts to draw out the loving adult she saw in him were to no avail. Has this happened to you?

Self-confirming behavior starts early in childhood. Do you remember what the adoptive mother said about the limitations her children placed on her ability to express her love for them and their ability to give love? *"They have both limited my expressions of affection and their own."* I want all you adoptees to *really* think about this. How many of you have felt as if your adoptive mothers were unaffectionate? If you are honest, do you think they just gave up after awhile? Of course as children you were not expected to understand your own defenses. There is no blame involved here. But as adults, it is imperative that, as daunting as it seems, you put an end to defensive maneuvers and begin to let love in, with your parents and with your partners. Please remember that being in a relationship is about being partners—on the same team—not adversaries, sparring with one another.

## A Crucial Element

I have spent so much time on emotional integrity because I believe it to be one of the most crucial elements of a good relationship. At the same time, it is one of the most difficult to attain, especially when one has suffered a paralyzing childhood trauma. Nevertheless, it is essential to strive toward, and, with both partners cooperating, it is attainable. However, there has to be a willingness to give up being the child. There has to be a willingness to stop being a victim and to become accountable for one's behavior. I will end by quoting Taylor and McGee again: "Emotional integrity is about loving, honoring, respecting, encouraging, and validating the full spectrum of our healthy feelings—and those of our beloved other." What more is there to say?

## Priority

One of the most discouraging aspects of couples counseling is the low priority many couples give to their relationship. Too often couples put everything else first: work, the kids, hobbies, T.V., the Internet, etc. There have been times while doing couples therapy, when I have assigned a 20–30-minute exercise for the couple to do during the week between sessions, that they have come in the next week saying they didn't have time to do it (or they did it on the way to the session!). It became obvious to me that the health of their relationship was way down on their priority list. How many of you take time to really talk to one another without allowing any interference? Is work more important? Are the kids too demanding? Is the Internet more interesting? Are you sure that both of you are okay with this? How about your kids? Won't they feel more secure if you place your relationship with each other a little higher on your priority list? Is interacting with a machine really more fun than interacting with a human being … especially one who loves you? If it is, perhaps it is time to get some help! If you enjoy the comfort of having someone around without having to interact with that someone, you are not assuming your responsibilities of being in a mature, reciprocal relationship. Think about it…

### Compassionate Listening

One of the exercises that I recommend and sometimes have had ignored by partners who were not yet ready to make their relationship a priority is one which teaches compassionate or empathic listening. It is an exercise I first learned about from a book called *Intimate Partners* by Maggie Scarf (1987). I thought it was an excellent exercise because it combined two important elements of a relationship in a kind of paradoxical fashion: It fostered a sense of the *individual as a separate person*, at the same time *encouraging connection* in the form of empathy and compassion. The exercise was simple: Go to a secluded place or make sure that the kids are asleep or away and turn off all phones, pagers, computers, and TVs. Set a timer for 10 (or later 15 or 20) minutes. (Get one that doesn't tick!) One person chooses a subject to talk about having only to do with him or herself. It is not to be about the other person or about the couple. Perhaps it could be about something that happened in sixth grade that you are still upset about, or perhaps it is about the dream you had of becoming a rock star.

Just to get you started, here are some subjects that could be enlightening as far as having a new understanding of your partner is concerned: 1. my basic philosophy of life, 2. my major aspirations and hopes, 3. my most fearful life experience, 4. my present spiritual beliefs, 5. current stressors in my life, 6. my secret ambition and why I haven't attained it yet, 7. worries I have about my parents, 8. my most shameful or embarrassing moment, 9. my worst childhood experience, 10. my most memorable holiday as a child. There are myriad topics you could talk about. Your level of trust will help determine which ones you choose. The more you trust your partner with your emotional life, the more intimate and revealing you will be. As you look at some of the topics I have listed, you can understand why trust is so important. It is hoped that doing this exercise on a regular basis will help build trust between you so that emotional intimacy can deepen. Whatever the person speaking decides to reveal, the other person is to listen *without judging or interrupting,* instead conveying an atmosphere of empathy and compassion. It is important to listen, not just to the story content, but to the feelings being conveyed in the telling of the story. When the timer goes off, the person talking finishes his or her sentence and stops (no cheating!). Then you switch roles. When you have finished the exercise, you are not to discuss what was said. You are simply to speak from the heart and listen with compassion, without judgment, and without further discussion.

What is the point of this exercise? Telling your partner something about yourself that you may never have told anyone else inspires empathy and intimacy. It makes you feel connected to one another in the emotional climate of the telling and listening. *You are talking from your heart and listening with your heart.* At the same time, it is making clear that you are separate people with separate histories and dreams. It gives you a better picture of your partner, communicating something unique about him or her, something which may never have been revealed before or perhaps even thought about for years.

Some people find it difficult to talk for 10 minutes or so without any feedback. Others find it difficult to listen without interrupting. Both can learn to do so. As it becomes easier, it is all right to extend the time to 15 or 20 minutes each, if both partners agree to this. The important thing is that both partners have equal time and equal attentiveness. This exercise can be helpful in other areas because it teaches one to be present, to pay attention, to be totally available to the other person. It teaches one to respect the other's choices, since the subject will be important to the speaker. Honoring the importance of whatever the partner wants to talk about and having compassion for the emotions it evokes inspires intimacy and empathy.

Scarf's exercise is an excellent one, and I would recommend that partners do it at least twice a month. (At other times, they should go on a date by themselves and just have fun ... no serious discussions.) Taylor & McGee recommend a similar exercise, except they don't exclude talking about one another or the couple. Their only caveat is that the couple cannot discuss any topic about which the speaker is angry at the listener. They claim that the key to deep listening is to have sessions on a regular basis with special sessions when needed. I concur. Doing this in a haphazard fashion is not useful and it negates the importance of the relationship. And while I certainly recommend having discussions about the relationship at a time when both people are feeling like adults, I believe that the usefulness of talking about oneself provides a safe place for intimate connections to take place. Intimacy doesn't mean disappearing into the other person. *Intimacy means having a deep emotional connection to the other person.*

## The Power Struggle

After the "bloom is off the rose" or the intoxication aspect of the relationship is beginning to wane, the power struggle begins. This, again, is part of all relationships whether the struggle is overt or covert. Sometimes the power struggle can consume many years of the relationship. This is too bad, because the stage that Taylor and McGee call "co-creativity," which follows the power struggle, can be the most rewarding.

The power struggle will be a part of every marriage. How long it goes on is up to the two people involved. Equality in a marriage or partnership is a relatively new idea. In our patriarchal society men have had the upper hand in almost all aspects of marriage except childrearing. This is no longer tolerable to 21st century women. Nor should it be. This does not mean that they equally divide up all the tasks, so that each does all of them some of the time. It means that they have to work out a fair distribution of tasks, making their wishes known. He might always take out the garbage and she might always do the cooking. But maybe not. It has to do with what they agree to. If she is a stay-at-home mom, she may do most of the household chores, while he is out earning the living. They have to decide together what seems fair.

### Equality in Childrearing

Equality means that both partners participate in the rearing of the children. Again, this doesn't mean the exact equal distribution of responsibilities. In the beginning of a child's life, the mother will be predominant in his care. This is as it should be, since she is the center of his life. Even when a child is older, the roles that mother and father play in his life may be different. Children need these different experiences. However, fathers may fall behind in their responsibilities as far as the care of their children is concerned. Sometimes the mother may be inadvertently playing a part in that phenomenon. It has been my experience in working with families, that sometimes, although the mother wants the father to be more involved, she also wants to control that involvement. Unless something abusive is going on, she needs to let the father have more control over his relationship with his children. Fathers cannot allow their wives' interference to be an excuse for them to be uninvolved. They have to be more assertive where the children are concerned. Whereas women sometimes back off on matters of finance, men sometimes back off when it comes to the children. A couple has to come to some understanding and agreement about their roles in the lives of their children. They have to be their children's parents, not their friends, and they have to be willing to sacrifice. Remember what I said: *Either we sacrifice for our children or we sacrifice our children.*

In an excellent article for the August 26, 2002 edition of *Newsweek* titled "In Search of a Grown-Up," Anna Quindlen, asks, "Is it the youth culture that suggested that no one really had to play the role of grown-up in the morality play that is life? Instead there is a thriving subculture of parents who act as if everything goes on as before. That's ridiculous. Having kids changes everything. Or at least it ought to." To that I say, "Amen." If this means that we have to sacrifice a promising career for awhile, then so be it. Our children deserve no less. As a nation, we have to stop believing that being a stay-at-home mom is a "less than" job. Oprah is always saying that being a mother is one of the most difficult yet important things a woman can do, and she is right. If we have kids, we can't be "good enough" mothers only if we want to. If we have a child, whether we planned on it or not, we have to begin to sacrifice for our children. This doesn't mean that as mothers we don't have a right to take care of ourselves. We *need* to take care of ourselves for ourselves, for our spouses, and for our children. We have to take the time to do things we like to do and go places we like to go, but without endangering the security of our children. This is possible.

Unfortunately, women have contributed to the myth that motherhood is less important than other occupations. Some of the early feminists contended that women were wasting their talent by "just staying home" with their kids. Nothing could be further from the truth. I have been told over and over again how important it was for me to have written *The Primal Wound*. I truly appreciate all those kudos, but I still believe that the most important thing I have done or will do is to be a "good enough" mother to my children. By the way, I have proven that one can be a stay-at-home mom and still have a satisfying outside career, or in my case two careers: teaching for 10 years, (before staying home with my kids for 20 years), and then up to the present time a combination of psychotherapy and writing (when the children were grown up). If I had stayed with teaching all during my children's childhood, not only would they have suffered and I have missed so many milestones in their lives, but, although I loved teaching, I probably would have been a raving lunatic after about 25 years. Of course the median cost of a house in the Bay Area wasn't $500,000 when I was staying at home. Couples today definitely have a more difficult time making this work, but many who could, don't. However, lately I have noticed a trend toward women wanting to stay home with their kids. Perhaps the glamour has faded from the fantasy of the corporate career. *Or better yet, perhaps we have begun to realize the importance we have in the lives of our children.*

Women are not the only ones who need to sacrifice for the children. How many men are absent fathers, not because they no longer live in the family, but because they work 60–100 hours a week or take too many business trips? They may say, "Well, in order to move up in the organization, it is necessary to work many hours overtime." That may be true, but is moving up what is best for your family? What are your priorities? Are you *living to work* or *working to live*? Does living include spending time with your family? Think about your priorities and the effect they have on the rest of the family. People should not have children (either by birth or adoption) unless they are willing to sacrifice for those children and the emotional welfare of the family. (By the way, after the last child has reached age four, it would be all right for dad to be the stay-at-home parent.) These are my own personal guidelines and might not be sanctioned by anyone else. I do believe that if it is possible, someone should be at home until the kids are in college. (Adolescence sure isn't the time to be away!)

*Financial Equality*

When it comes to finances, which is one of the most fought about subjects in marriages, both people have to know what is going on. How they distribute the day-to-day handling of the money is up to them and needs to be agreed upon. However, no matter how the distribution of monetary tasks is accomplished, both members of the partnership need to know *what is going on* financially. How many widows in the past have been completely thrown by their ignorance of the family finances when their husbands died? Of course, modern-day women may not be that ignorant, but do they know about all aspects of the family finances? Do they read the tax return or just blindly sign it? They need to insist upon a complete disclosure of the family finances.

Women have to take on that responsibility, even if it seems daunting. Knowing the true financial status of the family is the business of both partners (but not necessarily the children).

## A Tangent—Money and Children

I want to say something more about that phrase in parentheses. Too many parents make it the responsibility of young children not to spend too much money. Who's in charge here? Instead of just saying "No," they often make comments about the lack of money to make their point. If parents have been diligent about not allowing children to get the idea that they can have everything they want (or something every time mom goes shopping), they don't need to make these kinds of ridiculous comments. Little children should not have to bear the burden of a couple's financial situation. Although kids are bombarded these days with commercials and advertisements for all kinds of products, it is up to parents to curb their children's buying of these products *without* resorting to threats about how much money is available. Children should not expect to have everything they want, but neither should young children be concerned about the family finances.

When it comes to adolescence, however, it becomes time to teach kids about finances. It is amazing to me how many parents just give and give money to their teenagers without there being any accounting for it. Oh yes, there is the inevitable question, "What do you need money for?" but it is usually a rhetorical question. Most teenagers, even those with jobs, are not taught how to manage money. I have heard parents say they don't want to tie chores to allowances, that chores should not be paid for but are just part of being a member of the family. However, what I see in some cases is the reverse—*kids are getting allowances, but not doing chores.* Parents, you are forewarned: Colleges and universities are being paid to allow credit card companies to recruit your children as debtors. Will your children know how to use credit judiciously? Or will they do as so many have in the past few years, which is to run up a huge credit card debt that they will have to pay off at ridiculously high interest rates, in addition to having to pay off their student loans?

Whatever the case, it takes work and consistency for parents not to give in to kids' demands beginning early in their lives. It is by far healthier than using the fact (or fiction) that they don't have enough money as an excuse. Whether you are living from hand-to-mouth or don't have to worry about money, learn to say "No" and mean it! Kids don't have to have everything they want. If they want the "in-brands," let them pay the difference between a good pair of jeans and those with the current logos. And above all, don't substitute *things* for *time.* Although kids may give the impression that they are entitled to all the things you are buying for them or that they want you to buy for them, it doesn't appease their need for attention from you.

### Large Expenditures

One aspect of finances that often leads to acrimony is when one spouse spends large amounts of money without consulting the other. (In informal partnerships—outside of marriage—this might have a different connotation.) Although there is no set amount that is right for all spouses to adhere to, it is necessary for each partnership to come to some agreement about it. Certainly large expenditures, such as cars or luxury items, need to be made upon the agreement of the couple. This is true even if only one spouse is contributing to the financial earnings of the family. After all, if a woman is staying home with the kids, it is by mutual agreement, and therefore she should not be punished for this by having no say in the distribution of moneys. She is showing a great deal of faith in her husband by putting herself out of the job market and needs to be assured that it doesn't mean she is sacrificing her right to be involved in how the money is spent.

### His and Hers

Another difference between the "old days" and today is that today many couples keep their money separate. He has his account and pays for certain things, and she has her account and pays for other things. Sometimes they also have a joint "household" account, but they like to keep their money separate for the most part. I understand a woman's fear about having to stay in an abusive marriage with no way out, which may have led to this separation of moneys. However, if the couple has a good working financial plan that they do together, separate accounts may not be necessary. In any case, it is part of what they have to decide for themselves.

### Financial Savvy and Awareness

There are many aspects to financial equality in marriages. How much should one invest in the stock market? How much should be put aside for the children's education? Should there be an automatic savings account? How much should go to the church, charities, the vacation fund, etc.? All of this should be settled through discussion, compromise, and agreement. This means that both partners have to have some *knowledge* of financial matters, *not just opinions*. If either part of the couple does not want to bother becoming knowledgeable about the stock market or other such matters, perhaps he or she could agree to leave that aspect up to the one with more knowledge. This, again, would have to be agreed upon. Even if one person makes all the decisions about the stock market, the other should know what is going on (how their stocks are doing). If he/she doesn't want to learn more about it, however, there should be no complaints about what the other partner does.

A word about adult adoptees and money. Because many adoptees have a belief that they are undeserving, they sometimes manifest this belief in never allowing themselves to have very much or even enough money. This attitude is unnecessary for themselves, and can be devastating for a spouse and family. It is important for these adoptees to become aware of how this attitude may be influencing their job choices or other matters relating to money, and to rein in their sabotaging of their own and their family's financial security. When a person takes on the responsibilities of marriage and family, it is time to "give up childish ways," or to stop giving in to the fear that is paralyzing the child within.

## Sexual Equality

The other most argued-about subject in marriages is sex. Men and women don't necessarily see sex in the same way. One of the reasons recreational sex has been more or less of a failure for women is that many women feel the lack of an emotional connection as a deficit in a sexual encounter. Some men do, too, but perhaps not as many men as women feel this way. Having talked to many women who started out having one-night-stands and other sexual experiences, I agree with those therapists who report seeing many women who now feel used by the whole "sexual revolution." Feeling used doesn't mean that they blame the men. After all, casual sex is what they thought they wanted. It's just that when all is said and done, many of them feel it was an empty experience. For them there is no such thing as "free sex." One result that I've noticed is a kind of burn-out in the sexual arena. A great deal of casual sex in the early years may mean a less satisfying sexual experience when one is ready to settle into a committed relationship. "Been there, done that," seems to be some women's attitudes. What may be missing is intimacy. There can be sex without intimacy and intimacy without sex, but a combination of sex with intimacy is very satisfying. Intimacy implies that there is a deep emotional connection between the two people making love. Couples in a committed relationship should strive for the intimacy/sexual combination.

### Sex in Relationship

When a committed relationship is achieved, there may be a disparity in how often or what kind of sex to engage in. Whereas in the beginning of their relationship a couple may have had a mutually pleasurable sexual experience, as the relationship becomes more comfortable and the intoxication period is over, the discrepancies between their sex drives or their interest in sex may become more apparent. Most therapists believe that sex is only an excuse the couple is using for deeper problems in the relationship. This may be true, but I do believe that sex can be a problem in and of itself. Not every person feels the need to express her love for the other in a sexual way. A disparity in the amount of sex one wants doesn't necessarily mean that the relationship is in trouble in other ways. There *is* such a thing as sex drive, and it isn't always compatible between two people who truly love one another. When this is true, it is time to get some help.

## The Madonna/Whore Syndrome

Although it is generally assumed that men want more sex than women, I don't find this necessarily to be true. Contrary to what I said above, not all women have engaged in casual sex, and there appear to be many women in America who seem to be starving for a normal sex life. This doesn't necessarily mean that their husbands don't want sex; it may mean that they no longer want sex with their wives. Why? There is a phenomenon that is rarely talked about that I call *the post-children-incest syndrome.* What in the world does this mean? I am referring to couples whose sex life seems to, excuse the expression, peter out after the last child is born. For some reason, at this point in the life of the couple, the husband gets confused about the role of his wife: *Is she wife or is she mother?* If he sees her more as mother, then it may mean that having sex with her feels incestuous. There isn't any spark to it. It just seems wrong. That this is entirely in his imagination is of no consequence. He is impotent in her presence or at the very least is not "turned on" by her. He is, in fact, turned off. Some people refer to this split in the male perception of his wife as the *madonna/whore syndrome.*

However it is identified, it is more of a problem than most people understand. The man no longer sees his wife as a lover, but as "mother" or "madonna," in other words *untouchable.* That his wife should not take this personally will not play very well. It feels very personal. However, it really isn't. It is not about her, it is about *the role her husband has assigned to her.* That's why I think it so important for couples with children to take time out every week to focus entirely on one another as lovers. Some couples do this by having a date night. They go out to dinner, to a movie or play, or to the symphony, ballet, or opera. Perhaps they take a picnic lunch out to the park and just enjoy one another in the sunshine. It is all right to do this without the kids. In fact it is good for the kids. Children need their parents to be in love and strong in their relationship. I know some couples who always think that they have to do everything with the children.

Rather than this being *for the kids*, it might be a way to *avoid having to interact with one another.* While I don't recommend taking long vacations without the kids, or even short ones if the kids are under age three, day-trips or an evening out once a week would be good for everyone. Join a babysitting co-op and give several couples the opportunity to spend the night in a hotel once in awhile. If all activities except for work are focused on the kids, then seeing one another as mom or dad and not lovers may be inevitable. Don't let it happen to you!

### The Ho-Hum Syndrome

Becoming too routine is another complaint that couples have about their sex life after the first year or two. *Making love* becomes a perfunctory *having sex* after awhile. There needs to be a way to get the spark back. Remember what I said about chemistry—if it is really there, it will be retrievable. Think back to the beginning of your relationship. Were you hot for one another then? Familiarity does not have to breed contempt or even boredom. Familiarity can foster such a compassionate kind of caring that love-making can go on forever. (If your sex life has gone from sizzle to fizzle, go out and get Patricia Love's book *Hot Monogamy.*)

### Accentuating the Positive

A committed relationship is a transformative experience. This means that not only is the relationship transformed, but both individuals are transformed as well. There are stages of a marriage just as there are stages in other aspects of life. Just as we have to grow from childhood into adulthood, so does our marriage. A couple needs to keep evaluating the relationship and changing what needs to be changed. What seemed to work when they were age thirty may not be working today. Circumstances may have made change necessary. Wallerstein says, "A willingness to reshape the marriage in response to new circumstances and a partner's changing needs and desires is an important key to success." It means the couple has to grow in the marriage. They have to keep focused on their partnership and not on the adversarial aspects of daily life. They have to learn when to insist upon something, when to let the little things go by, when to laugh about something, and when to be silent. And they have to learn to forgive. It has been proven that marriages are more likely to succeed if both partners idealize the other a bit and emphasize the positive aspects of their partners, rather than always harping on the negative. It helps if they can laugh about one another's foibles. One woman in Wallerstein's study laughingly insisted that the key to a happy marriage is having a bad memory; in other words, not continually bringing up old grievances every time there is an argument.

Couples have to graduate from the intoxication stage into a more intimate and mature loving relationship. If one of the partners always needs to be in the intoxication stage, perhaps sex is being used as an analgesic, a way to either dissociate or sustain a euphoric feeling. This is an immature attitude and can be the death knell for a marriage. A truly good sexual relationship evolves into something strong and wonderful. This is a person you really know and care for and who really knows and cares for you. What can be more exciting than that?!

A good sex life doesn't have to depend upon how many times a week a couple makes love. It is more dependent upon the quality of that love-making. One problem is that people find it easier to engage in sex than to talk about it. This includes husbands and wives. Not everyone is alike in what feels pleasurable. Even though a couple knows each other very well, perhaps what feels good changes. Or sometimes we get forgetful. Does he forget that foreplay is important to her? Does she forget that he is getting older and needs more help to get the engine started? Do they both forget what an extraordinary thing it is to have an enduring relationship with such a long shared history, a shared history that encompasses such an important part of their lives? No one else will ever really know about that part of their lives. If they have been doing their best to be fair and compassionate in their relationship, their sex life can continue to be good.

## Trust

Trust is essential in any committed relationship. Without trust there can be no intimacy. Because of the experience of relinquishment, trust is difficult for adoptees. Although some trust may have been retrieved with the adoptive mother, trust is almost always an issue for adoptees in relationship. How can trust be re-established?

Again, it is a matter of paying attention to what has happened since that first "betrayal." If you think back in hindsight, most of you have been able or should have been able to trust your adoptive parents even if you didn't always feel trusting. It is not that they have always understood you or have not disappointed you, but they have been available to you as your parents. Even if "being there" meant some form of tough love, they were concerned and trying to help you. Some of the disappointment has been the disparity between your personality and theirs, and not knowing one another's biology—having no genetic markers. This may have hampered your relationship, but no one was at fault. It was difficult for all of you.

Perhaps it would be helpful for you to write about this. There needs to be a focusing in on the fact that your parents were there for you. It can't be some vague idea in the back of your mind. Some of you may remember very little of your childhoods. Others of you may remember only the bad things that happened, because sometimes things felt bad when they were just different. Concentrate, remember, write down, and integrate the experiences of connection and caring between you and your parents. In reunions it will be necessary to do this as well. The natural tendency to distrust the birth mother because she disappeared before has to be slowly overcome by your taking in her attitudes and actions in the present. This doesn't mean that you get to test her over and over again. But it does mean that each person in the reunion has an obligation to hang in there while the relationship is taking shape. These experiences have to be integrated into the limbic system as well as understood by the neocortex. This takes time, patience, and consistency.

Do the same thing with other relationships. Ask yourself questions about your relations with people. Do people usually respond positively to you? Do they seem to like you? *Are you paying attention to this?* Or have you been systematically sabotaging all others' attempts to show you what a wonderful guy or gal you are? Go back in time. Remember the people in your life from childhood on. Can you remember how much others wanted to be friends with you? Were you receptive to them? Or were you (unconsciously) "limiting others' expressions of affection as well as your own" to paraphrase that adoptive mom, who was so "right on" about how many adoptees react to others' attempts at affection. If you are blaming others for not being affectionate, please be honest about how receptive you have been to affection. Make an attempt to understand that others are not being wrong about you. They really value your friendship. They really believe you to be lovable. *Take that into your consciousness, believe it, and integrate it.*

This takes practice. Don't just think about it. Make a list of the people you know who made an honest effort to befriend you. Do you think they were all nuts? No. They valued an integral part of you that you may not even have allowed yourself to get to know. If you have been persisting in that old, tired, baby belief that you are unworthy, undeserving, or unlovable, *STOP IT!* Stop making all these other people wrong about you. What if *you* are wrong about you? You need to be able to trust yourself before you can trust others. Focus on your positive attributes and stop worrying about the monster you are afraid resides within you. It you gain control over the child—you, you won't have to worry about the monster. The monster is a creation of the child and *is only activated while you are acting from the child.*

Trusting others takes an effort when trust was destroyed at such an early age. Distrust has been imprinted on the neurological system and is not easily uprooted. In fact, it can't be uprooted; it must be overlaid with new trusting experiences. But those experiences have to be seen by the adult in you. You can't point to situations where you were disappointed in someone as a reason to distrust them. Grow up! We all disappoint and we are all disappointed. No matter how hard you try, you are going to disappoint and be disappointed by your wife, your child, your father, your friend, yourself. This is inevitable. This doesn't mean that you have to throw out the baby with the bath water. It means that you have to address your disappointment, make sure that you fully understand the situation, and realize that *no one* is always going to see things your way.

Trust doesn't mean never having to say you're sorry. Trust means that you can count on the other person to have your best interests at heart. This doesn't mean they will always agree with you. (If you make a habit of sabotaging yourself, *you* may *not* have your own best interests at heart!) Having your way and upholding your best interests may not be the same thing. Trust means that the important people in your life can be counted upon to share emotionally intense experiences with you. It does *not* mean that they are presently *experiencing* the same feelings neither does it mean they're not being compassionate. I have met adoptees who believe that if the other person does not actually *feel* the same feelings they are feeling, he is just not trying hard enough. People cannot manufacture feelings at another's insistence. However, others can tolerate your feelings and try to understand the source of them. This does not mean they have to tolerate bad behavior from you. That would not be in your best interest or theirs.

Respect is a big part of trust. You must first love and respect yourself, then you can love and respect others. Being loved and respected doesn't mean that everything you do will have the approval of those who love and respect you. If you are a Democrat and your wife a Republican and you both vote accordingly, that doesn't mean that you don't love one another or respect one another's choices. You don't have to agree, but you have to allow that the other has reasons for his or her choices. *You can trust someone who doesn't always agree with you.* In fact, if someone always agrees with you, this might be a reason to distrust that person. (Are you doing this—always agreeing with the status quo to avoid controversy? Should others trust this as authentic?) There is no way that two people who have different personalities and different life experiences are always going to agree. It is impossible. Trust gets broken if in disagreeing, you discount or in other ways invalidate the other's opinions or ideas. *Remember: life is not black and white; there are few absolutes.* If you have all the answers, please let someone know, because it will be a sensational phenomenon, a worldwide first!

### Assumptions—a Relationship Buster

There are many times when trust gets broken because of misunderstandings. I think one of the most insidious causes of problems in relationships has to do with assumptions. I have mentioned this before, but it bears repeating. Communication is a tenuous thing. Over and over again couples misunderstand one another. Ideas and opinions are not formed in a vacuum. They are products of our experiences in life and the value we place on these experiences. When we speak of something, we are speaking from these experiences and values. When someone else hears us, they are hearing us from their own experiences and values. *Everyone has a separate reality.*

Why is it important to know this? Because this is one of the greatest problems in relationships. People have a tendency to make assumptions when they are not quite sure of someone's intentions, and then they react and respond based on some belief they have, rather than on the true intention of the other. This, of course, happens between parents and children because children, with their different and limited experience, perceive things differently from parents. It also happens between men and women because they, too, experience the world differently based on the brain, hormones, and social acculturation. Different cultures have different values and traditions. So there are general differences based on age, gender, and culture. But there are also huge differences based on the more specific differences in personal history and experience. It's a wonder we understand one another at all!

The lower the opinion one has of oneself or the greater insecurity, the greater the chance of misunderstanding. Assumptions are made, based not on the other but on the self. In other words, we assume something about the other based on our own opinion of ourselves. People with high self-esteem have a better chance of understanding the true intentions of others because they don't have to try to fit them into a negative context. They don't have to reflect them back to some belief they have about themselves which they then hear coming from the other person. Did you ever notice after you learn a new word you seem to see that word all over the place? Well, the same thing happens when you have a belief about yourself: You see it all over the place, including in the opinions and intentions of others. *Check this out.*

### Beliefs as a Foil to Understanding

I believe that 80% of the problems in marriages could be solved if people would check out their assumptions. This involves checking out one's own beliefs and assumptions about oneself. Beliefs play a big part in our assumptions. If you have a basic belief that you are unworthy, then you are going to interpret a great many things that happen in your life as proof that this is true. You are going to see your partner, your colleagues, your friends as treating you in an unworthy manner. If it doesn't happen spontaneously, then you can always create a situation to make it happen. It is part of the child-self and is frustrating to your partner and friends. Remember that trauma creates a bias toward negative thinking.

If you find yourself always interpreting things in a negative manner, then it is time to check out your assumptions. How do you do this? You ask. For instance you can say, "It seems as if you are angry at me. Is this true and if so what did I do to cause you to be angry?" So simple!

It is easy for me to find people's Achilles' heels just by noting how they interpret other's seemingly innocuous remarks. This doesn't mean that there are not legitimate and accurate assumptions about others' motives. Perhaps the other person is verbally abusive or narcissistic himself. But if your friends and colleagues have a different experience of a person who is causing you problems, perhaps it is time to question your own assumptions and perceptions. Your perceptions are going to reflect your experiences and the value you place on those experiences. It is important to notice patterns. Are you constantly seeing others as undervaluing you? Is it possible that it is *you* who are undervaluing yourself and projecting it onto others? *Check it out!*

It is important for adoptees to remember that a great deal of how you assume others see you is going to be based on your experience of separation and the ensuing feelings of abandonment and rejection. If you have failed thus far to allow other possibilities into your consciousness, it is time to begin allowing in your experiences of those people who have not left you. You can begin with your adoptive parents. Are they still in your life? If not, is it their choice or yours? (If you left them, it isn't necessarily fair to see them as abandoning or untrustworthy.) Are your differences based on differences in your personalities (genetics) or on someone's (or everyone's) inability to accept these differences?

What about friends? Were you really betrayed in some of those relationships on which you slammed the door, or were you just disappointed? Be honest. Allowing that not everyone has to agree with you all the time, do you really think you couldn't trust those friends ... at least some of them? If you look back on their actions and your reactions, do you still see them in the same way? Could you have misinterpreted their motives or intentions? Did you check them out or did you base your reaction on your immediate emotional response to something the other person said or did? Remember that little rascal the amygdala: Because it wants so much to protect you from re-experiencing your separation trauma, it constantly causes you to react to anything vaguely resembling that trauma. The key word here is *vaguely*. It is up to you to begin desensitizing yourself to these responses. Take a second to engage the adult-you before responding. *This takes constant vigilance and self-control.* Take heart in the fact that it gets easier as you continue to do it—like practicing scales on the piano.

## Self-love

Over and over in this book you have been reading that you have to love and respect yourself. Loving yourself does not mean being selfish. Quite the contrary. Loving yourself is the key to being able to love others. Although narcissists seem to think only about themselves, they don't love themselves. Quite the opposite. Having been traumatized during the narcissistic stage of their development, they can act very selfishly because they see everything as being about them. If you claim to love others, but don't love yourself, you are fooling yourself because this is impossible. If you don't love yourself, all your demonstrations of love for others may really be an attempt *to get them to love you*. This may seem harsh, but look honestly at your feelings for others and your way of acting with them. Are you coming from fear, fear that they won't like you? Or are you genuinely engaged in the other person without any thought as to how she feels about you?

Without self-love you become co-dependent and self-destructive. You can't really trust your intuition or feelings. You won't be able to be assertive without being aggressive. You won't be able to be the person you want to be. Is all this worth keeping up the fallacy of "the defective baby," unworthy of love, unworthy of respect, unworthy of intimacy?

Always needing to have validation from external sources puts you at the mercy of others who may also be wounded. Adoptees have a handicap in the love arena. Because it was difficult for many of you to let in the love of the adoptive mother, you may still be seeking the validation that infants and young children need. Children need to feel cherished. In some cases the mother may have been incapable of instilling that love and validation, but in many cases you may have been incapable of allowing it in. At this point, it is useless to speculate which is true or if both are true. Remember that blame impedes healing. What matters is that you begin changing your attitude about yourself. Begin by validating yourself whenever you can. Let yourself know that you are a good person. Do not—I repeat—do not sabotage this!!

## Assessment

Make a list of your attributes. If you can't think of any!! ask your friends to list three reasons that they like you. But, honestly, most of you can think of ten things you like about yourself. Right? Remember that although as an adult it is important to assume adult responsibilities and perhaps to attain some kind of approval at work, it is not those responsibilities which really tell you who you are or why you are deserving of love. It is not the fact that you are a professor of physics. It is because you are a loyal friend. It is not because you can run the Bay-to-Breakers, but because you are kind, or respectful, or compassionate. It is not because you can impress people by bungee jumping, but because you are truly courageous if the need arises. Not only do you have to withdraw projections from your closest friends, relatives, and partners, you have to withdraw them from yourself ... the projections based on archaic, baby beliefs. Then you have to replace these projections with the *truth about yourself*. *Never* ask yourself, "Why would anyone like me?" but rather, "Why *wouldn't* anyone like me?" It's a much better question!

As your relationship with your partner progresses, continue your talks about your childhoods and the ways in which they are influencing your relationship with one another. You can then begin to withdraw your projections or transferences and stop taking out your grievances on each other. You can't really attain self-love without doing this. As long as you keep projecting the things you don't love about yourself or the perceptions you have about your family of origin, you will not be able to attain intimacy with anyone. Although many adoptees have heightened sensitivity to others, their intuition is often distorted by their separation trauma and the effect it has had on their own sense of themselves. Remember—what we don't love about ourselves, we project onto others. Could it be that neither you nor the other person deserves these projections??

*Wise Words*

Whether you are Christian or some other religion, I think you can begin to appreciate why Christ said, "Love your neighbor as you love yourself," and not "Love your neighbor *more* than you love yourself." He set the stage for us to have to attain self-love before we can really do what he is asking—love others unselfishly. Self-love also means that you have to see yourself as a separate person—connected to others, but not part of others. Remember what Kahlil Gibran says in *The Prophet*: "... let there be spaces in your togetherness/And let the winds of the heavens dance between you." You are unique; rejoice in that!

*Unconditional Love*

One word about unconditional love. Unconditional love does not mean unconditional approval. Although I talk about this in Chapter 12, it bears repeating. Your partner can love you unconditionally, yet not approve of everything you do. In fact, just as with parents, loving you unconditionally may mean disapproving of many things you do if you are being self-destructive or out to sabotage the relationship. Love can endure difficult behavior, but in adult relationships there has to be an effort on the part of the one being difficult to correct this behavior. Although some relationships begin as "rescue missions," that scenario gets old after awhile. If you are being the rescuer or being rescued, it is time to look at the relationship and begin making it more reciprocal. You can unconditionally love one another while this is happening, but you have to be prepared to confront one another over behavior that is the antithesis of a mature, intimate relationship. The insights and exercises in Taylor and McGee's book *The New Couple* will help you.

Self-love isn't selfish. Self-love is generous because it prepares you for being a truly loving, intimate, generous, compassionate partner in your relationship. Without self-love this isn't possible. It is time to get started!

## Healing Sibling Relationships

Sometimes adoptees have good relationships with their siblings and sometimes they don't seem to care if they ever see their brothers and sisters again. There are many reasons for these differences. Adulthood is a good time to reassess these relationships as well as those with the adoptive and birth parents. Whether the sibs are adoptive or biological, if there is healing that needs to take place, there is no time like the present.

### Adopted/Adopted Sibs

If you were reared with another adopted child, the two of you may have as little or less in common than you do with your adoptive parents. Although you had to relate somewhat while growing up, you may have never felt close. As adults, it just doesn't seem worth it to stay in touch. You have nothing to say to one another. But wait! Didn't you both grow up in the same household? Didn't you both experience being adopted by the same parents? Don't you have a childhood history together? Even if you perceived everything differently, you still experienced many of the same things. For instance, you both experienced the devastation of being separated from your first mothers and growing up without being genetically mirrored. You have both suffered as a result. Is the difference in your way of suffering what is causing you to abstain from a relationship now?

I have seen the compliant adoptee become very intolerant of the defiant adoptee and build up a great deal of self-righteous resentment and animosity toward that sibling. Disrespectful behavior toward the parents demonstrated by the acting-out sibling may have led to a real rift in the sibling relationship. While this may be understandable, especially in light of the need for the compliant child to keep the parents seeing him as loyal, it may be unfair. Remember that one of you had to be the defiant adoptee. It has nothing to do with personality or character and could have been you. Perhaps a bit of compassion for all the pain that your sib was in and may still be acting out wouldn't hurt. Read *The Primal Wound* again and realize that your sibling is in pain, not just trying to be difficult. Perhaps a reconciliation is in order and perhaps not. But it is important to explore the possibility.

On the other hand, if you are the acting-out adoptee, are you feeling resentful towards your sib who didn't act out? Do you think she has never known your kind of pain? Are you jealous of the relationship she had with your parents? Do you think she has had a better life? Think again! Both of you couldn't be the compliant one. Perhaps that role was already taken when you came along or perhaps your baby belief was that you could cope better with the pain of separation by being defiant, rather than compliant. For whatever reason, the role each of you assumed was out of your conscious control. Don't blame your sib for the fact that she "acted in" rather than acting out. She has had just as much pain as you, she has just expressed it differently—mostly by keeping it internalized. Perhaps you can learn to love yourself more and learn to love her, too. You have both experienced one of the most difficult traumas a person can suffer. If you could talk about it, it might help both of you to heal.

*The Adopted/Bio Combination*

The combination of a biological sibling or siblings and an adopted child can be difficult. Again, there may be very little in common so far as physical features, personality traits, or talents are concerned. There may be very little understanding of what makes the other tick. If the adopted child acts out, there will probably be some anger toward him from the bio sibs. If he is compliant, there may be jealousy. It is time to put away childish things, as the saying goes. All of you need to assess your relationship in the light of your adult wisdom and understanding. I believe we all have to forgive our own behavior when we were children as well as that of our sibs, no matter what we did. (There may be some forms of abuse toward the adoptee or from the adoptee to another sib that may be difficult to forgive. Sexual abuse is one of those. Repetitive physical abuse is another. Each case has to be evaluated individually as to the ability of the adoptee or other sib to forgive what took place. One clue may be if the abusing child acknowledges what he/she did and asks for forgiveness.) For the most part, children's behaviors are a form of communication about some feeling they are having for which they don't have words. Sometimes they can't even experience it as a feeling. They just know that something is wrong and need someone to "get it." As parents, often we don't. As sibs we just react. (Read about *projective identification* in Chapter 17.) The thing to remember is that *we are no longer kids.*

When a reunion takes place, sometimes the bio sibs or adopted sibs are afraid that the adoptee's biological siblings are going to take their place in her heart. They are not sure how much loyalty the adoptee feels toward the family, especially if the adoptee acted out. I have seen adoptees feel very drawn toward one of their bio sibs because of the similarities they find between them. It is quite "heady" to experience that genetic understanding when it has been absent your whole life. If the relationship with the sibs in the adoptive family was solid, after the reunion honeymoon period begins to wane, the relationship with the sibs in the adoptive family will get back to normal. There can be a good combination of bio and adoptive sibs in an extended family situation.

If the relationship between the adoptee and his sibs was difficult, calling everyone together for healing sessions might be in order. It might be necessary to do this with a mediator or counselor. However it is done, it is important to do for everyone's sanity. When there is alienation between one family member and another, it makes it difficult for everyone. There are very few transgressions that we perpetrate as children that can't be healed in some way when we become adults. If the transgressions took place during adulthood, everyone needs to be sure that he has the real scoop and isn't acting on assumptions. Remember that unsubstantiated assumptions is one of the great destroyers of relationships.

## Being Grown Up

I guess the key here is for everyone to act like grown-ups. Since almost everyone reading this book *is* a grown-up, this is only appropriate. It is the key to a great deal of what I have been trying to say in this book. We can't let the little kids in any of us run the show. This can be disastrous for everyone, including ourselves. However, it is also important to realize that everyone will have childlike feelings about different situations from time to time. That's okay as long as it is acknowledged that those feelings may have little to do with the present situation, but rather are vestiges from childhood. Then you can empathize with the inner child who is feeling afraid or threatened in some way, but *respond from the adult self.* Do not, I repeat, *do not* allow the child to be the one to respond! You would only be making a fool of yourself—not to mention compromising your health. Resentment and bitterness are debilitating burdens that none of you wants or needs to carry. And don't let anyone else in the family talk you into holding on to the burden of resentment. Loyalty should never be based on having to act disrespectfully toward someone else. Never!

What I am saying here is relationships that may have gotten off track during childhood or even during early adulthood may need some shaping up. Watch the movie "Secrets and Lies" again. (It's on video now.) What did making assumptions do to that family? How could it have been different if everyone had been honest with everyone else? Wouldn't it have been better if those sisters-in-law had confided their pain to one another and been able to be supportive with one another rather than feeling resentful and jealous toward one another? What a waste of time! What a waste of energy. So many family feuds are based on just that sort of misunderstanding. It isn't worth it. Shape up! Grow up! Talk to one another! And don't any of you take unfair advantage of the other's vulnerability! Instead, use your reciprocal vulnerabilities to bring you emotionally closer. This is what makes families fall in love. It beats anger, resentment, and bitterness every time!

*The Recalcitrant Sibling*

"But," you may say, "what if my sibling won't talk to me? What if no matter what I do, she doesn't want to have anything to do with me? What am I supposed to do then?" It has to be acknowledged that there are siblings, as well as birth and adoptive parents (and adoptees themselves), who are very difficult to reach. They are in an entrenched position and won't move. What can you do?

I have suggested writing a letter, rather than sending an e-mail or phoning. Definitely don't phone! A well-thought-out letter can be a good way to broach the subject of healing old wounds. You can be sure of what you are saying. Or can you? It is very difficult for the person writing the letter to write it without inserting blame somewhere. Somewhere deep in the message is a well-disguised, but nevertheless recognizable, angry statement about some attitude the other has. And believe me, the person to whom the letter is addressed will recognize that blaming statement right off the bat and probably won't remember anything else about the letter.

The key, then, is to write a welcoming letter without any trace of blame or resentment. Try it. Because there is anger and resentment on both sides, you will find it very difficult to do. Just as it is difficult for a birth mother or father to ask forgiveness for the relinquishment without adding "... but, ..." it takes a very secure and mature person to write to a sibling from whom she has been alienated for some time without including pieces of that anger and resentment somewhere in the letter. I have helped guide the writing of these letters for years, and I have *never* had a completely open and compelling letter cross my eyes. There has always been some modicum of anger there—something said that will be easily recognized by the recipient as "her real feelings." Can you do it? Can you write a truly welcoming letter without adding any resentful statements, no matter how well disguised they may appear? When I ask this, I realize that you may not be able to answer because many of you are completely unaware that you are making such statements. Most of the people whose letters I have proofread were unaware that they were sending any blaming messages in those letters. That's why it is important to have someone else, someone not emotionally involved, read the letter before it is sent, and then to follow his advice to the letter.

I say this, because even when it is pointed out that the statement might be construed as blaming and not very well received, the writer frequently doesn't want to change it. At least not *too* much. After all, isn't that the way she feels? Doesn't she have a right to her feelings? Yes, she does. But the idea is to keep the *goal* in mind. What is it you are trying to achieve? Are you trying to create the climate for a dialogue with your sib so you can heal old wounds, or are you just using the letter as an excuse to express old feelings no matter how unconsciously? You have to get an agreement to talk about healing before you can begin to have a dialogue. Don't sabotage it before you get to the mediation table!

If the first letter doesn't bring about the desired response, send another. Forget about pride. Forget about who did what to whom. Keep the goal in mind— getting together to talk about how you have each hurt the other. This includes reconciling and vowing to speak honestly, checking out assumptions in order to avoid misunderstandings in the future, and asking for and granting forgiveness. This means that you may have to let your sib know how much she means to you without knowing what you mean to her. It means making yourself vulnerable. This would be taking the high road. Even if she doesn't respond the way you want, remember that you were the one who reached out—who acted maturely. You can be proud of that!

## The Meeting

What if she finally agrees to meet? What then? How do you get started after so much time and so many hard feelings? First of all, it is important to agree to a set of guidelines for the meeting. This may include coming from "I statements," rather than blaming statements. It may mean allowing each of you to have your say without interruption, then allowing for the other to respond, also without interruption. It certainly should include the understanding that both of you were children (if this is true) when the hurtful behaviors took place, and neither of you understood the implications of your actions or words.

Neither of you should act defensively, even if you feel this way. This doesn't mean that you have to agree with the other's perception of what took place. But instead of saying, "You're nuts! That's not the way it was," you might try saying, "I would never have believed that you perceived it that way, Sally. No wonder you were hurt! May I tell you what was really going on for me?" As couples therapists are prone to ask, "Do you want to be loved or do you want to be right?" The goal here is to achieve a reconciliation, not to prove that you are the only one who clearly remembers your childhood. Neither of you has that kind of memory!

Always keep in mind that you are both adults now and you have to keep acting like adults. This is difficult where family members are concerned. Remember about *attractor states,* where everyone goes back to earlier roles in the family when they all get together. This can certainly happen if you and a sib get together. It takes diligence for you both to keep from being big sister/little sister or little sister/big brother, or whatever the combination is. As adults you are both equal and have to respect and respond to that equality.

If you keep these guidelines in mind, a reconciliation meeting can be a healing experience. If you use it to continue the disagreements, it will be useless. It is up to you.

## Relationships With Birth Parents

I have spoken about relationships between adoptees and birth parents in the chapter on Reunions, but some things are so difficult to integrate that they bear repeating.

### An Unnatural Process

The very nature of the process of relinquishment and adoption, often beginning with a birth that hasn't been completed because the mother wasn't allowed to hold and welcome her baby, is an unnatural process. A human baby is no more primed to be separated from his mother than any other mammal. No matter what the circumstances of the separation (which are based on sociology and culture, not biology) it feels wrong, wrong, wrong to both the baby and mother. Neither completely recovers from this abomination of nature.

This is brought home when an adoptee and birth mother meet, often for the first time postnatally. Although much of the experience feels right, the whole idea of having to get to know the person who gave birth to you or the person to whom you gave birth seems somewhat ludicrous. It is unnatural, happy, sad, connecting, confusing, full of distrust, full of hope, and anxiety-provoking. In other words, the feelings are intense and all over the place. Everyone is tiptoeing around in a mine field.

I won't repeat what I've said in the Reunion chapter, but I do want to emphasize that adoptees need both their adoptive parents who have shared their early personal history and their birth parents who share their biology. (The exceptions of truly abusive parents on either side of the fence does not exempt adoptees from this need, but it may prevent their achieving it.) Something is missing from their lives if either set of parents fails to be available to them.

### Tolerance Is Needed

In my experience, birth parents have less tolerance for the acting out adoptee than the adoptive parents have. Perhaps this is because they believe they are dealing with adults, rather than with children. However, when an adoptee is reunited with a birth parent, most of the time they will regress. Even those adoptees who plead with their birth parents not to treat them like long lost babies regress. This is evident in the testing behaviors, the distancing, the need to be in control, and the sometimes ridiculous requests that some adoptees present to their birth parents.

Two of the most difficult behaviors for birth parents to tolerate are the "abandoning the birth mother" scenario and the angry, disrespectful attitude and behaviors perpetrated upon her. Birth fathers are sometimes subjected to these behaviors, but it is usually the mother at whom the adoptee is most angry. Over and over again, I am asked by birth mothers, "How long am I expected to put up with this?" And over and over I say, "You cannot abandon him/her again."

### Divided Responsibility

However, since by reading this book you adoptees are a captive audience, I can say to you, "CUT IT OUT!" If you persist in either being disrespectful to or distancing from your birth mother, you are acting from your child-self. Don't allow yourself to do this for more than six months to a year. When I hear from birth mothers about this, they seldom have a clue as to the reason for the silence. They may or may not get a letter or e-mail saying that their child wants to break off contact. No reason. No explanation. Is this fair? No, but *it is what the adoptee once experienced.* Yet it isn't helpful to the adoptee either. It just prolongs the separation which is already too long. If there is a current and good reason for the distancing, then say what it is. Remember what I said earlier in this chapter about assumptions! Because both the adoptee and the birth mother are wounded, each is prone to making assumptions about the other. Either one who handles the situation by being secretive is playing games. This has to stop.

Somebody begin the dialogue. Use letters or e-mail, but not the telephone. Instead of just unloading upon one another, try to get to know the experience and feelings *of the other.* Try to get out from under your own need to be in control and open up a little bit. Adoptees, stop using anger to cover up how hurt you are that your mother didn't (couldn't) keep you. Although knowing you were hurt will break her heart, she will be better able to respond to this more honest feeling. Those of you adoptees who have birth mothers who have not recovered from their own abandonment or neglect in their families of origin will have a more difficult time of this. Your mothers will have a harder time being the mother and not the child. At some point (at the most after a year) you *both* have to grow up and act like adults.

*Birth Parents' Responsibilities Are Never Absolved*

Because the adoptee was relinquished many years ago some birth parents cannot believe they are still needed. After all, didn't the social workers tell them that their role was over, to stay away, and to get on with their lives? This message scared a great many birth mothers into being paralyzed as far as searching is concerned. I can assure you birth mothers that this is not true. A legal, sociological contract does not absolve you of your genealogical or biological responsibilities, not to mention the psychological, emotional needs that only you can fulfill. Most adoptees do not feel as if they fit in their adoptive families, no matter how much they are loved. They can better get that feeling of fitting if they have access to birth relatives who can mirror them. If you have never been without that mirroring, you won't appreciate how important it is. It is crucial to a sense of belonging. Adoptive parents can't give this to their children. Although they can make them feel wanted and connected to their adoptive relatives, they cannot make them feel that genetic connection that is so important.

## Hanging in There

*Birth parents: Do not abandon your child again!* I cannot emphasize this enough. Sometimes there is a great deal of activity at first and everything seems fine. Then at some point the birth parent backs off. This is what happens to the adoptee: She panics! She feels abandoned. She may regress in her other relationships. She will need more and more assurances that she is not alone. Yet she will feel alone when that contact is withdrawn. She may re-experience the confusion, terror, hopelessness, and helplessness that she felt at the first separation. She may become despondent and even suicidal. You, as the parent, simply must not do this. It is exceedingly cruel.

A second abandonment is sometimes instigated by a spouse or other children of the birth parent. I can sympathize with those on the periphery of the reunion process. It is tough. You feel like an outsider. You become afraid of the intensity of the emotions that are taking place between your husband/wife and the child. You demand less contact. Although your feelings are understandable, remember that you are older than the adoptee. You have the responsibility of containing your fear so that he doesn't have to feel so fearful. He may be regressed and unable to tolerate the withdrawal of his birth parent. The sense of abandonment and loss is tremendous. Please believe me when I say that it is greater than any feeling you may be having. You have to rise above your fears and allow some contact. How much can be negotiated, but *cutoff* is not an option.

If the reunion is relatively new, some contact should be maintained at least once a week. Remember that a newborn needs his or her parent to be available

24 hours a day. A newly reunited adoptee feels very similar to a newborn. Once contact is established, he cannot tolerate long silences. Please try to understand this. If you—the birth parent or spouse of the birth parent—are feeling overwhelmed by your feelings, *the adoptee is experiencing feelings that are 100 times more intense.* Please do the right thing and be the adult. You won't regret it. Your being the adult will earn you the sincere gratitude of both your spouse and his or her reunited child. No one should have to choose between a child and a spouse, yet some spouses of birth parents require just such a choice from their mates. Don't let that be you!

### A Lasting Relationship

A relationship with birth parents can be a lifelong commitment. If both parties assume a mature attitude toward reunions, they can benefit everyone including the adoptive parents. Neither the adoptee nor the birth parents should ignore the adoptive parents. After all, in most cases they have fulfilled their promise to rear this person to the best of their ability. No one is a perfect parent and adoptive parents have the additional responsibility of rearing a child who is not only genetically unconnected to them, but one who suffered a trauma before ever coming to them. They were not prepared for the impact of either. (Just as many of you birth parents are not prepared for the impact that the separation trauma is still having on *your* relationship.)

As I said in the chapter on Reunions, my idea of the ideal reunion is to include everyone in an extended family situation. While this may not always be possible, everyone concerned must be mindful of the importance of everyone else in the triad. None of you has more than a minute idea of the others' experiences. All of you have distorted memories of the past. It is time to start over in this new adventure. Without ignoring the past, use it to learn how to be in this new situation. Everyone is needed to fulfill the sense of wholeness that the adoptee has been missing—that the birth parent has been missing as well. And the adoptive parents, who may have been only too aware of the way in which their child has kept them at an emotional distance, may feel a new sense of togetherness with the adoptee and the birth parents. Most religions espouse love as one of their most important tenets. Let your spiritual life guide that love and let it extend to everyone important to the adoptee. If each of you can get out from under your childlike needs, everyone can benefit from a communal, spiritual love for one another.

### Summary

The severing of that first and most important relationship at the beginning of an adoptee's life has made all ensuing relationships more difficult for him. This is not a reason to blame the birth mother or the adoptive parents or anyone else. It was the way it was and everyone has to move on. Engaging in blame only hinders the healing process.

Adoptees have to realize how they may be sabotaging their relationships. They have to become aware of how they are affecting other people in their lives and change inappropriate behaviors. They have to learn that they are worthy of love and a connection to others. They have to be less secretive about themselves so that we can all get to know them. (Remember that the monster is in the child's imagination!) Whether the relationship is with a parent, partner, friend, or child, we no longer want to deal with the child-in-the-adoptee. We are worn out with the struggle. Besides, the mature adult is so much more interesting and appealing. I have met thousands of you over the years and I have never met one of you I didn't like. I have seen the authentic person beneath the fearful child and have rejoiced. Those of you who have managed to free yourselves from the tyranny of the child know what I mean. It means living in your own skin rather than always having to figure out how to be. It means freedom, connection, intimacy, and peace.

# CHAPTER 16

No Man Is an Island: The Spiritual Connection

---

*No man is an island, entire of itself ...*
*Any man's death diminishes me*
*Because I am involved in mankind ...*
*And therefore never send to know for whom the bell tolls;*
*It tolls for thee.*

*John Donne,* Meditation XVII, *1624*

John Donne wrote these words as part of a funeral sermon. He was telling us we are all connected and what happens to any one of us affects all of us. We ignore at our peril the universal connection among all people and the effect this has on what Carl Jung called the collective unconscious. Perhaps it is a particularly good time in history for us to remember this.

Jung once said that most of our issues can be traced back to a spiritual problem. Spirituality is certainly important in our lives. This doesn't necessarily mean connection to a church or any specific religion or denomination. It can mean any connection to something that gives meaning to life and to our part in it. It usually means having a belief in something greater than ourselves. In our culture, most people refer to this greater being as God. Whatever it means to each individual, there has been a spiritual aspect to our existence as human beings as far back as we can go in history. Many adoptees who have spoken to me about spirituality have voiced a concern about their lack of feeling connected to any spiritual life. Others have delved into a church or religious group with fervor and enthusiasm. For those who are having trouble in this aspect of their lives, what are the stumbling blocks to having a healthy spiritual life?

Spirituality is a word that is difficult to define. It is often confused with religion. What are the differences, if any, between these two words? In his book *Essential Spirituality* Roger Walsh says, "The word *religion* has many meanings; in particular it implies a concern with the sacred and supreme values of life. The term *spirituality,* on the other hand, refers to *direct experience of the sacred.* Spiritual practices are those that help us experience the sacred—that which is most central and essential to our lives—for ourselves" (Walsh, 1999). He claims that the ultimate aim of spirituality is awakening: "... to know our true Self and our relationship to the sacred." When we awaken to our spiritual natures, we discover that we are more than we thought we were, more than we imagine, more than we can imagine.

*Awakening*

What does it mean to awaken? Aren't we all awake, going in all directions, living at a fast pace? What if we are going in all directions in a trance? I am convinced that many adoptees spent their entire childhood in a trance, or, as adoptee Karyn Zilm describes it, a cloud. She talks about her experience of having to retreat to a safe distance from others in order to feel safe. This made it difficult to respond to others because it meant that there was a barrier between her and whoever was trying to communicate with her. She describes this phenomenon as it pertained to an incident in school which I think many adoptees will relate to. "For instance, when I was asked to come to the teacher's desk to receive some instruction from her, I experienced her request as an overwhelming encroachment and invasion of my personal space. I felt intruded upon. Being singled out and spoken to individually was more than I could bear." To cope with this situation, Karyn shut down, remaining physically present but being unable to receive the teacher's message. "I could not hear her words. I remained conscious that I was being spoken to yet I was not able to hear her. Because of my intense discomfort her voice was not audible to me. I was using all of my energy to repel and disassociate from the connection she was trying to make with me" (Zilm, 1999). I believe this phenomenon happens with adoptive mothers and their children as well. The fear of connection creates a barrier that makes communication impossible. Mothers think their children are being obstinate, but they are really not hearing what she is saying. The child is in a trance-like state, using all her energy to keep a safe distance.

Whenever we regress, we are in a trance-like state. In *Trances People Live*, Stephen Wolinsky says that we all experience this state at some times in our lives. Perhaps it is when a boss reprimands us and we feel like a child, or a spouse discounts something we have said. I believe adoptees live in the child-self/trance state a great deal of the time. It is time to wake up! Why is this so hard to do?

*Existential Concerns*

Part of the reason it is difficult to wake up is that trauma sets one up for dissociation or trance-like states. But also inherent in the adoption experience is the difficulty adoptees have with existential concerns. *The trauma of the separation from mother has interrupted the natural order of things.* Nothing makes sense. Innate in every infant is the knowledge that the person she needs is mother. And mother means the one who nurtured her in the womb and gave birth to her. Mother is home. Mother is the world. Nothing else matters. When she is gone, the world is shattered. Chaos reigns. One is plunged into the void.

While this may sound dramatic to some, thousands of adoptees assure me that this is exactly how they feel. They appreciate support groups where others understand about *the void*. As loving as their adoptive mother may be and as nurturing as their new environment was made for them, nothing makes up for the absence of mother. And the earlier the infant is separated from that mother, the more difficult it is. Newborns are fragile and are still a psychological extension of mother. Not only are they separated from her, but they feel severed from parts of themselves; they are no longer whole, but fragmented. And when they begin to put the pieces together, they are in another family with different personalities, traits, characteristics, propensities, etc., so they forge the emerging self as best they can in the image of this new family. Thus the false self is born.

What happens to the soul of these fragmented infants? Some adoptees describe their experience as *the death of the baby soul*. One woman described her soul as hidden in a cave under the mountain. Some just say that they died. Judith Herman says, "Long after the event, many traumatized people feel that part of themselves has died. ... Traumatized people suffer damage to the basic structures of the self. They lose their trust in themselves, in other people and in God." The overall feeling is a betrayal of the universe, of God, of the cosmos, of the infinite being. This was not supposed to happen. It is outside the realm of the natural order of life.

Not only does the baby begin to believe that he must be to blame for this thing that happened to him, but the interruption in the natural order of things has interfered with his right to his place in the world or in the universe. To make matters worse, babies who are born today are born into a world which seems to have lost its collective soul. Thomas Moore, author of *Care of the Soul*, reminds us that the ancients knew that our own souls are part of the world's soul, that we cannot separate ourselves from our nature, our culture, or the universe. Despite the appearance of an interest in religion, there is often a lack of soul in what we do, in the way we view or respond to each other, and in the way we view ourselves. In his book *Soul Making* Alan Jones, Dean of Grace Cathedral (Episcopal) in San Francisco, says, "Some people only *believe* they believe in God. There is no passion, no doubt, and no real movement in their lives" (1985). An active spiritual life involves all of those things—passion, doubt, and movement. The loss of soul within ourselves or in society can result in chaotic feelings and a variety of symptoms—obsessions, addictions, violence, and loss of meaning. In order for us to avoid being victim to our addictions and inner tyrannies, Jones says, "Soul making is a matter of choosing a certain paradigm or model. And the choice makes all the difference."

### A Paradigm for the Soul

Perhaps this is a good time to ask: What is the soul? It is not a thing, but, according to Thomas Moore, "... a quality or a dimension of experiencing life and ourselves. It has to do with depth, value, relatedness, heart, and personal substance." In our headlong rush toward independence and individualism, we have forgotten relatedness and connectedness, a sense of community, and those aspects of life which make life more meaningful and bearable. Jones says that we are in a process of forming our humanity through love, and he defines the soul as "... a metaphor for this process of transformation. We are, as it were, more or less 'human' insofar as we are in the 'school of love.' The only qualification required of pupils in the school is the willingness to wake up." Waking up is what this book is all about! Loving and being loved is the goal.

Jones says, "They teach us that love requires freedom, spontaneity, and the grace to stand back and allow another simply to be ... Here is the basic paradox of soul making: in order for me to be myself, I need to be able to be alone; in order to be myself, I need to be with others ... All questions concerning the making of a soul revolve around issues of identity (that's *me*) and unity (that's *you*)." We need to know who we are and we need one another. *We never reach the point where we are completely independent from one another.* Human beings need one another.

The first experience of connectedness, of course, is that between mother and child. As we progress from infancy through early childhood, we become more independent but there is a timing to this process and children have an innate sense of this. There is a story that a priest in France told of young children and their mothers enjoying a day in one of Paris' beautiful parks. The children were playing, some together and some alone, in the park, seemingly paying no attention to their mothers who were chatting nearby. However, if one of the mothers ventured out beyond a certain limit from her child, the child stopped what he was doing and watched her intently until she came back within the sphere he sensed as safe. Then the child went back to playing as if nothing were amiss. These children were very aware of their mothers' presence and had an intuitive sense of what was safe and what was unsafe so far as their proximity. What kind of anxiety is produced if mother is nowhere to be found? The adoptee's birth mother has gone beyond the limit of safety and has never returned. This has destroyed his faith that anyone can be counted upon to provide this safety. The adoptive mother gets the first stage of this mistrust. The child is afraid to connect with her because she may leave and leave for good. Yet connection is a key element in the search for the lost soul.

If adoptees feel that they have lost or hidden their souls, how do they get them back? We have talked about some ways in the chapter "The Search for the

Authentic Self." Another process, as has also been mentioned, is psychotherapy, where I have seen the "baby soul" re-emerge and grow and begin to blossom into the person who was meant to be and who was always there. Remember: *The seeds of the true self are within.* Eckhart Tolle speaks of "... the seed of enlightenment that each human being carries within ..." (*The Power of Now,* *1999*). The successful germination and growth of these seeds have to do with opportunity, encouragement, self-reflection, the absence of fear, and, according to Tolle, the absence of thought: "So the single most vital step on your journey toward enlightenment is this: learn to disidentify from your mind. Every time you create a gap in the stream of mind, the light of your consciousness grows stronger." He goes on to say, "Thinking and consciousness are not synonymous. Thinking is only a small aspect of consciousness. Thought cannot exist without consciousness, but consciousness does not need thought." His point is that most of the creations of the mind—the concepts, images, judgments, and words— interfere with relationship. They create a barrier to connection to other people, to nature, and to God.

When I think about this idea, I can identify with what Tolle is saying. Although not a Catholic myself, at one time during high school I was dating a Catholic boy and attended Mass and other religious observations with my boyfriend. I loved it because it was all in Latin. There was no need to pay attention to all the words. Although most people understood what the Latin words of the Mass meant, it was not the same as having to follow every word in English. There was a freedom about it and a feeling of experiencing the power of the ritual at an entirely different level than that of thought. I have never felt the same about the Mass since it has been said in English. For me, the mystery is gone. There was something numinous about the experience when it was in Latin that the burden of the English words obliterated. Some people will say, "Yes, but we can understand it better when it is in English," to which I say, "Maybe, but I *understood* it better when it was in Latin." There is understanding and there is *understanding.* Sometimes thought gets in the way of spiritual *understanding* or *knowing.*

Two other things that get in the way of our spirituality are pain and fear. Tolle says that all fear is ultimately the fear of death, the ego's fear of annihilation. Adoptees can certainly relate to that. To the infant, abandonment *means* annihilation. There is such a deeply imprinted fear embedded in the adoptee that to be free of that fear might seem like the loss of Self. According to Tolle, "There can be a great deal of unconscious ego investment in pain and suffering." Many times I have heard adoptees say, "If I rid myself of the false self and of my fear and pain, I won't know who I am." There is such an identity with the wound that it seems as if that is all there is.

It is sometimes difficult to separate psychology from spirituality. There has for too long been that mind/body split, separate boxes for the physical, psychological, emotional, spiritual, etc. When we begin to see that everything is connected, we can then begin to connect with everything and everyone. Finding soul is not the same as finding happiness. Happiness is only part of finding soul. Moore speaks of a soulful personality as "complicated, multifaceted, and shaped by both pain and pleasure, success and failure. Life lived soulfully is not without its moments of darkness and periods of foolishness." He urges us to drop the salvation fantasy in order to free us up to *the possibility of self-knowledge and self-acceptance which are the very foundations of soul.* This is much like Jon Kabat-Zinn's idea of mindfulness, which "... provides a simple but powerful route for getting ourselves unstuck, back in touch with our own wisdom and vitality." He says it is a way for us to be more in control of our lives by having more choice in the direction and quality of our own lives. This includes relationships—relationships within the family, at work, and in the greater world. It certainly means our relationship with ourselves as individuals and as a part of the greater world. In his book *Wherever You Go, There You Are,* Kabat-Zinn says, "The key to this path ... is an appreciation for the *present moment* and the cultivation of an intimate relationship with it through a continual attending to it with care and discernment." This is the opposite of taking life for granted or always regretting the past and fearing the future. Or, as Tolle says, "... the more you are able to honor and accept the Now, the more you are free of pain, of suffering—and free of the egoic mind." Living in the Now or Mindfulness is not a religion, although it has the same focus on the appreciation of the deep mystery of being alive and acknowledging being vitally connected to all that exists.

Adoptees, because mother was your whole universe, when you were separated from her, it *seemed* as if you were separated from everything—from the universe. That feeling persists for many of you, even though it is no longer—actually never was—true. The inability for traumatic events to be integrated as memories interferes with the normal process of getting on with life. The feeling of safety or basic trust is destroyed, and, as Herman reminds us, "Basic trust is the foundation of belief in the continuity of life, the order of nature, and the transcendent order of the divine." A sense of alienation and disconnection persists which pervades all relationships from, as Herman confirms, "... the most intimate familial bonds to the most abstract affiliations of community and religion." These are the feelings caused by trauma. It has nothing to do with reality, however. It is easy for each of you to see that for someone else. You can see that despite any trauma a person may have suffered, he is still part of his family, his community, and the universe. But what about you? The same it true for you. Jones says, "Soul making involves the willingness to cultivate a certain disposition towards the world and to other people; an attitude of receptivity and openness." This attitude of receptivity, connectedness, and openness needs to be a goal. I would ask you to accept this for a moment or at least act as if what I have been saying is true: *Your soul did not die, the true Self resides within you, and you are part of the collective—connected to all that exists.*

## Mindfulness and Acceptance

I am not asking you to ignore the pain of that separation and the effect it had on you, but to accept it as your reality. Tolle says, "The pain that you create now is always some form of nonacceptance, some form of unconscious resistance to what *is*." For adoptees and birth mothers that *"is"* is the fact of your separation. I often see this working against adoptees and birth mothers in reunion. Both resist accepting the fact of their separation and all that followed, which keeps them from enjoying one another in the Now. This is not to suggest that you have to resist the pain that you suffer, but as Tolle suggests, to cease giving it energy, stop thinking about it. This also means to stop fearing things that *might* happen. If you live in the Now, you won't keep anticipating that bad things are going to happen. You can enjoy the moment.

Another thing I am asking of you is not to ignore the ways in which the additional experiences in your life may have made you grow into a wiser, more compassionate, more diverse and interesting person. In order to do so, it is important to put the family situation into perspective because psychic pain can cause distortion in the way we perceive things. One of the cruelest myths of our time is that of the perfect family and perfect childhood. If our family, whether adoptive or biological, is not wonderful, we call it dysfunctional. Now, as a therapist I know that there are many dysfunctional families, but most families, although not perfect, are not dysfunctional. They are messy, chaotic, and confusing, but let's reserve the term dysfunctional for those family situations that are truly so. There are many ways in which children believe that they got a bad deal. For instance, every child believes that he deserved more attention than he got, or that he was smothered with too much attention and had no privacy, or his parents made him do too many chores, or wouldn't let him do "what all the other kids are doing," or something. This is not unusual. It is not dysfunctional. It is normal chaotic, sometimes disappointing, sometimes confusing, family life.

Adoptees will say, "Yes, but being separated from your mother and living with genetic strangers is *not* normal." And they are right. But within the context of living in an adoptive family, much of what went on was normal. While adoptees have a legitimate complaint in wanting their biological mothers, the ways in which some of them perceived their adoptive parents were distorted by that wish—some idealized, some demonized. To further confuse things, the impact of having a child who wouldn't quite connect with her had a tremendous influence on the ways in which the adoptive mother related to her child. Many adoptive mothers have told me that they didn't know themselves at times, that they seemed to be possessed by a being who seemed like a stranger, someone they had never seen before. Adoptees are quite skilled at getting other people to act out their feelings (see *projective identification,* Chapter 17). If the adoptee would like the adoptive parents to get to know who they truly are, rather than seeing them as the acting out/acting in coping behavior they displayed, I would suggest that they return the favor by trying to get to know their parents. All have in some way been strangers to one another. Jones says, "Soul making has to do with the removing of masks and with setting us free." *In order for souls to connect, we have to become real to one another.*

### Adoptees in Mythology and History

Even though the trauma of the adopted child impacted the whole fiber and dynamics of the adoptive family—making relationships either distant or difficult—it is important to consider that none of us in any family really got everything we wanted. But life is too short for us to spend the rest of our lives feeling like the victims of our families. We must, instead, look more realistically at the people and events which made up our lives and begin to relate to them in a more mature, compassionate, and spiritual way. Sometimes it even helps to consider myth as a doorway to a fresh look at things.

Those of you who are adoptees have many precedents for your experience in history and in myth. Thomas Moore relates:

Mythology from many cultures tells of the special child, abandoned by its parents, raised in the wild or by lowly foster parents. There is, in fact, an aspect of the child that is utterly exposed to fate, time, and conditions—not protected by being in a more personal context. Yet, this exposure is what allows the child to become someone new and powerful. Our own exposure to life is both a threat and an opportunity. In those moments when we feel particularly vulnerable, that child might appear as both defenseless and ready to be prepared for a special role in life.

Are you asking yourself what your special role in life is or are you bogged down by your feelings of loss, loathing, and lethargy? Elements of the divine are not strong in logic, so to ask "why?" or "why me?" serves no purpose. What has happened, happened, and the only thing to do is to live life to the fullest, no matter how painful the past has been or how unfair we feel our experience has been. As Jones says, "I don't know why it is, but there are some things that cannot be learned apart from suffering." It seems to be up to us to find meaning in our suffering.

Adoptees would do well to remember that Moses was an adoptee. If adoptees are "less-than" people, why would God entrust Moses with the Ten Commandments? Well, you may say, Moses' mother had to put him in the bulrushes to keep him from being killed. But as we know, dear adoptees, *the reason doesn't matter to the baby.* He just experienced her as missing from his life, just as you did your birth mother. Besides, your birth mother's reason was almost as compelling—to give her baby a better chance in life than she could provide for him; let a well-established couple give him a good home and life. At first Moses was responding to God from his baby mind and saying in essence, "I am not worthy to carry out your command, Father. You will have to find someone who is more worthy." But God persisted. He wanted Moses to carry out this important task of receiving the commandments and leading the Israelites out of Egypt. Why are some of you questioning God's wisdom in putting you here on this earth? Begin today by rejoicing in his wisdom, not questioning it. By continuing to believe that you don't have a right to exist on this planet, you are neglecting your need to find your purpose in this life. Don't use your relinquishment as an excuse not to begin taking care of your soul.

## Living in the Now

Tolle, Kabat-Zinn, and Moore all stress being in the present. Really being *here.* Moore says, "... care of the soul is quite different in scope from most modern notions of psychology and psychotherapy. It isn't about curing, fixing, changing, adjusting, or making healthy, and it isn't about some idea of perfection or even improvement. It doesn't look to the future for an ideal, trouble-free existence. Rather, it remains patiently in the present, close to life as it presents itself day by day, and yet at the same time mindful of religion and spirituality." Regretting the past or fearing the future allows us to avoid responsibility for the present. We need to focus on *what is,* rather than what should have been or what should be. We need to cease feeling responsible for the things over which we had no control in the past and take responsibility for those things over which we can have some control now and in the future. "To be truly free," says Jones, "we have to be accountable." We can become observers of our own lives and begin to appreciate everything which has gone into it. We can begin to live.

Jon Kabat-Zinn describes a *New Yorker* cartoon: Two Zen monks in robes and shaved heads, one young, one old, sitting side by side cross-legged on the floor. The younger one is looking somewhat quizzically at the older one, who is turned toward him and saying, "Nothing happens next. This is it." That's how you must learn to live your lives: This is it, this is your life, now live it.

*Finding the Sacred in Everyday Life*

Care of the soul is not a mysterious process about which we need to know secret or esoteric rituals or words. Care of the soul is finding meaning in everyday life. It is finding the sacred quality of everyday experiences. In some cultures there are no separate words denoting religion or religious experiences because religion is a part of everyday life. It is incorporated into every aspect of living. Sometimes we call these cultures primitive with a negative connotation. Yet what if primitive means closer to nature and our substance? What could be negative about being mindful of our connection to everything in nature so that we honor and protect it? How would the world be different if we were to see everything as part of our spiritual lives, part of the religious experience?

Life is sacred. Perhaps this is what we should aim for in our spiritual quests. Linda Sexson, in her book *Ordinarily Sacred*, puts it this way:

> Religion is not a discrete category within human experience; it is rather a quality that pervades all of experience. Accustomed as we are to distinguishing between 'the sacred' and 'the profane,' we fail to remember that such a dividing up of reality is itself a religious idea. It is often an awkward idea ... a confusion of part and whole, form and function. There are no inherently religious objects, thoughts, or events; in contemporary culture so much of our world has been 'contaminated' with the *mundane* we hardly recognize a quality of the sacred.

Again, it is the dichotomy of the dual aspects of spirituality as being either sacred or profane (inside or outside the temple) which gets us into trouble. When we divide up our natures as light and shadow, sacred and profane, we then begin to divide it into good and bad. In making a distinction between spiritual and material, we are able to pollute our earth, yet maintain that we are a spiritual people. After all, God is in His heaven, and all is right with the world. People whom we consider primitive believe that God inhabits the rocks, the soil, the plants and caves, so that everything is sacred and honored. Material things can be used, but should not be wasted, desecrated, or destroyed.

We can find the sacred within ordinary things and in ordinary tasks. It is important to find in seemingly mundane or secular experiences a sacred quality. We need to stop separating art from life, religion from culture, or the sacred from the profane. Who can stand in a redwood forest and not feel the sacredness of that place? The things which each person holds sacred have meaning within the context of his or her life. Sexson says:

The sacred quality of our lives is fabricated from the metaphors we make. We can discover or recognize the sacred within the secular, or the divine in the ordinary. We might say that our religious dilemma is not a secularizing dilemma, but a 'poetic' one. ... Religion does not reside in literal things but resides in them metaphorically. By metaphor, I mean the imaginal reality that gives depth and integrity to our lives.

She warns us that we need to distinguish between the sentimental, the monumental, and the truly religious. "Religion," she says, "is the desire for depth." Whether we call it religion or spirituality, it means looking beyond ourselves and at the same time feeling ourselves connected to what is beyond.

### Love as a Conduit and Connection to Others

No one can say what another's spiritual path should be. Each one of us has his/her own. For some it will be guided by an already established religious institution; for others it will be more personal, less structured. No matter what one's religion or spiritual path, one thing can always be applied, and that is *love*. But in order to love others, we first have to love ourselves lest we project our own shadows onto others. Adoptees who believe that they were a mistake run the risk of missing the meaning and purpose of their lives. (This belief can also be an excuse not to look for the meaning and purpose, thus to do nothing.) By seeing oneself as a mistake and therefore being unable to love oneself, one sets up a barrier to loving and truly caring about others. Remember: *If you do not love yourself, then everything you do for others isn't about loving them, but about getting them to love you.* There is no altruism without self-love. Think about it.

Jon Kabat-Zinn says, "Perhaps the most 'spiritual' thing any of us can do is simply to look through our own eyes, see with eyes of wholeness, and act with integrity and kindness." Sometimes it is that little extra step we take which gives a sacred quality to mundane acts. Daphne Kingma, writing in the Foreword to *Random Acts of Kindness*, suggests:

> ... it is when we step outside the arena of our normal circumstances, when we move beyond the familiar emotional and circumstantial boundaries of our lives that our kindnesses, too, move beyond the routine and enter the realm of the extraordinary and exquisite. ... To become the perpetrator of random acts of kindness ... means you have moved beyond the limits of your daily human condition to touch wings with the divine.

Kingma reminds us that these acts go beyond the *can, should,* or *must* of normal obligations we perform each day and set us free to give for the sake of giving. In so doing we can transform not only the world, but ourselves. We must never underestimate the impact of these acts. They can radiate like the ripples of a pebble thrown into a pond. Part of this process is *allowing others to do kindnesses for us,* which we can then pass on, rather than pay back. And we mustn't forget to perform random acts of kindness on ourselves.

## Getting Started

In order to get started upon your spiritual path or to put some new life into one that is already started, you can begin by doing several things. First look over this list to see which things you are already doing. Then decide which ones fit what you consider your spiritual or ethical life. Remember that these are only suggestions. You aren't expected to relate to all of them, and you may think of some that you want to add. This is about *your* spiritual life. I cannot know what that is. I can only make suggestions from the things that are important to me. Use this list only as a guide:

- Ascertain your own spiritual path. Take your time. Explore, experiment, and evaluate. Reach within yourself to ascertain your true beliefs, values, rules of conduct, principles, and ethics. These may change over time; just make sure they are yours.
- Discover the sacred in the ordinary. Taking a nature walk and really noticing what is around you is a good way to begin this process.
- Invent metaphors as conduits for the sacred in your life.
- Accept your history and make use of it both practically and spiritually. For some of you, this may mean looking at your life in an entirely new way. It will mean focusing on the positive in your life, rather than on the negative.
- Eliminate prejudice from your consciousness. Prejudice is a projection of one's insecurities.
- Erase all traces of arrogance associated with our culture. Not everyone has to do things our way. We can learn from other cultures, not just impose ours on others.
- Experience wholeness and interconnectedness directly, seeing that nothing is separate or extraneous. Once you begin to experience yourself as connected with everyone and everything, you will not feel alone.

- Remember that human beings are more alike than different.
- Maintain emotional integrity. (See Chapter 15.)
- Know the difference between truth and honesty. (Hint: What is your motivation?)
- Give the soul time and opportunity to reveal itself.
- Remember that contemplation of the soul includes complexities, confusion, and contradictions.
- Learn to live with paradox. It is all around you.
- Although it is best to act in the world as an adult, it is satisfying to see the world through the eyes of a child—with wonder, delight, and appreciation.
- Practice true humility. Humility is not self-negation. It is having respect and being courteous to everyone including yourself.
- Remember that true power comes from within and imposes nothing on anyone else.
- Practice acts of kindness. This means doing so without any thought of payback or benefit to yourself, yet remembering that we cannot truly help another without also helping ourselves.
- Engage in prayer or meditation every day.
- Be aware of opportunities to do good no matter how insignificant they may seem.
- Remember that even the tiniest act of kindness makes the world a better place. Think of the one flower that is blooming from a rock or the pavement: It is every bit as magnificent as the gardens of Versailles.
- Every day think of something for which you are thankful or grateful.
- Do not defile nature.
- Suspend judgment of others as well as yourself. Practice tolerance.
- Practice mindfulness or truly being in the present.
- Practice being wise, rather than right. (Being wise sometimes means admitting that you are *not* right.)
- Practice walking in the other person's moccasins.
- Practice the Golden Rule: Do unto others as you would have them do unto you.
- Have compassion, not pity, for self and others.
- If you are feeling sorry for yourself, go out and do something for someone else.

- Avoid acting like a victim. You can't control everything, but take charge of those things that you can.
- Participate in life; don't just sit on the sidelines being invisible.
- Live your life as if each moment may be your last. How do you want to be remembered?
- If you have a problem with someone, talk *to* him or her, not *about* him or her. Listen without interrupting to what he has to say.
- Learn the wisdom of forgiveness.
- Do not compromise your heart's wisdom.
- Love is the opposite of money in the bank—the more it is used, the more there is.
- Remember that everyone's number one fear is rejection and number one yearning is to be loved.
- Accept and love yourself.
- Love one another.
- Instead of searching for the meaning of life, *bring meaning into your life.*
- Keep in mind that life is a journey, not a destination. Enjoy the journey.

This is a long list. Remember that it is only a guide. You can make your own list. If you use this list, please don't try to do all these things at once! That would only give you an excuse to believe that you failed. Instead, first check off the things you believe are already happening in your life. Be honest with yourself. If there is room for improvement, then vow to improve. That might be the first order of business—tighten up those aspects of your spiritual life that need a bit of modification. Do you really treat *all* people with dignity and respect or are you selective? Did you insist that you were right in your last argument with your girlfriend, even though you knew half way through that you were not? Was that a wise thing to do? Do you keep so busy that your soul has no chance to reveal itself? Do you try to connect with people or does it give you some kind of satisfaction to believe that you can't?

Next decide upon one of the aspects that you have not been paying attention to. Make it easy on yourself. Take it slowly. Some of the things on the list are not easy to attain. It isn't a matter of just making up your mind to do them. Some of them may take some work on yourself. Others will be easy to strive for. Choose a new goal each week, each fortnight, or each month, one new thing to change or improve. Good luck!

Meanwhile you can begin to ascertain what your spiritual outlook is. Some people I've talked to have never really thought about this. They have accepted or rejected their parents' beliefs without replacing them or adding to them. Some have been living in a negative state: "This is what I don't believe in." That's not good enough. That's copping out. It leaves a vacuum. Many adoptees have filled that void in their lives with God. For others that doesn't seem to work. But please remember: *Everyone has a spiritual life*; it is up to you to define it so that you can better fulfill your own destiny. If spirituality has been a part of humankind from the beginning of recorded history, what makes you think you can escape? You can't; you can just avoid. This does not help you. It helps to know that spirituality can be a part of everyday life. It does not have to involve going to temple on Saturday or church on Sunday. Leading a truly spiritual life cannot be limited to certain days of the week or times of the day. Leading a spiritual life means *living a spiritual life* every second of every day. Will you always attain this? Probably not, but aspiring to do so begins to put meaning in our lives. It gives us purpose. What if we were put on this earth to learn to love and be loved? How are you doing with that? Jones calls love "... the wild card." He says, "Love is a kind of pain for which we are starved. ... Love, the wild card, comes to such a soul by first puncturing the hardened shell in which it has encased itself. ... Love, therefore, often comes as a terror—a threat to the self-protecting carapace under which we shelter." It is time to puncture that shell and play the wild card. Love and spirituality are intertwined in a sacred dance.

### Sacred Space

Some people find it easier to keep spirituality in their lives by having some kind of an altar or sacred place in their homes. This space can contain things that are meaningful to you. They don't have to mean anything to anyone else. I have seen some very beautiful altars which depict the spiritual values of the person or persons living in the home I was visiting. Some things I have seen on these altars are seashells, feathers, candles, figurines, crosses, pinecones, flowers, stones or crystals, certain fabrics, special sayings on scrolls, plants, bowls (some filled with water), photos of special pets or people, names of people who need special prayers, etc. The list is endless. And very personal.

Sometimes people will have a sacred place in their garden, a place where they go to meditate or pray. Even if you live in a small space, there can be room for a garden of some kind. Several pots of plants, trees, flowers, and a tiny waterfall on a balcony, deck, or even a corner of a room can become a garden. Sitting in a garden can be very healing. After all, you are surrounded by nature. The very act of planting and caring for plants is healing. It takes us back to something very basic and primal in our lives. It feeds the soul.

Spirituality cannot be separate from other aspects of your life. It must be incorporated into all other aspects of your life. Keeping mind, body, and spirit separated only confuses things. Wholeness and integration mean seeing these aspects as part of the whole and operating in life from that whole. Pay attention to your intuitive impressions as well as your rational thoughts. Live your life with love and strive for connectedness. No man is an island. We are all one.

# PART THREE

Attics and Basements

Exploring the dark, damp basement or the dusty, cobwebby attic can be frightening. There are creepy things lurking here. This is the reason that doing so with someone as a guide and witness is important—having someone with you makes it less scary. Many adoptees, having decided early on that they can "do it themselves," do not seek help. Although they believe that these rooms exist, they prefer not to explore them, even though the dampness and darkness seep through into the rooms above or below. Leaving these rooms unexplored can cause problems that at some time must be addressed if relationships are to be maintained. It is courageous, not cowardly, to ask for help in going down the stairs to the basement full of unknown monsters or up to the attic full of relics of the past. These last three chapters are written for those who might be able to help—parents, partners, and therapists.

The first of these three chapters, Hints for Birth and Adoptive Parents, can be helpful for adoptive parents rearing their children and birth parents in reunion. It can also be informative to partners of adoptees. One of the most important subsections, Projective Identification, will help explain the extreme feelings experienced by many people in relationship with adoptees. It will help keep these exaggerated feelings, which adoptees elicit, from becoming personal and overwhelming, and will provide tools for changing the typical reactions to calmer, more mature, and exemplary responses.

The second chapter sometimes addresses the therapists who work with adoptive children and families, and sometimes addresses the parents themselves. It is meant to be a guide for helping adoptees attain a sense of self, regulate the emotions which keep them feeling out of control, and become more cognizant of their effect on others. It is a plea for therapists to understand the differences between biological and adoptive families. Without understanding these differences, therapists will miss the aspects of an adoptee's pain—loss and the fear of abandonment—which have so much to do with the dynamics of the adoptive family.

This chapter is also very important for parents if they expect to keep their children from atrophying their true Selves in favor of adapting to the adoptive family's characteristics, no matter how different from their own. It is a manual for teaching compassion and empathy, and helping to regulate their children's emotional life. It requires a great deal from adoptive parents. But the more they can meet the challenges set forth in this chapter, the easier it will be for their children to flourish within the family. In adoptive families, bonds are formed through understanding, validation, and compassion, rather than gestation, genetics, and biology.

The third chapter in this part of the book is geared mainly for therapists and counselors. However, it should be read by anyone who is part of the adoption network. Adoptees are very often misdiagnosed if they are hospitalized or seek therapy. This chapter outlines the many similarities between the symptoms of separation trauma and those of people with borderline personality disorder. Relying only upon symptomatology to ascertain the diagnosis of any patient is a dangerous practice. In the case of adoptees, it has meant that many of them have had the "borderline" label pinned on them. In this chapter I explain how it is almost impossible for adoptees to be borderlines and why etiology is so important in diagnosing anyone in treatment.

In addition to traditional therapy, where the relationship with the therapist is tantamount and insight plays an important role, there are vignettes about some new therapies which can be helpful in breaking through the wall of denial and the belief systems which keep so many adoptees (and birth mothers) captive in their childlike selves. It sometimes takes a combination of different approaches to deal with such a profound and early wound as separation trauma. Talking alone will not break through the barriers that prohibit connection between people. It is important to get through the limbic system's stubborn firewall in order to facilitate these relationships. However, since relationships reflect the most difficult aspect of adoptees' issues, it is also in the relationship with the therapist that the limbic system can more readily be regulated and calmed. This is the reason that the person of the therapist and the condition of his or her limbic system are so very important.

So, go ahead and read this section, but be advised that the tone and emphases may be different from the first two sections. It is hoped that all the chapters in this book will help adoptees and those who love them, live with them, and work with them.

# CHAPTER 17
## Hints For Birth and Adoptive Parents

---

The following information will be especially helpful for adoptive parents as their children grow up in their families, and for birth parents in reunion. Because the trauma of separation happens so early in the life of the child, it is often difficult to distinguish the differences between his personality or character and the coping mechanisms caused by the trauma. It is important for parents who are trying to deal with certain behaviors to understand these differences, as well as for the adoptees themselves, as they are often puzzled by their own behavior. It is also important for birth parents in reunion to understand that the infant or child the adoptive parents took home with them was a traumatized child. Being separated from the birth mother traumatized the child, as well as the mother. Separation trauma added a dimension to the adoptive parents' child-rearing which otherwise would not have been present. Naturally, they were not given this significant information. In addition, the child and the adoptive parents were hindered by the lack of genetic markers, which in biological families aid in the interpretation of emotional needs and in the development of the child's self-esteem.

As mentioned before, adoption is still often seen by society as an altruistic act on the part of adoptive parents. This then precludes their perceiving the pain and difficulties which accompany this method of creating a family. This lack of understanding often isolates adoptive families in their difficulties. Believing separation from mother to be the ultimate loss, I tried in *The Primal Wound* to dispel the belief that adoption has little or no effect on children and, therefore, does not have to be addressed as a way of understanding these children's feelings or behaviors. Many adoptive parents lament the fact that when trying to get psychological help for their children, adoption is rarely considered as having anything to do with the problems they are experiencing with their children. Treatment usually focuses on the family dynamics without any true consideration being given to the impact which the child's original trauma might have had on him, his relationship with his adoptive parents, or any subsequent relationships.

Birth parents, also, are often ignorant of the impact the original separation had on the behaviors and emotional responses of their children. If they find out that the child had a difficult childhood, they often blame the adoptive parents. If the parents were insensitive, alcoholic, or abusive, that may be a partially accurate assumption, but many responsible adoptive parents have had children who have gotten into trouble or who have been very unhappy. It is important for all concerned to recognize that both the original trauma and the response to that trauma by the adoptive parents played a part in the outcome so far as the adoptee is concerned. And everyone has been bamboozled by the societal ignorance of all connected with adoption. It is time to start anew.

The topics covered in this chapter are attunement, projective identification, nature vs. nurture, the differences between personality and behavior, the dual reality of the adopted child, and a sense of belonging. Understanding their child's dual reality is a must for adoptive parents if the child is to retain a modicum of his own personality and not completely adapt to what he perceives to be the expectations of the adoptive parents. Wherever I go in the world, a sense of belonging seems to be missing from the adoptee's perspective. This appears to be connected to the lack of genetic markers or reflection of self, which all children who grow up without any biological relatives will face.

These concepts are also important for birth parents to understand because without the understanding of these issues they are apt to blame the adoptive parents for behaviors and attitudes which are a direct result of the trauma of separation and the way in which the neurons in the brain connected as a result of that separation. There doesn't have to be any blame assigned here – neither for the mother who surrendered the baby nor the mother who didn't recognize that the baby was grieving. To paraphrase Maya Angelou: We do the best we can, and when we learn more we do better. We are learning more and more every day, so we should be doing better and better.

We need to begin by allowing the biological mother to hold and welcome her new baby into the world and then say goodbye. The longer the mother can hold and interact with her baby, the better. A vulnerable newborn needs to feel safe in the arms and surrounded by the love of the mother who gave birth to him. The whisking away of the infant upon physical birth is an assault upon this new being. The stress hormones have not had time to recede and the birth is not complete. (This goes for any birth, not just those in which the mother and child are to be permanently separated.) Obstetricians need to be more sensitive to the baby in the birthing process.

### Attunement

Adopted infants and children come into the adoptive family traumatized by the loss of the first mother. They are grieving. Unfortunately, adoptive parents are not made aware of this significant information. This is not because of some malicious intent on the part of doctors and social workers, but because of the ignorance of everyone connected with adoption. What happens, then, is that the adoptive mother is not cognizant of the child's loss and need to grieve. She is not attuned to her child's emotional life. *Attunement* is very important for infants and young children, because it is the way in which they experience empathy from their parents and the way in which they learn to regulate their emotions. Babies cannot say, "You're a very nice lady, but I miss my mommy." However, for all the reasons I have talked about in my first book and earlier in this book, it is essential that adoptive mothers acknowledge, validate, and empathize with the child's loss and mourning process.

People are always asking me, "Do you mean to say that *all* adoptees experience that loss?" What does this question mean? Does it mean that perhaps some adoptees escape the natural experience of loss when their mothers disappear? Why would they, and which ones would they be? I believe that future brain scans will prove that all babies, regardless of whether they are relinquished, preemies, or infants whose mothers have died in childbirth, will have an acute emotional reaction to that loss. It has nothing to do with the adoptive parents, the nurses in the hospital, or anyone else. It just follows that when the mother is gone, the child will suffer. So, yes! All adoptees, all preemies, and other infants whose mothers were unavailable right after or shortly after birth will suffer this loss. If adoptive mothers don't recognize this truth, then they will miss one of their most important opportunities to connect with their children—*witnessing, empathizing, and aiding in their grief.*

The other important reason for the mother to be attuned to her child's emotional life is that *loss and fear of loss* are driving the ways in which the child integrates experience. A parent who is tuned in to those feelings can empathize with them, help the child to regulate his responses to them, and give him a different experience. A baby cannot self-soothe. It takes thousands of interactions between her and her soothing mother for her to learn to self-soothe. If a mother is unaware of her child's grief or fear, she cannot help regulate the child's responses to those experiences. We all need someone to bear witness to our emotional responses to life. It is the basis for compassion. It makes us able to empathize with others. And it allows us to learn to regulate our own responses to those feelings. A mother has to be attuned to her baby's emotional life because the baby has no words to tell her what her experience is. Adoptees who are regressed in reunion may need this same kind of attunement and empathy from their birth mothers. *Attunement is a key component in the intimate connection between mother and child.*

### Projective Identification

Understanding projective identification is probably one of the most valuable tools parents can have as a means to understanding their children. Because there is no verbal narrative for their feelings, children have to find other means of communicating those feelings. The most prevalent means, especially among acting-out adoptees, is that of *projective identification.* It is one of the most difficult manifestations of trauma for parents or significant others to cope with.

Projective identification is a defense mechanism, which means that it is unconscious so far as the one using it is concerned. There is no intent involved, only an unconscious need to defend against danger or pain. Its use by adoptees can cause even the calmest adoptive mother to rant and rave as if she were possessed by demons. Yet projective identification can be extremely valuable in identifying and healing pain.

Projective identification exists in feelings, thoughts, and behavior and is used to evoke in others feelings which are congruent with one's own feelings. In other words, instead of accepting dangerous feelings, thoughts, or behaviors, an adoptee may try to get rid of them by projecting them onto the recipient, usually the adoptive mother. If the mother is a mature, strong person, who can constructively reinternalize the projections, rather than defending against them, denying them, discounting them, or becoming out of control, she can set an example for her child. If, on the other hand, she acts out in reaction to the projections, she will confirm the adoptee's fear that the feelings were indeed too dangerous and unbearable to tolerate. His feelings, which may have originally been defenses against connection and the possibility of rejection, then become consolidated and may be labeled as pathological.

Projective identification serves several purposes. It is a *type of defense, a mode of communication,* and *a primitive form of object relations.* When used as a defense, it can offer safety by creating a distance between the adoptee and his mother or significant other, as well as creating a sense of distance from unwanted or dangerous aspects of the Self. This use of projective identification may often be observed after a mother and child have had an especially close experience. The close experience causes the child to begin to become uneasy, and he will create a certain type of behavior which will put distance between them. The mother, of course, is dumbfounded by this behavior because they just had such a wonderful day. If she can understand that the child, too, had a wonderful day, but that the feeling of closeness makes him fearful, she can allow him to have his distance without becoming defensive or feeling rejected herself. She may even help by putting words to his behavior: "We had a wonderful time yesterday, Jonathan, but it seems as if you need to have some space today. That's okay. I understand, and I'm here if you need me."

Adoptees use projective identification a great deal as a form of communication for preverbal feelings—feelings for which they have no words. They are able to communicate rejection, rage, helplessness, frustration, confusion, inadequacy, and so forth by projecting those feelings and making the other person feel them.

Any adoptive parent with an acting out child will recognize these feelings. They've probably had them all. It is often difficult to clearly identify the way in which the child sets the scene for the parent to feel these feelings, but they are extremely clever at doing so, albeit unconsciously. They don't plan it; it just happens. Many adoptive parents, especially when their children are adolescents, feel used by their children. But how can anyone be more used than a child who is completely cut off from his biological roots to satisfy the yearning of biological strangers for a child? It is exactly during adolescence, when a child is struggling with identity and finding it difficult to identify with his adoptive parents, that he projects *being used* onto the parents.

One of the easiest uses of projective identification for birth mothers to understand is when the adoptee suddenly stops all communication. Phone calls are not returned, letters go unanswered, e-mail is ignored, and holidays go by without even a card. The birth mother is going out of her mind trying to figure out what happened to the wonderful reunion she thought was taking place. How long is she supposed to wait for her child to respond in some way? As I've said in another part of this book, the adoptee is (unconsciously) trying to communicate to the mother how it felt to wait, and wait, and wait, and wait—without ever hearing from her. She is letting her birth mother know what abandonment feels like. Remember, it doesn't matter what the birth mother's intention was or what we call that separation, it felt like abandonment to the child. Now it is important for mother to know—to feel—what her child went through. If it is agonizing for the mother, she must understand and acknowledge how that endless waiting must have felt to a tiny, helpless baby.

Other behavioral problems, such as stealing and hoarding, needing to be in control, lying, etc., are equally understandable, when viewed in the context of the adoptee's traumatic beginning of life. Besides projecting his feelings onto someone else, he often creates on the outside what he is feeling on the inside. He feels chaotic inside, so he causes chaos outside; he had no control over what happened to him, so he desperately needs to be in control of every situation; he feels manipulated, so he manipulates; he is living a lie, so he lies; he feels stolen (which is preferable to feeling as if he had been given away), so he steals. Not only is he externalizing painful feelings, but he is at the same time calling attention to his pain. Parents should see his behavior as a metaphor for what is happening inside the child's psyche. Then they can name it, validate it, and allow the child to integrate it, rather than punish him for his feelings or the ways in which he acts them out. Too often children are told that they should not feel a certain way. This is confusing to children, because *it is the way they feel.* The message is: "You should not feel," so they shut down. What we must do instead is to acknowledge and name the feelings, then teach the child appropriate ways to express them. One of the ways to teach is by example. Adult adoptees, too, have to find appropriate ways to express their feelings without acting out. Poetry, art, metaphors, and other forms of expression can be helpful when ordinary words fail.

Sometimes projective identification is used as a primitive type of objective relations. This means the adoptee is trying to relate in a safe way to his adoptive parents and other significant others without risking too much. "If I don't love too much, I won't lose too much," is the belief. Having suffered a devastating trauma, she desperately needs to find ways in which to perceive, organize, and manage her internal and external experiences and to communicate them to those with whom she is close, such as the adoptive mother, spouse, or partner. The ways in which these important people respond to her relating in this way will help determine how well the adoptee is able to organize her internal and external worlds and her relations with significant others.

Because of the persistent use of projective identification, especially during childhood, it is not always easy for the mother to respond maturely. Thomas Ogden, who has taught me a great deal about the subject, gives this example in his book *Projective Identification and Psychotherapeutic Technique*:

> ... the child could exhibit persistently stubborn behavior in many areas of daily activity, by making a major battle out of eating, toileting, dressing, going to sleep at night, getting up in the morning, being left with another caretaker, and so forth. The mother might unrealistically begin to feel that she perpetually storms around the house in a frenzy of frustrated rage ready to kill those that stand between her and what she desires.
>
> *Ogden, 1982*

Every adoptive mother of an acting-out child will recognize the truth of that statement.

If the mother has not resolved her own conflicts about destructive impulses, she may react by either withdrawing from the child or acting violently toward him. If, on the other hand, the mother is able to integrate the projections by allowing herself to experience the feelings of confusion, frustration, anger, etc., without exhibiting any destructive behavior, projective identification can be useful as a means for psychological change and healing for the child. She can show him that feelings do not need to annihilate either oneself or others. If the mother fails to do this and instead acts destructively towards the child, no healing will take place and the adoptee will go on to use projective identification in other significant relationships, making those with whom he is relation feel manipulated, confused, frustrated, and furious. It is important that others in the life of the adoptive family also understand these phenomena, especially the adoptive father.

Because most of the feelings are projected upon the adoptive mother, fathers sometimes feel smug in escaping this projection, or critical of the mother for "provoking the behavior or letting it happen to her."

The best way to help the acting-out child is to identify and label the feeling that the child is evoking. "I'm feeling angry right now. Do you think you might be angry, too?" "Boy, Johnny, when you do that I really feel rejected. I'll bet you sometimes feel rejected, too." "When I have to leave you here (at the day care center, babysitter's or school), I feel very sad. Does it make you sad, too? I'll bet it may even make you feel scared." Or a teacher, when seeing a child is having difficulty, can put her hand on his shoulder and say, "You seem to be having a hard time right now, Bobby. Why don't you just put your head down for a minute, then see if you can finish the assignment." Instead of feeling like a bad kid, which is probably what he is used to, he can begin to feel understood. This lowers his anxiety and makes him better able to cope.

In dealing with this phenomenon in an adult adoptee, it is always important to make the person understand the impact this form of communication is having on the recipient. This needs to be done in a loving and non-threatening way. A birth mother, for instance, can write to her daughter and say that not hearing from her for such a long time has been very painful, and she wonders if the silence is a way to make her understand the devastation of the original separation. She can assure her daughter that she got the message, and wonders if they can begin to communicate again and that she would be glad to talk about how painful the experience was for her daughter. Sometimes, because this form of communication *is* unconscious, she may not have any response from her child. For those adoptees who are reading this, I urge you to stop the non-verbal form of communication and begin to respond in a more adult way to your birth parents. To continue this non-verbal communication (i.e., silence) keeps the relationship and you in a state of paralysis.

I cannot emphasize enough that as children and adults much of this type of behavior is unconscious. The types of defense mechanisms they use, by their very definition as defense mechanisms, are unconscious. The adoptee is not deliberately *doing something* to his parents, partner, or friend. Most adult adoptees are astonished to realize the things they felt as children and can't at all understand why they acted the way they did. If they are still acting this way as adults, they need to begin to own their feelings, take responsibility for their behavior, and work on responding to *situations*, rather than to the *feelings* themselves (which may be out of proportion to the situation—a trigger from the past).

Although projective identification is one of the most difficult aspects of adoption to deal with, it can be the most useful in understanding and validating the inner pain of the adoptee. It is important to remember that no matter how intense the feelings are for the recipients of the projections, they are *much more intense* for adoptees themselves. This is something most of us in relation to them would rather not know!

### Nature vs. Nurture

There has been a long-standing debate about the influences of genetics vs. environment on the development of personality. Because we as adoptive parents tend to believe that we have a great deal of influence over our children, many of us begin by believing that the greater impact is that of environment. Since many children are so good at adapting, this myth has remained a part of adoption lore. The exception may be the "personality" of the acting-out child, which is sometimes attributed to "bad genes."

One idea I want to retire once and for all is the "bad seed" or "inferior gene pool" theory. In the first place, if we are to determine good genes by one's socio-economic status, which seems to be the value system operating in this country at this time, many of the children placed for adoption in the past have come from middle class or upper middle class families. These are the families for whom an unwed pregnancy was shameful. When you meet most of these birth mothers, they may be depressed as a result of their unresolved grief at losing their babies, but they are not socially or educationally deprived individuals. They are your next-door neighbors. Socio-economic status may have something to do with opportunity, but it has nothing to do with the quality of those genes.

This does not mean that environment has no influence upon the development of the child. Matt Ridley, in his book *Nature via Nurture*, delights in this discovery: "To the extent that people are products of nurture, in the narrowly parental sense of the word, they are largely the products of early and irreversible events. To the extent that they are the product of genes, they are expressing new effects right into adulthood, and often those effects are at the mercy of the way they live," (Ridley, 2003). This is the reason that attunement is so important. One of those irreversible events for the adoptee is separation trauma. The ways in which the parents respond to that trauma can greatly affect his sense of Self.

Despite the fact that we do not remember most of the first three years of life, the experiences we have during those years play a big part in our overall attitudes and beliefs. Remember that the initial post-natal experience of the adopted child was one of separation and loss, and this has already had its influence on him. It has destroyed trust and made him hypervigilant. It has caused him to adopt coping behaviors in order to adapt to his new environment and situation (which includes the possibility of being abandoned again). All the while, the child is in an unresolved state of grief. Rarely do adoptive parents get to see the true personality of their child. What they see is behavior, the child's attempt to cope with his original loss and avoid another one.

This is important to understand because although genes may determine personality, aptitude, creativity, intelligence, and talent, how these attributes are employed may be influenced by the environment—nurturing—the ways in which each is recognized or unrecognized, encouraged or discouraged by the parents. The environment includes, as I already mentioned, the tremendously devastating experience of separation from mother and the lack of genetic markers. Adoptive parents do not get a tabula rasa that they can shape and mold when they adopt a child. It is incumbent upon adoptive parents to be very attentive to the genetic aptitudes and talents of their children and to encourage them in those talents, even if they themselves have hitherto had no interest in those particular aptitudes. If they are interested in their children, they will be interested in their children's aptitudes and talents. The child's talents and aptitudes may be predetermined by genes, but the development and nurturing of these talents are determined by the environment. In other words, parents have the responsibility to encourage, foster, and nurture their adopted children's genetically endowed talents, whether or not they themselves understand or value those talents. *All adoptive parents should value whatever talents their children display.*

Remember the story related earlier about the woman in New Zealand, who was good at athletics, winning many trophies and medals? Her adoptive parents never went to her meets because they were not interested in sports, nor did they think sports were important. It is unconscionable for adoptive parents to expect their adopted children to be like them and to refuse to encourage their children's particular talents and creative tendencies no matter how different from their own.

Birth parents, also, have to be careful about how they react to what their children are doing because we all have a cornucopia of aptitudes and talents which could be fostered and encouraged. (This has been confirmed by our studies of multiple personalities in which each "alter" has a different talent that has been developed.) The particular talents of adoptees that get attention may very well be determined by the adoptive parents. This doesn't mean that this is wrong. Since we don't have time to develop all our talents, those encouraged by the adoptive parents may be different from those which would have been encouraged by the birth parents. *As long as those talents are authentic to the adoptee, developing whatever that talent happens to be is fine.* What is *not* fine is forcing a child into something which seems totally alien to him. (I've seen many fathers, not necessarily adoptive, insisting that their artistically inclined sons play little league, for example. I have rarely seen athletically inclined sons forced into art classes!)

Nature or genetic codes appear to have a great deal to do with personality traits, proclivities, talents, and so forth, but the development of any of these attributes is determined by the environment. The environment includes not only our homes, schools, churches, and so forth, but all our experiences and the attitudes and perceptions we have toward them. Adoptive parents can help their children by honestly observing and encouraging their children's interests. It is irresponsible to do anything else. As adults, however, it is up to adoptees to discover and develop latent talents which they feel were ignored or discouraged during childhood. Sometimes this is difficult to determine because of the adaptations many adoptees have made as children. They have a dual reality, and, depending on the "match" between them and their adoptive parents, the genetic reality may be flourishing or almost extinct. Sometimes it isn't until a reunion with birth parents has been accomplished that the adoptee can recognize heretofore latent talents and aptitudes.

## The Dual Reality of Adopted Children

The adoptee has two realities, his genetic reality and his adoptive reality. The most real things about the adoptee, his bond with his birth mother and his genetic identity, have to be denied in order to assume the reality of the present situation, which is being the child of adoptive parents. The reality which is denied consists of genetic traits, birth parents, and the relinquished self. The denial of the adoptee's dual reality—adopted child/genetic child—plus his determination to be like the adoptive parents have survival value for him. His deeply felt sense is that they keep him from being abandoned again.

In some families the differences between an adoptee and his adoptive parents are overtly ignored and covertly confirmed. That confirmation is usually negative and the differences seen as unfortunate. Instead of saying, "Suzie is so athletic; it's refreshing to have an athlete in the family," people are more apt to say, "Suzie will never be as musical as the rest of the family." Suzie gets the idea that the real part of herself, the athlete, is not good and that she should at least make an effort—pretend—to be interested in music. The same applies if the adoptee is artistic and the parents are athletic and want to spend every weekend hiking.

The adoptive parents, in being as true as is possible to their own personalities, principles, ideas, talents, aptitudes, and opinions are not deliberately setting a trap for their children. They are just doing what most parents do—guiding their child's upbringing within their own principles. Their shortcoming is in not recognizing that it is natural for the child to be and feel different, and that there has to be permission for these differences. This is more often recognized in transracial/transcultural adoptions where the differences are more easily identified. But many adoptees who are of similar racial and cultural backgrounds as their adoptive parents may feel as if they, too, had been dropped into a foreign place. It was once thought that trying to match children and parents would be helpful to the adoptive situation, but the matching usually had nothing to do with character traits or temperament, but only with appearance. All this did was to allow and reinforce the denial of differences between adoptees and their adoptive parents. Adoptees who have similar coloring as their adoptive parents have said that they wish they had the "advantage" of the transracial kids, in that those kids aren't expected to be like their adoptive parents.

It is essential for adoptive parents to be aware of the differences between them and their children. Often what the parents see as real feels the least real to the child because it forces him to deny something fiercely primal and true about himself—his biological identity and connection to the birth mother. Is it any wonder that adoptees sometimes feel crazy? It is like being told that black is white and white is black, when he knows differently. Not only that, but he is expected to like and even feel grateful for this great deception. Some traumas, such as rape, have been blamed on the victims, but relinquishment/adoption is the only trauma for which a person is actually expected to feel grateful!

Adoptees spend a tremendous amount of energy trying to fit into a family in which they feel alien—where they are not reflected in those around them. Yet we fail to see what is really happening. Trying to sort out these two realities, one of which has been largely denied or ignored by society as having any significance, creates confusion for adoptees. We then label him as difficult and send him to therapy. Many children, of course, adapt very well. They are terrified not to. Their parents are completely unaware of the battle raging within them. These are the adoptees who give lie to the fact that adoption is difficult. They cause no trouble, so they seem untroubled. But often they are shut down. Their authentic selves are buried beneath the armor of the adaptive, compliant, false self.

Some adoptees have done such a good job of fitting in (adapting) that the parents are not the least bit aware that the child really doesn't fit. Yet how can she? She doesn't have one gene in common with the adoptive parents (unless it is an interfamilial adoption), and the basic personality is as much a part of our genetic coding as the color of one's eyes or the shape of the body. This reality is proven when an adoptee is reunited with her birth family, where not only physical traits are familiar, but there is often a better understanding of the adoptee's worldview, her humor, her talents, her way of functioning in the world. And the energy is right. She often feels that she has come home.

### The Difference Between Behavior and Personality

Behavior is different from personality, yet in many texts the two are used synonymously. Behavior is the result of experience and environment and is a form of communication. Difficult or withdrawn behavior is often the result of painful experiences. Behavior is what most adoptive parents observe about their children, whether they act out or act acquiescent. It is interesting that what many adoptive parents believe is the result of genetics (behavior) is actually the result of experience and environment (separation from mother and living in a non-biological family), and that the true personality or character of the child, which they believe they can mold and shape, is in fact genetic. The need to discriminate between personality and behavior became apparent to me whenever I talked to families that had more than one adopted child; they invariably had one who acted out and one who was compliant. It seemed implausible to me that adoption agencies would deliberately give the parents one of each, so there had to be another explanation.

What seems to happen is that the first child "selects" the coping mechanism which he believes will most help him deal with the unreality of calling one woman mother, when he has been born to a different woman who is also mother, and at the same time avoiding the trauma of losing the second mother the way he did the first mother. If the first child has chosen defiance as the means to avoid connection and the potential for loss, then the next child will chose compliance— or vice versa. Sometimes they trade back and forth. Children are exquisitely sensitive to feelings, so it isn't a big task for them to do this more or less instantaneously. Rarely are two children in a family in the same mode at the same time. What has to be understood, however, is that neither of these modes of behavior is the true Self of these children.

In order for parents to be helpful to their child, they must first discern between what is the true personality of the child—what seems natural to him—and what is a behavioral method of communicating his pain. Then they can encourage his natural tendencies, even if they are different from theirs. At the same time they can use his behavior as a means of understanding more about his pain. Behavioral problems, such as stealing, lying, battles for control, etc., are often metaphors for the inner reality of the child. If they can be named as such, instead of taken literally, healing can begin for both the child and his parents. Understanding of this kind is very important to the bonding process between adoptive parents and their children because they don't have the advantage of genetic markers showing them the way.

As for birth parents, some birth mothers are so sure that their child is going to be just like them that they are disappointed when he or she is his or her own person. It should be remembered that the birth mother and her siblings were not all carbon copies of their parents, so the lost child will not be exactly like her or the birth father. Although some habits and gestures are learned, it seems that many gestures, stances, gaits, facial expressions, and so forth are inherited from our biological parents and ancestors. The mirroring of these characteristics, which the adoptive parents cannot provide for their children, make children feel as if they fit into the family. This deficit, although no one's fault, certainly has a great deal to do with the difficulties the children may have in adjusting to their adoptive parents. So it is that birth parents, too, have to be vigilant about the expectations they have of their reunited children. They may be more like them than like the adoptive parents, but some gestures, attitudes, and so forth are also imitated. The adoptee may be a blend of both sets of parents.

### The Importance of Genetic Markers

What is the first thing we say when a baby is born? "Oh, he looks just like you!" And when we're going through family albums, "John is looking more and more like Uncle Richard. He even stands like him." Again, at family gatherings, "That twinkle in Katy's eye reminds me of when you were a little girl, Angela." Over and over again we compare one relative to another. Over and over we are reminded that we belong—that we look like someone, walk like someone, gesture like someone, talk like someone. Except for adoptees. Even if someone says, "Oh, yes, I can tell you are sisters. You look a lot alike," the adoptee knows this is not true.

It is difficult for adoptees to feel as if they fit when there are no genetic markers to indicate that they do. It doesn't do any good to make sure that blonde, blue-eyed parents get blonde, blue-eyed children because it's much, much more complex than that. Just ask yourself, "Do I feel as if I am related to everyone who has the same hair and eye color as I?" Of course not! It's about the feel of one's skin, the energy of one's body. It's about knowing things about the other person because he is like me.

The lack of genetic markers is difficult for adoptive mothers as well as for the adoptee. Both are trying to figure out *how to be* together. The mother doesn't have the genetic knowing about her baby that one does with a biological child—the knowing what to do for that particular child. She keeps trying to figure it out. She cannot mirror the child the way his or her biological mother could have done. The child does not feel reflected, and is constantly hypervigilant, trying to understand how to be in this particular family. Family means familiar, and nothing feels intrinsically familiar to either the child or the mother.

Looking up into one's mother's or father's face and seeing something familiar is the beginning of self-esteem: I am like them. "I am okay. I belong." Adoptees look, and see nothing familiar. They feel like the ugly duckling. "Something must be wrong with me." Those around them don't look like them, act like them, or think like them. Furthermore the rest of the family seem to be oblivious to what the adoptee is experiencing. No one understands. No one puts it into words: "It must be difficult growing up in a family where you don't see yourself anywhere." The child is full of doubt about his own identity. He begins very early to try to emulate his parents, to try to fit into the family so he won't be different and in danger of abandonment. The better he adapts, the more of himself he loses. The adoptee about whom it is said, "He is very well adapted," may be the adoptee who at age 35 doesn't have the slightest idea who he is.

Genetic markers play a key role in a person's feeling as if he belongs. Even if he doesn't like his relatives, he knows that he belongs there. He, therefore, can go on to feel as if he belongs in the community and in the greater society. This need to fit in and belong is one reason so many adoptees want to search for their biological families, for their roots. One of the first things they do is to compare physical characteristics, then personality traits, then speech patterns and body language—and on and on. Many see themselves being reflected only when they have their first child. This is such an intense and profound moment for them, it feels sacred.

We may not understand why it is so important to see ourselves reflected back, but it is. It seems to be instinctive and true for all cultures. It is something we need to think about when deciding whether to have open adoptions. It is very important for adoptees to have the same experience all the rest of us have—to see themselves reflected back—to know they are okay—to know they are not alone in who they are.

Genetic markers must be important because we talk about them from the time a baby is born. Yet adoptees are expected to be either oblivious to the absence of this important aspect of family life or to go along with the hoax of pretending that they are actually like members of the adoptive family. Whereas there are traits they may have in common with one or another member of the family, adoptees I have met from around the world speak of the lack of biological mirroring as a huge deficit in their capacity to feel as if they belong.

*Belonging—A Loaded Word!*

We know that belonging is something the adoptee rarely feels, yet it is something for which she is yearning. Belonging is what she is looking for when she begins to search for her birth family. She is *longing to be,* as one adoptee put it: *be/longing,* searching for Self. The authentic self is what we are before the environment begins to work on us, and it is what we need to redeem.

Living in one family while biologically belonging to another is an unnatural state, one which all adoptees of extra-familial adoptions experience. Biological mirroring is the beginning of self-esteem. A sense of belonging begins when that connection to the mother extends out to the father and the rest of the family, friends, community, society and the universe. Many adoptees say they never have a sense of belonging anywhere. They join churches, the armed services, cults, and other organizations searching for a feeling of belonging. Because adoptees, having experienced the tremendous and devastating surprise of separation, are ever vigilant, they are probably more aware than most people of the subtleties that make up the differences among people. They are very intuitive and observant. Therefore, they may be more aware than their adoptive parents of the differences that exist between them. Many adoptees have told me that their parents have never been aware of how much they don't feel as if they fit into the family.

This is not to say that they don't like being in the family. Many adoptees love their adoptive parents and relatives very much. In fact, upon meeting their birth parents, some adoptees are glad that they grew up in the family in which they did. That doesn't mean it was easy. There is a difference between loving their adoptive parents and feeling as if they fit in. There are other adoptees who feel so different and so alienated from their adoptive parents, either because of a very poor fit or because of an abusive relationship, that they don't feel as if they have anything in common or any reason to continue the relationship after they become adults. That is rare, but it does happen.

One young woman in describing her sense of not belonging in her adoptive family, put it this way:

> How I feel, have *always* felt like is that my adoptive family is one puzzle and that I'm a piece from another puzzle, and that society has placed me in the wrong puzzle. If you've ever done a puzzle in which sometimes a stray piece from another puzzle will sorta fit into the one you're doing—and though it fits in, it really doesn't. And you really won't notice it, unless either you're looking for it or you're right on top of the puzzle.
>
> It's the same thing with me. To society, I fit, so I'm "just as good as ..." and like the puzzle—like me—people won't notice by just looking. They won't notice until they start analyzing. I mean, sure it's a fit, though for me an uncomfortable one. And what happens when you need that one piece for the puzzle it really belongs in? You have a problem; that's what you have.

A sense of not belonging is one reason many adoptees act like chameleons. They are always trying to fit in by acting like whomever they are with or whatever group they are in. It is difficult to relate to them when they are doing this because they are not being true to themselves. Many do not even know who that self might be. It seems important to push that little puzzle piece into whatever space is available in whatever puzzle it happens to land on. Often it is only after meeting with the birth family that adoptees begin to realize just how much they have adapted during their lives. Many of them feel much more comfortable in the "right puzzle," where they don't have to distort themselves to fit in.

Unfortunately many adoptees, lacking a personal history with the birth family, have a difficult time feeling as if they fit into that family either. In one family there is a lack of genetic traits and in the other a lack of personal history. This should make us really think long and hard about the wisdom of taking children out of one family and placing them in another. We have to weigh the disadvantages of growing up with genetic strangers with the disadvantages of growing up with parents who have difficulty parenting them. It is a difficult choice, but the universal difficulties in fitting in or belonging will make it imperative that these issues be considered when the powers-that-be make these life-changing decisions.

A sense of belonging is something to which every child and adult should be entitled. Feeling as if one fits in is a very important aspect of emotional health. One way that adoptive parents can ease the problem for their children is to validate their feelings about it. In addition they should validate specific things about their children every chance they get. (Adopted children have a tendency to disbelieve general validations like "You are a wonderful child," but can integrate "I am very proud of the way you played the piano in the recital today.") When there is no genetic connection, the next best thing, according to hundreds of adoptees with whom I've spoken, is having adoptive parents who at least understand that this is a problem. Understanding, acknowledgment, and validation, in addition to love, are essential to a close adoptive relationship.

## Summary

Although most of this book is addressed to adult adoptees, this chapter is to help those *in relation to adoptees* understand what it may be like to be an adoptee—what makes them tick. However, I also hope that listing the issues in this chapter will enable adoptees to understand themselves better, both their behavior as children and some of that which continues into adulthood. I hope it will aid adoptive parents in their relationship with their adopted children, especially those with children still living at home. It should also help birth parents by explaining some of the reasons for the experiences their children had in their adoptive families in a more objective manner than their children remember through their lens of abandonment. It can also help them to understand and relate better to their children's behaviors in reunion.

The goal is understanding, which is essential to integrity, respect, and connection.

# CHAPTER 18
Working with Families

---

Parents of adopted children are often frustrated by the attitude of family therapists when it comes to seeking help for the family. Treatment usually focuses on the family dynamics without any consideration being given to the impact which the child's original trauma might have had on him and his relationship with his adoptive parents. Adoptee, clinician, and author Joanne Small, in an article in *Public Welfare* titled "Working with Adoptive Families," refers to these clinicians as "professional enablers" and claims that they often display co-dependent behavior in the manner in which they "... unwittingly engage in the same kinds of dysfunctional behaviors—avoidance, protection, covering up, and denial—with which adoptive families deny their differences" (Small, 1987), all the while ignoring the early experience of the child. When one considers the number of adopted children in psychiatric care, this attitude by clinicians is unconscionable, one we have waited too long to address.

Adoptees have consistently been over-represented in special schools, juvenile hall, and residential treatment centers. Adopted children have a higher incidence of juvenile delinquency, sexual promiscuity, and running away from home than their non-adopted peers. They also have more difficulty in school, both academically and socially. Many theories have been advanced as to why adoptees are at risk. Most of those theories treat adoption as if it were only a concept and not an actual experience of the child. Therefore, they fail to take into consideration what happened *before* the adoption took place in determining why adoptees are at psychological risk. Ken Watson, psychologist, independent consultant, and author, reminds us that adoption is *a legal and sociological* process, which fails to take into consideration the *biological and psychological* aspects of the child's reality. It is as if counselors (and sometimes adoptive parents as well) believe that the adoption papers and the revised birth certificate change the DNA of the adoptee and wipe out the experience of their separation from their mothers and their ancestry. Small says, "Becoming disconnected from one's ancestry is perhaps the loneliest experience known."

Adoption is not the main problem, although the experience of growing up without genetic markers takes its toll. Those of us who have not had to experience this deficit have no idea what it is like to exist day after day with no mirroring of our genetic characteristics—not being reflected back. It isn't until they experience the ease of being around their birth families that adoptees even begin to understand it themselves. Despite this difficulty, the main issue for adoptees is that of loss, the loss of the birth mother. If adoption is to be helpful to a child who needs parents, the adoptive parents as well as the professionals who work with them will have to first acknowledge the existence of the child's loss and the issues which ensue.

### The Usual Suspects

In normal family therapy, it is usually assumed that one of the children has been unconsciously designated as the IP or *identified patient*, and that the family is funneling their dysfunction through that child. The child is seen by the therapist as a scapegoat for the rest of the family's problems. In the adoptive family, although this may be one aspect of what is going on, there is another variable which needs to be addressed. It is that the child has come into the family with a great wound caused by a devastating trauma. That wound impacts everyone in the family and all other significant relationships throughout his life. Therefore, even highly functional, stable couples will sometimes end up becoming less stable or even dysfunctional. This is not the child's fault. He is simply frantically trying to prevent what he perceives to be the possibility of annihilation. The substitution of mothers for a baby is felt to be unnatural and will always have an impact on the child. It follows that it will also have an impact on the adoptive family. Many families who have had a couple of biological children and want to share their lives with a child from China, Korea, or Rumania have had their "ideal" families become chaotic and unmanageable. No one ever told them that love is not enough. I believe that this is changing somewhat. There have been enough failed adoptions among international adoptions that it has become apparent more education is needed for these parents.

## Good Beginnings: Working with Infants

Being aware of their new baby's emotional responses to the experience of separation from their biological mother is crucial to forming a secure attachment to adoptive parents. One of the most important things I learned in my international travels following the publication of *The Primal Wound* was that the adoptees who felt the most connected to their adoptive parents were those whose parents were the most understanding of their children's experiences and feelings. Love was not enough, but love coupled with understanding and validation helped form the bonds of the new family.

As an adoptive mother, I had not a clue in the beginning that a tiny infant knows her own mother and may be experiencing loss of the original mother as well as chaos and confusion about someone else assuming that role. Had I known in the beginning what I finally intuited after giving birth two years later,

I would have done many things differently right from the start. This is a litany that I've heard over and over from adoptive parents of children in their teens and twenties who have read my book. "Why didn't I know this sooner?" A question I always ask: "Would you have believed it sooner?" It is difficult to look into the face of a little baby and see anything more than an adorable little child whom we are primed to love and nurture. However, knowing what I know now, I would like to pass on to other parents and therapists some of what I have learned from the thousands of adoptees with whom I have worked and communicated, and from the latest in neurobiological research.

*Attachment and Attunement*

Therapists need to educate new adoptive parents in the idea that the two most important aspects of a mother's relationship with her new adopted baby are attachment and attunement. Encouraging and facilitating attachment with a baby who has been disconnected from her first mother is a daunting task. This is a baby who doesn't trust the permanence of the mother/infant relationship. She will be reluctant to attach. However, if the baby can attach, she will be inclined to attach to the person who is most available. Since the biological mother is out of the picture, the adoptive mother is no better a candidate than anyone else. It is therefore important for therapists to encourage adoptive mothers to stay home and be the caregiver with whom the baby attaches. This is the most important work she will do with her child and will be the blueprint for their future relationship.

*Facilitating Attachment*

In a lecture titled " Affect Regulation and the Repair of the Self," Allan Schore defined attachment as "… the regulation of biological synchronicity between organisms. Attachment is the dyadic (interactive) regulation of emotion." What then, of non-biologic attachment? Babies recognize their mothers through sensory cues—at first through smell, taste, and touch. For infants ages one to two months, smell is the key sense. A baby knows the adoptive mother does not smell right. His sense of confusion needs to be attended to by the adoptive mother. It would be my suggestion that all adoptive mothers request an article of unwashed clothing from the birth mother, so that the baby could first be comforted by her smell, then by blending her smell with that of the adoptive mother, gradually weaning the child from one to the other. Sheep ranchers learned this trick ages ago (mainly to fool the new mother by wrapping an orphan lamb in the skin of the ewe's dead lamb, but it can work both ways). These are only ideas, but the more evidence of the biological mother the baby can perceive (in addition to an article of clothing, a tape with her voice, perhaps) the less confused and anxious the baby may be. Also, the addition of the birth mother's sensory remnants commingling with the adoptive mother's sensory cues, may eventually allow the baby to accept the adoptive mother more readily.

Some adoptive mothers complain that their babies won't look at them. This gaze aversion is the baby's way of saying "You don't have the right face; you're not the right mom." Again, placing a photo of the birth mom next to the face of the adoptive mom might eventually allow the infant to accept the adoptive mom's face as being less of a threat and actually comforting, especially if the other sensory cues are also available. Babies are not easily fooled, and they know their own mothers—who she is and who she isn't. Placing babies at the left breast of the mother right after birth facilitates the bonding process as the baby gazes into the eyes of his mother. The distance between the breast and the mother's face is about the distance a newborn can see. Just because the relinquished infant never saw her mother's face doesn't mean that she won't recognize it. Teaching the infant to accept the substitution of mothers needs to be less wrenching and more gradual. Of course, the most beneficial would be for the actual birth mother to be available, to handle the infant in tandem with the adoptive mother. This would require a level of maturity and commitment to the welfare of the baby that most birth and adoptive mothers may not be able to actualize.

*Fine-tuning Attunement*

A mother's place in her child's life is very, very important. She is the container of her baby's emotions. She must, therefore, be aware of those emotions and a witness to them. Many adoptive mothers are unaware that the baby is suffering from the loss of the first mother and misses the cues to his pain. She cannot soothe the baby because she is not in tune with the baby's emotions. This attunement is crucial to the development of the brain and to the child's ability to learn to self-regulate. An infant can't self-regulate. It is up to the mother to provide a template for her child to regulate his emotions.

Why is attunement so important? In their book *Parenting from the Inside Out*, Siegel and Hartzell tell us, "... we as human beings are exquisitely social: our brains are structured to be in relationship with other people in a way that shapes how the brain functions and develops. For these reasons, attachment experiences are a central factor in shaping our development. ... When a parent's initial response is to be *attuned* to his child, the child feels understood and connected to the parent. Attuned communications give the child the ability to achieve an internal sense of balance and supports her in regulating her bodily states and later her emotions and states of mind with flexibility and equilibrium" (Siegel & Hartzell, 2003). A successful attachment depends upon attunement. Attunement between parent and child is the key to teaching a child to regulate her emotions. Brain research is beginning to point to an ability to regulate our emotions as a key component to good mental health. Because of the attending chemical reactions in the body, it is also important to good physical health. Positive emotions are more healthy than negative emotions. An anxious, depressed child will turn into an anxious, depressed adult unless the emotions are attended to early in the child's life. This is more difficult for adoptive parents because of the lack of genetic markers to help them understand their child's emotions.

As the infant matures, sight becomes the most important aspect of attachment. Visual stimuli take up more of the brain than anything else. This is the reason that a lack of genetic markers (in facial features, gestures, body language, and so forth) makes it more difficult for adoptees and will force both mother and child do the dance of learning *how to be* with one another. Adoptive parents must be aware of how difficult it is for the adoptees to try to fit into the adoptive family when genetic traits are not mirrored or reflected back. There is a constant need to be hypervigilant in order to try to fit in. This is equally true for the mother who is trying to discern the emotional climate of her child. In addition, the mother herself has to respond responsibly to her own emotions. This is not always easy. Mothers who are themselves poorly attached (to their own mothers) will have a more difficult time attaching to their infants. Being in touch with a therapist who understands what is going on can help give her support and, if need be, therapy. Finding a therapist who understands attunement and brain theory would be a good place to start. Meanwhile, parents and therapists should read *Parenting from the Inside Out* mentioned above.

## Working with Young Children

When I treat adoptive families with young children, I usually work with the parents to teach them how to parent their children, rather than working with the children themselves. A great deal of what I do with the parents may be more aptly named education than therapy. I educate them about the primal wound, the manifestations of that wound, and the ways in which they can help their child work through the resulting pain. If I think the child needs therapy, I recommend a therapist who works with the child and his parents.

I believe all work with children should include their parents. After all, it is a problem with the relationship to the parents that brings most children into therapy. Helping the parents to understand the underlying issues of their child, as well as their own, can facilitate the healing process. Certainly when attachment issues are a concern for adoptive parents, the healing should take place between the parents and child, not with the therapist and child. Certain neurological treatments may be the exception to this rule.

## Validating Feelings

The most important thing that parents can do is to *validate their child's feelings*. This is an extension of the initial attunement to the infant and is just as important. We can't be vigilant during infancy only to give up when the child hits the "terrible twos" and beyond. This means not reacting to outbursts, but calmly validating the child's experience. Let me give you an example:

> A mother of a six-year-old was having trouble getting her daughter to eat and get ready for school. The breakfast (which she had probably eaten for the past six months) was the wrong breakfast, and the clothes were the wrong clothes. Everything was wrong. What the child may have been sensing more exquisitely than usual was that this was the "wrong mother"—a non-biological mother. A typical thing for a mother to say at this point is "Patty, get up to your room right now and get dressed," or "Get in there right now and eat your breakfast." This adoptive mother, having had some counseling about her daughter's issues, said instead, "Patty, you're having a hard time today; you must be in a lot of pain." This caught Patty's attention because it was an intuitive, sensitive response to her outburst. This six-year-old's exact response to her mother was *"Mommy, you don't know all the pain that's in my heart."* Now, this is a statement to break a mother's heart, but it also exhibits trust in the mother's being able to hear it, validate it, and help her child contain this pain. As difficult as it was for this mother to hear, it was a gift of truth from her daughter. Although she would have been labeled the 'acting-out' child at the time, this young women is now a loving, productive, active 15-year-old who feels very secure in her connection to her mother.

Children will not give these gifts to mothers who are not ready to hear, validate, and contain them. And these mothers will say, "Joanne never even thinks about being adopted. She seems just fine." Perhaps Joanne is one of those children who has dissociated or is compliant, rather than acting out. Maybe Joanne knows that her mother doesn't want to hear anything negative about her adoption experience. Or she doesn't think her mother is strong enough to contain those feelings. Sometimes the children themselves are unaware that anything is wrong. Because they have experienced these feelings from the beginning of their lives, they consider them normal. Many adoptees have told me that they thought *everyone* felt anxious all the time. Or they didn't realize *they* were anxious until the anxiety lifted.

Parents also have to be very careful not to discount their child's feelings by reassuring them. Reassurance seems like a good, kind response. It may be surprising how often we do this. We want to make our children feel better, so we tell them "it's not so bad" or we tell them how *we* feel about it. Another example:

> A little boy from Mexico looked at his Caucasian mother and said, "Mommy, I wish I looked like you." His mother, wanting to reassure him, said, "Oh, David, it doesn't matter to me that you don't look like me. I love you so very much." What the mother just did, rather than reassuring him, was to discount what he was saying to her. He was not interested in what *she* was feeling, but was trying to tell her what *he* was feeling. What she could have said instead was, "Yes, David, it must be hard to grow up in a family where you don't look like anyone." Then David would have felt understood. He would have felt validated: "She understands me. She knows how I feel."

This is just one example of how we discount our children's feelings even though that is not our intention. We need to be more attentive to what they are trying to tell us and stop trying to "correct" those feelings by reassuring them or interjecting ideas of our own. This makes them more and more anxious. What we can do instead of discounting, reassuring, or correcting our kids would be to explore with them what they are experiencing. Never do this by asking "why," however. The word "why" may put them on the defensive. Besides that, these children don't usually know why they feel the way they do, but they may be able to tell more about their experience of it. Use, instead, phrases such as "Can you tell me more about that?" or "I'm curious about that ..." or "I'm wondering what that's like for you ..." Don't ask specific questions like, "What do you mean by that?" The questions need to be open-ended. The idea is to have a more accurate understanding of your child's experience. It may be coming from the right brain, rather than something specific from the left brain. Whatever he says may be painful for the parents to know, but hearing him out and trying to understand are the most useful means of connecting with an adopted child. As I mentioned earlier, during my travels the thing I heard over and over from adoptees who felt the most connected to their parents is that they felt as if their parents understood or tried to understand their feelings and experiences. Pretending that the relinquishment and adoption don't matter make adoptees feel alienated from their parents and alone in their pain.

A footnote here about the "David" story: Many Caucasian children of Caucasian parents think that transracial kids have it easier because they aren't expected to be like their parents. There is nothing more disconcerting for adopted kids than to have someone say, "You look just like your mother," when they feel so different from her. There are stages of development when children want desperately to be like their mothers or fathers, but that doesn't mean that they feel as if they are. This doesn't mean that it *is* easier for transracial or transcultural kids, but it does point to the idea that *looking like* is not the same as *being like*.

## The Importance of Play

Play is children's work. Unfortunately, these days too many parents and/or day-care providers interfere in that work by not allowing enough time for non-directed, creative play. Many children are over-scheduled and over-programmed to take part in directed activities. Not only does this create stress for the children, but it also creates stress for the parents who have to cart the kids around to all those activities.

Many of the thoughts and feelings for which children cannot find words can be expressed through play. Children are capable of working out complex psychological and emotional difficulties in their play. Bruno Bettelheim, in an *Atlantic Monthly* article, defined children's play as being "... characterized by freedom from all but personally imposed rules (which are changed at will), by free-wheeling fantasy involvement, and by the absence of any goals outside the activity itself" (Bettelheim, 1987). Little children should be free of any adult interference with their play activities unless there is true danger. Parents may observe their play in order to better understand what it is their children are trying to work out, but they *must not interfere in any way* in what the child is doing or how he is doing it. Their observation is for information only, not for direction.

Toys are very important in the play of little children. Dolls, puppets, cars, and trucks can all be used by the child to express feelings from the past or hopes for the future. Sometimes parents intercede with their own agendas based on religious or political beliefs. Children need to be free from these constraints in order to really work out their feelings of sadness, aggression, hatred, jealousy, and rage. One mother tells about how she was delighted when her son wanted a doll for Christmas. This played right into her feminist viewpoint of not treating boys like boys and girls like girls, but having a more androgynous approach to children's toys. You can imagine her horror when the first thing her son did when presented with the doll was to take a knife and cut its head off! One thing that day-care centers have done for children is to modify the belief that all masculine and feminine traits are learned. Give a little girl a couple of trucks, and she will have them talking to each other in a matter of minutes. Give a boy a doll and often he will use it as a bomb. In general, boys' play is more aggressive and manipulative than that of girls. It's hormones, folks!

However, dolls and puppets should be made available to both boys and girls. Dolls are wonderful instruments for allowing children to work out feelings about parents and siblings, teachers and classmates. Puppets allow the children to be once removed from the issues of jealousy, unworthiness, fear, or anger they may be experiencing as a result of some trauma in their lives or dynamics in the family. It is important for parents to remember that children see the family dramas through their own lenses brought about by their perceptions of their own experiences in life. They may not portray the events as the parents think they happened, but it is important to allow children to play out events as they perceive them, because that is how it affected them.

Not interfering does not preclude a parent's playing with her child. A mother's playing tea party or dolls can have a lasting impression on a child. She can model socializing behavior in a non-threatening way. For adoptive parents, playing with their children is a non-threatening way to connect with them. Children seldom feel the need to distance while playing as they might during other types of activities. The very nature of play lends itself to allowing for more closeness because, after all, it is make-believe. Bettelheim warns us that a parent should not play with her children simply out of a sense of duty, however. Nor should she play if the play is not the thing. In other words, if the purpose of playing is to educate, diagnose, distract, or entertain the child, the child will quickly perceive the parent's disinterest in the play itself and become offended by her pretense. Any benefit that playing could provide will be diminished.

Educational toys are not harmful in and of themselves, but if the parents insist on what the lesson to be learned is going to be, much of the benefit is lost. A toy, educational or not, should be used the way a child wants to use it. The lesson he needs to learn may not be the same as that conceived by the manufacturer of the toy. If a child is trying to work out some emotional difficulty, he must be able to use the toy as he so desires. Some of the best toys are puppets, toilet paper rolls, boxes, spools, and blocks.

What about playing with toy guns? I am not prone to provide kids with toy guns, with the exception of water guns on hot summer days. However, I don't think that every time a child points a stick or finger at another child and says, "Bang!" the parent ought to interfere. There are at least two things which can be learned from aggressive play, such as cops and robbers. If a child points a stick at a parent, for instance, and says, "Bang, you're dead," what the parent might do is to ask what that means to the child. The important thing is not so much the action as it is the child's intentions and feelings. It is not the time for a lecture on the evils of guns or war. The child is in the immediate present and needs an appropriate response from the parent. Some frustrations with the parent may be revealed. Children under age seven might not understand the permanency of death. (Remember that if the parent is actually playing *with* the child no questions should be asked.)

Aggressive feelings need an outlet so as not to become overwhelming. Sometimes the way children act out their aggressions may go against the parents' religious or political beliefs. These beliefs can be best taught to the child through the child's own method of play, such as talking about how he seems to be trying to understand the battle between good and evil. As Bettelheim says, "Serving the good is reinforced by the motivating force of a higher purpose. When a child acts out this understanding, he begins to appreciate a lesson that cannot be taught to him in a purely didactic fashion: to fight evil is not enough; one must do so in honor of a higher cause and with knightly valor—that is, according to the rules of the game, the highest of which is to act with virtue."

In addition to providing a way for children to work out their emotional or psychological difficulties, play is a way of socializing and civilizing our children. But we must trust them to know the lessons they need to learn and the means by which they will learn them. I remember when I was a child that setting up a play house was much more captivating than actually playing house. It took planning, creativity, strategy, and tenaciousness. When we provide a playhouse for a child, we deprive her of one of the most satisfying lessons in life: how to create something herself.

### The Rules of the Game

As children get older and begin to play with others, a great deal of their play is in negotiating the rules of the games or of the play. This is a very important part of learning because it teaches them how to cooperate, how to compromise, and how to reach consensus so that the game can go on. If adults interfere and suggest that they should hurry up and figure out what they are doing so that they can actually play the game, they will be hurrying the children through a very important part of their learning. With the great emphasis on team sports, where the rules are handed down from on high, this kind of negotiation is not available. Children will be deprived of opportunities to reason, judge what is appropriate and what is not, and how to reach consensus. Sandlot baseball is an important part of the learning process and might be more valuable to a child than Little League. Organized sports should not be started too young because they are competitive (even if the coach says that they are just having fun) and can be too frustrating for a young child.

Whether it is at home or in the therapeutic situation, play is an important part of a child's life, both for his psychological well-being and his socialization. Children learn by example, so we also must lead by our good examples. Children will emulate us and learn the lessons of the culture in which they live. Parents and therapists have to be patient observers and gentle guides in this process. Above all in this era of over-organization, children must be allowed to have the time and space for the very important work of play.

### Reprogramming the Cause-Effect Pathway

As mentioned before, the interruption of the natural order of life at relinquishment has caused a misfiring of the relationship between cause and effect for the adopted child. Thus, she has more trouble understanding consequences. Although the full impact of this deficit doesn't usually hit until adolescence, parents can't wait until then to begin the reprogramming process. Remembering that beliefs imprinted during trauma are the most deeply embedded, adopted children must be taught to recognize the connection between what they are doing and what will happen next beginning at an early age. Therapists can help by reminding the parents that their kids are not deliberately trying to do them in. Children really don't "get" the cause/effect connection. Therefore, every correction has to be *immediate* and *appropriate*. The parent should not say, "You cannot go to Jenny's house today because you didn't do your homework last Tuesday." The child will not remember this offence. If the child did not do her homework on Tuesday, then she should not have been allowed to watch television before going to bed Tuesday night, *even if it is more convenient for the parent to allow her to do so.* So many things parents let their kids get by with is because it is easier for them, not because they are trying to be nice to the kids. Therapists have to help parents be less intimidated by their children. An additional blow up today may mean a more respectful response in the future. Fairness and consistency are key here.

This training is extremely important for adopted kids, and adoptive parents must be diligent about it. The inability to discern cause and effect works in tandem with their aversion to being controlled. If they aren't taught about consequences, the kids may grow up to be very poor employees, arriving late for work, not wanting to do what they're told, etc. This extends into their other relationships making them unable to say yes to suggestions by their partners or friends because of a fear of being controlled.

### "Hey, That Hurts!"

Another neurological connection that needs reprogramming or repatterning is the "I have no impact" belief. This belief is deeply embedded in the limbic system and does not respond to neocortical input (talking about it). Experience is the better teacher. Again, it will mean that parents have to face the wrath of their children and let them know the impact of their words and behavior on them. This is important for therapists to remember, too, because it is characteristic for many therapists to be impassive in the face of their patient's outbursts. For adoptees, however, this may be counterproductive. They already feel impotent. They need to know that their behavior actually affects others. There is a difference between letting the adoptee know that they are affecting someone and rejecting them for it. The consequence for noncompliance should never be rejecting behavior on the part of parents.

Neither does this mean that parents should react with outbursts of their own. But they should let the child know that what they did or said hurt them. Remember what I said earlier that the failure of the infant's cries to get his birth mother back rendered him believing that he is impotent in his effect on others. This feeling or belief continues into childhood and adulthood unless another belief is superimposed upon the old belief. It takes thousands of experiences of the parents, other siblings, and friends letting the adoptee know that he is affecting them to finally make a dent in this archaic belief. Because most people simply resort to anger, this lets the adoptee off the hook. He can get angry back. If beneath the anger is a real experience of *being hurt*, that is what needs to be expressed. It is the foundation for his being able to understand his impact and form empathy for those he has impacted.

Rather than *telling* the child how she has affected the parent, it is more effective to *ask*, "Carol, do you have any idea how it makes me feel when you do/say that?" Saying the child's name first gets her attention. Wait for an answer. The child needs to connect her thinking about it to the emotion it brings up in her. Just telling her allows the impact to sail right by her consciousness. The appropriate facial, bodily, and emotional responses are also important. Cry, if you feel like crying. Just don't do anything disingenuous. A child can readily pick up anything false or fake. But real feelings are fine—real feelings of hurt, not the cover-up feelings of anger. I know that many adoptive mothers are deeply hurt by their children, but do their children know this or do they only see her anger? Teaching children how they affect others is one of parents' most important roles.

*Alternative Treatments*

In addition to play or attachment therapy, I believe that EMDR for children can be very helpful for adoptees. Their belief systems are so distorted as a result of that early trauma that they need to have a major "brain pattern adjustment" in order for things to change. For therapists working with children, it is necessary to take the EMDR general training first, then take workshops in working with children. Information about EMDR can be found on the Internet. A couple of good books on this subject are *Small Wonders: Healing Childhood Trauma with EMDR* by Joan Lovett and *Eye Movement Desensitization and Reprocessing in Child and Adolescent Psychotherapy* by Ricky Greenwald. Doing EMDR with children is different from doing it with adults, and special training is needed. It is well worth the effort as there are some things that cannot be changed with either talking, play therapy, or even attachment work. A key part of their recovering from trauma is the integration of the experience of separation from the birth mother so that it becomes a part of one's history, rather than an impending event.

## Living with Adolescents

When parents wait until adolescence to seek treatment for their children, the work can be very difficult. For one thing, adolescents don't take too kindly to being in therapy if they've never been in treatment before. They sometimes see it as proof that their parents think something is wrong with them. By adolescence, there have usually been years of difficulty between the parents and the child. The parents are convinced that the child is purposefully making their lives miserable, and the child is convinced that the parents are absolutely at fault for whatever is wrong. The parents feel battered by the child, and the child feels controlled by the parents. It is difficult to break through the belief system in either case. If at all possible, it is best to begin therapy before adolescence.

However, this may not have happened. Sometimes parents are loathe to give up and ask for help. Perhaps they feel like inadequate parents who are somehow responsible for their child's behavior. It isn't until adolescence, when the behavior becomes intolerable and perhaps dangerous, that parents finally realize that they are not going to be able to control the situation and they seek help. Perhaps they have sought help before and are being stonewalled by a therapist who carries confidentiality to the extreme by refusing to talk to the parents about their child. The therapist ends up colluding with the child in his distancing behavior toward his parents.

### The Myth of Rebellion

I'm not sure when Americans began buying into the idea that it is normal for teenagers to rebel against their parents. Perhaps it's when we began calling them teenagers instead of adolescents and assigned a certain behavior to them. It isn't that adolescents don't have to question the values of their parents and begin to forge some of their own, but it doesn't have to be through disrespectful and dangerous behavior. Other cultures don't condone this attitude. Why do we?

Perhaps it was during the "let it all hang out" seventies that parents began to think that expecting respectful behavior from their children would stunt their emotional growth. Some parents began to think that they had to be friends with their children, peers, as it were, rather than guides in their development. With more and more latchkey kids going home to no supervision, and parents arriving home several hours later, tired and moody, less and less attention was being paid to the attitudes and activities of these kids. Whatever the cause, the result has become an alienating and dangerous environment for both parents and their children.

How many parents really know what their children are doing? Do they know that they may be having group oral or anal sex (without condoms? "Yes, Mom! I'm still a virgin," might not be a lie, but it shouldn't bring too much comfort to parents of today's teenagers. Do they know that their kids may be going to keg parties at ages 12, 13, or 14 where parents aren't home? Do they really believe that their kids have never tried drugs? Do they know what the words of their kids' favorite songs really mean? Do they have any idea what kind of explicit sexual material they look at on the Internet? Do they know whom they are talking to in chat rooms? Are they sure their child hasn't met in person someone they met on the Internet? Do they keep track of how long their child plays violent video games? Would they even know how to find out? Do they really believe that they have no right to check on their child, to go into their rooms and look for drugs if they have reason to believe that their child is using? When did parents become so scared of their own children?

## The Second Family

I can hear it now: "Not my child. I know that Katie, James or Paul wouldn't do that. They tell me everything." Believe me, no teenager tells his or her parents everything. Did you? And these kids have much bigger and more dangerous secrets to hide. Ron Taffel, therapist and founder of the Institute for Contemporary Psychotherapy in New York is the author of a book titled *The Second Family*. He is alarmed at the change in teen behavior in the past ten years. He has interviewed hundreds of kids, parents, counselors, and teachers and has reached the conclusion that kids today consider their friends more important at this age than their parents. Taffel calls this the "second family." They hide all this behind a wall of silence, which their parents can't break. And they lie with impunity. Taffel says, "While kids have always lied to adults, never before have they lied with such ease, confidence, and lack of fear or remorse. Because of the distance between themselves and adults, they can afford to lie without qualms because they realize they are unlikely to get caught." He goes on to say that the problem is exacerbated by the facts that these kids are unsupervised by their overworked and overstressed parents and that they are living in communities where neighbors are strangers to one another. They attend large, impersonal schools where they have no sense of identity. Many kids feel unappreciated and unimportant to adults who "… are hardly aware of their existence, let alone what they are doing" (Taffel, 2001). Taffel cites a *New York Times* study which stated that in 1996 parents were spending 40% less time with their kids than they had been in 1966. The answer for these kids is to form a second family of friends and peers who seem to care about them more than adults do. They have essentially given up on the adults in their lives.

Adopted teens might have an even more pressing need to form a second family than others because they are at the height of their awareness of the differences between themselves and their parents. They feel like strangers to their parents. Unless the parents have been actively listening *as parents* to their children all along, unless the child really believes that his parents have tried to understand the way he feels, there is going to be even more alienation between teen adoptees and their parents than there was previously. Because identity is such as issue during these years, many adopted teens have a difficult time being in the presence of their adoptive parents. They spend as much time as possible with their friends. And the friends they bring home are not necessarily the friends they spend the most time with. These kids are always trying to fit in, and if they have low self-esteem, the kids they hang out with are going to be kids who also have low self-esteem and probably some other attitudes that the parents would not condone.

Cyberspace is a haven for adoptees because they can reinvent themselves all over again. They may have a difficult time knowing who they are, having lived without any genetic validation for so many years, and they can now become whoever they want to become via the Internet. They don't seem to understand that the people with whom they are chatting are also reinventing themselves. There is a lot of lying going on on the Internet

*The Silent Complicity of Parents*

Part of the problem, according to several avant garde therapists, is that parents are so intent on getting their kids to do this and that, they don't take the time to find out who their kids are, who their friends are, or what they are doing. They feel intimidated by their kids and are afraid to act like parents (i.e., in charge). Although the parents feel intimidated and often afraid of their kids, the kids themselves don't seem to feel as if they have much impact on their parents. Parents, often in the service of keeping the peace, don't let them know. According to Taffel, parents "... have bought in to the implicit ideology of the youth culture: kids are a world apart, with rights of perfect freedom and independence from adults." Let a kid know that you have every intention of checking her room every once in awhile, and you will be stunned by a diatribe about "my right to privacy and you have no right to get into my things." If a child is doing well and not causing any trouble, she has indeed earned the *privilege* of privacy. But if a child is ignoring her parents' inquiries about her activities (giving them the silent treatment)—constantly giving her parents trouble by being disobedient, irresponsible, and disrespectful—she has not earned that privilege. In any case, it is *not* a right.

Many parents feel guilty about the lack of time they spend with their kids. This may be true and regretful, but it is not a reason for these parents to act as if their kids are on the same level as they are. Parents need to expect respect from their kids. At the same time parents need to be respectful of their children. For instance, it is a good idea for parents to refrain from making rude comments about their teens' friends. Because these kids usually have a poor opinion about themselves, they identify with their "loser" friends, so that any derogatory comment the parents make about friends will immediately be construed as a comment about them. Besides, if parents were to really get to know these kids (the friends), they would probably find out that their baggy clothes, piercings, tattoos, and strange hair have very little to do with who they really are. It is crucial for parents to get to know their kids' friends, listen to their music, pay attention to the videos they watch—to discover their kids' worlds. They don't have to like it, but they should at least have some idea of what is influencing their children. Therapists should encourage the kids to let the parents into their world. Some therapists even encourage their patients to invite their friends to their sessions so that they can get to know them. After all, doesn't this make sense if the kids are spending so much time with them? Who are these kids who are having so much influence over this patient?

*A Balancing Act*

Parents have to find a balance between nurturance and expectations. They can't let guilt get in the way of their parental responsibility of preparing their child to be accountable as well as compassionate. As I've said before, this is more of a problem for parents of adopted teens or other teens who have been traumatized in some way because of the interruption in the natural order of things having made cause and effect or consequences more difficult for these kids to grasp. That is why persistence and consistency are so important. Failure to keep an agreement or an appointment, failure to do chores or homework, failure to be respectful or polite all need to be met with consequences. Parents who don't feel as if they deserve the respect of their kids need to get some help. Perhaps they don't, but why? And if they do feel they deserve respect, why are they not expecting it? Many kids, being without supervision for so many hours, feel unimportant to their parents. The parents' wavering on their expectations just reinforces this feeling.

Nurturance is also important. That may seem easy to do when the kids are little. But it is just as important when they are teens. Even if they sometimes seem indifferent about the love and attention of their parents, these kids need to know that their parents love them. One teen told me "Love is spelled TIME." Notice that she did not say, "Love is spelled Things." Too many parents are buying off their kids. "Well, I was too busy to spend much time with Junior for the past five years, so I will get him a car for his 16th birthday." This despite the fact that Junior hasn't been doing his homework and has been staying out later than his curfew. These kids might feel entitled to all the material things their parents are buying them, but they would rather have their attention—their time. As much as they whine about having to attend family gatherings, these kids really do want adult attention. They want to know that they *matter* to their parents.

## Split Personalities

It is difficult for many parents to know how their kids act in their "second family," because they act very differently than they do at home. They use different language, often wear different clothes, listen to different music, and have different values. While they may be fighting and raging against their parents at home, they may be quite compassionate and sensitive with their friends. Or they may be polite and quiet at home, but using foul language, using substances, and acting promiscuously with friends. These kids can be very good at keeping their roles straight. Adoptees can be especially good at these disguises, because they have spent their whole lives trying to fit in. They understand the chameleon. They can adapt.

## The Acting-Out Child

The kids most often brought into treatment, of course, are those who are acting out at home. They are brought in when the parents can no longer tolerate their behavior. This is true of non-adopted as well as adopted kids. There are some special considerations that adoptive parents and the children's therapists need to note. This is not to excuse the behavior of these kids, but only to offer explanations for that behavior. Most of the adoptive parents I've seen have never considered that the two most prevalent things operating in their child are *grief* and *fear*. Neither do many therapists. What they see is oppositional behavior and anger. What they don't know is that their child is attempting to mourn the loss of his first mother and to prevent the recurrence of that loss in this family. The oppositional behavior is the child's attempt to distance himself from his parents and thus save himself from more pain. His anger is often a cover-up for sorrow. He is not doing it *to them.* He is doing it *for him.*

Once the parents understand about the child's original trauma and that the behavior they are witnessing is an attempt to avoid another trauma, everything begins to make sense. They know, *even though it often feels like it,* that the child's behavior is not a personal attack on them, but a defensive device used to prevent further loss: "If I don't love too much, I won't lose too much." These kids are afraid of and puzzled by their own behavior. They are out of control, yet they won't tolerate anyone else controlling them. This is a dilemma for the parents because even the slightest suggestion is interpreted by the child as an attempt to control. Being controlled seems extremely dangerous for adopted children because they were not in control when they were separated from their mothers. This may also be true of children of divorce. They don't trust others to be in control of what happens to them, even for seemingly unimportant decisions.

### Handling Control

Even though having a heart-to-heart talk with teenagers is sometimes difficult, and more so with adopted teens, an attempt might be made to talk about the issue of control with them. This should be done when there is nothing volatile going on ... when calmness reigns. Approaching the "control issue" as a puzzle to be solved by both parents and child might work. Perhaps saying something like "You know, Johnny, it seems difficult for you to do things that we ask you to do. I've been thinking about this and I wonder if could be because you had so little to say about what happened to you in the beginning of your life—when you were separated from your birth mother and your first family. You were not in control then, and it may be scary for you to let others even make suggestions now. Have you ever thought about this?" Not many kids would have thought of this. They just think that their parents are trying to control their every move. And it doesn't mean that they will jump right on the band wagon now. But it is planting a seed. (I believe in planting seeds!)

If the child is receptive to continuing the talk, then there should follow a discussion about how he might distinguish between the parents just wanting to control him and their trying to help guide him into adulthood. Instead of going ballistic over some request that the parents make, they can ask him to tell them what he doesn't like about their request and perhaps compromise on a different pathway. It might be good if the teen would agree to notice the number of times during the day that he rejects the requests or suggestions of others. He probably has no idea how often this occurs. His becoming aware of this phenomenon can cause him to think about it and decide how he wants to handle this aspect of his fear.

Perhaps asking him to keep a log of the number of requests he truly believes are dangerous and those he might actually like to honor would be a good plan. He may be surprised to discover the number of times he puts the kybosh on things he would really like to do. So far as following the guidance of his parents, he would have to be willing to look honestly at each request and decide if it would be in his best interest or not. For instance, the suggestion that it might be time to start his homework might be seen as less threatening if he were to honestly look at his parents' motives vs. his own. If the parents convey the idea that what they have in mind is to make it possible for him to have more and more privileges, he might have an interest in doing something about this. If the child finds it difficult to have a face-to-face discussion with his parents, it might be a good idea to conduct this experiment through notes. Even if it doesn't seem as if anything is happening about this issue in the present, planting the seed about control having a connection to his relinquishment can create a window of opportunity for change in the future.

### Revisiting Cause and Effect

In emphasizing the relationship between taking responsibility for his actions and privileges, parents will still be instilling the relationship between cause and effect on their adolescent children. If the parents have been working on this for years, it should not be such a tough job during adolescence. If they haven't, it can be very frustrating. It is not that the kids are trying to be stubborn. They really don't "get" consequences the way other kids do. This makes giving consequences for non-compliance or unacceptable behavior more difficult, because the children do not project enough into the future to understand what will actually happen if they behave in a certain way. Again, it is very important to be *immediate, appropriate,* and *consistent* with consequences for the behaviors the parents want to correct. As I've said, it has to be taught over and over again. That part of the brain where the natural order of things turned to chaos is deeply imprinted in the neurological system. This is one reason that structure, consistency, and fairness are so important. It takes thousands of repetitions to change that limbic imprint. Hopefully, this repatterning began long before adolescence because by then the parents may have already lost the power struggle. If not, the parents have to form an alliance of strength to teach this lesson before the child goes out into the world.

*Fitting In*

It is also very important for these kids to be like everyone else. Find out what most of the kids are wearing to school and get those clothes for your kids. I always tell parents not to sweat the small stuff. Clothes and hair are small stuff. At certain stages in life, children like to dress in a manner that their parents won't like very well and do unusual things to their hair. Believe me, although it may seem like a big deal to parents who want a certain image, it is *not* a big deal. Drugs, alcohol, stealing, and sex are big deals. The image "thing" is especially important for adoptees because even though they love their families, they may not feel as if they fit. Fitting in is something they long for. Dressing and doing their hair like the kids they hang around with in school is very important to their sense of belonging.

*The Acting-In Adoptee*

Not all adopted children act out, but all adopted children have suffered loss. Instead of acting out, some children become detached, compliant, acquiescent, or clingy. Or as one adoptee in Vancouver, B.C., put it, "My brother acted out, while I acted in." All the pain is pushed down into the unconscious, where it festers and leaks out from time to time. All the while the acquiescent adoptee is walking the tightrope of trying to be perfect—trying to fit into the adoptive family, just as he perceives his adoptive parents want him to. Adoptees displaying either of these two responses need help, because neither is owning his true feelings: One is projecting the feelings onto the adoptive parents and perceiving these feelings as coming from them, and the other is burying them in the unconscious and becoming numb.

A therapist or parent has to be exquisitely observant to find out just what is going on with the "acting-in child." Daydreaming, especially at school, can be a sign that the child is dissociating. Watching too much television or spending too much time on the Internet can be a hint that something is wrong. Sometimes it is through her art work or poetry that hints are given as to her inner life. One mother of a cheerful, sociable 16-year-old adoptee came to me with her daughter's poetry. She couldn't understand how such a happy child could write such dark verse. The dark poetry (all about loss, loneliness, and the need for merger) was a more accurate reflection of her daughter's inner state of mind. The cheerful, exuberant teen was for public consumption. Other times it is through her relationships with her friends that hints about problems can surface. What is the nature of the friendships? How long do they last? What is the reason for their demise? Is this a pattern?

For the very young child, observing her play can be helpful, as I've mentioned. As she gets older, does she spend an inordinate amount of time in her room listening to music or reading? She may seldom talk about adoption and act as if being adopted doesn't bother her at all. Her method of distancing is to withdraw. She may spend more time with her pets than with friends. The withdrawn child is numb to her feelings. Her sole purpose in life is to make sure that she doesn't do anything to trigger a rejection. She is living the "false" or "partial" self. Reality is confusing, because the adoptee has to deal with a *dual reality*, half of which (the half that feels real) she wants to bury. Both the compliant and the defiant adoptee are living a dual reality. The first reality—his biological and genetic connection to his birth parents—is in competition with the second reality of being a member of his adoptive family. (An explanation of *dual reality* is found in the previous chapter.)

The challenge for the therapist with the acting-in adoptee will be to uncover the well-hidden feelings of these children. They have gone numb in their efforts to keep from feeling intolerable emotions. Dazed or being in a trance might be a good way to describe some of these kids. Although they walk through the activities of their lives seemingly unscathed, they are disconnected from their emotions, which is evident if one looks closely. It takes a patient and skilled therapist to break through the walls erected by these kids in order for them to feel safe. Why bother, parents may ask, when the child is not causing trouble? She seems fine. The child *isn't* fine. These same issues which plague the acting-out adoptee are also plaguing the quiet adoptee. They will seep out in her relationships regardless of her efforts to keep them hidden. They must be brought out into the light of day in a safe situation and worked through. These are the adoptees I most often see in therapy as adults. Failed relationships often bring them in, and the core issues of abandonment and loss are what must be addressed. As adults many of them suffer from the "disease to please," the inability to say no to people for fear of being disliked or rejected.

*Projective Identification*

Whereas the acting-out child's feelings seem to fly out in all directions, the more acquiescent child's feelings are buried so deeply as to be inaccessible. Both the acting-out child and the acting-in child may use projective identification as a means of communicating how they are feeling inside, but they are projecting different aspects of their pain. The acting-out child may project anger, hostility, chaos, frustration, and the fear of being controlled; while the acting-in child may project helplessness, fear of rejection, inadequacy, confusion, loneliness, and hopelessness.

*The Great Myths*

There are two myths which therapists need to purge from their understanding of adoptive families. Both myths perpetuate the adoptee's sense of unreality. These are the *chosen child* myth and the *grateful child* myth. Being told that he is chosen places a great burden on a child to be the perfect child of his parents. It also runs contrary to his feeling that he was *unchosen* by the birth mother. After all, it isn't true that he was chosen by the adoptive parents, as if from a row of available babies. It was not true when agencies were in charge of adoptions and chose who could be adoptive parents, nor is it true today, (except in those terrible Adoption Day circuses, where children are put on display like puppies at a pet store). Today it may be the birth mother who is choosing the adoptive parents for her child, rather than an agency. In both cases, it is the parents who are chosen, not the child. (In the case of adopting a child from a foreign orphanage, the child might indeed be chosen, but again, his experience is having already been unchosen by his birth mother.)

So far as being grateful, it is the parents who should more appropriately feel grateful, not the child. They wanted a child, and they got a child. It was a decision they made about which the child had absolutely no say. Why would a child be grateful for having been taken from his mother and all his relatives and given to genetic strangers? No matter how nurturing, loving, or affluent the adoptive parents may be, living with genetic strangers is a very hard life for a child; he has to spend tremendous amounts of energy trying to fit into a family in which he feels alien. Adoptees make very good mimics if they feel it is necessary to their survival.

# Treatment

*Getting Help*

At some point in their child's life, when parents of difficult teens decide that they've had enough, they want a therapist to "fix it." Some of them are genuinely interested in understanding their part in the alienation with their child and want to be involved in the therapeutic process. Others want to just drop their kids off and let the therapist deal with them. More and more therapists are realizing that this latter method doesn't work. Kids are too alienated from their parents already. They don't need another forum for alienation to take place—a kind of triangulation between the parents, therapist, and child.

So how should therapists deal with these kids? For the most part, I am not necessarily talking only about adopted kids here. I am talking about teenagers in general. As more and more kids are spending more and more time away from family members, there are more kids feeling disenfranchised and alienated from their parents. Who are these kids, and what can be done?

## Blurring the Boundaries

One of the problems today seems to be that many parents are not taking their role seriously. They are intimidated by their angry, foul-mouthed kids. They may yell back at their kids and complain that they can't get them to do anything, but they are not assuming authority in the family. This is confusing for teenagers. Jerome Price and Judith Margerum of the Michigan Family Institute say, "Our society isn't teaching them that while they are valuable individuals, they don't have the same authority as adults. ... As long as parents are reactive, and feel helpless and hopeless, the young person wields the power, dominates, controls, and simultaneously suffers" (Price & Mergerum, 2000). It is natural to have a power struggle going on, but the adults in the house have lived longer and *do* know more than their kids. They need to assume the leadership roles. Otherwise the kids don't feel safe. Or as Dr. Phil says, "It is hoped that you won't have to have an argument with your child, but if you do, be sure that you win." This, of course, is assuming that the parents are mature and fair in their interactions with their children.

Sometimes a power struggle arises when therapy is suggested by the parents. I have heard parents say, "Well, we'll start David in therapy and see how he likes it." Then if things aren't rolling along as fast as David wants them to (i.e., he's stonewalling), or if he finds it inconvenient to be in therapy instead of out fooling around with his friends, they allow him to quit. "He didn't seem to be getting anything out of it," they say. But what has changed at home to make these parents believe they can now tolerate his insolence and intimidation? Do *they* think their kid should quit? If not, why are they allowing it? Most of these kids don't trust anyone. It takes awhile for therapy to have any meaning for them. They need to stick with it and the parents should be the ones to see to it that they do. What Price and Mergerum suggest is to let the kid know that therapy will be going on with or without her and that the parents and therapist will be making decisions for her without her input if she chooses not to attend. That usually generates a little more interest in the process.

Therapists, too, fall under the spell of trying to be friends with the patient. While it is a good idea to try to get to know the kid before asking the hard questions, it is a mistake to make him think that he and the therapist will be buddies on one team and the parents on the other. The child isn't there to make another friend. He is there because he needs help. Instead of creating an atmosphere of "I'm here for you, kid, and I know your parents don't understand you," the therapist should include the parents in the process. After all, they have to live with him and he with them. It doesn't do any good for the therapist and patient to have a wonderful relationship if the parents are seeing the same old things at home. As I said, I don't believe in the "all teenagers are expected to be disobedient, disrespectful, and irresponsible" myth. Neither do I believe that they deserve to be disrespected, abused, and maligned.

Getting to know the patient before delving into difficult problems only makes sense. What are his interests, talents, favorite music, or favorite classes at school? How does he like school? Who are his friends? What do they like to do? Then some of the more "meaty" questions can evolve: What are his gripes with his parents? What specifically are they doing that he so dislikes? How does he think he might be contributing to the problems? Does he see any of this as being dangerous? Of course, some of this will be superficial at first, but sometimes it is the first time that someone has paid this much attention to the kid at one sitting. He gradually begins to believe that he is being taken seriously. I rarely have found that these kids believe in their own bravado. When they are listened to and taken seriously, they become more genuine and begin to see some of the ways they are sabotaging themselves.

The issue of confidentiality has to be seen in a different light. It needs to be made clear to the teen that although the therapist isn't going to divulge to his parents what he is saying, he will be discussing things he learns with them so that they can be more effective parents. Price and Margerum say, "We see teens alone at times, but almost never for a full session. We make it clear that we're closely involved with parents and we will use our judgment as to what we share with them." In many states, when working with minors confidentiality is held within the family, not by individual family members. Keeping the parents up to speed on things which directly affect family life makes for a more cohesive therapy. It is also very important for therapists to really know the parents of the kids they are seeing because teenagers have a skewed perception of their parents. I am not one of those therapists who think that everyone in the family needs a different therapist. I believe that this creates tunnel vision for the therapist and is a great handicap.

### Common Mistakes of Therapists Working with Adoptees

Price and Margerum list four mistakes that many therapists make when working with adolescents. The first is *courting the teenage client*, which has been discussed above. The second is *telling the parents to back off*. When the therapist gets too aligned with the teenager against the parents, he will often believe that what the patient needs is a little "breathing room." What Price, Margerum, and Taffel believe, and I concur, is that there is already too much breathing room between parents and their kids. What these kids need is *more* guidance, not less. When they are acting out, they may not have as many privileges or as much privacy or leniency as they want. They haven't earned it. It is important for the therapist to help the parents stand firm about this.

The third mistake is *relying on family communication.* Teaching communication skills is important in working with couples. However, communication is not the number one problem in most American families with teens—the power struggle is. Therapists have to help parents keep from getting into endless discussions about who is to blame and help them keep from thinking that they need to justify their positions. These kids are experts in refocusing the problem and making everything their parents' fault. For instance, if a mother confronts her son about the cocaine she found in his room, he will immediately start a diatribe about how she didn't have any right to go into his room and mess with his things and how now he can't trust her, and so on and so on ad nauseam. The whole issue has been diverted from his drug use to his mother's invading his privacy. Often the mother will get defensive and think that she has to justify herself. She loses all credibility if she does this. The very nature of what she found is her justification. She doesn't have to say a word. She can ask a question: "What did I find in there, Billy?" Then make him answer the question. At which point she can say, "End of discussion." Her son hasn't earned the privilege of privacy. (By the way, parents have to make clear to their kids that keeping drugs for their friends is punishable in the same way as keeping them for themselves—just in case there are any parents out there who still believe this old excuse.)

Price and Margerum also warn parents against telegraphing their strategies as to how they are going to handle certain problems. By the time parents get through telling their kids what they are going to do, the kids have figured out a way to get around their interference. They say, "Often, we actually coach parents to be more mysterious and indirect by keeping their knowledge and plans to themselves." They give an example of parents learning about an unsupervised party that their kids plan to attend. Instead of confronting the kids about it, they suggest organizing a group of parents to show up at the house and break up the party. They also suggest talking less and listening more to find out what their kids are up to. Whatever they do, parents have to stop justifying good parenting interventions. *Since when did parents have to justify being good parents?*

The fourth mistake therapists make is *succumbing to tunnel vision.* By this the authors mean that there are other people and agencies who can help parents with what is going on. Too often parents are embarrassed by what their kids are doing, and they are loathe to ask for help from family, friends, or authorities. This can be especially difficult for single parents rearing their children alone. If there is another adult in the household, he or she can be enlisted to help. It should be made clear to kids that the adults in the household all have an interest in what they are doing. Any, "You can't tell me what to do; you aren't my father," kind of remarks need to be discouraged. A parent should never allow any kind of abuse by another member of the household, but ordinary discipline and guidance should be every adult's responsibility. If we believe that "it takes a village to rear a child," then we can certainly start with all the people within one household.

The village can extend into the neighborhood. Many people have noted that neighbors don't know one another and therefore there is no help from them when trouble happens. Getting to know one's neighbors certainly seems like a good idea. We really do need to stop being so isolated in our communities. But another problem I have noticed with neighbors helping to keep an eye on other people's kids is that instead of appreciating others taking an interest in their kids, parents often deride the neighbors and tell them to mind their own business. Even when teachers discipline students, some parents immediately come to their child's defense without even trying to find out what really happened. This, I believe, is born out of parents' guilt about their own lack of discipline and control over their kids. This is a way they can connect with their kids—always defend them against others' accusations—us against them. This tactic simply reinforces a child's belief that he doesn't have to be accountable for his actions, and is unhelpful. Sometimes it is appropriate for parents to come to their children's defense. There are some people who have a strange idea of what is appropriate behavior for young people today, yet most people have some understanding of children. We need to begin helping one another. Our children need this.

It is important to remember that these kids, for all their bravado and offensive language, are vulnerable. They are very unsure of themselves. It doesn't help their self-esteem for the adults in their lives to ignore the things that are causing them problems. It doesn't make them feel more loved. They need our care and understanding, as well as our rules and regulations. But most of all they need our time and attention.

### The "Blank-Slate" Therapist

Kids today are so used to adults ignoring them that for a therapist to be neutral or unemotional in the face of some of their outrageous statements or incidents would be just reinforcing old patterns. Taffel tells about a 15-year-old boy who relates that he smoked dope in the band room at school. Instead of asking, "How does that make you feel?" Taffel shouts, "My God! That's crazy! What was going on that made you do a dumb thing like that?" This genuinely got the kid's attention, and after a thoughtful silence he said, "You're right. It was dumb." Taffel goes on, "Thus begins a real conversation ..." Kids are savvy about therapy—from TV, movies, or reports from their friends—and they can easily fool therapists who do nothing but ask about their feelings. These kids sometimes ask for advice. How do you think they feel when the therapist says, "Well, what would you do?" They don't *know* what to do. That's why they're asking. This doesn't mean that the therapist always has to tell a kid what to do, but it does mean that the options have to be explored, not just the kid's feelings about it. And sometimes they definitely need to be given advice about things they're afraid to talk to their parents about. It is also important for the therapist to work toward bringing the parents into the picture and helping the child and parent become more adept at attacking problems, not just each other.

*Expectations*

One thing many parents have problems with is expecting accountability of their kids. Kids want privileges without responsibilities. They don't see any problem with going out with their friends on Friday night, even though they were too sick to go to school that day. Teaching kids to be responsible is not the same as allowing them to have the same authority as adults. Therapists also have to help to teach accountability by insisting that the teenager, not the parents, call to reschedule or cancel appointments and, with rare exceptions, to insist on a 24-hour limit for doing so. Therapy has to be taken seriously. It cannot be seen as something to do if there is nothing else to do. There can be more flexibility in certain aspects of therapy with kids, such as length of sessions and location of sessions. It is sometimes easier for kids to talk to a therapist if they are taking a walk than if they are seated across from one another in a room. Sometimes this is good just for a change. It is also enlightening to allow for e-mail messages from these young patients. It might be easier for a teen to be more forthcoming in an e-mail message than face to face with the therapist. Of course, the therapist needs to bring up the subject of the message at the next session, but kids often find this easier than bringing it up in the session themselves.

*Narration*

For older children, some kind of narrative therapy is advised, even if the child is loathe to write. Narrative is very important in the development of the brain, and it is helpful in the effort to integrate painful events in one's life. These stories don't have to be factual, but may be symbolic. Sometimes writing about a fictional family can allow for more honesty about what is going on and how the child perceives her place in her family. This can be the more advanced version of using puppets. Listening to the child reading her story out loud is important, because she needs someone to bear witness to her experience, whether she presents it as her experience or not. She also gets more in touch with the feelings generated by the story in the reading than in the writing. Children should not be challenged as to the accuracy of their stories. Later, as adults, they can discover that not everyone saw the events in their lives in exactly the same way.

These are meant to be only some suggestions as to how to effectively treat adolescents. There are many therapists who are very good at working with this age group. It is important for these therapists to be aware of some of the special considerations that need to be taken into account when working with adopted teens. Without this knowledge, therapy can get off on the wrong track.

## Treating the Parents

If they are willing, I also treat the parents because by the time the parents bring the child in for therapy, the child has managed to tap into the parents' own abandonment and loss issues. If the parents act from that wounded-child place in their relationship with their child, the effectiveness of their parenting will be compromised. I try to help parents learn not to react to triggers. The degree of success I have with this will be determined by the parent's own emotional maturity. Maintaining emotional maturity is difficult with acting-out children because these children intuitively know their parents' Achilles' heels. Through the mechanism of projective identification they can make their parents feel their own emotions, thus causing many parents to act on feelings of rejection in frustration, anger, and hostility and sometimes with violence. If there are obvious loss or abuse issues that the parents have not previously addressed, it would be important for them to get some individual therapy, otherwise they will be constantly triggered by their child's issues and unable to maintain a strong parental position. It is crucial that parents control the expressions of overwhelming feelings, as difficult as it may be. And it *is* difficult. Only another adoptive parent can know how provocative these kids can be.

### Entitlement

Part of that provocation is difficult to pinpoint because it is in the subtle disallowing of the parents to be 100% the parents. As John Bowlby states when talking about children being raised by someone other than the biological parent, the child begins to act *almost* as if the caretaker is the parent. That "almost" can cause a sense of rejection, frustration, and anger in parents, even though they may not understand what it is they are reacting to. Some adoptive parents actually *expect* their children to be like them. They discourage any "aberration" from the family norm. The idea that their child has a genetic identity and may be quite different from them is something that never enters their minds. In this case, many tendencies the child has that the parents don't understand are interpreted as obstinacy and are criticized or punished by the parents. Their sense of entitlement is exaggerated because they extrapolate it to mean that the child has to be like them. They feel entitled to his very soul. This will backfire, as the child will feel misunderstood and will distance himself from the parents even more, even though the parents may be unaware of it. One can force one's child to *act* as if he is the child of those parents, but one can't force him to *feel* that way.

My advice for adoptive parents is to forget it. You cannot force a certain relationship, because the child is dealing with a dual reality that seems contradictory to him. It would be better to acknowledge the reality of the relationship and deal with the child from this reality. Sensitive parents know this and do so. This takes a great burden from the child, who consciously may want to *be* the child of the adoptive parents, but often feels different from them.

Parents are sometimes blamed because they don't feel entitled to their child. But that feeling is there because, although the child may be *with* that family, she cannot be entirely *of* that family. It is a feeling conveyed to the parents *by the child*. The child is unconsciously trying to preserve her sense of her genetic self. She cannot wholly become a member of a non-genetic family, even if consciously she may want to. She has a dual reality which cannot be denied, although there is often a great effort to do so for the purposes of survival. It helps just to know that being an adoptive family is *different from being a biological family* and accepting that fact. Neither legal papers nor ritualistic ceremonies change the DNA of the adopted child. Neither do they cancel out his loss.

*Pulling in the Mother*

The parent most often maligned in the adoptive family is the mother. She is the greatest threat to the child because she has the potential to re-enact the abandonment. She needs education and a great deal of support and encouragement by the therapist in order to cope with the almost constant (if she is dealing with the acting-out child) opposition and verbal abuse from her child. The father often blames her for the arguments that go on between her and her child because he does not see the subtle scenes which provoke her anger. The child needs to connect with the mother, but he must do it in a "safe" way (i.e., through anger and hostility, rather than affection and cooperation). Just asking the mother not to engage in the adversarial banter is not enough. There is a way in which these children drag her in kicking and screaming despite her resolving not to allow it. If she tries to disengage, the child finds a way to pull her back in. She is between a rock and a hard place, and it seems as if there is no way out. What this mother needs from the therapist are ways to respond to the child which keep the child both safe and connected. This is not easy, especially during adolescence, and it doesn't always work, but it's worth a try.

One of the things parents might do is to throw a barbecue party for their child and her friends. This is a way to get to know her friends and for these friends to experience a party in a safe environment. Even if the child at first doesn't want to (after all, no alcohol will be allowed and her friends might think she's square), if she is a part of the planning process, it might work. She might even be surprised that her friends actually welcome the idea. Some of these kids may be yearning for a caring, involved family. Another thing that a mother and daughter might want to do is to get their nails done together. The mother can let the daughter have any kinds of swirls and so forth on her nails that she wants. Fathers can take their sons to ball games or go fishing, ballooning, or rock climbing. They can do the same with daughters, if that is something that interests them. The parents can tap into their child's interests and do something together like attending a big league ball game or an art gallery opening. If they take their earplugs, they might even enjoy going to a rock concert with their kids. Kids sometimes get a big kick out of having their parents witness some of the outrageous behavior that goes on there. For some reason, it is usually easier to convince a teen to do these things with one parent, rather than with both. Perhaps it is because they are the center of that parent's attention for a few hours.

### How to Deal with Adoptee Intimidation

Therapists can help parents become more adroit at dealing with intimidation by their children. Because being controlled (i.e., responding positively to suggestions) is such an issue for adoptees, every instruction the parent gives can be the spark for an explosion from the child. Getting a handle on this needs to begin early. When children are young, it is helpful to validate their feelings before correcting their behavior. For instance, "I know that you are angry with me, Karen, but you will have to get ready for bed when this program is over." This validates the child's feelings without giving up parental authority. It shows that although the parent notices the child's feelings, it doesn't change the outcome of what is going to happen. In other words, having feelings about having to go to bed at a certain time is fine, but it doesn't mean that bedtime will be changed just because "a really good program" is coming up next. However, as the children mature into adolescence, validating their feelings just seems to make them angrier. Teenagers don't want parents telling them how they feel or that they understand their feelings. They don't think anyone understands their feelings. In a sense, they're right, but *they* don't understand their feelings either. When they get out of control, it scares them. They *need* their parents to rein them in no matter how difficult that may be. When parents become intimidated by their children's behavior and fail to address what is going on *while* it is going on, things will escalate. Yes, it will seem as if the situation is escalating at the time, but the parents have to remain firm and consistent. (It must be noted that the same thing happens in therapy sometimes; things may escalate before they calm down.)

What a mother must *not* do is to allow the child to hurt her then get off scot free. By that I mean that a mother may be so stunned by the ferociousness of her child's attack that she is left speechless. Five minutes later the child returns and says, "What's for dinner, Mom?" as if nothing had happened. (I hear this over and over from astonished mothers of teenagers.) The mother fails to see how she is contributing to this astonishing phenomenon. Even though she is still reeling from her child's attack, she does not want to start another altercation now that the child has calmed down, so she acts as if nothing happened five minutes ago: "Hamburgers and salad. Ice cream for dessert," she answers. The child, not understanding that she had any impact on her mother at all, goes about her business until another scene takes place. While everyone else may be aware that she is in fact setting up the dynamics of the entire family, she feels as if she is Casper the Ghost, leaving no impression. Because of the HUGE impact she has on the family as a whole and the adoptive mother in particular, it is very difficult to make these families understand that the child is unaware of the control she is exerting on the family dynamics.

What the mother (or father or sister or brother—and later partners and spouses) must do is to let the adoptee know *right then*—at the time of the abusive behavior—that he is having an impact. They must ask him if he realizes how much it hurts to have him say or do whatever it is he said or did. *Ask, don't tell.* He needs to take part in the exploration process of looking at his inappropriate and hurtful behavior. Sometimes those who are affected must just say "STOP!" and halt the "discussion" in its tracks. At other times, when one is truly hurting, it might be a good idea to cry if that is what one feels like doing. This will truly amaze the adoptee, who will have no idea that he was having such an effect. Every time the adoptee gets by with hurting others and not having it brought to his attention, it reinforces the belief that he has no impact. It is not a conscious thing. He is not thinking, "Oh, I guess I have no impact on this person." It is simply a belief way down in the depths of his being.

The problem is that the acting-out child is so intimidating no one wants to cause another problem when the crisis has passed and things seem to be going well. Therefore, no one wants to talk about the impact that the abusive behavior wrought. That's all right, though, because it should not be brought up at a later time. It can't be discussed later because the adoptee will absolutely not remember having done anything wrong. His perception is distorted by his belief that he has no impact, so he rarely remembers the transgression. It is therefore imperative to address the transgression at the time it is taking place. Never mind that things will escalate. It's bad already, so what's a couple more decibels? This is very important: *Offensive behavior must be handled at the time of commitment, and it must be consistent.* This means that the victim of the offensive behavior must respond with words of astonishment or disappointment, hurt or tears (not an angry, out-of-control reaction to the child, but an honest emotional response) immediately. Too many parents don't want to give their child the "satisfaction" of knowing that they got to them. This is a mistake. Letting them get by with it because the parents want to feel invulnerable reinforces the child's belief of having no impact. How can they take responsibility for their actions if they believe they don't matter? No matter how frightening and unappealing it may seem, allowing the problem to get worse in the moment will have better long-term results for the future. This is very important for relationships later because one of the most consistent complaints I hear from partners of adoptees is adoptees they don't seem to care how they affect others.

### Helpful Support

With the help and support of a good therapist, adoptive parents can find the courage to stand firm in the face of the intimidating behavior of the acting-out adolescent. The therapist has to truly understand the ways in which separation trauma has formed the core issues of the child. If not, he or she will have no idea how desperate these children are to be in control (or to not be controlled). Fear is at the core of their oppositional behavior. Even innocuous suggestions like being asked to put on their shoes seem like being controlled to these kids. It makes life very difficult for parents, especially when the kids do not take responsibility for their chores, homework, and other normal activities of family life. The difficulty they have with cause and effect exacerbates this problem because often they do not plan ahead. As bedtime creeps up and the homework is not done, a parent might suggest that it is getting late and it might be a good idea to begin the homework. The angry, hostile, intimidating responses that follow such innocuous remarks are truly amazing. These kids are masters of twisting the facts so that it seems as if the parents are to blame for whatever is going on. For instance, they may take no responsibility for the fact that the homework is not done, and instead redirect the attention onto the parents for trying to control them. Before therapists believe that these kids have extremely nagging parents, they need to walk in their shoes for a couple of days. This kind of behavior does not happen with people who are not important in the child's life, therefore most people are not witnesses to it. Neighbors or friends, who correctly find these kids charming and well-behaved, are loath to believe the parents' report of their at-home-only behavior. This is one reason support groups for adoptive parents are necessary—no one else will believe their stories, but they will validate and understand one another's. Parents need encouragement and support as they try to give guidance to children who are afraid of both connection and control.

## Caring for Siblings

When there is an acting-out adoptee in the family, biological children or the quiet adoptee may feel left out a great deal of the time. There is a feeling that the only way they could get as much attention as the acting-out child would be to sustain some injury that would make them handicapped. As easy as it would be to tell the adoptive parents that they have to attend to these other children, it is sometimes almost impossible to do because the acting-out child is in constant need of attention to feel as if she exists. Therefore, any inattention to her activities makes her *up the ante* until attention is paid. In addition, the mother is often preoccupied with trying to connect with this resistant child, so even when she is ostensibly paying attention to the other children, there is an air of disconnection in that interaction. This may make the other children feel less important than the acting-out child.

It is a good idea for the parents to have one-on-one time with the other children away from the acting-out child. Sometimes it is only in being away that their entire attention can be placed on the siblings. These siblings may be very angry at their acting-out sister or brother for causing the parents so much trouble and for taking attention away from them. They sometimes understand the reasons, but often do not, even if they themselves are adopted. Even if they do understand, being in the presence of this interaction day after day gets frustrating. Some of these kids need to be in therapy also in order to work through their experience of feeling less important than their sibling who is getting so much attention or about their anger and frustration with their sibling or parents.

## Saying "I'm Sorry"

Therapists can help adoptive parents learn to say they are sorry for the way the lopsided attention on the acting-out child has affected the other children. In the chapter on Reunions I tell birth mothers the same thing: It isn't enough to speak in the abstract. For adoptive parents, this won't do: "I'm sorry *you were hurt* by the attention I paid to your brother, but you know how much attention he demanded." Not only does this offer an excuse (or reason) for what the mother did, but it puts the onus on the child—*you were hurt.* He might think that if he had been a better or stronger child, he wouldn't have been hurt by his mother's inattention. The onus has to be on the mother: "I'm sorry *I hurt you.*" Period. No caveats, excuses, or reasons. The *child inside* has to hear the mother take responsibility for what she did without making excuses. The reasons are probably understood by the other children anyway. Yet no matter how distorted she believes the children's ideas of her motives are, there is something absolutely necessary about the mother's being able to take responsibility and apologizing for how her actions affected her children. I know first hand how difficult this is. There are many times during my daughters' childhoods when their perceptions were so far removed from what I intended that it stuns me. But it doesn't matter. We have to apologize for *their perceptions (how we affected them), not our intentions.* As difficult as this is, it works wonders.

Remember the quotation by Molly Layton about her emotional experience with her children? I believe it bears repeating, because it is so true:

> *The mother is the object, the bull's eye, of her children's feelings, some of which could stun an ox. She is intensely loved, hated, seized, ignored. I was thunderstruck by the blunt distortions my children made of my motives, and then at other times struck by their keen accuracy. In writing this, it occurs to me that they might say the same of me.*
> *Layton, 1989*

There are many misunderstandings in the rearing of children. Children don't perceive things the way adults do, yet it is their perceptions which shape their belief systems. Because we are the adults, it is up to us to apologize for our effect, no matter how good our intentions. Difficult, but necessary. When our children become adults, it is time to talk about some of the things that we may have done to mold their beliefs about themselves. If we are courageous and can say we're sorry, they will later be able to hear our interpretations of our motives. And, of course, when they become parents, they will begin to understand just how easy it is to have our intentions distorted by the minds of children.

### Choosing Good Therapists

Everyone will be changed by the addition into the family of a child who has suffered separation trauma. For therapists to work effectively with these families, they will have to acknowledge the differences between adoptive and biological families. They should be familiar with the latest in brain research because the way in which early trauma affects the neurological system is key to understanding adoptees. For therapists who have never thought of the differences between biological and adoptive families, it would be helpful to read "What Doctors Need to Know about Adoptive Families" and "What Adoptive Parents Can Do" in the Appendix of this book or on my Web site: www.primalwound.com. Adoptive parents and their children need understanding, support, and education, rather than blame and guilt. With the exception of those parents who are truly abusive, most adoptive parents really want to do what is best for their children. All parents—biological and adoptive—make mistakes with their children. In addition to dealing with the normal developmental issues of childhood, adoptive parents have to address issues related to their child's trauma while working without genetic cues. They often need help with this. There should be no stigma attached to asking for help. Good therapists, who truly understand the primal wound—the emotional, physical, neurological, and psychological manifestations of this wound—can educate the parents, so they can better help their children.

# CHAPTER 19
## Defining Adult Pathology

In my book *The Primal Wound: Understanding the Adopted Child,* I attempted to outline a realistic experience of relinquishment and adoption from the adoptee's point of view. The main point of the book was to validate the adoptee's experience and feelings as normal. Thus far in this book I have attempted to address the idea that adoptees' coping mechanisms, most of which have been in place since birth, need to be exchanged for the authentic, adult self. This involves not allowing the vestiges of the wounded child to influence her attitudes, decisions, and behavior, but to strive for a mature attitude toward herself and her relationships with others. Some of this can be accomplished by becoming aware of the differences between trauma-driven attitudes and behaviors and those of the authentic self.

However, reading my books, self-help books, or any other book is not the whole answer to gaining some control over the reactions to early trauma. It is like reading a book on gardening: You now have an idea what you want and some idea how to go about it, but in order to have a garden, work has to be done. It takes digging in and getting messy; it takes planting seeds and pulling weeds. It takes fertilizing, pruning, and transplanting. In other words, it takes work! It takes engagement. Healing, like gardening, is not a spectator sport. But unlike gardening, healing from separation trauma cannot be done alone. It began with the separation of two people and it has to be healed with the connection of two people.

### Getting the Right Help

Although much can be accomplished by following some of the ideas set forth in this book, there are certain aspects of separation trauma which need the help of another person. This is where therapy comes in. However, in order to be effective, a person has to have the right therapist and the right treatment plan. By that I don't mean that there is only one method that can be used, but that the right issues have to be addressed. Much of what is done in therapies that do not address the issues of *abandonment and loss* can be ineffective or even harmful. In most cases, the therapist does not consider what happened *before* the adoptive parents received the child. The health of the adoptee seems to depend upon his or her adaptation or lack thereof in the adoptive family—*whoever has the best false self wins!* Rarely do therapists see that the treatment of adoptees has to take into consideration the trauma of separation, which occurred before adoption took place.

Because many clinicians have not been aware that there is a difference between biological and adoptive families, it has been assumed that the substitution of mothers and the loss of biological heritage has had little or no effect on the adoptee. Their true experiences and feelings have been unacknowledged or discounted. As mentioned in the last chapter, in biological families the problems of the child are seen as projections of the problems of the parents—scapegoating. What happens then is that not only are the parents looked upon with suspicion, but the children are not helped and the family is not healed.

Many of the patients I see in my practice who have been in previous therapies have been incorrectly diagnosed and, therefore, have been receiving inadequate treatment. As children they were treated as simple cases of oppositional disorder, anxiety disorder, or some other cubbyhole diagnosis, without any consideration being given to the fact that they were living in a biologically alien family. Trying to figure out *how to be* in those families can be exhausting and frustrating. The acting out of the frustrated, angry adoptee, especially during adolescence, has sometimes resulted in their being placed in hospitals or treatment centers, where the staff had no idea about separation trauma or the difficulty in living in a family without any genetic markers. Adoptees spend years in therapy as children, then enter adulthood with the same core issues of abandonment and loss unresolved.

The issues of abandonment and loss result in symptoms which mimic borderline personality disorder or schizoid disorder thus predicating the wrong treatment. This is because the clinicians' bible, the Diagnostic and Statistical Manual of Mental Disorders (the DSM), presents symptomatology without etiology. In my opinion, this is dangerous and irresponsible because it can result in a particular treatment plan which might be counter-indicated for anyone suffering from separation trauma.

*Birth and Adoptive Parent Pain*

The adoptee is not the only member of the adoption triad who is suffering. The pain of the birth mother, who mourned the loss of her surrendered child in isolation, is frequently interpreted as pathological if the pain is uncovered by a therapist. Having been seen as unworthy of parenting her child and encouraged (read that coerced) to relinquish him to "more deserving" people, the birth mother is told, "But you did the right thing," as if that would eliminate her pain. This is unconscionable for therapists to say, because they, of all people, should understand the disparity between thoughts and feelings. The true experiences of the birth mother—her pain of loss, her trauma, her inability in many cases to conceive again, her being paralyzed in the emotional state of the time of her surrendering, and her difficulties in relationships—are not considered. Many of these women became numb as a defense against a society of unempathic people who wanted to believe that she could carry a child for nine months, give birth to him, surrender him to strangers, and then get on with her life as if nothing had happened. This, of course, is absurd. The fallout from surrendering a child to adoption is much greater than our society is willing to recognize, and birth mothers are suffering long and silently as a result.

The adoptive parents are often looked upon as the winners in the adoption scenario. Yet, the true experiences of many adoptive parents have also been overlooked. If they have a compliant child, everything seems wonderful (until they realize that there is a space that cannot seem to be bridged). If they have an acting-out child, other parents will think that if they just love the child more or discipline him differently, everything will be fine. Or maybe they shouldn't have told him he was adopted, as if the telling about being adopted is the source of the problem. Even many adoptive parents themselves aren't aware of what is going on, because they have nothing to compare it with. Their child's difficulty in bonding or even attaching to them, their feeling of not truly being entitled to the child, their difficulty in "reading" the emotional states of their child, and their feelings of inadequacy in not being able to eliminate or even alleviate the pain of their child are mysteries to them. Some of the hidden pain of adoptive parents come about in the same way as the hidden pain of the birth mother and the adoptee—each is ashamed of her inadequacy in being able to overcome her difficulties; therefore, each suffers in silence. All need to break their silence and seek understanding, compassion, and support in their suffering. It is hoped that some of that understanding and compassion can be directed toward one another!

## A Differential Diagnosis

### When Adult Adoptees Seek Help

When adoptees seek help it is usually because of problems in relationships. This makes sense, because the genesis of their issues was the severing of a relationship. Yet, in many cases the adoptee doesn't even let the therapist know that she is adopted, so the therapist has no awareness of that early trauma. Of course, as I stated earlier, because of the belief in our society about adoption being such a good thing, the therapist may not consider that the relinquishment and adoption have anything to do with her patient's relationship issues even if the adoptee does mention being adopted. In most cases, the therapist fails to take into consideration what happened *before* the adoptive parents got the child. Even if there are issues with the adoptive parents, and there are bound to be, the core issues of *abandonment and loss* have to be addressed first. Everything else, including the relationship with the parents, proceeds from the separation trauma. It would be a huge mistake to try to untangle the adoptee's relationship to the adoptive parents without an understanding of the lens through which the adoptee views them. All other relationships in the adoptee's life will be misunderstood as well. Something devastating happened to him which makes him distrust close relationships. That distrust colors the way he views others and his relationship with them. Although it may seem normal to the trauma-driven adoptee, nevertheless the distrust is unnecessary and is interfering with his relationships.

Without the understanding of separation trauma, the adoptee's normal response to her experience is seen as pathological, rather than as a *defense against further loss*. Instead of pathologizing society's penchant for separating babies and their mothers, we pathologize the victims of a grave wrongdoing. As mentioned above, this includes the responses of birth mothers, as well. We need to normalize the adoptee's and the birth mother's responses to this separation or at least come up with a better diagnosis, because what is happening is that inaccurate diagnoses are resulting in poor or harmful treatment.

## A Fresh Look

First of all, the adoptee's experience of separation from the first mother needs to be seen by therapists as an unnatural, abnormal experience, one no infant or young child should have to endure. Then the coping mechanisms and defense mechanisms which the adoptee employs need to be validated as good responses to a tremendous and devastating loss. But what also needs to be understood by the adoptee and addressed by the therapist is that *those behaviors and responses, although normal under the circumstances, have lost their effectiveness and are no longer serving the adoptee well. They are, in fact, doing the opposite—interfering with her adult relationships.* The problem is that the belief system, established by the infant adoptee in a valiant attempt to make sense of the confusing and chaotic thing which happened to her, is very difficult to change. The separation is locked into the implicit memory as an ever-occurring event, rather than integrated as a memory of something which already happened.

## What Constitutes True Pathology?

We need to take another look at just what is truly pathological. Many adoptees have been diagnosed with personality disorders simply as a result of the ignorance of the helping professions. Herman, in her excellent book on trauma, *Trauma and Recovery*, has little patience for these diagnoses, especially that of borderline: "The most notorious is the diagnosis of borderline personality disorder. This term is frequently used within the mental health professions as little more than a sophisticated insult." She goes on to tell that when a resident psychiatrist asked his supervisor how to treat borderlines, "... he answered sardonically, 'You refer them.'" Thus do borderlines strike terror into the hearts of clinicians! Adoptees are not borderlines.

In *The Primal Wound* I relayed the interesting phenomenon of adoptees either responding to their primal wound with compliance or defiance. These two types of coping mechanisms often translate into several behaviors which cause the person to be diagnosed as either borderline (acting-out) or schizoid (compliant, isolated, and withdrawn). Because the borderline label is the more prevalent, I would like to demonstrate why it is irresponsible to rely only on symptomatology and not to consider etiology when diagnosing patients.

*Similarities with Borderline Symptomatology*

On the surface, the adoptee and the borderline present with similar symptoms:

Primitive Defenses
- *Denial*
- *Splitting*
- *Projective identification.*
- *Avoidance*

Feelings
- *Helplessness*
- *Hopelessness*
- *Emptiness*
- *Loneliness*

Fears
- *Fear of abandonment*
- *Fear of engulfment* (borderline); *connection* (adoptee)

In therapy, both present with a *false self and difficulties in relationships.* They both report being *depressed and anxious.*

*Differences in Etiology*

The main difference between someone who suffers from separation trauma and someone who is truly a borderline personality is that of experience. The adoptee had a physical experience of separation from the mother, while the borderline's experience is intrapsychic (situated or occurring within the psyche).

| ADOPTEE | BORDERLINE |
|---|---|
| Problem with connection. | Problem with separation. |
| Abandonment/connection issues due to experience of separation from mother. | Engulfment issues: Sense that mother will not tolerate separation. |
| Failure to bond with adoptive mother at beginning of relationship. | Failure at rapprochement stage of development. |
| Afraid to connect. | Afraid to separate. |
| Strong ego: premature ego development | Weak ego: afraid to separate. |
| Low self-esteem: mother disappeared. | Low self-esteem: mother needy. |
| Symptoms are defenses: fear of recurrence. | Symptoms are part of pathology. |
| Splitting: Experiential (has two sets of parents) | Splitting: Intrapsychic |

It is in the etiology—or cause—that one finds the first difference between the two. For the borderline, the problem usually begins at the rapprochement stage of development(which usually begins around 18 months), when the mother fails in her job of allowing her child to experiment separating from her. For the adoptee, the problem begins with the actual disappearance of the mother, most often at the beginning of life. So, the major problem for the borderline is separation, while the major problem for the adoptee is connection (or reconnecting for fear of further abandonment). These issues ensue from the person's experience. For the borderline the experience is the sense that the mother will not tolerate individuation. For the adoptee there is the sense that to be connected is followed by abandonment.

Unresolved grief for both adoptees and birth mothers manifests as depression and is considered by mental health professionals as abnormal. Yet it is now confirmed by thousands of people who have suffered from the loss of a parent or child *by any means* that it may be impossible to entirely get over the disappearance of one's child or one's mother. If it is normal, then it may not be pathological, even though it may be affecting one's behavior or one's choices in life. It is simply the natural result of devastating loss. However, since these normal manifestations of trauma are interfering with adult choices in their lives, adoptees and birth mothers should take the steps necessary to make the kinds of changes which allow for a freer lifestyle. There are some adoptees and birth mothers who do in fact exhibit extreme behavioral reactions to this loss which may be considered pathological. A therapist needs to be careful in his conclusions about what constitutes true pathology in patients affected by adoption. An effective treatment plan depends on this kind of careful diagnosis. *There is a vast difference between treating pathology and helping a patient lower his defenses against connection/loss.*

Adoptees are often seen as having attachment or bonding problems. This we know is a result of the severing of the first bond with the birth mother. While many adoptees seem to attach, it is an anxious attachment completely devoid of the security needed to allow for bonding. This is a fear of abandonment following connection and is perpetuated into adult relationships as a fear of intimacy.

Borderlines have a fear of separation and individuation caused by the over-anxious or narcissistic mother who cannot allow her child to separate for her own pathological reasons. A child in the rapprochement stage of development is trying to separate from her symbiotic relationship with her mother. Remember that adoptees cannot have a symbiotic relationship to the adoptive mother, because it is too dangerous to allow for that kind of connection. The anxious (clingy) attachment of adoptees is not the same as symbiosis, although it may be mistaken as such. Symbiosis—the mother/baby fusion—is natural at the beginning of an infant's life. That wonderful feeling was severed forever for the adoptee when the first mother disappeared.

The normal process of individuation begins between the ages of 18 months and two years, when the child ventures away from the mother, only to return at intervals to assure himself that she is there when needed. If the mother encourages this venturing away by positive gestures and words, at the same time making herself available when the child wants to toddle back to her, the child will make a smooth transition toward individuation without anxiety. If, however, the mother seems nervous about the child's venturing away, always telling him to be careful, not to go too far, making him return to her before he is ready, or punishing him by withdrawing from him if he doesn't obey, the child will begin to sense that it is not all right to individuate. He will begin to fear being abandoned by the mother (her withdrawal), while at the same time fear being engulfed by her (not allowed to venture out).

### Differences in Ego Formation

Another difference between borderlines and adoptees is that of ego formation. Most adoptees have strong egos as a result of premature ego development.

Because the mother disappeared, making it impossible to have a symbiotic relationship with her, the infant was forced to form an ego or separate self much too soon. Adoptees will feel this as a sense that they are separate, isolated, cannot trust anyone else. They rarely ask for help, but can "do it themselves." Borderlines, on the other hand, rarely display that kind of independence. They have weak egos because they were not allowed to separate from their mothers and continued to operate under their mothers' egos. Both adoptees and borderlines have low self-esteem, however: the adoptee because his baby belief is that there is some intrinsic defect in him which caused his mother to reject him; the borderline because her mother is not trusting enough to allow her to individuate. The borderline fears disapproval of the mother if she tries to differentiate. The adoptee fears that the emergence of the true self (the bad baby who was abandoned) will trigger another abandonment. The adoptee's false self and low self-esteem often masquerade as a weak ego.

For the borderline, the symptoms are part of their pathology and intrapsychic phenomena. For the adoptee, the symptoms are defenses, which are in the service of avoiding a recurrence of the original abandonment experience. *Rather than being intrapsychic, they are experiential or contextual.* This is extremely important information for therapists

### Splitting

One of the symptoms which most confuses clinicians when trying to diagnose adoptees is that of splitting. Splitting is considered a red flag for borderlines. Splitting means seeing the self or others as either all-good or all-bad. This way of seeing people is phase-appropriate until age two or two and a half, when there is still idealization of the parents. If the child does not progress in his relation to the parents, in that he sees that his parents are not always good or right, this splitting continues to operate in the individual. Even though the child may begin to see that his parents are not always good, whatever is taking place at the time is his way of seeing them. In other words, if they do something he considers bad, he sees them as all-bad (not just the incident as bad). He does the same thing with himself. We call this intrapsychic splitting (or black and white thinking), and it interferes with ego development in the borderline.

In an unpublished doctoral dissertation entitled *The Adoption Syndrome: A Mimicry of Borderline Syndrome,* Joanne Whittington, a therapist in northern California, coined a phrase which captures the reality of splitting for the adoptee. She calls adoptee splitting "contextual splitting." Whereas the borderline splits his only mother into good mother/bad mother, the adoptee's internalization of two mothers is a reality. He *has* two mothers, the birth mother and the adoptive mother. He assigns good to one and bad to the other, often switching back and forth. This assignation interferes with his integration of love and hate. Contextual splitting involves what is real or not real for the adoptee: "real mother" vs. "substitute mother" and "real or authentic self" vs. "false or adaptive self." The adoptee's splitting of good and bad parent (usually mother) and the subsequent splitting of the good and bad self is confusing and frightening. Whittington states:

> *The adoptee has been required to internalize two separate sets of parents, one "real" and the other "not real." Usually the adopted child equates the "real" parent with "bad" (abandoning) and the "not real" parent with "good" (rescuing). These associations lead to a frightening paradox: What is real (about myself or my birth parents) is bad, and what is not real (about my adoptive parents) is good. This type of splitting may be thought of as "contextual splitting," since it is the task of the adopted child to separate this two realities in a manageable way.*
> *Whittington, 1989*

The adoptee has to deny the real, genetic self—abandon the flawed, relinquished baby—to become the good, rescued baby.

## Avoidance

One of the most difficult defense mechanisms to overcome for the adoptee is avoidance. It is his way of making sure that he isn't abandoned again. If you don't take any risks, you won't get hurt. In childhood this is manifested in a distant or superficial relationship with the mother. Although some adoptees seem to have a close relationship with her, often it is based in anxious attachment and is clingy, rather than secure. The acting-out adoptee, on the other hand, makes his fear readily known. He finds ways to keep his distance, even though he may desperately wish to connect with the mother. The different ways that compliant and defiant adopted children respond to this fear of connection have been discussed elsewhere.

As adults, adoptees would seem to have more control over those to whom they relate. They couldn't pick their adoptive parents, but they can pick their partners in adulthood. Yet they often don't do a very good job of making these choices. Because of the fear of intimacy, they often pick people who are unavailable either physically, socially, or emotionally. Thus we have the long-distance relationship, the relationship with a married person, or the relationship with a person also deeply wounded and emotionally unavailable. In these relationships there is a collusion to keep everything at a superficial level. Eventually, one partner in the relationship gets tired of it and leaves.

There is a great deal of sabotaging of relationships for adoptees. Besides the underlying fear of another abandonment, there is the problem of feeling unworthy or undeserving of a good relationship. When, perchance, an adoptee does choose someone who would be good for him, he may find a way to end the relationship simply because he doesn't feel deserving of it. Besides, there may not be enough drama in a good relationship for his need to feel alive—to experience chaos in his life. His lack of limbic regulation may make a tumultuous relationship seem more attractive than a calm one.

The defense mechanisms, which keep the adoptee in a state of disconnection with intimate partners and which she interprets as keeping her safe, need to be lowered. This would be much more helpful to adoptees than treating them for a personality disorder. The personalities of adoptees are buried beneath layers and layers of defenses and adaptations and need to be retrieved.

### Affect Regulation and Emotional Health

Some brain researchers have theorized that the key to good mental health (which I prefer to call emotional health) is good affect regulation (see Chapter 8). In a seminar on "Affect Regulation and the Repair of the Self," Allan Schore, citing Taylor et al., claimed that affect dysregulation is a fundamental mechanism of all psychiatric disorders. This, of course, would pathologize many more people than I have previously stated. When one considers that most people who get in trouble are those who cannot seem to regulate their emotions or their responses to their emotions, this makes sense. The enduring effect of early relationship trauma on the right brain has a tremendous effect on affect dysregulation and disorders of the self. Unfortunately, labeling many of the people suffering from affect dysregulation as having personality disorders seems to be the trend. Again, I emphasize that etiology, in addition to symptoms, is key in determining the diagnosis and thus the treatment for any individual.

## Treatment

As in any trauma there are several changes which need to take place during the course of the therapy. Patients will want to regain a sense of safety in their environments and in their bodies. In this sense they will have to deal with issues of passivity and helplessness. There must be some completion of the unfinished past. Uncovering memories will not be enough. Although this may be helpful for birth mothers, for most adoptees the early onset of trauma will prevent uncovering actual memories of the relinquishment. There will need to be a modified transformation from the hold the trauma has on them. This means putting it in its proper context and perhaps reconstructing it in a personally meaningful way. Very important to the success of the treatment are: being heard, being taken seriously, feeling understood, and having someone bear witness to one's pain. Finding some kind of personal meaning to one's experiences in life is critical. This doesn't mean that the meaning is always good. But the past cannot be undone. Yearning for it to be so will not make it happen. That's why meaning needs to be given to it. "What have I come away with from this experience that I can use in my present life?" The right kind of therapy can help with these puzzles, but this will happen toward the end of therapy, not at the beginning.

What is therapy and how can it help treat a wound so profound and so deeply imprinted as separation trauma? In *A General Theory of Love*, Lewis, Amini, and Lannon put it this way: "The first part of emotional healing is being limbically known—having someone with a keen ear catch your melodic essence." It is being limbically (or emotionally) known that is key for adoptees who have for the most part felt misunderstood all their lives. One has to be limbically known in order for limbic revision and regulation to take place. This coincides with Schore's theory that as therapists we have to connect with the patient where he is. It has to begin as a right brain to right brain connection. Schore says, "The self-organization of the developing brain occurs in the context of a relationship with another self, another brain." If that other self (mother) had no idea of the emotions the child was experiencing or the origin of those emotions, there would have been no communication, no help in the regulation of the child's emotions. Thus, these emotions may still be operating in the person today as formatively as they were when he was an infant. That's why therapy may be necessary—there needs to be a second chance to find help in learning to regulate affect. Otherwise the original relational wound will continue to create chaos in present relationships.

*Integrity in Treatment*

Being misdiagnosed is a further reinforcement of the wound, rather than a path to healing. Having outlined the etiological differences between borderline personality disorder and separation trauma as experienced by the adoptee, it should be clear why it is important to know the etiology, not just the symptoms of the patient. The treatment plans for borderlines and adoptees call for different sequences as well as oftimes diametrically opposed strategies.

I want to point out at this time that every adoptee, every birth mother, and every patient with any issues is an individual with a unique personality. I have never met two people who were alike, or treated two patients in the same way. It is crucial to maintain the integrity of each individual in treatment. However, that does not mean that there are not common issues which ensue from the common experience of separation trauma. It is helpful to keep in mind that it is the *experience of relinquishment and adoption* which is causing difficulties for the birth mother and the adoptee, not who they are. There is nothing wrong with who they are, but there *is something wrong with what happened to them* which has had a great deal of influence over much of the rest of their lives.

## Confronting Denial and Providing a Safe Place

The first thing to do with adoptees is to confront the denial and validate the profundity of their experience of abandonment and loss. It is important to interpret their genetic reality and validate the dual reality under which they have been living. The therapist must bring the patient back to his loss and sorrow and not collude with the false self. Although Daniel Siegel says that there is nothing "false" about a false self because it is a mechanism of survival, he does acknowledge that the false self lacks the ring of authenticity, since *the emotions caused by trauma mask one's true responses.* It is so very important that adoptees and therapists understand this, because adoptees have no idea that had they not been traumatized they would not be responding the way they are. Since most adoptees were relinquished at birth, it must be remembered that they have been operating from this adaptive version of themselves since the beginning of their lives and may be unaware of their over-identification with that aspect of themselves. There is no "before-trauma self" with which to compare the self they know and the self the therapist sees. The therapist has to be very careful not to collude with the false self, except to acknowledge that it has served to protect the adoptee from a sense of impending annihilation.

## The False Self and Dual Reality

Many experts in the treatment of borderlines believe that one must first treat the false self and address the splitting. Adoptees also have a false self, but it is formed differently from that of the borderline. Because they are taken out of one family and placed into another, adoptees have a *dual reality*—the reality of the genetic child and the reality of the adopted child. However, in most families that dual reality has been denied or ignored so that the adoptee's sense of reality is skewed. This has to be a heads-up for the therapist because the adoptee will want to safely focus on a symptom. Whatever the present symptom in therapy, it is probably long-standing, so the adoptee may have a great deal invested in it. As the patient focuses on the present symptom or invents new symptoms, it is up to the therapist to bring the focus back to the denied dual reality. That reality is difficult to accept because it entails acknowledging the impact of the loss of the first mother and the genetic self, and then experiencing the devastating sorrow which this brings up. If the therapist allows the patient to focus on the symptom without acknowledging the dual reality, the therapist will be colluding with the patient's maintaining the false self and denying the fact that he is different, both as an individual within the family and in the manner in which he entered the family.

The denial of the dual reality had survival value during childhood. The adoptee needed to deny his genetic self in order to become more like his adoptive family (and in ever-expanding circles, more like everyone with whom he came into contact—the *chameleon* is born!). To review, the reality which was denied consists of genetic traits, birth parents, and the relinquished self, which may have been simultaneously extinguished. With no genetic markers to let him know that the "inside self" is all right, the adoptee retreats further and further into the false self of an adaptive family member. As difficult as it may be for the therapist to see beneath the surface into the more authentic self of the adoptee, it is crucial that she do so. For, the authentic self is locked within the adoptee in the form of biological traits and independent thoughts and can be teased out with empathic and patient work on the part of the therapist. She will not be afraid of who is locked up there! If she colludes with the false self and simply tries to get the adoptee to accept this version of herself, she will be reinforcing the patient's belief that the true self is too dangerous to get to know.

Not getting caught up in the false self is important for another reason. Because so much of an adoptee's background is unavailable to her, reality must be discovered and maintained in the clinician's office. The adoptee herself may be almost completely identified with the trauma-driven self as exemplified by her behavior and coping mechanisms. It is very easy for some adoptees to convince the unaware therapist that they are very much "together" and that they just have crazy parents or unreasonable partners. Their bad relationships can be blamed on their parents or partners. It must be remembered that they have been operating from this false self for a very long time and are very good at it. It has seemed like a matter of life or death.

In their attempt to heal the trauma of separation, adoptees will create in their present relationships dynamics of the past. Unlike the treatment plan for borderlines, however, it is not usually helpful to work on these present relationships when in the beginning stages of therapy with adoptees. However, it is helpful to make note of the dynamics of these relationships as an example of the repetition of early patterns (the *repetition compulsion*). The therapist must bring the adoptee back to loss and sorrow and not collude with the false self (which, remember, can look very "together"). The real work can be in the transference, where the therapist can give the adoptee a different experience of trust and caring.

*Anxiety and Rage*

I will mention a couple of additional examples of the differences between treatment of borderlines and adoptees, then stick with the treatment of adoptees, which is what this book is about. Besides regression, which calls for opposite treatment plans for the two different etiologies, two other differences can be seen in the treatment of rage and anxiety. Whereas rage is discouraged in the borderline, it's source is identified and eventually worked through with the adoptee. Anxiety is encouraged with the borderline (at least according to my understanding of Masterson's techniques), but lowered with the adoptee. Both are encouraged to give up their child-like need for approval and develop a sense of self.

*Regression*

If one has any control over it, clinicians might do well to allow or even encourage regression in the adoptee, but not in the borderline. The reason for the difference is in their different experiences. Adoptees, having had their mothers disappear, do not trust others to be available to meet their needs. This will manifest in distrust in childhood and a lack of intimacy in adult relationships. It is, therefore, worthwhile to allow for a regression to that childlike state when the infant needed to be able to count on his caregivers. What looks like independence in many adoptees is really a fear of connecting. *This is a very important distinction.* (It is especially noticeable in young children, where independence is not age-appropriate.) Gaining an adoptee's trust may take a long time, and the therapist may tire of the endless tests to see if they are indeed trustworthy.

Regression is not encouraged for the borderline because the problem for the borderline is one of being able to individuate, not one of being able to depend on someone. Regression in borderlines can be very difficult to reverse. Borderlines can be very persistent in trying to force the therapist to take care of them—wanting to change their schedule often, being late for appointments, being unable to remember their appointment times, arguing about being charged for missed appointments, etc. However, instead of regressing in therapy, borderlines should be encouraged to work on their issues through the medium of their present relationships, including that with the therapist. Childlike behavior in the consulting room should be confronted and discouraged. Gratifying wishes is dangerous for the borderline because they need firm boundaries, something which was missing in their symbiotic relationships to their mothers. What they need verified for them is a belief in their ability to take responsibility for themselves—to be on time, to pay for missed appointments, to individuate.

The earliest stages in working with regressed adoptees creates a great challenge for therapists because if the patient regresses to infancy it will be necessary for a time to avail oneself to him on an almost 24/7 basis. Because almost no one can afford daily therapy, it may be necessary to allow short phone calls between sessions just to reassure the patient that the therapist hasn't disappeared. It will also be necessary to give the adoptee an itinerary of one's vacation plans and a phone number where one may be reached. (I have never had a patient call me while I was away, but having a phone number helps to relieve the fear that the therapist is lost.) A transition object (a handkerchief with one's perfume or aftershave lotion on it, for example) will help calm the anxiety about the therapist's absence, which may be interpreted as an abandonment on the part of the patient. The objective is to heal the abandonment wound, not to reinforce it by adhering to the rules which were established before anyone understood separation from mother to be a trauma, and before the impact of the trauma was understood to have anything to do with adoptees' issues. Upon returning from a trip, it is necessary to work through the feelings of abandonment created by the absence of the therapist. Many feelings and yearnings of the patient will be projected upon the therapist and will seem to be co-existing within the therapeutic relationship. This is known as transference.

## Transference

I have touched on transference in other parts of this book, but it is most understood in the context of psychotherapy, where the term originated. Transference deals with yearnings not realized in childhood or adolescence. It is the projection of those feelings onto another person, usually without realizing that it is a projection. It is a tricky phenomenon and one which is too often ignored or downplayed in the education of therapists who deal with family and relationship issues. Acting upon transference and countertransference feelings is the reason many therapists get into trouble with licensing boards. It is also the reason presidents get into trouble with interns.

If handled well in the context of therapy, transference can be a tremendous healing experience, albeit, a frustrating one at times. It is about love, but not all the love is really about the person upon whom the feelings are projected. John Sanford, a Jungian analyst, in his book *The Kingdom Within* (1970) has this to say about the transference:

A kind of uniting, healing love is visible in the phenomenon known as the "transference." While the term "transference" is a technical term deriving from psychotherapy, it is actually a psychological event which can occur between two people in widely varying circumstances. Usually existing between a man and a woman, it is characterized by very strong erotic feelings, often with sexual overtones. In psychotherapy both counselor and counselee may be aware of the existence of such feelings in the counseling situation. It may also occur between a patient and his doctor, a student and his teacher, a married man and the "other woman," or between two young people, in which case it is referred as "falling in love." The love which exists between the two people *is* love. But the extent that they are not aware of each other as individual human beings, with all the faults and frailties of human beings, but are seeing in each other only idealized images, the love is not personal, but "divine." Its source is the enormous attraction of the opposites which is constellated in the transference phenomenon. This is a different thing than one human being's coming to know, respect, and love the personality of another human being.

It is difficult for most people who are caught up in the transference to realize that most of what they are experiencing is not for the person upon whom the feelings are being projected. It certainly *feels* as if this were true. And because the patient is so adept at creating the proper (original) contexts for whatever happens in the therapeutic situation, it will seem as if it is indeed the therapist who is both the cause and the object of the transference feelings.

It has always been my belief that strong transferences should be interpreted for patients. Unbearable tensions (with strong eroticized transferences) or anxiety (with pre-object constancy transferences) can occur when visits are too far apart. Strong transferences are easier to manage on a day to day basis, as daily contact takes some of the charge off or reduces anxiety. Since not too many people can afford daily sessions, the tensions can become excruciating. This is not to say that the tension will be relieved by the interpretation of the phenomenon, but it can at least be understood.

Therapists who have not experienced the transference directly as a patient themselves may not have the resources to handle a strong transference. It is imperative that it be conscious on the part of the therapist. If not, it can turn out badly. In my experience, the positive transference (of love and affection) arrives first. However, sooner or later, the negative transference (of hostility and anger) will appear. This is inevitable. Sanford says, "... it will be necessary that they recognized both their own individuality and the individuality of the other person. To do this, each must be driven apart from the other in order to differentiate. Uncannily the unconscious will find a way to produce quarrels between them in order to facilitate this separation." In the therapeutic situation, accusations of uncaring, criticizing, or misunderstanding will create a distancing between the patient and the therapist. The patient will at this point be experiencing the therapist as the "unloving mother" or the "disapproving father." Unless there is a strong therapeutic alliance, the therapy may be terminated either by the patient or an unconscious therapist. If the therapist ends the treatment because of her inability to understand and tolerate the projected feelings of the patient, *the original wound will be reinforced instead of healed.* If the patient ends the therapy, the work will remain unfinished and the patient will be doomed to repeat the whole thing in the next therapy or in another relationship.

Boundaries are very important in the transference relationship. If the eroticized transference becomes sexualized there will be a tendency to want to concretize the emotions sexually. Sanford says, "They are driven by the supreme image of the kingdom of God, the *image of the wedding,* but as long as they are unconscious of this image, they may be compulsively drawn into a sexual relationship. Then the inner meaning of the experience is lost, because sexuality under these conditions is a regression to an unconscious, nonindividual event ..." This is what happens, not only in the "falling in love" of young people who really don't know one another and in some therapeutic situations, but in reunions between birth mothers and sons (and also daughters) and birth fathers and their daughters. In all cases, the "adult," the one having more authority in the relationship—parents, therapists, teachers, priests, presidents—have to take the responsibility of keeping the relationship from becoming sexualized. Sanford's solution:

> ... is to hold within oneself, and within the context of the relationship, all the affects, desires, feelings, and aspirations. The individual then becomes a crucible containing the elements of totality, and the intense feelings are like a heat which brings these elements through a process and into completion. The image of the kingdom as a wedding feast then works within all parties concerned, affecting them in the innermost levels of their being.

Only a Jungian analyst would say it so poetically! What it means is that it is important not to act on those feelings, but to protect and cherish them, allowing healing to take place in the safety of the *temanos* or consulting room. Interpretation becomes important in that the phenomenon becomes more clear, *less magical.* Interpreting transference phenomena as they come up and helping the patient to establish an observing ego is part of teaching one to become psychologically aware. Explaining the transference is a step toward correcting the balance of power in the relationship. Without this explanation, the patient is at the mercy of the therapist and the transference phenomena.

The transference can be an integral part of healing in the therapeutic relationship with adoptees, but it must be well understood by the therapist and interpreted for the patient. When patients are regressed, they are already at a disadvantage in the power structure of the relationship. While this may be all right for some time, eventually, without an understanding of the transference and the establishment of an observing ego, treatment can become unconscious, stagnant, and harmful. The patient must be allowed—and sometimes encouraged—to grow up in the relationship. Therapists must not keep the patient in a regressed state for their own gratification. Unfortunately, this happens sometimes, to the detriment of all concerned. Therapists who are not sure of themselves in the transference must immediately seek consultation with another therapist.

## Touch—A Touchy Subject in Therapy

Another therapeutic issue concerning severely regressed patients is that of touch. One of the deprivations of many adoptees is that of touch. Many of them were too afraid to allow the adoptive mother to hold or cuddle them, or she didn't feel right—wrong energy, wrong skin, wrong smell—or she wasn't an affectionate person. During the early stages of therapy, it may be important to find some safe way to touch the patient if she indicates that this would be helpful. This may mean simply holding a hand. (Touch should be avoided if the patient has been sexually or physically abused because it may create anxiety rather than relieving it.) Because touch is so much a part of early bonding and building trust, the lack of any physical human contact may create an impasse in the treatment. It is very important for therapists to have firm boundaries if they attempt any kind of touch, especially in cross-gender patient/therapist relationships. The patient is in a childlike relationship to the therapist and the responsibility to keep the therapy safe is *totally* that of the therapist. Any form of touch which could be construed as sexual must be avoided.

Later in the treatment, when trust has been established, it will be important to help the adoptee integrate the contextual split. This involves confronting the "baby belief" that the real or authentic self is flawed or bad, and to help the adoptee find value in that "defective baby." Because the belief is built into the neurological system during the first years of life, this is quite difficult to accomplish. It involves first discovering what is and is not authentic about the patient, then taking tiny risks in seemingly ordinary day-to-day activities, such as stating a preference for something before anyone else has or giving a different political opinion from those already presented. One of the most impressive techniques for permanently changing the belief system that keeps that bad baby going is EMDR (Eye Movement Desensitization and Reprocessing)—more about this later in the chapter. This technique accomplishes change at the neurological level.

All of these steps involve giving up the chameleon-like false self as a defense against what the patient believes is the bad, defective self. It means learning that it is not necessary to have everyone's approval. And it means discovering and practicing the authentic Self. It necessitates separating the person from the experience, by seeing how the beliefs and actions which have been perpetuated since infancy and childhood are not intrinsic to the true character of the adopted person, but are simply manifestations of his pain and defenses against its recurrence.

### Withdrawing Projections

As the therapy progresses, one can begin to use the present relationships of the adoptee to confront his use of projective identification. Projective identification is one of the most frustrating aspects of relating to an adoptee because he is unconscious of what he is doing. (See a discussion of this phenomenon in Chapter 17.) Because of the unconscious nature of this defense mechanism, he will need help in owning his own feelings and checking out his assumptions about the important people in his life. Parents and partners have all been the recipients of a great number of projections. This means that important people in his life will have to let him know when a feeling doesn't seem to be theirs, at least until he caused an event to evoke it. They will also have to let him know when his actions or words have been hurtful. As I've said before, letting these incidents go by only perpetuates his belief that what he says and does has no impact. It will also hamper any progress he may have made in his learning about cause and effect.

The patient will have to give up the victim role as he begins to assume more responsibilities and to empower himself. This is an important step because if the therapist continues to collude with the adoptee's perceptions of the parents and partners as those responsible for all his problems, the victim role will never be left behind. This collusion is important in the first part of the therapy, when the patient is regressed, because the therapist has to work with his perceptions. These early perceptions are what formed his responses to life. But children's perceptions are not always accurate and memory changes over time. At some time in the therapeutic work, these perceptions have to be challenged in order for him to grow up. Part of that growing up is in his ability to see his parents as having both good and bad aspects to their personalities, and for him to stop blaming them for whatever is wrong in his life.

Sometimes the opposite is true—the adoptee blames herself for everything. No matter how blatant the transgression on the part of someone else seems to others, the adoptee will take responsibility for whatever happened. Telescoping back to childhood, one can probably identify the blamers with the acting-out adoptees and the self-blamers with the compliant adoptees. Neither response is healthy or helpful. And both secretly feel responsible for their own relinquishment.

Splitting is detrimental to relationships because it is unforgiving. Many good friends have suddenly become bad because of some incident, often trivial but appearing to the adoptee as a betrayal. Some of those old "door slamming" incidents can be brought up in the therapy so that new meaning can be given to them. Was it really betrayal or only disappointment that occurred? Has the patient ever done anything similar to a friend? What was the outcome? Interpretation must be given to the ways in which the adoptee continually reconstructs the original abandonment or the adoptive family situation in every new relationship.

Just as with anyone else, many of the "shadow" aspects of an adoptee are projected onto those around her. The objects of those projections may be those with whom she is in relation, but may also include others who are on the periphery of her life. Adoptees can be very critical of others. It isn't until they have confronted and accepted these shadow aspects of themselves that they can begin to withdraw those critical projections from others and become more non-judgmental. It is wise to remember that envy can also be a projection of self, so that certain characteristics of those we envy may in fact be our own.

In addition to the therapist, an adoptee can enlist the support of parents and partners to help him withdraw his projections, to own his own feelings, and to take responsibility for his impact on those closest to him. If the adoptee thinks he has never been understood by his adoptive parents, he can be sure his parents are feeling the same way. From the first moment that every cell in his body screamed that the adoptive mother was the "wrong mother," he has been unable to see her as she really is. She may have been a good mother, but she has not been the "right mother," the mother to whom he was connected prenatally and to whom he expected to be connected postnatally. If the adoptee wants his parents to begin to accept his more authentic self, then as an adult it will be time for him to begin to see them as people in their own right. He will need to become more aware of their feelings and to check out his assumptions about them. Now that he is an adult, it can't be a one-way street any longer. The same is true with birth parents. Who are they really? All the fantasies have to be withdrawn—good and bad—and an attempt made to truly know and understand them.

A great deal of rage may have been displaced onto the adoptive parents, especially during adolescence. If it comes up in therapy and is projected upon the therapist, it can be worked through as the patient learns that this rage originates in his failure to get his mother to come back, and that the rage will kill neither the therapist nor himself. Neither will it cause the patient to be abandoned by the therapist. Although adoptees are encouraged to explore their rage and work it through, rage is neither encouraged nor explored when working with the borderline. Neither are borderlines treated directly for the abandonment depression, whereas adoptees are encouraged to explore more directly their feelings about having been abandoned. (There are some therapists who follow none of these protocols, but I am referring to protocols which have been the most prevalent.)

*Lifelong Habits and Beliefs*

It is important to understand the power of beliefs in the formation of our lives. Beliefs formed during the chaotic period right after mom left have been the basis of many of the perceptions an adoptee has about himself and others. As distorted as these beliefs may be, they persist because they have formed patterns in the neurological system and created attitudes and habits that seem to be a part of who the adoptee is. It is difficult to give up lifelong habits which seem to have been defining oneself or keeping one going. Yet this is the task of every therapist—to help the patient abandon those beliefs, attitudes, and habits which are keeping him in a victim role and holding him back from a more peaceful, productive, and meaningful life. This can be difficult because these habits have been perceived to have been helpful in coping with the losses, deprivations, and abuses earlier in life. However, today these habits simply get in the way of intimate relationships and a modicum of happiness.

What keeps patients from letting go of these habits and beliefs? One reason is that they are "old friends" which are familiar. One knows what to expect if one stays in the old ruts. Another reason is that there is an element of excitement connected with acting out old responses to feelings such as resentment, anger, and hostility which seems hard to give up. The negative excitement keeps the drama in their lives going and *assures them that they are alive.* This is no small thing! But it also causes them to distance themselves from others (or for others to distance from them). And, although it seems to them that they are acting out their feelings, a lot of what is going on is only drama, which instead *keeps them from responding to their true feelings.* Lewis, et al. say, "... a patient has to stomach the proposition that his emotional convictions are fiction, and someone else's might be better. Not everyone can do it. ... Early emotional experiences knit long-lasting patterns into the very fabric of the brain's neural networks. Changing that matrix calls for a different kind of medicine altogether." It is the work of the therapist to help the adoptee challenge those early perceptions and form a more helpful viewpoint.

That "different kind of medicine" is *limbic revision.* The problem is that the limbic system is a slow learner, unlike the neocortex. Furthermore, the limbic system and the neocortex do not speak the same language, which is the reason that insight isn't enough to permanently change old patterns imprinted in the limbic brain. Lewis, et al. say, "When a limbic connection has established a neural pattern, it takes a limbic connection to revise it." This is the reason that finding a therapist who has done his own work (i.e., had extensive therapy himself) is essential when seeking help with such exquisite pain. The therapist has to have a healthy, regulated limbic brain in order to healthily revise that of the patient. It is right brain to right brain work. The therapist will find himself responding to certain emotions of the patient. He should neither deny those feelings nor allow them to run amok. Instead, Lewis, et al. say, "He waits for the moment to move the relationship in a different direction. And then he does it again, then ten thousand times more. Progress in therapy is iterative. ... Therapy's transmutation consists not in elevating proper Reason over purblind Passion, but in replacing silent, unworkable intuitions with functional ones." I like their analogy about the limbic journey vs. insight: "Patients are often hungry for *explanations*, because they are used to thinking that neocortical contraptions like explication will help them. But insight is the popcorn of therapy. Where patient and therapist *go* together, the irreducible totality of their mutual journey, is the movie." With which I absolutely concur.

*Meanwhile, Back at the Farm ...*

Giving up old beliefs and habits means trusting in the therapeutic relationship and boldly starting on the path to emotional healing. Because this mutual journey is a long one—given the limbic system's stubborn hold on old beliefs—there needs to be a "meanwhile" in the life of people in therapy. Life has to be lived. There are certain things which *can* be changed behaviorally if they are known and the patient remains vigilant. The key here is *awareness*. One has to begin to become more aware of just what it is that one is actually doing in relation to others. What are the signs that one is once again sabotaging oneself, projecting one's feelings onto others, or rationalizing one's behavior? As the therapist and adoptee together go on their journey and look at what is going on in the therapeutic relationship as well as outside relationships, one can begin to see the signs. Then it is up to the adoptee to find the maturity and will to stop the behavior which will follow. Too often, one may say, "I can't help it. It is just the way I am."

To this I say, "Whoa! Stop!" When you do this, you are then doing what adoptive parents sometimes do—confusing genuine personality with trauma-driven behavior. Remember, behavior is a form of communication and has little to do with personality or who you are. It is time to communicate with words instead of behavior because that is what adults do. Often, however, the child-self gets in the way of an adult response, and a person will act out instead of talking it out. Although you can hope that people will accept your true essence, they certainly don't have to accept your behavior if it offends them. Confusing the two is self-indulgent. Expecting unconditional love from everyone is something mature people have to give up, especially if what they really mean is that others have to accept everything they do. This is magical thinking. Unconditional love and unconditional approval are two different things. Testing relationships is for children. Adults don't have to put up with testing from other adults. Remember that in relationships you are supposed to be on the same team, not in competition, not adversaries.

What is it that keeps one reacting to the old stimuli, enacting the old drama, resisting change? FEAR. Fear is the greatest growth-arrester known to man or woman. It paralyzes us or keeps us locked into old, destructive, repetitive ways of acting in the world. As mentioned earlier, it isn't justifiable fear which paralyzes us. When fear is appropriate, we can react by either fighting or fleeing. What most of us are reacting to or not reacting to is neurotic fear—fear of what *might* happen. Neurotic fear paralyzes and has no meaning. Instead, it keeps recreating old scenarios and hinders new ways of dealing with situations and people.

*A More Accurate Diagnosis*

This brings us to a more accurate diagnosis for what adoptees and birth mothers are suffering from—*post-traumatic stress disorder*. Some people are beginning to say that PTSD is becoming the latest pop diagnosis, the latest buzz word, like *borderline* in the 70s, *co-dependent* in the 80s, and *bi-polar* in the 90s. What I believe has happened is that up until recently we have not acknowledged how often or to what extent children have been traumatized, physically, emotionally, sexually, or psychologically. Just taking into consideration the millions of adoptees who have not been recognized as having suffered a trauma puts some perspective on the denial of the existence PTSD in our society. Calling it a pop diagnosis or a buzz word diminishes the horror of what has happened to children—how traumatized they may have been all along. Is it any wonder that as adults few people are able to achieve truly mature relationships? Everyone keeps reacting to all those old triggers. Trauma is based in reality. Unlike other psychological disorders, trauma is based on a true experience. In his work *Trauma and Memory*, Caruth says, "It is indeed the truth of the traumatic experience that forms the center of its psychopathology; it is not a pathology of falsehood or displacement of meaning, but of history itself" (Caruth, 1995). There is nothing untrue about the trauma and its effect, but it is in the repeated placement of it in the present which causes issues for trauma sufferers.

Therapists can help patients realize that as adults, experiences will not affect them in the same way as when they were children. Adults can be left, but they can't be abandoned. They are no longer helpless; they will not die. It just feels that way. That's the neurotic fear. This fear is maintained because it gives the illusion that one is in control: "I won't be abandoned if I don't connect. I won't be surprised by something if I don't take a risk." One won't have to confront the fear or to grow up and find adult solutions to problems so long as one can maintain one's childlike reactions to everything. Of course, one will also feel disempowered and victimized. Events in one's life have to be broken down into increments—what is really happening here? "Is the world really coming to an end, or did I just lose my job?" What are some interventions that can be applied? Bad things happen in everyone's life; it is how one handles them that shows one's true character. *One may have no control over certain events, but one should strive to have control over one's response to those events.*

## The Challenge of Adulthood

In order to grow up, to become empowered, therapists will have to help their patients begin to confront their fears and challenge their beliefs. They will have to honestly look at the ways the patients display their guilt and rage. Are these behaviors helping them to work through those feelings or are they, instead, perpetuating them? As described above, it is riding the limbic system in tandem with the therapist and her more healthy regulation of emotion that is one key. Sometimes there are adjunct therapies which may or may not be helping. Therapists need to look into what other forms of "help" their patients are getting. If a patient has been in a support group for five years and still feels just as guilty, angry, or hostile in the group as she did five years ago, perhaps she should quit the group. Sometimes these groups are not helping, and are only perpetuating the anger, guilt, or fear (tuning into the unregulated limbic brain of others in the room). They may be keeping the patient stuck in a childlike state. On the other hand, the patient has to ask himself the same question about the therapy? Is it keeping her stuck? What about current relationships? When one has come out of regression and is feeling more like taking on adult responsibilities, one has to be sure that one is moving forward.

When a person is in therapy, it is not always easy to tell if he is moving forward because so much of the changes are happening internally. I use the analogy of a long, dark tunnel. Many times in therapy the patient enters the tunnel. Because it is so dark he cannot tell if he is getting anywhere or not. However, weeks or months later, when the patient emerges at the end of the tunnel, he notices that he is not in the same place that he was before. Part of forward movement means plunging into the abyss, confronting the pain, going into that tunnel, and then the next one and the next one after that. If the patient wants to stop acting unconsciously, he will have to suffer—walk into the mouth of the tiger or drive unflinchingly into the tunnel. All that dancing around he has been doing all these years has been allowing him to avoid the reality of the past. It hasn't worked very well, so it is time to try something new. It is amazing how often people keep acting the same way and getting the same results, but never have the courage to change what they are doing. Changing it is dark and scary and takes a lot of courage, but it leads to someplace where he has never been before. Lewis, et al. put it this way, "… limbic connectedness of a working psychotherapy requires uncommon courage. A patient asks to surrender the life he knows and to enter an emotional world he has never seen; he offers himself up to be changed in ways he can't possibly envision." The life he is leaving is the life of the false self and the change is moving him toward a more authentic self. He doesn't have to do it alone. He *can't* do it alone. It is about limbic connectedness and has to be done in relationship. The therapeutic relationship with its *temanos,* crucible, or container may be the safest place to do it.

The heart of therapy for adoptees is in the relationship to the therapist. As Lewis, et al. say, "The *person* of the therapist is the converting catalyst, not his order or credo, not his spatial location in the room, not his exquisitely chosen words or denominational silences … the agent of change is who he *is.*" Who the therapist is must be a matter of research as well as intuition because if one has had a bad relationship with parents, that relationship is sometimes projected onto the therapist. The difference between intuition and projection is often a very thin line. Therefore, the reputation of the therapist is as important as the impressions of the patient. When the transference takes over, it is amazing how differently the therapist may be seen by each patient.

### Why Therapy and What About the Therapist?

Some people will ask, "Well, why can't I get the same results from a friend or a lover?" The answer is that to a certain extent you can if you are in relationship with someone who is acting from the authentic Self, who has good limbic regulation, is self-restrained and at peace with him or herself. There are two problems that come to mind, however. One is that the emotions of a friend, family member, or lover are entangled with the emotions of the adoptee. This makes healthy responses to behavior more difficult to achieve. The second is that most adoptees are attracted to others who are in pain like them. Their friends and lovers tend to have issues similar to or as difficult as their own. Therefore, the limbic brain is being influenced by woundedness, rather than wholeness. One of the wonderful responses that many patients have to therapy is that in the end they are attracted to healthier partners. It is difficult to figure out just how this happened because it often doesn't seem as if very much happened toward that end in the therapy. Limbic revision is a slow, almost imperceptible process. It is subtle and soft, but has dynamic results!

One hopes when one seeks help from a professional that the clinician will have more control over her limbic system than one's friends. However, as I mentioned when talking about the transference, that isn't always the case. It is crucial to be sure that the therapist has worked on her issues before beginning clinical work. One question to ask a therapist is "How much work have you done on yourself?" Or "Have you been in therapy as a patient and for how long?" Two years is a minimum. Some therapists may be put off by any personal questions being put to them, but you should consider this a professional question. It is as necessary as knowing that a physician has done his residency as well as having been to medical school. It is possible to get licenses to practice psychotherapy in many states without having done one's own therapeutic work. It is encouraged, but not required. Yet, the therapist's own personal therapy or analysis is crucial to his effectiveness in his clinical work. We are not dealing with a disease here. We are dealing with the soul. We cannot be too careful to whom we entrust our souls!

Therapy is time-consuming and costly. People ask, "But how long will this take?" Everyone hopes, of course, for a speedy recovery. People who grew up on television like to have things wrapped up in a nice, neat, sixty-minute segment. We are an impatient society. But we are not dealing with band-aids on the brain, we are dealing with almost impregnably imprinted neurological connections in the limbic brain that have to be changed. To quote Lewis, et al, "The neocortex rapidly masters didactic information, but the limbic brain takes mountains of repetition." The acquisition of emotional and relational knowledge "... requires an investment of time at which our culture balks" (Lewis, et al, 2000). Our culture is reflected in our insurance companies idea of how long therapy should take (which, I believe, is about six weeks!). Regardless, avoiding or putting off this process can be even more costly than doing it.

Plunging into the world of therapy takes courage and a willingness to stay for the long haul. It can be scary, messy, and at times tedious. But the result is being able to live in your own skin and the ability to make and sustain healthy relationships. Is it worth it? Human beings are meant to be in relationship. They are meant to give and receive love. Relationship has been basic to human existence since we lived in caves. If anything is getting in the way of that basic human need, something needs to change. Everyone deserves to live a full, meaningful life full of love.

*Heads Up for Therapists*

The treatment of adult adoptees is a very intense undertaking, one which challenges a therapist's skills, as well as the rigidity of traditional therapy. But the challenge is very different from that of working with borderlines in that there is an absence of the constant challenging of the therapist's competency or boundaries. Adoptees rarely question the therapist; they are much more apt to question themselves. Rather than boundaries being fluid, as with the borderline, they are more apt to be impermeable. The adoptee probably trusts no one and the therapist will be no exception. Connection seems dangerous and is avoided, except on a superficial level. Psychologically, this makes a lot of sense due to the patient's experience. Patience is needed on the part of the therapist.

Although Post Traumatic Stress Disorder (PTSD) is the closest diagnosis for those suffering from separation trauma, there are some problems with it as it is described in the DSM. That's because there is limited or no understanding of separation trauma, therefore no accommodation is made to include it in what constitutes PTSD. Please read J. Herman's *Trauma and Recovery* for a better understanding of the difficulties in using PTSD in diagnosing many traumas. Although she doesn't mention separation trauma, she does talk about the difficulties with the DSM diagnosis as it pertains to many different traumas.

Regardless of the diagnosis, the overall goal for the adoptee is to revive the baby soul and to discover and learn to love and accept the authentic Self so that she can learn to love and receive love from others. In order to do that, certain emotional responses must be modified via a revision of the limbic system. It is important that the therapist nurture the patient's growth from infancy to adulthood and not allow her to get stuck in infancy because of some need of his own. Only therapists who have had a thorough analysis themselves should work with adoptees in regression. The therapist has to be able to contain the bottomless abyss of sorrow as well as the tremendous rage of the abandoned newborn. Neither is easy to do. It requires an intimate knowledge of one's own vulnerabilities, as well as a faith in one's ability to withstand and contain the projections of one so deeply wounded.

## The Spiritual Component

I want to add a word or two about spirituality as it pertains to patients and their well-being. It is my belief that everyone has a spiritual life, even if he isn't aware of it. It does not have to involve any of the many religious faiths or denominations of the world. Sometimes it may be connected to a religion and sometimes it may not be. Having a spiritual life simply means believing in something other than the material or corporeal. A belief in the soul is in the realm of spirituality. Where do we get our ability to self-reflect? We don't need it for survival. Is that part of our spirituality, a part of the soul?

If it has not been happening all along, it will be time toward the end of therapy to explore the patient's spiritual life, whether it is defined as loved by God, connected to the universe, connected to all humanity, connected to nature, a known world view, a search for the meaning of life, a purpose in life outside the material realm, or caring for the soul. There is a need for adoptees to re-establish the sense of belonging, which may have disappeared along with the birth mother. Everyone's spiritual path is unique and each person has to find his own way. A therapist can help with this, but must not influence the direction of the pathway. There is a delicate balance between facilitating one's spiritual growth and directing it. That balance is essential to the well-being of the patient.

I have had patients from all the main religions except Hindu. I have had patients who abhor organized religion yet have a wonderful spiritual aura about them. I never try to change anything about their religious beliefs; I only try to get them to talk about how their spirituality affects them. I try to see how it may have influenced their lives. All religions encourage loving one another. Since love is essential to our well-being, perhaps we need to pay more attention to this aspect of religion. One can love and respect others without belonging to any denomination, and one can belong to a denomination and not show love and respect toward others. A great deal is in interpretation and how the individual places himself in the world.

In Chapter 16 on Spirituality, I explore in more detail what might be meant by spirituality and how it may help adoptees with their need for belonging. In this segment, I just wanted to alert therapists to the idea that spirituality means something to patients and it helps to know what that meaning is. A spiritual life can deepen and help nourish the soul.

## Treatment Methods to Explore

Before ending this chapter, I want to explore some alternative methods of treatment. There are many methods of treatment in psychotherapy. So long as the therapist understands the issues involved and has worked through most of his own issues, the method of treatment isn't so important. Every therapist has his own way of working in accordance with his specific personality and training. As I've said, the person of the therapist is more important than his methods. The important thing is to truly tune in to the patient and not just the false self. That being said, there are some specific treatments that have come on the scene recently which are interesting to consider when dealing with trauma. I will mention them here only in passing. A more thorough understanding can come from books or trainings dealing with each of these methods. A more extensive overview of the next four methods can be found in an article titled "Under the Microscope" by Mary Sykes Wylie in *The Family Therapy Networker*: July/August 1996, in which she looks at new approaches to treating PTSD.

*EMDR*

Since early trauma lacks visual or narrative memory, it is difficult to treat. Many of the behavioral or cognitive methods, although sometimes useful, will have no lasting effect on the beliefs which were imprinted as a result of trauma. In addition to limbic revision in the relationship with the therapist, one type of therapy which does seem to have a more permanent effect on those beliefs is Eye Movement Desensitization and Reprocessing (EMDR). This is a treatment discovered by Francine Shapiro of California. With this method, one visualizes the traumatic event or a representation of that event while one's eyes follow a back and forth pattern of finger motions by the therapist. This motion is believed to be similar to REM or Rapid Eye Movement—the motion of our eyes while dreaming.

The auditory form of this method is bi-lateral audio cueing, where one listens to a tone going back and forth between the left and right ears. I prefer this method to the eye movement type because it is passive and the full attention of the patient can be focused on the event, rather than on moving the eyes. Another sense, that of touch, can also be used in which a vibrating object is held in each hand. The point of bi-lateral cueing is to have more connection between the right and left brain. We know that the limbic brain and the neocortex do not agree much of the time when trauma has occurred. Even though we *know* that one thing is true, we may *sense or believe* that something else is true. For instance, an adoptee may know that he was not a bad baby, but still believes that he was. That belief has more "truth" to the adoptee than the cognitive knowing. What this bi-lateral work does is to challenge the limbic belief by allowing the understanding of the neocortex to permeate that limbic brain. Then the patient begins to not only understand something, but to feel it as well. In my experience, the easiest beliefs to change with EMDR are those based on guilt and shame. (I believe *Bi-Lateral Integration Process* would be a much better name for this therapy, except that its initials would be BLIP!)

This method can evoke rapid treatment effects because the neuronal bursts caused by a focused attention and alternative stimulation may interact with the limbic and cortical systems. This, in turn, can form a more integrated recognition of what is true. For adoptees, it can override some of the "baby beliefs" which still dwell in the limbic system and cause them to react inappropriately to stimuli that are no longer dangerous. For birth mothers, it can bring into focus the overwhelming pressures that went into their "decision" to surrender their children and allow them to begin to feel the reality of their situation, rather than their constant sense of guilt.

## TFT

A more puzzling form of repatterning of the brain's pathways is a finger tapping method called Thought Field Therapy (TFT), originating with a cognitive psychologist, Roger Callahan. With this method, which is based on the theory in Chinese medicine that energy flows along meridians and can be balanced and released by contact on acupressure points, one taps certain locations on the body corresponding to the part of the body which is holding the emotional pain or fear. The patient doesn't even have to talk about the trauma, but only tune in to it. Neither is it necessary to have any kind of rapport with the therapist.

This is probably the most controversial of the newer methods of treating PTSD because it defies any logical explanation for its success. In fact people who have been relieved of traumatic triggers often fail to credit TFT for having accomplished this feat, but find the relief of pain coincidental with the use of TFT! Coincidental or transformational, this method can make intense and overwhelming emotional responses to triggers seem like an event one is looking at in a scrapbook. It allows the patient to see the trauma as a snapshot of something, rather than as a recurring event. In other words, he appears to integrate the trauma as a memory with its proper place in history.

## TIR and VKD

Two other methods of treating PTSD are Traumatic Incident Reduction (TIR), founded by Frank Gerbode and Visual Kinesthetic Dissociation (VKD) based on Neuro-Linguistic Programming. In TIR the trauma is seen as never having been fully experienced, but resisted. The patient is thought to have *formed an intention* during the chaos of the event to fight it or escape from it, an intention which continues long after the event is past. This method depends upon the patient's being able "... to examine the circumstances and conditions—maybe forgotten—in which the old life-saving intention was made; examine it in light of new knowledge and let it go" (Wylie, 1996). It seems to me that there has to be a modicum of feeling in control for this method to work. In other words, it may work for birth mothers, but I have my doubts about its working for early childhood trauma.

With VKD there is a step-by-step process of "purposeful *dissociation* from the trauma, so that in the end the patient can view it from a distance and not become overwhelmed by it" (op. cit). Some things the therapist wants to know, after having established a rapport with the patient, are "... what he or she lost as a result of the trauma, what the client would like to have back and what he or she possibly gains by keeping the trauma alive" (op. cit). The client is monitored for physical reactions when thinking about the trauma and instructed to get in the "here and now" by making physical contact with the therapist or an object such as a chair and being told they are safe.

The client then retells the event, but this time seeing it as a movie the client is watching, the point being to gain some distance from the event. After a few more exercises, the client eventually realizes that he actually survived the event. This information is then transferred to the younger self of the patient "... along with any other reassurance, comfort and encouragement that might help" in order to ascertain what she did to survive and what she has done since. A shift has taken place in the client, and the traumatic event is seen in perspective. Again, I doubt that this method would be very effective with separation trauma, but I wanted to include it because it is very portable and fast. It may help with other traumas the adoptee may have experienced. All of the above treatments can be further explored in the July/August 1996 edition of *The Family Therapy Networker*—now called *The Psychotherapy Networker*—a journal for psychotherapists.

*The Decision Maker Belief Process*

The Decision Maker process was invented by Morty Lefkoe and is based on the idea that events have no inherent meaning, only the meaning our minds give them. As children we often give the wrong meaning to events, making ourselves largely responsible for them. Thus we end up believing that we are flawed in some way. His idea is to present a series of other meanings which we could have chosen instead, so that the meaning we've been living with all this time is challenged. It isn't that it is wrong, only that it isn't the only reason out there. Maybe one of the others is true. What if one of the others is true? Do we really have to live with the guilt and shame of our early interpretation when there are so many other alternatives?

Anyone can login to www.decisionmaker.com and find out more about this interesting approach to changing one's belief system. Although skeptical at first, I was impressed by a demonstration of Lefkoe's ideas. When one thinks about it, it is true that meaning is given to events, rather than their having inherent meaning. We can see this demonstrated when studying different cultures, where different meanings are given to the same events because of cultural differences.

This doesn't mean, for instance, that separation from the birth mother is not a devastating event for adoptees worldwide. It just means that the beliefs they formed as a result of that event—"I must have some kind of flaw or my mother would have kept me"—may not be the only interpretation of that event. And although many of you know that this is not the only interpretation, it is somehow different when done in a structured way in one of these sessions.

Check out the Web site. It may be interesting to you.

*Redeeming the Shadow*

Remember what Robert Bly said about how much of ourselves we lose—thrown into a mile-long bag we drag along behind us—when we perceive that someone disapproves of something we do? We are all born with a 360-degree personality and as infants can express "... the full breadth of our human nature, without editing or censoring" (*Shadow Work Seminars, Inc.*). Of course, I mentioned that adoptees, since their first postnatal experience is the disappearance of mother, don't even get to experience "the full breadth of human nature" at all. Immediately after they breathe their first breath, they are whisked from their mothers. So, right from the get-go they sense that they are not all right, not acceptable to their mothers. Ninety percent of themselves goes straight into the bag.

The idea of calling these repressed aspects of ourselves—which we can't directly know—*the shadow* began with Carl Jung. It is an apt term for all these unconscious, forbidden, repressed parts of the human psyche. How do you identify your shadow or begin to know what parts of yourself you have repressed if it is unconscious? One way is to notice what you *project onto others*. The traits we deny in ourselves we tend to project onto others. This can include "good" traits, as well as "bad" traits (envy as well as disgust). The feelings we have about that other person are neither neutral nor mild. There is a real charge behind our disgust or our envy. Bly says, "When one 'projects,' one is really giving away an energy or power that rightfully belongs to one's own treasury" (*A Little Book on the Human Shadow*, 1988). He suggests that we begin to retrieve those gold nuggets that are hiding in the mile-long bag we drag behind us.

Another way to discover your shadows is to notice things you find yourself doing involuntarily. Do you keep getting into relationships that are bad for you? Do you always arrive late for appointments? Do you ignore your good intentions about changing bad habits you have formed? On the other hand, do you find yourself at violin concerts, even though you don't believe yourself to be particularly musical? Are you drawn to art museums although you've never taken a painting class? Although you may claim not to like people, do you find people coming to you for advice? Perhaps you have talents that you have never allowed yourself to explore. This can be especially true for adoptees who are placed in a family where their particular talents are not valued. It is time to find the nuggets of gold in that long sack you are carrying around. Even the so-called "bad" traits that you keep projecting onto others can have value. And even if you can find no value in your vindictive side, for example, it is better to know that it exists in you than to always project it out to others. Acknowledging your own shadow can help you gain control over it, instead of allowing it to control you.

The point of shadow work is to explore the inner landscape and discover the gold that is hiding there. The false beliefs assumed by adoptees (and some birth mothers) can be challenged with shadow work. Shadow work can be done with a therapist familiar with Jungian psychology or in Shadow Work Seminars. It needs to be done gradually and in a safe place. Shadow Work Seminars, Inc. is a trademark for a particular method of working with the shadow. You can look on their web site for more information. You can also read Robert Bly's book *A Little Book on the Human Shadow* to gain a better understanding of this theory. I especially recommend the chapter called "Honoring the Shadow—An Interview with William Booth."

*Summary*

Although most of the feelings and behaviors evoked by separation trauma may not be pathological, they may be maladaptive and inappropriate in one's present life. If certain reactions and behaviors are getting in the way of a satisfying and meaningful way of life, they need changing. Because most adoptive mothers were unaware of their infant's loss and need to grieve, they were unable to help the child regulate his or her emotions surrounding that loss. This was a huge deficit for the adoptee and has often kept him in a perpetual state of anxiety and sorrow. The limbic brain connected in a certain way as a result of this trauma and may still need revising. This is a long and often painful process, but it can lead to a life which welcomes connection, intimacy, and love, rather than avoiding them. Some of the newer types of therapy may help speed up the process. I agree with friend and colleague Ruth Cohn, who says, "I now find that EMDR and in-depth psychodynamic work to be a winning combination. While there is no substitute for the painstaking work of developing the self and relationship capacity, I find that more quickly working through the experiences that have hindered or aborted those processes facilitates the relationship work" (Cohn, 1998). Although it is the relation to the therapist which can have the most permanent effect on relationship issues, that process can be expedited by some of the newer therapies which work more directly with the neurological system.

Being correctly diagnosed is paramount to getting the right treatment. Or, rather, not being diagnosed inaccurately is what is important. I don't care about a diagnosis except to satisfy insurance companies. Post Traumatic Stress Disorder is the closest diagnosis in the DSM, but it, too, comes up short. It is better suited to responses to events such as war or natural disasters. However, many of the criteria are true for adoptees and birth mothers, and some of the various treatment methods for PTSD can be helpful. It must be understood that adoptees suffer from both acute trauma (the separation from mother) and chronic trauma (living without biological mirroring). The second, although more prolonged, may be more easily treated.

The important criterion for treating adoptees is resurrecting the baby soul and/or the authentic Self. It means taking the adoptee out of victimhood into the realm of empowerment via withdrawing blame and taking responsibility for his impact on others. It means exploring a spiritual connection as well as guiding him in allowing a connection to others and welcoming love into his life.

# CHAPTER 20
A Call for a New Paradigm

Thousands of letters validating the existence of the primal wound and the lasting scars that separation trauma leaves on its victims point to the need for a new paradigm for adoption. The altruistic view that society has held for so long—the unaware baby, the chosen child, the grateful child, the rescuing parents—can no longer be sanctioned. Now that adoptees, birth parents, and adoptive parents are speaking out there is enough empirical evidence to cast doubt upon that cherished viewpoint. So what are we to do? Can we or should we eliminate adoption? There are people who believe this is the answer.

## Adoption Is Here to Stay

I don't think eliminating adoption is a realistic idea. There are too many children languishing in foster care who need permanent homes. I wish that with some help all the parents of these children could become adequate parents, but as a therapist I know too much to believe this to be possible. There are children who are neglected or severely abused in their biological homes. I have worked with some of them as adults. They would have been better off in good adoptive homes despite the pain of separation from their biological families. Having biological parents neglect or severely mistreat you your entire childhood is a chronic betrayal that children don't need. It is profoundly wounding.

I certainly believe that we can do more to help parents become good parents. I think there should be every bit as much money allocated for parenting classes for biological parents who want help as is allocated for the foster care system. Why pay strangers to take care of children if using the same amount of money could teach their own parents how to become "good enough" parents? There appears to be a punitive aspect to our current system in taking children away from their real parents. Perhaps knowing that the children are suffering from this practice and could do better in their own biological families if their parents had help will wake up those in charge of children's social welfare. We can only hope.

However, I know that there are some mothers and fathers out there, who, no matter how much help they are given, will never become parents who can give any kind of stability and safety to a child. Their children have been in the foster care system for years. They have been given chance after chance to visit their kids, to get help for their drug or alcohol addictions or their anger problems, yet they never come through. How long are these children to wait for permanency in their living situations? When a decision has to be made as to what is best for these children, sometimes adoption is the best solution.

### Euphemisms Don't Help

There have been suggestions made that the children could remain with a permanent family and the family would be considered legal guardians. The biological parents would have visitation rights when indicated. While there may be merits to this solution, I don't think it is the answer. Besides the fact that people wanting children may not be willing to do this, neither may the children. I have talked to many children who were in foster care most of their lives, some of them with the same foster parents. Every one of them wished they had been adopted. Even though most adoptees have trouble feeling as if they belong in their adoptive families, many know that their adoptive parents feel that they belong. It gives them comfort to be accepted and loved in this way. That might not be the case if the parents were considered only guardians. I do believe that all children should have access to their biological families and heritage. Open adoptions may be the answer if they are made binding—if the agreement is legalized and both sets of parents are held to the agreement. Binding open adoption may be harder on the parents, but it would definitely be better for the child.

The point is that there are always going to be children who cannot, for one reason or another, live with their biological parents. Trying to eliminate adoption by calling it something else is not the answer. Women who find themselves in the difficult situation of being pregnant out of wedlock need options, one of which may be adoption—hopefully open adoption. But we must make sure that these women have every opportunity to keep their children if they wish to. They should *never* be coerced into giving up their children! That decision should not be made before the birth takes place or when the mother is still under the influence of the birthing procedure or sedation. Eliminating adoption seems like one of those "fooling ourselves" things we do sometimes—calling something a by different name just to make us feel better.

## The Old Paradigm

If adoption is here to stay, we should at least create a new paradigm for it. Before doing so, however, we need to look at some of the aspects of the old paradigm and try to understand why we have been hanging on to them. We know that change is resisted in general. We see it in science, where old theories die hard, and in religion, where updating religious ceremonies is resisted. Adoption may be like a combination of both religion and science. Yet, perhaps neither the religion nor the science is sound.

## Society and Altruism

The old paradigm is based on myth and altruism. Deeply embedded in our culture is the belief that adoption is an altruistic act—that adoption rescues children from a terrible fate. Adoptive parents are seen as heroes in this scenario—selflessly plucking these children from a meaningless or difficult life. While this may be true in some instances, for the most part, this was not the case. A couple of years of help from social programs or from the parents of the young mother could have allowed many young women to have kept their children, thus avoiding the primal wound … for both of them.

## The Bias Against Birth Mothers

Being an unwed mother today does not have the same stigma that it did ten or twenty years ago. Young mothers have more options than they did in the past. This has resulted in a reversal of the 97%/3% ratio of young unwed white women giving up their babies. Yet there are still people today who are coercing young women into relinquishing their babies. There are many people who want to adopt babies and many attorneys who are anxious to accommodate them. This means that babies are at a premium. That there are still young women who feel ashamed or overwhelmed for having gotten pregnant makes for happy hunting grounds for unscrupulous adoption facilitators and attorneys.

And God help a young woman if, after having signed the preliminary papers, she dares to change her mind, even in the first few days or weeks. In the minds of many, this is considered the height of betrayal and subterfuge; she is chastised and vilified. Despite any progress we think we might have made in our humanity, the prevailing feeling in this country is that the birth mother is just an instrument though which another set of parents is to receive a baby. Some well-publicized cases in this country demonstrate just how biased people are against birth mothers and toward adoptive parents. What is it lurking in our psyches that make us so vindictive toward these young women?

Some states are making it more and more difficult for pregnant women to make an informed decision. They are asked (coerced) to sign away their rights to their children within hours of having given birth—when they are still fatigued from the birthing process, sedated, and in shock about the tremendous change in their lives. Sometimes they are asked to relinquished even before giving birth. Babies may not be real to some mothers until after birth. There is something punitive and cruel in this system—something dark, which needs to be addressed.

We must look into our consciences to better serve these young women. It needs to be stated and understood by all concerned that *no mother owes someone else her baby.*

*Adoption Myths*

There are many myths tied to adoption. One is that *the adoptive parents will be better parents than the biological parents.* At one time, it was deemed necessary for a couple to be married and the mother able to stay home with the baby to bring stability into the life of the child. A young mother was seen as unsuited to rear her own child if she was unmarried or too young. (At one time, she was considered mentally ill if she "got herself pregnant." No such label was placed upon the father—well, after all, she *got herself* pregnant!) In today's "adoption business" it isn't necessary to be married or to even have a partner to adopt a baby. People adopt kids and leave them in day care right from the beginning. There are a lot of people adopting (and giving birth to) children who really don't want to rear children. Or who don't have the time to rear children. I know of several people who have adopted, but haven't changed their singles life-style at all. They make no accommodation for the child they wanted so badly. I have nothing against single people adopting children if they are prepared to deal with the differences between an adoptive and a biological family and can be available to the child. Children will not attach to absent parents.

The *unaware baby* myth, although disproven by numerous perinatal studies, is still believed by many people. There is the belief that we can just willy-nilly substitute mothers and the baby will be none the wiser. I have talked about the awareness of babies in *The Primal Wound.* The new brain research should give us even more pause to consider the impact of these kinds of substitutions on the wiring of our children's brains. Adoption may be necessary; this is not a reason to ignore the difficulties it presents for the child. We cannot keep putting our heads in the sand about the impact that both the substitution of mothers and the absence of mothers have on the lives of children—adopted or biological.

The *chosen child* and the *grateful child* myths are two other beliefs that die hard. Although made to feel as if it were the case, most adoptees do not feel chosen so much as they feel unchosen—unchosen by their birth mothers. To be chosen by anyone else after that is anticlimactic. So far as being grateful, it is the adoptive parents who should be grateful. They are the ones pursuing the adoption. They are the ones who got what they wanted. No child would choose to be separated from his biological mother. That he may have to be separated from her is a different thing altogether. That is an intellectual, adult decision, not an emotional/sensual baby experience. Although grateful for many things his parents may have done for him, no child should be obligated to feel grateful for having a loving set of parents. That should be his right.

### Negating the Baby's Experience

The reason so many of these myths have hung on to our societal belief system is that no one is thinking about the emotional, psychological, or neurological ramifications of separating babies and mothers. I have always cringed when mention is made of contracts between surrogate mothers and the parents to whom the baby is going. Contracts are for commodities and services. *A child should not be considered a commodity.* And carrying a baby for someone else should not be considered a service. *These are human beings we are talking about!* We abolished slavery in 1865, yet we still think we can contract for the future of a human life—without the person who is most affected by it having any say in it.

All these contracts and agreements—don't get me started about the anonymous sperm and egg donor programs!—are made for the convenience or desires of adults. No one is thinking about how it is affecting the children involved. How is she feeling about having been separated from her mother? How is it affecting her emotionally? psychologically? neurologically? spiritually? There seems to be such a consensus in this country—by both men and women—for ignoring the importance of mothers in the lives of their children. And thus, we continue to ignore the emotional turmoil caused by the absence of mother. There is a great deal of hypocrisy in what we say. Some religious groups who believe that mothers should stay home with their children make exceptions of single mothers. "Get them off welfare and into the job market," is the cry. Well, forget about the mothers! What about the children? Why should the children of these mothers be any less deserving of having their mothers home with them than their more affluent neighbors? If having mother home is good for children whose mothers can afford to stay home, isn't is also good for children whose mothers are struggling? Why aren't we helping with this? Where is our compassion?

Even today, in the 21st century, society's main method of helping a young mother out of a dilemma is not by giving her the means and help to remain with her baby, but to give her baby to someone else. While sometimes this may be necessary, there needs to be some thought given as to how the children respond emotionally to what is happening to them. They do not experience separation and adoption the way the adults involved do. For them, it is a terrifying and confusing experience. They cannot take in what the adults are trying to do for them. Their emotions are flooding them, leaving them in a fog. We can no longer pretend that just because adults have good reasons for what they do, children do not suffer. Is anyone paying attention?

*Secrets and Lies/Smoke and Mirrors*

The idea that a child's identity changes when the adoptive parents take him home has to be challenged. A legal document does not change the heritage and identity of a child. Although experience and environment will act upon the genetic makeup of a person, it does not change the basic personality. The tabula rasa or malleable child is another myth to challenge. Not knowing one's heritage or ancestry means that the adopted child has no mooring, no anchor. It is one reason so many of them feel as if they are floating. There is nothing to shove off from—no way to anticipate the future. The secret of his birth family makes many adoptees feel ashamed. Schools' insistence year after year on the Family Tree project brings the impact of this secret to the surface for many adoptees. They know they are supposed to be members of their adoptive family, but they also know they are not related to them. Adoption may be necessary, but adoptees should always be able to retain their biological identity and have access to their own family tree.

Many of the myths that perpetuate the altruistic adoption picture are beginning to crumble. However, there are still too many people who have not educated themselves in the new research and continue to believe that picture. Those people who are more educated and enlightened must be ready to inform those living in the past of the new discoveries. It is time to consider a more humane approach to adoption.

# A New Paradigm

Several years ago, a resolution on adoption was drawn up by the Hague Convention. The first tenet of that resolution was "A child should not be considered for adoption unless he *needs* parents." This seems like a sensible enough idea. Yet this country did not sign this resolution for many years. Another tenet of the Resolution was "No mother should be coerced into giving up her baby." In this country, young mothers who changed their minds within a few days of having relinquished were told they were too late; the child belonged to the adoptive parents. Yet, clearly this was not a child who needed parents. Clearly having the parents at the birth ready to take the baby away was coercive. Both mother and child would suffer from that decision. Honoring the Hague Convention Resolution on Adoption is one of the first things we must do.

It is time for us to stop being naïve about the needs of children and begin to put their needs on the front burner. Sometimes this may mean that adoption is the right thing to do and sometimes it will mean that the biological mother just needs extra help. If grandparents or other relatives are acting as the caregivers for children, they may need and deserve as much financial assistance as foster parents do. Do we care about children or don't we?

It is my opinion that we need a new paradigm for children—period. Our capitalistic society and our denigration of motherhood have meant that more and more mothers are leaving their children in day care. However, working mothers are not the necessarily the problem. There are some mothers who are stay-at-home moms who spend as little or less time with their children than working mothers do. And where are the fathers? Fathers need to be emotionally involved with their children as well. This means spending time with their kids. Many children from different situations are feeling alienated from their parents and unappreciated. We are a society seemingly unwilling to make sacrifices for our children—real sacrifices, not the kind that means parents have to be running all over the place taking the kids to ten different activities a week. How much time do you as a family spend together—just being together, not necessarily going to some activity? not watching TV? not each going his own way? Do you ever talk about important things? Do you know what your child thinks about life? Do you know what his fears are? his hopes? his aspirations? How does he see you as a couple? as parents? How do you see yourselves as a couple or as parents? Have you changed your lifestyle for your children? I know that many of you have and do. But there are many children who are languishing, not in foster care, but in the care of their parents—biological and adoptive.

*Family Values*

Americans live in a materialistic society. This is no secret. But do we have any idea what this has done to our values? What has happened to integrity? How are the problems of companies such as Enron playing out in smaller ways in individual families? Are parents modeling *integrity* for their children? Are children being taught courtesy? Is *courtesy* being modeled in the home? What about *respect? honesty? fairness? generosity?* Are racial slurs being spoken in the home? What are the spiritual values being taught? Is religion being practiced one day a week, then ignored the other six days? Many children think that getting caught is the sin. Is your child one of these? Where did he learn this? Do your children know the difference between right and wrong as it pertains to their relationships with others? Children learn from their parents—from the way their parents live their lives, not what they are told. How are you doing with this?

For adoptive families, values should include being open to talking about adoption anytime the kids want to. This requires a certain attitude of openness on the part of parents. Children know when parents are just giving lip-service to allowing talk about birth families and other aspects of adoption. Children know if it is safe or not. They will not talk about it if they believe it to be unsafe. Being open does not mean making up things parents don't know. For instance, saying that "Your birth mother loved you so much she wanted you to have a good home," may or may not be true. In any case, it won't make any sense to the child. It is better to tell a child that someday he can ask his birth mother why she relinquished him.

Family values are important to all families. It may be more difficult to instill these values in adoptive kids, especially the acting out kids. It feels too much like control. The compliant kids will follow every rule. Adoptive parents should not let that fool them.

### Being Honest

There is no way putting a five-week-old baby in day care is not going to have an adverse affect on the child. It may be necessary, but it is not without consequences. We talk about our children not understanding consequences, but do we? as adults? as parents? We have a tendency to put our heads in the sand when it comes to situations for which we have no solution or for which we don't want to have to sacrifice too much for a solution. Are we willing to sacrifice buying a home or a bigger home, going on expensive vacations, buying an SUV so that our children can feel safe? Children don't care where they live as long as they live with mom and dad. Given a choice—a bigger house or mom at home—guess what most kids would choose. If it is necessary for both parents to work (or *the* parent in single-parent households) then there still needs to be an awareness and acknowledgment of the sacrifice the children are making for this—what it is costing them.

Educating adoptive parents is high on the list of things to do to reform adoption. If the adoptive mother fails to be told or fails to believe that her child is aware of the differences between his two mothers, she will be missing an honest connection with her child in favor of a myth—that it makes no difference to the child who the mother is, that he is not aware of the absence of his first mother, that he is not grieving. She will be unable to be attuned to him, to soothe him, and to help him regulate his emotions about this terrible experience in his life. He will be unable to find a way to truly connect to her. Adoptive mothers can do a great deal to help heal this loss for their children and to forge a real connection as a result, but they have to become realistic about abandonment and loss.

Before a couple (or person) even decides to adopt a child, there has to be honesty as to why they want to do so. Is it because a child is a symbol to them? Is it what everyone thinks they should do? Is it because the woman has a truly instinctive need to be a mother—or that both partners want to be parents? Do they really want to make the sacrifices necessary to rear a child? Children take a great deal of time and sacrifice. They cannot be a symbol for something missing in another person. They cannot be expected to live out the unrealized lives of their parents. They are individuals who have their own needs and characteristics, and, in the case of adopted children, those characteristics may be quite different from those of their parents. How will you deal with a child who is very different from you? How will you deal with a child who was traumatized in the first few minutes of his life? Are you ready?

## Children for Sale

Who will be facilitating adoptions? There is too much profit motive in adoption in this country. First of all, we must take money out of adoption. We should not be in the business of buying and selling kids. Anyone with money, regardless of their qualifications or their preparedness to parent, can adopt. Because agencies are no longer in charge of many adoptions, older women are adopting children or obtaining them through surrogacy—people who may not live long enough to see them graduate from high school or get married. Please don't try to tell me that they are doing this for the children. Adoptees, by their very definition, have already lost one set of parents. To be adopted by elderly parents—especially if the mother is over 50—will cause them a great deal of anxiety.

With the majority of adoptions being handled by attorneys, and with attorneys being a majority in most legislatures, taking steps to ensure that children have good parents is unlikely in the near future. Agencies were never perfect. Many social workers were just as naïve about the needs of infants and the toll separating babies and their mothers had on both as anyone else. Yet there was at least an attempt to interview and evaluate a couple's or person's suitability to parent. There was a modicum of regulation. Now, there is only money. People who have been turned down by several adoption agencies can adopt if they have enough money. This needs to be changed. *No one should be making money on the heads of little children.* What are we thinking?!!!

## The Best Interest of the Child Revisited

Any new paradigm needs to take into account more about the emotional well being of the child and less about the desires or convenience of adults. I have heard and seen so much nonsense done in the name of doing what is in the best interest of the child that I hesitate to even use the term. For instance, the courts are prone to divide the physical custody of children of divorce. I submit that rarely is this ever in the best interest of the child, especially young children. This is to placate the parents. Young children should always be in the physical custody of the mother, unless she is *truly unfit* to be a mother. Fathers will be upset at me for this statement, but I hold it to be true. Young children need their mothers more than they need their fathers. Fathers can and should be active in the lives of their young children, but kids should not be shifted back and forth like ping-pong balls between their parents. This is especially true if the parents have very different values and parenting styles. This means that children have to constantly be shifting the way they respond to parents. It can be confusing and exhausting. Parents should be making the adjustments and sacrifices, not the children.

I cannot imagine what court-retained psychologists are thinking when they recommend that joint physical custody be given for a 15-month-old child. I challenge them to have a brain study done to determine what this is doing to the wiring of this child's brain. Joint physical custody is not in the best interest of most children and young children need their mothers. If the children are older, then perhaps the father can be given physical custody. In fact, in the case of adolescent boys, this might be preferred. However, I don't think it is a good idea to have an adolescent girl living with her father unless he is married or in a committed relationship. I am not necessarily thinking about the danger of incest here (she might be in more danger from her mother's boyfriend), but of an adolescent girl's tendency to try to be the emotional support—"little wife"—for their fathers. Both parents, if they remain single after divorce (or single parents in general) need to be very careful that they don't rely on their child or children for all their emotional support. Children should not be their parents' confidants.

So far as adoptive parents are concerned, I have already stated that they have to be aware of the child's immediate history before coming into their home. This includes the separation from the birth mother. This history will come to haunt them if they ignore it and don't take the steps necessary to help in the healing process of their child. If possible, they should keep the lines of communication and their doors open to the birth families. Although it may seem harder, it is definitely in the best interest of their child to do so. Step families do it; so can adoptive families. There are, of course, some exceptions to this such as drug-addicted parents who are not fit to be with the child. In such cases, there need to be some biological relatives available to allow the child to be genetically mirrored in order to promote self-esteem and a sense of belonging.

*Education Is Necessary*

Adoptive parents can't be expected to meet the emotional needs of their child if they have no idea what those needs are. They have to be informed that adoptive families are different from biological families in important ways. They have to be given techniques and skills to be able to better meet the needs of their child.

Before that can happen, there has to be more of a consensus among professionals that relinquishment causes issues for adopted children that biological children may not have to face. So we first have to educate the professionals. When talking before pediatricians at Grand Rounds in several hospitals, I was amazed that this group of doctors, who administer to children, have almost no understanding of how rearing an adopted child may differ from rearing a biological child. This is important information because of the somatic reactions some of these children have to anxiety. Doctors are interested, however, and are willing to learn. (See "What Doctors Need to Know about Adoptive Families" and "What Adoptive Parents Can Do" in the Appendix.)

I find that many parents are also willing to learn. I have spoken to many pre- or new adoptive parents. Although they wish the primal wound didn't exist and that parenting their young children would be no different than it would be with biological children, many are now aware that this is a pipe dream. They are eager to understand the emotional lives of their children and to help them. But there are too few people educating them. I get calls from adoptive parents all over the country who want help. They find the helping professions lacking in their knowledge of adoptive families. We need to get the professionals up to speed about relinquishment and adoption, not only as pertains to the adoptees and their parents, but as to the pain of the birth mothers as well.

*Doing Our Best as Parents*

There are many wonderful parents doing a very good job with their children. Yet parenting is a daunting job. In a little aside titled "P.S." in her column, Ask Marilyn, in *Parade* magazine, Marilyn von Savant says, "Raising children is a lot like managing a portfolio of stocks: When you look back on what happened, everything you should have done seems perfectly clear, and you can't imagine why it wasn't obvious to you at the time" (von Savant, 2003). Isn't this the truth! What parent doesn't wish he or she could go back and "do it right this time"? Because even if we have six kids and should have it down pat, each child is unique, each child has a different perception of what is going on, each child requires a different style of parenting. So we are bound to make mistakes no matter how many children we have or how great we may seem as parents.

Parenting requires so many skills. It requires so much sacrifice. But is there anything more rewarding? Is there anything more important than guiding children to be kind, unselfish, loving, contributing, and compassionate people? When I watch some of the parents on Oprah or Dr. Phil, I wonder, "What are these parents thinking?" Yet I see a real wish to change, to become better, more effective parents. We need always to keep the child in mind, and that doesn't mean indulging our children—quite the opposite. It means loving them, cherishing them, respecting them, nurturing them, guiding them, setting boundaries for them, challenging them, and encouraging them. What else can we do to help our kids grow into adults with integrity, honesty, and respect for others? Part of the answer is that we can live that way ourselves.

*Summary*

The new paradigm for adoption has to include integrity, honesty, education, and intelligence. We cannot continue rely on wishful thinking and ignore the true experience of the children, the birth parents, or the adoptive parents. Adoption may be necessary, but it is not accomplished without trauma, confusion, and loss on the part of the child, as well as the birth mother. Adoption cannot be successful without sacrifice, attunement, love, and compassion. And it is not complete without the understanding and support from society as to the pain, complexities and intricacies of relinquishment and adoption—a realistic view, rather than an altruistic one—so that understanding, compassion, and support can be given to all members of the adoption triad. For so long each part of the triad has felt all alone in his/her struggles. No one outside adoption seemed to be able to understand what it meant to relinquish a child, to adopt a child, or to be relinquished and adopted. This is where the real paradigm shift has to come—in the hearts and minds of everyone.

# APPENDICES

## Appendix I

Questions To Ask Yourself—Chapters 3–7

*Fear*

1. Does my fear have anything to do with my present circumstance in life?
2. Am I afraid of every new situation, even before I know anything about it?
3. Do I fear situations, or do I fear that *I can't handle* situations?
4. Do I need to fear that my present partner will leave me—has s/he given me any reason to believe that s/he will? How might I be contributing to the reason, if there is one?
5. Is it necessary that everyone like me? (Do I like everyone?)
6. Do I understand that change doesn't mean something is wrong, only different?
7. Will my fear of intimacy make my partner stay or leave? Am I setting myself up for the thing I fear the most?
8. Is keeping myself secret keeping myself safe?
9. Do I believe that making a mistake will be catastrophic?
10. Am I willing to take risks instead of living a fear-based life?
11. Do I understand that not everyone experiences anxiety on a daily basis?
12. Am I using fear as an excuse to stay stuck in my life?
13. Do I want to change or am I comfortable as I am?

*Anger*

1. Is my anger appropriate to the situation going on now or is it out of proportion?
2. Is my response appropriate or is it over the top?
3. At whom am I really angry?
4. Is my anger covering up a feeling I don't want to have, such as fear or sorrow?

5. Does venting my anger have any long-term benefits or does it just feel good at the time?

6. Is my anger about my adult life or is it a vestige of my childhood trauma?

7. Is my anger adversely affecting my relationships with my spouse/partner and children?

8. Is the person making me angry really trying to denigrate me or am I overreacting?

9. Am I picking a fight because I want an adrenaline rush or am I truly upset?

10. Do I really think I can thoughtfully discuss what I am upset about while I am angry?

11. Do I want to endanger my health by using anger as a foil to more honest emotions?

## Guilt

1. Do I hold myself responsible for my own relinquishment?

2. Do I hold other adoptees to this same standard? If not, why not?

3. Do I feel guilty for things over which I had/have no control?

4. Do I take responsibility for things over which I *do* have control?

5. Do I understand that I could not help my behavior as a child and need to forgive myself for acting the way I did?

6. If as an adult I have offended or hurt someone, have I acknowledged this and asked for forgiveness? Will I now stop hurting others?

7. Do I expect my spouse/partner to pick up my IOUs from childhood?

8. Do I always have to blame someone for things that happen to me?

9. What can I do to let go of my shame?

10. Is my shame based upon false baby beliefs?

11. If shame is the underside of narcissism, how can I focus attention away from myself?

12. When I keep parts of myself hidden from others, do I realize that this practice is shame-based and will inhibit connection?

13. Am I avoiding close relationships because I don't believe I am worthy of love?

14. What *imaginary crimes* have I committed? What am I getting out of holding on to them?

15. Can I begin to believe others' ideas of me instead of retaining my baby belief?
16. As a birth mother, can I forgive myself for having given in to society's plan for my baby?
17. Do I understand that shame rendered me incapable of making my own decision?
18. Do I promise myself to separate healthy guilt from neurotic guilt, take action on the things I need to resolve, and let go of the rest?

*Sorrow*

1. Do I sometimes get angry instead of allowing my more honest feelings of loss and sorrow come up?
2. Has it ever occurred to me that I suffered a tremendous loss even before I had recall?
3. As a birth mother, have I ever mourned the loss of my baby?
4. Has it ever occurred to me that the birth father may also have felt loss?
5. As a birth father, have I allowed myself to feel the depth of my sorrow toward the birth mother and our child?
6. As an adoptive mother, have I recognized the sorrow I feel in not having connected with my child the way I want to?
7. Was I able to recognize sorrow in my child?
8. Do any of us realize that if we suppress any feeling, we are hampering our ability to experience all other emotions?
9. Have I ever had a witness to my grief or do I keep it a secret—sometimes even from myself?
10. Am I afraid to allow my feelings of sorrow to surface for fear that I will never stop crying?
11. Have I ever done anything that will help bring some kind of resolution to my grief?
12. What kind of a ritual could aid in the resolution of my sorrow?
13. Do I identify with my sadness and believe that in giving it up I will lose part of myself?
14. Do I understand that facing my grief and sorrow will allow me to feel other emotions?
15. When will I be ready to be honest about my grief?

*Joy*

1. Do I feel fearful or guilty when I catch myself feeling joyful?
2. What are my superstitions connected to feeling happy?
3. Do I know the kinds of places, activities, or people that make me happy?
4. Do I avoid joyful experiences in order to feel more in control?
5. Do I depend on a substance to feel happy? Is that real happiness?
6. When is the last time I did something just for fun?
7. How long did the feeling of happiness or joy last?
8. Do I believe that if joy doesn't last is isn't worth feeling?

# Appendix II

## What Doctors Need To Know About Adoptive Families

- An adoptive family is different from a biological family.
- An infant knows its own mother at birth: smell, voice, heartbeat, energy, skin, etc.
- He knows adoptive mother is "wrong mother" (not bad mother).
- The child comes into the family traumatized by the separation from the mother.
- Loss of bonding results in elevation in pulse rate, blood pressure, adrenaline and cortisol levels, lower serotonin levels.
- No matter what we call is (relinquishment, surrender) the child FEELS abandoned.
- Neurological connections are influenced by severing of bond with mother.
- The natural order of things is interrupted: later difficulty with cause and effect.
- Infant cannot make sense or integrate what has happened to him: world unsafe, chaos, confusion, existential difficulties.
- Child is grieving. Mother needs to notice signs.
- Signs of depression: unresolved grief, anxiety, fear of another abandonment, daydreaming, dissociation.
- Somatic responses to anxiety: irritability, gastro-intestinal problems, projectile vomiting, asthma, rashes, sleep disturbances, etc.

- Affect: rage, sadness, fear, numbness, dissociation, constriction, depersonalization.
- Adoptive family cannot mirror child as biological family could have. Child must adapt.
- Bonding with adoptive mother will be difficult: fear of another abandonment: Anxious attachment (clinging) not the same as bonding. Mother might misread this.
- Mother needs to be vigilant as to emotional state of infant and soothe his fears and grief.
- Lack of mirroring makes child feel as if doesn't fit in adoptive family.
- Child has no genetic markers for knowing how to be in the family. Hypervigilant.
- Child begins to adapt: in process begins to lose self. Becomes "chameleon."
- Family dynamics will be affected. (Families with biological children need to take note.)
- Child copes with pain of loss in one of two ways: compliance, acquiescence, and withdrawal, or aggression, provocation, and acting out. In two-child families: usually one of each.
- Behavioral methods of coping have nothing to do with basic personality.
- Behavior is not abnormal. Is normal way of responding to an abnormal event: separation trauma.
- Although child with each coping style needs help, usually parents of acting-out child only ones who seek help.
- Most of the child's difficulty will be with the adoptive mother: potential abandoner.
- Many parents, not understanding the issues, blame themselves. Feel isolated.
- Children will have difficulties around birthdays (separation day): fussy, sad, angry, ill.
- Symptoms will fit criteria for PTSD, but more complex.
- Because of trauma, many adoptees have difficulty in school due to problems with attention, distractibility, and stimulus discrimination.
- Adoptees have low self-esteem because often blame selves for abandonment: bad baby.
- When trauma occurs early, child, in trying to make sense of it, creates a set of beliefs, which become permanently imprinted in the neurological system.

- Children are not a "blank slate" at birth. Most of personality traits are genetic (but personality must be distinguished from behavioral coping style).
- Adoptive parents cannot expect the child to be like them.
- Core issues for adoptees: abandonment, loss, trust, rejection, intimacy, guilt and shame, control, and identity.

Important books: *The Developing Mind* and *Parenting from the Inside Out* by Daniel Siegel, *A General Theory of Love* by Lewis, Amini, and Lannon, *The Primal Wound: Understanding the Adopted Child* by Nancy Verrier, *Trauma and Recovery* by Judith Herman, *Building the Bonds of Attachment* by Daniel Hughes, and *Affect Regulation and the Origin of the Self* by A. Schore.

## What Adoptive Parents Can Do

- Deal with the reality of the adoptive situation: different from biological family: parenting plus!
- Attunement: Mother must be alert and empathic to signs of loss and grieving. Soothe infant.
- Mother's soothing important to child's achieving self-regulation. Thousands of repetitions.
- More difficult for mother to know what to do for this particular child: (1) no genetic markers and (2) separation trauma.
- If at all possible, stay home with child; he doesn't need one more disappearing mother.
- Brain research: First three years most important for neurological connections: Connections determined by child's perception of environment. Imprints during this time are lasting.
- Events of first year are imprinted in "implicit memory"—no recall, but tremendous influence on attitudes, behavior, emotional responses, and sense of self and others.
- Understand child's coping mechanisms: acting out or compliant. Compliant doesn't mean untroubled.
- Acting out child will demonstrate "wrong mother" idea by making adoptive mom wrong about many things. This interfaces with his need for control.
- Validate child's feelings. Do not defend against or reassure; he will feel discounted.

- For more info: Don't ask "why." Rather, "I'd like to hear more about that ..."
- Try to understand the difficulty of growing up without seeing oneself reflected anywhere.
- Celebrate birthday before the actual day. (Birthday often "separation day" for child.)
- Don't be late picking up child from school, activities, etc. (triggers abandonment fear).
- Fear sometimes keeps child from letting in love. Be patient. Not personal: not rejection of you.
- Tell child about being adopted before she knows what it means. Keep subject open for discussion.
- As she gets older, answer her questions honestly. Don't speak for anyone else (i.e. birthmother). Never say: "Your birthmother loved you so much she wanted you to have a good home." Even if true, it makes no sense to child: One doesn't give away what one loves. Always tell truth.
- Open adoptions preferable to closed adoptions. Child need genetic markers and secrets are toxic. Honor promises. (This also goes for birth parents.) Step families can do this; so can you.
- Learn to understand the differences between behavior (acting out or compliant) and the child's true personality. Behavior will often be different outside of family. Easier for others to see true personality. Child's true personality may enhance latent personality traits in adoptive parents' personalities.
- Acknowledge, respect, and value the differences between adoptee and other family members.
- Encourage child's talents and interests, even if they are different from yours or you previously had no interest in what he is interested in.
- Because the child will not be able to verbalize his pain, look for other forms of communication: art, poetry, music, play, projective identification (where child projects his pain onto parents).
- Behavior is often metaphor for beliefs: feels stolen, may steal; living a lie, may lie; people disappear, may hoard food, etc. Interpret for child.
- Recognize core issues: abandonment, loss, rejection, trust, intimacy, guilt and shame, control, and identity.
- Learn to understand child's anger as sometimes a cover for pain. Empathize with pain.

- Never threaten abandonment, no matter how provocative child becomes.
- Acknowledge child's feelings: Never say, "You shouldn't feel that way." Feelings come from the unconscious and are valid. Teach child to find appropriate ways to express those feelings.
- Allow child to be himself: Withdraw expectations which do not fit his personality or abilities.
- Do not try to take the place of the birthmother. She is real to him/her. You are a different person and very important in his/her life.
- Adoptees are often diagnosed with ADD. This is a result of the trauma and has nothing to do with intelligence. Hypervigilant: Trauma causes problems with attention, distractions, and stimulus discrimination. Difficult to focus on studies. Parents and teachers need to be patient.
- Prepare child for changes in routine. Fears surprises (like disappearance of mother).
- Because of interruption of natural order, child will not understand cause and effect or consequences as readily as other children. Especially difficult during adolescence. Consequences need to start early and be fair, immediate, and consistent. (Trying to repattern brain imprint.)
- Child needs strong boundaries and limits, even though may fight against them. Needs to feel safe, contained, and cared for. Is puzzled by his own behavior. Needs rational, stable parents.
- Father will not be having same experience as mother. Needs to empathize and support, rather than criticize her.
- Both need support group to compare notes with other adoptive parents and avoid isolation.
- Parents *very* important: Child desperately wants and needs your *love and understanding.*

Important books: *Parenting from the Inside Out* by D. Siegel & M Hartzell, *A General Theory of Love* by Lewis, Amini, and Lannon, *The Primal Wound: Understanding the Adopted Child* by N. Verrier, *Building the Bonds of Attachment* by D. Hughes, and *Magical Child* by J.C. Pearce.

# ACKNOWLEDGMENTS

This book was made possible because of the thousands of adoptees, birth parents, and adoptive parents who conversed, wrote, phoned, and e-mailed me following the publication of my first book *The Primal Wound: Understanding the Adopted Child.* The response to that book was overwhelming and led to my being invited to travel to many countries to speak about adoption. This offered me the opportunity to speak with many members of the adoption triad as well as professionals. The insight these conversations and other forms of communication brought me prompted the writing of this book. The willingness of so many of you to open your hearts to me educated me in the many areas of adoption that still needed to be dealt with. I thank all of you from the bottom of my heart for your courage, honesty, and trust.

I also want to thank my editors who kept me from getting too clinical (or at least tried to) and who often provided me with more understandable ways to explain complicated information. So, thank you Laura Keilin, Norma Eason, Darlene Gerow, and Monique Verrier for you keen eyes and helpful advice.

I am very grateful to my daughter's birth family, especially her birth mother B.J., for helping to form a healthy extended family to serve as a model for other families in reunion. How can I not love the birth mother of a daughter whom I also love? We have a great time when we can get together, and I highly recommend extending families in this way. Remember—*no one has too many people loving them.*

# BIBLIOGRAPHY

Atkinson, B. (1999). The Emotional Imperative. *Family Therapy Networker.* July/August 1999.

Bettleheim, B. (1987). The Importance of Play. *Atlantic Monthly.*

Bly, R. (1988). *A Little Book on the Human Shadow.* San Francisco: Harper.

Bodenhamer, G. (1995). *Parent in Control.* New York: Fireside.

Britten, R. (2001). *Fearless Living.* New York: Perigee. (2003). *Fearless Loving.* New York: Dutton

Bronson, P. (2002). *What Should I Do with My Life?* New York: Random House.

Campbell, R. (1989). *Psychiatric Dictionary*—Sixth Edition. New York: Oxford University Press.

Caruth, C. (Ed.) (1995). *Trauma and Memory.* Baltimore: Johns Hopkins University Press.

Cleary, K. B. (1995). *Before Attachment: The Effect of Infant/Mother Separation on Adopted Newborns* (unpublished dissertation).

Cohn, R. (1998). A Winning Combination: EMDR and Psychodynamic Psychotherapy. *Viewpoint: News and Views of the Psychotherapy Institute.* July/August 1998.

Collins, J. (1997). The Day-Care Dilemma. *Time.* February 3, 1997.

Dalton, P. (2000). Sexual liberation or liability? *Clove.* June, 2000.

Engel, L. & Ferguson, T. (1990). *Imaginary Crimes.* Boston: Houghton Mifflin.

Evans, P. (1992). *The Verbally Abusive Relationship.* Holbrook, NY: Adams Media Corporation.

Feuerstein. (1980). In "Speaking Their Language: Working with Students and Adults from Poverty" by Payne. *in focus.* Fall 1999.

Gibran, K. (1923). *The Prophet.* New York: Knopf.

Goldbart, S. & Wallin, D. (1994) *Mapping the Terrain of the Heart.* New Jersey: Aronson.

Goleman, D. (1995). *Emotional Intelligence.* New York: Bantam Books.

Gottman, J. (1999). *The Seven Principles for Making Marriage Work.* New York: Three Rivers Press.

Hendrix, H. (1988). *Getting the Love You Want.* New York: Henry Holt & Co.

Herman, J. (1992). *Trauma and Recovery.* New York: Basic Books.

Horner, A. (1989). *The Wish for Power and the Fear of Having It.* New Jersey: Aronson.

Jeffers, S. (1987). *Feel the Fear and Do It Anyway*. New York: Fawcett Columbine.

Jones, A. (1985). *Soul Making*. San Francisco: Harper & Row.

Kabat-Zinn, J. (1994). *Wherever You Go There You Are*. New York: Hyperion.

Kidd, S. (2002). *The Secret Life of Bees*. New York: Penguin Books.

Kingma, D. R. (1993). Foreword to *Random Acts of Kindness*. Berkeley, CA: Conari Press.

Layton, M. (1989). The Mother Journey. *Psychotherapy Networker*. September/October 1989.

LeDoux, J. (1996). *The Emotional Brain*. New York: Touchstone.

Lewis, T., Amini, F., & Lannon, R. (2000). *A General Theory of Love*. New York: Vintage Books.

Lifton, B.J. (1994). *Journey of the Adopted Self*. New York: Basic Books.

Meade, M. (1993). *Men and the Water of Life*. New York: HarperCollins.

Moore, T. (1992). *Care of the Soul*. New York: HarperCollins.

Morrison, A. (1989). *Shame: The Underside of Narcissism*. Hillsdale, NJ: The Analytic Press.

Nash, M. (1997). Fertile Minds. *Time*. February 3, 1997.

Ogden, T. (1982). *Projective Identification & Psychotherapeutic Technique*. New Jersey: Aronson, Inc.

Payne, R. (1999). Speaking Their Language: Working with Students and Adults from Poverty. *in focus*. Fall 1999.

Pearce, J.C. (1992). *Evolution's End*. San Francisco: HarperCollins.

Perry, B. (1997). In "Fertile Minds" by Nash. *Time*. February 3, 1997.

Pert, C. (1997). *Molecules of Emotion*. New York: Scribner.

Peurifoy, R. (1999). *Anger: Taming the Beast*. New York: Kodansha International.

Prescott, J. (1997). Essential Brain Nutrients, *Touch the Future*. Spring 1997.

Price, J. & Margerum, J. (2000). 4 Most Common Mistakes Treating Teens. *Networker*. July/August 2000.

Pynoos, R. (1991). Traumatic Stress and Developmental Psychopathology in Children and Adolescents. *The Textbook of Child and Adolescent Psychiatry*. Ed. By Wiener J. Washington, D.C.: American Psychiatric Press.

Ratey, J. (2001). *A User's Guide to the Brain*. New York: Pantheon Books

Restak, R. (2000). *Mysteries of the Mind*. Washington, D.C.: National Geographic.

Rowe, G. (2003). Author asks the big questions, *Contra Costa Times*. Jan. 23, 2003.

Ruiz, D.M. (1997). *The Four Agreements*. San Rafael: Amber-Allen Publishing.

Sanford, J. (1970). *The Kingdom Within.* Philadelphia & New York: J.B. Lippincott.

Ridley, M. (2003). *Nature via Nurture.* New York: Harper/Collins.

Scarf, M. (1987). *Intimate Partners.* New York & Toronto: Random House.

Schore, A. (1994). *Affect Regulation and the Origin of the Self.* New Jersey: Lawrence Erlbaum Associates. (2002) *Affect Regulation and the Repair of the Self.* R. Cassidy Seminars.

Seitz, K. (2000). *Journey Through Adoption.* South Australia.

Seligman, M. (2002). *Authentic Happiness.* New York: The Free Press.

Sexson, L. (1982). *Ordinarily Sacred.* Virginia: University Press of Virginia.

Siegel, D. (1999). *The Developing Mind.* New York: The Guilford Press.

Siegel, D. & Hartzell, M. (2003). *Parenting from the Inside Out.* New York: Tarcher/Putnam.

Small, J. W. (1987). Working with Adoptive Families. *Public Welfare.* Summer 1987.

Solinger, R. (1992). *Wake Up Little Susie.* New York: Routledge

Taffel, R. (2001). The Wall of Silence. *Psychotherapy Networker.* May/June 2001.

Tavris, C. (1982). *Anger.* New York: Simon & Schuster.

Taylor, M. & McGee, S. (2000). *The New Couple.* San Francisco: Harper

Thich Nhat Hanh (1987). *Being Peace.* Berkeley: Parallax Press

Tolle, E. (1999). *The Power of Now.* Novato, CA: New World Library.

Van der Kolk, B., McFarlane, A., Weisaeth, L. (1996). *Traumatic Stress.* New York: The Guilford Press.

Verrier, N. (1993). *The Primal Wound: Understanding the Adopted Child.* Baltimore: Gateway Press.

Von Savant, M. (2003). Ask Marilyn. *Parade.* June 20, 2003.

Walker, A. (1984). *In Search of Our Mothers' Gardens.* New York: Harcourt Brace.

Wallerstein, J. & Blakeslee, S. (1995). *The Good Marriage.* New York: Houghton Mifflin.

Walsh, R. (1999). *Essential Spirituality.* New York: John Wiley & Sons, Inc.

Watson, K. (1997). What Adoption Is and What It Isn't. *AAC Decree.* Summer 1997.

Whittington, J. (1989). "The Adoption Syndrome: A Mimicry of Borderline Syndrome." Unpublished thesis.

Wolinsky, S. (1991). *Trances People Live.* Las Vegas: Bramble Books.

# ABOUT THE AUTHOR

Nancy Verrier, M. A., is a psychotherapist in private practice in Lafayette, California, specializing in adoption issues. She is an internationally acclaimed lecturer on the effects of early childhood trauma and deprivation caused by the premature separation of mother and child. In addition to *Coming Home to Self*, Ms. Verrier has

Photo: Marianne Caldwell

written *The Primal Wound: Understanding the Adopted Child*, which has become a classic in adoption literature and for which Ms. Verrier was awarded of the Book of the Year Award from the Council for Equal Rights in Adoption in 1993 and the Emma May Vilardi Humanitarian Award from the American Adoption Congress in 2003.

Printed in the USA
CPSIA information can be obtained
at www.ICGtesting.com
LVHW010340120324
774177LV00022B/873